STILL ON THE CORNER
AND OTHER
POSTMODERN POLITICAL PLAYS
BY FRED NEWMAN

Still on the

and other
postmodern political plays by
fred newman

Edited by
Dan
Friedman

CORNER

CASTILLO CULTURAL CENTER · NEW YORK

CONTENTS

JEan Haskell

ACKNOWLEDGMENTS

This book is the result of a collective effort involving many dedicated and talented people. Diane Stiles, the managing director of the Castillo Theatre, served as the book's project manager, guiding it through all aspects of its production—from conceptualization, to design, to final printing. In addition, she brought her intimate knowledge of these plays (many of which she produced), along with her sharp political and artistic insights to her reading of the introductions, as did Gabrielle Kurlander, Castillo's producing director. Their critiques and suggestions were invaluable in correcting mistakes, deepening concepts and shaping the tone and form of the introductions. Dr. Phyllis Goldberg, who has co-authored two books of popular psychology with Fred Newman, lent her considerable copy-editing skills to the introductions. David Nackman, a leading Castillo actor and a talented graphic artist who designs virtually all of Castillo's posters, programs and ads, is responsible for the beautiful look of this collection. The cover is the result of a collaboration between Nackman, Stiles and talented graphic artist Lisa Anderson. Michael Klein, Castillo's sound designer and the most skilled researcher on its dramaturgical staff, served as our fact-checker. Jessica Massad, one of Castillo's lighting designers and producers, went over the entire contents of this book with me line by line and word by word, insuring that every period was in place and every change and correction was incorporated. She also worked tirelessly inputting cycle after cycle of the text's numerous revisions. As a proofreading team, Bruce Randall and Anne Resnick brought intense concentration and loving care to their work; Chris Street gave everything a last look before printing. Attorney Arthur Block made sure that all copyrights were respected and that all our legal obligations were met.

The production staff for *Still on the Corner and Other Postmodern Political Plays by Fred Newman* has spent many years working together building the Castillo Theatre and its sister organizations. In addition to being colleagues, we are friends who share a deep respect of and love for Fred Newman and his work in the theatre. Our friendships and shared histories have made the production of this book a gratifying, friendly, and fun experience. On behalf of all of us, I'd like to thank Fred Newman for working so hard to help maintain the vision/activity of a humane, democratic, and constantly developing world articulated so beautifully in these plays; for his remarkable courage in the face of all sorts of discouragement and attack; and for his creativity and inclusiveness which have allowed so many diverse people to work with him and with each other. All of which leads me to my final acknowledgment: to the hundreds of Castillo collective members, past and present, whose hard work over the last 15 years as fund raisers, producers, designers, and performers has made not only this book, but the plays of Fred Newman possible.

DAN FRIEDMAN
NEW YORK CITY, 1997

STORIES, PLAYS AND PERFORMANCES

A PREFACE BY FRED NEWMAN

My attitude is revolutionary, not theatrical. My world view is philosophical, not dramaturgical. My craftsmanship is that of the organizer, not the director. My view of subjectivity is far more developmental than clinical (although I am a social therapist). Yet my passion is for creative performance.

Whether as writer or director I do not create plays in themselves, but as performances. The very talented young Korean American novelist Heinz Insu Fenkl, the author of *Memories of My Ghost Brother*, sat on a panel which reviewed my play *Coming of Age in Korea*. He said that he was pleasantly surprised and moved by the performance, especially after reading the script. I was not surprised. My scripts are not written to be read. They are to be performed. If Heiner Müller is (as he says) his text then I am (or, more accurately, those with whom I create are) our performance.

Müller, a favorite of mine, is perhaps one of the greatest writers of the second half of the 20th century. He is an extraordinary poet. I am no poet at all. All the language in my plays consists of directions for performance. The words I write are not, in the language of the great Soviet psychologist Lev Vygotsky, tools for results, that is, tools (words) which gain expression in the play. Rather they are tools *and* results, components of a dialectical unity which (also in Vygotsky's terms) are completed (not expressed) in the collective performance.

Vygotsky's brilliant theory of the unity of thinking and speaking (speaking does not express what we were thinking, rather it completes a dialectical unity [thinking/speaking] in the performance [the activity] of speaking) informs my theatrical work as well as my therapeutic and political work. To look for significance in the meaning of the words (in themselves) of my plays is as metaphysical (in the worst sense of that ancient word) as the psychoanalytic attempt to discover social meaning in the unspoken thoughts (interpretations) of the so-called mind-in-itself (or Self).

Why then, you may reasonably ask, publish a book of plays to be read? They are not published to be read. They are published to be performed. Do not read them to see if they should be performed. Perform them to see if they should be read. Of course, you may do with them whatever you like. But this is my understanding (performance).

Growing up writing

I wrote plays (or parts of plays) when I was very young. In public school (P.S. 114) in the Bronx, I was in classes called OP4, OP5 and OP6. The OP stood for opportunity. Then in junior high school (J.H.S. 117), also in the Bronx, I was in a class called the SPs (SP stood for special progress). Following that I went to one of New York City's special high schools, Stuyvesant, when it was over on 15th Street and First Avenue in Manhattan (and all the students were boys). The schools and classes might have been special. I was not; an "underachiever" in the extreme, I barely made it through high school. But I did write some parodies.

In OP5 (somewhere around 1945 or 1946) we had the "opportunity" to work on a year-long "unit"—we studied radio in addition to our regular academic work. And we collectively created a play about radio called *Annie Get Your Radio*, a parody of Irving Berlin's recently opened *Annie Get Your Gun*. I wrote a parodic version of the Berlin song "The Girl That I Marry" called "The Radio I'm Buyin'." It included my favorite line: "'stead of seein' we'll be hearin' all the crowds at the stadium cheerin'." (I lived right across the street from Yankee Stadium.) In junior high school, in a social science class taught by Miss Dworkin (one of my earliest secret loves), I wrote my first full play—a parody of the Ellery Queen mystery novel—called *Celery King*. A little embarrassing to think about but, as far as I can remember, it was (if nothing else) anti-imperialist.

At Stuyvesant, where I flunked almost everything, I wound up as the art editor of the yearbook. I at least had the good sense to use the drawings of my assistant, a junior named Nick Megliola, who later changed his name to Nick Meglin and became a senior editor at *Mad* magazine. My "artistic" contribution was mainly to the senior poem written collectively by the editorial board. The traditional form was a rhyming last will and testament which left humorous fictional gifts to faculty members and administrators.

My stanza was for the head of the chemistry department: "Airwick to Mr. Schindelheim, whose name we find quite hard to rhyme. We leave this gift, we must confess, to rid the smell of H_2S." Not surprisingly, I was not "discovered" and wound up several months later in the U.S. Army for the next three years. An infantry private in Korea, I wrote little. But by 1957, the GI Bill in hand, I was a student at CCNY and elected to take a creative writing class—specifically a short story writing class taught by one Irwin Stark, who, I believe, had done some TV script writing.

What shall I major in?

There were about 15 students in the class. The star student (in the class and as well one of the top students in the whole college) was Ed Kosner, already a most-likely-to-succeed-in-the-writing-field type; he was editor-in-chief of one of the campus newspapers. He went on to become a major muck-a-muck in publishing, currently heading up *Esquire* magazine. The structure of the class was simple. We each wrote a story and then read it to the class (after Stark had looked at and graded them) in descending order of Starkian quality. In the first round of readings Ed Kosner, of course, read first. I read last. The other 14 students got either an A or a B. I got a C for a very, very short story called "Mr. Hirsch Died Yesterday." It would have been utterly humiliating except that in the class discussion Kosner (in particular) and most of the other students genuinely liked my story. That set the tone for the whole semester, during which we wrote about four stories each. Mine included another that I have spent the rest of my life with. It's called "The Store: One Block East of Jerome."

I became a philosophy major. By 1963 I had received a Ph.D. in philosophy of science from Stanford University but had essentially given up creative writing altogether. My passion for writing, however, remained intact.

Going back to school

My first post-Ph.D. teaching position was as an assistant professor of philosophy at a small Midwestern college located in Galesburg, Illinois—Knox College. My play *Left of the Moon,* written decades later, is set there. For me, the '60s took shape at Knox. I came out as a teacher, an intellectual, and a political person. My Stanford training, extraordinary as it was, was narrowly logical-analytic, philosophically speaking. But in the idyllic small town/small college atmosphere of Galesburg/Knox I was able to fraternize with young faculty types trained in a variety of disciplines and to create (formally and informally) cross-disciplinary contexts. I began to think about Dostoyevsky and Proust as much as Plato and Aristotle.

As a faculty member I felt freer to use the whole campus than I ever did as a student. I would wander somewhat aimlessly to the newly constructed theatre arts building and watch a student production of *Hamlet* in rehearsal. I would regularly attend colloquia featuring invited guests: Robert Creeley, the distinguished American poet; Archibald MacLeish, who wrote the extraordinary play *J.B.*; Jack Elliot, the virtuoso country guitarist; William F. Buckley. When Arnold Toynbee visited a sister college in Iowa (Grinnell College) I spent hours with him talking about his theory of history. In a way it was the liberal arts education I never really received at CCNY. My good friend Doug Wilson introduced me to Santayana's work and Mormon history. (The town of Nauvoo, in Illinois, one of the early Mormon settlements near where Joseph Smith was killed, was just 50 miles away on the Mississippi.) William Spanos, a brilliant and intense English teacher, talked passionately with me about existential literature. Ultimately Knox and I parted ways on unfriendly terms, after I became involved in an extended student/faculty protest over women's rights. But for a couple of years Knox College was, to me, a cultural haven. Even the political activity had a good cultural consequence (it also got me fired). I was honored to be selected by the students to deliver the address at what was called the Senior Convocation. Top administrators (who always attended these full community, full dress, cap and gown affairs) stayed away in droves on that late May day in 1965, but I wrote and presented (performed) a moving and poetic statement about the tragedy of human miscommunication. Ludwig Wittgenstein, the much misunderstood 20th-century philosophical genius, was the subject of my talk. In retrospect, it marked a major change in my philosophical thinking and style.

Taking action seriously

In September of 1965 (having just turned an untrustworthy 30) I returned to my undergraduate college, CCNY, as a faculty member. The anti-war, civil rights and women's movements were heating up and I became more and more politically involved. In the spring term of 1966 I got to teach an advanced course called "Theory of Action." The subject matter turned out to be sit-ins and Jean-Paul Sartre. I had just published a paper called "The

Origins of Sartre's Existentialism" and the rapidly politicizing atmosphere of the country and the school transformed the course into a lively ethical debate. During the last week of the term I met individually with the members of the class to discuss their final papers.

A student whose name I did not know (he had not been in class since the middle of the term) showed up at my office without a final paper. He asked if we could talk. I said okay—although, I confess, somewhat reluctantly. What he presented me with was his position on the war in Vietnam, the draft, and the theory of action class. He effectively argued that he should be given an "A" for the course since anything less than that increased the likelihood of his being drafted and sent to Vietnam to what he and I both felt was an immoral war. Indeed, he argued that a moral action for me would be to give everyone in the class (especially the draftable men) an "A." Now I had thought about the grading issue many times before. From a moral point of view, I did not like grading. Yet in teaching logic, philosophy of science, or classical philosophical texts it seemed possible to evaluate (objectively) how much someone had mastered the material and assign a grade accordingly. But philosophy understood as highly personal debate or discourse on important human issues of the day (which is what philosophizing was more and more looking like to me, in the theory of action class and elsewhere) seemed hopelessly impossible to grade. All that said, I was outraged by this student's request (and chutzpah). For all my liberalism/progressivism around students' rights, I had always been a very hard grader. I felt it was my responsibility, my moral obligation, as a teacher to be tough. But in the context of America circa 1966, in the context of the passionate ethical philosophizing that was the theory of action class, and in the context of my personal transformation regarding philosophizing and life, the argument of the "arrogant" absentee student stayed with me, hour after hour, day after day. He was right.

I have never given a (competitive) grade since. For two years (from 1966 to 1968) I taught at several colleges and universities and gave all and only A's to my students. (It seemed sexist and immoral to give only the men A's.) When this policy was discovered (and I did not hide it) I was summarily fired. In 1968 I left university teaching altogether to become a community organizer, an itinerant philosopher, a group therapist, a creator of performances and the principal architect of a development community which now numbers in the thousands across America and in which there is no grading. In contrast to '60s-style free schools—sometimes called "universities without walls"—we often refer, postmodernistically, to our developing development community as "walls without a university." Walls are of value on a cold day. Universities are problematic no matter what the weather.

A farewell address

In that theory of action class was another student (he came all the time) named Richard Strier. In some ways Richard was the mid-'60s analogue to Ed Kosner, who had supported my writing back in the 1957 creative writing class in which I was a student. Richard was a brilliant student of literature and the editor-in-chief of the CCNY undergraduate literary magazine, *Promethean.* Richard and I became good friends. (Kosner and I didn't.) Under his guidance I continued my "cultural development" begun at Knox; in particular he introduced me to the German author Herman Hesse. Richard asked me to write a piece for the Spring '66 issue of *Promethean,* which I was thrilled to do. It was my first piece of creative writing ever to be published. What I put together was a story/essay called "Mr. Hirsch, the Whore and Mr. Wittgenstein All Died Yesterday," combining the two short stories "Mr. Hirsch Died Yesterday" and "The Store: One Block East of Jerome" and the Wittgenstein talk I had given at Knox a year earlier.

In retrospect it was a farewell address—a farewell to academic life and its hypocrisy; a farewell to ivory tower philosophizing; a farewell to graded stories—and, in some ways, a return to the cold, dark streets of the Bronx where I had grown up as a poor working-class Jewish kid after my father's early death. It was a farewell to looking for a better life for myself (upward mobility) and the start of a self-conscious effort to help build a better world for all people. It was a farewell to my failed efforts to fit in. In a word, I became a revolutionary. Twenty years later Hirsch, the Store (the Whore) and Wittgenstein all returned. But by then I had organized, with thousands of others, an "ungraded" environment in which they finally made sense. They returned as performed—not as text, not as words, not as institutionally overdetermined tools for results, but as human-made tools and results.

Two decades of organizing

A couple of years ago I was chatting with a German playwright during an intermission in one of our productions at the Castillo Theatre in New York

City where I am the artistic director. He asked, "How long have you been writing plays?" I said eight years or so, that I had become a playwright in my early fifties. He said something like, "Oh, that's too bad. You are a very good writer. How come you started so late? What were you doing before you became a playwright?" I told him it took me 20 years to build the theatre. At that moment the little bell announcing the start of Act II tinkled and off he went to his seat looking bemused at what might have seemed to him my flippant answer. We never talked again. But my answer was not flippant. It was literal.

In 1968, after two politically transitional and tortured (and nomadic) years of giving all and only A's at five or six different schools from Cleveland to Los Angeles to New York City, I ended my academic career where I began it (at CCNY), as an adjunct professor of philosophy. In September about 10 of us began a completely unfunded and unaffiliated urban commune and free school called Centers for Change (after a whole list of other names that, for various reasons, were short-lived). Centers for Change (CFC) was essentially the anarchistic embryo out of which our development community grew. For 20 years virtually all of my political, intellectual and emotional energies went into nurturing this embryo.

It went through many stages, took on many shapes along the way, but CFC (the name is long gone) succeeded beyond our wildest dreams. It is now a school for development involving tens of thousands; ungraded; unfunded by outside institutions (private or public); and unfettered by institutionalized definitions of learning. By the mid-'80s, after 20 years of hard and glorious labor as an organizer, with the faith that the hundreds who made up the core at the time would continue to sustain and advance the project, I went back to school. What school? Our development school, of course. (There is no other school I would be interested in attending.) I became a student once again. I became a playwright. In 1986, at age 51, my lifelong passion for performance began to take specific shape in the writing and directing of plays.

Demonstration
Through the early days of the '80s the development community was largely involved in community/union organizing of the poor (welfare recipients, tenants, health consumers, low-paid social service workers); group therapy; and independent electoral politics. But somewhere around the middle of

the '80s a critical mass of community people in the arts (cultural types) began an informal dialogue about "cultural work." Significant numbers of artists (painters, actors and actresses, writers, poets, dancers, directors, producers) with a more or less shared critique of the political artists' movement (generally speaking, another phenomenon of the dying U.S. Left) eventually put together a more formal committee to consider the possibility of organizing a cultural project (of the evolving broader development community) which did not have all the objectionable elitist features of New York's established political arts movement. Assisted by financial support from the relatively wealthy family of one of the committee members, the group rented loft space at 7 East 20th Street in Manhattan and opened what eventually became the Castillo Center.

While the nascent political artists' grouping pretty much agreed on what they didn't like (culturally-politically speaking), there was not even a remote consensus of a positive sort. They began, therefore, with a radically eclectic approach which produced interesting dialogue (often furious fighting) but little quality performance. Some members of this cultural group urged me to become more directly involved as an organizer to help synthesize the diverse approaches and cultural influences. I began attending meetings of the organizing committee and going to more and more of the cultural events at Castillo. Break dancing, rap, labor theatre, anti-imperialist shows, Black and Latino art, avant-garde, gay performance, feminist comedy, left theatre and art exhibitions, and almost everything else in an uneasy mix yielded shows which were, in my opinion, sometimes thrilling and sometimes haphazardly awful. Was this alright? Did there have to be a synthesis? Could there be one? What was the relationship of this new cultural project to the rest of the development community? An intense debate went on among the artists over these kinds of questions.

From the outset the 20th Street space also included the very young school of the then five-year-old New York Institute for Social Therapy and Research (which was mainly a group therapy center located uptown on the West Side). At the time the school was actually a handful of classes held under the name of the George Jackson-Rosa Luxemburg Center for Working Class Education. Gradually, the Castillo cultural project began to become (like Jackson-Luxemburg) part of the social therapy institute. But the question of what kind of culture to produce remained unanswered. In that first year or so a lot of the work was producing "outside" artists. A consensus was reached that we needed to create more of our own art to better understand who we were culturally.

Two critical (for Castillo and for me personally) performance events emerged out of the chaos of the moment. The agreement to produce an event for International Women's Day in 1986 led to the creation of *A Demonstration: Common Women, the Uncommon Lives of Ordinary Women*. With various project members contributing elements, what was needed was a creative concept to tie them all together. One collective member, Maria Moschonisiou, a Greek lesbian feminist, a former producer and a good friend, urged me to come up with such a conception and direct the whole piece. I told Maria that I had no idea what a director did. Encouragingly, she offered to teach me, step by step. I accepted.

What resulted was an extraordinary theatre experience for many people, and surely for me. What I knew how to do was organize demonstrations. And so the centerpiece of *Demonstration* was a demonstration—actually two demonstrations. At the center of the loft theatre (with no seats) we created the fictional intersection of Christopher Street and Euclid Avenue. (For non-New Yorkers, Christopher is in the heart of Greenwich Village, the "home" of the gay and lesbian movement. Euclid Avenue is a major thoroughfare in working-class/poor Black Brooklyn.) The two demonstrations, one made up of Black women welfare rights activists and the other of middle-class lesbian activists, had a turf fight. The rest of the theatre/loft contained small sketches, poetry readings, video clips playing on monitors mounted on the ceiling, almost continuous '60s music, etc. in an agit-prop potpourri toward which the standing/moving/straggling audience, following the "directions" of an onstage stage manager on a ladder, drifted (or didn't). The chants of the competing Black welfare recipients and white lesbians often "introduced" and/or commented on the other pieces, ultimately resolving themselves into a women's unity statement. The piece was rough and fluid—truly more a demonstration than a theatre piece, but touching to most who participated. It seemed (at least for the moment) to answer the questions of what kind of art we were going to produce and what its relationship was to our broader community. In the meantime...I had become a director.

For the next season Maria asked me to write and direct a play. Once again she offered, and gave me, much support. And once again I turned to something I already knew—in this case, "Mr. Hirsch Died Yesterday." I reworked my old short story (one more time) into a one-act play. The first scene was simply a reading of the original story, set in a '50s working-class kitchen. (I performed Fred, a middle-aged Jewish man who read the short story.) Scene Two was a dialogue among seven created characters from the Hirsch story, played around a '40s-style Bronx candy store. For the most part the play within the play (Scene Two) followed the events depicted in the short story. But Fred (the author and storyteller) was (as a child in Scene Two) a young Black girl named Freda. Scene Three opened with Freda (the young girl from Scene Two), now a grown-up lesbian activist, wandering in the darkness until she came upon Fred sitting in his kitchen (Scene One). They began to speak to each other only to discover, to their utter amazement, that they had the same mother; they were "two different people with the same history." Ultimately, Freda showed the angry and possessive (of their mother) Fred that he was, in fact, liberated from his painful history by this bizarre turn of events. The structure and form of the play (not to mention some of the topics) have reappeared in many of my subsequent plays. For me, a play brings a story to life. Performance is the resulting relationship between the two (the story and the play). My performances, then, are demonstrations where stories meet plays, come together and then figure out what to do with each other.

INTRODUCTION

The publication of this collection of plays by Fred Newman makes available to a wide public for the first time a unique and ground-breaking body of dramatic work written between 1986 and 1997 and produced at the Castillo Theatre in New York City.

Fred Newman is one of a rare breed—a first-rate American playwright whose concerns are primarily political, not psychological. You can count his precursors on the fingers of one hand: John Howard Lawson and Mike Gold in the 1920s; Clifford Odets in the 1930s; Arthur Miller in the 1940s and '50s; Amiri Baraka in the 1960s. In the 1970s and early '80s political plays continued to be written by playwrights attached to a few small leftist theatre companies—Steve Friedman with Modern Times (New York City), Maxine Klein with the Little Flags Theatre Collective (Boston), and Joan Holden with the San Francisco Mime Troupe.

While American dramatic literature has been primarily psychological—and doggedly non-political—in its orientation, American political *theatre* in the last three decades has been decidedly non-literary. The emphasis of the radical theatre movement of the 1960s was on collective creation and per-formatory innovation. The American theatrical innovators of the last 30 years—Julian Beck and Judith Malina, R.G. Davis, Richard Schechner, Richard Foreman, JoAnne Akalaitis, Robert Wilson—have been primarily performers and directors, not playwrights. More concerned with creating a radical theatrical experience than a radical play script, the director, not the playwright, has shaped the American avant-garde in the second half of the 20th century.

Newman is part of this shift from the literary to the performatory. As a theatre person, he is first and foremost a director, a creator of performance experiences for actors and audience members. His view that performance— the uniquely human activity of being who we are not—is a powerful vehicle for development both builds on and extends the work of the performatory avant-garde over the last 30 years. He is not the first to point out that performance takes place offstage as well as on. It is his discovery of its potential as a means of development in day-to-day life that brings something new to the mix.

Newman's ground-breaking work on performance has implications that go far beyond the world of theatre. For if performance is an activity enabling ordinary people to "go beyond themselves"—that is, to step out of the societal roles that constrain us and thereby to develop—then it is not primarily a matter of aesthetics but of politics in the broadest sense of that word.

Which also means that Newman's plays are "political" in a new sense. The content of these plays is "progressive." Like his predecessors, Newman consistently takes the side of the underdog, the oppressed. For earlier political playwrights such content was what made their plays political—by exposing an evil, satirizing a corruption, inspiring resistance, and/or teaching a lesson. The form of their work was for them a secondary concern, tending to reflect the theatrical conventions of the time. For Newman, however, it is the form of performance that shapes our perception/construction of reality, and so the form—here he means not only the dramatic structure, but the approach to performance—must embody a challenge to our underlying assumptions not only about theatre but about life. That is, the content is simply a springboard for the more political/radical/developmental activity of creating a performatory experience.

The creation of these experiences is, for Newman, part of the long-term process of liberating performance from the theatre, a social institution that for thousands of years has served as an arena where irreconcilable social conflicts and contradictions have been given ritualized, illusionary resolution. As a stabilizing institution, theatre (and its progeny, film and television) has turned performance itself into the codified and commodified monopoly of a handful of specialists.

What Newman loves about the theatre is performance—the activity, not the commodity. As he sees it, his work *in* the theatre lies in liberating the developmental activity of performance *from* the theatre. As a playwright (and as a director) he is constantly exploring ways of making performance available to all of us as developmental adult play.

This is the angle from which the scripts in this collection are most productively approached—as elements in the creation of environments in which directors can help performers (onstage and off) to perform. Newman describes his work as "...theatre which *features* development—where the activity of creating performance determines the product, and not the other way around." That, in the most fundamental sense, is these plays' politic *and* their aesthetic. Newman, the director, became a playwright as part of the process of creating developmental performatory environments. He has used the scripts of others—including Bertolt Brecht, Aimé Césaire, Laurence Holder, Heiner Müller, and Yosef Mundy—toward the same end. His scripts are, on one level, artifacts of productions which came into being as both tools *for* and results *of* performatory experiences, and are offered here as tools/results for further performatory activity.

I met Fred Newman in 1981. I knew him first as the leader of the independent political movement in which I was then becoming involved. I have been a political activist since I was a teenager, and by 1981 I had worked with and in various Marxist groups for nearly 15 years. I was attracted to the movement Newman was building primarily because it had made significant inroads in organizing ordinary people—in particular the poor, the left out, the despised—to do something (politically, psychologically and culturally) about their pain.

Much of the progressive movement of that time—including the organizations in which I had been active—was overwhelmingly white and middle-class in its sensibility. Most progressives talked radical, but did little work in poor communities and nothing to challenge the status quo in any serious way. Newman and his followers not only talked the talk (although they talked a lot less than most of their leftist colleagues), they walked the walk, organizing in all strata of society, particularly among the poorest—the lower strata of the Black working class. They organized around traditional "empowerment" issues but, even more significantly as far as I was concerned, they dared to challenge some of the underlying philosophical and political assumptions of daily life. Although none of us had the language for it back then, what moved me was Newman's ability to organize environments in which the wretched of the earth could *perform* as something other than victims—in other words, environments that supported people to develop.

What was entailed in breaking out of victimized and oppressive societal roles, Newman realized, was not just politics (however radical); the oppressed need to participate in the creation of new ways of seeing the world (culture) and new ways of being, emotionally and otherwise, in the world (psychology). At the time, these views were virtually unheard of among progressives. That they are now more generally accepted is not because Newman has won some abstract political argument, but because he and his colleagues launched projects and built organizations that, in an ongoing way, have challenged—in practice—the institutions of psychology and culture, including the institution of the theatre.

Although Newman and his followers reached out to other leftists, Marxism was still approached by virtually the entire international Left as a dogma instead of a practice of method. Consequently, Newman (and those of us who worked with him) were attacked from all sides—but with particular viciousness by our fellow leftists. We were treated as heretics, which, I suppose, we were (and are). The content of these attacks focused on Newman's use of Marxist methodology in domains outside the traditional left political/economic arenas of union organizing, "educational" politics and protest marches. Newman's social therapy—a cultural/performatory approach to helping people with their emotional problems—was attacked as a technique for "brainwashing" people to be political, and, more specifically, to follow him. His work to create a developmental, inclusive performatory activity at the Castillo Theatre was dismissed as amateurish propaganda. Any mention of his theatre work—including the innovative plays gathered in this collection—was strictly forbidden in the left-liberal press. (New York City's *Village Voice* went so far as to write that Castillo didn't really have a theatre on the premises!) Behind these attacks (not very far behind) was the official Left's self-serving defense of its permanent niche in the American status quo: little beachheads (that is, jobs) in the "progressive" trade unions; within the institutions of psychology, education and social work; and in the Democratic Party. What Newman and his followers were building not only challenged the American Left's brand of dogmatic Marxism (i.e., its ideological rationalizations), its growing success jeopardized the Left's continued usefulness to the powers-that-be as the loyal (and harmless) opposition.

From the beginning, I was impressed by Newman's brilliance as a philosopher and political theorist, by his deep passion for and commitment to the oppressed, and, perhaps most profoundly, by the courage he demonstrated in taking "the path less traveled." One of the happy results of Newman's journey down this less traveled path are the plays in this collection.

When I became involved with the political movement (now perhaps more accurately described as the *development community*) led by Newman, I already had a Ph.D. in theatre history and dramatic literature from the University of Wisconsin. After receiving my doctorate in 1979, I decided not to pursue an academic career. Instead, I returned to New York City (where I had been born and partly raised) with hopes of building a professional-level political theatre whose audience would be based in working-class and poor communities. Over the next few years I led a number of unsuccessful attempts to create such a theatre. Then, in 1983, I got together with six other artists active in Newman's political movement to found the Castillo Cultural Center. The dream I brought with me to New York is now the reality of the Castillo Theatre—a grassroots-supported, artistically innovative, off-off-Broadway theatre with a diverse, non-traditional audience base. Castillo also became, over the course of the 1980s, the environment which nurtured Fred Newman as a director and playwright. It has also nurtured a design team remarkable in its ability to meet, and complete, the creative challenges constantly being offered by Newman. This team, which has evolved over the last decade, is headed by Diane Stiles and includes set designer and technical director Joseph Spirito, costume designer Emilie "Charlotte" Knoerzer, sound designer Michael Klein, lighting designer Charlie Spickler, Barry Z Levine, Castillo's videographer, musical director Dan Belmont, and gallery director Nancy Hanks. A number of other skilled and innovative directors—including Madelyn Chapman, Mary Fridley, Nancy Green, Gabrielle Kurlander and David Nackman—have also emerged at Castillo, as has an effective and resourceful production staff, and an ever-expanding acting ensemble too numerous (and too fluid) to be listed here, but whose names can be learned from the original cast lists which accompany each play in this collection. All but one of the plays in this volume have received at least one production at the Castillo Theatre, where Newman has been the artistic director since 1989.

The Castillo Cultural Center is a unique (anti-) institution. Each year it produces a full season of plays (including virtually all of Fred Newman's work). The theatre has grown up with other projects which utilize the same performatory approach to development, including the All Stars Talent Show Network—the country's largest and most successful anti-violence program for inner-city youth. Castillo does all this without relying on government or major corporate support. Instead, a dedicated corps of volunteers (approximately 150 people at this writing) work with the Community Literacy Research Project, Inc., the non-profit that funds Castillo, to raise money (through subscription sales and charitable donations) from the grassroots. It is Castillo's independence that has allowed it to survive and, indeed, to thrive as a progressive theatre in a period of political reaction and the constriction of arts funding.

It is also the means by which Castillo has built its large, diverse, non-traditional audience. A typical Castillo audience is likely to include residents from a city homeless shelter sitting next to a suburban couple from New Jersey sitting next to a Black church group from Brooklyn sitting next to some sophisticated downtown theatre types. Virtually all of these audience members are connected (directly or indirectly) to Castillo's productive activity, either by having contributed to it financially and/or by being involved in related development projects.

Castillo's history, Newman's history, and, indeed, my own history (I was the theatre's first artistic director and am currently its dramaturg), are closely interwoven. The compilation of this book has been a labor of love and of pride—love for Newman, who is one of my closest friends, and pride in both his pioneering accomplishments and the modest role I have been privileged to play in helping to create the environment in which he could write these scripts.

Newman wrote his first full-length play for the Castillo Theatre in 1986, at the age of 51. Born in the Bronx in 1935, a child of the Jewish working class, Newman was nine years old when his father's sudden death plunged the family into poverty. His early school career, marked by failure, culminated in a disastrous first semester at the City College of New York; a first love affair that ended unhappily precipitated his enlistment in the Army. After his discharge in 1956 (he spent nearly two years in Korea) Newman returned to City College on the GI Bill, eventually earning a doctorate in philosophy at Stanford University. Launched on an academic career, for the next few years he taught philosophy at several colleges and universities. In 1968 he left academia to devote himself full time to community organizing.

During his brief life as a professor of philosophy, Newman was fired from one university after another for giving all his students A's. (With the war in Vietnam raging, he was doing his part to prevent young men from flunking out of college and thereby becoming eligible for the draft; he gave his women students A's to avoid discriminating against them.) After leaving the campus for good in 1968, he applied his skills as a philosopher, teacher and organizer to building environments—cultural, political and therapeutic (he has been a practicing, albeit unconventional, psychotherapist for nearly 30 years)—in which individual and collective development could take place.

In 1978 Newman led the founding of the New York Institute for Social Therapy and Research (which has since evolved into the East Side Center for Social Therapy and the East Side Institute for Short Term Psychotherapy). In 1983, when the Castillo Cultural Center was launched, it was thanks to the financial and logistical support of the Institute, whose members recognized the need to engage not only traditional psychology and education, but the conventional production and distribution of culture as well. Castillo's first location was a tenth-story loft on East 20th Street in Manhattan where gallery shows, classes, and theatre performances were held until 1989.

The life and work of Otto Rene Castillo, a Guatemalan poet and revolutionary who had been tortured to death by the Guatemalan military dictatorship in 1967, were an inspiration to those of us who founded the center. His poem "To The Apolitical Intellectuals" demands: "What did you do when the poor/suffered, when tenderness/and life/burned out in them?" The activity of the center that we named in his honor is our answer to Castillo's burning question.

Newman was involved in the Castillo Cultural Center from the start, both as a founder and leader of the Institute and, increasingly, as an active participant in the creation of its gallery shows and theatre productions. Castillo's earliest years, before Newman came on board as artistic director, were marked by experimentation, floundering and fighting—and our inability to build a stable audience. Newman was a passionate proponent of getting the community directly involved in the creation of its culture. Toward that end, in the mid-'80s he began to write comedy skits and direct performance pieces at Castillo. Newman's growing involvement with the center was to have a profound impact on Castillo's subsequent development. Not only did he direct Castillo's first popular productions in 1986, but he began writing the plays which quickly became the mainstay of the theatre's work.

Newman became Castillo's artistic director in 1989, when Castillo formally separated from the Institute for Social Therapy and Research to establish itself as an independent cultural collective. That year Castillo moved to a larger space in SoHo (currently housing a 71-seat auditorium, with a small rotating stage flanked by two large video monitors mounted to the grid) and launched its unique fundraising model.

Most theatres in the United States, whether mainstream or avant-garde, commercial or not-for-profit, take the theatre market as given (for example: there are X number of theatergoers in New York City, from such and such cultural backgrounds and with such and such economic status…) and try to find their niche in it. Their working assumption is that if their product is good enough, it will attract an audience and/or the grants necessary to sustain it. Such an approach, Newman pointed out, makes the theatre vulnerable both to the whims of fashion and the marketplace, as well as to the conservatism of the grant-givers. (The very notion of "good," after all, is defined by the existing institutions.)

Under Newman's leadership, Castillo did something new—and possibly unique; it created its own market through community organizing. Along with its sister organizations and projects devoted to supporting human development, Castillo participated in the activity of expanding the broader "development community" of which it is part—a community that, among many other things, now supports a theatre. To accomplish this the members of the Castillo collective (whether they were actors, directors, designers, dancers, writers, audience members or whatever) committed themselves to the activity of grassroots fundraising.

A canvassing, street work and telemarketing operation was put in place which had Castillo collective members fanning out every evening and on weekends to neighborhoods throughout New York City and the surrounding suburbs, knocking on people's doors and talking to them about the work of Castillo and the All Stars Talent Show Network and asking for financial support for these independent cultural projects. Within a year after being launched in 1989, Castillo's canvassing operation was one of the largest in the New York metropolitan area, all the more remarkable for being staffed entirely by volunteers. Castillo's canvassing, street performance (which raises funds on the sidewalks of New York) and telemarketing operation have gone through many reorganizations over the last eight years, but the highly successful model of going directly to the grassroots for support has never changed. This is not simply an alternative *marketing* strategy, it is a *political* strategy fully in sync with Castillo's perspective that the building of community is the activity/environment most conducive to human development in general and to engaging how people perceive themselves and the world in particular.

As usual, Newman played a key role in this process. It is he who initiated the transformation of Castillo from a grouping of left-leaning artists into a collective of workers who took responsibility for the center's financial (as well as artistic) life. He led the research and development work and organized and trained scores of activists to take on the Herculean task of guaranteeing Castillo's financial independence.

The means by which Castillo was created and is maintained cannot be separated from what it has produced, including Newman's scripts. Self-conscious of the performatory nature of the mass organizing/fundraising work in which they were engaged, the Castillo artists/activists began to bring skills developed onstage to the street, the door and the phone and, conversely, to bring the performance of everyday life onto Castillo's stage. In so doing they brought out not only the news of Castillo, but the *actuality* of Castillo's performance to neighborhoods throughout the New York metropolitan area—and they created the activity/environment that helped make the developmental nature of performance clear to Newman. He continues to work with the collective to refine and develop its mass organizing/fundraising performance.

"The street performances, the performances door to door, the performances on the phone, give rise to everything we're doing," Newman has said. "That *is* our theatre performance. That's what political theatre in the United States in the 1990s *is*. Plays are simply one of many performances that we do at Castillo, only one of the things it means to make theatre." Fred Newman's plays grow out of, and are part of, this larger activity.

I discuss the particulars of each play in this collection, including its production history at Castillo, in individual introductions. Most of the scripts are also accompanied by an author's note by Newman, originally written for the program which accompanied the play's production at the Castillo Theatre. These notes reflect Newman's thoughts on the play at the time of production and have not been rewritten or revised for this collection.

Here I want to give an overview of Newman's dramatic writing. Newman's plays, taken as a whole, display certain common characteristics. Much more than the specific contents or production histories of the plays, these characteristics reveal the shape of performance (the form), and thus the politics, of Newman's work at Castillo. Including dramatic structure, approach to character, and dramatic language, these characteristics have come to be associated with what we at Castillo call "developmental theatre."

In a typical Newman play, the story is told a number of times from different points of view (or, perhaps more accurately, explored at different moments in history). The dramatic tension in Newman's plays is to be found not primarily within the plot (indeed, many of his plays don't have plots at all, and none are plot-driven), but arises from the conflict among the various versions of the narrative. In this sense Newman's scripts are analogous to cubist painting and sculpture; like cubism the plays give up single-point perspective (and the moralism implied in the "correct" way of seeing things) to show the same thing from a variety of perspectives at the same time. The aesthetic pleasure of both cubism and Newman's plays lies in the simultaneous perception of things from many points of view and in the appreciation of the tension/energy/possibility created by their juxtaposition. Still, the analogy is…an analogy. Theatre being a social activity, not a plastic art, it is the *conversation* among the points of view in Newman's plays that is important, not the points of view themselves. In this sense, his plays have no point. They are not "about" anything; they *are* their conversations. As Newman puts it, "For theatre to be developmental it must help us to go somewhere (emotionally, socially, physically, culturally) that we have not considered possible. The value of the experience lies in the journey, not the destination."

Newman's political theatre is thus neither moral (implying the "right" course of action) nor ideological (implying the "correct" or "real" or "progressive" conclusion). It is, if it is to be categorized at all, *activistic*—it deconstructs activity in various ways and leaves the audience not with a moral or an interpretation, but with an *experience* of the deconstruction.

One of the consequences of this approach is that Newman's plays characteristically lack resolution. After all, what is a resolution but the imposition of a particular point of view on the action?

Taken as a whole, Newman's writing for the stage also displays an unusual approach to character. In Newman's plays the line between "you" and "me" often seems to disappear. Characters in his plays sometimes appear to be more than one person at the same time, or two characters may appear to be the same person, or characters from different historical moments find their stories and their identities merging. In its most radical manifestation there are *no* characters in Newman's plays—at least not in the traditional sense of individuated, stable, socially/psychologically coherent units.

That isn't to say that there are never characters in Newman's plays, or to imply that traditionally trained actors have to be retrained in order to perform them. It is simply that Newman doesn't approach the individual as the object of interest onstage or, for that matter, anywhere else. As a theatre director, he looks at/works with the *ensemble*, not the individual actor. As a social therapist he doesn't try to help individuals to solve their emotional problems, but to lead the building of the *therapy group* as an environment/activity in which/through which everyone can get help. As a political organizer he does not look at/work with individuals or individual constituencies but at and with the *community*. And as a playwright, it is not *character* but the *interrelatedness* of characters, including the interrelatedness of the various aspects of the "same" character, which attracts him.

As with narrative, character in Newman's plays is viewed with a cubist sensibility—seen from a variety of historical and/or societal angles at the same time. Newman's characters, for the most part, don't resolve themselves into a stable, individuated unit (nor, for that matter, do they dissolve into fragments of a dysfunctional individuated unit); they are, instead, affected by conflicting (and interconnected) versions of themselves. They are who they are *and* they are who they are becoming. They are approached, at a fundamental level, as the embodiments of various versions of the narrative, not as psychological constructs called individuals. For lack of a more concise term, allow me to call this character-as-other-than-a-specific-one.

Not all of Newman's characters are other-than-a-specific-one. Some are stable, socially/psychologically coherent individuals. Yet in almost every case Newman's major characters struggle with a closed identity imposed by society or myth. This struggle, however, is not an internal conflict. Newman's characters don't have such things; they have historical others or historical choices which result (or can result) in their transformation. (Transformation has never been common in the theatre, where the individual as a stable unit is tacitly assumed to be the ideal.) While not every one of his characters actually changes in this way, it is Newman's interest in *transformation* (qualitative change emergent through activity) rather than psychology that informs his approach to character.

One way of understanding this approach—to dramatic structure *and* to character—is that in both instances Newman is providing his own deconstructions. The alternative narratives/characters can be viewed as deconstructions of each other, providing the audience/reader with a deconstructive experience which allows for the possibility of *re*construction.

What of the relations *among* characters onstage? Newman often provides a character, usually bearing a new version of the narrative, who acts as a catalyst for the transformation of others. This impact has nothing to do with the specific qualities of such characters. They are not smarter or more moral or more politically correct than the others. Rather, his characters' catalytic power (in political terms, their organizing ability) is connected to their embodiment/projection of a different version/vision/narrative from that of the characters who are (initially) so immersed in their societal roles that only some "other" can deconstruct those roles.

Possibility is opened up (for the characters onstage and, by extension, for the audience) by the alternative narratives/visions embodied in the catalytic character. The primary activity engaged in by Newman's characters is their joint creation—through a deconstruction of their old assumptions—of an environment of possibility. This is both why and how developmental theatre can make manifest the unique human ability to transform our environments even as we are determined by them. (This capacity is discernible, I think, even in these artifacts called scripts.)

Newman's approach to both dramatic structure and character grows from his understanding of history. For Newman history is not the "past" but the continuous, seamless activity of human life. Society, by contrast, is human life frozen in a particular time and place. We all exist in both history and society. Newman's ability to construct simultaneous versions of the same story (and/or the same character) stems from his working assumption that history (and thus the constant movement of deconstruction/reconstruction) is always with us and we with it. Identity—in the theatre this is called the "well defined" character—is for Newman nothing but a snapshot, so to speak, of the continuously changing, developing human being. His approach to dramatic structure and his portrayal of character-as-other-than-a-specific-one are both exercises in the methodology of deconstruction, and, perhaps more to the political point, affirmations of the historical dimension of human life.

If a stylistic label were to be stuck on Newman's dramatic language it would probably be "realist." However, such a label would misdirect our focus, for the "realistic" tone of Newman's dialogue grows not from any aesthetic commitment to verisimilitude but from Newman's conviction that conversation, as an activity, as a form of human social life, has the potential to be developmental. Conversation can, in Newman's words, "create new meanings—meanings rooted in the performatory, relational activity of collectively creating more and more differing and new 'forms of life.'" In other words, it is neither the content nor the style of the language (which in his scripts is often hauntingly poetic) that is of primary concern to Newman. Instead he is interested in its form—that is, the patterns of its movement, its activity. Newman has talked about "the loveliness of dialogue...that existential moment when human beings, who have been on their individual paths, touch one another." Whether the conversation *goes* somewhere, that is, whether it creates new meaning (onstage and off), is what interests Newman (onstage and off).

The major influences on Newman in regard to language come from outside the theatre—in particular from the early Soviet psychologist Lev Vygotsky, who understood language as *activity*, and from the philosopher Ludwig Wittgenstein, who viewed language as a form of human life. For Newman, it is not so much the *what* of speaking which is significant, but *that* we speak to each other. Newman is interested in language as social activity (at its best, a *completing* activity) through which people collectively and continuously create and re-create all sorts of things, including their relationships, their identities, their decisions, their selves.

These reflections on the commonalities to be found in Newman's work are made, of course, after the fact. Newman doesn't write his plays with a dramatic theory or a set of politically or aesthetically determined conventions in mind. Directors and playwrights should not construe these notes as a "definition" of developmental theatre. They are simply reflections on a continuously evolving process at a particular moment in its evolution.

While Newman is clearly part of the performatory, non-literary tendency in the American avant-garde, he has nonetheless, as this collection attests, produced a remarkable body of dramatic literature that touches on virtually all aspects of contemporary life. In light of that accomplishment, it may be helpful to take stock of the influences at work in his writing.

First and foremost one finds in the dramatic work of Fred Newman the presence of popular culture. Like most 20th-century Americans, Newman has been profoundly influenced by film, television, sports, the Broadway musical, and popular music. His writings reveal him to be, not surprisingly, a product of the American working class in the second half of the 20th century.

The "realism" of Newman's language makes his scripts immediately accessible to Americans from all walks of life. There is nothing "high-falutin'" or off-putting about his work. This accessibility is deliberate. Newman's working principle is that you have to reach people where they are, not where you want them to be. At the beginning, a Newman play usually seems to be "normal" (realist). It has the feel of something you have seen or heard before. However, Newman's commitment to reproducing the surface of "reality" ends there. What each play in its own way exposes—usually through the juxtaposition of alternative narratives and characters—is the socially constructed nature of "reality." The deconstruction of reality could not be accomplished as thoroughly if the "reality" were not first firmly established.

The popular culture that has so influenced Newman's writing is thus not only the culture appropriated from and then sold back to the people in film, television and records. It is also, indeed most importantly, the culture of everyday life; it incorporates the ways we modern Americans have come to organize perception. Popular culture is the framework of Newman's plays, even as the reconstruction of that frame is the activity of his theatre.

Within the broad flow of popular culture some movements and individual artists have particularly influenced Newman. Perceptible in his work is agit-prop (agitation and propaganda), the street theatre form that dominated radical political theatre in the United States (and much of the world) in the 1920s and '30s and which enjoyed a comeback during the upheavals of the 1960s. Agit-prop is ritualistic and dance-like. It is characterized by mass (choral) recitation and choreographed movement organized around simple political parables, its aesthetic very close to that of the rallies and demonstrations from which it originally emerged. Stylistically some of Newman's earlier work reflects agit-prop influences. However, taken as a whole, his work is a rejection of agit-prop's insistence on resolving the dramatic conflict in favor of the oppressed. For Newman resolution, regardless of its content, is dishonest, manipulative and non-developmental.

Another clear presence in Newman's writing is that of Bertolt Brecht, the German Marxist playwright, director and theorist who first came to prominence in the 1920s and who has been a major influence on political theatre ever since. Calling his work "epic theatre," Brecht sought to break out of realism's pretense that what was taking place onstage was "really" happening; he wanted to make his audiences aware that they were watching a play. This awareness, he maintained, could be engendered by "making strange" the activities onstage. (This has been translated—awkwardly— into English as the "alienation effect.") If the audience could be helped to stop "identifying" with the characters onstage, they might, Brecht argued, be able to think critically about what they were watching, and if they could see the social dynamics at work under the surface of reality they might do something about them in "real life." Toward this end Brecht rethought stagecraft at every level—creating his own approach to acting, music and stage design, introducing film into stage productions, etc.

Newman does not share Brecht's faith in the power of rationality and is critical of the German playwright's dualist assumptions in regard to thinking/feeling and theatre/"real life." Nonetheless, Brecht's challenge to realism on progressive political grounds has been vital for Newman's theatre. Brecht's emphasis on the *artificiality* of performance is also a premise of Newman's work. Newman's dramatic structure and approach to character cannot possibly coexist with the assumptions of conventional realism and are, to that extent, made possible by Brecht's pioneering work. Newman's use of narrator characters, direct address to the audience, and video sequences to interrupt and comment on the stage action all owe something to Brecht. For Brecht these devices were tools to "alienate" the audience so that they could *think* about the play's lessons. For Newman they are simply a part of the theatrical landscape in which he works and builds *experiential* environments.

Also present in Newman's work is Heiner Müller, Germany's leading avant-garde playwright, who died in 1995. Originally a disciple of Brecht, Müller had gone far beyond the simple political parables of his mentor. At first glance the work of Newman and Müller appears to be very different. Müller's work is intensely poetic and layered with literary and historic references. They are as German and European as Newman's are American. What Newman and Müller (who visited Newman at the Castillo Theatre in 1989) share is what might be called a postmodern Marxist perspective. Growing from that common political ground they both take a relentlessly non-psychological approach to character in their plays and reject linear plot and dramatic resolution. Since 1987 Newman has mounted more Müller productions than any other American director.

Finally, mention must be made of Caryl Churchill, the contemporary English Marxist-feminist playwright. While Churchill writes plays that are for the most part within the Brechtian tradition of epic theatre, her play *Cloud 9* prefigures Newman's work in some significant ways. Like many of Newman's plays, it contains parallel/conflicting narratives and characters-as-other-than-a-specific one. While Churchill didn't continue in her later work to explore the possibilities she introduced in *Cloud 9*, its impact on Newman is direct and has been gratefully acknowledged.

While Newman has been touched by these precursors, his work has not been overdetermined by them. He is not "of" any particular tradition. He is an innovator, and there is nothing formalistic or dogmatic in his writings. He entered the theatre not as an artist but as a community organizer, as a social therapist and as a political activist, and he has approached the writing of each play not with the goal of creating a "work of art," but as an experiment in performance. The results, integrating all sorts of influences, have broken new (and varied) ground.

This collection marks the emergence of Fred Newman as an original voice in the American theatre.

DAN FRIEDMAN

Mr. Hirsch Died Yesterday

Mr. *Hirsch Died Yesterday* (1986), the first full-length play written by Fred Newman, provides a preview of everything that is to follow.

In *Mr. Hirsch* can be found most of the political/philosophical/moral concerns which animate all of Newman's thought, as well as virtually all the aesthetic innovations that have come to characterize his work as a playwright.

It begins with the character Fred reading to the audience a story in the first person about the death of a Bronx candy store owner during Fred's childhood. The same story is then enacted by a cast of actors, except that the gender and race of the key character has changed. (Fred has become Freda.) The dramatic action of the play is the telling of the story/stories. The tension is not so much *within* the story as it is *between* two versions of the story, which literally confront each other in the final scene as the two characters (Fred and Freda)—one a middle-aged, white, straight Jewish man, the other a young Black lesbian—fight over whose story (history) this is. The two most obvious (and most radical) aesthetic characteristics of *Mr. Hirsch Died Yesterday*—the juxtaposition of stories (and the consequent conflict/dialogue between them) and characters who are who they are while being someone else as well—are to be found, in increasingly sophisticated forms, in almost all of Newman's subsequent work for the stage.

The fact that Fred is Jewish and Freda African American is, of course, not incidental to the play or to the concerns of the playwright. The relationship between Blacks and Jews—two of history's most persecuted peoples, who have met on American soil under sharply unequal circumstances—is a central concern of Newman's. It is a concern that he brought to the theatre from his work as a political organizer, and which he has continued to explore in many subsequent plays.

The painful similarities and equally painful differences between Blacks and Jews make their interactions a highly effective arena for exploring and challenging the notion of identity itself—whether it be ethnic or individual. It is, after all, identity that Fred and Freda fight about ("She's *my* mother!") and it is identity as a sociological and philosophical category that Newman explores in almost every play in this collection. Taken together Newman's dramatic work—from *Mr. Hirsch* to *Life Upon the Wicked Stage*—questions the concept of identity and the notion of the self that everywhere accompanies it.

Newman was 51 years old when he wrote *Mr. Hirsch Died Yesterday*, and already the leader of the nascent independent political movement. Earlier he had written and co-authored a few skits for comedy nights at Castillo and, in 1986, had collaborated with other writers on *A Demonstration: Common Women, the Uncommon Lives of Ordinary Women* and *From Gold to Platinum*. Both, directed by Newman, were sprawling, large cast, political epics with roots in traditional agit-prop. *Mr. Hirsch Died Yesterday,* not only marked his emergence as a playwright but proved to be a significant turning point in the evolution of the Castillo Theatre. Since then Newman's statement as playwright—quite distinct from the agit-prop and Brechtian elements that had most influenced Castillo's earliest work—and Castillo's evolution as a theatre have been intimately bound together.

Mr. Hirsch Died Yesterday is also Newman's most explicitly autobiographical play. Born in 1935 in the Bronx into a working-class Jewish family, Newman was the youngest of five children. After his father's death when Newman was nine, his mother Sadie eked out a living for herself and her two youngest sons by taking in boarders and running a floating poker game to supplement a meager welfare check. Mr. Hirsch and Mr. Hoffman were the owners of a candy store in the neighborhood.

While elements of Newman's Bronx childhood and later life appear throughout his work, it is in *Mr. Hirsch Died Yesterday* that the playwright offers himself and his personal history most directly to the audience. So straight-ahead is this offering—the main character is called "Fred" and the playwright performed him in the original production—that *Mr. Hirsch* can be viewed as a transitional form/activity between memoir and play.

Mr. Hirsch Died Yesterday opened under Newman's direction at the Castillo Theatre's first location on East 20th Street in Manhattan in December 1986 and ran through the end of January 1987. It was revived, again directed by Newman, but with David Nackman in the role of Fred, in March of 1991 at Castillo's current location on Greenwich Street in SoHo. For the second production, the opening of the play was changed. Instead of starting with Fred reading the story to the audience, the story was told as mutual reminiscences by three men—the adult versions of the children in the story, including Fred—sitting around a bar. The rest of the script remained the same. In May 1992 *Mr. Hirsch* became the second act of *Dead as a Jew (Zion's Community)*. The first act of *Dead as a Jew* was another early Newman play, *No Room for Zion (A Kaddish by a Communist Jew)*, first staged in 1989, and the third act was a version of *The Store: One Block East of Jerome*, which had first been produced by Castillo in 1991.

We present here the original 1986 version of *Mr. Hirsch Died Yesterday*. Of the three versions, it most effectively stands on its own and most clearly establishes the dramatic structure and approach to character that would come to characterize Newman's plays.

D.F.

Mr. Hirsch Died Yesterday was first produced at the Castillo Theatre (Nancy Green, managing director) in New York City in December 1986. The cast, in order of appearance, was as follows:

FRED . . . . Fred Newman
GABRIELLE . . . . Gabrielle Kurlander
IRIS . . . . Madelyn Chapman
FREDA . . . . Pam Lewis
HOFFY . . . . Dan Friedman
MR. HIRSCH . . . . Roger Grunwald
SADIE GREENBERG . . . . Doris Kelly
ESTHER DUBROW . . . . Ellen Korner

Fred Newman, director; Maria Moschonisiou, producer; Patience Higgins, saxophone; Wilton Duckworth, set and lighting design; Elena Borstein, scenic design and slide photography; Jennifer Ruscoe, costume design; Kenneth Hughes, production stage manager.

Mr. Hirsch, the candy store man, was murdered at Auschwitz. But will he ever die? *Mr. Hirsch Died Yesterday* tries to ask whether any can live *after* the 20th-century concentration camps of Central and Eastern Europe, South Africa, Israel, Latin America, Asia, the U.S. of A. Or, indeed, can any of us die?

But it is not a postmodern play about "good and evil." It is a simple, post-revisionist communist, working-class learning play about nice and nasty; the very ordinary human emotional concentration camps in which all of us have been forced to live by the capitalist gods (Bush & Co.) who produce, direct and act out a viciously violent and racist *immorality play* sponsored by the world's oil companies and other such deities.

It is dedicated to Sheila Pyros, who every day teaches us how to live, and the Reverend Al Sharpton, who every day teaches us why to live.

MARCH 1991

CHARACTERS
(in order of appearance)

FRED

GABRIELLE

IRIS

FREDA

HOFFY

MR. HIRSCH

SADIE GREENBERG

ESTHER DUBROW

Scene 1

FRED sits reading aloud.

FRED: When I was young I *liked* Hoffman, the candy store man. Grown-ups used to say he was "good with kids." I didn't much like the grown-ups, but I liked Hoffman, anyway. We all hung out in his candy store talking about (as best I can remember) Joe DiMaggio, Joe Louis, Hitler, Mussolini, Tojo, and underwear. We ate penny candies and read his ten-cent joke books for nothing. Sometimes he got pissed off at us and told us to "Get the hell outta here." But we kids, who were "good with grown-ups," knew he didn't mean it. We liked Hoffman. Everybody liked Hoffman.

Hoffman's partner was his brother-in-law. His name was Mr. Hirsch. Nobody liked Hirsch. Why? It didn't make a difference. Nobody liked him. People liked Hoffman and hated Hirsch. Period. This was a long time before we knew from "why." The day after Hirsch died I was talking to my friends and they didn't seem very sad about it.

"But Hirsch died yesterday," I said to Ira.

"Yeah."

"What do you mean, 'Yeah'?"

Ira shrugged and spat...poorly. (The saliva didn't hang together...it sprayed.)

I was sort of sad about Mr. Hirsch. I kept thinking about him. He was short and bald. I thought he must have been that way all his life. One day me and my friends were talking about what our parents and *other old people* we knew must have looked like when they were young. I said "Mr. Hirsch" and everybody cracked up; me too. Hirsch was not a little child kind of person. He never seemed to shave. We used to kid him because he never shaved. He was grumpy and...unshaven. Hirsch wore a dirty old gray jacket in the store and we all said he must have slept with it on. Unlike Hoffman, who smiled even when we didn't pay, Hirsch frowned when we did pay.

The chocolate covered marshmallow candy with the cherry syrup inside was the best. I remember once I was in the candy store, sitting on the last stool, reading "The Human Torch." The guy who delivered the candy was talking to Hirsch and Hoffman—now I remember, we called him "Hoffy." But it was Hirsch who barked at the delivery man in Yiddish, "Don't forget the marshmallow candy! The kids like it!" The cherry marshmallow candy was good alright, but everyone hated Hirsch.

Once, Ira's mother forgot to leave him lunch money. He went to the store—I was with him—and asked Mr. Hirsch (Hoffy wasn't there) if we could borrow a dollar. Hirsch really frowned and gave the money. Ira said, "I hate the way he stares." He belched. Ira and I had lunch. After lunch, we came back to the candy store and used up the money that was left on marshmallow candy. Hirsch gave us a dirty, dirty look when we gave him back "his" money.

My mother and Esther, her best friend, were talking about Hirsch once. Esther, who was president of the Ladies Auxiliary of the Synagogue, said that Hirsch gave money to charity. My mother said he gave it so that everyone would say nice things about him, but that he *really* didn't want to give it at all. Like I said, nobody, not even my mother, liked Hirsch.

Many years later, at my mother's funeral, I was thinking about Hirsch. Nobody liked my mother much either. She wasn't very nice. But, like I said, this was childhood, long before we knew from "why." The world was simpler then. There were nice people and not so nice people. Simpler, yes, but not so nice for the not so nice people. I stood in the light drizzle at my mother's graveside and I remembered Hirsch. "Short and bald man," I thought in an almost childlike voice, "everybody hated you. I don't know what to think about you anymore, Mr. Hirsch. You got the candy we liked, but nobody cared. You gave money and my mother said, 'show-off.' I don't hate you, Hirsch, and I don't like you, but I didn't like them saying all those things about you. You're dead, Hirsch, and so now is my mother and it was hard to be one of the not so nice people in that simple and ugly world of my childhood. You're dead, Mr. Hirsch. That's enough."

Scene 2

A brightly lit candy store scene. Stage right, away from the store, are ESTHER
DUBROW *and* SADIE GREENBERG *in a pool of light. The other five characters—*
HOFFY, HIRSCH, FREDA, IRIS *and* GABRIELLE—*are in the candy store.* FREDA, IRIS
and GABRIELLE *are seated at counter stools reading comic books.*

GABRIELLE: *(Very dramatically)* The Human Torch. The Human Torch. The
Human Torch.

IRIS: What about the Human Torch? What about 'em, Nutso?

GABRIELLE: I mean he's made of fire.

IRIS: So what? So he's made of fire. So what?

GABRIELLE: I mean…I mean…how d'ya feel up someone made of fire?

IRIS: Geez, Gabrielle, geez. You got some heavy problems there. Maybe he
don't do nuthin'? Maybe he's a weirdo…like you.

FREDA: *(Looking up from comic)* First thing to mind. "X." How about "X"?

IRIS: X-ray machine.

FREDA: "T." Gimme a "T."

GABRIELLE: Tits. Yeah. Tits.

IRIS: Does your mother know you talk dirty like that?

FREDA: A "B." Try a "B."

GABRIELLE: Brassiere. That's good, huh. Brassiere.

IRIS: Jesus Christ. You're a damn sex fiend.

(Pause.)

FREDA: *(Sings)*
Dunno why
There's no sun up in the sky
Stormy weather…

IRIS: That's nice, Freda. That's very nice.

GABRIELLE: What about Lena *as a kid*?

IRIS: *(Sings to the tune of "Stormy Weather")* Why? Mommy, why, why, why, why? Mommy, Why, why? *(Speaks.)* What about Gary Cooper?

FREDA: Yup, yup, yup, Mommy. Yup, yup, yup.

IRIS: Brassiere? Holy shit. You're a pervert; a damned pervert.

FREDA: Yup, yup, yup…

IRIS: BRASSIERES. TITS. Gabrielle, what kinda family you come from?

HOFFY: *(Warmly as always)* Alright you kids, get the hell outta here!

GABRIELLE: Aw, Hoffy, I didn't finish the comic book yet.

HOFFY: Spend a dime maybe, and buy the book?

GABRIELLE: C'mon, Hoffy.

(Pause.)

HOFFY: Where'd ya get that red hair?

IRIS: *(Jokingly)* Who's got red hair?

GABRIELLE: Shut up, Iris.

HIRSCH: Stop that, you two.

IRIS: Her hair ain't red.

HIRSCH: Don't talk back to me; don't talk back to me. *(IRIS mumbles.)* What did you say?

FREDA: She didn't say nothin', Mr. Hirsch. *(To IRIS and GABRIELLE.)* Why don't you two cool it before we get thrown the hell outta here?

HOFFY: You three beauties wanna buy somethin'?

HIRSCH: Did the marshmallow candy guy come yet?

HOFFY: I don't think so…Red, you want that book?

HIRSCH: We need the damn cherry marshmallow candy.

IRIS: Yeah, where's the cherry marshmallow?

FREDA: *(Quietly)* Cool it, Iris.

HIRSCH: What did you say?

FREDA: Nuthin', Mr. Hirsch, nuthin', nuthin' at all. Just that we like the cherry marshmallow candy. I mean, you know that…I know you know that. Nuthin', we weren't saying nuthin'.

GABRIELLE: Hoffy, can I borrow a half dollar to buy a hamburger at the luncheonette? My mother'll pay you back.

HOFFY: Does your mother know you're borrowing money?

IRIS: Her mother doesn't care. She's rich.

GABRIELLE: Hey, Iris, I told you to stay out of my hair.

IRIS: Listen, you ketchup head.

FREDA: Jesus Christ, you two.

HIRSCH: Here's two quarters. Now get outta here.

GABRIELLE: Do I have to go now?

IRIS: Hey, can I get a couple of quarters, too?

FREDA: Jesus Christ, Iris, cool it!

HIRSCH: Hoffy, these kids are driving me crazy. They make me crazy.

HOFFY: Alright you three, outta here. Out. Out. Out!

(*IRIS, FREDA and GABRIELLE return comics to rack and head for the door.*)

IRIS: I hate that Hirsch. He looks like my father when he's on the toilet in the mornings!

FREDA: What the hell you doin' lookin' at your father on the toilet?

IRIS: I ain't lookin'; I ain't lookin'. He's just sittin' there with the door open.

GABRIELLE: I'll bet you're not lookin'!

IRIS: Listen, carrot-top, you gonna give me half that burger?

GABRIELLE: I wouldn't give you shit, you blond bombshelter.

FREDA: Jesus, you two creeps are drivin' *me* crazy, too.

GABRIELLE: Oh, listen to the goody-goody kid with the black curly hair.

IRIS: Who the fuck you think you're talkin' about, Red?

GABRIELLE: *(Backs off)* Yeah, okay, okay, we'll all share the burger.

FREDA: Leave Hirsch alone, you two clowns. The poor bastard's a sicko.

IRIS: He gives me the creeps. And he gives Miss Creamsicle here a half buck. Jesus Christ.

FREDA: Iris, you're really light on brain power today.

IRIS: Maybe so. But Hirsch is a creepo. He's fuckin' dead. I tell ya he's dead. Hoffy's cool. Hirsch is dead.

GABRIELLE: Yeah. Iris is right for one time. Hoffy's cool. But Hirsch is dead. D-E-A-D. Dead.

FREDA: Hoffy's okay. But he don't give nuthin' much but a big smile and a pat on the head and…sometimes…a pat on the ass.

IRIS: Yeah, well, whatta ya want?

GABRIELLE: Yeah, whatta ya want?

FREDA: Let's go stretch out the burger, you two clowns.

(The three girls exit. Enter SADIE and ESTHER.)

SADIE: You know my boarder Margie?

ESTHER: Yes. She's a lovely woman.

SADIE: Some lovely woman. She stole my sheets.

ESTHER: Margie stole your sheets?

SADIE: Yes. That's what I just told you. Margie stole my new sheets.

ESTHER: How do you know? Margie stole your sheets?

SADIE: I found three of my new white sheets hidden under her bedspread.

ESTHER: What did she say?

SADIE: Nothing. I just called her a thief and told her to get the hell out.

ESTHER: Margie's gone? You have no boarder? I just saw her yesterday. Margie's gone?

SADIE: Yes. I told you. I threw her out…No thief's gonna stay in my apartment.

ESTHER: Margie seemed like a lovely woman, Sadie.

SADIE: Esther, goddammit, I told you she's a thief.

ESTHER: I'm so shocked. It's terrible. I know you need the money. You have no boarder, Sadie?

SADIE: I have. I rented to Harry the bookie. He gives me twice what Margie gave.

ESTHER: So fast you rented…that's…wonderful, Sadie.

SADIE: Harry always said he liked that room.

ESTHER: He's a quiet man. It's nice you have a boarder…Where did Margie go?

SADIE: I don't know. I don't care. She's a crook.

ESTHER: Why would she steal your sheets? Why would she hide sheets under the bedspread? For three sheets she'd steal?

SADIE: Stop already, Esther. She stole the damn sheets. Whattya think, *I* put them in her room?

ESTHER: You could have made a mistake, Sadie.

SADIE: Get away, get away, you dummy!

(*SADIE storms angrily out of the store and off.*)

HIRSCH: Mrs. Dubrow, whatta you want?

ESTHER: (*Quietly*) Sadie…Sadie put the sheets under her bedspread; under Margie's bedspread.

HIRSCH: What did you say, Mrs. Dubrow, c'mon, speak up. You want something. You want something. Speak up.

ESTHER: Mr. Hirsch, you still need a shave, you know.

HIRSCH: Dubrow, it's your business?

ESTHER: Why can't you be nice, Hirsch? Why can't you be nice?

HIRSCH: I'm not nice, Dubrow. Hoffman's nice. You're nice. Not me, Dubrow. I'm not so nice. Now what the hell do you want? What can I get you, my very *nice* friend, Mrs. Dubrow?

HOFFY: Esther, what happened to Sadie? She stormed outta here like a crazy woman.

ESTHER: She's a crazy woman, Hoffy, a crazy woman…Can't you get Hirsch to shave once in a while?

HOFFY: *(Laughs)* He's a crazy man, Esther Dubrow. He's a crazy man.

HIRSCH: What are you two, psychiatrists or somethin'? You want an egg cream? What do you want? I'm a candy store man, not your patient. Just a candy store man.

ESTHER: Give me a little ice cream please, Mr. Hirsch. Just a little ice cream.

(FREDA, IRIS and GABRIELLE re-enter candy store.)

GABRIELLE: Hello, Mrs. Dubrow.

IRIS: *(To GABRIELLE)* Creep!

FREDA: Cool it, Jesus Christ, you two.

HIRSCH: What are you three doin' here again? Ain't there no school today?

IRIS: It's a holiday. It's Armistice Day. Weren't you in the Army, Hirsch? What'd they do, throw ya out for not shavin'?

ESTHER: Don't talk to Mr. Hirsch like that.

HIRSCH: That kid's gonna grow up no good…wait and see.

IRIS: You won't be around to see it, Grumpo.

FREDA: Shut up, Iris. Just shut up.

ESTHER: I was just with your mother, Freda. She told me about Margie and the sheets. She told me Margie left. It sounds terrible.

FREDA: Well, Mrs. Dubrow, you know my mother. What can I tell ya?

ESTHER: Margie didn't steal the sheets, did she, Freda?

FREDA: Hey look, I dunno. My mother says so. My mother says she did. What can I tell ya?

GABRIELLE: You have a new boarder, Freda?

IRIS: What's it to *you,* Red?

GABRIELLE: I just asked. Jesus Christ. I just asked.

FREDA: Yeah, we gotta new boarder. Harry the bookie.

GABRIELLE: Harry the bookie's livin' in your apartment, Freda?

FREDA: I mean, Red, even a bookie's gotta live somewhere, ya know.

IRIS: Red. You're a creepo, a real creepo.

FREDA: Cool it, Iris, cool it.

ESTHER: Hoffy, give all the children an ice cream. I'm buyin'. What kind do ya want?

FREDA: Hey, thanks, Dubrow. Yeah, thanks a lot.

GABRIELLE: Yeah, thank you very, very much, Mrs. Dubrow.

IRIS: Shut up…Thanks Esther…you're okay.

FREDA: Ya know, Hirsch, you *could* use a shave and a new jacket.

GABRIELLE: You could use two shaves.

HIRSCH: I could use a lot more than a shave, a lot more than a jacket…and a lot less noise from you three.

IRIS: Popsicle!

GABRIELLE: Fudgsicle!

FREDA: Creamsicle!

HOFFY: There's your ice cream. *(Warmly, as always.)* Now, get the hell out of here.

FREDA: Okay, Hoffy, we're goin'. Yeah, thanks again, Dubrow. Thanks again.

(Kids exit.)

HOFFY: *(To HIRSCH)* Are you alright?

ESTHER: Yes, Mr. Hirsch, are you alright?

HIRSCH: Leave me alone. I'm alright. Leave me alone.

HOFFY: I don't like how you look. You're sure you're okay?

HIRSCH: No one likes how I look. Leave me alone.

ESTHER: Hirsch, Hirsch. You and Sadie…I've known both of you for so many years. You're my friends. But it's so hard to be nice to you two; so hard.

HIRSCH: I'll be dead soon enough, Dubrow. Then I won't be such a bother to you.

HOFFY: God forbid, Hirsch. Why did you say that?

ESTHER: I don't want you dead, Hirsch. *I* don't want you dead.

HIRSCH: Mrs. Dubrow, it don't make a damn bit of difference what you want.

(HOFFY puts arm around ESTHER. Lights up outside store, on SADIE and ESTHER.)

SADIE: Hirsch is a phony, Esther. Hirsch is a phony.

ESTHER: But he gives, Sadie. He gave a big donation to the Ladies Auxiliary.

SADIE: He's a phony, Esther. I tell you he's a phony. He does it all for show. I understand Hirsch. He's a miserable bastard. He could drop dead tomorrow and nobody would care. Maybe you'd care and maybe Hoffy …a little. But no one else.

ESTHER: I'd care. I'd care a lot.

SADIE: I know, Esther Dubrow, I know. *You'd* even care if *I* dropped dead tomorrow.

ESTHER: Why are you saying that, Sadie Greenberg? Why are you saying that?

SADIE: Because you're too nice, Esther Dubrow…too damned nice.

(They enter store; only HOFFY is there.)

HOFFY: Hirsch is dead, Mrs. Dubrow. He died yesterday.

ESTHER: Oh my God; oh my God.

SADIE: How did he die? *(No answer.)* How did he die?

HOFFY: He slit his throat. Yesterday night. He slit his throat.

ESTHER: Oh, my God; oh, my God!

SADIE: He was alone?

HOFFY: He was always alone since my sister died.

ESTHER: He slit his throat?

HOFFY: With a razor.

SADIE: What a phony bastard.

ESTHER: Sadie, stop it. How can you say that? He's dead. Mr. Hirsch is dead. He slit his throat with a razor. Mr. Hirsch is dead.

SADIE: He was a phony. Lived a phony; died a phony.

HOFFY: Why do you say that? Why are you so unkind? Why won't you be nice?

SADIE: Was he nice? Was Hirsch, the old bastard, nice? No. He wasn't nice and I'm not nice and if he was gonna slit his throat with a razor, why didn't he do it sooner and spare us all his miserable life? Me, I'm gonna wait until cancer eats me all away. But if I was gonna kill my miserable self I'd have done it long ago. Hirsch, that son-of-a-bitch, was a phony.

ESTHER: Stop it, Sadie, stop it. *(Now screaming and hitting SADIE.)* Stop it. I can't stand you. Stop it. Stop it. Stop it.

(Enter three kids.)

FREDA: What's goin' on here?

IRIS: Where's Hirsch?

HOFFY: Mr. Hirsch is dead. Mr. Hirsch died yesterday.

IRIS: Holy shit! How'd he die?

SADIE: He slit his throat with a razor. The old bastard finally shaved.

HOFFY: Mrs. Greenberg, stop it. Stop it.

ESTHER: Sadie Greenberg, stop saying those kind of things!

GABRIELLE: Oh, my God, Mr. Hirsch is dead.

IRIS: Holy shit! The creep slit his throat.

FREDA: Cool it, Iris.

IRIS: But your mom said the same…

FREDA: Cool it, Iris! I said cool it.

SADIE: (*Embracing FREDA*) Whattya think of that, darlin'? The old bastard slit his throat.

FREDA: Yeah, Mom, Hirsch is dead.

SADIE: You're not gonna get rid of me so easy, darlin'. No way.

FREDA: Easy, Mom. Easy.

IRIS: Hirsch slit his damn throat.

GABRIELLE: I feel sick.

ESTHER: Sadie Greenberg, how can you be so cruel?

HOFFY: Please, everybody, stop it. Mr. Hirsch is dead.

SADIE: (*Laughing now maniacally*) The old bastard finally shaved it clean. Finally shaved it clean. The phony bastard.

FREDA: C'mon, Mom. Let's go home. Let's go home. (*FREDA walks with SADIE to a pool of light stage right. SADIE freezes.*) Many years later, at my mother's funeral, I was thinking about Hirsch. Nobody liked my mother much, either. She wasn't very nice. But, like I said, this was childhood, long before we knew from "why." The world was simpler, then. There were nice people and not so nice people. Simpler, yes, but not so nice for the not so nice people. I stood in the light drizzle at my mother's graveside and I remembered Hirsch. "Short and bald man," I thought in an almost childlike voice, "everybody hated you. I don't know what to think about you anymore, Mr. Hirsch. You got the candy we liked, but nobody cared. You gave money and my mother said 'show-off.' I don't hate you, Hirsch, and I don't like you, but I didn't like them saying all those things about you. You're dead, Hirsch, and so now is my mother, and it was hard to be one of the not so nice people in the simple and ugly world of my childhood. You're dead, Mr. Hirsch, that's enough."

Scene 3

Scene begins in total darkness; characters are lit as they appear.

FRED: Who's that? Who's there?

FREDA: Huh?

FRED: Who's that? Who's there?

FREDA: Calm down. Take it easy. Who the hell are you? Whatta you doin' out here in the dark in the middle of nowhere?

FRED: *(Cautiously)* Who wants to know?

FREDA: Just relax, man, relax. My name's Freda. This is kinda weird. Said my name's Freda. You're…

FRED: Fred, I'm Fred.

FREDA: You live around here, Fred?

FRED: *(Nods)* Yeah. I live around here. What are you doing here?

FREDA: I dunno. I mean, I dunno exactly how I got here. I was walking and thinking about stuff. Remembering my mother and my old neighborhood.

FRED: Uh huh.

FREDA: Yeah, I was walkin' and thinkin'. Stuff about my mother… She died a while back, my mother.

FRED: A long time ago?

FREDA: Yeah. A long time ago… of cancer.

FRED: I'm sorry. I'm sorry.

FREDA: She suffered a lot. She was sick a long time. I was thinkin' about that.

FRED: That's hard.

FREDA: I was thinkin' about her. She wasn't very nice, my mother.

FRED: Oh? You want a coke or something?

FREDA: Yeah. Thanks. I've been thinking a lot about her, lately. And the others in my old neighborhood where I grew up. A candy store guy named old Hirsch. Creepy bastard. Not so nice, either.

FRED: Hirsch? A candy store guy?

FREDA: Yeah. Hirsch.

FRED: What candy store?

FREDA: The old candy store in my neighborhood near my buildin'. In the South Bronx. Between Gerard and Walton on 161st.

FRED: What was your mother's name?

FREDA: Sadie. Sadie Greenberg.

FRED: *(Draws back...wind knocked out of him, stunned, mumbling)* Sadie Greenberg? Sadie Greenberg was my mother. Hirsch was my candy store man...Who the hell are you?

FREDA: Whatta you talkin' about? Whatta you sayin'?

FRED: I'm sayin' that what you're saying can't be! Sadie Greenberg, Mr. Hirsch. Th-that's my story! Who the hell are you, anyway?

FREDA: What do you mean, that's your story?

FRED: That's my story!

FREDA: This is nuts!

FRED: Why did you come here?

FREDA: Look, Mister, I don't know what this is about, but it's late and I don't want to bother you, so I'll just go...

FRED: No! Don't go anywhere!

FREDA: How the hell do I get out of here?

FRED: Don't go! Please. Don't go.

FREDA: Jesus Christ, what is this? Listen, Fred, just calm down, man.

FRED: You've got my story. Sadie Greenberg, Mr. Hirsch. And the others... Mrs. Dubrow...

FREDA: Yeah, old nicely-nicely Esther Dubrow. She was my mother's best friend, Mrs. Dubrow...

FRED: You see, that can't be! Mrs. Dubrow was *my* mother's best friend. This can't be. You've got my story.

FREDA: Look, let's just calm down, alright? Let's figure this one out. I mean, we're two sensible people, Fred. Let's figure this thing out. (*FRED nods, more stunned than angry, and sighs.*) Now, you're saying that you're from the Bronx, too. That you knew old Hirsch, and Dubrow and Iris and all that. That's what you're sayin'?

FRED: Yeah, that's what I'm sayin'! It's right here in this story I wrote. I was readin' it just before.

FREDA: How do you like that! You're a writer, huh? I always thought I'd like to take up writing sometime. This story you wrote is all about old Hirsch?

FRED: It's...about Hirsch. And the others.

FREDA: This is incredible. It's kinda like Twilight Zone only it ain't so scary.

FRED: Anyway, this is my story, so maybe you can understand how I feel about you coming here and saying it's yours.

FREDA: Well, let's not fight about it, man.

FRED: It's not so easy as that.

FREDA: How come?

FRED: Well, who the hell are you?

FREDA: Let me see if I get this straight. If...if you know Hirsch, and Hoffy and, and the rest, and *your* mother is Sadie Greenberg and *my* mother is Sadie Greenberg…well…it seems like we have a lot in common; I mean, a hell of a lot. How could we be such strangers?

FRED: I think I'll leave that to the philosophers. But it's my story.

FREDA: *(Hurt)* Jesus, man. You make me feel like a thief in the night.

FRED: I'm sorry. I don't mean to.

FREDA: Well, let's just figure this out, okay? Relax.

FRED: Alright.

(*Pause.*)

FREDA: Makes me think of that guy—Solomon. King Solomon—remember him?

FRED: Solomon?

FREDA: Remember these two ladies come to him, and they're both claiming that the kid's theirs…remember, and they're making this whole scene? And Solomon says—"I'll fix this" and he says, "bring me my sword and I'll cut the kid in two and you can each have half."

FRED: Huh?

FREDA: I mean, who wants half a kid?

FRED: I don't get it.

FREDA: I mean, who wants half a kid? And who wants to divide up one lousy mother. Ya get it?

FRED: She wasn't much of a mother…but I loved her a lot. I dunno if I wanna divide her. She was my mother.

FREDA: Yeah. Sadie Greenberg was somethin' else. 'Member when she planted those sheets under poor old Margie's bedspread?

FRED: *(Agitated)* You read that in the story!

FREDA: It wasn't in the story, man. It wasn't in the story…Sadie Greenberg did bad shit to people…bad shit.

FRED: But I loved her. I loved her. She was my mother.

FREDA: She led a hard life…a hard life. She was miserable and she made everyone else miserable. Her and Hirsch and Iris. Didya know Iris died in a big car crash?

FRED: Yeah. I know. I know…Freda…are we the same person?

FREDA: Well…I dunno. Maybe. Let's see, I'm a Black lesbian in my mid-twenties.

FRED: Well…I'm a straight white Jewish man in my early fifties.

FREDA: That's rough, brother; that's rough.

FRED: It doesn't look like we're the same, does it? I mean, even for a dream …or an allegory or whatever…I don't think we're the same, Freda. I don't think we're the same.

FREDA: But, ah…what about Sadie Greenberg and Mr. Hirsch?

FRED: I dunno what to tell ya. I mean, maybe we're two different people with the same history!

FREDA: That can't be, can it?

FRED: I didn't think so until a few minutes ago.

FREDA: I mean, if we have the same history, how could we turn out so different? I'm Black, you're a Jew. I'm a woman, you're a man. I'm gay, you're straight. Lots of differences.

FRED: But she was *my* mother. She was *my* mother. She was *my* mother.

FREDA: My oh my oh my. You gotta lotta "my's" there, don't you, brother? Ya know, in the old King Solomon story the real mother said, "Don't chop the kid in half…give it to the other lady." And Solomon knew then who the real mom was. With you, all these "my mother, my mother" scenes makes me think Sadie Greenberg ain't your mother at all. I mean…she was in such pain…was so hurt…was so miserable… hurt so many people…Why do you possess her so? I ain't no damned philosopher, or even a writer. But this "my, my, my" shit is a bigger difference between you and me than Black, Jew, gay, straight, woman, man…ya know what I'm sayin'?

FRED: She's *my* mother. That's what I'm sayin'. She's *my* mother.

FREDA: Easy, straight. Easy.

FRED: Ya can't change that history, sister.

FREDA: Not with you clutchin' at it that way, brother. Not with you clutchin' like that.

FRED: It's my history, goddammit. It's mine. I need it. It's mine. She's my mother and she ties me to my roots…ugly, miserable, insane…but mine…my roots. She's *my* mother.

FREDA: You don't need her no more, brother. Let that miserable old mother of ours die already.

FRED: *(Sobbing)* But she's *my* mother. She's *my* mother. She's *my* mother. She's *my* mother.

FREDA: Let go of her. Let go of her. We'll both be a whole lot freer. We can have the same history and still be so wonderfully different…but not if you insist that she's your mother. White boy, give up that mother. White boy…she's dead…White boy…that's enough. That's enough.

))))

Carmen's Community

With excerpts from *Carmen*:
music by Georges Bizet, words by H. Meilhac and L. Halevy;
translated by Deborah Green

In *Carmen's Community* (1987) Newman again tells the same story twice.

Instead of presenting the stories sequentially, as he did in *Mr. Hirsch Died Yesterday,* in *Carmen's Community* Newman cuts back and forth between scenes (including selected arias and duets) from Georges Bizet's romantic 19th-century opera *Carmen* and scenes from the life of Carmencita. A contemporary New Yorker who lives in a housing project behind Lincoln Center where the opera is being performed, Carmencita and her friends are great fans of the opera. As she sees her life spinning dangerously close to the plot of *Carmen*, Carmencita must decide whether to give in to her attraction to fate—thereby winding up another victim of male rage—or to challenge fate by trying to change the "inevitable."

The attempt to do something innovative with *Carmen*—the most performed opera in the world—is not new. There have been a number of American adaptations of *Carmen.* Oscar Hammerstein's *Carmen Jones* (1943) shifted the story's location from 19th-century Seville to South Carolina during World War II, and staged it on Broadway with an all-Black cast. In the Ridiculous Theatrical Company's 1995 adaptation, Carmen was played by a man and Don José was played by a woman. But none has questioned the underlying social, political and aesthetic assumptions of Bizet's opera.

Newman, however, is not concerned with "updating" or "making relevant" an old play. He is interested in challenging the social and cultural attitudes embodied in the original—attitudes still very much with us on the eve of the 21st century. Newman's juxtaposition gives the audience (and the reader) a chance to see *Carmen* with two sets of eyes at the same time—to appreciate its power and beauty while at the same time questioning its commitment to romantic love and tragic fate.

Bizet's *Carmen* marked the theatrical emergence of a new kind of woman. Before this opera the role of the outlaw, the rebel, the heroic breaker of social convention, had been strictly reserved for men. Suddenly Carmen, self-consciously and courageously defying the conventions of society and the control of men, appeared onstage. She dies for it, of course. But she dies a heroine's death, unbending in her resistance, stubbornly refusing to give up her freedom.

Carmen's insistence on her independence is part of what has made her such a beloved character over the last 120 years. However, her death at the hands of her scorned lover resolves the story's conflicts in favor of the status quo. It is this resolution that Newman's script challenges. As in *Mr. Hirsch*, the dramatic tension is not primarily within one or the other story, but in the conflict between the two. *Carmen's Community* is thus a dialogue between the 19th and 20th centuries, between the emerging modern woman of Bizet's time and the emerging postmodern woman of our time. It is also a stylistic dialogue—tense and inharmonious at times—between the conventions of opera and the informality of American life. And it is, at the "deepest" level, a dialogue—and a struggle—between fate and development.

The developmental catalyst in *Carmen's Community* does not come from any of its primary characters—Carmen/Carmencita, Don José/Don, Escamillo/Escamil, all of whom move along parallel tracks until the very end—but from the chorus of Tenth Avenue prostitutes. In this sense, it is the *community* of *Carmen's Community* that is the star of the play. It is this chorus of women that encourages Carmen to rebel against fate, to do something outside the parameters of the opera (and society), to *act* instead of merely *behaving*. Equally to the point, the women of the chorus can only play this developmental role because of their relationship to the opera. The cigarette girls of the original *Carmen* can warn our heroine to avoid her fate, but they cannot offer an alternative activity. It is the ability to watch their own/not their own story that allows the women of *Carmen's Community* to see beyond the immediacy of their situation.

The location of development in the group, as opposed to the individual, has long informed Newman's political and therapeutic work as well as his playwriting. In *Power and Authority*, a book on psychology and politics written in 1974, Newman writes: "…the human mind is a mass mind—not an individual mind. It is a spiritual, collective mind. It is a mind capable of dialectically discerning contradiction. For in being aware of contradiction the human being has an awareness of her or his connectedness with the dialectical historical flow of history." This dynamic of group development is evident in much of Newman's work—in addition to *Carmen's Community,* it is particularly explicit in *Left of the Moon*—but nowhere in Newman's theatre oeuvre is the connection of the "group mind" to "the dialectical historical flow of history" clearer than in *Carmen's Community*.

The language in *Carmen's Community* is very different from the dialogue heard in most of Newman's other plays. Taken as a whole, Newman's language is casual, conversational, functional—poetic realism that does not draw attention to itself. But in *Carmen's Community,* the language—perhaps taking its cue from the formality and hyperbole of the opera tradition—is elevated, polemical, propagandistic.

"Dearest Carmencita, our sister, our comrade," says Woman #3, "We need you. You're our leader, not their whore. You're beautiful but you're not free. This place we live in must be Carmen's community, not Carmen's whorehouse, not Carmen's scene, and not Carmen's cemetery." To which Carmencita replies: "I love you, my sisters. You are wise women. I love you …It is a great struggle for me. But I must try to learn what you teach."

While the elevated language can, presumably, be traced back to the tone of Bizet's *Carmen* and Newman's attempt to bridge the gap between the formality of classic opera and the expectations of a contemporary American audience, it is also coherent with the polemical intent of the play. *Carmen's Community* is one of Newman's most didactic stage works—it even ends, agit-prop style, with a song that "teaches" the play's lesson. Like all of his dramatic work, *Carmen's Community* is, at least on a structural level, a dialogue, a conversation. But one side of this dialogue—the romantic notions of love and fate—is set in Bizet's text. The response to the ideological assumptions embedded in *Carmen* (and much of popular culture) therefore becomes far more polemical than conversational. *Carmen's Community* is, in this sense, also Newman's most backward-gazing play. Not only is it responding to 19th-century opera, but it looks back—in terms of didactic content, polemical language and, to some extent, form—to the agit-prop of earlier eras.

In addition to its polemical intent, Newman wrote *Carmen's Community* out of a deep love for the beauty of classical opera and a desire to share it with the Castillo audience—and, by extension, all those alienated from classical opera. After all, although opera has been expropriated by a cultural elite in America, it started out as a popular theatrical form with a large working-class following, particularly in Italy. As Newman put it, "Opera is too beautiful to reject." The question is, how do we make it ours again? *Carmen's*

Community is, among other things, an attempt to answer that question in practice.

Carmen's Community was first produced under Newman's direction in March of 1987 at Castillo. The original cast included Daphne Rubin-Vega (who would go on to star in the mega-hit *Rent,* a decade later) in the role of Carmencita. It has since had three other productions, in 1989, 1992 and 1995, each under Newman's direction. The 1992 production was staged with a mix of professional opera singers and young rappers from the All Stars Talent Show Network, who wrote the raps that were inserted into the community scenes. The 1995 production returned to the original script, which appears here.

D.F.

Carmen's Community was first produced at the Castillo Theatre in 1987. The version presented here was produced at the Castillo Theatre (Fred Newman, artistic director; Gabrielle Kurlander, producing director; Diane Stiles, managing director) in New York City on April 28, 1995. The cast, in order of appearance, was as follows:

WOMAN #1	L. Thecla Farrell
WOMAN #2	Magdalena López
WOMAN #3	Gloria Strickland
CARMENCITA	Connie Embesi
LIEUTENANT COCONUT	Roger Grunwald
OFFICER DON	Stephen Alexander Velez
ZUNIGA	Michael Narváez
DON JOSÉ	Robert Turner
SOLDIER/GYPSY	Omar Ali
SOLDIER/GYPSY (UNDERSTUDY COCONUT)	J.B. Opdycke
CIGARETTE GIRL/FRASQUITA	Madelyn Chapman
CIGARETTE GIRL/MERCEDES	Lisa Linnen
CARMEN	Karen Ann Cholhan
ESCAMIL	Louie Leonardo
ESCAMILLO	Andrés Perez
STANDBY FRASQUITA	Cathy Rose Salit
STANDBY SOLDIER/GYPSY	David Nackman

Fred Newman, director; Diane Stiles, producer; Vicki Lane, musical director/piano; Don Hulbert, flute; Joseph Spirito, set design; Elena Borstein, scenic design; Charlotte, costume design; Jessica Massad and Beth Peeler, lighting design; Michael Klein, sound design; Barry Z Levine, video design/cinematography; Brenda Ratliff, production stage manager.

In her well-named book *Opera, or the Undoing of Women,* Catherine Clément says:

The most feminist, the most stubborn of these dead women is Carmen the Gypsy, Carmen the damned.

Just the same, this woman who says no will die too. This woman who makes decisions all alone, while around her the men keep busy with their little schemes as brigands and soldiers. She is the very pure, very free, Carmen. My best friend, my favorite.

I have always heard permanent ridicule heaped on this opera; no music has been more mockingly misappropriated. Toreadors, blaring music, and a gaudy Spain… They always forget the death. When mockery becomes involved I get uneasy; something in me wants to understand. Wherever laughter takes hold, some unrecognized truth is lying low; surely we have not been reading Freud all this time just to forget his lessons. But Carmen's music, ridiculed by the North, in the South of France has become the symbolic and ritual theme for bullfight entrances, for paseos where, dressed in silk and gold, the still-intact toreros parade. This is one of opera's inspired and unconscious transferences: music devoted to a woman convokes virile heroes, and the heroes are just as brilliant and combative as Carmen, playing with the lure and the animal with horns as if they were daggers.

Carmen, whose music is the echo of living it up for generations of children who were taken to the races; Carmen, in the moment of her death, represents the one and only freedom to choose, decision, provocation. She is the image, foreseen and doomed, of a woman who refuses masculine yokes and who must pay for it with her life.

Carmen's Community, a postmodern deconstruction, asks whether we can hold on to the charm, the beauty, the seductiveness of *Carmen* (and, more generally, of classical opera) even as we engage the sexist exploitativeness of its form and content. Why bother? Perhaps because Carmen's story remains the sad narrative of real life even in a supposedly liberated culture.

Ultimately, I believe, if culture is not radically transformed, politics may be "prettied up" but will remain fundamentally untouched. But the opera is too beautiful to reject. What, then, is to be done? Let the community, not Fate, decide.

This production of *Carmen's Community* is dedicated to Don Hulbert, a founding member of Castillo and a talented classical flutist, whose contributions to our work, including, most significantly, his decency and humanity, are a permanent feature of our cultural activity.

APRIL 1995

CHARACTERS

On the street

WOMAN #1

WOMAN #2

WOMAN #3

CARMENCITA

LIEUTENANT COCONUT

OFFICER DON

ESCAMIL

In the opera

ZUNIGA

DON JOSÉ

MEN (SOLDIERS, GYPSIES)

WOMEN (CIGARETTE GIRLS, GYPSIES)

CARMEN

ESCAMILLO

FRASQUITA

MERCEDES

Act I, Scene 1

The play is set mainly on a long metal staircase which leads from backstage of the Metropolitan Opera House to Amsterdam Avenue and the working-class neighborhood in back of Lincoln Center. Beyond the staircase we see the backstage area of the opera house where Carmen, *the opera, is performed.*

WOMAN #1: Hey, Carmencita! They're playing your opera—they're playing *Carmen*—at the Lincoln Center Opera House tonight. That's beautiful, Carmencita, that's beautiful!

CARMENCITA: *(Jokingly)* Yum dum dum-dum-dum da-da-da dum.

(Women laugh and joke and dance around singing Carmen *arias with* CARMENCITA. LIEUTENANT COCONUT *enters.)*

COCONUT: Cut out that damned noise. Stop your goddamn playin' around. Go the hell home already. Don't you kids know what time it is? The opera's about to begin.

WOMAN #2: *(Sneeringly)* Hey, Lieutenant Coconut, we are home. This is our neighborhood. What'sa matter with you? You busy lookin' after Mr. Lincoln's Center tonight? Be cool, Lieutenant Coconut, be cool.

COCONUT: Quiet, you whorey bitch. I am lookin' after this neighborhood. I'm protecting it from scum like you.

WOMAN #3: *(Taunting)* Well, you piggy officer, we can look after ourselves, thank you.

(COCONUT moves to physically apprehend WOMAN #3. CARMENCITA steps seductively between them.)

CARMENCITA: Easy there, my Lieutenant Coconut.

COCONUT: Oh, it's you, Carmencita; the ringleader of these beauties here. The head of the Amsterdam Avenue whores. Well, you're certainly nice to look at so maybe we'll take you down to the precinct and run you through the lineup once again.

CARMENCITA: *(Seductively)* But Lieutenant Coconut, then we'd all miss hearing the beautiful opera music out here in the cheap seats, here in the moonlight, here on the city streets where us poor folks live.

COCONUT: I won't miss anything, Carmencita. I'll have the new rookie cop take you in. It's your old neighborhood buddy, Don. *(Blows police whistle and OFFICER DON appears.)* Officer Don, take this "beautiful Gypsy" over to the precinct and book her for prostitution. *(Pause, then whispers.)* But don't keep her there for too long.

CARMENCITA: *(Laughing)* PROSTITUTION? PROSTITUTION? Lieutenant Coconut, everyone knows you're the only whore in the neighborhood.

(COCONUT makes a menacing move and then exits.)

DON: Cool it, Carmencita. *(Grabs her.)*

CARMENCITA: Don't put your dirty hands on me, you lousy sell-out.

DON: Quiet, bitch. I'm makin' it out of this cesspool community. I'm gonna make some cash outta my street shit. I'm gonna be the MAN. You understand, Carmencita? I'm gonna be the MAN!

CARMENCITA: You are the pig. You are the goddamned pig. *(CARMENCITA stares hard at DON. Then slowly takes flower from her hair, becomes more seductive.)* Hey, Don, I wanna hear my opera tonight. I need to hear my opera. We could be friends again, Don. Like old times. You remember. Don't take me to the precinct. I must hear *Carmen*, my opera. Okay? The Lieutenant was only kidding anyway. You know Coconut. He's always jokin' around.

DON: *(Long pause)* I'll get into lots of trouble for this.

CARMENCITA: I am trouble, Don. You know that. I am trouble. But trouble can be a good fuck.

DON: *(Apprehensively releases CARMENCITA)* I get off duty at midnight. We'll meet here? By the steps.

CARMENCITA: We'll meet. After my opera, Don. After my opera.

Act I, Scene 2

Overture. Barracks on one side, cigarette factory in the distance. Onstage are ZUNIGA *and* DON JOSÉ. *Spoken dialogue.*

ZUNIGA: Don José, they say there are a lot of pretty women working in that factory there. Is that true?

JOSÉ: Yes, sir. They also say that those cigarette girls are of very easy virtue!

ZUNIGA: Yes. But at least they are pretty?

JOSÉ: Sir, I wouldn't know. I don't pay attention to women like that. Well, here they come now. You can judge for yourself.

(Sound effect of factory bell ringing; square fills with cigarette girls; soldiers come out of barracks. JOSÉ *indifferently busies himself with the chain on his saber.)*

SOLDIERS/TOWNSPEOPLE: Here they come, those flirtatious factory girls, puffing away on their cigarettes! But we don't see "la Carmencita."

CIGARETTE GIRLS: There she is! There she is! There is la Carmencita!

SOLDIERS/TOWNSPEOPLE: At last! We've been waiting for you! Carmen, how long will you go on teasing us? When will you give us your love?

(Musical intro: two bars of recitative, then aria.)

CARMEN: *(With a glance at* JOSÉ, *sings)*
When will I give my love? Who knows, it's hard to say!
Perhaps not at all, tomorrow I may. But one thing is sure: Not today!

("Habanera")

Love is free as the wayward breeze,
It can be shy, it can be bold.
Love can fascinate, love can tease,
Its whims and moods are thousandfold.

All at once it arrives and lingers
For just how long can't be foretold.
Thus it deftly slips through your fingers,
For love's a thing no force can hold.

L'amour! L'amour!
L'amour! L'amour!

A heart in love is quickly burned,
It knows no law except its own desire.
If I should love you and you spurn me,
I'm warning you, you play with fire!
If I'm in love with you,
Don't ever, ever try to spurn me.
My friend, remember, if I love you,
you play with fire!

Wait for love and you wait forever
Don't wait at all, it comes to you.
Try to grasp it,
It's far too clever,
It flies away into the blue.

Love has so many forms and shapes,
Each day it wears a new disguise.
Think you've caught it and it escapes
To catch you later by surprise.

L'amour! L'amour!
L'amour! L'amour!

(A pause. The soldiers surround CARMEN, who looks at them one by one.
Then she breaks through the circle and goes straight to JOSÉ, who is still busy
with his little chain. Spoken dialogue.)

CARMEN: Hey, friend, what are you up to?

JOSÉ: I'm fixing the chain that holds my saber.

CARMEN: (Laughing) Fixing the chain that holds your saber? Really, is that
all you want to hold? Look! Here's something to hold on to!

(CARMEN throws the flower in her hair at JOSÉ and runs away. He jumps
up. The flower has fallen at his feet. Outburst of general laughter. Factory
girls surround JOSÉ, with CARMEN singing "A heart in love is quickly
burned..." The factory bell rings again. CARMEN and her friends run into

the factory. Soldiers go into guard house. JOSÉ is left alone; he picks up the flower.)

JOSÉ: What a hussy! The way she threw that flower at me—it hit me like a bullet! But how pretty and fragrant it is! And the woman…If there really are witches, she's certainly one!

(Sound effect: commotion offstage, girls screaming.)

ZUNIGA: *(Enters)* What's going on over there? José, take two men into that factory with you and see who caused all that commotion!

(JOSÉ exits into factory with two soldiers. We hear/see the cigarette girls shouting, taunting the soldiers, pushing each other out of their way. JOSÉ collars CARMEN and brings her onstage. ZUNIGA speaks, CARMEN sings.)

ZUNIGA: What have you got to say?

CARMEN:
Tralalalalalalala
You can cut me or burn me,
and silent I'll stay.
Tralalalalalalala
You may beat me or torture me,
It doesn't matter!

ZUNIGA: Spare us your songs, and since you've been told to answer, answer!

CARMEN:
Tralalalalalalala
I will never betray what I keep in my heart!
Tralalalalalalala
There's one man I adore,
and for him I would die.

ZUNIGA: Since that's your attitude, you can sing your song to the prison walls.

CARMEN:
Tralalalalalalalalala
lalalalalalalalala
lalalalalalalalalalalala

ZUNIGA: *(To JOSÉ)* Corporal, take her away!

CIGARETTE GIRLS: Oh no! Not to prison! Not to prison!

> *(A brief pause. CARMEN raises her eyes and looks at JOSÉ. He turns, withdraws a few paces, then comes back to CARMEN, who has been watching him all the while. Spoken dialogue.)*

CARMEN: *(To JOSÉ)* Where are you taking me?

JOSÉ: To prison. You heard the order—I do as I'm told.

CARMEN: Very well, but I know you'll help me escape no matter what your captain says—because you love me!

JOSÉ: I? I, love you?

CARMEN: Yes, José! The flower I just gave you, you know, the witch's flower— you can throw it away now. The spell is working!

JOSÉ: Don't talk to me any more! You hear me? Say no more! I forbid it!

CARMEN: *(Speaks, while music goes on)* Very well, mon capitan, very well! You forbid me to talk, so I won't talk. *(Sings.)*

("Seguidilla" and Duet)

Close to the wall of Sevilla,
Lives my old friend Lillas Pastia.
I'll dance to a gay seguidilla
And I'll drink Manzanilla,
At the inn of Señor Lillas Pastia.
But when a girl goes out to dance,
She wants to have some company.
So I don't want to take a chance,
I'll take the man I love with me.
(Laughing) The man I love?
What am I saying?
I told him yesterday we're through.
My heart is free, longing for someone,
Eager for love with somebody new.
There are so many who adore me,

But I don't care for any one.
With one whole Sunday free before me,
Who wants my love? He'll be the one.
Who wants my heart?
Who comes to claim it?
Here is your chance, it still is free.
You can have it for the asking.
With my new love I'm on my way.
Close to the wall of Sevilla,
Lives my old friend Lillas Pastia.
I'll dance to a gay seguidilla
And I'll drink Manzanilla.
I will meet my love at Lillas Pastia's!

JOSÉ: *(With severity)* Enough! For the last time I forbid you to talk!

CARMEN: *(With simplicity)*
Who said I spoke to you?
I sing for my own pleasure,
I sing for my own pleasure!
And I'm thinking!
Since when are people not allowed to think?
A certain young man's on my mind,
A certain young man's on my mind,
Who loves me, and I confess,
Yes, I confess that I could love him too.

JOSÉ: *(Sings.)*
Carmen!

CARMEN: *(Pointedly)*
He's not a colonel or sergeant,
Really his rank is quite low.
He's only a corp'ral but
That's good enough for a Gypsy girl.
I'll be happy with him, I know.

JOSÉ: *(Agitated)*
Carmen, I can bear it no longer!

If I free you, if I surrender,
Will you promise to keep your word?
And if I love you, Carmen,
Carmen will you love me?

CARMEN:
Yes.

JOSÉ:
At Lillas Pastia's?

CARMEN:
We both will dance the seguidilla.

JOSÉ:
I have your word?

CARMEN:
And we will drink Manzanilla.

JOSÉ: *(He unties the rope)*
You'll keep your word!

CARMEN:
Ah!
Close to the wall of Sevilla,
Lives my old friend Lillas Pastia.
We'll dance to a gay seguidilla
And we'll drink Manzanilla,
Tralalalalalalalala!

ZUNIGA: *(Returns, to JOSÉ)* Here's the order; off you go now. And keep a good lookout.

CARMEN: *(Aside, to JOSÉ)* On the way I shall push you, as hard as I can…let yourself fall over…the rest is up to me.

Act II, Scene 1

CARMENCITA and women friends are seated on the staircase. Enter ESCAMIL.

ESCAMIL: Hey Carmen, baby, I ain't seen you for a while. You still like this opera shit? You still like hearing them sing the fancy music over at Lincoln Center?

CARMENCITA: Listen, you crazy boxer. Are you still punch drunk? You still like people hittin' you in the mouth? You like people kneeing you in the balls? Boxing is ugly, man. Ugly. This is beautiful music, you welter head…or is it welterweight?!

ESCAMIL: But Carmencita, I'm gettin' paid for bein' beat up. And I'm gettin' out of this dump we grew up in. I'm gonna be the champ someday. Escamil—welterweight champion of de world.

CARMENCITA: Maybe a champ, maybe a chump Escamil. *(Pause.)* But you're a very beautiful guy. I always liked you. At least you're not the pig.

ESCAMIL: *(Seductively)* Yeah, Carmencita. One day maybe we make it together, eh? I'll buy one of those opera records and some wine and fancy cheese and maybe we go over to my place? Whattya think?

CARMENCITA: Maybe, Escamil, maybe.

(Enter DON.)

DON: Carmen, why are you talkin to this punk—this small time pug? Don't forget our date tonight. I'm gonna get you to go straight, Carmencita; I'm gonna clean up your act and make you my wife.

CARMENCITA: Listen here, Don, the brother, Escamil, is no punk and I ain't no cop's wife. You don't make me nothin'. I dig your body, Don, and I'll fuck you. But I won't live off of you bustin' people's heads. At least Escamil's got no tin badge. He fights fair. You're the MAN now but you're still a coward, Don. A fuckin' coward.

ESCAMIL: *(Menacingly)* Yeah, brother, take off that tin badge and let's go at it right here.

CARMENCITA: *(Interceding)* Easy, you two macho clowns!

(Enter COCONUT.)

COCONUT: What's all this damn screamin' about? *(Notices CARMENCITA and DON.)* What the hell is Carmen doing here? I told you to take her down to the precinct. What's she still doin' on the street?

DON: I thought you were kiddin', Lieutenant.

ESCAMIL: *(To DON)* Asshole! Asshole! God, you're an asshole. You don't even know how to be a cop. Asshole.

COCONUT: Listen, rookie. Your fuckin' ass has had it. Now you go down to headquarters and turn *yourself* in. Confine *yourself* to quarters. I'll take care of you in the morning. *(Turns seductively to CARMENCITA.)* Why don't you and I meet after the opera and make some music, Carmencita? It's time you stopped hangin' out with punks and queers.

WOMEN: *(In opera-style chorus, semi-singing, taunting)* Who you gonna listen to, Officer Don? Carmen or the Coconut? *(Repeat twice.)*

DON: *(Full of himself, confronts COCONUT)* Lieutenant Coconut, I'm in love with Carmen. We have a date tonight. She's not yours, Lieutenant Coconut. She's mine, all mine.

COCONUT: No way, Don José. Down to the precinct or you're finished.

DON: Then I've got to go with Carmen. I'm forced to go with Carmen and the neighborhood riff-raff, and leave the goddamn police force. *(Throws his badge down.)*

(CARMENCITA and friends shout "Bravo! Bravo!" and dance around singing refrain from Carmen.*)*

ESCAMIL: *(To DON)* Still an asshole! Always an asshole.

COCONUT: *(Goes after DON)* You punk. You can't do this to me. Nobody quits on me. I'll throw your ass out, but you don't quit on Lieutenant Coconut. *(Women surround COCONUT and stop him.)* Get the fuck off or I'll lock up the whole goddamn bunch of you. *(Women persist; drag COCONUT offstage screaming.)* You're in big trouble now. Carmen, tell these broads to let me go. Goddammit, Carmen, tell them to get offa my ass!

(ESCAMIL walks off after women who are carrying COCONUT off.)

ESCAMIL: Shit! This is better than Saturday night wrestlin'!

(DON and CARMENCITA are left alone sort of embracing.)

CARMENCITA: *Forced* to be with me? You're saying you're forced to be with

me? Not very romantic, Don José. But I guess it's got to be good
enough for a Hell's Kitchen soap opera.

(*They embrace passionately, though, in* CARMENCITA'S *case, somewhat
artificially.*)

Act II, Scene 2

The tavern of Lillas Pastia. CARMEN *is with her Gypsy friends and soldiers.*
CARMEN *sings.*

("*The Gypsy Song*")

CARMEN:

    The stillness at the end of day
    Is broken by a lazy jingle,
    The sleepy air begins to tingle.
    The Gypsy dance is underway!
    And soon the tambourines of Spain,
    And strumming of guitars competing,
    Continue on and on, repeating
    The same old song, the same old strain,
    the same old song, the same refrain!
    Tra lalalalalalala!

(*Chorus sings "Tra lalalalalalala," or musicians play this vocal line.*
CARMEN *dances with friends.*)

    The copper rings the Gypsies wear
    Against their dusky skins are gleaming,
    With red and orange colors streaming,
    Swirling skirts billow through the air!
    The music guides the dancing feet
    With ever more compelling beat.
    Quite timid first, but soon the master,
    It drives them on, and growing faster,
    It starts to rise and rise to fever heat!
    Tra lalalalalalalala!

(Chorus sings "Tra lalalalalala," or musicians play this vocal line. CARMEN dances with friends.)

The Gypsy men play on with fire,
Their tambourines loudly whirring!
The pulsing rhythm fiercely stirring
Enflames the Gypsy girls' desire.
Their passion carries them away,
Their agile bodies turn and sway
In burning frenzy and abandon.
On and on they dance madly driven
Like a whirlwind no force can stay!
Tra lalalalalala!

(Chorus sings "Tra lalalalalala," or musicians play this vocal line. CARMEN dances with friends. Spoken dialogue.)

ZUNIGA: Your soldier boy—the one they sent to prison on account of you—he's free now.

CARMEN: Don José's free? *(Carelessly.)* Oh. That's nice.

CHORUS: *(Offstage)* Hurrah! Hurrah for the Toreador! Hurrah! Hurrah for Escamillo!

ZUNIGA: It's the winner of the Granada bullfights. *(To ESCAMILLO, who enters surrounded by a cheering crowd.)* Will you drink with us, comrade? To your past and future triumphs!

("Toreador's Song")

ESCAMILLO:
Thank you all, you gallant soldier-heroes,
And in return I drink to you tonight!
Long may you share a common joy,
The thrill of the fight!
Crowds are swarming in the great arena,
Excitement fills the atmosphere.
Ev'ryone waiting, loudly debating,
Wild with impatience,
They raise a thunderous cheer!

Shouts and stamping become contagious,
Till at last it's like a thunderstorm.
Day of fame for men of soul courageous,
Day of fame for men of heart!
It's time, Torero, come on! On guard! Ah!
Toreador, fight well and hard,
Proud as a king!
Yours is the ring!
And, after you have won the victor's crown,
Earn your sweet reward,
Your señorita's love!
Toreador, your sweet reward is love!

(Chorus sings or musicians play this vocal line.)

Toreador, fight well and hard, etc...

ESCAMILLO:

All at once, the crowd is silent.
What are they waiting for?
And what is happening?
Breathless expectancy
Hushes the gallery
Through the gate the bull is leaping out into the ring!
Rushing on, he charges madly,
A horse goes under, dragging down a picador,
"Come on, Torero!"
They roar like thunder.
Then, like a flash, the bull turns 'round,
Charging once more!
The lances stab his bleeding shoulder,
And blind with rage he runs.
The sand is red with blood!
Clear the ring, ev'ryone take cover!
Just one man stands sword in hand!
It's time, Torero, come on! On guard! Ah!

(CARMEN refills ESCAMILLO's glass. Spoken dialogue.)

ESCAMILLO: *(To CARMEN)* What is your name, señorita? When I fight again, your name will be on my lips!

CARMEN: Carmen, Carmencita! It makes no difference. *(Pause.)* And now, gentlemen *(to soldiers and ESCAMILLO)*, out with you! The chief of police wants the inn closed for the night!

(All leave the tavern, except CARMEN and her Gypsy friends, at least two women and two men.)

CARMEN: *(Ironically)* Well, friend, you were saying you need me on your next job?

MAN: Indeed, Carmen my love, we require your services. When it's a question of smuggling, trickery, deception and thieving, it's always good to have a sexy woman around!

CARMEN: *(Laughing, to girlfriends)* Go with him if you like—I won't go this time!

WOMEN: But why, Carmen? At least tell us the reason.

CARMEN: I'm in love!

MEN: See here, Carmen, be serious!

CARMEN: Head over heels! My friends, don't be annoyed, but love must come before duty this time.

WOMEN: But who is this man? Perhaps he'll come with us, too?

(Dragoon d'Alcala music comes up.)

CARMEN: *(Running to window)* Here he comes, my handsome soldier.

MAN: So this is the lucky man! We could use him on our side!

CARMEN: I doubt he'll join us, but it's worth a try.

("Dragoon D'Alcala Song")

JOSÉ: *(In the far distance, singing)*
    "Who are you? Someone new?
    Soldier, who goes there?
    Where are you going to?

Soldier, tell me where?"
"Looking for my rival,
I intend to meet him,
Fight him and defeat him."
"Since the case is so
Freely you may go.
Honor's stern command,
Affairs of the heart,
Those are things apart.
Soldiers understand."

(Exit men and women. JOSÉ enters. Spoken dialogue.)

CARMEN: So it's you! Just out of prison?

JOSÉ: Carmen! I'd do it all over again, if it were for you!

CARMEN: You love me, then?

JOSÉ: I adore you!

(Duet and "Flower Song")

CARMEN: *(Gaily)*
Now that you're here, I'll dance for you
For you alone, señor
And even more than that, I'll sing and play my music.

(She makes JOSÉ sit down.)

You sit right here, Don José *(With a serio-comic air.)*
You're the audience!

(CARMEN sings and dances accompanying herself with the castanets. Near the end of the dance bugles are heard behind the scenes.)

JOSÉ: *(Stopping CARMEN)*
Just one moment, wait,
Only one moment, I beg you!

CARMEN: *(Surprised)*
And just why, may I ask?

JOSÉ:

> In the distance I hear…
> Yes, our bugles are blowing,
> Sounding the retreat.
> Now, don't you hear them too?

CARMEN: *(Gaily)*

> Bravo, bravo! That's even better!
> It's not so easy a thing to sing and dance without music,
> But now we have some music which has dropped from the sky.

(She resumes her dancing. The sound of the bugles dies away.)

> Lalalalalala.

JOSÉ: *(Again stopping CARMEN)*

> You do not understand, my love!
> That was the signal,
> I must be back, in camp,
> In my quarters by night.

CARMEN: *(Stupefied)*

> Back in camp? For the night?
> *(With an outburst)* Ah, how could I be so stupid!
> I took no end of pains.
> I tried my very best,
> My very, very best,
> To entertain señor!
> So I sang and I danced,
> (May heaven forgive me)
> I was almost in love!
> Taratata!
> He hears the blasted bugle!
> Taratata!
> Dear me, and off he goes!
> Back to camp, stupid fool!
> Here! *(throwing his shako at him)*
> Take your belt, your saber and your helmet,

And go back to your camp, my boy!
Hurry back to your quarters!

JOSÉ: *(Sadly)*
You're very wrong, Carmen,
To mock me as you do!
It's painful leaving you,
No woman I have known
Has so affected me.
Never before, no never in my life,
Has any woman ever
Moved my soul so deeply!

CARMEN:
It's painful leaving me,
No woman you have known
Has so affected you.
Never before, no never in your life,
Has any woman ever
Moved your soul so deeply!
Taratata! "My God, retreat is sounding!"
Taratata! "I'm going to be late!"
Oh my God, there are the bugles,
I'm afraid I'll be late!
So he forgets me, runs off,
That's the end of his love!

JOSÉ:
And so, you don't believe my love is real!

CARMEN:
I don't!

JOSÉ:
Well then, you do not know!

CARMEN:
What more is there to know?

JOSÉ:

> Listen to me!

CARMEN:

> You'll keep them waiting!

JOSÉ: *(Violently)*

> Yes, I say you will!

CARMEN:

> No, no, no, no!

JOSÉ:

> I want it so!

(He draws from the vest of his uniform the flower which CARMEN *threw at him and shows it to her.)*

("Flower Song")

> Through ev'ry long and lonely hour
> In prison there, I kept your flower,
> and though its bloom was swiftly gone,
> Its haunting fragrance lingered on.
> In the darkness, as I lay dreaming,
> Its perfume consoling, redeeming,
> Recalled your image night and day,
> And my despair would fade away.
> At other times, I would berate you.
> I swore to detest and to hate you!
> Of what nemesis am I the prey?
> What whim of fate sent you my way?
> Then I knew I was lying:
> There could be no doubt, no denying,
> One burning hope was all I knew,
> One sole desire inflamed my heart!
> To see you, my Carmen,
> To see you!
> Carmen, the magic of your glances
> Cast a spell around my heart,

Luring me on like an enchantress,
Oh, my Carmen!
You took possession of my heart!
Carmen, I love you!

(End of duet. Spoken dialogue.)

CARMEN: You don't love me!

JOSÉ: What did you say?

CARMEN: No, no, if you loved me, you'd prove it by coming away with me. You'd take me up behind you on your horse and carry me far across the mountains!

JOSÉ: Ah! Carmen, stop!

CARMEN: Think of it! No officers to obey, the open sky, the wandering life, all the world our home! No bugles telling lovers when to part!

JOSÉ: I won't listen to you! To desert—that's shameful!

CARMEN: Alright, then, go!

JOSÉ: Carmen, I implore you!

CARMEN: No! How I hate you!

JOSÉ: Listen!

CARMEN: No! Goodbye forever!

JOSÉ: Alright! Goodbye forever!

(JOSÉ hurries towards the door; just as he reaches it, somebody knocks.)

ZUNIGA: Hello there, Carmen, hello, hello!

JOSÉ: Who's that knocking? Who's there?

CARMEN: Keep quiet!

ZUNIGA: *(Forcing door)* I'm opening up myself, and coming in. *(Sees JOSÉ; to CARMEN.)* Ah, shame, my lovely lady! This isn't a happy choice; it's demeaning to take the soldier when you've got the officer. *(To JOSÉ.)* Off with you! Get moving!

JOSÉ: No!

ZUNIGA: Get out—there's the door!

JOSÉ: I shall not go!

ZUNIGA: *(Striking him)* You bastard!

(JOSÉ and ZUNIGA go for each other, drawing swords.)

CARMEN: *(Throwing herself between them)* Help! Help! *(Gypsies appear from all sides. CARMEN points to ZUNIGA and they hurl themselves upon him and disarm him. CARMEN speaks to the tied-up ZUNIGA.)* My fine officer, love has played a nasty trick on you. Your arrival is most untimely; too bad, but we are compelled to detain you...for at least an hour.

ZUNIGA: *(Tied up)* Your invitation is a most convincing one. But later on, watch out!

MAN: All's fair in love and war!

(Music comes up—the following is sung, once.)

CARMEN: *(To JOSÉ)*
Have you at last made up your mind?

JOSÉ: *(Sighing)*
I have no choice!

CARMEN:
Ah, that does not sound too kind.
But no matter! For soon you will see
What life can be!
Happy to roam the open spaces,
All the world for our home,
We obey our will alone.
Best of all, a priceless possession.
Our life is free!

Act III, Scene 1

Women, CARMENCITA, DON.

WOMAN #1: We locked the Lieutenant in the furnace room.

WOMAN #2: Yeah, you shoulda seen the look on Coconut's face, Carmencita.

WOMAN #3: How's your opera goin', Carmen?

CARMENCITA: Beautiful. Just beautiful.

DON: You jokers locked up the Lieutenant? Jesus Christ, Carmen. You and your friends are in big trouble now and I'm a goddamned accessory. Holy shit! What the hell am I doin' here tonight?

CARMENCITA: Stop yappin' away, Don. You and me and the rest of us, we've been in big trouble our whole fuckin' lives, but at least you're free as a bird now.

DON: Free! Bullshit. I'm off to jail with you and your women friends. Carmen, I'm doin' all this out of my love for you. Do you understand that? *Do you understand?*

CARMENCITA: At least you're not a pig anymore, Don José. That's freedom. There's a freedom here on the streets.

DON: Goddamned women. Carmen, you're ruining my fuckin' life.

CARMENCITA: Stop being such a coward, Don. Stop being such a coward. (*CARMENCITA moves to speak privately with her women friends.*) I don't like it, my sisters. Something bad's gonna happen. Not with the lieutenant. He's an asshole but we've got so much shit on him that he won't fuck with us. But something else is going on here tonight— something I just don't understand.

WOMAN #1: I'll tell ya what I think, sister Carmencita. It ain't cops and it ain't boxers and it ain't lieutenants that's our problem…it's just MEN …it's the whole stinkin' lot of 'em.

WOMAN #2: I hear you, Sister Alma. But our problem's not too much MEN. Our problem is too little WOMEN! MEN have too big a goddamn role and us women—we have too small a role, too weak a role, too victimized a role. In an opera, in a community, in this whole fuckin' world.

Everywhere. "Carmen" is a sister's name but it's always all about MEN, Carmencita.

WOMAN #3: Tell it, my sister. Carmencita, those bad omens you keep talkin' about all the time are not oMENs, they're plain MENs. Dearest Carmencita, our sister, our comrade. We need you. You're our leader, not their whore. You're beautiful but you're not free. This place we live in must be Carmen's community, not Carmen's whorehouse, not Carmen's scene, and not Carmen's cemetery.

CARMENCITA: I love you, my sisters. I love you dearly. Yet I do not understand you sometimes. Because you speak of men and women but you do not mention Fate. But do we not know that Fate is our master?

WOMAN #3: Fate, like love, is indeed our master. Still another man. Truly a rebellious bird, a macho vulture. But you must not be Fate's whore. Far more than Escamil and Don José and Coconut, Fate and his hand-servant ROMANTIC LOVE are the real MAN, the macho sado-masochist who turns all of our people, women and men alike, into low-paid prostitutes, Carmencita.

CARMENCITA: I love you, my sisters. You are wise women. I love you. *(They embrace passionately.)* It is a great struggle for me. But I must try to learn what you teach. *(They embrace again.)*

DON: What are you, fuckin' lesbians?

CARMENCITA: Shut your mouth, Don.

DON: *(Grabs her angrily)* Don't tell me to shut my mouth. I've given up everything for you tonight, Carmencita. Everything.

(Women move to protect CARMENCITA, but before they can, ESCAMIL enters.)

ESCAMIL: Get your pig hands offa her. She's too good for you. She's too good for anybody around here...but me. I've always loved her since we were kids and no scummy ex-cop is gonna touch her.

(ESCAMIL and DON fight: DON pulls a knife; CARMENCITA saves ESCAMIL; Women stop the fighting altogether.)

WOMAN #1: Stop this fucking fighting. You macho bastards are gonna get us all arrested for real.

DON: (*To* CARMENCITA, *menacingly*) Carmen. I'll never leave you. You'll never be rid of me, no matter what. You fall for this boxer here and I'll kill you, I swear it. I'll fuckin' kill you.

CARMENCITA: You do not scare me, ex-cop. You don't scare me, Don José.

(*DON exits as entr'acte music begins.*)

Act III, Scene 2

In the smugglers' camp. Spoken dialogue.

MAN: Rest here for an hour, comrades; meanwhile I want to make quite sure there are no surprises—we must get our goods past the guards.

(*During the scene,* CARMEN *and* JOSÉ *enter. Some of the Gypsies light a fire, near which two Gypsy women seat themselves. The others wrap themselves in their cloaks, lie down and go to sleep.*)

CARMEN: (*To* JOSÉ) Why do you stare like that?

JOSÉ: I'm thinking about what I have become—a smuggler, a renegade, a deserter!

CARMEN: Well, then, why don't you go straight? This Gypsy life means nothing to you. You might as well leave us—the sooner the better!

JOSÉ: Go away and leave you?

CARMEN: Precisely!

JOSÉ: Leave you, Carmen? Listen, if you say that again...

CARMEN: You would kill me, perhaps? What a look...you don't answer... What do I care? After all, Fate is the master.

(*CARMEN crosses to the two women by the fire, who are dealing cards and telling their futures. She sits down and picks up the cards. Sings.*)

Let's see what the cards hold for me. (*She starts to turn up the cards.*) Diamonds! Spades!

(Aria)

It's death! It is plain.
First for me, then for him.
But all the same, it's death!
You can't evade the truth the cards are saying clearly,
No matter how you try.
No use to deal again, they're telling you sincerely,
The cards will never lie!
If Fate saved you a happy page within its book,
No need for anxiousness.
You know you'll get a lucky card before you look,
Your fate is happiness.
But if your time has come and you are evil-starred,
And if the end is near,
You can try twenty times, the unrelenting card
Will reappear once more; if you are evil-starred,
If there is death in store,
The unrelenting card will reappear once more!
(Turning up the cards.)
Once more, once more,
There's death in store.

(Gypsy men enter. CARMEN turns to them. Spoken dialogue.)

All clear?

MAN: All clear! We'll get through, while we have the chance! José, you're on guard. Shoot on sight if need be.

(Everyone exits. JOSÉ follows, to the edge of the stage, gazing in the distance. He sees something, aims his rifle and fires.)

ESCAMILLO: *(Enters, examining the hole in his hat)* A little bit lower and it would have been all over for me.

JOSÉ: Your name, answer!

ESCAMILLO: Hey, easy now, friend! I'm Escamillo, Toreador of Granada!

JOSÉ: Escamillo! I know your name, you're welcome here; but really, my friend, you were foolish to take so great a risk!

ESCAMILLO: You may be right. But you see, I'm in love, and any man worth his salt takes his chances in love!

JOSÉ: The girl you love is here?

ESCAMILLO: Right you are. A most exciting Gypsy girl.

JOSÉ: Her name?

ESCAMILLO: Carmen.

JOSÉ: Carmen! (*Menacingly, pulling a knife.*) You know, we don't let our Gypsy girls go without a fight!

ESCAMILLO: Ah, I understand! The deserter I heard about that she loved— or rather *used* to love—is you, then.

JOSÉ: Yes, I'm the one!

ESCAMILLO: (*Draws his knife*) I'm delighted, my friend. Now I know where I stand!

(*JOSÉ draws his knife and they both wrap their left arms in their cloaks. They fight. ESCAMILLO slips and falls. Enter CARMEN and the other Gypsies. She rushes forward and stays JOSÉ's hand.*)

CARMEN: Stop, stop, José!

ESCAMILLO: (*Getting to his feet*) Really, I'm overjoyed that it should be you, Carmen, who saved my life!

MAN: Enough, enough, no more quarreling! We must get going. (*To ESCAMILLO.*) And you, my friend, good night!

ESCAMILLO: Till we meet again, I bid you all farewell.

(*ESCAMILLO bows to CARMEN and leisurely exits, to strains of "Toreador's Song." JOSÉ tries to attack him but is held back by Gypsies.*)

JOSÉ: (*To CARMEN*) Take care, Carmen, don't drive me too far!

MAN: (*To JOSÉ*) And you, my friend, you should be on your way!

CARMEN: Go on! Go on! It's better this way. You never did belong with us.

JOSÉ: You're telling me to go so that you can run after your new lover! No! I won't go! Death alone can part us!

GYPSIES: It will be your death, José, if you don't go now. José, take care! Don't tempt Fate.

JOSÉ: *(To CARMEN)* You are mine and mine you'll stay. Destiny links your fate with mine!

(Gypsies force him at gunpoint.)

GYPSIES: Ah, take care, Don José!

JOSÉ: *(To CARMEN)* Have your way, I'm going, but we shall meet again!

(JOSÉ hurries off. We hear the "Toreador's Song" in the distance, sung by ESCAMILLO.)

Act IV, Scene 1

CARMENCITA, WOMEN, ESCAMIL.

ESCAMIL: Carmencita, how will this thing end? How will it end? How will this fuckin' fight end? I kinda dig this opera. It's kinda like our lives here on the streets. Tell me, Carmencita, how does it end?

CARMENCITA: Listen to the music, Escamil, listen to the music. Maybe the music will tell you the ending or maybe, just maybe, we'll make our own ending this time.

Act IV, Scene 2

The fourth act opening music is playing over the crowd scene taking place in a square in Seville, with the walls of the bull ring in the background. A bullfight is about to take place and there is great excitement in the crowd, which is milling about. At last ESCAMILLO appears, accompanied by a radiant and magnificently dressed CARMEN. He and CARMEN sing.)

ESCAMILLO:
    If you love me, Carmen

Then today, of all days,
You will be proud of me,
If you love me, if you love me.

CARMEN:

I am yours, Escamillo,
And may God be my witness,
I never loved a man with such passion before!

TOGETHER:

How I love you, how I love you!

(ESCAMILLO *leaves.* FRASQUITA *and* MERCEDES *enter. Spoken dialogue.*)

FRASQUITA: (*Approaches* CARMEN) Carmen, a word of advice, don't stay here.

CARMEN: And why, may I ask?

MERCEDES: Don José is here! He's hiding among the crowd; look!

CARMEN: Yes, I see him. But I'm not afraid of him. I'll wait for him here.

MERCEDES: Carmen, believe me, take care!

CARMEN: I'm not afraid of anything!

FRASQUITA: Take care!

(FRASQUITA *and* MERCEDES *enter the arena with crowd, and in withdrawing reveal* JOSÉ, *leaving him and* CARMEN *alone downstage. They sing.*)

(*Final Chorus*)

CARMEN:

José.

JOSÉ:

Carmen.

CARMEN:

Frasquita and Mercedes both told me you were near,
That you would look for me.
And they even believe my life will be in danger.
But I have courage and decided to stay.

JOSÉ: *(Gently)*
> I do not mean you harm.
> I beg you, I implore you,
> What used to be is done,
> The past is dead, it is over.
> Yes, we'll start life anew.
> It will be a new existence,
> Far away, just you and me.

CARMEN:
> You are talking like a dreamer.
> I won't lie, I won't pretend!
> What was between us is over;
> Once and for all this is the end!
> You know, I never lie,
> Once and for all, this is goodbye!

JOSÉ:
> Carmen, oh let me persuade you,
> Yes, life is still before you.
> I beg of you, please, come away with me,
> For I adore you.
> *(Passionately)* Ah Carmen, come away with me,
> We both can be happy still!

CARMEN:
> No, I have made my decision,
> And I know that this is the hour.
> But come what may, I do not care, no, no!
> No. I will not give in to you.

JOSÉ:
> Carmen, life is still before you...

CARMEN:
> There's no use at all imploring,
> My heart holds no love for you.
> No, my love for you is dead.
> I will not hear what you say.

There's no hope for you.
My love is dead, you hope in vain.
I won't go with you,
Never will!

JOSÉ: *(Anxiously)*
You don't love me at all?

CARMEN: *(Tranquilly)*
I love you no more.

JOSÉ:
But I, I love you more than ever.
Carmen, I worship and adore you!

CARMEN:
What's the good of that?
Your words are pointless now!

JOSÉ:
Carmen, Carmen, I adore you!
Alright, I will remain an outlaw,
I'll rob and steal for you.
I will do anything, yes, all you ask,
If only you will come with me Carmen!
Those golden days, have you forgotten them?
How much we loved each other!
(With desperation) O Carmen, do not leave me now!

CARMEN:
Carmen will never yield!
Free I was born, and free Carmen will die!

(Hearing the cries of the crowd in the amphitheatre applauding ESCAMILLO, CARMEN makes a gesture of delight. JOSÉ keeps his eyes fixed on her. When CARMEN attempts to enter the amphitheatre JOSÉ steps in front of her. Musicians play through chorus part.)

JOSÉ:
Is it he?

CARMEN:

Let me go!

JOSÉ:

That is your fine new lover
Applauded by the mob!

CARMEN:

Let me go, let me go!

JOSÉ:

Never, never, you will not run to him!
Carmen I'll make you follow me!

CARMEN:

Let me go, Don José, I'll never go with you!

JOSÉ:

You're on the way to him, Carmen.
(Furiously) You love this man?

CARMEN:

I love him!
Defiant in the face of death,
With my dying breath,
I shall love him!

(*CARMEN* again tries to enter the amphitheatre but is stopped by JOSÉ. *Strains
of "The Toreador's Song" are heard.*)

JOSÉ: *(Violently)*
And so I have lost my salvation.
I am damned to hell, so that you
May run to your lover, you harlot,
And in his arms jeer at my despair!
I swear to God you shall not go.
I say, you are coming with me!

CARMEN:

No, no, I won't!

JOSÉ:

Once again, time is getting short!

CARMEN: *(Angrily)*

Go ahead, kill me at once!
Or let me go inside!

JOSÉ: *(Madly)*

For the very last time, Carmen!
Will you come with me?

CARMEN:

No, no! *(Tears a ring from her finger.)*
Remember this ring?
The ring that you once gave me! Here! *(Throws ring away.)*

JOSÉ: *(Rushing towards CARMEN)*

By God, then die!

(CARMEN attempts to escape, but JOSÉ catches up with her at the entrance of the amphitheatre. He stabs her; she falls and dies. JOSÉ, distraught, falls on his knees beside her. Offstage ESCAMILLO sings, or orchestra plays through this choral part.)

Toreador, fight well and hard,
Proud as a king,
Yours is the ring,
And after you have won the victor's crown,
Earn your sweet reward,
Your señorita's love.

(The crowd re-enters the stage.)

Toreador, your prize is love!

JOSÉ: *(In utter despair)*

I have killed my own love!
I killed the one I love!
She is dead!
O my Carmen, how I loved you!

Act V, Scene 1

WOMEN, CARMENCITA, ESCAMIL

ESCAMIL: *(Embracing CARMENCITA)* Carmencita, I saw what happened to Carmen. That's some heavy shit…heavy shit. But don't you worry about that creep Don, ya know. I won't let him harm you.

CARMENCITA: I'm not afraid of Don, the rookie pig. And I can take care of myself.

WOMAN #3: Beware, Carmencita. The force of the opera is strong. You know that. Don't confuse your arrogance with your power. And surely do not confuse a man's love with your security.

(CARMENCITA reaches out to WOMAN #3 to hold hands while also holding ESCAMIL's hand. Enter DON, insane with rage.)

DON: Here you are between another man and your fuckin' lesbian friends, Carmen. *(Pulls a gun and points it at CARMENCITA.)* You are a whore—a dirty whore and yet I love you and so you have ruined my life. But still, still, I adore you and I will never let you go to this fool of a boxer or these perverted women.

ESCAMIL: *(Throws himself in front of CARMENCITA)* You will not kill her, ass-hole. This is no opera bullshit. This is real life.

(ESCAMIL jumps DON and they battle for the gun. The women and CARMENCITA pull them apart, grab DON's gun and surround the two men.)

WOMAN #2: You men will never again determine Carmen's fate.

WOMAN #1: Fate. *(Laughs.)* Fate, I have learned from my sisters, is the authority of men disguised as religion. It justifies the privilege of men. And it justifies the rape of women.

WOMAN #3: Carmencita, fate is for the victimized. Power, only power, is a woman's passion.

CARMENCITA: *(Runs to CARMEN lying "dead" on opera stage)* But my opera, my beautiful opera. What of my opera? What of my Carmen? What is Carmen's fate?

WOMAN #3: Bring her here, Carmencita. It is your opera now; it is our opera now. We lay claim to it; it can no longer control us. Bring it here to Carmen's community. You have the power, Sister. You have the power. The world is our stage. Bring her here.

(*CARMENCITA lifts CARMEN to her feet and the two CARMENS walk out to the staircase with the opera cast following; they sing a new version of "Habanera"; the street gang joins opera cast in singing and dancing.*)

(*"Habanera"*)

Love's a bird
A macho bird,
At times it's noisy
And at times unheard.
Love and Fate,
When those two mate
Their sex is sordid
And filled with Hate.

ARISE
ARISE
OH, SISTERS,
WE MUST
ARISE!

Hear us sisters
Our time has come.
We can't be victims
And we can't be dumb.
The MAN will kill us
If we do not rise.
With FATE as
Master
All of humankind dies.

When man is king
And Love's their thing
A woman's life
Is dangling on a string.

Our Fate is cast—
The Whore's life,
A low grade prostitute,
A high grade wife.

ARISE
ARISE
OH, SISTERS,
WE MUST
ARISE!

Hear us sisters
Our time has come.
We can't be victims
And we can't be dumb.
The MAN will kill us
If we do not rise.
With FATE as
Master
All of humankind dies.

Our Power sings
The women's day
With passions powerful
Not grabbed away.
We'll change the world
With Carmen's might
No sad seductiveness
No petty fight.

ARISE
ARISE
OH, SISTERS,
WE MUST
ARISE!

Hear us sisters
Our time has come.
We can't be victims

And we can't be dumb.
The MAN will kill us
If we do not rise.
With FATE as
Master
All of humankind dies.

When women rise
To lead the class
No more will
Fate and Love
Make us the Ass.
So join us men
Who know the score
Who fight for Justice
And not L'amour.

ARISE
ARISE
OH, SISTERS,
WE MUST
ARISE!

Hear us sisters
Our time has come.
We can't be victims
And we can't be dumb.
The MAN will kill us
If we do not rise.
With FATE as
Master
All of humankind dies.

〉〉〉

No Room for Zion

(A Kaddish by a Communist Jew)

No *Room for Zion (A Kaddish by a Communist Jew)* (1989) began as a magazine article/story. It first appeared in the August 1989 issue of *Stono*, a journal of culture and politics published by the Castillo Cultural Center. It was an analysis of the sociological, economic and political changes in the Jewish American community since the Second World War and a polemic, from the left, against Zionism.

The play remains a sociological analysis and a political polemic. It is also (like *Mr. Hirsch Died Yesterday*, written two years earlier) a performed memoir. The setting of *Zion* is the old neighborhood in the Bronx, two months after Hirsch killed himself. Fred, again one of the play's characters, and his wife Rie talk about Hirsch's suicide, discuss other friends from the neighborhood (several of them—Esther Dubrow, Harry the bookie, Hoffman— appeared or were also mentioned in *Mr. Hirsch Died Yesterday*), and worry about what's becoming of their community. Although the play is set in the late 1940s, it is not the adolescent Fred whom we meet, but the middle-aged man projected back to the neighborhood as it had been nearly 50 years earlier.

It is this neighborhood—Jewish and working-class—that is the real subject of the memoir. The neighborhood, and the community, were disintegrating. The Jewish community of Newman's youth was leaving the Bronx en masse, moving to the suburbs, climbing the ladder of American upward mobility, and, in the process, abandoning the radical, inclusionary politics of pre-revolutionary Russia and Depression-era America for post-Holocaust anti-communist Americanism and Zionist chauvinism. For Newman, something precious and profound, something fundamental to Jewishness itself, was being lost in the transition.

Analysis, polemic, memoir—*No Room for Zion* is all of these, and it is as well a "secular prayer" for the dead. The subtitle of the play is, after all, "A Kaddish by a Communist Jew." Here Kaddish, the Jewish prayer for the dead, is not being said for an individual (although surely Mr. Hirsch and Fred's father are included in it); the death(s) it commemorates are far more tragic—the death of Jewish progressivism, the death of Jewish community, the death of the Jews as a people. As Fred puts it in the play, "…international Jewry, which bravely survived German fascism, succumbed to American capitalism."

The prologue of *Zion* establishes the setting and provides us with two very likable characters, Fred and Rie. Together they recite the Kaddish, which consists of two parts. The first—the bulk of the performance—is text taken directly from the article; the second is a free verse poem which Newman wrote after his first trip to Europe in 1989. The two parts flow seamlessly into each other, and in performance it is virtually impossible to separate the poetry from the polemic.

This is the most polemical of Newman's plays, although it differs radically from the agit-prop tradition of reducing complex issues and conflicts to simple dramatic parables. It is also unlike those "socially-conscious" plays of the late 19th and early 20th centuries which overlay their argumentation with the veneer of "realism." Rather, *No Room for Zion* directly presents a complex and sophisticated political analysis onstage. The fact that much of it takes the form of stories about the old neighborhood helps to personalize the political while in no way covering up or simplifying it. In this sense, *No Room for Zion* is a performed polemic as distinct from a polemical play.

Indeed, by most definitions *No Room for Zion* is not a play at all. It has no plot, no character development, very little dialogue. Perhaps more than any other of his scripts, *No Room for Zion* reveals the experimental nature of Newman's work. As a playwright and director he has never been interested in meeting the criteria of drama nor in conforming to (or even "playing with") the conventions of the theatre. In fact, Newman considers defining itself to be anti-developmental. Instead, all of his scripts are experiments designed to help create performatory experiences, and the hybrid *No Room for Zion*—a mix of memoir, polemic, Kaddish, poem, and play—is the most obviously experimental.

No Room for Zion is the only Newman play (perhaps the only play, period) to contain within it an analysis of another of the author's plays. Appropriately, the play discussed is *Mr. Hirsch Died Yesterday*, to which *Zion* has so many connections. As part of the discussion of *Mr. Hirsch,* it also contains the first of Newman's writings on dramatic theory: "*Hirsch* is not a representation, and, as such, is not about anything. Rather *Hirsch* is an activity or perhaps a guide to an activity; not a play that teaches, but a play that learns (we teach it; it does not teach us)." Besides shedding light on *Mr. Hirsch*, this concise statement can serve as a manifesto (if any is needed) for developmental theatre as it has emerged at Castillo under Fred Newman's direction.

No Room for Zion was produced twice at the Castillo Theatre, first in October of 1989 and again in December of 1990. Both productions were directed by Newman and featured him in the role of Fred. Reflecting Newman's practice of writing roles for specific actors, Rie was played in both productions by Gabrielle Kurlander (whose nickname is Rie). Castillo's producing director and one of its leading actresses, Kurlander has been in a close personal relationship with Newman for nearly a decade.

D.F.

YIDDISH GLOSSARY

KADDISH: Jewish prayer for the dead.

YAHRZEIT CANDLES: Candles lit on the one-year anniversary of a death.

DAILY FORWARD: In the first half of the 20th century, a daily Yiddish-language socialist newspaper based in New York City, the largest circulation Yiddish paper in the U.S. Today, it is a Zionist weekly published in English.

YIZKOR: Colloquial term for the Kaddish, literally the first two syllables of the prayer.

TANTA: Aunt.

REBBITSIN: A rabbi's wife.

YISGADAL V'YISKADASH...: The beginning of the Kaddish.

SHUL: Literally, "school." Used informally as a term for a synagogue.

MINYAN: A quorum of 10 Jewish men over the age of 13 needed in order to hold Jewish religious services.

BAR MITZVAH: A religious confirmation service held for Jewish males at age 13, as a ritual of transition into manhood.

KOSHER: Jewish dietary law, which among other strictures, forbids the eating of pork and shellfish, and requires the separation of meat and dairy products in cooking and eating.

BROCHAS: Blessings recited in Jewish religious services; a boy performs these for the first time at his Bar Mitzvah.

HAFTORAH: A chapter from the book of the Prophets, read weekly. Bar Mitzvah boy reads from this.

MITZVAH: A good deed. Jews are commanded to do these.

No Room for Zion (A Kaddish by a Communist Jew) was first produced at the Castillo Theatre (Fred Newman, artistic director; Gabrielle Kurlander, producing director) in New York City in October 1989. The cast was as follows:

FRED . . . . Fred Newman
RIE . . . . Gabrielle Kurlander

Fred Newman, director; Emmy Gay, producer; Wilton Duckworth, set and lighting design; Jennifer Ruscoe, costume design; Rhonda Robinson, music design; Michael Klein and Diane Stiles, slide design; Kenneth Hughes, production stage manager.

A NOTE FROM THE AUTHOR

No Room for Zion (A Kaddish by a Communist Jew) is a prayer for the dead. The Jewish people, abandoned by so-called white civilization in our holocaust, were in its aftermath victims of the Zionist hucksters who profited from the mass genocide. I viewed this deadly process as a child/young man, from the vantage point of a poor Jewish family on welfare in the South Bronx who did not "make it" to Long Island. My father died in the forties even as Israel was born (and Zionism was "reborn"). But Israel's creation and the accompanying evolution of the assimilated American Jew, the middle-class Zionist Jew, was in no way a real birth. For its middle-class Zionist midwives made a political deal with the capitalist devil for our collective soul. Our people died, the Jewish people were buried alive, even as Long Island, USA became a hotbed of Zionism, a stage for the vulgar "catered affair."

No Room for Zion explores the sadness, the tragedy, the pain and the outrage of our death in a prayer, a Kaddish, which has no god.

OCTOBER 1989

CHARACTERS
(in order of appearance)

FRED
RIE

A kitchen with a table covered by a white lace tablecloth. On the table are a menorah and books; around it are three wooden chairs. There is a radiator (with cover) near a window. More books are stacked on the floor. On the table and the radiator are three Yahrzeit candles. Through a window, a New York winter sunset can be seen. To the right is a lectern with a light to read by; next to it is a little table or stool with a Yahrzeit candle. Music plays from a radio on the radiator. There is a coffee pot and a plate of halvah on the table. RIE, *dressed in simple, working-class 1940s style, is seated at the table reading the* Daily Forward.

FRED: *(Offstage)* Rie. Rie?

RIE: *(Looking up from the newspaper)* Whaddya want, honey?

FRED: *(Still offstage)* Do we have time for sex?

RIE: *(Short pause)* I don't think so, honey. The sun's almost down. After dinner we'll have sex.

FRED: Okay, baby... is it time yet to say Yizkor?

RIE: *(Back to reading the* Forward*)* Almost, honey, almost.

> *(*FRED *enters, wearing a flannel shirt and khaki pants. He carries a yarmulka which he puts on the table. He hugs and kisses* RIE *lovingly from behind, and sits down at the table.)*

FRED: Baby, are we goin' to see Tanta Hinda this week... or next week?

RIE: I dunno, honey... next week, I think. Next week. *(*FRED *picks up a book;* RIE *continues to read the paper. Pause.)* How much do you love me, honey?

FRED: I love you more than anything in the world.

RIE: We'll have sex after dinner?

FRED: *(Jokingly)* Don't ya hafta wait an hour?

RIE: *(Swats* FRED *playfully)* That's for swimming, wise-ass.

FRED: Okay, okay, baby. Listen, when I say the Kaddish I'll make up a little prayer for especially good sex tonight.

RIE: *(With a show of mock indignation; half serious, half joking)* That's a terrible thing to say. That's terrible.

FRED: Why? God knows about sex. I'll bet God is sexy as hell.

RIE: …I'll bet *she* is.

FRED: But I'll bet she's not as beautiful as you.

(Pause.)

RIE: Ya know, it's been almost two months since Hirsch died?

FRED: I know.

RIE: …I can't go near his old candy store. I keep thinking of him with his throat slit, bleeding to death, the razor by his side. Why did he do it, honey? Why?

FRED: I don't know, baby. I don't know.

RIE: It's becoming a very sad neighborhood, honey…a very sad time.

FRED: Mr. Kover is getting more and more crazy. And Mrs. Kover, so sweet and so sad.

RIE: Rabbi Zion and the rebbitsin seem more and more bewildered.

FRED: And Esther…well, Esther is Esther.

RIE: Harry the bookie…lonelier than ever. Stella has a little money now. She seems silly. Even Hoffy doesn't smile anymore.

FRED: And Yussie. Yussie won't make it, baby. Yussie won't make it.

(Pause.)

RIE: I think it's time for the Kaddish, honey. *(FRED picks up a prayer book and puts on the yarmulka. He walks toward the window and radiator. When he's almost there, he turns to RIE.)*

FRED: *(Smiling warmly)* Sex after dinner, baby?

RIE: Do the Kaddish, my honey. Do the Kaddish, my love. *(Pause.)*

FRED: Yisgadal, V'Yiskadash, sh'm…(*Scene fades to black. Lights up on* RIE.)

RIE: Fred's first play was called *Mr. Hirsch Died Yesterday*. I was in it. It is about discovery and the shockingly ordinary process and circumstance that give rise to it. It is about working-classness as some few people lived it in a Jewish community in the South Bronx in the '40s and early '50s. It is easy to misunderstand *Hirsch*. Progressive-minded people with their liberal morality are particularly prone to missing the point. They would often say after a performance, "I get it. Hirsch and Sadie are not *really* bad and Hoffy and Esther are not *really* good." But Hirsch and Sadie *are* bad enough and Hoffy and Esther *are* pretty good. It is just that good people do bad things and bad people do good things and being bad doesn't make you sub-human and being good doesn't make you a god, etc., etc.

Mr. Hirsch is also about Jews and what has become of Jews, the sellout of Jews by the international community and the sellout by Jews of the Jewish community. "Why, where is all that in *Hirsch?*" some people ask. Well, *Hirsch* is not a representation, and, as such, is not formally about anything. Rather, *Hirsch* is an activity or perhaps a guide to an activity, not a play that teaches, but a play that learns. (We teach it; it does not teach us.) But, says the liberal representationalist, "What did you *want* it to say? What is it *about*?" Heiner Müller, the East German playwright, speaks. He says, "If I know what I want to say, I say it; I don't have to write it." Danke, Herr Müller, danke. The play is neither outside of history, nor is it a product of history. It is a *maker* of history. It is the form and not merely the content which is political (as Müller also insists, citing Godard). And what of *Hirsch*'s disheveled form? I do not know its form. Indeed, I do not care to know its form. For not only must the form be radical but form itself must be radicalized. Rather I (and hopefully some others as well) will seek to form it. It is, to use Lev Vygotsky's term, a "tool and a result." And in Fred's words, "a tool to make a tool to make a tool…" And in one forming of it, *Hirsch* is *informally about* Jews and our abandonment: by others, by ourselves and of others.

Fred always comes home to write.

FRED: Rabbi Zion and his wife (the rebbitsin) came to our neighborhood from Eastern Europe in 1946, just after the war. The small wood-framed walkup shul he took over was just a dry cleaning store away from the rundown two-story house—also wood—that he and his family lived in. I was eleven in 1946, still shocked by my father's sudden death the year before and the family's ensuing plunge from the edges of the lower middle class to the heart of welfare poverty. In that first year of mourning I came to know the very un-American Rabbi Zion and his tiny shul reciting the Kaddish each evening. "Yisgadal, V'Yiskadash…," whispering from a fading transliteration of the mourner's Kaddish written on a blue-lined sheet of yellow paper which I slipped into the funny-smelling prayer book each service. Rabbi Zion was a good man, a poor man, a man who made the altar at which he stood and the Torah behind him seem a little less forbidding. The congregation of Rabbi Zion's synagogue in the winter of 1946 was also poor…and small. The Rabbi walked the cold streets as the sun fell beneath the empty Yankee Stadium searching for men to make a minyan (I was of no help since I was not yet Bar Mitzvahed). Miraculously he always found 10 so I never discovered what would have become of my prayer if the requisite number failed to gather. But Rabbi Zion didn't fail. In his worn-out coat, collar up, shawl wrapped around his neck, he made his minyan and as the Jews of my Bronx working-class neighborhood slowly dragged their feet up the stairs to Zion's shul, I placed my transliterated Kaddish into the old book. "Yisgadal, V'Yiskadash…"

The Kovers were the neighborhood's weirdos. Mr. Kover, a plumber by trade, was a short and frenzied man, fanatically orthodox, who in most of his public existence sped through the community on his way to Zion's shul or back home again making little social contact. Mrs. Kover was a dear woman, kindly and gentle, subserviently attending to her kosher home, her neurotic husband and her three children with a grace and simplicity that totally denied the objective pain of her oppression.

The oldest child, as is often the case, was an ill-mixed combination of his parents. Yussie Kover, who became my best friend as I became poor (and as *my* family became the neighborhood's other weirdos), was physically his father in miniature. Emotionally, his basic structure was orthodox male, but his mother's capacity to love had somehow touched him and Yus was able to give even if he never did learn how to be given to.

It was Yus, already fluent in Hebrew at 11, who transliterated the Kaddish for me. A couple of years later, in fact, Yus and I pulled off the "Miracle on 158th Street" when he taught me by the method of transliteration all the brochas and the haftorah (admittedly short!) necessary for me to perform at my Bar Mitzvah at Zion's little shul. (And in 1948, in Zion's still uncrowded workplace, when the confirmation ended I whispered to Yus, "Today I am a minyan maker.")

The little Jewish working-class neighborhood in the South Bronx in the late 1940s had many characters. Dave the butcher. Hymie the chicken plucker. Harry the bookie, and Esther (remember, from *Hirsch*) and her ceaselessly barking little black dog. Stella who pretended she was middle-class until one day she was, but she never stopped pretending. A Runyonesque collection of Yiddish-speaking Jewish Americans who for the most part had suffered the Holocaust in the relative safety of America. But the very European Rabbi Zion and his family (who lived through the Nazi genocide in Europe), the Kovers, and my misshapen family were, in many ways, the extremes of the community. And while the more "sane and solid" citizens of Gerard and Walton Avenues did their fair share of brutalizing the members of the social periphery, there was in this *working-class Jewish community* room for everyone. "Isn't dis vat is community after all?" Rabbi Zion would say in his broken English, with his thick accent. "In community, in our Jewish community, der must be room for all." So said this simple working-class rabbi at my Bar Mitzvah in June of 1948. There must be room for all.

RIE: This gentle man who had lived through the murder of our people by the Aryan scum had as well survived the spiritual outrage of abandonment by Jews and non-Jews alike, in Europe and America, in the face of Hitler's big dollars and gas chambers. Oh yes, there were those who did not abandon. There were those who helped, those who risked. But there were also Nazis who didn't kill. Indeed there were Nazis who helped. It does not diminish the crime of genocide. Nor does the fact that some helped mitigate the moral crime of cowardly abandonment. And this crime of abandonment of Jews by others and of Jews by Jews, and eventually of others by Jews, is called Zionism and Israel, both deadly and destructive products of the 20th century, lawful if tragically painful reactions by and to a dying European civilization thrashing out first to scapegoat the handful of world Jewry and, finally, the masses of the world's people of color in its decadent demise. Sick European civilization, even in its heyday, had nothing but loathing for the Jew (and not even that for people of color!). When it was not attempting an inquisition it was finding functions for the non-Christians which further exacerbated the image of the Jew as fundamentally, i.e., spiritually, inferior. The dirty Jew, after all, is not hygienically filthy but spiritually so, and could never be saved, indeed is not even a candidate for salvation. It has always been dirty work for the dirty Jew. That Jews have survived and even flourished over centuries is no thanks to the Euro-Christians any more than the survival and creative contribution of the African American people is to be attributed in any way to white racist America. Dirty work for the dirty Jew. It has always been so.

But European civilization, born out of feudalism, royalty and thievery reaches its pinnacle (and therefore begins its decline) under capitalism, and in this tragic century Nazi Germany combined all these elements to produce a violent insanity directed against the Gypsy, the homosexual, the communist and, as always, the Jew. It was new and it was not new. The decline of European civilization and the structural crisis of capitalism were *newly* recognized. Hence the viciousness of fascism and the moral bankruptcy of liberal democratic abandonment were qualitatively and quantitatively new in form and content. But still it was the same old Jew and the Jew was to be persecuted. And together with the Gypsy, the homosexual and the communist, persecuted we were. And in the face of such persecution and more startling still with worldwide acceptance of such persecution—in the face of *abandonment*—the Jew, the eternal *outsider* "inside" European civilization, said a simple, lawful but pathetic Kaddish. "Is there work for me to do? Do not annihilate me. Find for me, the dirty Jew, some dirty work so I may survive. Find for me a job that will be so useful that my assimilation will be secured as it was not in Germany. Find for me such work and I will do it, no matter what, I will do it. I will sell my historical Jewishness, my very soul. For if I do not there will be no soul to sell. I am the dirty Jew and I have always done your dirty work. What is it now? What ugliness is your Christian civilization into now? What filth? I, the dirty Jew, will help to clean. Just do not kill me. Do not kill me. I will sell my community, which is my soul, in order to survive."

Rabbi Zion did not approve of this new prayer, yet, like a disease, it came into my community. And it was called Zionism.

FRED: The New York Yankees of the late '40s and early '50s, as talented a grouping of white Christians who ever played on grass, lived in Rabbi Zion's and my neighborhood. Baseball had yet to make it out of the feudal epoch and into liberal capitalism. Hence many players, even the brightest stars, rented apartments or even rooms for the summer during the baseball season. My friends and I often delivered groceries to Yogi and Carmen Berra, who were, as best as I can recall, good tippers. Between 1949 and 1953 the New York Yankees set an all-time baseball record (it still stands) by winning five consecutive world championships. To me and to many in my neighborhood and elsewhere, that was by far the most important occurrence of the half-decade. Of course it wasn't. Much of extraordinary importance was going on throughout the world. But as it turned out it wasn't even the most important thing happening in my neighborhood—which was, after all, in the world even if it sometimes didn't seem so. Between 1949 and 1953, as Casey Stengel and my mother began to talk more and more alike, Yussie Kover and his family, Rabbi Zion and his family, Sadie Newman and her family, and millions of Jews the world over were being abandoned once again and were abandoning ourselves and others in a mass *suicide* that was the painfully symmetrical companion piece to Der Führer's mass genocide. It was the American Jew being assimilated. It was the American Jew, a small but significant element of the U.S. working class, moving into the middle class. It was the Long Islandization of the New York working-class Jew.

"Now," you ask me, "what could be wrong with that?" Nothing is wrong with that, nothing at all. Nothing except the price tag. The dreadful price tag. Our soul. Our community. "But wait, wait, wait a minute. What you say is ridiculous, an ugly distortion, a cheap commie-Marxist criticism. Zionism and Israel have brought the Jewish community together. Never have we been safer. Never have we been more religious. Never have we been more Jewish. You are a self-hating Jew." Between 1949 and 1953, while Mr. Berra convinced the world that "it wasn't over till it was over," Rabbi Zion's community and neighborhood transformed. First it got cleaned up—a little. Then it was abandoned—completely. Rabbi Zion's little shul, where only a few years earlier one could barely find 10 men for a minyan, was suddenly filled with Jews-on-the-make, savoring the mitzvah of upward mobility and selling seats in the synagogue for the High Holy Days by openly admonishing the startled and still-poor elements of the community that they *must* raise money for Israel and the United Jewish Appeal or their prayers would not be heard. So said the new-Jew, the becoming-middle-class Jew, the *nouveau* Zionist, to Mr. Kover who had been coming every day to Rabbi Zion's *shul* for many years before there even was an Israel and before Israel and Zionism had become profitable.

RIE: There was no room for Zion in Zionism, American-style. The poor rabbi was once again abandoned. "But there must be room for all," he said, even as he and the rebbitsin and the children, now teenagers, were told in 1953 that a *newer* rabbi was needed, a more American rabbi. "There must be room for all." Yes, Rabbi, in a community, yes. But not when the *business of assimilation* has taken over, not when our working-class soul is being gentrified by Zionist leaders opportunizing off our fear and trembling and dread, and not when middle-class means a "new respectability" which "cleanses" the dirty Jew by selling our community, our soul, to the very people who sat by and watched as the gas fumes sifted up our nostrils and into our disbelieving eyes. The middle classizing of the American working-class Jew was not about upward mobility pure and simple. Nothing is pure and simple for the Jew, just as nothing is pure and simple for the African American. Anti-Semitism and racism make sure of that. There was a price tag on Jewish upward mobility. The little blue and white ticket was stamped ABANDONMENT. Having been abandoned by an uncaring world, the enterprising Zionist hungered, indeed salivated, over the opportunity to sell what was left of our people and our Jewish soul to those with the big dollars, the truly filthy who had written a new Bible for a new religion which preached that wealth makes you cleaner. And so the "dirty American Jew," petrified by the close call with annihilation in Europe and therefore vulnerable to the hucksters of Zionism, moved upward in the Bronx and, eventually, moved ever further *upward and eastward* to Long Island.

The sociologists have described the phenomenon to death. But their literature does not speak of Rabbi Zion and the Kovers and Sadie Newman, who were abandoned because there was no longer room for all in the *new Jewish community*. For it was, in reality, *no community at all*. In the temples of Hicksville and Levittown and even Great Neck and Lawrence the American Jew was being cleansed; the American Jew was being middle classized. *Zionism* was the new religion. Israel was the apparent cause; anti-communism was the politic, and there was no longer room for all. Some of the most orthodox Jews stayed in New York's "inner city" and cried out against the Long Islandization with a fanatically right-wing voice. But it was liberalism's day and the conservative extremists had never been open to a broad sense of Jewish community in any case. It was the '50s, the Cold War, Rabbi Zion, Yussie Kover, Sadie Newman and Ethel and Julius Rosenberg.

The Zionists themselves were allowed to orchestrate the cultural conversion of Judaism from a working-class ethno-religion to a middle-class media show. Bourgeois political science teaches that it is always best to have the mercenaries "come from" the ethnic and/or religious group that is being sold down the river to a new master. But high politics is too important to be handled by the comprador. Jews or Blacks may be the players—even the stars—but the box office is always as white as green! The Rosenbergs' murder was nothing more than the state teaching its filthy politics to the American Jew, listening carefully and furtively from their not yet furnished and not yet paid for homes in Hicksville. The message to Ethel and Julius Rosenberg was explicit: publicly condemn the Soviet Union's treatment of the Jew and you will not be electrocuted. The message to American Jewry was no less clear: your working-class love affair with communism is over. What the anti-Semitic always identified as the "disproportionate number of Jews in the Communist movement" was to be a dead statistic. The political price of Jewish-American middle-class assimilation and upper-class Jewish influence was anti-communism here and abroad. American post-war foreign policy was, purely and simply, a strategic consolidation of the U.S. empire in the light of the extraordinary American advantage yielded by World War II and the Bretton Woods agreement. Anti-communism at home and throughout the world was the tactical companion piece. And there was an important role—a piece of dirty work—for international Jewry, and most particularly for the American Jew. What was the role? On the surface, in the most deceitful Madison Avenue manner, the role of the American Jew was—seemingly sensibly enough —to support the Jewish homeland, Israel. But the money given at synagogues throughout America in the 1950s to "make the prayer count" had more to do with capital and America than with prayer and Israel. THE MYTH MUST BE PUNCTURED ONCE AND FOR ALL. The American Jew was only marginally helping Israel to survive. As a well-paid client state, Israel's function was always to defend Washington's politics and American capital in the Middle East. The dirty role for the American Zionist Jew, the new Jew, was to support *Washington's advance and survival* and to *use* Israel as a bargaining chip in the ongoing political poker game that was postwar, Cold War politics. The *new* Zionist American Jewish community was to "offer up" Israel to the new American ruling elite, much as some of the new African American "leadership" currently seeks to "sell" Black Africa to white Washington in exchange for political and economic advantage for the new Black upper middle class in the U.S. Here at home the Zionist-controlled "Jewish community" (as sinful a misnomer as has never been atoned for) was peddling anti-Sovietism (succumbing to the right-wing, CIA-organized campaign in support of Soviet Jewry), participating in domestic Cold War politics to prove the loyalty of the new American middle-class Jew, even to the point of betrayal of the Rosenbergs and other progressive working-class Jews.

FRED: And why not? After all, betrayal of the Jew *by* the Jew for political and economic gains has *always* been the corrupt *modus operandi* of the Zionist. In Europe Theodore Herzl's followers played the subtle game of sacrificing the European Jew to Nazism in order to help create a better postwar political environment for the land grab of the Palestinian homeland, a land grab that a PR firm on 38th Street dubbed "the return of the Jew to his historic homeland." Note well that the Native

American's *justified* claim to land stolen only a few *hundred* years ago is invariably related to in a smugly "that's the way the cookie crumbles" fashion by the white international ruling class, especially its U.S. contingent. But seemingly the Judeo-Christian God, long controlled by finance capital, authorized the murder and dislocation of the Palestinian people. Israel's right to exist is actually capitalism's might-makes-right to create whatever the hell it needs and the Zionists' right to buy and sell on the political "free market" to serve their own economic and political ambitions. The so-called Jewish Lobby which, myth has it, spends and works feverishly to maintain U.S. support for Israel, is an insult to Jewish intelligence and, especially, Jewish entrepreneurial skills. For it is very bad business to spend money to make happen what will happen in any event. No. The job of American and international Zionism is not to support Israel. It is rather to keep international Jewry in line and fully in support of Washington, D.C.-led international capitalism. And as capitalism's and D.C.'s positions have worsened—witness the staggering U.S. debt and balance of trade crises—the demand on international Jewry to carry out more and more dirtier and dirtier work intensifies.

American Jewry, long a mainstay within the liberal-progressive coalition, did not so easily abandon just causes even as it caved in to the witch-hunts of the '50s and switched from the red star of communism to the blue star of Zionism—in reality the red, white and blue star of loyal Americanism. Thus the '60s saw Jewish American participation in the liberal civil rights and peace movements. Blacks and Jews worked side by side in Mississippi. But as Black nationalism lawfully expressed itself and, what was of equal importance, as J. Edgar Hoover red-baited the Black movement to its death, liberal Jews, caught between a middle-class assimilationist rock and a historically progressive hard place, came to see the "real deal" they had made with capitalism. From the West Bank to the West Side of Manhattan, international Jewry was being forced to face its written-in-blood deal with the capitalist devil. In exchange for an unstable assimilation, Jews under the leadership of Zionism would "do-unto-others-what-others-had-done-unto-them." The others to be done unto? People of color. The doing? Ghettoization and genocide. The Jew, the dirty Jew, once the ultimate victim of capitalism's soul, fascism, would become a victimizer on behalf of capital-

ism, a self-righteous dehumanizer on behalf of capitalism, a self-righteous dehumanizer and murderer of people of color, a racist bigot who
in the language of Zionism changed the meaning of "Never Again"
from "Never Again for anyone" to "Never Again for *us*—and let the
devil take everyone else."

"Der must be room for everyone in our community," said Rabbi Zion.
And the simple working-class rabbi with an almost instinctive sense of
Jewish universality *meant* everyone. For while he understood community as "Jewish community," his understanding of "Jewishness" and of
"community" did not exclude, was not a Zionist commodity, was not a
political weapon, a gun for hire pointed at those Jews who did not con-
form, and would not disdain, despise, and decimate people of color in
the name of our Holocaust. But there was no room for Zion, no less
community, no less communism, in Zionism. And international Jewry,
which bravely survived German fascism, succumbed to American capitalism. Zionism was the hit-man. I was there, in the late '40s, when it all
began. The Zionists do not like me. I know who they are.

RIE: Wandering
       across
       a cruel Christian sea
       my poor parents
       crossed
       before the Czar
       was buried deep
       by Bolshevism; a
       Jew, a revolutionary
       going home
       to pogrom
       and concentration
       camp. God
       knows why.

FRED: With two
       Jewish comrades,
       a terrified troika,

reciting by our
journey
a mourner's Kaddish
for our
people…crying tears of blood for
all whom
we have murdered
as we died
Yisgadal
V'Yiskadash
Yisgadal
V'Yiskadash
Yisgadal
V'Yiskadash

RIE: Travelling with us
Rabbi Zion and
the rebbitsin,
Crazy Mr. Kover and dear
Mrs. Kover and
Yussel, dearest Yus, my friend,
a skinny
muscled, angry Jew…
and Sadie Newman
who told terrible,
terrible lies
and spewed out
hatred everywhere.

FRED: But Sadie, my mom,
she weren't no
fuckin' Zionist,
She weren't no
fuckin' Zionist.
Mr. Hirsch died
yesterday; no
hero, Hirsch,

Simply a
man destroyed, merely one
of a people
destroyed.
But it is not enough to say
that's enough.
For Hirsch
and Zion, and the rebbitsin
and Yus
and Jackie
and Rie
and our Palestinian
sisters
and
brothers
and our Black
sisters
and brothers.

RIE: For people
of color
the world
over
we, communist
Jews,
offer our bodies
and minds
in your struggle.
We have no soul
but we offer
you our history.
Please forgive
us. No
one survived
our Holocaust.
Even without
soul

we must
die
trying to prevent
yours.

))))

Off-Broadway Melodies of 1592

(The 400th Anniversary of the Centennial Celebration of Columbus' So-called Discovery of America)

Book and Lyrics by Fred Newman,
music by Fred Newman and Annie Roboff

Off-Broadway Melodies of 1592 (The 400th Anniversary of the Centennial Celebration of Columbus' So-called Discovery of America) was produced in 1992 as the Castillo Theatre's contribution to the 500th anniversary of Europe's "discovery" of America.

Its immediate inspiration was *Broadway Melodies of 1492*, a political revue by Jura Soyfer, a Jewish communist who died at Buchenwald. In the early 1930s Soyfer—a performer and painter as well as a playwright and songwriter—was part of Vienna's lively political cabaret scene. This performance tradition, which had its counterpart in Germany before the Nazi victory, survived in semi-legality under Austria's home-grown fascist government until Germany annexed the country in 1938. *Off-Broadway Melodies* is a tribute to both German political cabaret and to the American musical theatre of the first half of the 20th century. At the same time it pokes fun at both of them. *Broadway Melodies of 1492* is a satire of American popular culture and its influence on Europe; *Off-Broadway Melodies of 1592* shifts the focus to lampoon Eurocentric views of the quincentenary in particular and of European pretensions in general.

Off-Broadway Melodies is Newman's first full-length musical production. Like those which were to follow—*Still on the Corner, Sally and Tom (The American Way), Coming of Age in Korea,* and *Carmen's Place*—it was written with composer Annie Roboff, a songwriter currently living in Nashville whom Newman has known for 15 years. Roboff's early credits include the movie, television show and soundtrack of *Fame*, a stint singing on the streets of New York with the well-known a capella group the Bondinis, and several years composing themes for all of the major broadcast and cable networks. She has written songs recorded by numerous pop, R&B and country artists, including "Maybe It's Love" on Trisha Yearwood's album *Everybody Knows*.

By 1992 Newman and Roboff had been writing songs together for a number of years. In fact, some of the songs included in the revue were originally written for other occasions. "Sadie's Song," named for Newman's mother, was originally written for *Dead as a Jew (Zion's Community)* (not included in this collection) earlier that same year. "I'm Black, I'm Strait, and I'm Gay" was written for *Billie, Malcolm & Yusuf* (an early version of *Billie & Malcolm: A Demonstration*) in 1991. "Black Child, Black Woman" and "Black and Country" were both written for "Pam Kansas," a showcase for country-western vocalist Pam Lewis produced by Castillo in the summer of 1992. (Pam Lewis, the national producer of the All Stars Talent Show Network, grew up in Kansas and sings under the name of Pam Kansas.) Like these songs, the skit "These Ships Ain't No Fools" was written earlier. It was first done for a night of comedy skits at Castillo in the mid '80s. It was included in *Off-Broadway Melodies* because it fit in with the general theme of the European penetration of the Americas.

Off-Broadway Melodies, like most American musicals until the early 1940s, is essentially a framework for a series of related (or not-so-related) songs and skits. It was not until Jerome Kern and Oscar Hammerstein's *Showboat* in 1927 that a coherent plot and consistent character development were introduced to the American musical—a process that reached fruition in Richard Rodgers and Hammerstein's *Oklahoma* in 1943. It is within this revue tradition that the premise of the first act of *Off-Broadway Melodies*—the trip of the Merman sisters to Europe in 1592—is completely (and abruptly) dropped at the top of the second act with a single line: "The Merman sisters were never heard from again." Equally abrupt is the sudden emotional shift two scenes later from the farcical to the tragic with the song "What Kind of Men are You?"

Off-Broadway Melodies is, among other things, Newman's salute to the American popular culture he loves so much—particularly (and appropriately given the show's form) to vaudeville and the early musical stage. It contains characters (three of them) based on Ethel Merman, the Marx Brothers (also three) and Bruce Springsteen (just one) and references to a host of other stars of stage and screen including Bette Davis, Marlene Dietrich, and Noel Coward. The Descartes skit, which ends with a raucous fight, harks back to Edward Harrigan's "Mulligan Guard" plays which so enthralled New York's Irish immigrant audiences in the 1870s and '80s and which almost always ended with a raucous—but somehow good natured—brawl.

Newman often uses the people around him as the basis of his characters, and this intimate connection between the ever-expanding and ever-fluid Castillo ensemble and Newman's writing is perhaps more obvious in

Off Broadway Melodies than in any other play. I have already mentioned Pam Lewis—her character, Pam Kansas, appears not only here but in *Billie & Malcolm: A Demonstration* and *Still on the Corner*. The character of Santa Maria in the "These Ships Ain't No Fools" skit was written for a Greek Marxist (Maria Moschonisiou) active with Castillo at the time. Kate, the Dutch girl in the Holland scene, was created for Kate Henselmans, a Castillo activist from Amsterdam.

The connection he frequently makes between a written "character" and a "real life" person is one of the factors that has led Newman to speak of performance as a dialogue between the character-as-written and the performer-as-she-or-he-is-developing, a dialogue which results in the actor creating something other than (and beyond) her or himself—and other than (and beyond) the written character as well. This creative, developmental process can come into play no matter what the particular performer's relationship to the playwright and the creation of the script. Thus while Pam Kansas, Santa Maria, Kate, and many other characters in this and Newman's subsequent plays were written with specific performers in mind, that in no way limits their appropriateness for others. (Shakespeare, after all, also wrote some of his greatest characters for particular actors in the Globe Theatre company.)

Off-Broadway Melodies also reveals something—through its use of many inside jokes—of the close and friendly relationship between the playwright and the Castillo audience. Most of Newman's plays (at least the lighter ones) contain jokes that can only be fully appreciated by a regular Castillo audience member or someone from the broader development community of which it is a part. Not getting these jokes doesn't get in the way of appreciating the play; however, knowing the inside reference adds a second layer of enjoyment. For example, in *Off-Broadway Melodies* the "ZPD-500" ray gun used by Muckerex to transport the performers and the audience back 400 years is a reference to the "zone of proximal development," a phrase first used by early Soviet psychologist Lev Vygotsky to describe the interaction of adults and very young children that enables the children to perform beyond themselves and learn, for example, how to speak. Vygotsky is a major influence on Newman's own theories of development and his practice as a therapist. Those familiar with Vygotsky, or who have worked with Newman in other capacities, or have read the scholarly books that he has written with developmental psychologist Lois Holzman, would get a chuckle from the reference. To those who have never heard of the ZPD, the "ZPD-500" is just a mock-scientific name for a standard science fiction device. Another inside joke in the play is the remark by the Pinta (in "These Ships Ain't No Fools"), "I think I need boat therapy…short term boat crisis normalization." "Crisis Normalization" was the name given to a program developed in the mid-1980s in an attempt to mass market social therapy. The exchange in which Bethyl Merman asks her sister, "Did you speak to the Left?" and Methyl replies, "You can't talk to those guys. They're so caught up with their macho proto-proletarian Europeans that they don't even know if they support the Mohawks" alludes to the contemporary struggles of the Mohawk Nation with the Canadian and U.S. governments, which Newman had actively supported; at the same time it takes a swipe at the orthodox Left, which has consistently snubbed the political tendency that Newman leads.

Off-Broadway Melodies was produced at Castillo in November of 1992 under Newman's direction.

D.F.

Off-Broadway Melodies of 1592 (The 400th Anniversary of the Centennial Celebration of Columbus' So-called Discovery of America) was first produced at the Castillo Theatre (Fred Newman, artistic director; Gabrielle Kurlander, producing director) in New York City in November 1992. The cast, in order of appearance, was as follows:

SIR MALCOLM MUCKEREX .... Allen Cox
LADY LADY ETHYLETHYL/METHYL MERMAN/
HARPA COLUMBUS/THE PINTA .... Marian Rich
SIR WE'RE GONNA HANGEMHIGH/PAGE VI .... Kenneth Hughes
DR. LITTLE LADYBUG/ETHYL MERMAN/SINGER .... Cathy Rose Salit
DR. FRANÇOIS LE NICKNACK/FRANÇOIS LE SPRINGSTEEN/
CHRISTO MARX AKA GROUCHO COLUMBUS .... David Nackman
DR. STRAIT GAYGGLE/THE NINA/EMMY STRAIT .... Emmy Gay
PROFESSOR HENRI DESHORSE/RENÉ DESCARTES .... Roger Grunwald
PROFESSOR BOLSH RED/SINGER .... Gabrielle Kurlander
LADY LADY MERMANMERMAN/BETHYL MERMAN .... Ellen Korner
DR. NEBRASKA KANSAS/SINGER/PAM .... Pam Lewis
DR. SCHULTZIE DUTCH/KATE .... Kate Henselmans
SISTER SADIE/SINGER UNDERSTUDY .... Janet Weigel
PROFESSOR ZEPPO CHICO/CHICO COLUMBUS .... Ron Connor
THE SANTA MARIA .... Maria Moschonisiou

Fred Newman, director; Mary Fridley and Emmy Gay, producers; Ron Connor, musical director; Wilton Duckworth, set design; Michael Mitchell and Judy Penzer, scenic design; Charlotte, costume design; Linnaea Tillet, lighting design; Michael Klein, sound design; Barry Z Levine, video design/cinematography; Diane Stiles, production stage manager.

A NOTE FROM THE AUTHOR

Off-Broadway Melodies of 1592 is an anti-imperialist, anti-Columbus, pro-human musical comedy in the traditions of Brecht, Weil, Soyfer, Brel, et al. and, hopefully, the best of American vaudeville. It is also in the tradition of Castillo—pro-people of color, pro-women, pro-gay, pro-working class, pro-revolutionary, and (at least we try to be) pro-fessional. In it we deal harshly with European civilization, though not nearly as harshly as European civilization has dealt with the rest of the world. We neither mean to suggest that *all* Europeans are the greedy, plundering bastards that we portray nor that Europe has contributed nothing positive to human evolution. Rather, we are implying that the Frankensteinian European *weltgeist* appears to varying degrees in all (even the non-European) and that the positive contributions of European civilization have been commodified and "well paid for."

This play is dedicated to my dear comrade Sema Salit, who died on October 24, 1992. Sema had asked to be in *Off-Broadway Melodies*. You are, Sema, you are.

NOVEMBER 1992

CHARACTERS

Onstage
SIR MALCOLM MUCKEREX
METHYL MERMAN
BETHYL MERMAN
ETHYL MERMAN
PAGE VI, a page at Queen Elizabeth's court
RENÉ DESCARTES
FRANÇOIS LE SPRINGSTEEN, a peasant at DESCARTES' class
KATE, a Dutch girl
CHICO COLUMBUS
HARPA COLUMBUS
CHRISTO MARX aka GROUCHO COLUMBUS
THE NINA
THE PINTA
THE SANTA MARIA
SINGERS
PAM, a country singer
EMMY STRAIT, an itinerant comedienne

On video
SIR MALCOLM MUCKEREX, LADY LADY ETHYLETHYL, SIR WE'RE GONNA
HANGEMHIGH *(pronounced "Hang 'em High")*, DR. LITTLE LADYBUG, DR.
FRANÇOIS LE NICKNACK, DR. STRAIT GAYGGLE, PROFESSOR HENRI DESHORSE,
PROFESSOR BOLSH RED, LADY LADY MERMANMERMAN, DR. NEBRASKA KANSAS,
DR. SCHULTZIE DUTCH, SISTER SADIE, PROFESSOR ZEPPO CHICO, ANNOUNCER

NOTE:
This play contains both live scenes and video sequences.

Act I, Scene 1

Proscenium-style stage. Vaudeville-style, surrealistic, avant-garde backdrop and props are seen. The stage is empty. Two video monitors are at stage left and right.

Video begins. It is a PBS-style show, opening with funny space-age/electronic music and graphics that zoom in and whirl into place.

ANNOUNCER: PBS presents this week's edition of "Discovery" featuring, as always, your host, Sir Malcolm Muckerex.

(Graphics and music cross-fade with the logo of "Discovery," then dissolve into the scene: A panel of noted academics and experts in their fields (the company in weird contemporary dress) seated in a semi-circle with SIR MALCOLM MUCKEREX slightly to the side.)

MUCKEREX: Good evening, ladies and gentlemen in our PBS audience, and welcome to our distinguished panel. Thank you for joining us for this week's special edition of "Discovery." Tonight we are going to explore the emergence of what is now well-known the world over as European civilization or the European personality or European ideology…in a word we cast our eyes this evening on…THE EUROPEAN.

(Illustrations and graphics accompany MUCKEREX's narration.)

Coming out of their Middle Ages, with the total consolidation of Catholicism, Europe was, through much of the 15th century, a primarily agrarian economy; the largely peasant population lived in a feudal civilization, ruled for the most part by royalty—kings, princes, dukes and barons sharing control of varying parcels of land with the church. In the course of the 1500s, however, from roughly 1492 when Christopher Columbus sailed the ocean blue *(a little laugh)* for Spain's King Ferdinand and Queen Isabella, Europe in general began to take shape as a new kind of civilization. What evolved was a new economics based on exploration and exploitation in Africa and the so-called New World—South, Central and North America. New navigational techniques, new technology was coming onto the scene which in turn triggered new sciences. For instance the study of the stars—the advent of astronomy—further advanced navigation; the invention of the printing press by Gutenberg profoundly developed communication, and so on. What began to emerge in the 16th century was a new mode of production—Mercantile Capitalism (better known as rip-off or trickle-up economics)—which itself transformed within a couple of hundred years into Industrial Capitalism—an entirely new form of producing. The dominance of agriculture slowly started to turn to the dominance of exploration, plundering and then manufacturing. *(Panel is seen in varying states of self-absorption and somnolence.)* Simultaneously, the ideology necessary to rationalize and justify these new developments—actually new and more sophisticated forms of plunder—to give a secular basis for all these events began to evolve. Great struggles over ideology emerged between 1492 and 1592 involving many so-called reformers, identifiable as protesters, that is, Protestants, including Martin Luther. Many challenged the orthodox scholastic views of the established Catholic church. Of course there were non-Christians as well. Muslims were brutally oppressed as were Jews. Gypsies, homosexuals and non-believers were often violently murdered. A new European world was taking shape based primarily on stealing other people's gold to fill the coffers of reigning queens and kings—and further developed in urban centers where primitive forms of manufacturing were taking place—a new form of profiteering off the exploitation of human labor. We see as well the beginnings of so-called European humanistic views deriving from the new sciences and broadened world view challenging the traditional dogmas of Rome. The 16th century, more precisely 1492-1592, was not merely the century following Columbus' trip across the Atlantic; we might say it was the birth-century of so-called European Civilization. By 1592 the European had arrived.

ETHYLETHYL: Brilliant statement, Sir Malcolm. As always, I completely agree with your assessment.

MUCKEREX: Well, Lady Ethylethyl, I think we can back this all up with some hard facts...

ETHYLETHYL: Oh, but of course, Sir Malcolm. As a matter of fact—a very,

very well-known fact, actually—it was in 1492 that Ferdinand and Isabella drove the Moors *(glances at DR. KANSAS and DR. GAYGGLE)* completely from the Iberian peninsula. And 200,000 Jews were expelled at the same time. Just from Spain alone. In that one year. Can you imagine?

MUCKEREX: You have something, Sir Hangemhigh?

HANGEMHIGH: Yes. As I'm certain you all know…just to illustrate what you said, my dear boy, about the beginnings of the new manufacturing. The first English paper mills were opened as early as 1494…April 16th I think it was.

MUCKEREX: Dr. Ladybug.

LADYBUG: And it's well-known—a very well-known fact—that in 1496, the Jewish people were completely expelled from Portugal.

MUCKEREX: Dr. Nicknack.

NICKNACK: I'm sure we all recall that in 1498, Vasco DeGama…even the children remember him…traveling around southern Africa, reached India, opening up vast trade opportunities with the East.

MUCKEREX: Yes…vast. Sir Hangemhigh?

HANGEMHIGH: Oh dear…The cities were pigsties. In 1499 London was 500 years old and the Plague—the so-called Black Death—broke out. Just barbaric.

MUCKEREX: Horrendous. Dr. Gayggle.

GAYGGLE: Here's something barbaric for you. 1510—it's the date of the first trans-Atlantic slave shipment and the beginning of the transition from Mercantile to Industrial Capitalism. *(Pause.)* Pretty smart, eh?

MUCKEREX: A well-known fact, Dr. Gayggle, a well-known fact. Professor Deshorse.

DESHORSE: 1513! Ah, 1513. What a date in literary and philosophical circles. Machiavelli authored *The Prince* in…1513…laying out the intrigue, and vile human machinations—giving the imprimatur of civilization to sicko backroom wheeling and dealing called European politics. Mr. Clinton and Mr. Bush are America's own prickly Princes.

MUCKEREX: Yes. Professor Red!

RED: In 1517, you know, Luther, an Augustinian friar, nailed the 95 Theses onto the door of Wittenberg Palace Church—beginning the Protestant Reformation.

ALL: *(In general hub-bub, including MUCKEREX)* Yes, yes, of course. A well-known fact indeed. Hear, hear.

MUCKEREX: My dear Lady Mermanmerman.

MERMANMERMAN: And in 1519, I believe, yes, that's the year, Zwingli brought the Reformation to Switzerland. A fact, my good friends. A fact!

MUCKEREX: Dr. Kansas.

KANSAS: In 1519, Cortéz arrived uninvited to Mexico where his behavior was so macho and foul everyone thought he was a God.

MUCKEREX: That is well-known. Dr. Dutch. How fortunate you could be here today.

DUTCH: As this distinguished body comprehends all too well the peasant uprisings took place in 1524-25. 200,000 peasants massacred. Now there's a hard fact for you.

MUCKEREX: How interesting, Dr. Dutch.

DUTCH: Luther was the most conservative—the "official" protester. He didn't support the peasant uprising: cut a deal so as not to lose his backing. Perhaps he was the first sold-out reformer.

MUCKEREX: Yes. Quite. Lady Ethylethyl…

ETHYLETHYL: *(Cutting him off)* Rome was sacked *(MUCKEREX and others murmur in recognition)* in 1527 by the Germans and the Spaniards. And that ended the Italian Renaissance. Now there's a fact for you.

HANGEMHIGH: *(Jumping right in)* The weavers (without Pete Seeger) rioted in Kent, England, in 1528.

MERMANMERMAN: In 1531 Zwingli was killed. Dear me, what a loss.

MUCKEREX: Yes, a turning point. Yes? Dr. Ladybug.

LADYBUG: *(Sings)* He was Hen-er-y the 8th he was, Hen-er-y the 8th he was, he was. *(Speaks.)* The pig established the Anglican Church in 1535. Thomas More, of course was against it and they popped his bloody head off. *(Laughs.)*

MUCKEREX: Oh yes, yes, yes. Sister Sadie.

SISTER SADIE: Calvin set up a theocratic government in Geneva in 1541. A fact, my friends, a fact.

GAYGGLE: Did you know that in 1582 when the Gregorian calendar was adopted 10 days were dropped, and London workers rioted, afraid they'd lose 10 days' pay?

MUCKEREX: Right on, sister, right on!

HANGEMHIGH: That old Black Plague killed over 15,000 in London in the year 1592 alone.

MUCKEREX: Yes, unthinkable…

NICKNACK: In 1501, Gutenberg's by then well-known rapid method of printing books reached a level of significant production and distribution.

MUCKEREX: Professor Chico!

CHICO: 1509—that was a de first a year that doctors a needed a license to a practice medicine. I think at a first it was a dog a license.

KANSAS: Copernicus—a very well-known white European—put out the heliocentric theory in 1512! He said that other than himself the sun was the most central element in the universe.

NICKNACK: Galileo was born in 1564. A seven-pound, three-ounce bouncing baby boy.

RED: In 1534, Michelangelo was painting the Sistine Chapel. Marvelous. Simply marvelous. I think he was painting it off-purple.

MUCKEREX: So. To sum it up. We're saying *(becoming more "street")* that these sicko white guys, check this out…were looking for new and more hip ways of kicking the shit out of other people, poor people, people of color. Yeah, that's it, that's the straight deal. Kicking the shit out of African people, so-called Native American people. Basically getting down with stealing the Asian people blind, and the Indian people. And dig this! Not only were they perpetrating this shit, but these mothers were callin' it civilized and forcin' everybody to eat this shit. Man, what a bad scene these Europeanies were into.

ETHYLETHYL: Sir Muckerex! Aren't you going just a little too far!

MUCKEREX: Word up! These Europeanies got a righteous bullshit rationalization for that kind of murder, that kind of rape, that kind of lowdown dealing.

MERMANMERMAN: Really, Sir Malcolm.

MUCKEREX: Hey, this is the straight shit.

HANGEMHIGH: But really, Muck, not quite the way to put it old man.

LADYBUG: Sir Muckerex, this is PBS after all. What about our sponsors?

GAYGGLE: Our sponsors? I thought we didn't have sponsors!

(*Everybody laughs.*)

DESHORSE: EuropExxon Corporation! Oh, God yes. They've paid several million to put on this show. Sir Malcolm, please try to rephrase things quickly. We may still be able to salvage things. Consider the Board of Directors.

MERMANMERMAN: Such a crude way of putting it, my dear Muckerex. Perhaps you're not feeling too well.

KANSAS: Hey Malc…be cool, brother.

MUCKEREX: No, no, no. This is how it happened, how it went down…you can't clean this up! The European hit the stage of history with a vengeance…that's right, with a vengeance!

NICKNACK: Sir Muckerex.

MUCKEREX: Look folks. You gave the well-known facts real good. This is a very distinguished panel. You've been just fine. But real history—people's history—is all about little-known facts! They are what makes history, sisters and brothers. What gets into the history books are the biggies, the official facts. But we gotta get down with the little-known facts. That's the real deal. That's the music we need to hear. To hell with PBS. PBS—that's petit bourgeois shit—(*PANELISTS gasp*) we're talkin' people's TV and people's music and people's facts. Lighten up panelists, we're gonna make a little history tonight. (*Pulls out a ray gun.*) This is my new time machine. A ray gun. A ZPD-500. It shakes up official history and gives us the real deal. I'm gonna lay it on us, my friends …so hold on tight…we're goin' on a big old trip.

PANELISTS: (*Screaming*) No! No! No!

(*Weird music comes up, images flash on screen, then images flash onstage where cast appears in costume, looking at themselves, bewildered as video fades.*)

MUCKEREX: (*Offstage; with echo*) Welcome back to "Discovery!" Part II: The Emergence of the European. 1492-1592: The Little-Known Facts. Via our extraordinary ZPD-500 Time Machine, we present to our viewers tonight those who have not made it into the history books, those who have made the little-known facts that show us the real deal. Please, panelists, let us sing together tonight's theme song—THE EUROPEAN.

(*Music begins, and MUCKEREX speaks the first lyric, in rhythm.*)

(*"The Europeans"*)

Europeans are obscene in their essence;
They invented the word "effervescence"
To describe the bubbles
Which cover up all the troubles
Caused by Europe's prolonged adolescence.

COMPANY: (*Sings*)
It's invalid to overly generalize,
But when you peer into a European's glassy eyes
There is greed
There is plunder
The look of loud thunder
A Wagnerian gaze meant to hypnotize.

WOMEN:
But strictly between us

It's really the penis
Which captures the European core
Which explains what is grandly
Defined as most manly
To psychotically lust for MORE…and MORE…and MORE!

SISTER SADIE:

So, Attila the Hun is a novice.
There's a rumor he rested on Shabbos
But so completely obsessed
With the gold and the breast
The European, on the Lord's Day, will rob us.

WOMEN:

But strictly between us
It's really the penis
Which captures the European core
Which explains what is grandly
Defined as most manly
To psychotically lust for MORE!

ALL:

So beware of the European common line—

MEN:

Board your windows, hide your daughters,
It's Frankenstein!

WOMEN:

As Voltaire once said
As he lay in his bed;
"It's the best of all possible worlds."
But Voltaire wasn't one of the girls.

Act I, Scene 2

Backdrop of ocean, docks, etc. A prop canoe is at a dock, against a blue sky back-
*ground. Onstage are the Merman sisters (*BETHYL, METHYL *and* ETHYL*) dressed*
identically as Annie Oakley. They are carrying signs: R.E.A.D.Y.A.I.M.F.I.R.E.

SAYS COLUMBUS WAS AN IMPERIALIST! LET'S GO "DISCOVER"
THEM! BRING THE CRAP BACK TO EUROPE! etc. They are loading the
canoe with crap: wooden shoes, the New York Times, etc. They are taking back
to Europe all the shit the Europeans brought over here. At the instant the lights
come up the three sisters realize there is an audience, drop their picket signs and
melodramatically break into a gusty rendition of "There's No Business Like
Show Business."

MUCKEREX: *(Offstage)* Ladies! Ladies. That's the wrong show. The wrong show. Pleeeeease, Ladies. *(They stop, and go back to picketing and loading the canoe.)* Little-known fact. In the year of our Lord 1592, the great, great, great, great, great, great, great, great, great, great grandmother of 20th-century musical star Ethyl Merman and her two sisters Bethyl Merman and Methyl Merman organized the world's first feminist "Native American" support grouping. The grouping was called R.E.A.D.Y.A.I.M.F.I.R.E. In that critical year, 1592, the centennial of the Columbian Plague, of Christopher's tyrannical travels to what became known as America, the R.E.A.D.Y.A.I.M.F.I.R.E. decided in a Central Committee vote of two to one to borrow a canoe from their Mohawk friends, travel across the Atlantic, "discover" Europe and bring back all of the crap that the Europeans had been bringing over here since 1492. They departed at 4:23 pm on August 3rd 1592, exactly 100 years to the minute from Columbus' sailing.

BETHYL: Not many people showed up to our demonstration.

METHYL: Did you give out all the leaflets?

BETHYL: Yeah. I gave 'em all out. Did you speak to the Left?

METHYL: You can't talk to those guys. They're so caught up with their macho proto-proletarian Europeans that they don't even know if they support the Mohawks.

ETHYL: Would you two shut up already? We're ready to go.

BETHYL: Ethyl, can we sing now?

ETHYL: Allll right. In the canoe. C'mon. Here we go.

("1592")

MERMAN SISTERS: *(Sing)*
    It's 1592,
    One hundred years since you
    Came with three ships from Spain
    Drove folks insane
    Inflicted pain.

    Now it's our turn at bat
    A time to show you that
    They're not your Indians.
    We're bringing back, your macho smack.

    It's the centennial
    Of your perennial destruction.
    Now we'll discover you
    To show you how
    We feel about abduction.

    We've had enough of white,
    Red folks are quite alright.
    So take your alcohol
    And soccer ball
    And shove it all!

    We're loading up canoes
    With British tea and wooden shoes.
    We want to see
    If you've got
    Anything worthwhile.

    Our hopes are low,
    But here we go
    On a holiday
    Of the centennial
    Of your perennial
    Destruction.

Act I, Scene 3

MUCKEREX: *(Offstage)* Little-known fact! The Merman sisters, Ethyl, Methyl and Bethyl, in one single tiny birchbark canoe, made it to Europe in 309 days. On the trip they sang "There's No Business Like Show Business" 14,611 times. They landed tired, but not hoarse, in Portsmouth, England, and in two weeks' time traveled overland to London which at that very moment was preparing to celebrate its 600th anniversary. On June 26th of 1593 they arrived to return the unwanted goods at Queen Elizabeth's court. The court of Queen Elizabeth has been portrayed in 1930s American movies as quite beautiful, and the queen, as portrayed, for example, by a young and snobby Bette Davis, as squeaky clean. Not so. The court, in fact...little-known fact...made the dungeons in the Roman Colosseum look like Saks Fifth Avenue. In a word—it stunk!

(MERMAN SISTERS enter with picket signs. They are bickering and carrying a soccer ball, tea, etc.)

ETHYL: Shut up and put those signs down!

BETHYL: I wonder if I can get a deodorizer somewhere?

(They are working-class friendly; PAGE VI is neurotic and allergic. The queen is a cardboard cut-out.)

METHYL: I can't believe how smelly it is! Yuck!

BETHYL:...I thought this was the civilized court of her hotshit majesty, Queen Elizabeth?

PAGE VI: Oh Sisters of Merman. You are the Merman sisters?...I bid you all welcome to Her Majesty's court. Please excuse the mess.

ETHYL: Jesus, man, this place stinks. How d'ya stand it, pal? I mean this joint makes Buffalo Bill's Wild West Show smell like Marlene Dietrich.

PAGE VI: I try to keep a stiff upper nostril.

METHYL: It really stinks here!

PAGE VI: Yes, ma'am!

BETHYL: Holy cow. This is supposed to be civilized. We're supposed to be the rural stinkers.

PAGE VI: It's all a big lie madam, but please don't tell the queen I said so. I'm just an office temp.

METHYL: Oh, no, brother, my lips are sealed.

ETHYL: My nose, too.

BETHYL: Is that the queen?

PAGE VI: Yes, milady.

BETHYL: Listen, pal. I think you should pack it in and a...go to law school or somethin'. This job stinks.

PAGE VI: We British always try to accept our station in life, milady.

BETHYL: Well dat ain't nothin' to be so proud of, pal. The only good reason I can see for you havin' your nose in the air is that it keeps the smell out a little.

PAGE VI: Yes, milady.

BETHYL: And ah...I ain't your lady. Actually I ain't anybody's lady.

PAGE VI: Well, we do have a proper respect for class over here...what is it that you wish to return, madam...May I call you madam?

METHYL: *(Not so loud)* Yeah. That's okay. Call me madam—call us all madams. We're returning this English language you folks brought over. *(Drops newspaper on the floor.)*

ETHYL: Yeah, we don't like talkin' this funny way y'all do.

BETHYL: Yeah, pal, take this Queen's English and shove it.

PAGE VI: Shall we dance? *(They dance a minuet, then PAGE VI sings.)*

("Queen Elizabeth's Court")

Queen Elizabeth's court,
Not quite what you'd expect.
It's filled with filth and slimy bugs
Large rats and other "dreck."

London town is a mess;
Six hundred years of slumming,

Of dirty streets
And rotted meats
And medieval plumbing.

BETHYL:

The Britishers look down their nose
At continental lederhose.
They think that only they are civilized,
But Shakespeare notwithstanding
It's just upper-crust grandstanding
And snootiness is not the same as wise.

You city folks are a trip.
Marx thinks we're rural idiots,
But cultured style
Can't hide the bile
That Queen Elizabeth emits. *(Holds nose.)*

PAGE VI:

Bette Davis is a cinema hussy,
The real Liz, much more puss-y.
Your movie hits with Zazu Pitts
Hide all the crap with fussy.

We Brits hide our barbarity
Beneath our pseudo-insincerity.
We think we all resemble Noel Coward.
But in the 16th century
Europe's finest penitentiary
Was known to one and all as London's Tower.

Henry "Eight" was her dad,
Women did not get him mad
He murdered wives
De-valued lives.
The son of a bitch was bad,
But in England he was merely a cad.

Act I, Scene 4

MUCKEREX: *(Offstage)* The Merman sisters, having dropped what was left of their British accents, made their way across the English Channel, by canoe, to Bologne, France and then by oxcart to the University of Paris. Little-known fact! They arrived in early September on the very day that René Descartes, that most extraordinary French philosopher whose insights to this day rationalize much of solipsistic white male-supremacist Euro-American psychology, publicly delivered his famous third meditation. Only yards away from where Abelard had been castrated 210 years earlier, Descartes is about to deliver the lecture in which he attempts to justify Europeans' doing whatever the hell they feel like doing.

(Paris. The MERMAN SISTERS in front of a backdrop of a huge crowd at L'Université de Paris. FRANÇOIS LE SPRINGSTEEN, a peasant, and RENÉ DESCARTES, a philosopher, are present.)

DESCARTES: *(In a ridiculous French accent)* I have spent many long hours, peering at a wax candle in my darkened room, to see if I could discover the most fundamental truth of all—an indubitable truth—to see if I could discover what it is that makes the European the only truly existent person in all of the world. I stared, and I stared at my shrinking candle with the eyes and the mind that God has bequeathed to me as a member of the European intellectual elite. It became plain to me that what is most fundamental to real existence is European thinking. At first I said aloud—right after I exclaimed, "Eureka!"—"the European thinks, therefore, the European is." Then I said, "Wait a minute, René, that might not be sufficient. After all others might say, 'the African thinks, therefore, the African is.' No. I must say, 'I think, therefore, I am.' And then be ready to kick the shit out of anyone else who says it." Pretty brilliant, n'est-ce pas? *(Rumblings are heard among the crowd.)*

VOICE IN THE CROWD: Hey, Descartes! Who do you think you are, man?

DESCARTES: Who said that? *(Silence. He continues.)* So. I was really getting off on this magnificent Eurocentric "discovery" when…

VOICE IN THE CROWD: Yo, Descartes, who do you think you are, man?

VOICES IN THE CROWD: *(Growing louder, more unified)* Yeah, Descartes, who made you God? Yo, Descartes, get a job! Who do you think you are, man? Go back to your wick, man! Who do you think you are?

MUCKEREX: At that moment…little-known fact…the great, great, great, great, great, great, great, great, great, great, great, great grandfather of Bruce Springsteen, François Le Springsteen, leaped to his feet, mandolin in hand, to lead France's first student/peasant/workers uprising.

(LE SPRINGSTEEN sings as DESCARTES comments.)

("Mr. Descartes, Who Do You Think You Are?")

ALL:

Mr. Descartes	DESCARTES:
Who do you think you are?	Prof. Descartes
Mr. Descartes	
Who do you think you are?	C'est moi

LE SPRINGSTEEN:

Meditation	DESCARTES:
Your creation	Vraiment
Made you overnight sensation	
Talkin' French	
Philosophy	Correct
What you think	
Is what you be	
Cogito ergo sum	
Sounds okay	
But said to whom?	Picky, picky

ALL:

Mr. Descartes	DESCARTES:
Who do you think you are?	Le professeur!
Mr. Descartes	
Who do you think you are?	

LE SPRINGSTEEN:

Just because
It comes out Latin

It won't fly   DESCARTES:
In Upper Manhattan   Manhattan?
If you are
'cause you think   you got it…
What are we
'cause we stink?   Peasants.
Mr. D. rationalizin'
Royalty imperializin'   Long live Louis whoever

ALL:

Mr. Descartes   DESCARTES:
Who do you think you are?   Silence…
Mr. Descartes
Who do you think you are?

LE SPRINGSTEEN:

Folks say
You made up   DESCARTES:
Analyt' geometry   Nice job, eh?
That's mighty cool
My French friend   Merci
I'm told
They're usin' it
To make the cannons fire
And we're the fodder   Tough break, mon ami
In the end

ALL:

Mr. Descartes   DESCARTES:
Who do you think you are?   Ze European
Mr. Descartes
Who do you think you are?   Down with ze masses.
Mr. Descartes
Who do you think you are?
Mr. Descartes
Who do you think you are?
Mr. Descartes
Who do you think you are?

Mr. Descartes
Who do you think you are?

(The final chorus deteriorates into a raucous brawl.)

Act I, Scene 5

MUCKEREX: *(Offstage)* In the early competition for imperialist control amongst the vicious and violent Europeans, some won, some lost. Some of those who lost early on, realized that they would do well to get themselves a good PR firm both to cover over their failures and to make it appear as if they'd never participated in the entire ugly imperialist business. Noteworthy in this kind of cover-up is an element of the bourgeoisie known to us these days as the Dutchman, or its variant, Dutch Schultz.

(Holland. The backdrop is a beautiful blue sky, with a windmill, tulips in the sun, the dikes in the background. KATE, a Dutch girl in a starched outfit, is picking flowers. Enter the MERMAN SISTERS, who are, as usual, bickering among themselves.)

BETHYL: *(To her sisters)* Hey. Look at this beautiful place. This is really different than everything else we've seen here in Europe. It's kinda like the Catskills.

KATE: *(Very cheerful)* Hello! Welcome! I'm very pleased to meet you!

BETHYL: *(To her sisters)* This is nice. *(To KATE.)* You seem to be—what—planting flowers?

KATE: Yes, I am planting tulips. We always have beautiful flowers, tulips, daffodils. Would you like some flowers? *(Offers them flowers.)*

BETHYL: Isn't that lovely. *(To her sisters.)* You see? Everything in Europe isn't that bad…*(To KATE.)* Thank you so much for the flowers, dear. *(Takes flowers.)* And those buildings with those things turning around. They're so interesting, so beautiful. What are they called?

KATE: Windmills. They are called windmills. Aren't they beautiful?

METHYL and ETHYL: They're very nice. Yeah, they're very nice.

BETHYL: Do they have a function, my dear?

KATE: They grind flour.

BETHYL: They grind flour! *(Nods at her sisters.)*

KATE: We make bread for all the people.

BETHYL: This is a lovely, lovely place, bread for all, beautiful. What do you call this place ?

KATE: This is the Netherlands.

BETHYL: The Netherlands. And the people are called Netherlanders?

KATE: We are the Dutch.

BETHYL: The Dutch! What a marvelous name. What a relief.

METHYL and ETHYL: It's nice. Yeah, it's very nice.

KATE: We are very happy, very healthy, very clean.

BETHYL: This is simply beautiful. You see, girls? I mean not all Europeans participate in this foul…*(To KATE.)* Well, you see we were in Queen Elizabeth's court…you heard of Queen Elizabeth's court *(KATE nods)* and it was really gross and disgusting, and then we met this professor René Descartes at the University of Paris…you know about the U. of P. *(KATE nods.)* Well, he was just a pig…

KATE: No. Not the Dutch. We have no need to be nasty. There is plenty to go around. Plenty of flowers, plenty of bread, plenty of canals, plenty of blue skies…

BETHYL: I can't tell you how happy we are to have run into you. We were starting to think everything here in Europe was ugly and dirty. But this is just so lovely. What are these flowers called again?

KATE: Tulips.

BETHYL: Tulips. Beautiful. Just beautiful. We'll be on our way, you are a charming, charming young girl, such a lovely accent. *(To METHYL and ETHYL.)* She speaks English so beautifully—not like Queen Elizabeth. Thank you so much.

METHYL and ETHYL: Yeah. Thanks a lot. Very beautiful.

KATE: Thank you. Thank you so much. Very charmed.

BETHYL: Well we'll be going now, dear. We'll leave you to your gardening. *(They begin to exit.)*

KATE: That will be $10.95, please.

BETHYL: *(Pause. Puzzled)* I beg your pardon, dear?

KATE: That will be $10.95.

BETHYL: I don't understand. $10.95? For what? What are you talking about?

KATE: For the five-minute tour.

BETHYL: What tour?

KATE: The tour, the tulips, the windmill, the blue sky, das spiel…the starched apron. It's the five-minute tour. $10.95, please.

BETHYL: But, I thought that was just friendly conversation…the nerve of you!

METHYL and ETHYL: Very nice. Yeah. Very nice.

KATE: I am the flower child tour guide! Do you think we give free tours here in the Netherlands? What are you, cheap ugly Americans?

(The three chase KATE offstage.)

BETHYL: Get outta here…get outta here. *(Sings.)*

("Don't be Fooled by the Dutch")

They seem less crass than the others.
The Dutch are like our sisters and brothers.
Their PR is pretty girls skating,
Hans Brinker waiting
To save the city from flood.

The Dutch are different than the Germans;
These folks are not the Prussian vermins.
Canals that freeze in the cold—

Rembrandt of old
Was peaceful we're told.

BETHYL, ETHYL and METHYL:

But these are Europeans,
Not one bit less obscene,
Stole Manhattan for 24 beans.
These are Europeans
And as such
They can never have too much.

BETHYL:

So don't be fooled by windmills
Or flower pots on white sills.
Behind all of that beauty
Was the businessman's duty
To plunder and rob.

BETHYL, ETHYL and METHYL:

For these are Europeans,
Not one bit less obscene,
Stole Manhattan for 24 beans.
These are Europeans
And as such
They can never have too much.

For these are Europeans,
Not one bit less obscene,
Stole Manhattan for 24 beans.
These are Europeans
And as such
They can never have too much.
They can never have too much.

Act II, Scene 1

In darkness, MUCKEREX is heard.

MUCKEREX: *(Offstage)* The Merman sisters were never heard from again. Yet their extraordinary adventures on the celebration of the centennial of Columbus' vile invasion has led to a serious reconsideration of the Myth of Columbus. Even Russell Baker, in the prestigious *New York Times,* says we have finally seen through the Genoan pirate, who had long been glorified in our textbooks as an illustrious hero. In fact, he was a lout, a drunkard, a no-goodnik, unfaithful to his wife, a petty, sexist, thieving entrepreneur. But—a little-known fact. Christopher Columbus was also the great, great, great, great, great, great, great, great, great, great, great, great, great grandfather of the world famous 20th-century comedian, star of *Coconuts, Horsefeathers* and *Duck Soup,* Groucho Marx. Yes. Christo Marx, or Groucho Columbus, as he was often called, and his sister and brother, Harpa and Chico, spent endless hours in the obscenely filthy bars of downtown Madrid, getting drunk out of their wacky minds before Christo/Groucho left on his now-famous voyage early in August of 1492.

(A dive in Madrid where HARPA, CHICO *and* CHRISTO MARX *aka* GROUCHO COLUMBUS *are seated at a table getting very drunk.)*

CHICO: I'ma tella you Christo, I'ma tella you once, I'ma tella you a milliona times da earth isa flat. Isa nota round, isa flat.

(HARPA honks.)

CHRISTO/GROUCHO: No, no, it's round, I'm sure it's round. Every time I look at it from a distance I see it's round.

CHICO: Whatta you talkin? Seea froma distance. What distance? Youa drunk alla time, thas how coma you think isa round. But isa flat. I'ma tella you once I'm a tella you a million times you getta youself ina serious trouble, Christo, seriousa trouble. *(HARPA honks three times.)* Hey! Shut uppa you! *(To* CHRISTO/GROUCHO.*)* You go arounda sayin' you think isa round, you tella Isabella anna Ferdinanda isa round, dey lay soma money ona you…*(HARPA honks twice.* CHICO *shoots a look at* HARPA, *continues)*…you go on a boats and isa flat anna you come back anna dey gonna putta you ass in jail for years anna years anna years. *(HARPA honks twice.)* I tolla you shuttup! I'ma talkin. *(To* CHRISTO/GROUCHO.*)* Dey are de king anna de queen you dummy. You no messa wit dem, whasa matta wit you? Sometimes you sound like our old a buddy, I saw hima coupla months ago when I was back ina Genoa... you know, Amerigo Vespucci. Amerigo is a dummy allatogether. Cuz he went toa college ata Padua University... (*He mispronounces Padua: Pa-doo-ah.*)

CHRISTO/GROUCHO: (*Interrupts*) That's Padua.

CHICO: Atsa what I said: Pa-doo-ah.

CHRISTO/GROUCHO: Padua, Padua!

CHICO: Pa-doo-ah, Pa-doo-ah.

CHRISTO/GROUCHO: (*Rolls eyes.*) Now you've got it.

CHICO: ...anna he thinksa dat de world isa round, too. But dat a bozo Amerigo—hea say you notta gonna reacha India you gonna find a new landa datsa called Amerigo. (*HARPA honks repeatedly.*) Fora oncea you right! (*To CHRISTO/GROUCHO.*) So I'ma say to him, "Amerigo, you dummy, you bozo, howa you figure Columbus' agonna find a new land witha you name on it?" So he says a to me "wait and see." What a dummy!

CHRISTO/GROUCHO: Don't worry, I tell you, it's round. I'm a lousy sailor but I got 20/20 vision especially when I'm drunk...and I'm always drunk. As for Amerigo, God bless him, does he like Japanese food? Besides if it's flat all that can happen is I'll go over the edge. My wife says I've been over the edge all my life...so, what's to worry. Either this world is round or my compass has stopped. Chico, play "Melancholy Baby" for me as a goodbye gift. Or, better still, play me the theme song from "Goodbye Columbus."

CHICO: (*Goes to piano*) I'ma gonna play you "My name isa Capt. DaGama de a African Explorer." It's a de only songa I know.

(*"Christopher Columbus"*)

CHRISTO/GROUCHO: (*Sings*)
I'm Christopher Columbus,
The European explorer.
You'll need a chonahorah
When I come to your port.

I sailed from Spain in summer.
My wife said, "You're a bummer."
When we ran out of rum, her
Words seemed like a tort.

On the lead ship St. Maria
I got the sickness sea-a.
No dramamine for me-a,
But I'm-a feeling out a-sort.

I'm sick of the sea.
Between you and me,
If the world isn't round
I'm gonna spend a decade
Locked up on the ground.

Amerigo Vespucci
Who is wearing shoes by Gucci
So I'll bring him back some sushi
This shouldn't be for nought.

I'm such a lousy sailor
I should have been a tailor
Then they wouldn't need a jailer
To hang me when I'm caught.

I'm sick of the sea.
Between you and me,
If the world isn't round
I'm gonna spend a decade
Locked up on the ground.

I'm Christopher Columbus,
The European explorer.
You'll need a chonahorah
When I come to your port.
I come direct
From Isabella's court.

Act II, Scene 2

MUCKEREX: *(Offstage)* Columbus set sail nine days later, presumably drunk as a skunk. History books tell us about the rebelliousness of the crew, and of Christopher Columbus' heroism. But—little-known fact—the crew's mutiny paled in comparison to the rebellion by Columbus' three ships, the Pinta, the Nina, the Santa Maria.

(The sound of the ocean is heard in darkness. As the lights come up we see the NINA, the PINTA, and the SANTA MARIA in a triangular formation with the SANTA MARIA at the apex. The PINTA and the NINA are talking to each other. They wear sandwich boards with cut-outs of ships. PINTA is played by the actress who played HARPA.)

NINA: Hey, sister Pinta, listen up for a minute. What do you think of this bullshit about sailing west to get to the east?

PINTA: *(Very neurotic)* East, west, that's the least of my worries. I'm scared shit of falling off the edge. I mean what in the hell am I doing here in the middle of the goddamn Atlantic Ocean being sailed on by a lunatic explorer who's working for the king and queen of Spain. I think I need boat therapy, Nina, short-term boat crisis normalization.

NINA: Be cool, Pint *(pronounced to rhyme with "mint")*. I agree, this bastard Columbus makes Bill Clinton look like a feminist. But at least you don't gotta put up with his racism. Whoooeee—this guy makes Pat Buchanan look like a Black Panther. You know what I'm sayin'? I hope wherever we're going there ain't no people of color there because Columbus is a man on a white horse when it comes to colored folks. I mean you've heard of the Knights of Columbus, haven't you?

PINTA: *(Always melodramatic)* Nina, I think we need help. We're in deep water, sister, deep water. Do ya think our classical Greek friend Santa Maria will talk to us today? The Greeks are smart. They know all about this navigational stuff. Pythagoras invented the right angle didn't he? And wasn't it someone named Isosceles who invented the triangle altogether? I'm scared, Nina. Let's try to talk to Santa Maria one more time, please.

NINA: Okay Pint, before you have a nervous breakdown. Let's mosey on up and try to rap with the Greek.

(*They slowly, cautiously, paddle their way up to* SANTA MARIA. *As they get close she turns sharply to them.*)

SANTA MARIA: (*Sternly*) What do you two want?

PINTA: Santa Maria, I'm very, very scared. Are we going to fall off the edge of the world? I don't want to be eaten by a dragon.

SANTA MARIA: (*Sarcastically*) Don't worry, dragons are vegetarians!

NINA: C'mon Santa Maria, don't you see the sister's in trouble? You're the leader here. Why don't ya stop being so classical and help her out?

SANTA MARIA: (*Pauses*) Alright, Pinta. Stop worryin'! You won't fall off the edge (*aside*) though you might go over the deep end.

NINA: How come you're so damn uppity Santa Maria? How come you're always reading books and won't talk to us ordinary workin' ships. Ya hear what I'm sayin'? I understand you folks invented rationality and logic and all that shit but that don't mean you can't just shoot the breeze with us common types once in a while.

PINTA: Yeah, Santa Maria, us ships gotta stick together out here alone on the high seas with Chris Columbus and his all-male crew. Why won't you be a little less classical and get tight with the sisters?

SANTA MARIA: Alright you two. I've been listening to this classical Greek shit for weeks now and I'm tired of it. All Greeks are not classical. I'm a Greek. I'm not classical.

NINA: Hey sister Maria, that syllogism doesn't follow. It's invalid. I'm surprised at you! Goddamn.

SANTA MARIA: Not bad, not bad. Right you are sister Nina. But I'm not a classical Greek. I'm a progressive Greek! You know…a socialist…a revolutionary. And the reason I stay away from you two is that you're too damned self-centered. All you ever talk about are your mainsails or your starboard bows. About your bein' ship shape! You never think about the rest of the world, about wagons or stars or even classes of people. This joker Columbus walks around all day singin' "Popeye the Sailor Man" and "I'm Christopher Columbus, the European Explorer," smoking a cigar and flicking his damn ashes all over the deck, wringing his hands in anticipation of the plundering and raping he hopes to do in what he calls the New World. That's why those creeps Isabella and Ferdinand sent him—to rip off some shit from the folks who already live there—Indians, I think the Europeans will call them someday. Now if you wanna worry about something, why not worry about that!!! Why not worry about them?

(NINA and PINTA look somewhat sheepishly at each other. As they do, we hear CHRISTO/GROUCHO coming, singing "I'm Christopher Columbus..." He enters.)

CHRISTO/GROUCHO: What are you three broads doing talking to each other? Get back to your places Nina and Pinta. *(Points to SANTA MARIA.)* And as for you sister remember you're Santa Maria, not Comrade Maria, so far as I'm concerned. So get to work you three or you'll all sleep with the fishes...was that from one of my movies?

NINA: Look here Columbo, if we don't keep on chuggin' along it's you and your sexist crew that's gonna be fish stew. I don't know about this communism stuff...I mean boats of the world unite sounds a little fishy but Santa Maria makes sense when she talks about what a scurvy bastard you are.

PINTA: Did you make up all those stories about going off the deep edge just to keep us in tow? *(Honks twice and makes HARPA face.)*

CHRISTO/GROUCHO: Don't I know you from somewhere?

SANTA MARIA: Of course he did. The truth is that the Spanish monarchy is broke—flat broke. And they hired Cristobal Colon over here to go and rob and plunder to bail them out. Ain't that right, Chris baby?

CHRISTO/GROUCHO: Quiet commie. I am the European. I think therefore I am. I am therefore you're not. You Greeks lost to the Romans, the Catholics beat the Romans and then we Europeans beat the Catholics. So now we're the Super Bowl champs. Get it gals?

SANTA MARIA: Quiet, blowhard. You're just a capitalist lackey. A common thief. And Groucho, Chico, Harpo, Zeppo and Gummo will be ashamed of you someday.

NINA and PINTA: Right on, Santa Maria!

CHRISTO/GROUCHO: You three are beginning to sound a little like my crew— I mean mutinous. So just cut this shit out, lay back and float your asses due west.

NINA: Hey Colon, are there people of color in this place we're going to?

CHRISTO/GROUCHO: We're goin' to India and there will be Indians there to rob blind in the name of the Spanish Empire.

PINTA: I don't want any part of robbin' Indians.

NINA: What color are Indians, Chris?

CHRISTO/GROUCHO: Well…they're not white like me. I'll tell ya that.

NINA: Then count me out. These Indians are my sisters and brothers.

SANTA MARIA: Right on, Nina.

CHRISTO/GROUCHO: But you can't be counted out, you dumbo ships. This is 1492 and Columbus is sailing the ocean blue and you three, Nina, Pinta and Santa Maria—you three are too. It's history, a well-known fact, you can't change it. So shape up and move the hell out!

SANTA MARIA: Sorry Chris but we can change that well-known fact into a little-known fact. Nina, Pinta, let's throw this bastard overboard.

(*They pick up* CHRISTO/GROUCHO *and swing him back and forth preparing to throw him overboard.*)

CHRISTO/GROUCHO: Wait, I'll change course. I don't wanna drown. We'll go to a different place. We'll go to Hollywood. I know some movie moguls. Anything but don't throw me overboard. (*Strikes a Groucho pose, held up by the ships.*) Besides, don't I look lovely like this, ladies?

(*They throw him offstage.*)

SANTA MARIA: Sorry Chris. But we're going on without you. The three of us are headin' to New York City. We're gonna have a few drinks at a little women's bar on West 76th Street on an avenue between Amsterdam and Central Park West now called...

NINA: Oh, you mean Colum...

SANTA MARIA: Not any more, sisters. Now it's called Sister Maria Avenue.

NINA and PINTA: Right on, sister Maria.

Act II, Scene 3

A bar in a club, somewhat modern, somewhat surreal. The SINGERS are all dressed in black.

MUCKEREX: *(Offstage)* The Europeans have invented many, many things. Some few have even been helpful. But mostly they have created a very special brand of brutal oppression, of rape, of murder. For 500 years what they've produced is unbelievable amounts of pain. They have hurt and destroyed trillions all over the world, from the African people who they enslaved, to the Jewish people who they murdered, to Native American people who they annihilated, to Asian people who they plundered, to women who they raped, to gay people who they tortured.

("What Kind of Men are You?")

SINGER:

The tears of our women
Meant nothing to you.
The rage of the sisters
Meant nothing to you.
The rape of our children
Never did touch you.
The death of our mothers
Never did touch you.

What kind of men are you
Who passed through
Our lives without
A human sensibility?
What kind of men are you

Who threw a knife into
Our life
And raped us all?

The fears of our women
Never moved you.
The fright of our children
Left you cold.

The death of our people
Never bothered you,
And now we are sad
And growing old.

What kind of men are you
Who passed through
Our lives without
A human sensibility?
What kind of men are you
Who threw a knife into
Our life
And raped us all?

(*"Sadie's Song"*)

SINGER:

Sadie,
Where are you?
Are you wandering
As you always do?
Are you sad-eyed
Crying inside?
Trying hard to hide
A life that had to die.
Trying hard to live
Without a reason why?

Golden stars
Reflect in your eyes
Lighting up the dark

Of their night.
Sadie, Sadie,
You were the light
That will never shine again.
They closed your eyes, my Sadie,
Never shine again.

Sadie,
Where are you?
Are you wandering
As you always did?
Are you wondering
The way you always used to do
Or my Sadie
Are you gone forever now?

Sadie,
Where have you gone?
Sadie,
What have they done?
Sadie,
What were we here for?

("*Black Child Black Woman*")

SINGER:

Black child,
Country home,
Daddy's playing music,
Mama's on the phone.
Kansas was my childhood,
Sort of lonely and sad.
When my daddy died a young man
Lost what happiness I had.
When my daddy died a young man
Lost what happiness I had.

Girl child,
Sister to my brothers.

Growin' up singin'
Playin' songs for others.
Thinkin' of my daddy,
Gonna keep his voice alive.
Then I left my home in Kansas
Just to see if I'd survive.
Yeah, I left my home in Kansas
Just to see if I'd survive.

New York town,
New York sounds,
How's a tiny country girl to live?
All alone
With my song.
Daddy's not with me anymore
To teach me right from wrong,
Right from wrong.

Black woman,
Made this city mine.
Singin' urban country
Kansas doin' fine!
Papa's got a new tune
With his little darlin's voice.
Daddy's makin' music,
Daddy's makin' Black music,
Daddy's makin' country music,
And the music's all mine.

Act II, Scene 4

MUCKEREX: *(Offstage)* The Columbus myth is fraught with disinformation and misinformation. Myth has it, for example, that Columbus landed in the Caribbean, in the Bahamas. Little-known fact…Columbus actually landed in Harlem, USA…little-known fact…on 125th St. right near the Cotton Club.

(PAM, a country singer, and EMMY STRAIT meet in West Harlem. They are clothed in weird medieval/modern entertainer costumes.)

PAM: How ya doin', sister Emmy?

EMMY: Oh, I'm doin' okay, just hangin' out. *(Points to dock.)* You see those strange boats that landed here yesterday?

PAM: Those three old boats with all these white guys jumpin' off and on? Yeah, I seen 'em.

EMMY: Whattya think it's all about?

PAM: I dunno. Looks like *Brothers From Another Planet* to me.

EMMY: It's sure weird. I jus' keep away from that kinda stuff.

PAM: Say, you workin'?

EMMY: No, I ain't got work. How 'bout you, you workin'?

PAM: Yeah, I got this crazy gig, in an Off-Off-Off-Off-Santa Maria Avenue show called *Billie & Malcolm*. I play this itinerant comedienne who goes to heaven and she's hangin' there with Billie Holiday and Malcolm X. I sing this funny song. Actually, I was wondering, I mean, you know something about this comedy stuff, could I just run it by you, Emmy?

EMMY: Hit it, sister Pam.

("I'm Black, I'm Strait and I'm Gay")

PAM: *(Sings)*
Well, I'm Black, I'm Strait and I'm gay,
I wouldn't have it any other way.
It may come from my genes
Or some weirdo teenage scenes,
But I'm as Black as anybody in the 'hood…

(EMMY has been watching incredulously as PAM belts out the song.)

EMMY: *(Interrupting)* That's my song, Pam. I sang this song before. Shit. I lived this song. I know this song, sister Pam, maybe from another life or death…or somethin' like that. *(EMMY and PAM sing together to the end of the number.)*

And I'm proud to be Black and to be gay.
Hey, I'm hangin' out with Malcolm X
And Lady Day.
Don't tell me it's unnatural;
It couldn't be more factual,
So, brother…come on back and join this play.

Oh yes, I'm Black, I'm Strait and I'm gay,
I wouldn't have it any other way.
Don't criticize my preference
'Cause I won't show no deference
To anyone who does that macho sway.

I'm Strait, I'm gay and I'm Black.
I ain't no prince or princess,
Just a plain old workin' hack,
But no one makes a joke of me
In Cleveland or in Galilee
And if they do I'm gonna pay 'em back.

We gotta all rejoin that good ole human race
Before that New World Order puts a boot heel in your face.
Us Black folks straight and gay
Gotta lead 'em all the way
To make this spinnin' ball a better place.

I'm Black, I'm gay and I'm Strait, ya see
It's time we got together
And wiped out white supremacy
'Cause fightin' 'mongst each other—
Hey, I'm your sister, you're my brother,
There's something here on which we all agree.

Well, I'm Black, I'm Strait and I'm gay,
I wouldn't have it any other way.

PAM: STOP THE MUSIC! This song *is* you, Emmy. You take the job. I'm
gonna give you the gig. You're the one who should be doin' this.
Besides, I'm lookin' to git the hell out of vaudeville. I want to break

into Black country music. I want to sing my country song at the Apollo.
I want to work for the Harlem rodeo.

EMMY: There's a rodeo in Harlem?

PAM: (*Á la Groucho*) There's a Nina, Pinta and Santa Maria in Harlem?

(*EMMY exits. PAM sings.*)

(*"Black and Country"*)

Workin' for the rodeo in Harlem
Singing country melodies uptown
Wearin' a cowboy hat on Adam Clayton Boulevard
Thinkin' 'bout Malcolm X
And his Omaha sound.

Came to New York City on the night train
Black as I could be but Kansas-grown,
Wonderin' if the great man from Nebraska
Worried if he'd ever make it on his own,
Worried if he'd ever make it in this town.

Black and country,
Black and country's what I am.
Black and country,
And not knowing if I can
Sing my song at the Apollo
As a Black and country woman.
Black and country,
Black and country's what I am.
Black and country,
Black and country's what I am.

I'm gonna do the right thing for my people.
Black is Black—that's true the whole world 'round.
I come from the country and country Black's my sound.
So I'm working for the rodeo in Harlem-town.
Yes, I'm working for the rodeo in Harlem-town.

Black and country,
Black and country's what I am.
Black and country,
And not knowing if I can.
Sing my song at the Apollo
As a Black and country woman.
Black and country,
Black and country's what I am.
Black and country,
Black and country's what I am.

Call me a rodeo rider,
Got a horse that's black and white.
Call me a Harlem cowgirl,
Hear my hoofbeats in a Harlem night.

Black and country,
Black and country's what I am.
Black and country,
And not knowing if I can
Sing my song at the Apollo
As a Black and country woman.
Black and country,
Black and country's what I am.
Black and country,
Black and country's what I am.

(The entire company comes onstage to congratulate PAM. There is a lighting effect similar to that of the opening scene; the company exits and the action returns to the video monitors. MUCKEREX and the company appear in modern dress, incorporating costume elements of their period counterparts.)

MUCKEREX: So. That's the real story. That's what really went down.

ETHYLETHYL: *(Sings)*
Curtain up, light the lights, we have nothing to hit but the heights…

HANGEMHIGH: Most extraordinary. Most extraordinary.

GAYGGLE: *(Sings)*
>   I'm Black, I'm Strait and I'm gay and…

KANSAS: *(Sings)*
>   I'm singin' country music up in Harlem everyday.

DESHORSE: I think…I think…I think…I recognize some of those folks.

NICKNACK: *(Sings to the tune of "Born in the USA")*
>   Cogito Ergo Sum, Cogito Ergo Sum, Cogito Ergo Sum.

MERMANMERMAN: *(Sings)*
>   There's No Business Like No Business.

RED: Wow! All power to the Soviets…wherever they are now.

LADYBUG: *(Sings)*
>   … Starting here, starting now, honey everything's coming up tulips…

ALL: It's astounding! It's incredible! It's hysterical. It's historical!!

(Musical intro, to MUCKEREX reading start of "The Europeans." They sing.)

(Reprise: "The Europeans")

MUCKEREX:
>   Europeans are obscene in their essence;
>   They invented the word "effervescence"
>   To describe the bubbles
>   Which cover up all the troubles
>   Caused by Europe's prolonged adolescence.

ALL:
>   It's invalid to overly generalize,
>   But when you peer into a European's glassy eyes *(All scream.)*
>   There is greed
>   There is plunder
>   The look of loud thunder
>   A Wagnerian gaze meant to hypnotize.

WOMEN:
>   But strictly between us
>   It's really the penis

Which captures the European core
Which explains what is grandly
Defined as most manly
To psychotically lust for MORE…and MORE…and MORE!

SISTER SADIE:

So Attila the Hun is a novice
There's a rumor he rested on Shabbos
But so completely obsessed
With the gold and the breast
The European, on the Lord's Day, will rob us.

MERMAN SISTERS:

But strictly between us
It's really the penis
Which captures the European core
Which explains what is grandly
Defined as most manly
To psychotically lust for MORE!

ALL:

So beware of the European common line—

MEN:

Board your windows, hide your daughters,
It's Frankenstein!

ALL:

As Voltaire once said
As he lay in his bed,
"It's the best of all possible worlds."

WOMEN:

But Voltaire wasn't one of the girls.

Billie & Malcolm: A Demonstration

Original music by Dan Belmont, Fred Newman and Annie Roboff, lyrics by Fred Newman

Structurally, *Billie & Malcolm: A Demonstration* (1993) is more complex than *Mr. Hirsch Died Yesterday* or *Carmen's Community*. But like them it can be viewed as a series of narratives—not strictly parallel, but all having to do with racism and violence—which eventually interact and impact on each other.

The first act provides, if not a narrative, an impressionistic vision or memory of the 1960s and the painful consequences of the failure of that era's social movements. This vision is juxtaposed with Act II, set in heaven and consisting of four narratives. None of the Act II narratives has anything directly to do with the '60s, and yet when experienced together they shed light on (provide a new way of viewing) the first act. Malcolm X tells his story; Billie Holiday tells her story; Walter, a young Black man shot by a cop in the 1990s, tells his story. Each of these tragic narratives of African American life (and death) is contrasted with the comic narrative of Emmy Strait, a fourth-rate Black comedienne, who has also been shot dead by a racist but unlike the others doesn't relate to her own death as tragic. She thereby challenges, however unintentionally, the politics of monumentalization, that is, the attitude, all too common across the political spectrum, that approaches leaders (and ideas) as unchanging, idealized things-in-themselves, thus constraining their development. In so doing, Emmy allows the 1960s—an era characterized by, among other things, radical challenges to prevailing monuments—back into the play.

While it is the group that remains the unit of change in *Billie & Malcolm*, as it was in *Carmen's Community*, Emmy Strait emerges as the catalyst in the group's transformation. Strait—through her contrasting narrative/vision/attitude—becomes the agent of change. In political terms, she is the play's "organizer." This organizer figure, the character who creates the conditions for the group to transform, will reappear in later Newman plays—most notably as Holiday Hill in *Left of the Moon* and Carmela Petrelli in *The Store: One Block East of Jerome*.

In this regard, it is important to note that Strait is not smarter or braver or more insightful than Malcolm X or Billie Holiday or Walter. In fact, it is Strait's fourth-rateness, her lack of "street smarts," her ordinariness, that allows her to disrupt the static politics that have turned Billie and Malcolm into icons. Being hip is, after all, a social adaptation, a means of surviving/ thriving in the world as it is. That Strait is not hip, not cool, gives her the least investment in things as they are and allows her to challenge every monument in the play—Blackness, Maleness, Heterosexual Romance, Talent.

Not only is Strait not hip; she is sacrilegious. What else can you call a character whose first lines when she "wakes up" in heaven are: "Alright! I know where I am. *Where the hell is God?* ...I am ready to meet my maker. I hope the *bastard* is ready to meet Emmy Strait." Newman has called sacrilege "the condition for escape"—in this case from heaven and in a more general sense from every one of the social and historical prisons in which we find ourselves. His entire enterprise, onstage and off, can be viewed as sacrilegious, a challenge to the various orthodoxies—religious, philosophical, political and psychological—which define our moment in history.

It is worth noting that Emmy Strait is a comedienne and that *Billie & Malcolm: A Demonstration*, despite its serious concerns, is a comedy. For Newman, humor—the ability to step outside the immediate situation and to appreciate its absurdity—and sacrilege are closely related. Without humor we are trapped by our egos, hopelessly caught up in circumstance, fully committed to and determined by our worship of idols/icons/heroes. While only two other Newman plays—the musical revue *Off-Broadway Melodies of 1592* and *Outing Wittgenstein*—can be called comedies, all his plays contain humor and imply its liberating qualities. It is Emmy Strait's combination of ordinariness, sacrilege, and humor that makes her a catalyst for change.

Billie & Malcolm is the first of Newman's plays to include dead characters. His belief that the dead are with us, not in the pre-modern sense of ghosts or spirits, but in Marx's sense that nothing is lost in history, is a feature of many subsequent plays.

The evolution of *Billie & Malcolm: A Demonstration*—a creative process that stretched over eight years—reveals much about how Fred Newman works and how his development as a playwright has been intimately interwoven with the production history of the Castillo Theatre. Newman has said that he has "trouble" with the notion that a play ends. By this he means not only that he questions the assumption that there is a fixed boundary separating performance and non-performance marked by the moment when the curtain comes down, but also the assumption that a script, once written, is a finished product. *Billie & Malcolm* is a good example of how Newman approaches a script not as a finished work of literature but (to borrow a word from the military and politics), as an artistic *tactic;* it changes in ways that are consistent with its own internal logic/integrity and is, at the same time, part of the play's ongoing interaction with a constantly changing world.

Billie & Malcolm: A Demonstration began as two separate plays, each of which went through a number of productions, and significant reworkings, before being brought together as a single play in 1993. The synthesized script was reworked yet again (for a production the following year) into the version included here. This version has had two productions. It was directed by Newman in 1994 and by Castillo's producing director, Gabrielle Kurlander, in 1995.

The evolution of *Billie & Malcolm* began with the 1986 Castillo production of *A Demonstration: Common Women, the Uncommon Lives of Ordinary Women,* the first piece ever directed by Newman. As the title implies, the production was a conscious attempt to blur the distinction between a play and a political rally. The performance centered around two demonstrations—one of radical lesbian feminists (mostly white), the other of women welfare activists (mostly Black)—which run into each other at the corner of Euclid Avenue (the heart of Black Brooklyn) and Christopher Street (the main drag of Greenwich Village, the center of New York City's gay community). In "real life" they are many miles (and a social world) apart, but the historic intersection of these two thoroughfares was crucial in the building of the independent political movement in New York City, which by the mid-'80s Newman had been leading for a decade. The performance ended—in traditional agit-prop style—with the actors/dancers rising from the floor to a militant rebirth in the 1980s.

Two years later (under the title of *Demonstration!*) the performance piece was restructured and restaged—with a cast of more seasoned Castillo performers and considerable upgrading of production values—both at Castillo's 20th Street space and at Aaron Davis Hall on the Harlem campus of the City College of New York. The first act of *Billie & Malcolm: A Demonstration* can be traced back to these two productions.

The second act had its origins in Newman's *Billie, Malcolm & Yusuf*, first produced at Castillo in November of 1991. Like *Common Women*, *Billie, Malcolm & Yusuf* grew directly out of Newman's political concerns— in this case the murder of Yusuf Hawkins, a 16-year-old African American youth killed by a white mob in the Bensonhurst section of Brooklyn in August 1989. Every Sunday for nearly a year Newman, along with the Reverend Al Sharpton, Dr. Lenora Fulani and attorneys Alton Maddox and C. Vernon Mason, led large demonstrations through the streets of Benson-hurst, demanding justice for Yusuf Hawkins' murderers. The young work-ing-class character who found himself in heaven with Malcolm X and Billie Holiday in 1991 was called Yusuf Hawkins.

Billie, Malcolm & Yusuf was the first play Newman wrote after an extended nine-month run at Castillo of James Chapman's *Our Young Black Men are Dying and Nobody Seems to Care*. Chapman's piece documents the ways in which young Black men are being killed—by the police, AIDS and each other. Newman was eager to present a work about the crisis in the Black community that didn't focus on—or end with—death. The writing and production of *Billie, Malcolm & Yusuf* also coincided with the hoopla surrounding the release of Spike Lee's film, *Malcolm X*. In response to the increasing iconization (and commercialization) of Malcolm X and other Black political and cultural leaders, Newman wanted to challenge the process of monumentalization, a theme he had already explored to some extent in 1987 in *The Collected Emotions of V.I. Lenin* (an early version of *Lenin's Breakdown*) and would return to in a number of later plays—*Sally and Tom (The American Way)*, *Risky Revolutionary*, and *Stealin' Home*—all of which are included in this collection.

The 1991 production of *Billie, Malcolm & Yusuf* began with a funeral procession in the lobby of the Castillo Theatre at its current location on Greenwich Street in SoHo, which had been dressed to resemble a funeral home. (The tone of Act I in *Billie & Malcolm: A Demonstration* is much closer to this funeral procession than it is to the celebratory feel of *Common Women* and *Demonstration!*) A coffin was ceremoniously borne into the theatre, followed by the audience, which then found itself not at an earthly funeral service but in heaven. Emmy Strait popped out of the coffin after

Billie's first song. In addition to Billie Holiday standards and Emmy's songs, the script contained a number of raps for Yusuf, who was portrayed as a charming young hip-hopper, although less mature than the "Walter" character who emerged in the later version of the play.

The most significant difference between *Billie, Malcolm & Yusuf* and the second act of the later *Billie & Malcolm: A Demonstration* is the ending. In the 1991 production, as Malcolm, Billie and Yusuf realize that they have been monumentalized and begin to come off their pedestals, the television monitors hanging above the stage come alive with news reports of massive demonstrations—a virtual revolutionary upheaval—on Earth. The characters—led by Emmy and full of the fear and trepidation that come with hope—venture through an onstage door, leaving heaven behind to re-enter history. This is a far more "optimistic" ending than the later version of the play, contained here, which concludes with two melancholy songs, "Nobody Sees Nobody" and "Will It Ever Happen?" In *Billie, Malcolm & Yusuf* it *does* happen, and as with *Common Women*, the play ends in the rebirth of progressive social motion. In this regard, it remained firmly within the agit-prop tradition of resolving social conflicts onstage in favor of the oppressed.

What we see in the 1994 version of *Billie & Malcolm: A Demonstration* is the beginnings of Newman's refusal to use the stage to resolve social contradictions that can not be resolved in society, either on behalf of the oppressed (as in agit-prop) or the status quo (as in most traditional plays). Since the only resolutions that can be imagined are overdetermined by the world as it currently exists, resolution itself is conservatizing. Newman's later plays are neither "hopeful" nor "despairing." His refusal to resolve conflicts onstage is perhaps his most radical break with the institution of the theatre—"progressive" or otherwise—and has become a distinguishing feature of his writing for the theatre. It is the lack of resolution in his plays that Newman has identified as one of their most important "developmental" aspects. The evolution of *Billie & Malcolm: A Demonstration* thus shows an aspect of Newman's journey from agit-prop to what we now call developmental theatre.

D.F.

Billie & Malcolm: A Demonstration was first produced at the Castillo Theatre in 1993. The version presented here was produced at the Castillo Theatre (Fred Newman, artistic director; Gabrielle Kurlander, producing director; Diane Stiles, managing director) in New York City on February 4, 1994. The cast, in order of appearance, was as follows:

COPS . . . . Doug Balder, Kenneth Hughes

DRAG QUEENS . . . . Jeff Aron, Allen Cox, Howard Edelbaum,
Kate Gardner, Creston Rice

BLACK PANTHERS . . . . Lawrence Davis, Lisa Linnen,
Michelle McCleary, Jamela Stevens

FEMINISTS . . . . Jill Battalen, Madelyn Chapman, Julie Kinnett,
Luvenia Suber, Gayle Weintraub

BLACK PANTHER/PAM KANSAS . . . . Pam Lewis

OLD HOMELESS BLACK PANTHER . . . . Doug Miranda

BILLIE HOLIDAY. . . . . Cece Waterman

MALCOLM X . . . . Emmitt H. Thrower

WALTER JOHNSON. . . . . Cuffee

EMMY STRAIT . . . . L. Thecla Farrell

NEWSCASTER (ON VIDEO). . . . . Michael Mitchell

Fred Newman, director; Diane Stiles, producer; Amy Pivar, choreography; Joseph Spirito, set design; Elena Borstein, scenic design; Charlotte, costume design; Linnaea Tillett, lighting design; Michael Klein, sound design; Barry Z Levine, video design/cinematography; Ellen Korner, production stage manager.

Billie & Malcolm: A Demonstration is a work of fiction about, among other things, two enormously important people, Billie Holiday and Malcolm X. Who were the real Billie and Malcolm? I do not know. There are probably as many real Billies and Malcolms as there were people moved by these extraordinary human beings. Millions.

What is the truth of their lives and deaths? I do not know. Indeed, I make no claim to be a truth-teller, merely a completer (in Lev Vygotsky's sense) of stories. The play intends no insult to anyone. It does, however, wish to provoke. For it is a play about betrayal in general and, in particular, betrayal by and of our own people. Such betrayal is, in my opinion, the tragic essence of this despairing century. *Billie & Malcolm* is the companion piece to my play *Dead as a Jew*, which provocatively engages Zionism's betrayal of the Jewish people. It is a companion piece as well to Heiner Müller's brilliant work *The Task* (a play I had the pleasure to direct earlier this year), which engages the tragedy of revolutionaries' betrayal of revolutionaries.

Recently I had the honor of personally meeting and dialoguing with Minister Louis Farrakhan, the leader of the Nation of Islam. We discussed, among other topics, the relationship between Blacks and Jews. He is an extraordinary man, in my opinion, who will never betray either his people or his spirituality. He is a good friend to the Jewish people—a much better one than many of our self-professed buddies from Roosevelt to Reagan to Clinton. For over a decade I have counted myself a fan and pal of the Reverend Al Sharpton. We have often disagreed. We have both worked not to betray each other in any way. I deeply value what we have built together. My very closest political friend is Dr. Lenora B. Fulani. Many who disagree with her a good deal love and respect her because betrayal is no part of this remarkable African American woman. *Billie & Malcolm* is dedicated to these three Black leaders (and the millions who follow them), who have not betrayed their independence, their capacity to grow, and, thereby, their commitment to humanity.

FEBRUARY 1994

CHARACTERS

Onstage
DEMONSTRATORS from movements of the '60s
(drag queens, Black Panthers, feminists)
PAM KANSAS, a Black Panther
OLD MAN, a former Black Panther
BILLIE HOLIDAY, a blues singer
MALCOLM X, an orator
COP, a racist cop
WALTER JOHNSON, a college student
EMMY STRAIT, an itinerant comedienne

On video
NEWSCASTER, a media representative

NOTE:
This play contains both live scenes and video sequences.

Act I

The stage is dressed as a street scene in 1968. A park bench; perhaps some posters advertising '68 movies or other products; McCarthy and/or Bobby Kennedy posters, etc. Also barricades (and a cop or two) indicating a demonstration is near. A single '68 song—maybe Stevie Wonder—begins to play. Otherwise the stage is empty; video screens flanking the stage are dark. Two demonstrators walk slowly on—one Black, one white, with a banner saying "All People's Unity Day, 1968." They hang the banner as the music changes to, perhaps, Dylan singing "Blowing in the Wind." As they complete the banner hanging, several more demonstrators carrying placards, etc. wander on from three different groupings—Black Panthers, including PAM KANSAS *and* OLD MAN, *feminist women (Black and white); and drag queens (Black and white). As the stage fills with demonstrators, the monitors show a '60s music and action montage. As the video plays, demonstrators (in a choreographed walk/dance) continue to get ready for the demo (they set up the microphone; talk/argue with cops; finish painting signs; practice a chant). Video continues, but sound comes down as* BILLIE HOLIDAY *and* MALCOLM X *(wearing wings) enter upstage.*

MALCOLM: Sister Billie, I can't get used to nobody bein' able to see me.

BILLIE: Or hear you either, Brother Malcolm.

MALCOLM: How come, Billie, when ya dead ya can't be seen no more?

BILLIE: Hey, I dunno, Brother Malcolm. That's how it's always been. When ya dead you can still see and hear what's goin' down, but no one sees you. That's just how it is.

MALCOLM: But it don't make no sense. Look…

BILLIE: *(Interrupting somewhat angrily)* What you mean it don't make no sense? This is how it is. This is what dead is. This is the Man's way, Brother Malcolm.

MALCOLM: I guess so, Sister Billie. I guess so. *(Pause.)* Where are we now,

Sister Billie? *(Looking at silent video and live actors setting up demo.)* Where in history are we?

BILLIE: Hey. We're just out takin' a little walk. That's where we are, Brother Malcolm. Just relax.

MALCOLM: No. No, Sister Billie. You know what I mean. Where…where… in history are we? 'Nother thing I can't get used to is us bein' able to go anywhere in history that we want to. Just my damn luck; now that I can go anywhere I want, nobody can see or hear me.

BILLIE: You doin' a lot of complaining today, Brother Malcolm. A lot of complaining. Why don't we just walk and enjoy ourselves. I just needed some fresh air. I been feelin' a little cooped up lately, ya know. Heaven's a little too peaceful and slow movin' even for me sometimes.

MALCOLM: Hey, I wanna know where we are Billie. What's goin' on down here?

(Black and white demonstrators [buddy-buddy] brush by MALCOLM; not noticing him, of course, but pushing him slightly and inadvertently.)

MALCOLM: *(Yells after them)* Hey there, you two. Be careful. Y'all might think you're buddy-buddy nowadays, but you better watch where you're walkin'. Youngsters have no manners anymore, Sister Billie.

BILLIE: Be cool, Brother Malcolm. They don't even see ya. Can't ya get that straight? No one sees ya…no one hears you or me anymore. We're invisible, Brother Malcolm. That's the deal. Ain't no way outta heaven. Ain't no way we ever gonna be seen or heard again. You gonna just have to get used to that.

MALCOLM: I think it's the late '60s. Look there, Billie. Look at that banner …says 1968. We're in the late '60s, Billie. Ain't that something? They're gettin' ready for a demonstration. Let's us get on in there with 'em, Billie.

BILLIE: Malcolm X, will you behave yourself, Brother? You are dead. You can't get in there with 'em. You are dead as can be.

(Video visual continues; contingent of Panthers stands up on bench and begins rhythmic "All Power to the People" chant [along with Panther rally

*on video]; MALCOLM jumps up on bench with them. BILLIE pulls him
down.)*

BILLIE: Brother Malcolm, will you behave yourself? No one can see ya anymore.

MALCOLM: *(Reluctantly)* Okay, Sister Billie. Okay.

*(Rally continues; drag queens begin walking around the bench chanting in
unison with Panthers, "All Power to the People.")*

MALCOLM: *(Sort of embarrassed)* What d'ya think about that, Sister Billie? I
mean as a woman, ya know. What d'ya think about men dressin' up like
that...ya know, like girls?

BILLIE: Hey, Brother Malcolm, I never have cared much about what people
are wearin'. Hell, you and me walkin' around now with wings sproutin'
outta our bodies. We ain't exactly cool no more, Red. *(She smiles at him.)*

MALCOLM: Yeah, Sister Billie, but we ain't go no choice. *(Pointing to wings.)*
This here's the uniform.

BILLIE: Hey, Brother Malcolm, who knows how much of a choice they have.
Did you choose to be Black? Did I? Besides, I'm sure if you wanted to
apply for a transfer—ya know, go to hell with yourself, get a new uniform—that someone upstairs could accommodate you. I mean, Malcolm, you were well on your way to the big Furnace before you straight-
ened up in those last 10 or 15 years on the planet Earth. *(Points to the
drag queens.)* Hell, that's a fine lookin' outfit there. Makes old Billie
look kinda drab.

*(Feminists begin to march around chanting "All Power to the People." At
one point they all simultaneously reach under dresses or blouses and take off
their bras. They hold them on high and continue chanting.)*

MALCOLM: Now, Billie, that's wrong. I mean it's undignified. It's unwom-
anly. Maybe that's okay for white women. But not for sisters.

BILLIE: Malcolm, where in the hell did you go when ya went to Africa anyway? With all due respect, Brother Malcolm, to the Muslim sisters, ya
got a few Black women back home in Africa who ain't been wearin'
bras for quite a while. You know what I'm sayin'?

(*MALCOLM stares at* BILLIE *very skeptically; demonstration now reaches a crescendo of "All Power to the People."* BLACK PANTHER *stands on the bench.*)

BLACK PANTHER: Brothers and Sisters. Listen up now. Let's bring a million people out to Chicago next month. (*Crowd responds.*) Let's show that honky Mayor Daley and his Democratic Party cronies what we the people mean by democracy. (*Crowd responds.*) Let's rock that damn convention hall to the ground. (*Loud response.*) "The People United Will Never Be Defeated."

(*The crowd repeats new chant, "The People United Will Never Be Defeated." The song, "El Pueblo Unido" begins to play. Video continues; the crowd, led by Panthers, marches off leaving only* BILLIE, MALCOLM *and* PAM KANSAS, *who stands at a distance from* BILLIE *and* MALCOLM. *Music fades; video out.*

PAM *slowly gets up on bench. She takes off Panther outfit—beret, leather jacket. She becomes 1990s in costume, as increasingly contemporary music accompanies her costume change. Recorded music fades as live piano introduction begins to "Who Made All the Lies Fit." One* COP *remains.* OLD MAN *sits against wall throughout.*)

("*Who Made All the Lies Fit*")

PAM: (*Sings*)
Where were we standing
When Malcolm was lying
When Martin was dying
When children were crying?

With Birmingham bleeding,
What were we feeling?
When Detroit was flaming,
Who did the framing?

Who named them Black riots?
Who made all the lies fit?
Who wrote up the story?
Who stole all the glory?

Who sat on the jury?
It wasn't you and I.

Now in this moment
Of torture and torment,
Who is deciding?
What are they hiding?

Who named them Black riots?
Who makes all the lies fit?
Who writes up the story?
Who steals all the glory?
Who sits on the jury?
It isn't you and I.

And one day we might make it ours,
And one day we might make it ours,
And one day we might make it ours,
Make it ours.

Who named them Black riots?
Who makes all the lies fit?
Who writes up the story?
Who steals all the glory?
Who sits on the jury?
It isn't you and I.
It isn't you and I.

MALCOLM: I don't think we're in the '60s no more, Billie.

BILLIE: That sister sings mighty fine, don't she, Brother Malcolm?

MALCOLM: (Nods) She remembers me. That makes me feel real good. But it looks like the '60s didn't make it happen, Billie. Where we now, ya think? '80s? '90s?

BILLIE: Somewhere around there, I guess.

PAM: (Still standing on the bench; naturally, contemplatively) Hey, what did it all mean? What did those '60s really mean? Lots of folks demonstrated— lots of demonstrations, Black folks, Fannie Lou Hamer, Rosa Parks,

Selma, Birmingham, white people, civil rights, anti-war, feminist, gay, Dr. King, Malcolm X, Huey P. Newton, Stokely Carmichael, Rap Brown, Fred Hampton. Lotsa people killed, dead in the streets, people locked up and murdered in jail…George Jackson was my favorite. But are we better off? Is there justice? Do our people have jobs? Homes? Good education? Are we more poor or less poor? What did we demonstrate? We had demonstrations—I went to the Black demos *and* the lesbian demos and the anti-war…*but what did they demonstrate*? That's the question that keeps coming up for me. Did we demonstrate our power? Our pride? Our rage? What did we demonstrate? I wonder.

We're more proud. Maybe so. But what are we proud of? Oh yeah, it's good that we took on the MAN—the white MAN. THE POWER STRUCTURE. But have we really made any headway? In terms of what our children need? Young Black men and women are still dying. We still fight with each other. Gay people fight with straight people. Puerto Rican people fight with Black people, people of color fight with white people. Working-class people fight with middle-class people. Men and women still fightin'! We can't seem to find a way to stop fighting with each other. Civil rights were won—then lost. Oh, yeah, some people are better off. There's a tiny Black middle class; middle-class women got some new jobs; there were some cultural changes—all of that was good. But revolution? Changin' the basic structure—shit—people don't even believe you can do that anymore. Lotsa people think that the best we can do is a honky from Arkansas and Yale named Bill Clinton. *Why did we demonstrate? What did all the demonstrations demonstrate?* What does Black history demonstrate? Sure it shows that we are a courageous people; we've gone to the streets; some of us have risked a great deal. Many have been killed. The Panthers—Bobby Seale, Elaine Brown—were my heroes and heroines. Malcolm was a great man; Dr. King was a powerful leader. People gave their lives. Rosa Parks, Fannie Lou Hamer, the children in Birmingham, gave a hell of a lot. What'd they give their lives for? To have a movie made about them; to have a song written about them; to have a play written about them?

What's gone wrong? Thirty years after James Farmer appeared with Malcolm on TV and all but laughed in his face, he comes back on TV and says that Malcolm was right after all; that he, Farmer, had naively underestimated the depth of racism in this country. Now Malcolm's a monument to be respected. Back then Farmer and lots of others tried to put him down—make a fool of him. But so what! What's happening right now that takes seriously the depth of the racism in this country? Who's gonna cure racism—Al Gore, Bill Clinton? Jesse Jackson? Is that what Jesse's doing? Black kids are still getting killed by white cops, and by Black cops. Rodney King is brutally beaten up on live TV, and then the cops get acquitted. What were the '60s all about? Did they mean anything to us? Who was Malcolm X? What did he really do?

We all talk about Black history. At least we talk about it in February. That's when it's official to talk about Black history. We all talk about the '60s like some freaky thing that happened a hundred years ago. But what is history? What does it mean to those of us who lived through it? What does it mean for those of us who came after? I mean the real power that the Big Guys have is that they control how we understand history. They put it into *their* structures, their categories. They give us *their* interpretations and call it truth. They got the big money to make movies and TV shows about it. They control the public schools and the publishing houses that put out the books. So we never understand who we are. We never understand our own history. Everything that happens gets transformed into them telling us who they need us to be, who they want us to be. They still decide who we are because they decide where we came from.

(*Angry.*) Look what's still goin' on! Has anything changed? Look. We gotta take a good look. *It's still goin' on dammit.* It's still goin' on!

(*WALTER enters alone, kind of in a cloud; brushes ever so slightly against COP.*)

COP: Alright asshole, what's your name?

WALTER: My name is Walter Johnson.

COP: What the fuck ya doin' here, boy?

WALTER: I said my name is Walter Johnson.

COP: Listen, asshole, to me you're just another nigger boy lookin' to make trouble.

WALTER: I ain't makin' no trouble.

COP: Then what are you doing here? You don't belong in this neighborhood.

WALTER: I gotta friend of mine who lives here.

COP: *(Laughing)* You gotta *white* friend?

WALTER: Yeah, I got a white friend.

COP: What's his name? What's the nigger lover's name?

WALTER: It's a girl friend. Her name's Sheila Cohen.

COP: You got a white girl friend; a Jew girl friend?

WALTER: Yeah, she's Jewish.

COP: You fuckin' her? Are you fuckin' her, boy? Fuckin' Jew girls really love Black cock, don't they? That's what's wrong with this country. Are you fuckin' her?

WALTER: That ain't none of your damn business.

COP: Oh, oh, oh. It ain't none of my business. You wise-ass nigger. I just asked you a simple question…you know, man to man.

WALTER: I ain't a wise-ass and I don't want no trouble. I'm just on my way to the subway. I'm just on my way home.

COP: You play basketball, boy?

WALTER: Yeah. I play basketball.

COP: You any good?

WALTER: I'm okay. Nothin' too special. I ain't no Michael Jordan. But I start for my college team.

COP: But you're good enough to fuck a white woman…*(laughs)* even if she's a Jew.

WALTER: Look, officer, I don't want no trouble. I just wanna get home.

COP: Where d'ya go to school?

WALTER: I go to City College—up in Harlem.

COP: Mainly Black kids there now, huh? Used to be mainly Jews. I pay taxes so you can go to that school. You know that, Walter?

WALTER: Yeah. I know that. My folks pay taxes that pay your salary. You know that?

COP: (*Slight laugh*) Walter, you are a wise-ass. You people goin' to college and gettin' smart ass and uppity…I don't know…

(*OLD MAN interrupts, drunk, down and out.*)

OLD MAN: What you doin' to that young man, officer? You messin' with him? Boy, is this pig botherin' you?

COP: Get the fuck outta here, you drunken old coot. Get back in your hole.

OLD MAN: (*In COP's face—COP holds off OLD MAN with stick*) You know who I am, pig? You know who I am? I was a Black Panther. I knew Eldridge and Bobby out in California back in '70. I was one of the organizers of the Philly convention. (*Moves close to WALTER*) Is this pig botherin' you? Back in Oakland we'd go around with shotguns. And if the pigs bothered anybody in the neighborhood we'd kinda hang there with our guns pointin'. Pigs ain't so wise-ass when we had guns, boy. You hear what I'm sayin'?

(*COP grabs OLD MAN by the left shoulder and turns him around.*)

COP: Get your ass outta here, you rummy, before I run you in. This young fella is a college man, you old nigger, and he's fuckin' Jewish ass. Now get the fuck outta here before I bust your Black head wide open.

WALTER: C'mon, officer. Leave him alone. He's just a drunk old man.

OLD MAN: Fuck you, college boy. I can take care of myself.

WALTER: Listen old Panther…you're gonna get us both in trouble. Now go on home. Get outta here. Let's all go home.

OLD MAN: I ain't got no home. But I don't bow down to no pig.

(OLD MAN steps back and to left, slowly pulls finger out of pocket, raises arm. COP pulls out real gun. WALTER jumps in front of OLD MAN and COP shoots WALTER through the heart—dead. OLD MAN holds up finger; COP looks.)

OLD MAN: What? What? Wha...

COP: You dumb fuckin' asshole. *(Pause.)* I shot the kid. You made me shoot the kid.

OLD MAN: Is he dead?

COP: You're dead, man. You're dead. *(COP shoots OLD MAN.)*

(Blackout. We hear PAM's voice. Lights come up to reveal her sitting on the bench. COP, WALTER, and OLD MAN are gone.)

PAM: It's still goin' on, dammit. It's still goin' on. *(She sobs hysterically.)*

MALCOLM: *(Goes to comfort her)* Hey, Sister, it's gonna be alright. Yeah, it's gonna be alright.

BILLIE: She can't hear ya, Malcolm. She can't hear ya.

MALCOLM: *(Very angry)* Well, what in the hell's goin' on down here? The sister's right. Nothin's changed. They're still killin' our people. There ain't no damned unity. Young Black men are dying. Gettin' murdered. Murderin' each other. What's goin' on? When's it gonna end? Is it ever gonna be different? Will it ever happen?

(PAM gets up from the bench and walks "toward" BILLIE. She seems drawn to her even though she does not see or hear her.)

("Will it Ever Happen?")

BILLIE: *(Sings)*
Will it ever happen?
Will it ever happen?
Will it ever happen?
Will it ever happen?

PAM:

> From the '60s
> To the '90s
> Nothin' much has
> Changed and so,
> I know, yes, I know
> There's a long, long way to go.

MALCOLM:

> Will it ever happen?
> Will it ever happen?

BILLIE:

> Up in heaven,
> Down on Earth,
> Nothin' different,
> Same old show,
> So I know, yes, I know
> There's a long, long way to go.

MALCOLM:

> Will it ever happen?
> Will it ever happen?

BILLIE and PAM:

> Yes, we know
> That life goes on,
> But we hope
> When we're all dead and gone
> Maybe there'll be a rebirth
> If we fight for all we're worth
> And a little heaven here on Earth.

BILLIE, PAM and MALCOLM:

> Will it ever happen?
> Will it ever happen?
> Will it ever happen?
> Will it ever happen?

Act II

In heaven, a month later—Earth time. EMMY *is sitting on a stool, covered by a funeral cloth;* WALTER, BILLIE, MALCOLM *are also on stools. There is a lectern onstage.*

MALCOLM: So, Lady Day…you singin'? You gonna sing for our new arrival here? *(Motions to black cloth covering* EMMY.*)*

BILLIE: I…ah…I ain't feelin' so good today…I don't feel like singin' so much. *(Pause.)* Tell you the truth…I ain't felt much like singin' lately, Brother Malcolm. Ya see…I dunno why I'm singin' anymore…you know? I've been depressed since we took that walk from the '60s to the '90s.

WALTER: Please sing, Miss Holiday.

MALCOLM: *(Facing* BILLIE*)* Sister Billie. You sang for me so many years ago when I first got here. I hadn't seen you since that time downtown at the Onyx Club. I remember you were so sick then. But you sang beautiful. You sang for young Brother Walter when he got here. We need you to sing for this new *(laughs),* I dunno yet…brother or sister. And further-more *(laughs harder),* I just love to hear your voice, Lady Day. There's… well, there's never been another like it, you know.

WALTER: I mean there ain't much else happenin' around here, Miss Holiday. Please sing.

BILLIE: My head is hurtin' me…Godamighty! Ain't nothin' gonna happen, Malcolm. I'm tired, I…just ain't got it in me today. That was a nice sis-ter we saw on our walk last month. But there ain't a lot like her, I don't think…I'm afraid I made a damn fool of myself. *(Pause.)* Who'm I sin-gin' to, Brother Malcolm? I was *never sure* who I was singin' to, you know. But *now*…now I dunno at all. Ain't nobody hearin' me. White folks didn't really ever know what I was singin' about. And Black folks don't wanna hear about it no more. So who'm I singin' for, Brother Malcolm? *(Pause.)* I used to sing for me. I loved how it felt. I loved the music, ya know…I loved to be around music…I loved to make music. But they killed me, Brother Malcolm X. The white folks killed me; the Black folks killed me; the men folks killed me; I killed me. Well…now

I'm long dead. I don't feel the music no more. I don't feel nothin' no more. It ain't never gonna happen, I don't think, Brother Malcolm.

MALCOLM: Maybe you'd feel better, Sister Billie, if you just sang a little bit. I know what you're sayin' though, Lady. I dunno sometimes who I'm talkin' to anymore. I don't think anyone is listenin'. And I dunno if our people are feelin'. I mean, I know we're still hurtin' bad...but I dunno if we're feelin'. Maybe we been hurtin' so much and for so long that we can't feel no more.

BILLIE: *(Slowly stands)* Okay, okay, okay, I'll sing...I know at least you two ...uh, maybe three *(points to EMMY's stool)*...will hear me.

(BILLIE comes down to footlights and sings "Strange Fruit.")

MALCOLM: Ah, Sister...that was exquisite. You are still the *epitome* of song, you know. Thank you, Sister Billie. Thank you.

WALTER: Now I know why my folks loved to hear you.

BILLIE: Well, thank you, thank you, Brothers. Like I said, I thought you two might...appreciate a song...so...*(she gestures toward the cloth cover)* who else did I have the honor of singin' for here today?

(WALTER stands; pulls cover off EMMY STRAIT. EMMY stands up. She is in a weird costume; jacket, funny hat, etc. She's a fourth-rate stand-up comedienne who is almost always doing some kind of comedy routine. She looks around and immediately starts in.)

EMMY: Alright! I know where I am. *Where in the hell is God?*

(BILLIE, MALCOLM and WALTER look at each other, shocked, nonplussed.)

EMMY: Where is he? Someone point him out to me. Which one of you... *(peering suspiciously at them)*...which one of you know where I can find him? *(Pauses for response.)* Go ahead. Show me the way. I am ready to meet my maker. I hope the *bastard* is ready to meet Emmy Strait.

MALCOLM: Wait. Wait a minute, Sister. "Where is God?" *(Laughs.)* Nobody asks, "Where is God?"

BILLIE: Yeah, hush now, Sister. Hush now.

WALTER: *(Seated, amused)* Calm down, Sister. Calm down.

EMMY: *(Disregards them completely)* Where...the hell...is God? Who is he? I've got all day, I figure, and we are gonna be here until I get my answer.

MALCOLM: Who in the name of Allah do you think you are talking about, may I be so bold as to inquire?

BILLIE: Say! You know where you are? It ain't right what you sayin', Sister. I mean I know you probably had a rough week...I remember what dyin' was like...but still, young Sister, you just can't talk like that around here.

EMMY: I don't give a good goddamn about your holier-than-thou ways. I ain't never *played* heaven before. I just need to know, where's God? Where's the damn manager around here?

MALCOLM: Hey...listen up and learn! You're out of line, my Sister.

EMMY: What the fuck is your problem? Why don't you just tell me where he is?

(All speaking at once.)

WALTER: Shit! Who is this?

MALCOLM: What you're doing, it's not done here. I mean downstairs they make out like they're *talking to God*. But...it's not done up here, ya see.

BILLIE: Yeah, listen to the brother. Just relax, baby...hold up, honey.

EMMY: *(Even more exasperated)* Listen, what's the story? Tell me where God is. I demand to know. I demand to know. *(Waits stubbornly.)* I have my civil rights! *(Clenches fist in the air.)*

WALTER: *(Smiling)* This is deep.

MALCOLM: Ummm, yes. We all know about Dr. King's civil rights stuff. Though, as I have often pointed out *(MALCOLM is "speechifying")* you'd be better off talking about human rights, Sister, but...

BILLIE: *(Interrupting MALCOLM's "speech")* Who in the hell IS this?

EMMY: For the last god-damned time, WHERE-IS-GOD? Where-is-God?

MALCOLM: Okay. Just a minute now. Calm down. Just calm down. Let me ask you something, my Sister. What happened to you? *(Pause.)* I mean, how'd you die?

EMMY: Oh sure, now y'all trying to distract me. You ain't God. I dunno who in the hell you are. But I know y'ain't God. Listen up...I ain't sayin' nothin' till I get what I came here for...can y'all dig that?

BILLIE: Hey, darlin'...take it slow and easy and...c'mon tell us who y'are. Tell us what happened to ya.

MALCOLM: What happened to you? How did you die? Did someone kill ya? Seriously, Sister, tell us how it happened.

EMMY: Well...ya see...Well...Okay. I'm Emmy Strait...stand-up comedienne *par excellence*. Been in the business about...oh...15 years now. Okay, I travel around, a lot, you know, city to city, club to club—sometimes I work a campus—never a dull moment. It's work, ya know...It's Wichita, Phoenix, Spokane, the circuit, Kalamazoo, Akron. (*Pause.*) So I'm doin' Cleveland last Tuesday. And I gotta admit I'm havin' a good night. I'm loose and the audience—small audience—but they're laughin' pretty good. Little club, downtown Cleveland, right on Euclid, near where Western Reserve meets the Hough...maybe 15 people in there and, like I said, they're having a good time...I mean I'm pretty good and this night...I'm loose. It's an okay crowd. Anyway, there's this thing I almost always do at the end of my act, particularly when it's nice and loose. I go out into the crowd at the end and I play a little game of guessing who people are. And I do little one-liners...like—funny guesses. Like I'll say to a young sister sittin' with this older guy— "Where'd you find this dude, Sister, in a pawn shop?" Well, last Tuesday night, I'm at the Lido, in Cleveland, and I'm sort of going around the room doin' these one-liners, and there's this guy in there, sitting in the back...in the corner. Real cracker type, white as snow, black leather jacket hangin' on the chair, boots, tattoo on each arm, crew cut, shades. But I mean, he's there in the club, maybe a medical student, so what the hell. I mean sure he looks tough...but...hey, I'm tough, too...so I go right up to this dude, and I say to him (*she acts it out*) "Let me see, let me see, let me see...I know, YOU'RE the local FASCIST!" (*Slight pause.*) *And he whips out a .45 and blows my fuckin' head off.*

(*All three stand—brief freeze—in shock. Another overwhelming story of murder. TOTAL SILENCE. EMMY continues.*)

Yeah, so that's what happened, this son of a bitch just calmly pulls out a .45 *(pause)* and then BOOM! Off goes my head. Bang, zoom! That's the whole story, that's it. Next thing I know I'm sittin' under this black cloth. My head's back on. I hear this real nice singin'. We didn't have no singer at the Lido. Sooo, I figure I'm in heaven or hell or whatever ...*I know it ain't Cleveland. (Pause.) So here I am*. That's my story. My mama always said that one day I'd tell a real bad joke and I'd get hurt. *(Pause.)* Now, where's God? *(Pause.)* Anyway. Who in the hell are you folks? I ain't doin' any guessin' no more...if you know what I mean.

MALCOLM: *(Laughs)* That's good thinking, Sister. My name is Malcolm X. It's nice to meet you, Sister Emmy Strait.

EMMY: Jesus Christ, Jesus Christ! *(Whispers.)* Jesus Christ, man. You're Malcolm X? I mean the real Malcolm X? Holy shit. You ain't fuckin' with me? You're really Malcolm X?

BILLIE: My name's Billie, Sister, Billie Holiday. That's some story you got there. Yeah. Welcome, Sister...welcome.

WALTER: I'm Walter Johnson. I'm sure you never heard of me.

EMMY: Billie Holiday? Billie Holiday? Holy shit. How'd I wind up in this part of town? I don't play no big clubs. *Billie Holiday! Damn! DAMN!* Malcolm X, Billie Holiday. Those are class acts. Hey, you're heroes. I mean, what in the hell am I doing here? I mean, I'm just Emmy Strait, i-tin-er-ant stand-up Black comedienne, *par excellence*...but, really, you know...*(whispers)* I'm just a workin' stiff *(laughs at her own joke)*...a hack...you folks are class. Jesus Christ. What am I doin' here? Hey, I *gotta* speak with God. I've been sent to the wrong part of town.

MALCOLM: Just settle down, Sister Strait, it's good to have you here... you're pretty funny, Sister, pretty funny. And we can always use a few good jokes up here.

WALTER: Yeah. Brother Malcolm's right on time. It's good to have you here.

BILLIE: Emmy Strait...hmm. Sister Strait...a pleasure. Always nice to have another Sister in the 'hood. *(Reaches to shake hands.)*

MALCOLM: *(After a pause)* So, *Strait*, what...

EMMY: One second, Brother Malcolm...I'm sorry about this, but my *name* is Emmy Strait. Hey...look, I'm real honored to meet you all. I mean no disrespect. But, Brother Malcolm...I don't like being called Strait 'cause *(pause)* well...I'm gay. *(Pause.)* Let's get this cleared up right away. You with it, brother? I'm gay.

WALTER: Your name is Emmy Strait, but you're gay?

BILLIE: Yeah, that's what she said. Emmy Strait is gay. She just told ya. Jest be cool, Walter, be cool.

WALTER: Emmy Strait is gay? *(To* EMMY.*)* Is this some kinda dumb joke?

MALCOLM: Listen up, Walter. Her name is Strait but she's gay. That's cool. I mean...up here...that's cool.

WALTER: *(To* EMMY*)* It's unnatural, number one...and it ain't so funny, number two.

EMMY: *(Angrily)* It ain't meant to be funny, Brother. I'm Emmy Strait...and I'm gay...and now I'm dead...that's the deal.

MALCOLM: *(In an uncharacteristic attempt at reconciliation...and stand-up humor)* You gotta admit, Sister Strait, it does sound a little bit like Abbott & Costello or somethin' kinda white like that. *(*MALCOLM *laughs a little at his own joke.)*

WALTER: Now wait a minute...wait a goddamn minute. There ain't no lesbos, no queers in this part of heaven. So Strait, *"who's gay,"* is outta here...or I'm outta here!

MALCOLM: Whoa! Who're you tellin' who's outta here? Since when you began makin' these decisions?

BILLIE: Yeah, Walter, be cool. I remember when you "arrived" even though I'd seen ya shot down I said to myself, "Whatta we doin' with a young college boy up here?" But you know...you here for a reason. Well, Sister Strait must be here for a reason too.

EMMY: Listen up, I'm Black, I'm gay AND I'm Emmy Strait AND I am here—reason or not, AND I want to know...where is God?...AND what am I doin' with y'all? *(Addressing* BILLIE *and* MALCOLM.*)* With you, and you. (*To* WALTER, *less angry; more in control.*) Even you, my straight-assed young brother. Shit…I don't even know if you're old enough to know what in the hell you are!

WALTER: (*Macho posing—turns his back on* EMMY) Emmy Strait, who is a lesbo, you are ridiculous.

EMMY: Ridiculous? Ridiculous? Ridiculous? I'll show you ridiculous. (*Breaks into vaudeville song a cappella.*)

("*I'm Black, I'm Strait and I'm Gay*")

Well, I'm Black, I'm Strait and I'm gay,
I wouldn't have it any other way.
It may come from my genes
Or some weirdo teenage scenes,
But I'm as Black as anybody in the 'hood.

And I'm proud to be Black and to be gay.
Hey, I'm hangin' out with Malcolm X and Lady Day.
(*To* WALTER) Don't tell me it's unnatural;
It couldn't be more factual,
So Brother Walter…come on back and join this play.

Oh, yes, I'm Black, I'm Strait and I'm gay,
(Like I said)
I wouldn't have it any other way.
Don't criticize my preference
'Cause I won't show no deference
To anyone who does that macho sway.

I'm Strait, I'm gay and I'm Black.
I ain't no prince or princess,
Just a plain old workin' hack,
But no one makes a joke of me
In Cleveland or in Galilee
And if they do I'm gonna pay 'em back.

Maybe we gotta all rejoin that good ole human race
Before the New World Order puts a boot heel in your face.
Us Black folks straight and gay

Gotta lead 'em all the way
To make that spinnin' ball a better place.

I'm Black, I'm gay and I'm Strait, ya see,
It's time we got together
And wiped out white supremacy
'Cause fightin' 'mongst each other—
Hey, I'm your sister, you're my brother,
There's something here on which we all agree.

(*EMMY speaks to the others*) C'mon, let's try that last verse together. C'mon now. C'mon, Sister Billie and Brother Malcolm and you too, Brother Walter.

(*MALCOLM, WALTER and BILLIE resist; but EMMY insists and leads the others in singing the last verse together. They then all laugh heartily.*)

WALTER: Y'know, Sister Emmy Strait…*who's gay*. (*Laughs; tells story to EMMY.*) I'm kinda like you in a way. I mean what am I doing in this fancy, famous neighborhood? I ain't no Black monument. Maybe God put me in the wrong place too. I was twenty-one—an engineering student at CCNY. And I was minding my own business, comin' home from a date with my girl friend Sheila. I meet this macho racist cop who starts fuckin' with me…and then this old Black guy comes along—also macho as hell—and the next thing I know I'm dead. Shot right through the heart. Sister Emmy Strait…*who's gay*, I mean, check it out—I never did nothin' heroic. I never won nobody's heart like Sister Billie over there. I never gave a speech or moved anyone to do things, like Brother Malcolm X. I was just a young guy goin' to college. A little macho myself…but shit…not enough to get killed over. And come to think of it, Emmy Strait, since I been here, I ain't met no one named God, either. So where is this God? And, yeah, what are Sister Emmy Strait…*who's gay*, and me, plain old Walter Johnson, what are we doin' here? Sister Billie, Brother Malcolm, you been here the longest… you're the oldest and wisest and you are…well, *no offense*, but you are the real monuments…the big shots, the honchos, the class acts…whatever. *What's the deal?*

BILLIE: No, no. I ain't no monument, Walter. I ain't no monument. Well, I maybe touched some hearts. I sang, people fell in love, but no one ain't *never* really loved Billie…y'see I was always starring in someone else's play…the sultry torch song beauty, the bearer of dreams for those cool white jazz buffs up in Harlem. But hey, I ain't no monument, Walter. I'm tellin' y'all about deep slow *pain.* It's mighty ordinary, Walter. Ain't nobody really understood what it meant to be loved by millions, and never really held by no one, to be scorned and beaten by the Black man for playing to the white folks. Y'know it's okay for the Black man to play to the white folks. But not the Black woman. No, not the Black woman. When she plays for the white folks she's a…castratin' bitch and nobody loves no castratin' bitch so nobody would have me, really have me…not the white man or the Black man. Walter, I was no monument. Well…I was just a whore, a prostitute on a pedestal. No man loved Billie. No man loves a whore…no man really loved me.

(BILLIE sings "Lover Man.")

MALCOLM: *(Shows BILLIE a picture)* You remember when you and me took this picture downtown at the Onyx? *(To EMMY and WALTER.)* Last time I seen Lady Day alive. Dope and heartbreak stopped that there heart as big as a barn and that sound and style that no one successfully copies to this very day. Lady sang with the soul of Black folks from the centuries of sorrow and oppression. What a shame this proud, fine Black woman never lived where the true greatness of our race was appreciated. *(Puts arm around BILLIE.)*

BILLIE: So, long before I got here I lived in a cloud…white powder…had to kill the pain, worse, always worse…and then, well, you know, I died. This is where I been since then. Ain't no one told me what I'm doin' here, either.

EMMY: So, Bro Malcolm *(stands and walks towards MALCOLM)*, I guess that leaves you. Whatcha got to say for yourself? What's the real deal around here? Is this Monument City, or what?

MALCOLM: I…became a threat.

EMMY: You're damn right, you did, Brother. I read your autobiography, man.

MALCOLM: No, Sister Emmy. You don't understand what a threat I was to *our* people—to Black people. You don't understand at all. Young Brother Walter here was killed by a white racist cop. That's a tragedy. But he wasn't killed by his *own* people. You, Sister Emmy, were killed by a crazy white fascist from Cleveland. It's a sad story you tell. But you weren't killed by your own people. But I was killed by *our* people; by Black people, because I was a threat to some of our people—to Black people. You know why I was a threat? I'll tell you, Sister Emmy Strait. Because centuries of white supremacy have *destroyed our people.* (*Lights change, he goes to lectern.*) When I was a young minister in Boston, I would talk about the ugly reality of slavery like it really was. "Not even in the *Bible* is there such a crime! God in His wrath struck down with *fire* the perpetrators of *lesser* crimes. *One hundred million* of us black people! Your grandparents! Mine! murdered by this white man. To get fifteen million of us here to make us his slaves, on the way he murdered one hundred million! I wish it was possible for me to show you the sea bottom in those days—the black bodies, the blood, the bones broken by boots and clubs! The pregnant black women who were thrown overboard if they got too sick! Thrown overboard to the sharks that had learned that following these slave ships was the way to grow fat! Why, the white man's raping of the black race's woman began right on those slave ships! The blue-eyed devil could not even wait until he got them here! Why, brothers and sisters, civilized mankind has never known such an orgy of greed and lust and murder…" That's what I told the brothers and sisters back in the 1950s. Slavery and white supremacy have destroyed our people, Sister Emmy and Brother Walter and Sister Billie. It has made us into liars: it has made us into cheats and pimps, always vulnerable to being used. I knew the lyin', thievin' life…*I lived it.* I lived it on the prison of the streets of the ghetto and I lived it in the prison of the Man, like we all live it in the prison of America. And I escaped from those prisons by trying to speak the truth to our people, Sister Emmy. And because of that I was *loved* by our people and hated by the white man. But I did not become a threat to *our* people until I realized that I was still in prison—that the scams and the lies of the streets become even bigger and uglier and more destructive of our people when they are turned by phony smooth talkin' Black folks into THE TRUTH and slickly and hypocritically passed along to our people by self-appointed phony SPEAKERS OF THE TRUTH; by the HYPOCRITES. And I was *used* by these hypocrites. Because I had been destroyed by those streets and I was vulnerable. And I spoke loudly of this, I threatened not the masses of our people, not the ordinary folks, who loved me then and love me still, but those amongst our people who pimp off of the degradation and destruction of our people; who opportunize off of the needs and weaknesses of our people; who do the white man's job by keeping our people liars and pimps—even though they preach against lying and pimping—because *they themselves* are models of *successful* liars and pimps. And when I refused to stay imprisoned, those who had the most to lose from my close ties to the masses of our people—the white pigs always looking after their racist, white supremacist system—the FBI, the CIA—and the rich Black pimps got together and murdered me that cold February day at the Audubon.

(Pause. BILLIE, WALTER and EMMY are spellbound and shocked.)

WALTER: Brother Malcolm…it almost sounds like you sayin' I was sort of lucky to be killed by a white man? I mean, I love you, Brother…now that I know you you I love you even more than ever. You are truly our Shining Black Prince. But I felt so humiliated takin' that racist shit from that white cop and then watchin' that fool old Panther get us both killed. You know what I'm sayin', Brother Malcolm?

MALCOLM: I know, Walter. I hear ya. Our people have been killed by the white man by the hundreds of millions and we all have to suffer not only that unbelievable cruelty but the sickening stupid grin of the white man as he does it. For the *privilege* of the white murderer is not only his criminality; not only his capacity to benefit from his murder and rape and plunder of Black folks; but his ability and willingness to laughingly turn his rape and murder into self-righteous *truth and morality*. Yes, Brother, you died tragically as hundreds of millions of our people died—with the white man laughing at you. No, Brother Walter, I can never deny that tragedy…your tragedy…my tragedy. Still the Black man who would benefit and pimp off of our pain…who would prefer we remain enslaved if he may live off of our destitution; the mercenary who would murder his own people for a price and the hypocrite who would justify this pimping with self-righteous rhetoric—he must be strung up alongside the white supremacist murderers for he is no different than they are.

EMMY: Brother Malcolm…folks are still pimpin' off of you. Lotsa people makin' money offa your name, each one sayin' that they know best who you really were. This one makin' a movie, that one complainin' about it —ya know what I'm sayin'? I don't need ta mention no names—but you know what I mean?

MALCOLM: I know, Sister Emmy. I know. *(Laughs.)* But how could they know for sure who I was when I never knew for sure? I kept on changin'…I'm still changin', I ain't no monument. I'm still growin', I'm still tryin' to tell a little truth, Sister Emmy. Jest like you. Jest like Brother Walter and Lady over here. When I returned from my pilgrimage to Mecca in 1964 I shocked the world by saying: "In the past I have permitted myself to be used to make sweeping indictments of all white people…" We must never let ourselves be used as monuments or as anything else. I have always tried to face facts and to accept the reality of life as new experiences and knowledge unfold it.

BILLIE: You makin' me wanna sing, Brother. You know that? *(Laughs, just a little.)* It's so good to hear you speechin' again. It's just fine.

(BILLIE sings "Crazy They Call Me"; mostly to MALCOLM.)

WALTER: That's good, Sister Billie. That's real good.

BILLIE: You know people always said that nobody sang the words "hunger" or "love" like I do. All I've learned is wrapped up in those two words. You've gotta have something to eat and a little love in your life before you can hold still for any damn body's sermon on how to behave, Brother Malcolm. Ain't that right? You know my dream? It's always been to have a big place out in the country where I could take care of stray dogs and orphans; kids that didn't ask to be born; kids that didn't ask to be black, blue or green or something in between.

WALTER: You're a fine sister, Miss Holiday. And you too, Miss Strait…who *is* gay. *(Laughs warmly; turns to MALCOLM.)* So, Brother Malcolm. You sayin' there ain't no monuments here at all. That the monuments are bein' made by the fat-cat monument builders downstairs who are makin' some quick bucks offa you and Sister Billie. Do I have it straight? *(To EMMY.)* No offense, my gay comrade…The monument makers like the temple builders are grabbin' the bucks while our people are dyin'. Yeah. I believe it, Brother Malcolm. I believe it.

MALCOLM: You've got it young Brother.

EMMY: Hey, this is good. Yeah, real good. I'll tell you, Brother Malcolm, *with all due respect,* I always wondered what I got or my family got or just plain ordinary folks got off of the *Malcolm Monument.* Like Sister Billie said, folks need something to eat and some love…and I would add, they gotta laugh a little. I mean, I'm just a simple joke-teller, Brother Malcolm, but I never bought in on a whole lot of bullshit.

MALCOLM: Sister Emmy…

WALTER: Who's gay…*(they all laugh.)*

MALCOLM: You're a genuine speaker of the truth.

EMMY: Okay, okay, Brother Malcolm. That's good, that's good…but, what about God? Where in the hell is he?

MALCOLM: *(Stands)* I dunno. I ain't never seen him, either. Been here over thirty years now…ain't heard a word. As a Muslim it don't exactly surprise me…but that's the deal.

(Suddenly sound comes from the video monitors for the first time in Act II. It's a news broadcast on WGOD. WALTER and EMMY watch stage right, BILLIE and MALCOLM watch stage left.)

NEWSCASTER: Good evening ladies and gentlemen. WGOD brings you the evening news. *(Pause.)* This gruesome story just in from the Midwest. Last Tuesday evening Miss Emmy Strait, a Black woman stand-up comedienne, was shot and killed at the Club Lido in downtown Cleveland, Ohio. *(Pictures of EMMY appear on screen.)* Miss Strait was just finishing her routine when a young white medical student from Case-Western Reserve, disconsolate over failing grades, fired seven shots into her head and chest. Miss Strait, who hailed from Irishtown, New Jersey, began her career in the late 1960s appearing in anti-war theatre while a student at Antioch College in Yellow Springs. Her one-woman show, *What in the Hell Did Malcolm X Ever Do For Me?*, won her an award as Black woman feminist comedienne of the year in 1976. But in recent years Strait had fallen on harder times…Meanwhile, in Anchorage, Alaska, two dermatologists have…

(Video sound fades out.)

MALCOLM: Well, Sister Emmy…*What in the Hell Did Malcolm X Ever Do For Me?*

EMMY: *(Embarrassed)* Hey…I'm sorry about that, Brother Malcolm.

WALTER: *(Very excited)* Chill out you two. How come that TV is talkin'? Y'all ever heard it make a sound before?

BILLIE: I ain't never heard it before.

MALCOLM: Me neither. Never heard no news up here before. *(Pause—takes a step toward EMMY.)* Who in the hell are you, Emmy Strait? Who in the hell are you?

EMMY: Look here, Brother Malcolm, I told you who I am. I mean I didn't mention that feminist stuff 'cause I…ya know…I had it a little wrong back then. Shit, Brother Malcolm…I ain't been to Mecca but I've done a little growin' too.

BILLIE: *(Comforts EMMY)* That's alright, Sister Emmy. Brother Malcolm… don't you be unkind to Sister Emmy here.

WALTER: Yeah, Brother Malcolm…be cool with our *gay* sister.

MALCOLM: Hell, I hear you. Look. I agree. Sister Emmy is real cool; real fine. But ever since she's been here *strange things* have been happening. Good things, I think. But I just wanna know who she is.

EMMY: But Brother Malcolm, I've told you who I am, remember? *(Begins to sing.)* I'm Black, I'm Strait and I'm Gay…

BILLIE and MALCOLM: *(Together stopping EMMY from continuing the song)* Yes, yes, Sister Emmy, we…we, uh, all remember.

MALCOLM: I'm thinking that maybe we don't need monuments no more …that monuments are killing us; that our enemies pay for those monuments. Some people used to say that my problem was that I couldn't resist a platform. Well, maybe I don't need a platform any more.

EMMY: And maybe *Lady* doesn't need a stage. Doesn't need to be no prostitute on a pedestal. *(To BILLIE.)* Lady, you can just straight out sing the blues, Sister, like no one else can.

(BILLIE sings "God Bless the Child"—mainly to EMMY and WALTER. EMMY and WALTER applaud loudly.)

MALCOLM: Allah be praised, Sister Billie, Sister Emmy, Brother Walter, now I got it. Now I know where God is! WE ARE THE GODS! We are the idols; the false idols. And that is how the Man keeps us dead, Sister Emmy. You see, we get turned into Gods and monuments and then we're dead forever and for sure. But I don't think we have to be dead, Sister Emmy. I don't think we need to be monuments. I think maybe we can be *seen* again and *heard* again.

BILLIE: Brother Malcolm...has you gone crazy or somethin'? How we gonna get outta here? How we not gonna be dead? No one's gonna see us or hear us no more.

WALTER: Yeah, Brother Malcolm, you hear a little sound on that TV and you ready to try and leave heaven? I dunno, Brother, I dunno. It was hard enough gettin' out of the ghetto. I dunno if we can slip this joint, Brother Malcolm.

EMMY: Now wait a damn minute. I think Brother Malcolm is right on. I mean there's a door over there *(points to offstage door)*—I believe we can just walk the hell out of it. *(As a comical preacher.)* I believe it...I do believe it...*(MALCOLM, BILLIE and WALTER all stare at her; MALCOLM reaches over to stop her.)* Sorry about that.... I used to do this Black lesbian preacher bit. This monument shit is heavy...heavy...I'll tell ya. Whoo-whee...

MALCOLM: But Sister Emmy is right. We can walk out of here. Right through that door. Billie and I done that before. But I believe we can be seen and heard again.

BILLIE: Like I always said, I'll try anything once, you know.

WALTER: Sister Emmy...you lead the way, okay?

EMMY: *(Walking toward the door)* If we make it the first thing I'm doin' is to pick up my check from the Lido...

(Everyone starts walking to the door.)

MALCOLM: Sister Emmy, lead us all to Cleveland...and beyond.

(Suddenly the door opens and OLD MAN comes staggering in with PAM.)

EMMY: Who the hell are they? Who are you, old man?

BILLIE: Yeah, old man, who are you? Hey, hey. Ain't you the sister we saw down at that demonstration back in the '60s and the '90s?

OLD MAN: I'm just an old Panther. Just an old homeless Black Panther.

WALTER: *(Loudly)* Shit. That's him. That's the old son of a bitch who got me killed, Brother Malcolm, you remember? *(Very agitated and angry.)* Hey old man, you got me killed...you bastard. D'you remember? You old son of a bitch.

MALCOLM: Be cool now, Walter. Be cool. He's just passin' through.

OLD MAN: *(Facing MALCOLM)* Whatta ya mean? You sayin' I can't hang out with you all? I'm too dirty for ya? You don't want me in your neighborhood? Y'all won't touch me? Where y'all think you're goin' anyway? There ain't nothin' out here. Heaven and Earth...it's all the same for us. It's all the same for everybody. Nobody sees nobody. Nobody hears nobody. Nobody touches nobody.

BILLIE: Maybe so. Huh. Maybe so. Maybe he's right, Sister Emmy and Brother Malcolm. *(To PAM.)* Whatta you think, Sister? Whattaya think?

("Nobody Sees Nobody")

PAM: *(Sings)*
Nobody sees nobody,
Nobody hears nobody,
No one touches anyone,
In heaven or on Earth.

We are deaf
And we are blind.
It's impossible to find
Anybody
But the me who's always hangin' on my mind.

Hey, listen, I don't know,
It could happen, maybe so
If we can simply
Get away from time.

Then maybe we could see
Right through eternity
And touch each other
That wouldn't be no crime
But till then…

Nobody sees nobody,
Nobody hears nobody,
No one touches anyone,
In heaven or on Earth.

We'll stay deaf
And we'll stay blind.
Doesn't matter, never mind,
All alone
Until the end of time.

Yeah, it's a mighty funny life
Filled with sadness, filled with strife
Painful, with a little bit of joy,
But maybe we could be
A little kinder to another me
And live together,
That would be just fine
But till then…

Nobody sees nobody,
Nobody hears nobody,

No one touches anyone,
In heaven or on Earth.

We'll stay deaf
And we'll stay blind.
Doesn't matter, never mind,
All alone
Until the end of time.
All alone
Until the end of time.

WALTER: *(Still angry)* I didn't have to die!

MALCOLM: Be cool, Walter. I know it can change. We can change it. We could see and hear each other. We could touch each other. Didn't you hear what the Sister said *(referring to PAM)*? Listen, everybody. Listen up.

OLD MAN: *(Touches MALCOLM's shoulder)* So you're Malcolm X. Hey, will it ever happen? Will it ever happen, Malcolm?

MALCOLM: Yeah…it might. *(MALCOLM puts arm on OLD MAN's shoulder.)* It just might. It just might.

(PAM leads demonstrators, etc. into "heaven" and PAM and BILLIE sing "Will It Ever Happen?")

PAM and BILLIE:
Will it ever happen?
Will it ever happen?
Will it ever happen?
Will it ever happen?

From the '60s
To the '90s
Nothin' much has
Changed and so,
I know, yes, I know
There's a long, long way to go.

Will it ever happen?
Will it ever happen?

Up in heaven,
Down on Earth,
Nothin' different,
Same old show,
So I know, yes, I know
There's a long, long way to go.

Will it ever happen?
Will it ever happen?

Yes, we know
That life goes on,
But we hope
When we're all dead and gone
Maybe there'll be a rebirth
If we fight for all we're worth
And a little heaven here on Earth.

Will it ever happen?
Will it ever happen?
Will it ever happen?
Will it ever happen?

》》

Still on the Corner

Book and lyrics by Fred Newman, music by Annie Roboff

Fred Newman's plays have always incorporated music. The first production of *Mr. Hirsch Died Yesterday*, for example, had a live jazz saxophonist onstage who improvised throughout the performance. Newman's second full-length stage work, *Carmen's Community*, made use of arias and duets from Bizet's opera *Carmen*. The early Newman performance piece *Common Women* (which eventually evolved into the first act of *Billie & Malcolm: A Demonstration*) was woven together with recorded rock and roll and folk music. *Billie & Malcolm* utilizes Billie Holiday standards and three original songs to set the mood for scenes in what is, essentially, a speaking-play.

Still on the Corner (1993) is Newman's first full-fledged musical. (*Off-Broadway Melodies of 1592*, written and produced the previous year, was a musical revue; that is, it didn't have a through-story or set of characters.) To date he has completed three other book-musicals—*Sally and Tom (The American Way), Coming of Age in Korea,* and *Carmen's Place (A Fantasy)*— all of which are included in this collection. In each case Newman has collaborated with Annie Roboff. Newman and Roboff's collaborative process is rich, fluid, and, since they live thousands of miles apart, intense. When they begin work on a musical, Roboff flies to New York City from her home in Nashville and over a period of a week (or frequently less) she and Newman sit around a piano trying out musical ideas. Their songwriting, in which Newman primarily contributes the lyrics and Roboff the musical composition, is truly a joint activity. In their most recent collaboration, *Carmen's Place,* Newman himself has written two of the melodies. It is an indication of both the range of Newman's talents, and of his desire to intersect American popular culture, that he is one of the few playwrights in American theatre history who has successfully written both "straight" plays and books for musicals—Arthur Laurents, Terrence McNally and Neil Simon being among the handful of others.

The evolution of Newman's musicals mirrors the evolution of the American musical form itself—from nearly plotless song-and-comedy revues to works with increasingly coherent plots and serious themes. *Off-*

Broadway Melodies was a string of farcical skits and songs. In *Billie, Malcolm & Yusuf*, which preceded *Still on the Corner* by two years, Newman was already experimenting with the use of song (and rap) in a play. *Still on the Corner* is Newman's first musical with an extended plot, characters that are other than comic stereotypes, and a serious theme.

The songs in *Still on the Corner* are used in a number of ways traditional to the American musical: "Song of the So-Called Homeless" and "Still on the Corner" set the scene and provide exposition; "Crazy Charlie," "Black Child, Black Woman," "Streets of the City," "Never Be The Same," and "Social Worker's Lament" reveal and deepen character; "Never Again" moves the conflict forward; "White Ain't All It's Cracked Up to Be," harking back to the revue form, adds comic relief. In each case the music is used to heighten or extend the emotionality of the scene, as is customary in the American musical (and the European operetta and opera), not to distance the audience from or comment on the action as in the Brechtian tradition.

Still on the Corner is also the first Newman play to make extensive use of dance. As a director, Newman had begun to explore his interest in dance with the 1992 Castillo production of Heiner Müller's *Explosion of a Memory (Description of a Picture)*. Choreographer/dancer Amy Pivar, who had worked with him on *Explosion* and *Billie & Malcolm: A Demonstration*, went on to choreograph (and dance in) the first production of *Still on the Corner* in 1993 and, that same year, collaborated with Newman on *Requiem for Communism*, a dance theatre piece which featured Bill T. Jones as V.I. Lenin and Pivar as Rosa Luxemburg. (*Requiem* was produced at Dance Theater Workshop, one of New York City's premier venues.)

While the songs in *Still on the Corner* are used for a variety of dramatic purposes, the dances all have the same basic function—to set the tone for the scene which follows. Each scene in the play begins with what the script describes as a "Hallmark holiday card pose," that is, a sentimental, conventional Christmas-time image, and a popular Christmas carol. As the recorded carol continues, the pose becomes a dance of the interaction between the stylized grace of the well-to-do residents of Manhattan's Upper West Side and the determination/desperation of the "homeless" panhandlers. From the early 20th century's idealized middle-class picture of the holiday, the stage is transformed into the bleak, conflicted reality of a late 20th-century urban Christmas. There are eight such poses/dances, each a variation on a theme. These dance sequences are key to establishing the tone of the particular scene, and trained dancers are recommended.

Unlike Newman's earlier (and much of his subsequent) work, *Still on the Corner* has a single linear plot (there are no parallel or contrasting narratives) and individual characters with conventional borders around their identities. Lacking the window of possibility provided by parallel/contrasting narratives/characters, *Still on the Corner* is also one of Newman's gloomiest plays. Nothing changes except that one more person—Pam Kansas—joins the ranks of the destitute. Cecilia, who briefly "makes it" in show business, can't shake the madness of and loyalty to the street and winds up "still on the corner." The play ends with "Will It Ever Happen?" (Newman also used this song to close *Billie & Malcolm: A Demonstration*.) Given the sense of inevitability inherent in a linear plot and the lack of change or development among the characters in the play, the song takes on a far darker tone on New York's Upper West Side than it does in heaven.

Still on the Corner has received two productions at Castillo—the first in November/December 1993 and the second in December 1994/January 1995—both directed by Newman. There were slight changes in the lyrics and dialogue in the second production to keep the play topical. The 1994-'95 version is included here.

D.F.

Still on the Corner was first produced at the Castillo Theatre (Fred Newman, artistic director; Gabrielle Kurlander, producing director) in New York City on November 19, 1993. The cast was as follows:

BROTHER DUGY . . . . Doug Miranda
CECILIA HARDY . . . . Cece Waterman
SISTER T-LA . . . . L. Thecla Farrell
CRAZY CHARLIE . . . . David Nackman
EMILY . . . . Emmy Gay
DANCER . . . . Madelyn Chapman
DANCER . . . . Almalyn Largey
DANCER . . . . Amy Pivar
MRS. HERMAN . . . . Cathy Rose Salit
MRS. ROSEN . . . . Gabrielle Kurlander
MR. WOODY . . . . Roger Grunwald
PAM KANSAS . . . . Pam Kansas
CAMERAPERSON/INTERVIEWER (ON VIDEO) . . . . Kenneth Hughes
STANDBYS . . . . Kelly Drummond *(Dancer);* Marian Rich *(Mrs. Herman);*
Jonathan Riseling *(Dancer);* Cathy Salit *(Mrs. Rosen)*

Fred Newman, director; Diane Stiles, producer; Dan Belmont, musical director; Amy Pivar, choreography; Joseph Spirito, set design; Elena Borstein, scenic design; Charlotte, costume design; Linnaea Tillett, lighting design; Michael Klein, sound design; Barry Z Levine, video design/cinematography; Ellen Korner, production stage manager.

Still on the Corner is a postmodern Christmas carol. The form is inspirational; the content hopelessness. *The streets of this city* wore Pam Kansas down. *It will never be the same—even if nothing ever changes* sings Cecilia Hardy. Yet people continue to live with and within hopelessness. People continue to laugh and play even as they are worn down. The middle class (the dancers, wonderfully choreographed by Amy Pivar) symbolizes whatever privilege remains in a world no longer growing. The street people still remember the music of life. But the words speak more and more of death. To be sure, there are profound social and class differences. But *Still on the Corner* is no Dickensian tragedy set in the spirit of hope. It is about hopelessness within the reality of life. Ultimately we are all still on the corner. "Will it ever happen?" sings the ensemble at the end of our play. Will it ever change? Maybe not. Still we sing and dance; still we laugh and make jokes. Postmodern life is still on the corner.

This production is dedicated to my dearest friends, Gabrielle Kurlander and Jacqueline Salit, who, as I grow older, hang out with me (and put up with me) on the corner still.

DECEMBER 1994

CHARACTERS

The "Homeless"
BROTHER DUGY, a slightly older, militant African American man
CECILIA HARDY, the leader of the "homeless" grouping
SISTER T-LA, a more austere nationalist
CRAZY CHARLIE, insane and eccentric
EMILY, the young street comedienne

The Middle Class
MRS. HERMAN, a conflicted middle-class woman
3 or 4 DANCERS

•

MRS. ROSEN, a social worker
PAM KANSAS, an African American country singer
MR. WOODY, her aggressive and provocative agent
CAMERAPERSON

On video
ANNOUNCER
ENTERTAINMENT REPORTER

NOTE:
This play contains both live scenes and video sequences.

Act I, Scene 1

The stage is almost dark and the cast is in a frozen pose. The stage has two levels. The lower level [downstage] is an outdoor scene—Riverside Park (near 93rd Street) as viewed from New Jersey. The "homeless" are gathered around the bench in various poses. The higher level [upstage] is a platform, which forms the bottom of a large window of a Riverside Drive middle-class apartment. To one side of the window is a staircase which leads into the street [onto the lower stage]. Three or four middle-class people are posed behind the window. As the lights come up—as day breaks—the cast remains in a holiday card pose. Christmas carols play. It is a "homeless" holiday card. We call this the Holiday Pose.

Then, everyone begins to move. The middle class comes into the streets with strollers, etc. and the "homeless" begin to ask for money. We call this the Interaction Dance. It is the Christmas season. The weather is cold. The Christmas carols continue.

The "homeless" are five in number. CECILIA HARDY *is the social leader of this "homeless" grouping. She is young, talented, beautiful and deeply loved by her people.* CRAZY CHARLIE *is insane and eccentric, but an accepted member of the "homeless" family.* EMILY *is a young street comedienne.* BROTHER DUGY *is a slightly older, more militant African American man.* SISTER T-LA *is a more austere nationalist. Two or three dancers and the more conflicted middle-class woman,* MRS. HERMAN, *are the white middle-class people in the window.*

There is a two-to-three minute Interaction Dance between the "homeless" and the middle class. The "homeless" use the following "pitches," among others:

T-LA: Do you have some money for a proud poor Black woman down on her luck? *(or)* Spare change. I must have something to eat. Would you help me, please?

DUGY: Could you spare some change? *(or)* Help a brother out with a dollar, my friend.

CHARLIE: I need just a little help, okay? *(or)* I haven't eaten for a week, or is it a month…I don't know. Help me out…wouldya?

CECILIA: Could you help me out with just a few pennies…please.

EMILY: Gotta buck or so, pal…I'm only kidding…spare change *(said comically)* spare change.

(All of these "pitches" are said in a barely audible voice and repeated together with other one-liners consistent with the character. The middle-class people sometimes give; sometimes they walk by ignoring the "homeless"; other times they are more nasty. There is no consistency in their response.

The Interaction Dance—begging for money and the middle-class response— is stylized and culminates in the stage getting darker and darker [it's twilight]; and the middle class going home. The "homeless" gather near the bench and count their money. They sing.)

("Song of the So-called Homeless")

DUGY:
> The liberals,
> From across the street, on Riverside Drive,

CECILIA:
> …Call us "homeless."

DUGY:
> Why don't they simply say we're
> Dirty and crazy and weird and mad?
> But no,
> Our liberal neighbors

CECILIA:
> …Call us "homeless,"
> And sometimes they even add
> "Not hopeless."

DUGY:
> But that's really bullshit,

T-LA:

> Because life
> On the streets of New York
> Is awfully bad—
> And always sad
> With no *hope*
> And only a liberal
> Dope
> Would think
> Otherwise.

CECILIA:

> Otherwise.

CHARLIE:

> We, the homeless, so-called,
> Have been had. We *have* been had;
> It makes us mad.
> But we don't—we don't speak it—
> To a liberal.
> A homeless person cannot speak
> Because they provide the change
> The quarters and the dimes
> That in these desolate times

CECILIA:

> …Buys a burger
> For a psychotic Black lady
> On a freezing cold night
> While our liberal neighbors
> Sit at home
> And talk about
> Their group therapy.
> They've seen the light.
> They do not feel the cold.

DUGY:

> The liberals, from across the street,
> Say that we're not "hopeless,"

CECILIA:

And they are right.

DUGY:

We are far beyond hopeless,
Far beyond the night.
Our darkness never leaves;

T-LA:

We're permanently mad,
Crazy, insane, weird,
Not homeless, not even bitter,

DUGY:

...Simply filthy and mad.

EMILY:

Thank you
For the dime. We never ask
The time.

CHARLIE: *(elongated and weird)*
Soon...

CECILIA:

...Everything will be just fine.
*(laughs)*But there is no soon.
There is no soon,
Only
That next dime.

Act I, Scene 2

Holiday Pose #2 (a new Christmas carol, etc.) and the Interaction Dance repeats. Suddenly EMILY and CHARLIE cross downstage center; the others exit quietly.

CHARLIE: *(Sort of stammering)* Do it, Emily. Do your performance. People will give a lot of money to see you perform, Emily. Please do it. You're famous around here. Do it, Emily, do it.

EMILY: Okay, Crazy Charlie. You gonna help me do it?

CHARLIE: Oh yeah, Emily. Yeah. Yeah. I'll help you. Yes, I'll help you. (*EMILY steps up on the park bench. CHARLIE stands in front of the bench, now a makeshift stage.*) Ladies and Gentlemen, I wanna introduce to you...um ...I want you to...um...meet...Miss Emily, the street comedienne... who...um...well, she...um...

EMILY: C'mon, Charlie. Get it over with.

CHARLIE: Oh, yes, Emily. Here's the famous street comedienne: the hilarious homeless lady...Miss Emily...(*He applauds.*)

EMILY: Good evening, Ladies and Germs...oh, I'm sorry, I mean Gentlemen. We're the germs around here. Ha, ha, ha. Nice to see you here today in the 'hood. (*A small crowd—one person—starts to gather.*) Well, I'll tell ya. A funny thing happened to me a couple of years ago as I was walkin' down the street. (*Looking angrily at CHARLIE.*) I said...ah...a funny thing happened to me a couple of years ago as I was walkin' down the street.

CHARLIE: (*Wakes up*) What's that, Emily? What happened?

EMILY: I started livin' here.

CHARLIE: Where?

EMILY: On the street, Charlie. Don't you get it?

CHARLIE: Oh, oh, yeah. I get it. That's funny, Emily. I think that's very funny.

EMILY: Well...I mean...you people (*a second person has joined the audience*) with homes don't realize what a burden they are. I mean homelessness is a great way of life. I mean it. You poor folks with homes. Jesus, we should be giving you money. I mean you got all these bills for heat and electricity and rent. And ya got these nasty landlords. And sometimes ya gotta go on a rent strike. Not out here in the park, on the street... shit...the homeless never have a rent strike. Oh yes, and by the way if you're on one of those rent strikes and you're not payin' the rent...you know the rent money's in...ah...whatta they call it, *escrow*. Listen, if you want me to hold it for ya...here's my card. (*Pretends to give card, crowd is gathered.*)

CHARLIE: Emily, Emily, Emily, tell 'em the story about our fashion shows. *(Laughs loudly.)*

EMILY: *(Sarcastically)* Oh, yeah. Thank you, Charlie. We street folks have fashion shows just like y'all do. We like to see who's got the dirtiest outfit…and we decide on a foul *smell* for the season. And what color trash is in this year. And whether we're wearin' our rags short or long…and whether Black homeless people have more soul than white homeless people…and…

(DUGY and T-LA enter and lift EMILY off the bench.)

DUGY: Okay. The show's over. Please give some money. Okay.

T-LA: Yeah. The show's over. Thanks for comin'.

CHARLIE: Whattsa matter?

EMILY: Yeah. Whattsa matter? You don't like the act? As soon as I say the word "Black" you gimme the hook.

T-LA: Be cool, Sister Emily. Be cool.

CECILIA: *(Comes over)* It's alright Sister Emily. T-La and Brother Dugy are just lookin' out for ya. They mean no harm.

EMILY: But I was just makin' some jokes to make a little change.

CECILIA: I know, Sister Emily…and that's cool. You're a wonderful comedienne.

(CHARLIE jumps up on the bench.)

CHARLIE: Can I do a show, Cecilia? Can I?

CECILIA: Sure, Charlie. You do a show. We'll all watch ya.

("Crazy Charlie")

CHARLIE: *(Does a little dance on and around the bench, then sings)*
I'm a crazy, crazy man.
I'm a Brooklyn Dodger fan.
I suffer from dementia;
Giuliani musta' sent ya
To take me back to Bellevue.

It's one helluva swell view.
I'm a crazy, crazy man.

I'm as mad as the proverbial loon.
I'm singing a very weird tune.
I am labeled depressive
Perverted, obsessive
Altogether a mess,
I'm a crazy, crazy man. *(Jumps off bench.)*

See me, see me,
I'm really a person
Just like yourself.
See me, see me,
Don't put a label
On me
On your shelf.

I'm a crazy, crazy man.
My hat is a frying pan.
I don't have a nickel;
My life's in a pickle.
I'm a crazy, crazy man.

See me, see me,
I know that
You don't wanna be me
But see me, see me.
I'm really a person
Just like yourself.

I'm a crazy, crazy man.
My hat is a frying pan.
I don't have a nickel;
My life's in a pickle.
I'm a crazy, crazy
Crazy, crazy
Crazy, crazy
Man.

Act I, Scene 3

Holiday Pose #3; then a two-to-three-minute Interaction Dance. DUGY, T-LA *and* CECILIA *cross to downstage center.*

DUGY: *(To CECILIA)* Sister, you are the only really nice person I have ever known. Most nice people I don't believe at all. I always find out they're bullshittin'. Nationalists or whatever…it's all the same. But you, Sister Cecilia, you are a mighty decent person.

T-LA: It's true, Cecilia. I mean I'm nice sometimes. Brother Dugy's nice… well…I remember him bein' nice one time. *(Laughs.)* But you're the best.

CECILIA: Would you two cut it out. Y'all as nice as could be. And you know I ain't so nice as ya think. I can be nasty as all get out.

DUGY: When was you ever nasty?

T-LA: Yeah, Cecilia. I never seen you nasty.

CECILIA: Hey, we needa raise some more money. It's gettin' dark. Let's do it. It's cold out and it's Christmas time. White folks are a little kinder around Christmas…for a day or so.

T-LA: That's Kwanzaa, Cecilia, Kwanzaa.

CECILIA: Right on, Sister T-La. Kwanzaa, Hanukkah, Christmas. Whatever, we need the money. It's cold and a bowl of hot soup sounds good to me. *(She points.)* I'll grab that corner over there.

*(*DUGY *and* T-LA *cross upstage and* CECILIA *moves to the "corner," downstage right.* CECILIA *sings.)*

("Still on the Corner")

Christmas 1994
Still livin' mighty poor
Out on the streets
Of this town.

Still without a home
In a world so alone.
Cold and sadness
All around.

And when I start to think about
How my people have been so kept out,
I'm still on the corner.
I am on the corner still.

Christmas time
Seems far too white
In the slush
Of silent nights.

All this time has passed.
Always near the very last,
Poor and poorer
Is our way.

And when I start to realize why
My people all know how to die.
I'm still on the corner.
I am on the corner, still.

Temperature droppin',
Temperature droppin',
(It's) gettin' mighty cold.
Temperature's droppin',
Won't be warm until
I'm old and buried.

I'm still on the corner.
I am on the corner, still.
I'm still on the corner.
I am on the corner, still.

(Enter MRS. ROSEN, stage left.)

MRS. ROSEN: Cecilia, how ya doin'? How's the singing going? Yeah, how's it goin'?

CECILIA: Mrs. Rosen. Good to see ya. How's the social work business? Everything's lookin' good, Mrs. Rosen. Ya know—things ain't never as bad as they seem. No. They ain't never as bad as they seem.

(Enter CHARLIE and EMILY.)

CHARLIE: It's Mrs. Rosen, my social worker. Did Mayor Giuliani send ya to deal with my dementia? Which day of Hanukkah is it, Mrs. Rosen?

CECILIA: Charlie, stop giving Mrs. Rosen a hard time. She's our friend.

EMILY: Hiya, Mrs. Rosen. Ya wanna hear a good joke?

MRS. ROSEN: Hiya, Emily. Always lookin' for a laugh. Lemme hear.

EMILY: Why did the homeless person cross the road?

MRS. ROSEN: Why, Emily, why?

EMILY: To see how things look from the other side…Ha, ha. Get it?

CHARLIE: That's funny, Emily. That's really funny.

(T-LA and DUGY come downstage.)

DUGY: Hey, Rosen, long live the PLO.

MRS. ROSEN: Right on, Brother Dugy. Long live the PLO. And *mazel tov* to Yasir Arafat.

T-LA: Rosen, you about the nicest Jew I know. *(Laughs.)*

MRS. ROSEN: Thank you, Sister T-La. Thank you. I love you, too. And *mazel tov* to Louis Farrakhan.

DUGY: What's the damn city payin' you these days, Rosen?

CECILIA: Brother Dugy, that ain't none of our business.

MRS. ROSEN: Oh, about $30,000.

T-LA: Is that all? Jesus. You deserve a lot more than that for workin' with us creeps. *(Laughs.)*

CHARLIE: Thirty thousand a day?

MRS. ROSEN: No, Charlie, a year—a year.

DUGY: Rosen, we gonna get welfare bonuses for Christmas this year?

MRS. ROSEN: I'm afraid not, Brother Dugy…I'm afraid not. None of us are gettin' any bonuses. The city's broke as usual.

T-LA: You're okay, Rosen. You're okay.

MRS. ROSEN: You know, it's goin' down to 10 below. Can I get you guys set up in a shelter tonight?

CECILIA: Oh no, Mrs. Rosen, don't bother. We'll be okay. We *live* here on Riverside Drive and 93rd Street. Not in a shelter. We're not homeless.

CHARLIE: Yeah, Mrs. Rosen. This is very family, very family. We're not homeless. We may be hopeless. But we're not homeless. *(He laughs.)* Get it? Get it? Hopeless but not homeless!

EMILY: Yeah, Mrs. Rosen, you gonna drop over for Christmas dinner? Bring your own seat. *(Laughs.)* Get it? Bring your own seat. *(Laughs hysterically.)*

CECILIA: Mrs. Rosen don't wanna hear all those bad street jokes, Emily.

DUGY: Yeah. And neither do we.

T-LA: Rosen, we'll be fine tonight. We're still on the corner like Cecilia says. But we know how to be cold. Thank you for askin', Rosen, yeah. Thanks for askin'. You're a good person.

EMILY: Mrs. Rosen, do you ever talk to your own family about us? You tell 'em we're your friends?

CECILIA: Mrs. Rosen, we like ya. We voted you the best social worker in New York City. *(Laughs gently.)*

DUGY: Hey, everybody, talkin' with our social worker ain't makin' us no money. Excuse us, Rosen, but business responsibilities is callin'.

MRS. ROSEN: Take care. Take good care.

("Homeless" leave MRS. ROSEN, *who sings.)*

("Social Worker's Lament")

Who am I
To speak of them?
We live so many miles apart.
Every day I come to them
And talk words
To their broken hearts.

I can't really change a thing.
Nothing happens in a world
In which we cling to

A hopeless dream, a foolish scheme
Where everything is exactly
As it seems.
A hopeless dream, a foolish scheme
Where everything is as
Bad as it always seems.

Who are they?
They never say.
They don't trust me,
Even though I care.
And who are we?
Just hangin' on to life
In a world that isn't fair.
I sometimes scream but nothing's gonna happen
As we stand around and cling to

A hopeless dream, a foolish scheme
Where everything is
Exactly as it seems.
A hopeless dream, a foolish scheme
Where everything is as
Bad as it always seems.

I'm just a social worker, friend.
Gettin' 30 thou a year,
And even if I get that raise
I couldn't even care.

A hopeless dream, a foolish scheme
Where everything is
Exactly as it seems.
A hopeless dream, a foolish scheme
Where everything is as
Bad as it always seems.

Act I, Scene 4

Holiday Pose #4 leads again to the Interaction Dance. PAM KANSAS *enters with* MR. WOODY, *her very aggressive and provocative agent. He is pulling her by the hand.*

MR. WOODY: Please, Kansas, you gotta do what I say. I'm the damn agent. I know what New York is all about. You're a country girl from where… Montana…oh, no, I forgot, from Kansas…that's how you got that hokey name. But it's okay. Black country music! What an idea. Joe Franklin'll love it. We'll make a fortune. But ya gotta do what I tell you to do.

PAM: Mr. Woody, I appreciate all you're doin' for me and all that, but do we hafta do a promo with people livin' on the streets? I mean it seems like imposin' on folks who are havin' hard times enough.

MR. WOODY: Imposing? Whataya crazy? They'll love it. What else they got to do? I mean helpin' out a young Black sister—an' all that kinda stuff. They'll love it. This is New York, Kansas. The Big Apple. Take those country manners of yours and bury 'em. Manners don't go over in Manhattan, Kansas.

(MR. WOODY, still holding PAM by the arm, approaches EMILY and CHARLIE.)

MR. WOODY: Hey there, excuse me, but a…This here is Pam Kansas, the famous Black country singer…

PAM: *(Interrupting)* Mr. Woody, I'm not exactly famous…uh…

MR. WOODY: *(Whispering)* Quiet, Kansas—whatta they know?

CHARLIE and EMILY: Hello, Pam Kansas, can ya spare a quarter?

MR. WOODY: Listen, you two, I'll give ya five dollars for about half an hour of your time. All you need to do is let Kansas over here sing a tune or two to ya.

KANSAS: What did you say, Mr. Woody?

MR. WOODY: A tune or two to ya. We're gonna video it and use it to show people whatta nice person Pam Kansas is. *(Pulls out paper form.)* You'll just sign these releases and I'll go get the cameraman from the truck. Okay?

EMILY: I don't think we can do that unless Cecilia says it's okay.

MR. WOODY: Who's Cecilia?

CHARLIE: Cecilia's the one who tells us what we can do.

MR. WOODY: Kinda like a street boss? Jesus, *everyone's* got a boss.

EMILY: I'll call her…Cecilia, Cecilia…

(*CECILIA comes to them.*)

CHARLIE: This is Cecilia.

MR. WOODY: Hi there, Cecilia. Look, I'm Pam Kansas' agent. You hearda Pam Kansas. She's the famous Black country singer. (*Turns to* PAM.) Pam Kansas…This is…uh…(*He can't remember her name.*)

EMILY: Cecilia.

MR. WOODY: Yeah, Cecilia.

CECILIA: It's very nice to meet you.

PAM: Oh yeah. It's great to meet you. (*She semi-whispers.*) Look, I don't wanna be no bother to y'all.

MR. WOODY: (*Overhearing*) Bother? We won't be no bother. We just wanna do a little promo piece with Kansas and…uh…some of…uh…you… uh…homeless people.

CECILIA: Oh, that would be lovely. If this is of help to you, Miss Kansas, it'll be fine.

PAM: Well, I really appreciate it, Cecilia. It's really good to meet you.

CHARLIE: We're gonna be on TV?

EMILY: Can I tell a couple of jokes?

CECILIA: C'mon now, you two, this is for Miss Kansas here. We're helpin' her out.

PAM: I mean call me Pam. That's my real name. (*Laughs.*)

MR. WOODY: Listen, I'm gonna go get the camera guy. Be back in a minute. You all get to know each other. (*MR. WOODY exits.*)

CECILIA: Pam…are you really *from* Kansas?

PAM: Oh yeah. Hey, lemme tell y'all about it. *(Sings.)*

("Black Child Black Woman")

Black child,
Country home,
Daddy's playing music,
Mama's on the phone.
Kansas was my childhood,
Sort of lonely and sad.
When my daddy died a young man
Lost what happiness I had.
When my daddy died a young man
Lost what happiness I had.

Girl child,
Sister to my brothers.
Growin' up singin'
Playin' songs for others.
Thinkin' of my daddy,
Gonna keep his voice alive.
Then I left my home in Kansas
Just to see if I'd survive.
Yeah, I left my home in Kansas
Just to see if I'd survive.

New York town,
New York sounds,
How's a tiny country girl to live?
All alone
With my song.
Daddy's not with me anymore
To teach me right from wrong,
Right from wrong.

Black woman,
Try to make this city mine.
Singin' urban country

Kansas doin' fine!
Papa's got a new tune
With his little darlin's voice.
Daddy's makin' music,
Daddy's makin' Black music,
Daddy's makin' country music,
And the music's all mine.

CHARLIE: Wow! That was great, Miss Kansas. That was great.

CECILIA: That's mighty fine singin', Pam.

(*MR. WOODY returns with* CAMERAPERSON.)

MR. WOODY: Okay. Okay. (*He arranges* EMILY, CECILIA *and* CHARLIE *in a group behind* PAM.) Now, Kansas, sing that a...that anti-white song.

PAM: It ain't anti-white!

MR. WOODY: Hey listen, Kansas. I don't care if it's anti-white...Long as it's pro-green. (*Laughs.*) Y'know what I'm sayin'?

PAM: But it ain't anti-white. It's just makin' fun the way all country music does.

CECILIA: Sing it, Pam. We wanna hear it.

(*"White Ain't All It's Cracked Up To Be"*)

PAM: (*Sings*)
White ain't all that
It's cracked up to be,
Even though in
The dark of night
You're easier to see.
I ain't no racist
But I hope you'll all agree,
That white ain't all that
It's cracked up to be.

When I was a little child
My mother said to me
White folks are no bargain

Even though they "set us free."
(Now) I don't mean no disrespect
It's just sociologically correct
(To say) White ain't all that
It's cracked up to be.

White-on-white shirts
Seem plain silly.
White gets dirty
Willy-nilly.
Whites get red-faced
When they run too fast,
And I'm not sayin'
Black is better
But in very sunny weather
We don't have to put
All that lotion on!

White ain't all that
It's cracked up to be,
Even though in
The dark of night
You're easier to see.
I ain't no racist
But I hope you'll all agree,
That white ain't all that
It's cracked up to be.

White folks think
That white means
Virtue
That whites are good
And they won't hurt you.
I know some who'll
Surely question that.
Now some whites can be
Mighty decent
Especially in

These times recent
Nonetheless I gotta tell you that

PAM and CHARLIE: *(In harmony)*
    White ain't all that
    It's cracked up to be,
    Even though in
    The dark of night
    You're easier to see.
    I ain't no racist
    But I hope you'll all agree,
    That white ain't all that
    It's cracked up to be.

CHARLIE: Hey, Ms. Kansas. I'm white. And I really like that song...Did you know I was a Brooklyn Dodger fan...

CECILIA: Okay, Charlie. That's cool. Be cool.

EMILY: *(To MR. WOODY)* Would you like to hear Cecilia sing? She sings just beautiful. Just like Sister Pam does.

MR. WOODY: That's real nice. But we gotta get goin' now. *(Reaches for $5 to give to CECILIA.)*

PAM: *(More assertive than usual)* Hey Woody, we got a minute. They listened to me. Let's hear Cecilia.

CECILIA: Oh no, Pam. It's your show. Not mine.

PAM: Hey...I really wanna hear you.

EMILY: Yeah, Cecilia. Sing that song about the willows that you sometimes sing late at night when we all can't sleep.

(PAM nods supportively and CECILIA sings "Willow Weep For Me." At the end of the song, MR. WOODY is in shock. A moment of silence.)

PAM: That's incredible, Cecilia. That's just beautiful. I mean you sound like Billie Holiday. My dad always played Billie Holiday records. That's unbelievably beautiful.

EMILY: Yeah, she's wonderful, huh?

CHARLIE: She sings lots of songs real nice.

MR. WOODY: *(Finally coming out of shock a little)* Where did you learn to sing like that? You got an agent?

CECILIA: No, I ain't got no agent, Mr. Woody.

PAM: She should get some kind of audition right away, shouldn't she, Mr. Woody?

MR. WOODY: This kid don't need no audition. She's got it.

CECILIA: Hey, look now, this is Pam Kansas' show, not mine.

MR. WOODY: No problem. You two ain't competin'. There's room for both. Holy cow! Whadda day. Whadda day! Whadda day!!

Act II, Scene 1

The scene is the same as at the opening of Act I except that PAM *is now among the street people and* CECILIA *is not.* MRS. ROSEN *is with them. Act II begins with Holiday Pose #5 leading into an Interaction Dance, which is interrupted by video monitors coming on. The onstage action goes into a soft freeze as all watch the video, a very commercial variety show.*

ANNOUNCER VOICE-OVER: And now, ladies and gentleman, what we've all been waiting for. *Christmas Special, 1996* is proud to present America's most sensational newcomer, the young woman who has come from nowhere in just two short years to steal the hearts of everyone with her voice and her charm, the sensational *Cecilia Hardy*. *(Huge applause; she appears and sings a bluesy holiday song. Monitor goes black.)*

(The street scene comes back to full action.)

CHARLIE: *(To EMILY)* Did you see Cecilia? Was that really her?

EMILY: I think so. Yeah, it was her.

MRS. ROSEN: It's incredible. Just wonderful. Maybe something good could happen for everyone.

CHARLIE: *(To PAM)* Wasn't Cecilia good, Pam? Wasn't she?

PAM: She was fantastic, Charlie. And it couldn't happen to a nicer human being. I'm really happy for her.

CHARLIE: Will you sing for us later, Pam?

T-LA: (*Annoyed*) Quiet, Charlie. You ever heard from that sleazeball Mr. Woody, Pam?

PAM: Oh no. I guess he's pretty busy with Cecilia, ya know.

DUGY: That bastard dropped you like a hot potato, didn't he?

PAM: Ya know, Brother Dugy, I just didn't have it. I don't wanna blame Woody. Hey man, he found me a place to live and some fine friends.

EMILY: Yeah, Pam Kansas, yeah. That's funny.

PAM: (*To CHARLIE*) I'll sing later. Yeah, Charlie, I'll sing for you later. These streets are somethin' else... somethin' else. (*Sings.*)

(*"Streets of the City"*)

The streets of this old city
Wore this country girl down.
I don't want no one's pity
I've always tried it on my own.

Now I'm down, yes, I'm down.
It wore this girl down.
The streets of this city,
It's a sea in which I drowned.

When you're poor in the country
There's an open field to roam.
When the city runs you over
You don't have no place that's home.

Now I'm down, yes, I'm down.
The city wore me down.
The streets of this city,
It's a sea in which I drowned.

Let me tell you, sisters and brothers,
I'm afraid to look ahead.

Who's to say or sing, what another day will bring
Or whether we're already dead?

Country music left me homeless,
Guess I never had a chance.
No more singin' 'bout my homeland,
There are no steps in my dance.

Now I'm down, down.
It wore this girl down.
The streets of this city,
It's a sea in which I drowned.

And let me tell you, sisters and brothers,
I'm afraid to look ahead.
Who's to say or sing, what another day will bring
Or whether we're already dead?
Or whether we're already dead?

Act II, Scene 2

Lights up on Holiday Pose #6, leading into the Interaction Dance. MRS. HER-
MAN *comes down the steps and walks through the scene, stopping and talking to*
DUGY *and* T-LA. *On her walks throughout the play* MRS. HERMAN *is snooty but
always surreptitiously gives dollar bills to everyone. So the street folks sort of like
her. At a minimum, they want her to keep giving money.*

MRS. HERMAN: *(To* DUGY *and* T-LA*)* Did you all see Cecilia on TV last night?
Wasn't that extraordinary? Now that's what you all need to do. Make
something of yourself. Doesn't Cecilia inspire you? She's a credit to
your race. She's a credit to all of us. It makes all the money I've given to
you over the years worthwhile.

DUGY: Well, Mrs. Herman, we're certainly glad for Cecilia. I mean, she's a
wonderful person. I don't sing quite as good as her though. Ya know
what I mean?

MRS. HERMAN: Now don't be making fun of me. You know what I mean.

T-LA: What do you mean, Mrs. Herman? What do you mean?

MRS. HERMAN: Well, I mean no disrespect. I'd just like to see you all off the streets and living decent and good lives. That's all I mean.

EMILY: *(Crossing to be part of the conversation)* That's a very good idea. I'm waitin' for David Letterman to discover me, Mrs. Herman.

DUGY: I can give you 10 good reasons why he won't.

PAM: Easy now, Brother Dugy.

MRS. HERMAN: You're pretty new, aren't you?

PAM: Yeah, I'm pretty new. Maybe a couple a years out here. You've always been nice to us, Mrs. Herman. The street people like ya.

MRS. HERMAN: Well, I hope that doesn't mean you all plan to stay forever.

PAM: We ain't got too many plans, Mrs. Herman.

(The video monitors suddenly come on; it's an interview with CECILIA on her way to perform at a gala Christmas Benefit for the Homeless.)

ENTERTAINMENT REPORTER: *(On video)* Look who it is. The sensational new TV and recording star, *Cecilia Hardy*. Ms. Hardy, Ms. Hardy, can we have a minute of your time? *(She stops.)* Whatta career. Whatta they call you—"The Star Who Came From Nowhere"? Well, you're one helluva talent; you're extraordinary, Ms. Hardy.

CECILIA: *(On video)* Thank you very much.

ENTERTAINMENT REPORTER: *(On video)* And it's great to see a new mega star like yourself coming out here tonight for this Christmas Benefit for the Homeless. I mean as busy as you are…just takin' this time to be here is real fine. You don't hardly need the promo, Ms. Hardy. What are your thoughts about homelessness in this city?

CECILIA: *(On video. Somewhat discombobulated)* I…ah…I think it's terrible that people are living out in the cold…ya know…It's…ah…it's just terrible. I have friends who are still living on the streets…

ENTERTAINMENT REPORTER: *(On video)* You do! Whattya mean you have friends still living on the streets?

T-LA: She shouldn'ta said that! She shouldn'ta said that!

MRS. HERMAN: You're right, Sister T-La, she never should of said that.

ENTERTAINMENT REPORTER: *(On video)* Well, Ms. Hardy, what did you mean by that? You have homeless friends?

CECILIA: *(On video)* Well…uhm…just that I have people who I know and love who have been…uh…living on the streets for many years.

ENTERTAINMENT REPORTER: *(On video)* How do you know them? How did you get to be their friends?

DUGY: *(Screaming)* Leave her alone, you son of a bitch!

PAM: Yeah. Leave our sister be.

ENTERTAINMENT REPORTER: *(On video)* Ms. Hardy…Uhum. Did you ever live on the streets? Is that what you're saying? Is that what you're telling us?

MRS. ROSEN: Say no, Cecilia. Say no.

PAM: Where the hell is Woody?

CECILIA: *(On video)* I sort of don't…uh…I don't wanna talk about it.

ENTERTAINMENT REPORTER: *(On video)* Well, Ms. Hardy, you raised it. I mean, it's no disgrace. If you were one of the homeless…well, Ms. Hardy, that's a *great* story…a helluva *great* story.

CECILIA: *(On video)* Whattya mean "It's a great story"? It's not a story at all. *(She's getting angry and on the verge of "losing it"…going crazy.)* T-La's not a story, goddammit. She's my friend. We hugged each other for hours so we wouldn't freeze to death in Riverside Park back in '89. She's no damn story. Brother Dugy's no story. You dumb son of a bitch. Y'see Brother Dugy *(laughs crazily)*, I told you I could be nasty. *(To ENTERTAINMENT REPORTER)* You stupid bastard. Homeless people *have* homes. We live on the goddamn streets. Crazy Charlie, Emily, Pam Kansas…those are real people, real people. Cold and hungry and sad and hopeless…But real people. *(By now she is screaming and swinging her arms about madly.)* WHY DON'T YOU UNDERSTAND THAT? WHY WON'T YOU UNDERSTAND THAT?

CHARLIE: Did ya hear, Sister Emily? Cecilia said our names on the TV. Did you hear?

T-LA: This is bad news. She's in big trouble; big trouble.

CECILIA: *(On video)* I DIDN'T COME FROM NOWHERE. I WAS POOR. DIRT POOR. I'M FROM THE STREETS. MY PEOPLE ARE CHARLIE AND EMILY AND T-LA AND DUGY AND PAM KANSAS. I AIN'T DOIN' NO DAMNED BENEFIT FOR THE HOMELESS. I AM THE HOMELESS. AND DUGY, AND EMILY, AND T-LA, AND CHARLIE AND PAM KANSAS—IF YOU'RE LISTENIN'…I SOLD Y'ALL OUT. YEAH. I DID. I SOLD Y'ALL OUT. I LEFT YA OUT THERE ON THE STREETS. I OUGHTA BE WITH MY PEOPLE. AND THAT'S WHERE I'M GOIN' RIGHT NOW…YOU STUPID, STUPID MAN…*(She slugs him and runs away.)*

Act II, Scene 3

Holiday Pose #7 leading to Interaction Dance. CECILIA *is back among the street people.*

T-LA: *(Embraces her)* You doin' okay today, Cecilia?

CECILIA: Yeah, T-La. *(She's unsteady; less certain than before.)* I'm okay.

PAM: *(Comes over)* Hey, Cecilia. I'm gonna get a little vegetable soup over on Broadway. I'll bring you some back, okay?

CECILIA: I ain't raised no money yet, Pam. I'll get some on my own soon.

PAM: Hey, Cecilia, what's the big deal? You'll get some for me later, ya know.

CHARLIE: That was nice when you and Pam sang for us last night, Cecilia. That was beautiful.

CECILIA: Well, I'm glad you liked it, Charlie.

CHARLIE: So many people loved how you sing Cecilia. So many people, ya know. I mean *real* people.

CECILIA: You're as *real* as any of them, Charlie.

EMILY: Hey, Cecilia, that was funny when you *hit* that announcer guy on TV.

DUGY: Be quiet, Sister Emily. Be quiet.

CECILIA: It was funny, Sister Emily. It really was.

EMILY: Hey, Brother Dugy, I know it was a bad thing that happened to Sister Cecilia. I ain't no damn fool. But it was funny. Did you see the look on that honky's face? Shit, it was funny as hell.

CECILIA: Right on, Sister Emily…hey, a funny thing happened to me on the way to bein' *rich* and *famous*.

EMILY: *(Laughing)* What's that, Sister Cecilia? What's that?

CECILIA: Well…I realized I was *poor* and *unknown*.

CHARLIE: That's not so funny, Sister Cecilia. That's not so funny. I don't even think I get it.

CECILIA: You're right, Charlie. I never could tell a joke. I better leave the humor to Sister Emily over here. *(She crosses to stage right alone and sings.)*

("Never be the Same")

It'll never be the same
Once you've *touched*
A dream.
It'll never be the same
Once you've *felt*
A life.
It'll never be the same,
But nothing ever changes.
It'll never be the same.

But it doesn't make a difference.
No, it doesn't make a difference.
No, I'll never leave this place,
Still it feels as if it'll never be the same.

I thought I went away,
I was livin' for a minute.
I thought I went away,
A new play and I was in it.

I thought I went away,
But I never left at all.
I thought I went away,
But now I can't recall.

No, it doesn't make a difference.
No, I'll never leave this place.
Still it feels as if
It'll never be the same.

Everybody tried to tell me
I was made to go somewhere,
But somethin' musta told me
I had to be right here.

No, it doesn't make a difference.
No, I'll never leave this place.
Still it feels as if
It'll never be the same.

Act II, Scene 4

Holiday Pose #8 leading to Interaction Dance. MRS. HERMAN *stands on the stairs watching the street scene more intently—and sadly.* MRS. ROSEN *sees her from across the stage and begins to talk to her; a fight develops.*

MRS. ROSEN: *(Upset, angry)* You know, Mrs. Herman, what I never understood about you liberals is how come you pay hundreds of dollars for tickets to Broadway shows like *Les Miserables* which are all about poor people and street people and then come home to 93rd Street and Riverside and look down your noses at people livin' on the street right across the way? What's the story? Street people from 1848 are okay but not from 1996? Actors performin' like street people are okay but not the real thing? What's the story, Mrs. Herman? What's your goddamned story?

CECILIA: Hey, Rosen, be cool. Don't talk to Mrs. Herman that way. It don't do no one no good.

DUGY: Yeah, Rosen, she ain't the worst of 'em anyway.

T-LA: Calm down. Whatsa matter, you need a social worker, Rosen?

MRS. ROSEN: It sucks. The whole damn society sucks. And I'm sick of it… Anyway, butt out of it. This is a thing between us white middle-class assholes. (*She walks across stage to bottom of stairs.*) So, Herman. What the hell ya got to say for yourself?

(*MRS. HERMAN and MRS. ROSEN sing.*)

(*"Never Again"*)

MRS. HERMAN:
> Mrs. Rosen,
> You have chosen
> To be a social worker.
> So, Mrs. Rosen,
> Work some magic,
> Put an end
> To all that's tragic.
> I can't look anymore,
> What are social workers for?
> Mrs. Rosen, Mrs. Rosen,
> Make *them* a better life.

MRS. ROSEN:
> Mrs. Herman,
> They're not vermin
> And I don't know a trick.
> So, Mrs. Herman,
> Beg your pardon, but
> This world is mighty sick.
> You can't look anymore?
> Well, sister, shut your eyes.
> Mrs. Herman, Mrs. Herman
> Would you have the poor arise?

TOGETHER:
> I don't think we really need to fight.
> You and I find bedrooms every night.
> I can feel the sadness of their pain.

MRS. HERMAN:
> I'm a Jew, Mrs. Rosen.

MRS. ROSEN:
> I am too, Mrs. Herman.

TOGETHER:
> We say "Never again."

> We're Mrs. Herman
> And Mrs. Rosen.
> We have chosen
> To care about the poor,
> But what frustration
> This is a nation
> That will not fight this war.
> So we're standin' on the street
> Before we start, already beat.

MRS. HERMAN:
> Mrs. Rosen,

MRS. ROSEN:
> Mrs. Herman,

TOGETHER:
> What were we chosen for?

CECILIA and PAM:
> Mrs. Rosen and Mrs. Herman
> That song is mighty funny.
> But Mrs. Rosen and Mrs. Herman
> It don't make us any money.
> Never again can sound just fine
> But isn't yet complete
> Cause Mrs. Rosen and Mrs. Herman
> We're still living on the street.

DUGY: *(Joking)* Goddamn, I thought we were the chosen people.

T-LA: *(Joking)* Yeah, we are. Rosen, Herman, we are the chosen people.

PAM: Well, whatta we been chosen for?

CECILIA: Hey, Pam Kansas, you were chosen to come to the city.

PAM: I guess so, Cecilia, I guess so.

("Will it Ever Happen?")

T-LA, DUGY, MRS. ROSEN, MRS. HERMAN: *(Sing)*
> Will it ever happen?
> Will it ever happen?
> Will it ever happen?
> Will it ever happen?

PAM:
> In the country
> In the city
> Nothin' good is
> Goin' on.
> So I know, yes, I know
> It's a long, long way to go.

COMPANY:
> Will it ever happen?
> Will it ever happen?

CECILIA:
> Days you make it,
> Days you don't.
> Nothin' good is
> Goin' on.
> So I know, yes, I know
> It's a long, long way to go.

COMPANY:
> Will it ever happen?
> Will it ever happen?

CECILIA and PAM:
> Yes we know
> That life goes on,

And we know
When we're dead and gone
Another kinda day,
Another kinda way,
For our children may be won.

COMPANY:

Will it ever happen?
Will it ever happen?

(Repeat from top, with entire company singing together.)

))))

Lenin's Breakdown

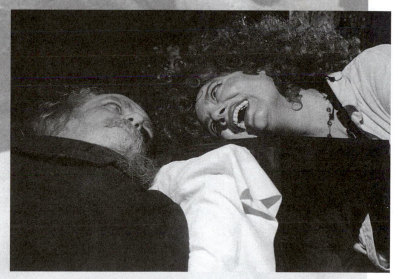

By Fred Newman and Dan Friedman

Except for the musicals, Newman has collaborated as playwright on only one play. That play is *Lenin's Breakdown* (1994), and I'm honored to say that I am the co-author.

The idea for the play was Newman's. He presented it to me in the summer of 1986 and, as I recall, he had already thought through all the elements of Lenin's encounter with a series of characters, fictional and historical, "somewhere in history." Although by then Newman had directed a number of productions, he had not yet written *Mr. Hirsch Died Yesterday*, and didn't see himself as a playwright. I had been writing plays for over a decade, so when he came to me to translate his idea into a script it seemed a logical division of labor. I completed the first draft in 10 days (a record for me), Newman read the script, suggested some minor changes, and in short order the Castillo Theatre had a play with which to open its 1986-'87 season. The play—containing all the scenes of Lenin's encounters "in history" but none of his dialogues with the psychiatrist at Bellevue Hospital, which were added later—was called *The Collected Emotions of V.I. Lenin*. Newman directed it at Castillo in October 1986. With different casts and slightly altered scripts he directed it there again in June and December of 1990.

The Lenin of the title is Vladimir Ilyich Lenin, the leader of the Russian Revolution of 1917 and the founder of the international communist movement. On one level *The Collected Emotions of V.I. Lenin* was an attempt by two American Marxists to come to terms—our terms, of course—with Lenin and his legacy.

(A theatre history note: *Lenin's Breakdown* appears to be the only American play ever written in which Lenin is the central character—or at least the only one ever printed. Lenin was a character in *Requiem for Communism*, the 1993 dance theatre piece performed by Amy Pivar Dances and Bill T. Jones, for which Newman wrote the text. Lenin also appears in Newman's *Life Upon the Wicked Stage*. In fact there are very few plays in English in which Lenin appears as a character, Robert Bolt's 1977 *State of Revolution* being a notable exception.)

Newman and I were aware of the deadly betrayals and failures of the communist movement; at the same time we viewed communism as the only serious attempt in modern times to empower poor and working people. Seeing/believing both of these things was/is very painful. The play—in both the earlier and later versions—deals with the shift in revolutionary activity from Europe to Africa, Asia and Latin America; the misguided dependence of the communist movement on ideology; its underestimation of the role of culture in social transformation; its repressed attitude toward sex (including its homophobia); and its exclusion from the revolutionary process of those most stunted and destroyed by the capitalist system. At the time we thought of the play primarily as a polemic against monumentalization (a theme Newman also explored in *Billie & Malcolm: A Demonstration* and would return to in *Stealin' Home*). *The Collected Emotions of V.I. Lenin* was our effort to demonumentalize Lenin, to get him off his pedestal and back into living history.

By 1994, when Newman restructured the play into *Lenin's Breakdown*, Lenin was, of course, no longer on a pedestal. The house he had built was in collapse and his monuments dragged through the streets of Eastern Europe by the very people he had hoped/claimed to be liberating. The real question for serious Marxists had become whether anything positive and growthful could be salvaged from the ruins of communism. For the 1994 production, which was staged at the Castillo Theatre under the direction of Gabrielle Kurlander, Newman wrote scenes in which a deranged, elderly street person named Lenin wanders into the mental ward of New York City's Bellevue Hospital and tells his stories of the revolution to a psychiatrist on duty that night. These new scenes, juxtaposed with the scenes from the old *Collected Emotions,* cast them in a very different light and created a whole new theatrical and political experience. No longer primarily a polemic against monumentalization, the play had become a sad conversation about a failed movement and an exploration of how to go on when the way forward has been completely lost. It's that 1994 script which is included here.

The other big change was in the play's ending. In *Collected Emotions* there had been a character—a hustler, former prostitute and ex-convict (called Lower Strata Person)—who entered after Trotsky. She was the catalyst who reorganized the entire grouping of characters and allowed them to enter history. Put another way, she created the conditions for the qualities of the various characters to be synthesized into a unified revolutionary for the late 20th century. The first production ended with wild laughter that spread from Lenin to the others. The next two productions concluded with the entire cast dancing to Motown music and inviting the audience to join in onstage (which they invariably did).

The end of *Lenin's Breakdown* presents a far bleaker picture. Lenin lies sick and probably dying in the mental ward, with a prostitute—a friend of his from the streets—futilely trying to revive him. The "historical" characters are left stranded (in history, or in what Lenin now says might instead be "memory…dream or fantasy"). There is no transformation onstage, no development, except perhaps for the psychiatrist who, it is suggested, may learn something about his own life by talking with Lenin. The Lower Strata Person has become Edie, the prostitute, who does not galvanize the characters into history; she merely wants to drag Lenin back to the corner of 104th Street and Broadway.

Most of the political issues in the earlier form of the play remain in *Lenin's Breakdown*. But with the new structure and new ending the play loses its polemical contours and becomes far more personal *and* far more historical. Its central metaphor—breakdown—refers simultaneously to the failure of the revolutionary process initiated by the historical Lenin and to the mental exhaustion of Lenin, the street person.

The Collected Emotions of V.I. Lenin/Lenin's Breakdown is the first of Newman's plays to be set "in history"—not in the past, but in what Newman has called the "continuous, ongoing flow of human life." While society is like a snapshot of the here and now, history is *movement*—and is therefore not bounded by time or space. Since the actions of every human being who's ever lived are with us, even when they are physically dead, there is no death in history.

The corner of Euclid Avenue and Christopher Street in *Common Women* implied this conception of history, as did the encounter between Fred and Freda in *Mr. Hirsch Died Yesterday*. But it was with *The Collected Emotions/Lenin's Breakdown* that history-as-setting became explicit, and its dramatic and political possibilities more thoroughly (and playfully) explored. Many of Newman's subsequent plays, and particularly *What is to be Dead? (Philosophical Scenes), Risky Revolutionary, Stealin' Home,* and the final scene in *Sally and Tom (The American Way),* would employ history in this way.

Lenin's Breakdown also shows a new sophistication in Newman's dramatic structuring. His 1994 rewrite of *The Collected Emotions of V.I. Lenin* transformed it from a Brecht-like political parable which neatly and romantically resolved its contradictions into *Lenin's Breakdown,* in which the play's dramatic tension no longer resides primarily in the conflicts between Lenin and the characters who come to visit him, but between the two Lenins and their contrasting narratives/realities. As with *Billie & Malcolm: A Demonstration* there is no resolution in *Lenin's Breakdown*. Ultimately, Newman's refusal to resolve the play's conflicts is the most significant political/aesthetic statement of this very political play.

D.F.

Lenin's Breakdown was first produced at the Castillo Theatre (Fred Newman, artistic director; Gabrielle Kurlander, producing director; Diane Stiles, managing director) in New York City on March 18, 1994. The cast, in order of appearance, was as follows:

PSYCHIATRIST . . . . Kenneth Hughes
VLADIMIR ILYICH LENIN . . . . Fred Newman
DETROIT . . . . Doug Miranda
ELIZABETH K. . . . . Cece Waterman
"RED" EMMA GOLDMAN . . . . Marian Rich
LEON TROTSKY . . . . David Nackman
EDIE . . . . Vicky Wallace
VLADIMIR ILYICH LENIN UNDERSTUDY . . . . Roger Grunwald

Gabrielle Kurlander, director; Fred Newman, production design; Diane Stiles, producer; Don Hulbert, flute; Joseph Spirito, set design; Sheila Goloborotko, scenic design; Charlotte, costume design; Jessica Massad, Beth Peeler and Linnaea Tillett, lighting design; Michael Klein, sound design; Jeff Aron and Beth Peeler, stage turners; Phyllis Goldberg, dramaturg; Ellen Korner, production stage manager.

Lenin's Breakdown is not intended to be *about* V.I. Lenin—twice over. Firstly, I try not to write plays that are about anything. For when language is primarily *about* another thing we lose something of the *activity* of speaking and creating. Secondly, if this play *is* about anything, it is about aging within a dying civilization. The main character, an old man who (like V.I. Lenin) was born in 1870 and (unlike Lenin) is still alive in 1994, looks back on his (or Lenin's) youth and is shocked by the illusion of immortality that permeates all of our days before old age (very old age). This illusion is manifest primarily in the self-assurance and egoism of our youth (approximately age 10-80). It can be recognized as well in Lenin's deadly and moribund motivation, commitment, and obsessiveness.

But Lenin is not unlike the rest of us. We all shape ourselves, it seems to me, in accordance with others' designs for or upon us, even when the plan of others is for us to design *them!* "They all loved my intensity," says old man Lenin, "and I became a mass murderer." Haven't we all become something we rather hated because everyone loved us doing some of the things that we were doing? And hasn't a civilization based on alienation made us all into the product(s) of others' transference? And mustn't we all find a way to move beyond alienation if we are to develop further?

Such is the political psychology of *Lenin's Breakdown.* The play has nothing to do with V.I. Lenin and everything to do with all of us living in the ruins of a dying civilization.

APRIL 1994

CHARACTERS
(in order of appearance)

PSYCHIATRIST
VLADIMIR ILYICH LENIN
DETROIT, an auto worker
ELIZABETH K., Lenin's mistress
"RED" EMMA GOLDMAN, an American anarchist
LEON TROTSKY
EDIE, a prostitute

Scene 1

The emergency ward at Bellevue Hospital. Dimly lit. It's between 3:00 a.m. and 4:00 a.m. It is winter, some time in the 1990s. A very, very old man, obviously a street person, is sitting on a bed while a somewhat kindly (though reserved) psychiatrist behind a desk interviews him, at first in a totally pro-forma fashion.

PSYCHIATRIST: *(Reading an administrative form)* Your name is Lenin? Is that right? Is that how you pronounce it, Mr. Lenin? And you spell it L-E-N-I-N?

LENIN: *(Stares at him pathetically; his words stumble out slowly)* Yes...yes. That is my name.

PSYCHIATRIST: Have you been here at Bellevue before?

LENIN: No. No. I never...*(his voice fades.)*

PSYCHIATRIST: Well, why did you come here, Mr. Lenin?

LENIN: I don't know. I needed a place to sit for just a minute.

PSYCHIATRIST: You live on the streets, Mr. Lenin?

LENIN: I suppose so. Yes. I live on the streets.

PSYCHIATRIST: Are you sick?

LENIN: Yes, I am sick.

PSYCHIATRIST: Well, what do you think is wrong with you?

LENIN: I have grown completely tired of life. I no longer care about anyone or anything. I see no reason to do anything. I see no reason to answer your questions, to talk at all, to go anywhere. To move my hand *(he gestures with his hand)* one way or another.

PSYCHIATRIST: Then why do you answer my questions, Mr. Lenin?

LENIN: I am polite...even if I can no longer think of any reason to be so.

PSYCHIATRIST: Are you...uh, on any drugs, Mr. Lenin?

LENIN: I do not use drugs. I never have. Maybe I should. What do you think, Doctor?

PSYCHIATRIST: How old are you?

LENIN: I am very old. It seems I cannot die. I have lived this whole century.

PSYCHIATRIST: You are in your nineties?

LENIN: Even older than that.

PSYCHIATRIST: What is your first name, Mr. Lenin?

LENIN: Vladimir. My first name is Vladimir.

PSYCHIATRIST: *(Pause)* Your name is Vladimir Lenin? *(Laughs slightly.)* Are you a relative of the famous Russian revolutionary?

LENIN: *(Pause; stares at PSYCHIATRIST)* No. I am no relative of his.

PSYCHIATRIST: Have you always been so uninterested in life, Mr. Lenin? What did you do when you were younger?

LENIN: I cannot remember what I did. I think I did my duty. I did whatever had to be done. Everyone wanted me to be someone for them. So I tried to do whatever they wanted me to do.

PSYCHIATRIST: So you were never motivated to do what you really wanted to do?

LENIN: *(Just a little agitated)* Oh, no. They all wanted me to be very motivated. So I was. I was more motivated than most anybody. I think that's why they liked me so.

PSYCHIATRIST: But you're saying you weren't really motivated...is that right? You were motivated because they—the others in your life— wanted you, needed you, to be motivated?

LENIN: I don't know. I never could tell. Maybe I was motivated to be who they all wanted me to be. Can someone be motivated to be motivated, Doctor? What does Sigmund Freud have to say about that?

PSYCHIATRIST: I don't know, Mr. Lenin. I don't know. *(Pause.)* But I think I understand what you are talking about. *(He walks pensively across the room, then back to his desk and picks up a family picture.)* Do you want to lie down for a little while, Mr. Lenin? It's almost four a.m.

LENIN: Are you going to psychoanalyze me?

PSYCHIATRIST: *(Laughing)* No, Mr. Lenin. Though you are an interesting man. No. I'll just finish up this report. You can sleep the night here. We'll discharge you in the morning.

(LENIN lies down; PSYCHIATRIST works on his report, looks again at the family picture.)

LENIN: *(Free-associating)* The Black worker from Detroit. That Black worker with the strange drawing of me…

PSYCHIATRIST: What about him, Mr. Lenin? What about him?

Scene 2

A brightly lit early 20th-century study. A more youthful LENIN enters and sits at his desk writing. A worker—DETROIT—enters and approaches him.

DETROIT: Excuse me, Lenine, I don't want to bother you.

LENIN: No, not at all. I was just reworking a talk I have to give tomorrow. Please, please come in.

DETROIT: I could come back another time.

LENIN: No. It's fine. I could use a break anyway. Have a seat.

(They sit quietly staring at each other for a long moment.)

LENIN: What have you come for, comrade?

DETROIT: I have come to see for myself that you are white. That your face is white. V.I. Lenine, the greatest revolutionary of all, is really white.

LENIN: I was born a European. Yes, I am white.

DETROIT: Yes.

LENIN: Yes.

DETROIT: Yeah.

LENIN: My skin color is a problem for you?

DETROIT: Of course, it's no fault of yours. But for me, yeah, it's a problem.

LENIN: Why?

DETROIT: (*Reaching into his pocket,* DETROIT *takes out a folded leaflet, which he unfolds carefully*) Look at this. (DETROIT *flattens the leaflet on* LENIN'S *desk.*) I'm a pretty good artist. I don't mean to brag or nothin'…I'm not a professional, but among us communists in Detroit, I'm considered one of the best.

LENIN: Yes. It's good. It's very good.

DETROIT: When we decided to form a study group last winter I was asked to draw a picture of you for the leaflet. But whenever I sat down to draw you, you kept comin' out Black.

LENIN: (*Examining the leaflet*) I do, don't I?

DETROIT: I drew you over and over again, but I couldn't make you look white. It got to the point where I thought maybe you were really Black. So I came to see ya. But, uh, you're not. You're white.

LENIN: So what is the problem, comrade?

DETROIT: Many problems, Lenine. One is that when I read your writings, when I hear about what you did in Russia in 1917, I feel you're very much like me. But you're really not.

LENIN: We're both communists.

DETROIT: I'm a Black communist. You're a white communist.

LENIN: Granted. That is a difference.

DETROIT: I want to follow you. I want the other workers in my shop to follow you. But with all due respect, Lenine, I don't want to follow a white man.

(*A pause;* LENIN *is nodding.*)

LENIN: Do the bosses see me as a white man?

DETROIT: When they look at a photograph of you, they do.

LENIN: You think the bosses see a difference between the Black Lenin you drew and the white Lenin of the photographs?

DETROIT: Sure. I do.

LENIN: I think, perhaps, you are right. When they see with their white racist eyes. But when they stare with their greedy bank accounts in mind and look with their private property-possessed egos, they see only rebellious communists who want to take everything away from them.

DETROIT: But the workers see a difference. To those in my shop, you're the same color as the boss.

LENIN: When they are on strike together or, better yet, fighting at the barricades, is that distinction of color so clear?

(*DETROIT becomes a little more agitated.*)

DETROIT: Yeah. Look, I know that the issue of color is trivial; that class is the real deal. But here's the important point, Comrade Lenine. The white worker is no longer at the barricade. The white revolution is over, Comrade Lenine. Millions of your white workers in the Soviet Union and Eastern Europe have abandoned the barricades for capitalism and Christian democracy. We are Black communists. Communists of color. We are Black revolutionaries. And we will not be fooled by your white workers. We have been abandoned. The white guys have been bribed. You are a symbol of white workers; of a white revolution. And it's dead. So, Comrade Lenine, what of you?

(*A pause; LENIN is thoughtful.*)

LENIN: I have been abandoned, too. The vision of our revolution has been bleached by a corruption whiter even than white skin. You are right, my Black comrade. The white revolution is indeed over. But I am no symbol of white workers; any more than you are a symbol of Black workers; any more than your drawing here is a representation of you or me or anyone else. I am no symbol. I am no monument. You are no symbol; no monument. We are revolutionary workers. Our duty is to make revolution. And it is our flesh and blood duty, which defines us, dear comrade. Let Stalin, the bastard, be the monument to our failures.

(*DETROIT peers at LENIN and breaks into a little grin.*)

DETROIT: You do seem a little less white, Comrade Lenine. (*Laughing.*) Do you think it's the lighting? Say, what is this strange lighting anyway? Where in the hell are we, Comrade Lenine?

LENIN: We're deep in history, comrade. (*A thoughtful pause.*) Or maybe we are in a memory or a dream or a fantasy. Now in history we're both the same color.

DETROIT: What do you mean, we're in history?

LENIN: This is where revolutionaries permanently reside. In history. We have no zip code. We are of no society. In the light of history we are the same red color. A young Indochinese fellow came to visit me a while ago. He was a cook on a French freighter and he wanted to know how he could take these "European" ideas back to Asia. I told him the kitchen of a freighter seemed as good a way as any to travel through history. His name was Ho Chi Minh. And a young Cuban, Fidel Castro, came by to see if "Leninism"—isn't that what you call it!—would work in Latin America. A small boat made history there.

DETROIT: Very interesting, Lenine. But what if this is a memory or a dream or a fantasy?

LENIN: Then…then we are finished. Then we are truly dead. Then you and me and the others mean nothing. Or we are all madmen. Very possible, my friend. (*Pause.*) But it is a sunny day and those are dreary thoughts. Please, have a drink. (*Pours DETROIT a glass of wine.*)

DETROIT: (*Sips; looks at his drawing*) Then you think this is an alright picture?

LENIN: I think it is fine. It's just a picture. Only a picture. A very nice picture, Comrade Detroit…but only a picture.

Scene 3

Bellevue Hospital. LENIN sits up suddenly.

LENIN: Why did I have to say those words? They seem so foolish and empty now. Why did I have to speak that way? So full of myself and self-assured.

PSYCHIATRIST: They seemed appropriate words, Mr. Lenin. Caring and kindly words.

LENIN: Did I say them because Detroit, my old comrade, needed to hear them? Is that it, Doctor?

PSYCHIATRIST: Is there something wrong with that, Mr. Lenin?

LENIN: There is, but I still can't tell what it is. *(Pause.)*

PSYCHIATRIST: This fantasy you have of being V.I. Lenin, the long dead Russian revolutionary talking to a Black worker you call Detroit...it is recurring...I mean do you have it frequently?

LENIN: I don't believe I ever had that fantasy at all.

PSYCHIATRIST: You mean this was the very first time?

LENIN: You think it is impossible that we were in history, Doctor? That Detroit and I were really in history? That it was not a fantasy?

PSYCHIATRIST: To me it seems impossible, Mr. Lenin.

LENIN: So then I am mad...a lunatic. I have wound up a fantasizing lunatic. If you live too long, Doctor, I think you become a madman.

PSYCHIATRIST: There is something to that, Mr. Lenin. I believe there is.

(PSYCHIATRIST looks again at his family picture.)

LENIN: That is your family, Doctor? That is a picture of your family?

PSYCHIATRIST: Yes. It is.

LENIN: Has it also grown too old, Doctor? Forgive me, I do not mean to pry. I mean no disrespect.

PSYCHIATRIST: No, Mr. Lenin. I hear none. Perhaps we have all grown too old. Perhaps the world has grown too old.

LENIN: I have been too old all my life, Doctor. Too stuffy. Too formal. Elizabeth always told me so.

PSYCHIATRIST: Elizabeth? Your wife?

LENIN: No. My mistress...a long time ago. *(LENIN lies down on couch.)*

Scene 4

Lenin's study.

ELIZABETH: *(Offstage)* Vladimir, darling!

(*ELIZABETH K. enters.*)

LENIN: Elizabeth?

(*ELIZABETH crosses to* LENIN *and embraces him at his desk; she is oblivious to* DETROIT.)

ELIZABETH: Of course, darling, who else?

LENIN: *(Disengaging himself from her embrace)* Elizabeth, this is a comrade from, uh, Detroit.

ELIZABETH: *(Shaking DETROIT's hand)* Detroit? How interesting.

LENIN: Elizabeth is a, uh, friend. We met many years ago in Petersburg.

ELIZABETH: And what times we had, didn't we, Vladimir Ilyich?

LENIN: *(Pulling himself together)* Yes. We've had some wonderful times. And what have you come for today, Elizabeth?

ELIZABETH: I've come to take you to a play, Vladimir Ilyich.

LENIN: A play? What a nice idea, but I can't really. I have work to do.

ELIZABETH: You always have work to do. You act like such an old man. *(Grabbing his hand.)* Let's go.

LENIN: No, really, Elizabeth. I can't leave tonight. I have an article to finish.

ELIZABETH: Can't it wait until tomorrow?

LENIN: No, actually, it can't. It goes to the printer in the morning. The local mill workers are waiting for it.

ELIZABETH: Oh, let them wait another day.

DETROIT: But if Comrade Lenine says he has to work...

ELIZABETH: Nonsense, I came all this way, and I won't take no for an answer.

LENIN: You must.

ELIZABETH: Oh, Vladimir Ilyich, really. This is such a play! It's Chekhov's latest. Stanislavsky is starring and it's very political. It really is. It's about a financially ruined aristocratic family who won't face up to their situation and they have their estate bought by a vulgar bourgeois friend. That's who Stanislavsky plays. He has plans to cut down their beautiful cherry orchard and sell lots for bungalows. *(Slight pause. She looks at LENIN for a reaction. He has none.)* Don't you see? It's all about the transition of Russia from semi-feudalism to capitalism! It's onstage just like you write about it in your pamphlets. But, oh! Chekhov is such a poet.

LENIN: It sounds very interesting.

ELIZABETH: It is! And I do so want to see it with you. I saw it last night with such philistines. The whole thing went over their heads. They wept for the family's estate as if the play were a cheap melodrama. It's actually a comedy. Very clever, you'll see that. Please, Vladimir Ilyich, I long to have an intelligent discussion of this play! There are so few intelligent people in this world.

LENIN: Elizabeth, I can't, not tonight.

ELIZABETH: When then?

LENIN: I don't know.

ELIZABETH: This is just like the time in Stockholm when your Bolsheviks were having some kind of congress and I came to spend some time with you. Out of a month, you could only see me twice.

LENIN: Elizabeth, I'm sorry. I know how unpleasant that was for you. But I do have my work.

ELIZABETH: Yes, you certainly do. You old fuddy-duddy. Is this communism business really going to work anyhow?

DETROIT: Hey, c'mon now. It's extremely important work, the revolution depends on him.

ELIZABETH: *(To DETROIT, impatiently)* Yes, yes. I know all that. *(To LENIN.)* Vladimir Ilyich, you're such a brilliant man. There's so much you could do. So much you have to offer the world, and there's so much the world could offer you. But you're so single-minded, so obsessed with this revolution of yours.

LENIN: It's true.

ELIZABETH: Well, it makes you boring.

DETROIT: Am I boring?

ELIZABETH: I don't know you, friend.

DETROIT: Lenin is boring like a worker. Doing the same thing over and over. That's what I do all day, you know, in Detroit. A chassis comes along; I lean over and add three bolts. It moves down the line. Eight hours a day. It makes me sweaty and pretty boring.

ELIZABETH: Yes, but you have no choice; he does.

DETROIT: Maybe that's part of what makes him so great.

ELIZABETH: That he chooses to be boring?

DETROIT: No. That he chooses to work like a worker.

ELIZABETH: (Laughing) Yes, yes. I suppose you're right. But it's infuriating. He's so obsessed. I remember once I was playing Beethoven's "Appassionata" Sonata for him. It's a very beautiful piece. And he had me play a particular part over and over. And when I asked him why, he said it reminded him of the revolutionary hymn of the Jewish Socialist Bund.

LENIN: It is very similar. I've been meaning to ask this guy at the Bund if they got their melody from that passage. It would be nice for the Bolsheviks to have our own song, don't you think, comrade?

DETROIT: Yes. Music can be very organizing.

LENIN: We've never been able to organize a composer into the Party...

ELIZABETH: I should think not. When would he have time for music?

LENIN: Elizabeth, please...

ELIZABETH: (Trying again) How about tomorrow afternoon? There's an exhibit of new French paintings. They call it cubism. It's fascinating; they've broken with single-point perspective. It's the most radical transformation in painting in 300 years. A revolutionary like yourself must see it.

LENIN: You're such an interesting woman, Elizabeth. It's a pity you're not a communist.

ELIZABETH: You're an interesting man yourself. It's a pity you are only a communist.

(They both laugh very loudly, holding hands.)

Scene 5

Bellevue. LENIN *sits up startled; sort of hysterical; a mixture of laughter and torment.*

LENIN: I am only a communist. Wow! And that is boring. Wow! Or is it only a dream, a fantasy, a memory? Can a boring man have interesting fantasies, Doctor? Isn't that what Professor Freud proved? My maternal grandfather, like Freud, was a Jewish doctor. Not a psychiatrist. Just a general practitioner. I think Elizabeth was right, Doctor. I was only a communist. Isn't it unhealthy to be only something…whatever it might be? Now I am only a bum, an old man, a street person. Maybe when I die I can stop being only one thing. What's my problem, Doctor? What is your diagnosis?

PSYCHIATRIST: You are too old to be psychoanalyzed, Mr. Lenin. Far too old.

LENIN: But perhaps I will never die.

PSYCHIATRIST: If you think that then you are too mad for psychoanalysis.

LENIN: *(Slightly agitated)* Is it true then that Dr. Freud's psychoanalysis works only for middle-aged, middle-class women of modest madness?

PSYCHIATRIST: I do not wish to fight with you, Mr. Lenin. Whoever you are, your dreams, your fantasies, your memories, or, perhaps, even your history are more fascinating than my life. *(Takes a whiskey bottle from his desk drawer; pours himself a drink.)* Would you like a drink, Mr. Lenin?

LENIN: *(Pause)* Yes. I would. I am sad to hear about your life, Doctor. You seem to me a good man.

PSYCHIATRIST: Yeah. I'm only a run of the mill postmodern neurotic. *(Pause.)* You sure you're not related to V.I. Lenin?

LENIN: Why?

PSYCHIATRIST: Oh, I dunno. The stuff you're telling me seems so intimate— not like something you'd read in a book—and, at the same time, it sounds like real memory. I dunno. *(Pause.)* Do you have any memories— or whatever—with famous people?

LENIN: Like who, for example?

PSYCHIATRIST: Let's see. Uh…what about Emma Goldman? Yeah. What about Red Emma.

LENIN: You know crazy Red Emma?

PSYCHIATRIST: No. But I've heard about her. My father was an anarchist, an old Wobbly.

LENIN: Red Emma was crazy. If you listen carefully, I'll bet you can still hear her screaming. *(They pause and we do hear RED EMMA screaming.)*

EMMA: *(Offstage)* Comrade Lenin!

Scene 6

Study. EMMA rushes up to LENIN.

LENIN: Comrade Emma?

EMMA: Look at you!

ELIZABETH: Who is this woman?

EMMA: You call yourself a revolutionary, but you look like a damned Philadelphia lawyer.

LENIN: Well, I was a lawyer.

EMMA: Oh, for Chrissakes, Lenin, you never practiced law in your life. One of the smartest things you ever did was to not practice law. How can you talk to the workers about liberation when you go around in a three-piece suit?

ELIZABETH: I beg your pardon, how should he dress, like you?

EMMA: Who are you? I'm talking to Lenin here.

LENIN: Excuse me. This is the famous Red Emma, an anarchist comrade from the United States. *(To EMMA, laughing.)* Ah, I take it you're still an anarchist, Emma?

EMMA: What a question! I wouldn't take up with those stuffy bourgeois intellectuals, Marx and Engels, if...

LENIN: *(Cutting her off)* Yes, well. This is a comrade from Detroit.

EMMA: What's happenin'?

LENIN: And this is Elizabeth.

EMMA: Are you one of his Bolsheviks, too?

ELIZABETH: Certainly not!

LENIN: Elizabeth and I are, uh, friends.

EMMA: "Friends"?

LENIN: Yes, Emma, we are friends.

EMMA: Oh! You two are lovers. *(She finds this very amusing.)* That's wonderful, V.I. I didn't know you had it in ya.

LENIN: Please, Emma, this isn't something we need to talk about.

EMMA: It's exactly what I came to talk about, Comrade Lenin. I want to know where sex is in your revolution.

ELIZABETH: *(Laughing)* Well, I was sort of asking a similar question.

LENIN: I don't see what sex has to do with the revolution.

EMMA: I didn't think you did, Lenin. That's why we have to talk.

LENIN: The oppression of women is explained by Engels in his book, *The Origin of the Family, Private Property and the State.* Of course, we'll abolish bourgeois marriage right after the revolution.

DETROIT: We will?

EMMA: Lenin, we know all that.

DETROIT: We do?

EMMA: I guess what I'm really saying is—you're not sexy. *(To* ELIZABETH.*)* No offense, sister.

ELIZABETH: Not at all. I like your style.

DETROIT: Wait a minute. Wait just one goddamn minute. You come in here and tell Lenine, *LENINE,* the leader of international communism, that he's not sexy? What in the hell are you two talkin' about?

EMMA: It's exactly because he is the leader of international communism that it matters. I mean, you're not so sexy either, brother, but who cares?

DETROIT: Comrade Lenine, would you like me to, uh, get rid of her?

EMMA: You and what army?

LENIN: No, of course not. Sex, like color, is important not in-itself, but for our class, in history.

EMMA: The workers *(giving* DETROIT *a dirty look)*, at least the ones I know, demand to know where sex is in your revolution. They want to know what Lenin means by pleasure. If there's no dancing in your god-damned revolution, I don't want any part of it.

ELIZABETH: And I want Chekhov in the revolution.

EMMA: Who's he? A Menshevik?

ELIZABETH: No, a playwright.

> *(*LENIN *gets up, goes to a corner of the playing area, and begins to do acting warm-up exercises: rolling his head, his shoulders, shaking his arms and legs out, stretching his face muscles, blowing air through his lips like a horse, etc. The others watch him, baffled.)*

DETROIT: Are you alright, comrade?

LENIN: I will be, yes. I'm just doing some exercises that an actor friend taught me. They help me relax before a speech.

EMMA: Am I making you tense, Comrade Lenin?

LENIN: Oh, yes. There are some very hard questions being asked about the revolution these days.

DETROIT: Would you like us to leave?

LENIN: No. Please. We must talk about this. I have been living in my pamphlets for too long. I am boring. Revolutionaries are concerned with life. Sex is part of life. We need to talk about it.

ELIZABETH: You make it sound like an obligation.

LENIN: I don't mean to.

EMMA: Well, you do give that impression.

LENIN: Do I? (*LENIN finishes his exercises, walks back to his writing table, sits down, blows air through his lips like a horse again.*) Okay, Emma. It's true, I don't know much about sex. But I sense a certain lack of seriousness on your part.

EMMA: I'm deadly serious. Sex and joy and life and emotions are things you communists don't take seriously.

LENIN: Emma, what I'm questioning is your seriousness about revolution.

EMMA: (*Icy*) I've dedicated my whole life to the revolution, comrade.

LENIN: To a revolution where you can dance. But what if you can't? What if your legs are shot off by the bourgeoisie?

EMMA: There's nothing I can do about that. What I'm concerned about is— what if my legs are shot off by the proletariat?

LENIN: And what if they are? What if all our legs are shot off by the proletariat? Would we still be for the revolution? (*EMMA and LENIN look at each other steadily.*) It's a hard question, Emma. A revolution is not cappuccino and talk in a Greenwich Village cafe; it's not writing an essay or choreographing a dance; it's not a lecture series, and it's not even a strike or a demonstration. (*To DETROIT.*) It's one class using every means at its disposal, including the most unpleasant, to overthrow another. If it succeeds it changes everything, including how we dance and how we make love. When revolutionaries make love we don't do it simply for the fun of it, or to procreate the species, or even primarily to express our love for another individual. We make love for the revolution. We don't make the revolution in order to make love.

Scene 7

Bellevue.

LENIN: *(More agitated than before)* Why did I talk that way? We had some good minds at the beginning. I assure you. I had a very good mind. But I became so motivated and so obsessed. I became a truth-teller and a pragmatist. A truly deadly combination. The philosophical profile of a mass murderer, if you want to know. Emma was too crazy; Elizabeth too trivial. But they knew better than me. I could have been almost anything. I did not wish to be a statue. But I was obsessed with being obsessed. They loved my intensity and I became a mass murderer—not like Stalin; worse than Stalin. He was a narrow-minded fool. I was a genius. *(Pause.)* That was Red Emma. What do you think?

PSYCHIATRIST: Yeah. I liked her. She was a little like my Aunt Ellen. *(Pause.)* These fantasies you have are nightmares, aren't they? But if they are history—your history—then you have lived one helluva life. Maybe no one could have done any better.

LENIN: Then maybe it shouldn't have been done at all. "What is to be done?" I asked. Perhaps the answer was "nothing." Too motivated; too committed; too boring. Trying too hard to make my will determine history. That's the fantasy of it. I do so want to die.

PSYCHIATRIST: *(He stands up)* Stop forcing things so much and perhaps you will!

LENIN: Oh, Dr. Psychiatrist. You do have some wisdom after all. That was a good comment. You are psychoanalyzing me, Doctor. I see you are a dialectician. Good. Very good. I must pay you a proper fee. Let me see. Who else would you like to know about? Stalin? H.G. Wells? Gorki? Who?

PSYCHIATRIST: *(He sits again)* Tell me about Trotsky. Leon Trotsky.

LENIN: Mainly he and I fought with each other. You know Leon was terribly, terribly aggressive. No one ever screamed out my name as he did.

Scene 8

Study. TROTSKY begins offstage, then enters during his first speech. He is reading an article by LENIN intensely. He has a pamphlet stuck in his back pocket. He is agitated and totally absorbed in the article and has bustled in unaware that anyone other than LENIN is in the room or that he might be interrupting anything.

TROTSKY: Lenin, Lenin, Lenin! This is imprecise. Certainly we can speak of our Soviets as "Soviets of Workers, Peasants and Soldiers," but it's sloppy, and inaccurate to write of the "democratic dictatorship of the proletariat and the peasantry." A peasant dictatorship would have to be reactionary. The proletariat rules. There can be no such thing as a "democratic dictatorship of the proletariat and the peasantry."

LENIN: Trotsky, I have guests.

TROTSKY: *(Looking around for the first time)* Ah, excuse me, comrades. I was absorbed in this article that Comrade Lenin wrote.

EMMA: *(Extending her hand)* Good evening, comrade.

TROTSKY: And whom do I have the pleasure of addressing?

EMMA: They call me Red Emma.

TROTSKY: *(Shaking her hand warmly)* This is indeed an honor. I was an avid reader of your journal *Mother Earth* for the brief time I lived in New York City.

EMMA: You read an anarchist journal, Comrade Trotsky?

TROTSKY: And why not?

LENIN: This is a comrade from Detroit, Michigan…in the United States.

TROTSKY: *(Very interested)* Detroit? I hear that your city is a center of the automobile industry.

DETROIT: Well, it was…once upon a time.

TROTSKY: We must talk later. I'm very interested in how the automobile industry is organized.

LENIN: And this is Elizabeth K.

ELIZABETH: You've held meetings in my apartment.

TROTSKY: Yes, and a beautiful apartment it is—such high ceilings, and the parquet floors. And your samovar makes such tea! It's a wonderful machine.

ELIZABETH: Why, thank you.

TROTSKY: *(Speaking with even more aristocratic gentility than usual)* No, no, no, no, no, no, thank you. Thank you for the service you have rendered the revolution.

ELIZABETH: Comrade Trotsky, are you patronizing me?

TROTSKY: I'm not.

DETROIT: I think y'are. I mean does this sister mean anything more to you than her parquet floors and high ceilings and—what did you call it—a samovart?

TROTSKY: Yes, of course, she's Comrade Lenin's friend.

ELIZABETH: And if I wasn't Lenin's "friend"?

TROTSKY: Well, I don't think we would have met if you weren't Lenin's friend, now would we? *(To LENIN.)* Comrade Lenin, can we talk now?

LENIN: I suppose, comrade, if you don't mind company.

TROTSKY: No, not at all. Our struggles should be open to the whole working class—and others friendly to the revolution. I welcome the participation of the rank and file in every aspect of our work.

EMMA: *(Sarcastic)* How democratic of you, Comrade Trotsky!

TROTSKY: But, of course.

ELIZABETH: And what of me?

TROTSKY: And you too; you are a friend of the revolution.

ELIZABETH: From a friend of Lenin to a friend of the revolution, I suppose that's what you folks call progress.

LENIN: Elizabeth, please…

ELIZABETH: No, really V.I. I'm quite sick of it. Red Emma is right. Your sexist patronizing is quite boring. I know what you all think of me. You think I'm nothing but a wealthy whore. And do you know why they think that, "Comrade Lenin"? Because that's who you've told them I am.

LENIN: Elizabeth, I would never say something like that…

ELIZABETH: Do you think the only way you say things is with your words or in your pamphlets? You treat me like a charming and superfluous embarrassment. I'm so witty and cultured, aren't I, Vladimir Ilyich? But when it comes down to it, my raison d'etre is to lure you away from your "important work." It's gotten so that even I believe that's who I am. But I really don't want to do that anymore.

(*ELIZABETH pauses, looks around. Everyone, including LENIN, is staring at the floor.*)

EMMA: (*Looks up*) Elizabeth, there's no need to overstate the case.

DETROIT: She's not overstating anything. You know how we've all been lookin' at her, including you, Emma. We've been looking right through her. Wishing she wasn't there. She was just something that had gotten in the way, between us and Lenin.

ELIZABETH: (*Speaks quietly; she is surprised and moved*) Thank you, Detroit, thank you.

DETROIT: Well, shit, I know real well what it feels like to be invisible, to have people make believe I'm not there, to make them uncomfortable simply by existing.

LENIN: I'm sorry, Elizabeth.

ELIZABETH: You were sorry about Stockholm, too, if I'm not mistaken. Your apologies are also patronizing.

DETROIT: (*To LENIN*) Hey listen, V.I. It might not be a bad idea to see those paintings, either, the ones without single-point perspective that she was talking about. I don't know that much about them, but I do know how important culture is.

ELIZABETH: Oh, you should know about cubism, Detroit. It's dialectics brought to the graphic arts. It shows a thing from opposite sides at the same time. You communist workers would love it.

DETROIT: I'd like to. In Africa they've never used single-point perspective.

ELIZABETH: I didn't know that.

DETROIT: No, I guess you wouldn't. There's a lot of culture out there you know nothing about. I'd really like you to hear Motown sometime, Elizabeth.

ELIZABETH: Motown?

DETROIT: It's the kind of music that I grew up with. Great for dancing.

ELIZABETH: I love dancing.

DETROIT: Oh yeah? Well, maybe we can go out dancing sometime.

ELIZABETH: Detroit!! Well…that sounds like fun. It's a strange word, this "motown." Is it African?

DETROIT: (Amused) No, no. It's called Motown because most of it was recorded in my hometown, Detroit, the "Motor City," Motown, get it?

ELIZABETH: I love the way you Americans shorten everything.

TROTSKY: Comrade Lenin, can we have our discussion now or not? I could come back, but it is rather pressing.

LENIN: If you feel it's important, Leon.

TROTSKY: Theoretical struggle is always a priority.

LENIN: Yes, of course, even, I suppose over dancing to "Motown" music. Well, what are we "struggling" about today, Leon?

TROTSKY: Imprecision, Lenin, your imprecision. This reference to a "democratic dictatorship of the proletariat and the peasantry."

LENIN: The peasantry makes up the vast majority of our population. Should we ignore them?

TROTSKY: Lenin, setting me up as a strawman is beneath you. I'm obviously not saying we should ignore the peasantry upon whose broad shoulders Mother Russia has been built. But I am saying—let us not elevate the peasantry, petty-producers that they are, to equal partnership in the Soviet state. Socialism is the rule of the proletariat; Marxism, the ideology of the working class.

LENIN: Without the support of the peasantry, the proletariat, in a backward country such as Russia, cannot retain power.

TROTSKY: Yes, yes, of course, we all know that, Lenin. But the precise, the accurate, the scientific formulation is the "dictatorship of the proletariat relying on the peasantry."

LENIN: It's really not worth arguing about.

TROTSKY: Not worth arguing about the precise nature of our revolutionary government?

LENIN: We agree on the nature of our revolutionary government. That's not the question. What you don't seem to understand is the difference between a tactical formulation and a scientific statement. Our government is the rule of the proletariat in alliance with the peasantry. That's the fact. To call it a "democratic dictatorship of workers and peasants" in an article for a journal directed mainly to peasants, makes good sense.

TROTSKY: Maybe in a purely situational or pragmatic sense.

LENIN: Exactly. That's how I write, pragmatically.

TROTSKY: And if it's incorrect?

LENIN: *(Slight shrug)* Then it's incorrect.

TROTSKY: This is a problem of yours, Lenin. Everyone looks upon you as the great theoretician of the communist movement, yet you are incorrect on some very important points. And what's most frustrating, is that you don't seem to care. Moreover, you seem to care less and less. What's gotten into you? You have, on a number of occasions, written one thing and then done just the opposite! You have a responsibility to be more precise.

LENIN: I have only a responsibility to make the revolution.

DETROIT: *(To TROTSKY)* What the hell are you talking about?

TROTSKY: Well, for one thing, comrade, take the notion of permanent revolution. On paper, Lenin still rejects it, while in practice, he leads it. *(Pulling his pamphlet from his back pocket.)* As early as 1904, I wrote *(he reads his pamphlet aloud),* "it is possible for the workers to come to power in an economically backward country sooner than in an advanced country. To imagine that the dictatorship of the proletariat is in some way automatically dependent on the technical development and resources of a country is a prejudice of 'economic' materialism simplified to absurdity. This point of view has nothing in common with Marxism." *(Putting pamphlet back in his pocket.)* 1904, 1904, comrade! Up until February of 1917 you, Lenin, were still writing that Russia first had to have a bourgeois revolution and an epoch of development before it could have a socialist revolution. You have never publicly printed a retraction.

LENIN: I should think that my practice would suffice.

TROTSKY: Ah, but it does not! You have a responsibility toward posterity.

LENIN: Posterity will know far better than either of us the nature of our state.

TROTSKY: Perhaps, but the workers need correct theoretical leadership.

LENIN: You want to be correct? Be correct. You want to be right? You're right. Leon, Leon…I can't take you anymore.

TROTSKY: Thank you. But as the leader of the revolution it is imperative that you correct your theoretical errors once you realize them.

LENIN: As the leader of the revolution, I have absolutely no interest in "correcting my theoretical errors." Revolutions were never led by people with the correct line. "Correctness" is determined by the future. You can't be right and make a revolution. Stalin was not right when he exiled you from the Soviet Union. Nor was he right when his agent drove an ice pick into you. The Stalinists were never right. More importantly, your petty bourgeois preoccupation with being right was no match for them. Your rightness is your insanity!

TROTSKY: We made a revolution in Russia with my rightness.

LENIN: For all your correctness, Comrade Trotsky, it is you who came to me in 1917, not the other way around.

TROTSKY: I came to you because you had finally come around to the idea of permanent revolution.

LENIN: That surprises me. I thought it was because I was leading the revolution.

TROTSKY: It was. But you were able to lead the revolution precisely because you had come around to the idea of permanent revolution.

LENIN: I had not come around to the "idea" of permanent revolution, or any "idea" for that matter. I was working in history, and history had come around to revolution in Russia. Yes, Leon, I am a pragmatist, not a purist.

TROTSKY: What happened in October was a clear case of combined and uneven development. We skipped the bourgeois stage of the revolution.

LENIN: How do you distinguish between "skipping a stage" and something you just didn't know would happen? What if the bourgeois stage is still in the future? What if there is no Soviet Union in 80 years?

TROTSKY: But I did know, I've just quoted from my 1904 pamphlet, "Results and Prospects." What you say is preposterous!

LENIN: The bourgeoisie, since their rule is based on lies and illusions, always try to cover their stupidity. Communists don't have to rationalize. We shouldn't have to hide our stupidity. What's wrong with our stupidity?

TROTSKY: Are you calling me stupid, Comrade Lenin?

LENIN: I'm calling all of us stupid, comrade. What I'm calling you is administrative. You try to administer history. The "correct theories" you care so much about are nothing but the rules you set up for the administration of history. The "theoretical" battles you waged so doggedly with Stalin and the others were over which set of rules history will be made to follow. It was clear that you would lose out to Stalin's authoritarianism. History doesn't follow our rules; it's the other way round.

TROTSKY: Your characterization of history seems to me rather Hegelian…

EMMA: Oh, for crying out loud, would you two stop all the Bolshevik talk, already? It puts me to sleep.

TROTSKY: It's the language of science.

EMMA: Yeah, maybe, but I got news for you, comrade. Analysis doesn't make revolution. Passion does. People don't go to the barricades because they've understood the correct line. They go out of hate; deep, centuries old, smoldering hate of the bosses. And they go out of love; love of the working class, love of all humanity.

ELIZABETH: I hardly think Trotsky would deny the role of passion, Emma. I have heard him give speeches to the workers, and there is no more passionate orator in all of Russia. But in providing leadership, I would imagine, there is a certain need for analysis.

TROTSKY: Thank you, Comrade Elizabeth. But Red Emma and the others have a basic misconception about who I am just as they do with you. They think I'm a repressed petty bourgeois intellectual who's spent his whole life in the library, whose only passion is for abstraction and whose only love is dialectics. They think I have the personality of a pen, a mouthful of dust, and a crotch of polished marble.

EMMA: Very poetic, Trotsky. Very poetic.

TROTSKY: You talk about passion, Emma, you talk about sex, you talk about intimacy. But your sex is only the romantic kind between a man and a woman, your intimacy goes only so far. Do you know who Lenin and me are? Are you open to this? (*TROTSKY walks over to LENIN, kisses him passionately on the mouth.*) Does that passion count? This man and I have made a revolution. We have lain together in the cold hallways of the Winter Palace as the masses of the Russian people mounted the stage of history. I have comforted him in his moments of greatest fear. And our love is as filled with sexuality as any can be. I am Leon Trotsky: a gay Jew from Yanovka in the Ukraine, and I have truly loved in my lifetime only the revolutionary motion of working people and this man, V.I. Lenin. Can you understand that, Emma Goldman?

EMMA: I don't know that I can.

TROTSKY: You thought you were the most radical person in this room a few minutes ago, didn't you? *(EMMA nods.)* You see, I too have a deep passion. Will you hold me tightly, Vladimir Lenine?

(TROTSKY begins to cry, softly; LENIN comforts him.)

Scene 9

Bellevue.

LENIN: That was Trotsky. He lied to Emma, of course. He mainly loved himself.

PSYCHIATRIST: Did you have sex with him?

LENIN: Why do you ask such predictable questions? *(Pause.)* I don't remember. It was the night of the October revolution. I awoke that morning in hiding. Russia's most wanted criminal. By midnight I lay with Trotsky in the hallway of the Winter Palace, leader of the largest country in the world. It was too much for me. I grew dizzy. Trotsky, you know, suffered his whole life from something the doctors then called "chronic catarrh of the digestive tract." He was always dizzy…and nauseated. But I could never be allowed to be faint for even a moment. On that night we slept together. He comforted me. A memory? A fantasy? History? Homosexuality? I don't know.

PSYCHIATRIST: Trotsky wanted only to be right.

LENIN: I was no better. I wanted only to do right. We both murdered millions in the name of our obsession.

PSYCHIATRIST: Stalin did worse.

LENIN: That is of no comfort to me.

PSYCHIATRIST: You are Lenine, aren't you?

LENIN: I don't know. You are my psychiatrist. You must tell me who I am.

PSYCHIATRIST: No. So stupid I am not. I must go home to my family, my mid-life crisis and my postmodern despair.

LENIN: And where will I go?

PSYCHIATRIST: Sleep here until morning. Then you'll be discharged, Mr. Lenin. The day doctor will sign you out. There will be no second session. (*PSYCHIATRIST laughs slightly and extends his hand in a handshake.*) It was good to meet you, Mr. Lenin. Have a good death.

(*They shake hands. PSYCHIATRIST exits. The stage is dark. LENIN lies down. He begins to snore. A figure is seen in the dark. A street woman. A prostitute. EDIE.*)

EDIE: (*In a whisper*) Is that you, Lenin? Are you in here? Lenin, is that you over there?

LENIN: (*Sits up startled*) Who's that? Who's that?

EDIE: (*She comes closer to the bed*) Goddamn, it is you, Lenin. What in the hell are you doin' here? (*She admonishes him.*) This is Bellevue Psychiatric, goddammit. Why'd you come down here, Lenin? Are you crazy or somethin'?

LENIN: What are you doing here, Edie? How'd you find me?

EDIE: When you weren't there on the corner, ya know, up at 104th, ya know, I thought you was dead or something. So I started lookin' around. Bernie, my old pimp, said he heard you'd come down here. What the fuck you comin' here for? Are you some kind of nut case? Jesus, man.

LENIN: Why'd you come after me, Edie?

EDIE: I like workin' the street corner with you, Lenin. Yeah, man, I like those wild stories you tell about them revolutionary types. I like those stories. Yeah. I like you, Lenin. You're okay. So why'd you split like that and come down here to this shit house? I mean what's your fuckin' problem? You don't like the 104th Street crowd no more? We ain't good enough for ya? You don't like me no more? Whaddya come here to get psychoanalyzed, Lenin? Shit, man, I like those stories better than any shrink could. You been talkin' to a shrink, Lenin?

LENIN: Yeah, Edie. I have been. I'm sorry.

EDIE: Hey, man. That's okay. You can talk to whoever ya want. You don't belong to me. But I like ya. Ya tell great stories man, great stories. They keep me warm at night. Did ya talk about Emma Goldman, Lenin? Did ya tell the shrink about Red Emma. I dig Red Emma. She's my favorite.

LENIN: Yeah, Edie. I talked a little bit about Red Emma.

EDIE: I'm sorry I missed that. Did the shrink say anything interesting about Emma?

LENIN: No, Edie. He didn't have much to say about Emma.

EDIE: Was ya feelin' bad, Lenin? Is that why ya came here?

LENIN: Yeah, Edie, I was feelin' sick. Kinda tired. Wanting to die.

EDIE: Now why'd ya wanna go ahead and get into that old bullshit? I told ya I like you. I told ya I like your stories. Ain't that enough for ya? Whaddya want, a fuckin Valentine's card? Lenin, man, you're an old fuckin' guy, but I like ya. Like I said, those long nights on the street, ya need stories, man. And you got the best. Emma and Trotsky and Elizabeth and Detroit. Those are great stories, y'old son of a bitch. Vladimir Ilyich. Yeah. That's a helluva name. Vladimir Ilyich Lenine.

LENIN: I'm tired, Edie. I'm very tired.

EDIE: You wanna touch my tits? C'mon, touch my tits, Lenin.

LENIN: I don't know, Edie, I'm…

EDIE: C'mon, Lenin. I don't give away free tit action to everybody. Gimme your hand. (*Grabs* LENIN's *hand and puts it on her breast.*)

LENIN: That feels nice, Edie. It feels very nice.

EDIE: Now tell me somethin' about Red Emma. Ya know, somethin' juicy.

LENIN: You're better than Red Emma, Edie. Way, way better.

EDIE: Stop that bullshit, Lenin! Don't fuck with me. How could I be better than Red Emma? She's in one of your revolutionary stories. Goddammit, Lenin, sometimes you can be an awful sap. But at least y'ain't boring. *(Pause.)* Ya wanna touch my pussy? *(EDIE puts his hand on her crotch.)* We should get goin' before it gets light, Lenin. *(They stand and EDIE leads LENIN quietly toward the door.)* I can't believe it, a man of your age, comin' to get his head shrunk. Shit. Didn't the doctor tell ya you was too old to be *(in a funny voice)* psy-cho-ana-lyzed?

))))

Outing Wittgenstein

Outing Wittgenstein began in the spring of 1992 with a request to Fred Newman from Mary Fridley, a longtime lesbian activist and builder of the Castillo Theatre, that he write a play on a gay theme for Castillo's next season.

A year later Castillo produced two such plays by Newman. Both explored the issue of identity (sexual and otherwise) and both had the Vienna-born philosopher Ludwig Wittgenstein as a central character. *Yes! We Have No Bananas and Other Contradictions in the Life of Ludwig Wittgenstein* was produced in May 1993 under Newman's direction. *Outing Wittgenstein (or Sunday in the Park with Ludwig)* went up a month later, directed by Fridley and this writer.

They were both full-length comedies, with roots in the skits Newman had written for Castillo's "comedy nights" in the mid-'80s. More immediately, they built on his musical comedy revue *Off-Broadway Melodies of 1592* which had been produced at Castillo the previous season. *Bananas* was a full-throttle farce—a nearly plotless series of encounters between Wittgenstein and some of his relatives, friends and acquaintances within the framework of a television show called "This is Your Death," which brings dead people back to life to appear as guests of the Dolly Parton-esque hostess, Sally McNally. The second play, *Outing Wittgenstein,* starts out as a contemporary realistic comedy set in New York City's Central Park the day after Wittgenstein appears on "This is Your Death." The TV show acts as the stimulus for a series of comic "outings," with the play ending as farcically and absurdly as *Bananas*. Newman originally had in mind a Wittgenstein trilogy. Instead, for the 1994 season he combined the two plays (with *Bananas* becoming the first act and *Outing* the second) into a single script. It is that two-act version of *Outing Wittgenstein,* produced at Castillo again in 1995 with Fridley directing, which is included here.

Outing was the first play Newman wrote with the explicit aim of exploring a "gay theme." However, gay characters have always been part of

Newman's stage world. Freda, in *Mr. Hirsch,* is a lesbian whose very existence challenges the identity of her straight male counterpart, Fred. *The
Collected Emotions of V.I. Lenin* "revealed" the sexual nature of the relationship between Lenin and his fellow revolutionary Leon Trotsky. In a
similar vein, the later play *Risky Revolutionary* would explore the love
between Fidel Castro and Che Guevara. Emmy Strait in *Billie & Malcolm:
A Demonstration* sings about being Black and gay, and all the characters in
What is to be Dead? (Philosophical Scenes) are, at least in some of their
manifestations, gay.

The presence of gay characters in Newman's plays is not a matter of liberal pluralism. His work in the theatre—as in politics and therapy—has long
been informed by the conviction that gayness, whatever else it may be in
terms of nature and/or nurture, is also a social/political activity. Gay relationships challenge—in practice—the assumptions of institutionalized (hetero-
sexual/patriarchal) roles and relations. In short, gayness is progressive to the
extent that it shows that life can be lived differently.

What is not progressive or developmental about gay identity,
Newman argues, is *identity*. Along with its broader social expression, identity politics, identity is conservatizing, according to Newman, in that it ties
us down to being who we *are* (individually and/or as members of a particular group). It thereby prevents us from being who we are not (that is,
what we can *become*).

As a social therapist, Newman repeatedly challenges what he considers
the inhibiting effects of prescribed identities on individual development. As
a political leader, he has opposed organizing primarily around the identities
of various oppressed groupings, seeking instead to create environments for
the practice of "relational politics," which includes all sorts of people (and
peoples) in mass democratic activities that shape/create/re-create their
world. Newman approaches the theatre itself as just such a relational mass
activity.

Newman's concern with identity runs throughout his plays. It is, at least
in part, what informs his fluid approach to character. In a Newman play it is
very often not clear just who a character is. From Fred and Freda in *Mr.
Hirsch Died Yesterday* to Sprintze/Mrs. Golub and Pearlie/Hinda in *What is
to be Dead?,* Newman's characters are best understood/approached not as
psychologically defined, primarily static entities, but as historically shaped

and primarily emergent. They are not characters who can, with the certain knowledge of Popeye, say, "I yam who I yam"; they are, at one and the same time, who they are *and* who they are becoming.

In addition to the questioning of identity inherent in Newman's approach to character, a number of Newman's other plays—*Mr. Hirsch, Lenin's Breakdown* and *What is to be Dead?*—explicitly tackle the philosophical/political/psychological issues inherent in identity. In *Outing Wittgenstein* it is sexual identity, in particular, that is challenged.

Wittgenstein, a major influence on Newman's development as a philosopher, easily lends himself to this enterprise. Wittgenstein's deconstruction of the representationalist view of language and, in particular, his notion of "family resemblances" inform much of Newman's subsequent thinking on identity. At the same time, Wittgenstein, who was ruthlessly honest in his intellectual work, lived his life as a closeted homosexual. The idea of bringing Wittgenstein "back to life" to deal with this contradiction by utilizing some of his extraordinary philosophical insights "to move about and around" his personal life, tickled Newman's funny bone, and has given the thousands who have seen *Outing Wittgenstein* a good laugh as well. It is worth noting that no prior knowledge of Wittgenstein is needed to appreciate the play, yet no one is likely to leave a performance—or a reading—without having at least glimpsed something of Wittgenstein's biography and philosophical thought.

To deal with Wittgenstein's contradictions, Newman divides him into two characters, Wittgenstein and Wittgenstein's Gay Alter Ego. This two-in-one approach to character is reminiscent of Shen Te and Shui Ta in Brecht's *Good Woman of Setzuan*. As in the *Good Woman,* the divided character in *Outing* is, at least in part, a response to a societal environment which makes honesty impossible.

Another important element of *Outing Wittgenstein* is its satirical treatment of mass culture in general and of television in particular. When combining the two one-acts, Newman added the scenes in which the producers of "This is Your Death" plan the show and react to its popularity. These scenes serve not only to tie the two "stories" together, but add another level of satire and caricature. The play in its current form is, among many other things, a satire of our society's propensity to commercialize anything and everything—including gayness and philosophy.

As in all classic comedy, the conflicts in *Outing Wittgenstein* are resolved happily (if absurdly) in the end. Such resolution is atypical of Newman's scripts. What is characteristic is the structure of the play. The combination of *Yes! We Have No Bananas* and *Outing* into one play juxtaposes two very different approaches to Wittgenstein and the issue of identity, providing the double (or triple) vision with which Newman sees.

D.F.

Outing Wittgenstein was first produced at the Castillo Theatre (Fred Newman, artistic director; Gabrielle Kurlander, producing director; Diane Stiles, managing director) in New York City on June 3, 1994. The cast, in order of appearance, was as follows:

HERMAN . . . . Roger Grunwald
DAISY FIELDS . . . . Diane Stiles
STAN . . . . Jeff Aron
OLLIE . . . . Omar Ali
SALLY McNALLY . . . . Cathy Rose Salit
LUDWIG WITTGENSTEIN/WITTGENSTEIN OF EARTH . . . . David Nackman
MRS. BEVAN . . . . Howard Edelbaum
GAY ALTER EGO/WITTGENSTEIN OF WITTGENSTEIN . . . . Kenneth Hughes
MARGARETE (GRETL) VON STONBOROUGH . . . . Cathy Rose Salit
ADOLF HITLER . . . . Maggie Zarillo-Gouldin
BERTRAND RUSSELL . . . . Dan Friedman
CARMEN MIRANDA . . . . L. Thecla Farrell
MR. MIRANDA . . . . Doug Miranda
GAILIE GAILIE . . . . Gail Elberg
ALAN SILVER . . . . Richard Mann
EDDIE THOMAS . . . . Emmitt H. Thrower
CAROL SILVER . . . . Madelyn Chapman
DIANE WRIGHT . . . . L. Thecla Farrell

Fred Newman, director; Diane Stiles, producer; Joseph Spirito, set design; Charlotte, costume design; Jessica Massad and Beth Peeler, lighting design; Michael Klein, sound design; Barry Z Levine, video design/cinematography; Ellen Korner, production stage manager.

Outing Wittgenstein concludes with the money-hungry madmen (and woman) who produce and write the prize-winning TV show "This is Your Death" screaming "Commercialism Über Alles, Commercialism Über Alles." The weekly show has achieved astronomical success following the recent appearance of the philosopher Ludwig Wittgenstein. (Each week another dead person is brought back from "the beyond.") Actually, both Ludwig Wittgenstein *and his gay alter ego* are what sent the ratings off the charts on Sally McNally's (she is the hostess) TV extravaganza.

The "outing" of Wittgenstein, the long-dead Viennese genius, is what "turns on" America's TV audience. For in our "sick" society, "gayness" is as commercial as hell even as gay people, real people, die of AIDS by the hundreds of thousands and far too little is done about it; even as real gay people are battered and bashed; even as real gay people are vulgarly discriminated against. "Gayness" sells while gay people are related to as immoral and worse.

The vulgarity of how "gayness" is "identified" and exploited on Earth is in sharp contrast to what happens on the planet Wittgenstein. There, everyone is gay. And anyone (from somewhere else) who isn't is welcome. As the mad producers drool over their "ultimate commercial success," their cast of characters is heading home to Wittgenstein. Ludwig, it turns out, is not merely "out"—he is "out of this world."

JUNE 1994

CHARACTERS
(in order of appearance)

HERMAN, a TV announcer
DAISY FIELDS, a TV writer
STAN, a TV producer
OLLIE, a TV producer
SALLY MCNALLY, a TV show hostess
LUDWIG WITTGENSTEIN, a philosopher, aka WITTGENSTEIN OF EARTH
MRS. BEVAN, Dr. Bevan's wife
GAY ALTER EGO, aka WITTGENSTEIN OF WITTGENSTEIN
MARGARETE (GRETL) VON STONBOROUGH, Ludwig Wittgenstein's sister
ADOLF HITLER, an old acquaintance of Wittgenstein
BERTRAND RUSSELL, an old friend of Wittgenstein
CARMEN MIRANDA, an entertainer
MR. MIRANDA, Carmen Miranda's father
GAILIE GAILIE, a beatnik
ALAN SILVER, an English teacher
EDDIE THOMAS, a TV repairman
CAROL SILVER, Alan's wife, an unsuccessful novelist
DIANE WRIGHT, a hypochondriacal believer in spirituality

NOTE:
This play contains both live scenes and video sequences.

Act I, Scene 1

Two producers, OLLIE and STAN, the writer, DAISY, and the announcer, HERMAN, in a "smoke filled room."

HERMAN: Who the fuck is Ludwig Wittgenstein? *(He pronounces "w"s as exaggerated "w," not "v.")*

DAISY: That's Lud*v*ig Vittgenstein, Herman. The "W"'s pronounced like a "V"…like in Vagner. It's German, schmuck. Where did you go to announcing school, y'asshole?

HERMAN: Listen, Daisy, I don't need your shit today. My stomach's killin' me. Alright. Who the fuck is Ludvig Vittgenstein? Is dat better, you pumpkin head writer? When was the last time you thought of a good line?

STAN: Would you two cut it out already? Wittgenstein is a philosopher; a Viennese philosopher…

HERMAN: Isn't that Wiennese?

OLLIE: Shut up, Herman. Go on, Stan.

STAN: Thank you, Ollie. He died in the early '50s and he's got kind of a cult following. He was an odd duck, kind of a recluse.

DAISY: He was a Class A genius.

OLLIE: And everyone says he was gay.

DAISY: His family was loaded with dough.

OLLIE: There's been some art movies about him and a bunch of books. But can we get him for the show? I mean can we bring him back from the dead?

HERMAN: We never had no philosopher before. Why do we want a philosopher with a funny name? You know I have trouble with funny names.

DAISY: It'll add some class, asshole. You have trouble with words altogether. You're the worst damn announcer on TV.

HERMAN: Stop callin' me asshole. You're the dumbest writer since Dwight Eisenhower.

DAISY: You mealy mouthed schmuck.

STAN: Cut it out, goddamn it, cut it out. We desperately need a show for June 12th. George Armstrong Custer can't come back until the week after.

OLLIE: Amelia Earhart…we can't find her. Alexander Graham Bell doesn't look good on TV.

DAISY: How's Sally gonna work with Wittgenstein?

HERMAN: That bimbo can't work with anybody. So what's the difference?

DAISY: Sally's no bimbo, you sexist pig.

HERMAN: Are you kiddin'? Suddenly you're a feminist. Sally's Miss Bimbo of the century.

OLLIE: I think Wittgenstein's gotta be our guy for June 12th.

STAN: Can "tech" get him back to life on time?

DAISY: Listen, if we can keep Herman alive, we can bring back Wittgenstein …(to HERMAN) that's Vittgenstein, with a "V," creep.

HERMAN: Daisy…(sarcastically and in announcer voice) I've always loved you madly.

STAN: Then it's "Ludwig Wittgenstein—This is Your Death" for June 12th.

OLLIE: Look, we'll put him up in some cheap hotel and if he wants…

Act I, Scene 2

A TV studio, CSTO, with TV cameras, tech equipment and video monitors right and left of the stage. The stage is the set of the "prize-winning" show "This is Your Death"—obviously a take-off on "This is Your Life." There are two chairs stage center and a bench or couch upstage.

HERMAN: *(Bounces with obviously phony energy onto stage)* Hi there. Good to have you here tonight. Welcome to the prize-winning TV show, "This is Your Death." For those of you who have never seen the show—shame on you—anyway, here's what happens. Famous people, notorious people, dead people are brought back to life and into our studio audience. But this famous person doesn't know that they are going to be the star of "This is Your Death." That's right. There's someone dead and very famous sitting out there with y'all right now who will soon be picked out as tonight's star. Our mystery guest. How do we bring them back from the dead? Here to tell you—Ms. Death Warmed Over herself—Daisy Fields.

DAISY: Thanks, Schm…er, Herman. We bring 'em back by a process called "Past Transfo." It's really just a speed o' light space/time ship that catches up with our dead subjects' light waves and kryonizes them. Ya know, freezes them and brings 'em back here to the studio for a melt down right on time.

HERMAN: Thanks, Daisy, you dumb bit…sorry about that. Meanwhile, we've spent months talking to significant people in the life of our mystery guest, some of whom we'll bring out on this stage to meet her or him—in many cases they haven't seen each other in decades. I'm not gonna tell you who tonight's guest star is. We'll leave that for the award-winning hostess of our prize-winning show, Sally "I said I ain't no Bimbo" McNally. Hey, let me hear you folks applaud. *(Gets them to applaud.)* Not bad. Not bad. I'm gonna need your applause during the show—so keep one good eye on me—I'll be holding up cue cards for clappin' or booin' or keepin' cool during a commercial break…just follow me and the cards. Okay. Have fun, everybody…welcome once again…we'll be on the air in exactly 15 seconds.

(Pause, theme music begins.)

OFFSTAGE VOICE: Hello America! Live from New York—it's the prize-winning TV show, "This is Your Death." The show that asks the question "Are you worth remembering at all?" Now…ladies and gentlemen… *(music builds up)* the award-winning star of our show…the woman who brings "This is Your Death" to life. Msssss. Sally McNally!!!

(HERMAN holds up applause sign; loud applause as SALLY bounces onto stage and video monitors.)

SALLY: Hello, hello, hello! Welcome to "This is Your Death." I know y'all can't wait to discover who this week's mystery guest is…but you'll have to…No, no, no. I'm just kidding. You know old Sally. Tonight, on "This is Your Death," we are just jumpin' for joy to have with us a man who's given genius a new meaning. For the first time ever "This is Your Death" has us a philosopher—but not just any old philosopher—one of the greatest wisdom worshippers of this here century. We got ourselves a god-damned thinker tonight. Born in Vi-en-a Austria in 1889 this dude came from a big old wealthy family that started out Jewish but by the time he came along they wuz Cath-o-lics. Big family. He was the youngest of eight kids. Lotsa musical talent in the family. But as a kid our guy was more interested in buildin' things. Liked workin' with his hands. Got into learnin' about aer-o-nau-ti-cal engineerin'. Then he got a hankerin' for what they call pure mathematics. Y'all know what pure mathematics is? Well, Sally sure as hell don't. But our mystery man did and no sooner was this son of a gun of a genius learnin'…pure mathematics and somethin' called foundations of mathematics…when he wrote a gol'darn book tellin' everybody what it was. Well, he wrote this little ole book with a funny Latin title—I won't even try to pronounce it—and then he gives up his workin' in the field *(laughs)*, says his book answered all the interestin' questions. He's no sooner started and he's all done with it. Son of a bitch—kinda like how my old man relates to sex!!! Slam, bam, thank ya Ma'am. Sorry about that *(makes funny face)*. Anyhow, our guy packs a rucksack and takes off for the hills …he's kinda a recluse…ya know what I mean. Fella's sort of weird. Likes livin' alone in a shack in northern Finland or somethin'. Strange guy. But after awhile the philosophy crowd wants our man to come on back and make up some more stuff. And eventually he does. Our mystery guest gives away his whole gosh darn inheritance—provin' that geniuses ain't so bright—and goes to Cambridge, England where they give him a Ph.D. in about an hour and a half and then they put him to work teachin'. Well our man hates snooty old English academic life but he's a doin' it anyway. And guess what? Our guy discovers in a few years that everything he thought was right-on in that ole Latin book he wrote

...was wrong—I mean all wrong. So he starts fillin' up notebooks with what's right—what he now thinks is right. I mean everyone else—an outfit called the Vi-en-a Circle—is still gettin' off on the first shit— whoops, pardon me—but our genius is makin' up new stuff. Well he pretty much hangs there in jolly old England, bein' a genius, doin' a little teachin', actin' kinda weird, writin' in his notebook, till he gets himself cancer and crumps out in 1951. Then his philosophy buddies really get into publishin' his notebooks and sayin' that he's the greatest philosopher of the century. Maybe so. I ain't got no other candidate myself. Nowadays he's kind of a cult-figure. Anyway, we are proud as hell to have him here tonight and we're gonna give him a big old American welcome...*(music build up)* LUDWIG WITTGENSTEIN... THIS IS YOUR DEATH!

(Spot on LUDWIG *in audience; he is aghast...but silent; theme music; applause; general pandemonium.)*

SALLY: Come on up here, Mr. Ludwig Wittgenstein, THIS IS YOUR DEATH. We're gonna find out if you're really worth rememberin'. LUDWIG WITTGENSTEIN...THIS IS YOUR DEATH. C'mon everybody *(to audience)* let's bring Ludwig on up.

(Ushers bring him onstage. He remains nonplused. SALLY *embraces him and reveals a big book,* The Book of Wittgenstein's Death, *with his picture on it. As he comes up video monitors show a series of stills of* LUDWIG's *life.)*

HERMAN: *(Speaking onstage with hand microphone to accompany video)* When Wittgenstein first learned from Dr. Bevan, his physician, that he had cancer, he expressed an extreme aversion and even fear of spending his last days in a hospital. Dr. Bevan then told him that he could come to his house to die. Wittgenstein was deeply grateful for this remarkable offer. He remained at Dr. Bevan's until his death. When Wittgenstein came to live with the Bevans, Mrs. Bevan was at first frightened of him, but soon became devoted. They took many walks together. As she told me, his influence over her came to be great, even in little things. For example, she had bought a new coat to wear to a party, and before leaving the house, went to show it to Wittgenstein. He scrutinized it carefully, said "Wait!" in a peremptory tone, took a pair of scissors and, without asking permission, cut several large buttons off the front. And she liked the coat better that way! On Friday, April 27th, he took a walk in the afternoon. That night he fell violently ill. He remained conscious and when informed by the doctor that he could live only a few days, he exclaimed "Good!" Before losing consciousness he said to Mrs. Bevan (who was with him throughout the night), "Tell them I've had a wonderful life!" By "them" he undoubtedly meant his close friends. When I think of his profound pessimism, the intensity of his mental and moral suffering, the relentless way in which he drove his intellect, his need for love together with the harshness that repelled love, I am inclined to believe that his life was fiercely unhappy. Yet at the end he himself exclaimed that it had been "wonderful!" To me this seems a mysterious and strangely moving utterance.

(*MRS. BEVAN's theme music comes up.*)

MRS. BEVAN: (*From offstage, heard through sound system, as are all guests before their entrances*) Hello there, Professor Wittgenstein. Hello, dear. I still have that old coat with the buttons cut off. I'll keep it forever. You were such a dear. I do hope you don't mind my having made up that silly business about what a wonderful life you had. You may recall that your actual last words were more like, "Mrs. Bevan…get me a goddamn bowl of soup." You were a bit cross. But when Mr. Malcolm, your biographer, rang me up about your death for his book I thought it would be grand if you had said something…oh, you know…profound and mysterious… yes, that's it…profound and mysterious. Professor Wittgenstein, I do hope you don't mind. It was just a little lie.

SALLY: Ludwig Wittgenstein, do you recognize that voice?

LUDWIG: It's Mrs. Bevan. Dear Mrs. Bevan.

SALLY: Is he a genius, or is he a genius? I ask you, ladies and gentlemen.

(*Enter MRS. BEVAN, accompanied by her theme song. Audience applauds; LUDWIG and MRS. BEVAN gently embrace.*)

MRS. BEVAN: How are you today Professor Wittgenstein?

LUDWIG: I'm feeling…Okay.

MRS. BEVAN: Do you mind that little fib I made up, Professor Wittgenstein? It's become rather…a famous story. Are you upset with me, sir?

LUDWIG: Perhaps it wasn't quite right to do, dear Mrs. Bevan. But…well, I surely forgive you. Anyway, I did have a wonderful life.

MRS. BEVAN: Really? Oh, my God. Well, then it wasn't a lie.

LUDWIG: Oh no, Mrs. Bevan. It was still a lie because I didn't say that… until just now. But your lie included a proposition, namely that I had a wonderful life, which was true.

MRS. BEVAN: Is that worse than lying or better than lying, Professor Wittgenstein?

LUDWIG: Now, Mrs. Bevan, that's very difficult to say. Perhaps those British chaps at Oxford—some of those fool ordinary language types who claim to follow me—could answer that. But now you mustn't worry about it.

MRS. BEVAN: Well, I meant no harm. It's just that it seemed to me it would be too bad if such a great man as yourself had as his last words, "Get me a goddamn bowl of soup."

LUDWIG: Sorry I was so grouchy, Mrs. Bevan. But those actual last words would have been just fine to leave to posterity…yes, just fine.

SALLY: Was that there business about lyin' you just did…was that philosophy talk, Ludwig?

LUDWIG: I suppose so, Ms. McNally.

SALLY: Oh, call me Sally.

LUDWIG: Fine then, Sally. However did you get me here?

SALLY: Clever, huh? Ms. Daisy Fields takes care of that. It's called "Past Transfo."

LUDWIG: "Past Transfo"?

SALLY: And thank you, Mrs. Bevan, for being with us on "This is Your Death." Have a seat right back here. (*Leads her to the bench.* SALLY *reads now from* The Book of Wittgenstein's Death.) Ludwig Wittgenstein, your personal life, like your philosophical life, was tormented and tortured. You were sexually repressed, conflicted. Some have even written that you were homosexually promiscuous. That for years you hung out in Prater Park in Vienna, where Bartley, another of your biographers, says "rough young men were ready to cater to you sexually." Now, Ludwig, is there any truth to this?

ALTER EGO: *(From offstage, in a loud, somewhat effeminate, British-accented whisper)* Ludwig...oh, Ludwig...have you told them yet that we're homosexual? C'mon, LW, say it out loud...just once. I mean, for someone who's so caught up with language, why can't we just one time say "I'm gay." C'mon, Wiggy...say it: "I'm gay..."

SALLY: Ludwig Wittgenstein, do you recognize that voice?

ALTER EGO: *(Still offstage)* Ludwig, don't be pigheaded, you silly fool. There's no getting around it. We are gay!

LUDWIG: That's me. That's me speaking.

SALLY: Right again! Your alter ego...your homosexual self.

(ALTER EGO's theme song comes up.)

ALTER EGO: *(Entering)* Ludwig, now let's do try to have a civil conversation this evening. Let's kiss and get our act together, darling boy.

LUDWIG: You're up to your same old tricks. Can't you ever lay low? Can't you stop tormenting me?

ALTER EGO: Oh, Wiggy...you terrible hypocrite. Tortured honesty in our philosophical writings and lying through our teeth about sexuality. Believe me, Ludwig, there are things about our life much less pretty than our gayness. Now you know that.

LUDWIG: Please let me do this, this...ah...TV show...without any of the ugly business.

ALTER EGO: But, Wiggy, sweet thing, we are not ugly. Sexuality is not ugly. That stuff that Bartley wrote about us in Vienna. Well...it's absurd. Sexually promiscuous. Not a word of truth. But even we wrote in our coded private notebooks—oh, that was so cute—about our love for

David and Francis and Ben. Stop hiding us, Ludwig. Everyone knows we're gay.

LUDWIG: But love is not sex! Sex is dirty. SEX IS DIRTY!

ALTER EGO: Oh, LW, stop that Otto Weininger shit, already. What year is this ...1994. My God, we're 105 years old. It's time we gave up that adolescent nonsense. Wiggy...for cryin' out loud, Weininger was a Nazi even before there were Nazis. Really, old man.

SALLY: Who was this fella, Weininger...what's his first name?

LUDWIG: Otto...Otto Weininger. He was also a Viennese philosopher.

SALLY: Well, guys...who was he?

ALTER EGO: He was a silly self-hating Jewish homosexual who wrote this awful, awful book called *Sex and Character* back in...let's see...1902. My God, how time flies. Then, in 1903, he went to Ludwig von Beethoven's old house and commits suicide...shoots himself to death. Well... Strindberg, after Weininger blows his head off, calls the book "awe-inspiring" and the next thing you know there's a silly old Weininger cult. This man hates women...hates Jews...hates everything modern. I mean he's a classical elitist Viennese aristocrat. What's wrong with you? Why are you still so turned on by that nutcase, Wiggy?

LUDWIG: But we are Viennese aristocrats!

ALTER EGO: I mean, that's where we came from. But we don't have to be that forever...do we? Wiggy, goddammit...there's nothing wrong with sex!

SALLY: Look guys...it's apparent that you've been at this for...ah...quite awhile...like a century. But we have to move on now. Mr. Wittgenstein *(pointing to ALTER EGO)*, would you like to go sit over there with Mrs. Bevan and...

ALTER EGO: *(Offended)* Why should I go up there? *(Pointing to LUDWIG.)* I'm as much Ludwig Wittgenstein as he is. What's this? Is "This is Your Death" anti-gay? Now really.

LUDWIG: Please, Ludwig, please. Do what she says.

ALTER EGO: Well...I won't go!

SALLY: Okay. Okay. Both of you stay here. Stagehand, honey...get me another chair.

ALTER EGO: *(Embraces LUDWIG)* Oh, we can sit together on this one!

LUDWIG: Stop it. Stop it. *(Chair arrives.)*

ALTER EGO: Okay. We'll sit here right next to each other.

SALLY: *(Opens the book and reads)* Ludwig Wittgenstein, you were born to a very, very wealthy Catholic Viennese family on April 26, 1889, the youngest of eight children. Your father, Karl, was a leader in the iron and steel industry and a devoted patron of the arts. Musical evenings attended by Brahms, Mahler and Bruno Walter were not uncommon at your palatial home. Your family lived at the very center of Viennese cultural life. Sounds pretty classy, Wiggy. But suicide was at least as fundamental to the Wittgenstein family as culture. Your three oldest brothers, Hans, Kurt and Rudolf all committed suicide. That's some tough family shit, Ludwig, er, ah...Ludwigs.

LUDWIG: Father was stern.

ALTER EGO: So was mother.

(SALLY exits quietly as Ravel music with Paul Wittgenstein playing piano begins.)

LUDWIG: That's Paul playing Ravel's concerto for left hand. *(Then, to SALLY, not realizing she has left the stage.)* My brother, Paul, was a marvelous pianist who lost his arm in World War I. Ravel wrote that piece especially for him...where is Sally?

GRETL: *(Offstage, played by the same actress who plays SALLY)* Ludwig...Paul could not make it tonight, my darling. But I, as always, am here for you.

ALTER EGO: It's Gretl. It's our dear sister, Gretl.

(Klimt portrait of MARGARETE (GRETL) VON STONBOROUGH comes up on video monitor.)

ALTER EGO: There's lovely Gretl's wedding painting by Gustav Klimt. Ludwig, look...it's Gretl. Now Gretl never thought that sex was bad. She was kind of a Freudian, you know. She actually helped old Sigmund get the hell out of Vienna in '38. He barely made it. Freud was a terrible, terrible gay basher. But at least he gave sex a liberal twist. *(To the absent* SALLY.*)* By our bizarre reactionary family standards Gretl was a bonko radical. *(To* LUDWIG.*)* Where is Sally?

GRETL: *(Offstage)* Ludwig, Ludwig. How good to hear you again.

*(*GRETL *appears, looking exactly like painting…and just a little like* SALLY*!)*

ALTER EGO and LUDWIG: *(Jumping up from seats)* Gretl!!! *(All three embrace.)*

GRETL: You look so wonderful. Are you well? Tell me, have you ever gone into psychotherapy? You were such a happy little child. *(Laughs.)* Actually you never even bothered to speak until you were four. But then you became so unhappy…so contorted, so troubled. All those suicides and then the war. As Austria unraveled, Ludwig, so did you, dear child…so did you. We were indeed a family of genius—a civilization of genius…but reaction…indeed fascism…was no small part of that genius.

ALTER EGO: Gretl, Gretl…you were always my favorite…always.

GRETL: *(Laughs)* Maybe I had the most liberal politics. But I was the worst musician. I had the least genius. Ludwig, do you still whistle so well?

LUDWIG: Yes, dearest Gretl…sometimes. *(Pause.)* Where is Sally…our hostess? Where is she? Gretl, did you see her? Did you see her when you were offstage?

MRS. BEVAN: *(Waves her hand)* Hello, Gretl. I'm Mrs. Bevan. I was with your brother Ludwig when he died.

GRETL: *(Waves hello; turns to* LUDWIG*)* No. I saw no one.

ALTER EGO: Do you know, Gretl, you look a good deal like Sally McNally?

LUDWIG: You do, dearest Gretl. You really do.

GRETL: Sally McNally. I look like Sally McNally? *(Longish pause; changes back to* SALLY *character.)* Well, Sally's my alter ego, guys.

*(*ALTER EGO *and* LUDWIG *do double-takes; blackout onstage; spotlight on* HERMAN.*)*

HERMAN: *(Very English voice)* And now a word from our sponsor. *(HERMAN continues in German voice)* Franz Kafka, the man who made torment into a household word brings you a new all-natural insecticide, KafkaEsque. Just spray KafkaEsque on roaches and in twenty seconds they turn into human beings. Then you simply ask them all to leave. It's the civilized way. KafkaEsque. Put an end to the torment of household pests. Call 1-800-KAFKAAA. Don't forget…there's not a single cockroach left in all of Eastern Europe. That's 1-800-KAFKAAA…today!

(Theme music comes back up; applause card, etc.)

SALLY: Welcome back to "This is Your Death, Ludwig Wittgenstein."

LUDWIG: Sally…*(looking back at couch)* where's Gretl?

SALLY: I dunno, Ludwig *(slapping both LUDWIG and ALTER EGO on knee)*, alter egos come and go in this business—ha, ha, ha. *(She reads from the book.)* Ludwig Wittgenstein, you sure as hell hung out with a lot of famous people in your day. But for one year when you was a teenager attending somethin' called the Realschule *(butchers word)*—how was that, guys?—in a place called Linz—is that in New Jersey?—you was a school mate with a dude who quite a few people in this world got to know and hate…the man with the unruly hair and the little mustache …*(HITLER's theme music comes up loudly.)*

HITLER: *(Offstage)* Ludwig! Ludwig Wittgenstein! Mein alte Freund, my old friend…Ludwig Wittgenstein! *(He enters in HITLER garb, giving Nazi salute.)*

(HERMAN prompts audience to "BOO" loudly.)

ALTER EGO: *(To SALLY)* You brought Adolf Hitler here? That's kinda weird, Sally.

SALLY: Well, he said he was an old friend! Look, I ain't the goddamned producer.

LUDWIG: We were at the Realschule together but I think I saw him one time.

HITLER: Ludwig. Ludwig. What do you mean? What do you mean? We were the best of friends, Ludwig. We studied Otto Weininger together. Weininger was the only good Jew I ever heard of. As soon as he realized that Jewishness was irretrievably ugly he killed himself. Good man, Otto Weininger. Don't you remember, Ludwig?

LUDWIG: We never spoke, Hitler. We never spoke.

HITLER: Stop it, Ludwig. Remember one time you and me and Stefan Sweatbelter did a choral reading of Weininger's *Sex and Character*? Oh, I can hear Weininger like it was yesterday *(quotes from Weininger)* "...this modern era is a time of communistic ethics, of the most foolish of historical views, the materialistic interpretation of history; a time of capitalism and of Marxism; a time when history, life and science are no more than political economy and technical instruction; a time when genius is supposed to be a form of madness; a time with no great artists and no great philosophers; a time without originality and yet with the most foolish craving for originality."

ALTER EGO: Adolf Hitler, you're a mean old son of a bitch. This is just one more big lie, you anti-Semitic homophobic bastard.

HITLER: Oh, Ludwig. I know you've always been uptight about those Jewish grandparents of yours. Oh, yes, I know your family paid off my SS people so they wouldn't be classified as Jews under the Nuremburg Laws. I knew it then. I let it go, Ludwig. We were old friends. I was always a reasonable man.

LUDWIG: You are a liar and a mass murderer. I am conflicted about being a Jew; I am conflicted about being a homosexual; I am conflicted about sexuality altogether. I admit I was deeply moved by Otto Weininger. Perhaps I still am. But I am not a mass murderer. And I did not know you at Linz and *(to SALLY)* I don't want him on my show.

MRS. BEVAN: Won't anyone else ever come sit here? It's very lonely.

LUDWIG: *(Sternly)* Please be quiet, Mrs. Bevan.

MRS. BEVAN: *(Raises voice)* You're yelling at me again, Mr. Wittgenstein.

ALTER EGO: Please, Mrs. Bevan. Please.

SALLY: Well, Mr. Hitler, I'm afraid I'll have to ask you to leave. Ludwig is the boss.

HITLER: Don't worry, it happens almost everywhere I go. By the way, that's nice strawberry blond hair you got there. You are an Aryan, yes?

SALLY: You'll have to go, Führer, you'll have to go. *(Begins to run him off the stage.)*

HITLER: *(Stupidly; to audience)* Okay, kids. It's back to Paraguay.

(HERMAN gets audience to boo him off; HITLER exits; music back up.)

SALLY: *(Reading from the book)* In 1911 you became more interested in philosophy through the work of Gottlob Frege. He suggested that you contact the distinguished mathematician-philosopher, Bertrand Russell, and so you went off to Cambridge where you and Lord Russell met. *(BERTRAND RUSSELL's theme music comes up.)*

RUSSELL: *(Offstage)* Ludwig Wittgenstein, you were quite a bright fellow! The closest thing I've ever seen to a genius. And I told you so. I've read that it was my telling you that you were a genius that kept you from committing suicide. Well, I'm glad I did, old man; glad I did.

(Music. RUSSELL enters.)

LUDWIG: Bertrand Russell.

RUSSELL: Ludwig!

LUDWIG: Bertrand. You old Victorian intellectual sell-out.

RUSSELL: Why do you persist in calling me a sell-out, Ludwig? I was always kind to you. It's becoming a bit tiresome, you know.

LUDWIG: Being kind to me has nothing to do with it. Indeed, that you think it does is the very problem, Russell; the very problem.

RUSSELL: Why? How so? What have I done? I mean, I did write the introduction to the *Tractatus* for you, didn't I? I thought that was rather nice of me.

LUDWIG: I always thought the Russell paradox had to do with sets which were members of themselves. But I was wrong, dear Lord Russell. I was quite wrong. The Russell paradox is, in reality, your compulsive need to make philosophy—which is, by its very nature, inaccessible—accessible to "the masses" as you and your liberal friends might say.

RUSSELL: And you would insist that philosophy is only for the highbrow? The specialists? What is so righteous in that unliberal position, Wittgenstein?

ALTER EGO: Well, in all fairness, Lord Russell, it was you who told me that I had a genius for philosophy.

RUSSELL: Surely it doesn't follow that only geniuses should participate in philosophy? Oh, you Austrians.

LUDWIG: Why would one choose to do philosophy except out of a sense of duty? And why would you encourage the notion that doing philosophy is of some instrumental value?

RUSSELL: Now wait just a minute, Wittgenstein. It was you yourself who insisted that your students—for example, Malcolm—had to learn something of value for their lives-as-lived if philosophy was to be worth studying at all. I read that in Malcolm's biography. Yes, I did indeed.

LUDWIG: Indeed, that's true, Lord Bertrand Bolshevik. But I never suggested that philosophy was worth studying! What I say is that if you must study philosophy, then get something practical out of it. But there is no good reason why you must study philosophy. Remember, Bertie, the contrary to fact/conditional!

RUSSELL: But I believe learning philosophy is of value.

LUDWIG: And I believe that getting rid of philosophy is of value. And that is precisely why I consider you a soft-headed sell-out. Brilliant as you were as a young logician, Russell, you wound up as Lord Liberal. And it offends me…not to mention your foul and pompous essays on free love.

ALTER EGO: Now wait a minute. (To LUDWIG.) Wait a damn minute. Gretl talked with us about free love long before Russell wrote about it. I appreciate what you're saying about philosophy, Wiggy, but you don't know shit about sex and politics. Russell's problem was insisting that his popular writings about sex and politics were also philosophical.

MRS. BEVAN: Hello, Lord Russell. (She waves.) How are you? I'm Dr. Bevan's wife.

RUSSELL: I'm just fine, Mrs. Bevan. Just fine.

SALLY: Lord Russell, can you join us at this evening's party after the show? And could you go sit with Mrs. Bevan, for now?

MRS. BEVAN: Oh, please do, Lord Russell, please do.

RUSSELL: Well, I'd love to…if Mr. Wittgenstein will have me.

LUDWIG: Of course, Bertrand Russell, of course. You're not Adolf Hitler, merely a ruling-class liberal…and a Brit at that.

ALTER EGO: Please stay, Russell. Please stay. Don't mind Wiggy.

(*RUSSELL goes to couch with* MRS. BEVAN.)

SALLY: (*Resumes reading from the book*) Ludwig, you have always been an eccentric. Your tastes, like your philosophy, are filled with contradictions. You detest English culture, opting instead for a strange combination of Austro-German high culture—Beethoven, Mozart, etc.—and American popular culture. You loved American musicals with Betty Hutton and Carmen Miranda. Really, Ludwig? I knew there was something I really liked about you.

(*Video of* CARMEN MIRANDA *with Latin music; enter* CARMEN MIRANDA *dancing.*)

CARMEN: (*With mock irritation and Brazilian accent*) Ludwig Wittgenstein. I always wanted to meet you. Why you watch me so much in the movies, huh? I know you used to sit in front row and peer at me. You think I am sexy or something?

LUDWIG: Well, it's a pleasure to meet you, Miss Miranda, after all these decades. You are, as I understand it, in the movies to be watched.

CARMEN: Wittgenstein, don't give me that philosophy bullshit. You know perfectly okay what I mean, yes?

LUDWIG: No.

ALTER EGO: Yes, of course, Miss Miranda, we understand. But I can assure you we meant no discourtesy.

CARMEN: (*Glances at* ALTER EGO) I mean you're a big smarty pants, Wittgenstein. How come you don't watch fancy art movies? How come you sit in the front row and watch me do the Brazilian hootchy-kootchy dance?

LUDWIG: I never have liked fancy art movies, particularly British ones. I really don't like much of modern culture at all. I like your movies. I like you. You're quite lively, Miss Miranda, quite alive.

CARMEN: What are you...dead?

ALTER EGO: We're worse than dead. We're a genius...and a Class A European smarty-pants.

CARMEN: Well, I'm dead now, too, Wittgenstein. But I've never been as dead as you.

(*Enter* MR. MIRANDA *from the audience; no music; grabs* CARMEN.)

MR. MIRANDA: Is this that Mr. Wittgenstein you talk about? The Euro-letch who sits and stares at you wiggling your ass, Carmencita?

ALTER EGO: Who is this man?

CARMEN: He's my father. Mr. Wittgenstein, meet Mr. Miranda.

MR. MIRANDA: Are your intentions honorable, Mr. Wittgenstein?

ALTER EGO: I assure you, sir, they are disgustingly so—at least relating to your daughter! (*LUDWIG makes a face.*) Oh, Wiggy—I was just joking.

CARMEN: Are you a gay caballero, Wittgenstein?

MR. MIRANDA: You're gay!!! You're a gay, Viennese-born philosopher who went to school with Hitler, studied with Bertrand Russell, gave away a fortune, had three brothers who committed suicide, lived for years alone in one-room shacks in the frozen tundras of Scandinavia...and you like to watch my daughter, Carmen Miranda, wiggle her ass?

LUDWIG: I'm afraid so, Mr. Miranda. I'm afraid so.

(*Offstage we hear bongo beats and inaudible chanting.*)

CARMEN: What's that, my music cue?

SALLY: (*Picking up the book*) No, Carmen, it's our final guest.

RUSSELL: (*Lecherously*) Carmen Miranda, please come here and sit with us.

LUDWIG: Russell, watch yourself. Mr. Miranda, you'd best sit between your daughter and that aristocratic sex fiend.

MR. MIRANDA: Goddamn, Wittgenstein. I think I like you.

ALTER EGO: Oh, that's very nice, Mr. Miranda.

CARMEN: *(Hands on hips)* Well, da-dee. I think he is very cute, too.

LUDWIG: That's nice. I think you are…very…sexy.

ALTER EGO: Wiggy! What are you saying?

RUSSELL: Please come sit next to me.

MRS. BEVAN: Mr. Miranda, I have room here, next to me.

SALLY: *(Exasperated)* Alright, you guys, would you let me finish the show. We'll all party later. *(SALLY gently sends CARMEN and MR. MIRANDA back to the couch as bongo music comes up louder. SALLY reads from the book.)* Ludwig, in the 1950s at the beginning of the beat era, your early writings—that damn Latin book…

LUDWIG: It's called the *Tractatus Logico Philosophicus.*

SALLY: Anyway, those words of yours were heard all over Greenwich Village in New York as well as on Paris' Left Bank and in London's Soho. As the beat generation was emerging, the Kerouacs, the beatniks were playing bongos in San Francisco's North Beach and reciting mystical propositions from your Latin book. Now in her middle seventies, one of the most famous of the Beatnik Wittgenstein Bongo Brigade—Gailie Gailie.

(GAILIE GAILIE enters playing the bongo and reciting.)

GAILIE GAILIE:
Logic fills the world.
Wittgenstein said,
Logic fills the world.
Cool, man, cool.
Logic fills the world.

LUDWIG: Oh, this is just terrible. I rejected all of that.

ALTER EGO: Be quiet and listen, Wiggy.

GAILIE GAILIE: *(Reciting)*
The solution of the

problem
of life is seen
in the vanishing of the
problem.

LUDWIG: This is bizarre!

ALTER EGO: Be cool, LW. Be cool!

GAILIE GAILIE: *(Still reciting)*
Is not this
the reason why
men
men to whom after
long doubting the
sense of life became
clear,
of life became clear,
could not then say,
not say,
wherein this sense consisted?

ALTER EGO: Are those our words, Ludwig? I always liked them better as poetry than as philosophy.

GAILIE GAILIE: *(Reciting)*
There is indeed the inexpressible.
Indeed the inexpressible.
This shows itself; it is,
this shows itself it is,
it is the mystical!
The mystical…
Whereof one cannot speak,
thereof one must be silent.
One must be silent.
Silent!

SALLY: Thank you, Gailie Gailie, for bringin' this fine sound to "This is Your Death." Sit yourself down, Gailie Gailie…oh yes, the floor would be fine. And speaking of silence, we're about to run out of time. Ludwig

Wittgenstein, this has been one hell of a show. One hell of a show. What are we to say about this guy…ah…those guys? *(Both LUDWIG and ALTER EGO stand.)* Audience, is Ludwig Wittgenstein worth remembering? *(Reacts to crowd.) (Theme music up.)* Thank you, Mrs. Bevan and Lord Russell and Carmen Miranda and Mr. Miranda and Gailie Gailie…and as for you, Adolf Hitler—man, you sure can lie. And, oh yes, to my alter ego, Gretl Wittgenstein *(Klimt picture on video monitors)*—all I can say to you, darlin', is *(SALLY takes off wig to display GRETL look and sings in GRETL'S voice)* Yes, we have no bananas. We have no bananas today…

HERMAN: Good night all. Tune in next week to "This is Your Death." *(Theme music up and out. OLLIE and STAN walk onstage.)*

OLLIE: Okay everyone…That's a wrap.

STAN: Yeah. Good show. Real good show.

Act II, Scene 1

It's the morning after "This is Your Death" with WITTGENSTEIN. HERMAN, DAISY, STAN and OLLIE in the smoke-filled room.

STAN: Whatta show. We've gotten 18,000 post-show phone calls overnight. It's unheard of.

OLLIE: The greatest. This Wittgenstein guy is unbelievable. A marketable philosopher. Unbelievable.

DAISY: Why'd you call me "death warmed over" on national TV, you asshole?

HERMAN: I've called you worse.

OLLIE: Would you two cool it? This Wittgenstein business could be the biggest thing ever.

STAN: I've gotten three calls already this morning from station management about Wittgenstein having his own show. Maybe something like "This is Your Philosopher." Whatta ya think, Daisy?

HERMAN: I thought the son of a bitch—both of them—was other-worldly.

DAISY: What's that supposed to mean, asshole?

HERMAN: I dunno. He didn't seem like all the other stiffs we brought back from the dead.

OLLIE: Who cares, Herman. We're lookin' at billions of dollars here. We'll all retire on Wittgenstein.

HERMAN: *(To DAISY)* Will ya still love me so when I'm a trillionaire?

DAISY: Listen, schmendrick, I wouldn't love you if you were the last man on Earth.

HERMAN: *(Romantically, mockingly)* You never called me schmendrick before.

Act II, Scene 2

It's midday in Central Park, New York City, near the reservoir and the running track around it. People in jogging outfits walk by a small grouping of three joggers—ALAN SILVER, EDDIE THOMAS and CAROL SILVER—who are sitting and stretching on a bench and the grass. It's June 13, the day after WITTGENSTEIN'S appearance on "This is Your Death."

ALAN: That's bullshit, Eddie...just bullshit...man...why do you make these things up? Ludwig Wittgenstein wasn't gay. That's crazy, Eddie... you're full of shit.

EDDIE: What are you so excited about? I mean first of all he was gay. But... whatever...what's the big deal? What are you so agitated about? You don't want him to be gay? Okay. So he's straight. No big deal, man.

ALAN: But that misses the whole point, Eddie. Calling someone gay is serious. People get bashed bad...people get killed for being gay. You know what I'm saying? It's like fucking around and calling someone Jewish—who isn't, or even who is—in Vienna in 1939. It's just fucking irresponsible.

EDDIE: But Wittgenstein's dead, for cryin' out loud. And he was gay, goddamn it...he was gay.

CAROL: What's with you two today?

EDDIE: I don't know why your husband is so damned upset about my saying that Ludwig Wittgenstein was gay. What's with him?

CAROL: What am I, his mother? You're his oldest friend and you got him into this Wittgenstein business in the first place, Eddie, remember?

ALAN: It's not a "Wittgenstein business" and I don't appreciate being condescended to, Carol…I really don't. *(He gets up and jogs off.)*

EDDIE: What in the fuck was that all about? Has he been like this a lot lately?

CAROL: What…now I'm his shrink? This Wittgenstein course you two are taking at the New School…don't they know if he's gay or not? Doesn't the teacher know if he was gay?

EDDIE: I mean, I think it's clear that he was, but Wittgenstein was a recluse and very morally tortured. He led a very private life. A lot of his personal stuff…ya know, what he did…it's kinda unclear.

CAROL: Well, does it make a difference?

EDDIE: I think it makes a difference.

CAROL: Like what? What difference does it make?

EDDIE: I dunno. I mean Wittgenstein was a very passionate philosopher. His sensibilities—even when he's doing very technical philosophy…ya know, philosophy of mathematics or logic or language—are deeply moral and aesthetic and personal; subjective. So his sexual and emotional attitudes are real important to understanding him. Does that make sense? Ya know what I mean? *(CAROL laughs loudly.)*

EDDIE: Whatya laughin' about, Carol?

CAROL: I don't know really. It's just kind of funny to hear you talking about a philosopher…and talking so intellectually. I mean for twenty years all I ever heard you guys talk about with each other was football and basketball.

EDDIE: *(Smiling; getting the humor)* And baseball.

CAROL: Yeah. And baseball.

EDDIE: Well ya know, Carol, I'm improving my mind. *(Laughing slightly.)* Now that my body is cavin' in I figure I'd better do something about my brain. I mean how many slam dunks can ya get turned on by in one lifetime, Carol? But, Alan…I mean he was always a head-guy. He's a high school English teacher. He's been thinkin' ever since I knew him. What's he so goddamn upset about? Maybe he doesn't like me talkin' smart talk? Maybe he doesn't like me doing that? Ya think so, Carol? Whattya think?

CAROL: I don't know. I don't think so much anymore. Maybe I should start. My body's caving in, too.

EDDIE: Bullshit. Your body won't ever stop, Carol. Believe me. Believe me.

CAROL: Oh, Eddie…you working-class Romeo. Stop handing me that sexist line…that you know I love to hear.

(*EDDIE and CAROL laugh warmly together. Another jogger and friend, DIANE WRIGHT, a woman of color, joins EDDIE and CAROL.*)

DIANE: Hey, you guys, did you run yet?

EDDIE: I did speed laps, Diane. But I'm gonna go another few miles.

CAROL: (*Gets up; hugs DIANE*) How ya been? I haven't seen you all week. You haven't called. What's doin'?

DIANE: Oh, I've been feeling like shit again. I didn't work all week.

EDDIE: What's wrong? You been to the doctor?

DIANE: No. I think it's the flu or something. I'll be okay. It's gettin' better.

CAROL: Is there something bothering you? You seem kind of down, Diane. Are you okay?

DIANE: I don't know. You know…(*she breaks into tears.*)

CAROL: (*Embracing her*) Hey. Hey, Diane. What's going on, darling? What's the matter?

EDDIE: Yeah. What's up? Your white honky old man been fuckin' with you again?

CAROL: (*Playfully*) Shut up, Eddie. What's going on, Diane?

DIANE: (*Hesitantly*) I got a little lump…in my right breast. I don't think I ever had a lump like this before. I'm feeling scared.

CAROL: Have you been to see your doctor?

DIANE: No…I think it's okay. I really do. I think it's okay.

EDDIE: Whatta you mean "you think it's okay"? You gotta see a doctor.

DIANE: I spoke to my therapist about it. She says it's nothing. You know… she thinks I'm a screamin' hypochondriac. And I think she's right.

CAROL: Well, have you and she been through this before?

DIANE: Oh, yes. We have. *(To CAROL.)* You remember last summer? I had that funny feeling in my left breast.

EDDIE: Well, I still think you should see a real doctor.

DIANE: No, I don't think so, Eddie. I get scared but I think my shrink is right. It's in my damned head. I'm just crazy about these kind of things. You know what a crazy lady I am. *(Laughs.)* Hey…what were you two talking about? And…where's Alan?

CAROL: We were talking about Ludwig Wittgenstein and how our bodies are crumping out.

DIANE: Well, I can get into that.

EDDIE: Do you know Wittgenstein…you know anything about him?

DIANE: Yeah, I do. One thing…there's a new movie out…a British film…I just read a review. I couldn't understand a word of it. But then last night I was watching the Sally McNally show…you know, "This is Your Death"…and Wittgenstein was the mystery guest. What a great show. He's some wild, spiritual kind of dude. I really dug him. Kinda crazy, like me.

EDDIE: Diane…you watch Sally McNally? You watch that bullshit "This is Your Death" show?

DIANE: Why is it bullshit, Eddie, huh? Why is it bullshit?

CAROL: Yeah, Eddie…just because you don't like it doesn't make it bullshit. Men, Diane, men.

EDDIE: Now wait a minute. The damned show is a fucking hoax. They claim that they're bringing back dead people and putting them on TV. That's crazy. It's a fucking hoax!

DIANE: Well, who are they on the show? Who are they? Last night they had Wittgenstein and Hitler and Bertrand Russell. Who are they, Eddie? If they're not the real people...who are they?

EDDIE: Whattya mean who are they? Are you crazy? They're actors, god-damn it. They're goddamned actors. That's who they are.

CAROL: But they claim they're real. That they came back from the dead. And the FCC has done two investigations and they haven't found a single actor...or actress...who says they ever played a role. And they uncover stuff that no one else knew. You don't think there could be some new electronic/spiritual technique...

EDDIE: It's a *HOAX*. What are you two, crazy? You can't bring people back from the dead, Carol...I don't believe this. Do you watch Sally McNally on "This is Your Death," too?

CAROL: Sometimes. Yeah, sometimes. And frankly, Eddie, I don't like your ...well, your sexist attitude. You're talking to me and Diane like we were two bimbos. I mean, lots of strange things are going on in the world these days, Eddie.

EDDIE: Well, "frankly" I think you're talking like two bimbos. I mean, this is completely crazy. I mean McNally is straight out of the *Enquirer.*

DIANE: I think the show is authentic. And I spoke to my spiritual advisor about it and he thinks so, too.

EDDIE: Your spiritual advisor? What in hell am I hearing here today?

DIANE: Eddie, I've had a spiritual advisor for years.

CAROL: Yeah, Eddie...and you've known it. We've talked about it many times. Maybe you haven't been listening. Maybe you've been too tied up with the "spirituality" of Duke, Michigan and the NCAA to bother listening to Diane. Now all of a sudden you're a damned intellectual... taking a course on Wittgenstein at the New School...and so Diane and I become bimbos.

DIANE: On Sally's show last night they actually had Wittgenstein and his homosexual self—kinda like his alter ego—both on the show. It was astounding. Fantastic stuff. I believe it. I really do.

EDDIE: They had what? Wittgenstein and his homosexual self? Two...ah... different people? On the show? Those fuckers have no shame.

CAROL: But it does show that he was gay. I'd think you'd be pleased, Eddie. You're right about Wittgenstein. He was gay. And we all know how important being right is to you. Alan was wrong. You were right.

EDDIE: I ain't right because that floozy Sally McNally and her cockamamie TV show "This is Your Death" says so. They're a bunch of hucksters and nutcases and so are you two. I can't believe this. I've known you for twenty years. Is this some kind of a bad joke? You're puttin' me on, right? You...(*He is interrupted by* ALAN, *who returns at this moment.*)

ALAN: What are you all so agitated about? I could see you jumpin' up and down for a quarter of a mile, Eddie.

EDDIE: You won't believe this, Alan. I know you won't, but Diane is a "follower" of Sally McNally and that crazy "This is Your Death" hoax. Did you know that? (ALAN *shrugs with liberal nonchalance.*) And your wife— your Radcliffe graduate wife—agrees with her. Carol agrees with her. She watches the show sometimes, too. Did you know that? This is crazy. I can't believe this!

ALAN: Well, what's the big deal? Who knows what's possible these days? You always have to have all the answers? First you're telling me for sure that Wittgenstein is gay. Now you're tellin' us for sure that the Sally McNally show is a hoax. Jesus, Eddie, how'd you get so smart all of a sudden? I remember when you were just a dumb high school dropout trying to earn a buck fixin' TV's and toasters.

EDDIE: Is this what you teach your kids in school? Is this stupidity what they call postmodern? Hey, if this is postmodern, give me modern. Fuck... give me ancient.

DIANE: Listen, Alan, Wittgenstein is gay. Eddie is right about that. Wittgenstein's homosexual self was on the McNally show last night. I taped it. I really liked Wittgenstein. He's very nice.

ALAN: (*Shocked*) What do you mean his homosexual self was on TV? What the fuck does that mean, Diane? What are you talking about?

EDDIE: Oh, now listen to you. Suddenly you're a skeptic. You fuckin' hypocrite.

ALAN: Quiet, asshole. Quiet.

CAROL: There were two Wittgensteins on the show...Right, Diane? Wittgenstein...the straight Wittgenstein...and his homosexual alter ego. Isn't that right, Diane?

DIANE: Yeah, Carol. That's exactly right. And they talked to each other. I liked how they talked. Wittgenstein's alter ego is a lot nicer than mine.

ALAN: You have this...ah...conversation on tape, Diane?

DIANE: Yes, I do.

ALAN: Can we see it? I mean right now. Can we see it?

EDDIE: What are you saying, Alan? You're gonna watch Sally "Asshole" McNally?

ALAN: Let's all go to Diane's place and watch it. Right now. Right this minute.

EDDIE: Are you crazy? Are you nuts? I got laps to do. I got important things to do. I ain't gonna watch that dumb TV show.

ALAN: C'mon, Eddie. You said he was gay. Well, let's take a look. Maybe you're right.

EDDIE: "This is Your Death" don't prove nothin'!

DIANE: C'mon. I got fresh bagels.

CAROL: Yeah. C'mon, Eddie. Let's go see the gay Wittgenstein.

EDDIE: (As they all pull him to his feet) You guys are crazy. I can't believe this.

ALAN: Maybe it's time for you to "come out," Eddie. (ALAN, EDDIE, CAROL, DIANE all exit.)

Act II, Scene 3

DIANE's sparsely furnished apartment. There's a picture of an Indian spiritual leader on the wall and a TV in the middle of the room. ALAN, CAROL and DIANE enter "dragging" EDDIE; DIANE leads the way.

DIANE: Here, sit down on these mats. I'll put some bagels and cream cheese out.

EDDIE: *(To DIANE)* Well, you certainly went from being depressed to being kinda cheerful in a big hurry.

DIANE: This is exciting. It's spiritual. Besides...that's how I always am.

CAROL: Yeah, Eddie. Haven't you ever noticed?

EDDIE: Where's your old man? Where's George?

DIANE: He's in Eritrea working with a UN team making sure the elections are honest.

CAROL: *(Sarcastically)* Oh, that's interesting.

DIANE: C'mon, sit down. *(She puts out the bagels and cream cheese.)* I'll go get the video tape. *(She exits.)*

ALAN: *(To EDDIE)* You hadn't heard about this show? When was it on?

CAROL: Just last night.

ALAN: You saw it? Where was I?

CAROL: Yeah, I saw it. You were in the bedroom watching the NBA playoffs.

ALAN: How often do you watch this show, Carol? *(To EDDIE.)* Was there anything on the news about this? Was it in the papers?

EDDIE: No one covers this hokey show. No one...at least I thought no one ...takes it seriously.

CAROL: Millions of people watch it.

EDDIE: Millions of people watch "Superman." Millions of people watch wrestling. But no one believes it, goddamn it. It's not news. It's fantasy ...and dumb fantasy at that.

ALAN: *(To CAROL)* So when Eddie and I were arguing before you thought he was right, huh? You think Wittgenstein is gay too?

CAROL: Yeah. I thought he was right.

EDDIE: And that whole thing about "doesn't anyone at the New School know if he's gay…" that was all bullshit in a way. How come you didn't tell me then about the McNally show? How come you didn't say you saw it? And that you thought he was gay?

CAROL: How come? How come? Look at how crazy you two are. Look at this reaction. I don't tell you or Alan most of what's happening in my life anymore.

ALAN: *(Somewhat hurt)* What do you mean, Carol?

CAROL: Well, we never talk very much these days. I don't think you really know me very well anymore. I don't think I know you very well.

EDDIE: But you and I are buddies, Carol. You've always confided in me.

ALAN: What's that supposed to mean?

EDDIE: Oh, Alan, stop being a schmuck.

CAROL: Would you two stop it already!

DIANE: *(Enters with video tape)* Here it is. I have it set at where the homosexual Wittgenstein enters.

(She puts the tape in the VCR. Video is a real-time recording of the indicated portion of Act I, and can be seen and heard by the audience and the actors. It begins with SALLY'S introduction of the gay ALTER EGO, and runs continuously through the entrance of GRETL. Act II characters respond to it as indicated.)

EDDIE: Oh, God. Look at that bimbo McNally.

CAROL: I really resent that kind of talk, Eddie. And you wonder why I can't confide in you.

DIANE: Quiet, everybody. Quiet.

ALAN: Yeah. Keep quiet.

(On video, ALTER EGO enters.)

EDDIE: They don't even look alike.

DIANE: Well, why would they?

ALAN: Quiet. Keep quiet.

(Tape continues.)

EDDIE: *(To ALAN, after Weininger remarks in video)* Did they say anything about…what's his name, Weininger…in the New School course?

ALAN: No. Keep quiet.

DIANE: I think it's really Wittgenstein's two selves. I really do. My spiritualist talks about our different selves all the time.

ALAN: Shhhhhh!

CAROL: Alan, don't tell Diane to keep quiet in her own house.

ALAN: I'm sorry, Diane. I just want to hear this.

EDDIE: *(As ALTER EGO refuses to go sit in the back)* Well, I guess at least it proves he was gay. They wouldn't put it out that way if he wasn't. I mean it seemed pretty well researched. But what hokey fucking acting. Did you see how effeminate that clown alter ego played Wittgenstein? Jesus Christ.

DIANE: I don't think they were actors.

CAROL: I don't know. Sally had Harry Houdini and his wife and child on last month. I was sure it was really them.

ALAN: It only proves he was gay, it seems to me, if you accept that it was really Wittgenstein and his alter ego, Eddie.

EDDIE: That's preposterous! Alan, you've got an M.A. What kinda stupid thing is that to say? I mean I think they did good research maybe. The teacher at the New School is mainly talkin' about Wittgenstein's technical philosophy. But it don't mean that McNally's hoax "This is Your Death" is for real. That's nuts, Alan. That's nuts.

DIANE: *(Excited)* Hold on a second, you guys. Watch this part where Sally turns into Wittgenstein's sister, Gretl.

CAROL: Oh, yeah, yeah…watch this. There's this old painting of Gretl Wittgenstein by someone named Klimt. It looks exactly like Sally. Watch this.

(Video continues to blackout on SALLY. DIANE turns off the VCR.)

ALAN: *(To DIANE and CAROL, condescendingly)* That's interesting. *(Back to EDDIE.)* Listen up, Eddie. I didn't think Wittgenstein was gay. You did. I was wrong. Okay? I was wrong. Now I see that he was gay. But there's no way I got that from some good research. No fucking way. Besides, I thought you hated this McNally show. You said it was a goddamn hoax. How'd they suddenly get to be doing "good research"?

EDDIE: I mean they could have a good research department. They probably need one to hold down the libel suits. *(Long pause. EDDIE, CAROL, DIANE eat bagels. ALAN jumps up and walks around very nervously.)*

ALAN: I'm gay. Alright. I'm gay. *(Everyone is shocked.)*

CAROL: What do you mean you're gay? We've been married for twenty years. What do you mean you're gay?

ALAN: I'm gay. I mean I'm gay. For 10 of those 20 years—the last 10—I've been seeing a man...living with him when you've been away...travelling with him on most of my trips. Loving him. Loving him as much as I love you. That's what I mean. I'm gay.

CAROL: Did you know about this, Eddie?

EDDIE: No. I...I...didn't know anything about this. I didn't know.

ALAN: I couldn't talk to either of you about it.

CAROL: *(To ALAN)* What's his name?

ALAN: Jim. His name is Jim. He's Black. *(EDDIE is startled.)* We're very careful. We're tested regularly. We're negative. *(To CAROL.)* You're safe. There's no danger. He's a TV actor. You've probably seen him. He's not very famous. He knows all about you. He says he loves you. *(Slight laugh.)* I think he does. I think you might love him. He's much nicer than I am, Carol, much nicer. He's been wanting me to tell you for years. He carries your picture in his wallet. I think sometimes he tells people you're his wife.

CAROL: I don't believe this is happening.

EDDIE: Alan...I mean...I can't believe you never told me. It's...hard to believe you've had this other life for years...that you've had a gay lover and I never knew. It's almost impossible…it's almost impossible to believe.

ALAN: Lots of things seem impossible to believe, Eddie…don't they? Wittgenstein was gay. Maybe that was him on TV telling you so. I'm gay. You've got no research on me…but I'm gay. Believe me.

DIANE: I'm a lesbian. I have been my whole life. I'm a lesbian. It's time I told all of you.

EDDIE: Is this another one of your fantasies, Diane?

CAROL: Stop it, Eddie. Stop it. You can't talk to Diane that way.

DIANE: I've never spoken to my therapist or spiritualist about it. They wouldn't approve. George doesn't know anything about it. I love him. We have good sex. I've hardly talked to anyone about it. It makes me crazy…not telling anyone. It makes me crazy.

ALAN: Carol, did you know about Diane?

CAROL: *(Reaches for and holds DIANE's hand)* Yes. I know about it. *(Pause.)* We've been lovers…on and off…we've been lovers for years.

EDDIE: What is this? Is everyone gay around here except me? We've been the best of friends all this time and…and…and no one talks to hardly anyone about who we are…what are we doing here? Jesus Christ, man. Maybe Sally McNally is the only sane person in this whole fucking city!

ALAN: *(To CAROL)* I always thought you were a lesbian. I'm glad. Yeah. I'm glad. *(To EDDIE.)* Hey, man. Now that we have this gay stuff out all we've got left to decide is whether we're all dead or alive. *(Slight laugh.)*

EDDIE: You're a crazy motherfucker, Alan, a crazy motherfucker.

DIANE: Anybody want more bagels and cream cheese?

EDDIE: Put that tape on again, Diane. Please. Put that tape on again. I gotta take another look at this shit.

(DIANE rewinds quickly and video begins with ALTER EGO's entrance.)

Act II, Scene 4

A week later at the same spot in Central Park. ALAN, EDDIE, CAROL *and* DIANE *are in jogging outfits and seated and/or lying together on the grass.*

EDDIE: *(To DIANE)* Is George back from Africa yet?

DIANE: No, not yet. I think he's coming back later this week.

ALAN: *(To EDDIE)* What did you think of Professor Muller's lecture on the *Tractatus* last Thursday?

EDDIE: I didn't think it was very good. I think I'm getting bored with his course. Actually I'm getting sick of the New School. But I'm not getting tired of Wittgenstein, that's for sure. I've been re-reading Bartley's biography. *(To ALAN.)* Have you read it? It's wild.

CAROL: *(To EDDIE)* Did you watch "This is Your Death" last night?

EDDIE: *(Little pause)* I did. Yes, I did. *(Jokingly.)* I admit it.

DIANE: I'm sure we all watched it…yes? *(They all nod.)*

DIANE: *(To EDDIE)* What did you think?

EDDIE: I dunno. They still seem a little like bad actors to me…but it…I dunno…it…uh…it seemed different from before. That old guy really sounded like Custer.

ALAN: How was it different?

EDDIE: I dunno. Maybe I'm different. Jesus Christ…I mean, in about one hour last Sunday I found out that three of my best friends are gay and that…well…maybe Ludwig Wittgenstein is really two people…and, they both appeared on live television. That's like pickin' nine straight at Belmont.

CAROL: How was everybody's week?

DIANE: I told my therapist and my spiritualist about the Sally McNally show and Wittgenstein and about all of us and last Sunday…they both hate that I'm a lesbian. They think I'm sick. I thought they were both creepy. I walked out on them. Both of them. It felt great. I haven't felt this good in years.

CAROL: That's great, Diane. Right on. That's great. I had a helluva week too. I started working on my novel again. I haven't written a word in years. I mean I could hardly remember where I'd put the manuscript… and what it was about. But I read the first hundred pages or so and I liked it. I'd forgotten about this, Diane, but there's a Black lesbian character in the book.

DIANE: Oh, yes?

CAROL: Yeah. A lovely character…I mean it's you. I think I wrote her in when we first started having sex together. (ALAN *looks slightly shocked at the openness of* CAROL'S *remark.*)

ALAN: I told Jim about what happened last Sunday. He wants to meet everyone. He said maybe Sally McNally can only bring back gay dead people on "This is Your Death."

EDDIE: That's crazy… (*he stops himself.*) I'm sorry. But doesn't the show have straight people on it?

ALAN: Jim said maybe everybody's really gay.

EDDIE: Hey, look, I don't mean no disrespect or nuthin' but I'm not gay and …uh…I know quite a few ladies who aren't either.

DIANE: Hey, Eddie, maybe you're the only straight man in the world. The last straight man on Earth.

EDDIE: (*Playfully*) And maybe you're Cleopatra.

DIANE: (*Playfully*) No. No. No. Sally had Cleopatra on her show a few months ago…and it wasn't me. But I think I might be Rosa Luxemburg.

EDDIE: Who in the hell is Rosa Luxemburg?

DIANE: She was a Polish-Jewish Marxist economist and revolutionary who got herself murdered in the 1920s.

EDDIE: (*Sarcastically*) Well, that certainly sounds a lot like you.

(*Stage has been slowly but continuously darkening during the entire scene and there has been a whirring noise growing louder and louder.*)

ALAN: Doesn't it seem to be getting a little dark for *(looks at watch)* 3:30 in the afternoon?

CAROL: I think so, Alan. It is getting dark. And what's that noise? Does anyone else hear it?

DIANE: Yeah. I hear it.

EDDIE: Me, too. And…and…uh…it is getting dark.

ALAN: Yeah, I can hear it. *(Noise grows louder; strange lighting.)*

EDDIE: What in the fuck is going on here?

DIANE: I wonder if this has anything to do with the Sally McNally show?

(Noise grows very loud and lighting intensifies; a space ship in the shape of Wittgenstein's head appears onstage to very big sound and light effects. We cannot see inside the space craft yet. Noise diminishes; weird lighting continues; ALAN, EDDIE, CAROL and DIANE stand utterly astounded.)

ALAN: The shape of that…that…uh…space ship?…is like…it's like, uh… Ludwig Wittgenstein's head.

CAROL: This is astounding…no, it's much more than astounding.

DIANE: God, I'm glad I got rid of my therapist and spiritualist.

EDDIE: I think I believe in the Sally McNally show!

CAROL: Should we do something? Like should we do those musical notes from *Close Encounters*? You remember, that old movie with Richard Dreyfus?

ALAN: I don't think so.

DIANE: I think we should just be cool and wait. *(Doors or curtains in space ship open and the two WITTGENSTEINs come out.)* It's them! It's the two Wittgensteins from the Sally McNally show.

EDDIE: I do believe in the Sally McNally show! *(He crosses himself.)*

WITTGENSTEIN OF EARTH: Good afternoon. I'm sorry we made things so dark but we put something of a drain on solar energy levels…particularly for the descent. We're Ludwig Wittgenstein. Did any of you happen to catch us on Sally McNally's show last week?

DIANE: I did. And I loved you, Mr. Wittgenstein. You were sensational.

CAROL: Yes. I saw you also…uh…Mr. Wittgenstein.

EDDIE: Where…uh…where are you from? Where did you come from?

WITTGENSTEIN OF WITTGENSTEIN: We're from the planet Wittgenstein. It's 283 light years from Earth. Actually it's the closest planet to yours which has human-type life. You know…or do you?…that there are only 17 humanoid planets in the entire universe. And who are you?

(Pause to take in WITTGENSTEIN OF WITTGENSTEIN's speech.)

ALAN: I'm Alan Silver.

CAROL: I'm his wife, Carol.

EDDIE: I'm Eddie Thomas.

DIANE: I'm Diane Wright. We're all friends. *(They all nod.)*

WITTGENSTEIN OF WITTGENSTEIN: And your sexual preferences? What are they? *(ALAN, EDDIE, CAROL, DIANE are slightly shocked.)*

EDDIE: I'm straight…

ALAN, CAROL, DIANE: We're all gay, Mr. Wittgenstein. We're all gay.

WITTGENSTEIN OF EARTH: Well, we're gay…that's been cleared up…as you probably saw on Sally's show.

WITTGENSTEIN OF WITTGENSTEIN: *(To WITTGENSTEIN OF EARTH)* Oh, Wiggy. You're being somewhat tentative.

WITTGENSTEIN OF EARTH: Well, it's still a little new to be talking about it so openly.

WITTGENSTEIN OF WITTGENSTEIN: *(To ALAN, EDDIE, CAROL and DIANE)* You see on the planet Wittgenstein everyone is gay.

EDDIE: *(Shocked)* Everyone? Everyone? Well, then how do you have children?

WITTGENSTEIN OF EARTH: I'm not so sure that's any of your business.

WITTGENSTEIN OF WITTGENSTEIN: Oh, Wiggy. It's perfectly alright. You see *(pointing to WITTGENSTEIN OF EARTH)* he's actually an Earthling. Quite a genius as I'm sure you all know...but an Earthling. Well, back in the early days of your 20th century...so called...he invented this extraordinary rocket ship...he was into aeronautical engineering back then—did you know that?—and he arrived one day on the planet Wittgenstein. Of course, we were all delighted. I fell immediately and madly in love with him. He and I came back here together in your 1930s—our planetary PR people made up that silly story about him teaching children in southern Austria—and created "Wittgenstein's later works"—*The Blue and the Brown Books* and *Philosophical Investigations.* Then in 1951 I got a message that my dear mother wasn't well. So we ourselves made up that little prostate cancer performance and went back to Wittgenstein. We hadn't been back here on Earth until Sally rang us up three weeks ago. Oh yes—how do we have children? We've mastered the lower phyla activity of binary fission. Rather good fun, too. We actually "do it" collectively. It's a gas.

DIANE: Everyone is gay. My God. How extraordinary.

CAROL: There are...uh...there are lesbians?

WITTGENSTEIN OF EARTH: Of course there are!

CAROL: I meant no insult, Mr. Wittgenstein...really.

WITTGENSTEIN OF WITTGENSTEIN: Oh, don't mind Wiggy. He's touchy like you Earthlings tend to be.

WITTGENSTEIN OF EARTH: Well, really *(to WITTGENSTEIN OF WITTGENSTEIN)*, it is rather insensitive to ask if we have women on Wittgenstein, don't you think?

WITTGENSTEIN OF WITTGENSTEIN: But how could they know?

WITTGENSTEIN OF EARTH: Well, they think they know it all. These damned Earthlings have an explanation for anything and everything. We tried to teach them about that in our later writings. *(Turning to ALAN, EDDIE, CAROL, DIANE.)* The point is not to explain or interpret things—it's to do things, change things, create things. I mean Karl Marx told you all of that over a century ago! But these "educated" Earthlings never learn; never develop. *(Turning to EDDIE.)* You look like one of those types who knows everything. Yes? You're the straight one. Is that correct?

EDDIE: Well, yes, Mr. Wittgenstein. I'm afraid that's so. But I could tell from your later writings that you were gay. I mean I got that. Alan didn't. But I did.

ALAN: Jesus, Eddie, I don't think that's the right thing to say.

WITTGENSTEIN OF EARTH: Well, how did you know?

EDDIE: *(Giving ALAN a dirty look)* Well, there's this sensibility that's not so damned macho...not so rigid and...you know...well like you say...not having to know everything. Not so caught up with truth and right and wrong.

ALAN: *(To EDDIE)* You mean, not so much like you?

EDDIE: Yeah, you've got it...not so much like me.

WITTGENSTEIN OF WITTGENSTEIN: Oh, that's wonderful. Wiggy, did you hear that? Isn't that wonderful? This gentleman's got it...he's gotten something from us.

WITTGENSTEIN OF EARTH: Yes. I think so. You're not a philosopher, are you?

EDDIE: Oh, shit no, Mr. Wittgenstein. I'm a TV repairman part-time and a computer programmer the rest of the time. Just a working man. Mr. Wittgenstein...just a working man. And...uh...I love Carmen Miranda like you do. *(He smiles.)*

WITTGENSTEIN OF EARTH: *(Smiles broadly)* That's good. Yes...That's very good. You're not anti-gay, are you?

EDDIE: Well...uh...no, I don't think so.

DIANE: Just a little, Eddie. Maybe just a little.

EDDIE: *(Begins to argue)* Well, I don't agree...I think...

WITTGENSTEIN OF WITTGENSTEIN: *(Interrupts)* Now wait one minute, Eddie old boy. Just wait one minute. None of that is necessary. None of that. *(WITTGENSTEIN OF WITTGENSTEIN puts his hand on EDDIE's shoulder.)*

EDDIE: Okay. I'm sorry. Forgive me, Mr. Wittgenstein.

CAROL: Everyone is gay on the planet Wittgenstein? That's incredible.

WITTGENSTEIN OF WITTGENSTEIN: It's actually very, very pleasant. Straight sexuality is so tied to so many of your other Earthling vices.

DIANE: So no man on Wittgenstein has ever slept with a woman and no woman has ever slept with a man? You've never slept with a woman, Mr. Wittgenstein.

WITTGENSTEIN OF EARTH: I must say that's rather forward of you.

WITTGENSTEIN OF WITTGENSTEIN: Wiggy, cut it out. *(To DIANE.)* Actually, I sleep with lesbians quite frequently. Indeed, so far as I can tell I am a lesbian. Gayness to us on the planet Wittgenstein doesn't mean sex with the same sex—it means sex without definition. There is no "opposite" sex. Therefore, there is no "same" sex. And when you take away "opposite" and "same" then sex is quite a different matter.

WITTGENSTEIN OF EARTH: It's rather like the idea of "family resemblances" that we talk about in the *Philosophical Investigations.* There are "sexual resemblances"—not definite sexes. Surely some people are biologically identifiable as women and others as men. But why should we identify ourselves—biologically or otherwise. Identity is such a vulgar Earthlike idea.

EDDIE: No one has any identity? I mean…uh…how do you know who anyone is?

WITTGENSTEIN OF EARTH: Well, presumably our so-called identities are based on who we are. So we must have a capacity to know who we are logically and historically prior to having identities. It's like any code. You have to know what something means before you encode it. Now some codes have positive value. Identity—human identity, Earthling identity—has none.

DIANE: So then, Mr. Wittgenstein, I wouldn't be Black?

WITTGENSTEIN OF EARTH: Well, you are Black. You simply wouldn't be identified as Black.

ALAN: It's kinda like everyone is the same.

WITTGENSTEIN OF WITTGENSTEIN: Oh no, dear boy. It's rather like everyone's different. It's those categories of identity which makes everyone the same—in a sense. Actually on Wittgenstein "same" and "different" have no real meaning. That's why we're all so bloody gay.

CAROL: But isn't saying that "everyone is gay" giving an identity?

WITTGENSTEIN OF EARTH: No. Not at all. Something or someone must not be gay in order for gayness to be an identity. But everything and everyone is gay on Wittgenstein.

EDDIE: *(Jokingly)* I guess there's no gay liberation movement.

WITTGENSTEIN OF WITTGENSTEIN: There's no liberation movement on Wittgenstein. Wittgenstein is a permanent liberation movement. Old Leon Trotsky Wittgenstein taught us that.

CAROL: I love it. Jesus Christ, Alan. There is some value to philosophy after all.

WITTGENSTEIN OF EARTH: No. I don't think so. Philosophy has no value. What has value is the activity of philosophy. And the proper activity of philosophy is, of course, getting rid of philosophy.

WITTGENSTEIN OF WITTGENSTEIN: Wittgenstein, our dear, dear planet, has no philosophy. *(Looks lovingly at WITTGENSTEIN OF EARTH.)* I think Wiggy has finally seen that and now he's more at peace. Sally's show was of enormous help to Wiggy. She's such a dear.

EDDIE: Exactly who is Sally McNally in all of this, Mr. Wittgenstein? She seems...uh...well, she seems so...uh...unsophisticated, you know, so...uh...

DIANE: Well, say it, Eddie. You think of her as a bimbo, a floozy, a dumbo, a fool.

EDDIE: Well, I used to...uh...last week. But...

WITTGENSTEIN OF WITTGENSTEIN: Sally McNally. A dumbo? Oh no. *(Points to WITTGENSTEIN OF EARTH.)* Sally is Wiggy's therapist. Has been for years. Even back when Sally was Wiggy's dear sister Gretl. Did you see that on the show? Wasn't that adorable? Sally is extraordinary. She's absolutely unidentifiable. She's a...what do you Earthlings call it...oh, yes, yes...she's an unidentified flying object—a UFO—that's Sally McNally.

WITTGENSTEIN OF EARTH: Sally is who you should be studying. Not Wittgenstein at the New School but Sally McNally.

ALAN: *(To WITTGENSTEIN OF EARTH)* Then Sally and you were just pretending not to know each other on "This is Your Death?"

WITTGENSTEIN OF WITTGENSTEIN: Wasn't he wonderful? What a performance. He's a genius.

WITTGENSTEIN OF EARTH: Please, Ludwig. Yes. We were just pretending.

(At this moment MRS. BEVAN, BERTRAND RUSSELL, GAILIE GAILIE and MR. MIRANDA jog onto the stage led by SALLY MCNALLY. MR. MIRANDA hands CARMEN MIRANDA's headpiece to DIANE. She puts it on.)

SALLY: Hi guys…and gals. Can we all go home to Wittgenstein now? I'm ready for the ride. I do need a break from commercialism.

WITTGENSTEIN OF WITTGENSTEIN: Yes, Sally. We were waiting for you. We're about ready to blast off.

CAROL: You're all from the planet Wittgenstein? You're all gay? And Diane …uh…Carmen…you're one of them?

WITTGENSTEIN OF WITTGENSTEIN: Yes, dear. We are. And we're goin' home. You all wanna come along? We have plenty of room.

MR. MIRANDA: *(To WITTGENSTEIN OF WITTGENSTEIN)* It's good to see you again.

EDDIE: Well, I guess you all could go. I'm not eligible.

WITTGENSTEIN OF WITTGENSTEIN: Oh, no way, Mr. Eddie. You are absolutely welcome on Wittgenstein. We'd love to have you all. Back where I'm from we say, "This is Your Wittgenstein." Get it? Isn't that cute? C'mon. Let's go. You'll have a ball.

RUSSELL: *(To EDDIE)* Yes, you will. Do come along.

MRS. BEVAN: *(To EDDIE)* The Wittgensteinians are such lovely people.

GAILIE GAILIE: *(To EDDIE)* You do hear the beat of the drum. You do hear the beat of the drum.

DIANE (CARMEN): *(In accent, to EDDIE)* Eddie, this is your life. Do it.

SALLY: *(To EDDIE)* C'mon, buddy. Join the rest of us bimbos.

EDDIE: *(Hesitantly)* Yeah. Yeah. I'm comin'. I'm comin'. This is one hell of a cure for a mid-life crisis.

(They all cheer and enter the space ship. Loud noise. Takeoff lighting effects; fade.)

Act II, Scene 5

OLLIE, STAN, DAISY and HERMAN are in a total frenzy.

OLLIE: We've now gotten 1.5 billion calls off the Wittgenstein show in the last week. It's incredible. It's the biggest commercial success in human history.

STAN: Have you spoken to Sally today?

OLLIE: No. I haven't. She's worth a trillion dollars now. After the Wittgenstein show all the world wants to see is "This is Your Death." Three quarters of the world's viewers watched the Custer show last night. Can you believe it? It's unbelievable.

DAISY: And no one even likes Custer.

HERMAN: The Sally McNally Wittgenstein show...it's the ultimate takeover of commercialism.

STAN: We're taking over the world! We're taking over the world! Commercialism Über Alles!

ALL: Commercialism Über Alles! Commercialism Über Alles!

(By the last exclamation, they are all doing Nazi salute. They freeze as lights fade.)

))))

Left of the Moon

Like *Mr. Hirsch Died Yesterday*, *Left of the Moon* (1994) is, among other things, an autobiographical piece.

In 1962 Newman, his doctorate from Stanford University newly in hand, was hired as an assistant professor of philosophy at Knox College in Galesburg, Illinois. At the end of his second year there he was informed that his three-year contract would not be renewed; in other words, he was being fired. An excellent teacher already with a published book to his credit, the "problem" with Newman was that he had become a troublemaker. During his first semester at Knox, a student in one of his classes—a young, working-class woman from Chicago—was expelled for repeatedly violating the curfew, to which only women students were subject, and came to him for help. Newman, repelled by the hypocrisy of the college administration, was outspoken in her defense. It was his first political act of consequence. The student left Knox, but her expulsion became the catalyst for student-faculty protests that rocked the campus for the next two years. Newman remained at the center of the storm, choosing principle over prudence. In retrospect, he was taking the first steps on a road that, by the end of the decade, would lead him out of academia and into full-time community organizing.

Obviously, then, there are parallels between the playwright and the character of Professor Paul Heller, although they are far from exact. (Newman, for example, didn't wind up hospitalized.) The character of Holiday Hill is inspired by the "real life" student who came to him after she was expelled. The three mental patients—Hannah Cohen, Ted Little and Rylie Shall—are inventions. There was no mental hospital near Galesburg.

Yet these fictional psychotics are key to Newman's play. *Left of the Moon* deals with a central concern of Newman's—the relationship between emotionality and society. The activity of reorganizing that relationship is the crux of Newman's social therapy. In *Left of the Moon* he explores dramatically the beginnings of a period in U.S. history when society was in flux to such an extent that the norms of behavior and perception had begun to shift and the organization of both emotionality and society was being challenged.

Newman implies in *Left of the Moon* that in moments such as the 1960s (vital in his own development as a political and cultural activist), society goes mad. That social madness, although tremendously painful, is vital to continued human development. When the times are out of joint, new ways of seeing and being can move center stage.

Newman—perhaps the least polemical of political playwrights— explores all this not through agit-prop-type grand pronouncements or parable-like lessons in the Brechtian tradition, but by putting an odd mix of ordinary people together in a small town to converse about a small controversy at a small college. Newman's belief that conversation has the potential to be one of humankind's most developmental activities is perhaps demonstrated nowhere more clearly than in the unfolding conversations that make up *Left of the Moon*.

Although this play, like virtually all of Newman's work for the theatre, is far more conversational than action-driven, there is nonetheless more plot, in the conventional sense, here than in any other Newman play, with the possible exception of *Coming of Age in Korea*. Each of the characters in *Left of the Moon* makes an important decision and, as a result, changes the circumstances of her or his life. Moreover, the decision made by Professor Heller has an impact not only on his own life but on the lives of everyone else in the play. His student, Holiday Hill, is the play's catalytic character; by coming to Heller and asking him to practice in real life the ethics that he preaches in class, she sets in motion a series of events that impact on Heller, on Knox College, and, in a small but emblematic way, on American history.

Unlike many of Newman's plays, *Left of the Moon* has a linear plot. Yet this plot, far from overdetermining the structure of the play, is but one element in it. As in many Newman plays, the same story is told over and over again. In the case of *Left of the Moon* the story is told through the dramatic action onstage, through the Narrator, and, in the 1994 production under Newman's direction, through the play's opening video.

This and *Life Upon the Wicked Stage* are the only Newman plays to have narrators who function outside the internal action of the play and from that vantage point provide the audience with background and commentary on the action. (Madison Hemings in *Sally and Tom (The American Way)* serves a similar function, although by the end of the play he and the rest of the characters find themselves onstage together in history.) The Narrator in *Left of the*

Moon is very clearly an authorial voice speaking not in the dramatic mode but the narrative (epic) mode. "Dallas is 12 months away," the Narrator tells the audience, "yet the motorcade is already moving." She or he (the Narrator was played by a man in the 1994 production and by a woman in the 1996 production directed by Laurence Holder, both at Castillo) is, among other things, the voice of history talking not only *to* the audience but *with* the other elements of the production—the dramatic story line and the video.

With *Left of the Moon,* video takes on a new dimension in Newman's plays. Like virtually all elements in Newman's mature dramaturgy, video was there from the start. *Common Women* used film clips of the Black Panthers as part of its theatrical montage. In *Billie, Malcolm & Yusuf,* a video newscast interrupts the live action to report on an uprising on Earth, thus playing a vital role in the unfolding of the plot, and a fictional television broadcast was used in a similar manner to advance the plot in *Still on the Corner.* In *Dead as a Jew*—a 1992 production which interwove portions of *Mr. Hirsch, The Store* and *No Room for Zion*—Newman, as director, experimented with video as a performance element independent of the plot, running videos of professional wrestling throughout much of the play as a comment on and counterpoint to the stage action. He also put an entire scene of the play *No Room for Zion* on video. That same year Newman's production of Heiner Müller's *Explosion of a Memory (Description of a Picture)* made extensive use of video, including a tape of Müller reading the text in English from the rooftop of the Deutsches Theater in Berlin as part of the seven-hour performatory deconstruction process that *was* the play. In *Yes! We Have No Bananas and Other Contradictions in the Life of Ludwig Wittgenstein,* which later became the first act of the second version of *Outing Wittgenstein,* the Castillo Theatre was transformed into a mock television studio, complete with two cameramen and a TV director in the theatre. Two monitors hanging over the stage showed different shots of the live action taking place onstage. The use of a camera in the theatre to provide alternative shots of the live action was carried over into the 1994 production of *Outing Wittgenstein.* That production also featured video clips to introduce each of the characters who were supposed to be guests on the television show "This is Your Death." Mock television documentary footage was used to open and close Newman's 1994 production of Laurence Holder's *Red Channels,* a play set in the early 1950s.

By the early '90s Newman, using video in a wide variety of ways, had made it an integral feature of most of his productions. This extensive and rapidly developing use of video was the product of Newman's creative collaboration with Barry Z Levine, Castillo's talented resident videographer. Unlike most theatres, Castillo has a video production studio on the premises; it attracts a regular stream of student interns from Europe and throughout the United States. Two large video monitors hanging from the grid, facing the audience, have become a permanent fixture of Castillo's stage architecture. Newman does not use video (as Piscator and Brecht used film clips) to bring the world into the theatre; it is, instead, a means of bringing the theatre into the world. As Newman puts it, "Almost every room in America has a television set. How could Castillo not?"

With *Left of the Moon* video became, for the first time, more than background, commentary, or even a plot element, but central to the play's dramatic structure. The 1994 production began with a 15-minute video of the playwright talking about the incidents in his life that inspired the play. Thus the audience knew the whole story before the play began. The same story, transformed into drama, was then acted out onstage and also told/commented upon by the Narrator. *Left of the Moon,* in the original production, consists of three takes on the same characters, the same period, the same issues, the same conflicts. The dramatic tension is not within any one of these elements. (How much tension can there be if you already know the story and how it ends?) Instead, as in most of Newman's plays, the tension is among the different/same narratives. What is new in this production of *Left of the Moon* is that one of those versions is provided by the video. Thus *Left of the Moon* is the first of Newman's plays to bring together all the structural and technical elements that have come to define the mature Newman play.

D.F.

Left of the Moon was first produced at the Castillo Theatre (Fred Newman, artistic director; Gabrielle Kurlander, producing director; Diane Stiles, managing director) in New York City on November 4, 1994. The cast, in order of appearance, was as follows:

MAN PLAYING THE PIANO . . . . Dan Belmont
MAN SINGING IN CAFE . . . . Fred Newman
RYLIE SHALL. . . . . Alice Rydel
HANNAH COHEN. . . . . Maggie Zarillo-Gouldin
TED LITTLE . . . . Doug Miranda
GEOLOGY MAJOR . . . . Omar Ali
HOLIDAY HILL . . . . Gabrielle Kurlander
NARRATOR . . . . David Nackman
PROFESSOR PAUL HELLER . . . . Kenneth Hughes

Fred Newman, director; Diane Stiles, producer; Dan Belmont, piano; Fred Newman with Madelyn Chapman, choreography; Joseph Spirito, set design; Elena Borstein, Michael Mitchell and Joseph Spirito, scenic design; Charlotte, costume design; Jessica Massad and Beth Peeler, lighting design; Michael Klein, sound design; Barry Z Levine, video design/cinematography; Ellen Korner, production stage manager.

"East of the Sun (And West of the Moon)," written in 1934 by Brooks Bowman, is about as good an example of Great Depression music as there is. The marvelously haunting melody is joined with sappy lyrics. With almost half the country starving, Bowman says that we're "living on love and pale moonlight." By the 1960s, lyricists like Bob Dylan create fine poems to go with strident and eerie sounds. But though the product is perhaps aesthetically better, American culture in the '30s, '60s, as well as today, remains mysteriously distant from the real (historical) lives of the American people. Why? Because first and foremost, genteel American popular culture is entertainment. It is designed and produced to obscure the lives of our people; to cover up not only harsh realities but their underlying causes and reasons.

In our play, Hannah Cohen, Ted Little and Rylie Shall—all longtime inmates at the local mental asylum—create new words for "East of the Sun." Their song, "East of the Hump and Left of the Moon," is specific to a moment in their lives. Neither a message nor a palliative, it is, simply, their lives. *Left of the Moon* is a slice, a moment, of mine. It is not about madness. It is about *my* madness. It is meant to be neither genteel nor entertaining, but I do hope it speaks to you.

This play is dedicated to Nancy Green, whose creativity, hard work and profound decency have led Castillo's cultural work from the very beginning.

NOVEMBER 1994

CHARACTERS
(in order of appearance)

RYLIE SHALL

HANNAH COHEN

TED LITTLE

GEOLOGY MAJOR

HOLIDAY HILL

NARRATOR

PROFESSOR PAUL HELLER

Scene 1

The scene is a cafe some 10 miles out of Galesburg, Illinois, home of Knox College. It is the early 1960s. Country music plays on the jukebox. The cafe, called "The Moon Cafe," is inhabited at this late hour of the night mainly by a few local people, farmers, etc; a handful of students from Knox College (who are, in the case of the women anyway, in violation of dormitory curfew) and a few inmates from the state mental asylum a mile and a half away. (These patients are also in violation of the asylum's 10 p.m. curfew.) Seated at one table are three mental patients:

TED LITTLE, a Black man in his early fifties. He is a former janitor at Knox College who "went mad" when his wife committed suicide many years ago.

HANNAH COHEN, a 42-year-old Jewish woman originally from New York City. Her entire family had escaped the Holocaust by leaving Germany in the mid-1930s, only to be destroyed in a tenement fire in New York in 1943, while HANNAH was away at college at Knox. She "went mad" when she received the news and attempted to throw herself off the main building (the site of the fifth Lincoln-Douglas debate). The school institutionalized her and she has been a mental patient ever since.

RYLIE SHALL, a local farm girl who was sexually molested in a "famous incident" by a group of Galesburg toughs. She has been in and out of the asylum since then, some 12 years or so.

A piano player plays "East of the Sun (And West of the Moon)." The three mental patients are playing cards, speaking and drinking at their table when HOLIDAY, a far out, beatnik-type Knox student enters. They see her and become very excited.

RYLIE: (*Stands up, shouting somewhat weirdly*) Holiday. Holiday. Over here, Holiday. Come here. Sit here with us.

HANNAH: Yoo hoo, Holiday. Beautiful, beautiful, Holiday. Shaina Holiday. Sit here, Holiday. Rylie, it's Holiday.

TED: Come over here, Holiday, darlin'. Sit with us.

RYLIE: Holiday, come here. Sit here with your friends. *(Excited.)* Oh, Ted, it's Holiday. It's Holiday.

GEOLOGY MAJOR: *(Making a provocation of her name)* Yeah, Holiday, go sit with your "kooky" friends from the mental hospital.

HOLIDAY: *(Turns toward GEOLOGY MAJOR)* Fuck you, asshole.

GEOLOGY MAJOR: You're as fuckin' crazy as they are.

(HOLIDAY gives the finger to GEOLOGY MAJOR and crosses to sit at the table with TED, HANNAH and RYLIE.)

TED: That guy givin' you a hard time, Holiday?

HOLIDAY: Oh man, Ted, don't worry about him. He's a goddamned geology major from Peoria. The son of a bitch wants to spend his life fuckin' with rocks and he comes from a goddamned town that prides itself on throwin' out Black folks by sundown everyday and he says we're crazy. *(To GEOLOGY MAJOR)* Go fuck yourself, rockhead.

HANNAH: It's a Jewish holiday soon, Holiday. You're not Jewish, I know, but the holiday is. That's funny, Holiday, yes? That your name is Holiday, yes?

RYLIE: What Jewish holiday, Hannah?

HANNAH: I dunno. Maybe Simchas Torah or Succoth? I dunno. My mother knew all the Jewish holidays. But she's dead now. Everyone in my family is dead. They all burned in a fire. Do you remember, Holiday?

TED: Hannah! How could Holiday remember? That was over 20 years ago. We've only known Holiday for about a year or so. Are you crazy, Hannah? Stop actin' crazy.

RYLIE: Oh yeah, Ted. She's crazy. Remember, we're all crazy, Ted. We all live together in the mental asylum down the road and…

TED: Dammit, Rylie, I *know* that. I know that.

HOLIDAY: *(Calms them down caringly)* What you three been up to?

RYLIE: Ted's teaching us to play Hearts.

TED: *(Quietly, but somewhat defensively)* Just for match sticks, Holiday. Not for real money.

HANNAH: We don't have any real money.

HOLIDAY: Well, that's nice. What you three been doin' with yourselves?

HANNAH: I've been eating chocolates.

HOLIDAY: Where'd ya get chocolates, Hannah?

TED: I think she stole them.

RYLIE: She didn't steal them.

TED: How do you know she didn't steal them?

HANNAH: I didn't steal them.

RYLIE: I told ya, Ted.

HOLIDAY: Well, dearest Hannah, where'd ya get the chocolates?

HANNAH: Someone sent them to me in the mail. I got a package.

TED: Who sent you a package? You never get mail. You have no family, no friends, except us.

RYLIE: Maybe *my* sister sent them to Hannah. She really likes her.

HANNAH: Yeah. It was from Rylie's sister, Stella. There was a note.

TED: Well, why in the hell didn't you say so, Hannah?

RYLIE: Ya never gave her much of a chance, Ted.

TED: Whattya mean? (*He turns his head away annoyed.*) Jeez, you two are nuts.

RYLIE: We're all nuts, Ted, remember? We live in the asylum…

TED: (*Interrupting and even more annoyed*) Dammit, Rylie. I know we do. But stop sayin' it. You know we're not supposed to be here this time a night. Be cool, Rylie, dammit, be cool. Don't be such a damn hick.

HOLIDAY: Now c'mon, you three. Stop arguin' so much. You're the very best of friends. Stop this silly fightin'. Okay?

TED: Okay, Holiday, okay. How are you doin', darlin'?

HANNAH: Why do you call her "darlin'," Ted? Holiday's not your darlin'.

HOLIDAY: Oh, I don't mind, Hannah. *(Then jokingly)* Besides, how d'y'all know that I ain't Ted's darlin'? *(She playfully touches* TED's *head. He's embarrassed.)*

RYLIE: Well, Holiday, he's old and he's Black…and he's crazy like me and Hannah…

HOLIDAY: Shit, Rylie. None of that bothers me. Black and old and crazy's as good as anything else, darlin', don't ya think?

(RYLIE nods.)

HANNAH: At least he's not Jewish, Holiday. I'm Jewish. My whole family died in the Holocaust.

TED: No they didn't, Hannah. They died in a fire in New York City. Where did they live, on Rivington Street? In a tenement on Rivington.

HANNAH: Yeah, Ted. You're right. It was a fire. *(She looks sad.)*

RYLIE: *(Comforts HANNAH)* It's alright, darlin'. It's alright. Maybe Stella sent you the chocolates for the Jewish holiday. I mean Stella's a Methodist, but she knows about all religions. Stella's very smart.

TED: Can I please find out how Holiday's doin? How's old Knox College… my alma mater?

HANNAH: You didn't go to Knox College, Ted. I went there, but you didn't.

TED: Well, I worked there as a janitor for 15 years, darlin'. That makes it my alma mater. Now do you mind if Miss Holiday speaks?

HOLIDAY: Oh, Ted, everything's fine. Takin' a course with this new philosophy teacher named Professor Heller. Seems like a nice guy. We're studyin' about Plato. Y'all know Plato? He's this Greek dude. Lived over in Athens a long time ago.

RYLIE: I heard of him. There was a guy at the asylum a while ago, said *he* was Plato. He wore a white sheet and he asked everyone a lot of questions. I remember him. You remember him, Ted?

HANNAH: He said he was Moses, too. And Christ. He talked a lot. Remember?

TED: I remember the son of a bitch. He stole my goddamn keys. Crazy son of a bitch.

(*RYLIE, HANNAH, TED and HOLIDAY freeze.*)

NARRATOR: Welcome to our play tonight. Its opening scene is set in 1962 in a small roadside cafe called "The Moon Cafe" about 10 miles outside of Galesburg, Illinois. Galesburg, back in the early '60s, was a small city of about 36,000 people. When the "welcome wagon" came around to greet folks who just moved into town in those days, they told you that Galesburg was famous for having the world's largest "railroad hump." What's a railroad hump? Well, a railroad hump is what they used to use to uncouple and re-couple trains—it's kind of a man-made hill—and Galesburg, being about 170 miles due west of Chicago, was where they "re-did" the Southern Pacific trains going west and coming in from the west. Locals back in '62 used to say, proudly, that they were probably way up on the Soviet's atomic bomb hit list because of "the hump." The country around Galesburg is mainly farmland and Galesburg is the local urban center…the home of Montgomery Ward, Sears Roebuck… and Knox College, once a denominational school, but by '62, a non-sectarian, non-denominational college. About 2,000 students. Let's see, what else can I tell ya. Oh yeah. Knox College, more specifically, the steps of the main building, was the site of the fifth Lincoln-Douglas debate. And Galesburg, before the Civil War, was a stop on the Underground Railroad which, as I'm sure you all know, was an escape route for Southern slaves who wanted to come north or go all the way to Canada. The town of Galesburg and Knox College had an abolition-ist-fundamentalist-liberal history.

(*A spotlight on* TED. *He gets up and walks, somewhat mindlessly, up the aisle as the* NARRATOR *continues.*)

That's Ted Little. Galesburg had a small Black population—mainly descendants of escaped slaves who stayed on. Many worked for the local Admiral TV factory. Ted was a janitor at Knox College. Then about 15 or so years ago, Ted's childhood sweetheart who became his wife, Ellie Little…she killed herself. Outta nowhere. Just a short time after the war…she cut her veins open one day with one of Ted's razors and bled to death. Ted discovered her when he got home from work at the college. He lay down right next to her for three days before anyone found them. Then for almost two years he sat outside their old house on Poplar Avenue staring off into space. They put him into the asylum about 12 miles outside of Galesburg—Western Illinois State Mental Hospital. He's been there ever since.

(By this time TED has returned to his seat and his freeze. Spotlight comes up on HANNAH, who stands and walks up the aisle.)

That's Hannah Cohen. She's an inmate at Western Illinois also. Hannah was a student at Knox in 1943. Her extended family—her mom and dad, brothers, a sister, Grandma Hinda and cousins—had escaped the Holocaust by somehow getting out of Germany in 1935. They settled in New York City's Lower East Side. In October 1943— during the war—they were all killed, 11 of them, in a tenement fire. When Hannah got the news she began to scream and never stopped except when she slept, for over a year. She had no place to go. The college institutionalized her at Western Illinois. Almost 20 years later, Hannah sometimes still speaks of going back to Knox to get her degree.

(HANNAH has returned to her seat and freeze. Spotlight comes up on RYLIE, who stands for her walk up the aisle.)

That's Rylie Shall. R-Y-L-I-E, Rylie. Rylie Shall. Everyone around Galesburg knows about Rylie. She's a local girl...a farmer's daughter. When she was about 15...right at the end of the war...she came into town one Saturday—into Galesburg—to buy a new dress. She went over by Third Street to browse in the record stores and three "toughs" grabbed her, pushed her down the alley-way by the barber shop and raped her. They ripped off all her clothes, tied a rope around her belly and made her walk stark naked down Main Street till the cops came and then they ran off. They were never indicted. Rylie went catatonic for almost a decade. Last several years she's learned to talk again. She's lived at Western Illinois since her mom died about 12 years ago.

(RYLIE has returned to her seat and freeze. Spotlight comes up on HOLIDAY. She walks up the aisle.)

That's Holiday Hill. She's a junior at Knox. From a working-class family in South Chicago. Kind of a beatnik turning into a hippie. Comes to

"The Moon" almost every night. Says it's the only place she can study. Hates the dormitories, but it's the rules that you have to live there. It's also a Knox College rule that women—not men—have to be back there by curfew—11 p.m. weekdays, 1 a.m. on Saturday. But Holiday always breaks that one. Her "rep" is that she's "loose." Whatever that means. Maybe so. Anyway, the few mental patients from Western Illinois who sneak over to "The Moon" late at night love Holiday. She spends a lot of time talkin' with 'em. That's Holiday Hill. She kinda cares about people.

(*HOLIDAY goes back into a freeze, then the scene continues.*)

HANNAH: I'm gonna come back to Knox someday, Holiday, and finish my degree. You know, I used to go to college at Knox, Holiday. You know that, don't ya?

HOLIDAY: Oh, sure, Hannah. We've talked about that. You should do it.

RYLIE: Hannah's Jewish and from New York City. She's very smart. But they killed all those Jews in Germany. Wasn't *that* crazy, Holiday? I think *that* was crazy.

TED: That was fascism, Rylie. Like they killed millions of Black folks, too. That's fascism…(*his eyes wander*)…and my Ellie, my darling Ellie, she killed herself. She lay there and the blood flowed out of her. My darlin' Ellie. She left me all alone in this ugly, ugly world.

HOLIDAY: (*Reaches for TED's hand*) Why, Ted? Why did she do it?

TED: Oh, Holiday. The world was just too ugly for her. Ellie was too beautiful for such an ugly world. That's what happens, Holiday. Only the ugly keep on livin' in such an ugly world. That's why I worry about you, Holiday. You're too beautiful for such an ugly world. Like my Ellie. Too beautiful, darlin'. Too beautiful, Holiday.

HANNAH: When my folks burnt to death I screamed. I screamed for a very long time. I screamed…I screamed…until they took me out of this ugly world. I screamed…I…a…I…a…I…thought I would…a…I thought I would scream…forever. Ya know, I wanted to scream…forever. My family…my Jewish family was burnt alive.

RYLIE: I couldn't talk...after they ripped off my clothes and made me walk
like an animal. I could never speak again, Holiday. Do you understand?
I'm not smart like Hannah or a strong Black man like Ted or beautiful,
Holiday, like you. No. I was just a farm girl. And they ripped off all my
clothes and made me walk naked up Main Street in Galesburg...by the
Sears Roebuck store. I am dumb, Holiday, I could not speak. Just a
dumb farm girl. A dumb farm girl, Holiday. I just wanted to look at
some new records. And they beat me up. Why, Holiday? Why?

HOLIDAY: I dunno, Rylie. I dunno.

Scene 2

*The Knox College campus, near the "Gizmo," a campus coffee shop. The sound
of Petula Clark singing "Downtown" comes from within. Professor PAUL
HELLER stands reading Plato's* Republic. *HOLIDAY walks hesitantly toward him.
A freeze.*

NARRATOR: It's about one month later. Early November 1962. That's the
Knox College campus you're looking at. The gray-haired guy over there
reading is Professor Paul Heller. Remember him? He's Holiday's philosophy teacher. He's reading Plato's *Republic* in preparation for his
lecture next hour on Greek political philosophy. He's standing outside
the campus coffee shop—a place called The Gizmo. That's Petula
Clark—remember her?—singing "Downtown." Kennedy is president.
There's a crisis in Cuba. But the country lives for a moment in a strange
hiatus. The '50s are dead. Nixon was defeated in 1960. It is not
Camelot. It is not the profound change of John Kennedy's Peace Corps
rhetoric or Jackie Kennedy's pillbox style. Still there is a sense of
dreaminess in the air: a sense of anticipation. Something will happen.
The dream turns out to be a nightmare. But America doesn't quite
know that yet. Kennedy will be dead in a year. Dallas is 12 months
away, yet the motorcade is already moving. Knox has a basketball game
at home tonight against Grinnell College. The basketball team's star is
a local kid named Otie Little: a Black sophomore, one of only five
African Americans enrolled at Knox. Otie is Ted Little's nephew. But
Ted, once a great sports fan, won't be at the game tonight. Somehow,
coming to the Knox campus makes him crazy. It's a sunny fall day, ordi-

nary in its sounds and colors. It's the Midwest in the middle of our century waiting for the end to begin.

(*HOLIDAY and HELLER break the freeze.*)

HOLIDAY: Professor Heller…excuse me…I don't mean to interrupt your reading, but…it's important…if I could just speak with you for a moment.

HELLER: Oh no…no problem. Not at all. You're Miss…uh…Let's see… Miss Hill. Yes. You're in my Greek philosophy class. Yes. Back row… far right. I mean as I face you…ya know. Let's sit down…and talk. What can I do for you, Miss Hill? What's your first name? It's unusual, isn't it?

HOLIDAY: It's Holiday. Yeah…it's sort of unusual. Holiday Hill. Thank you, Professor Heller. I appreciate you takin' the time.

HELLER: No problem. No problem at all. What's up?

HOLIDAY: Well…Professor Heller…I've been…uh…I've been…thrown out of school. I just met with the Dean of Women and she told me I've been permanently…whatever you call it…thrown out.

HELLER: Well, that's terrible, Miss Hill. That's upsetting. What happened? I mean, what did you do? Is there an appeal possible? I mean…what exactly happened?

HOLIDAY: I've consistently violated the dormitory curfew. I've been warned again and again. But…uh…well, I just kept stayin' out after hours and …well…finally the Dean called me in and said the student-faculty committee on morals had decided to expel me without appeal.

HELLER: What are these dormitory curfews? I mean I've only been here a couple of months. I don't know these rules, ya know. I mean I taught for 10 years before I came here at NYU—New York University. It's a big urban school. There are no dorm hours as far as I know. I mean the school's in the middle of Greenwich Village. What's this business with curfews?

HOLIDAY: All the women have to live in dorms—unless you're married. And there are curfews: 11 p.m. on weekdays, 1 a.m. on Saturday. I think it's

real stupid. And men have no curfews even if they live in the dorm…
and they don't have to. It's a bunch of bullshit if ya ask me. Anyway,
they threw my ass out…pardon my language, Professor Heller.

HELLER: Ah…no problem, Miss Hill. Don't worry about your language.

HOLIDAY: Call me Holiday, Professor Heller. Please call me Holiday.
Everybody does.

HELLER: Look…uh…Miss Hill…uh…Holiday. This doesn't seem quite
right to me. I mean…I dunno much about these matters. You know,
I'm new and I know nothing about Knox College tradition and regulations…but this doesn't seem quite right.

HOLIDAY: Would ya speak to somebody? I mean can ya do anything, Professor Heller? I'd really appreciate it.

HELLER: Well…I dunno. I don't like getting involved, you know. I'm so new
here. I'm just an untenured associate professor of philosophy, Holiday.
I dunno.

HOLIDAY: Don't you teach Ethics? Don't you teach about morality? I don't
mean to be nasty or a wise-ass. But, Professor Heller, this is gonna
really hurt my mom and dad. They've worked their asses off so I could
come to this damn school. Maybe you could do something.

HELLER: Well…uh…listen…I hear what you're saying and…uh…you're
right. I mean…listen…I do take what I teach…and, yes, I do teach
morality…seriously. It's not just…ya know…some abstract stuff to me.
It's about truth and morality. Yeah…hey listen, you're really right, Miss
Hill…uh, Holiday. I'm gonna talk to someone. I'll see what I can do. Hey
…look…we'll do something. I can't imagine that nothing can be done.

HOLIDAY: Thank you, Professor Heller. (*She begins to cry. He reaches over
and touches her gently on the arm.*)

HELLER: Hey listen…don't be upset. Tell me about it…tell me about yourself…yeah, tell me about yourself.

HOLIDAY: Don't you have your Greek philosophy class now? Shouldn't you
be getting over to the classroom?

HELLER: I'll miss it today. Or we'll do it here. (*He smiles.*) I'll talk with you about morality…about this foolish business. Yeah. Okay? That's what we'll do. Okay? Don't be so upset. It's gonna work out, Holiday. It's gonna work out.

(*Freeze.*)

NARRATOR: Professor Heller, of course, was completely wrong. It didn't work out for Holiday Hill. Knox College's morals committee made mincemeat of Plato and his spokesperson Professor Paul Heller. Holiday's suspension was upheld. Yet it was a strange time—the barest beginnings of the '60s. And if nothing was *really* ever going to change, some people's lives at least were profoundly affected by the *illusion* that something could change. To be sure many people were looking to get out of lives that they were trapped in. The '60s gave them permission to leave. Holiday Hill was Paul Heller's ticket to a new life. Three weeks later on the Knox campus—just before the 1962 Thanksgiving break.

(*HELLER and HOLIDAY break the freeze.*)

HOLIDAY: (*Agitated*) It's over, Paul. There's no other appeal. You've done everything…everything. If you do more they'll "expel" you—they'll fire your ass. And what good would that do?

HELLER: I just can't accept that. The administration has been…well, they've been unbelievably arrogant and self-righteous and insensitive. I can't stop, Holiday. I'm gonna push it all the way, Holiday. I don't know what to do. But I must go on.

HOLIDAY: What does your wife Ruth say?

HELLER: Ruth says what she always says. She says I'm crazy. She says we didn't come out here to Galesburg, Illinois…to Knox College to have a no-win political fight with self-righteous, pious Midwestern liberals. And she's right. Ruth's always right. She says lots of the students will support me loudly and that some of the younger faculty will stand with me for a while. But she says they'll all bail out down the road and in the end I'll be the one that's fired. And she's right. I know she is. But I can't stop, Holiday. I know it's madness. But I know I'm mad.

HOLIDAY: Paul, I can't be responsible for this.

HELLER: You're not. No one's responsible, Holiday. I'm a madman. I'm crazy. But I can't keep taking librium and sleeping pills. I can't keep spending my life at once afraid that I will die any moment and wanting to die every day. If I am mad then I must be mad. Jesus, Holiday, let the madness mean something. Let my insane life mean something. My wife is right. I am crazy. But that is precisely who I am. So I will continue this insane fight—not for you and not because we can win and not for some political principle. I will continue because I am mad.

HOLIDAY: Will you come with me to "The Moon" tonight, Paul? I want you to meet my friends before I leave. Before I go home. Please come with me tonight. Come with me to "The Moon."

("East of the Sun" is heard on piano.)

Scene 3

Back in the "The Moon Cafe." HELLER, HOLIDAY, TED, HANNAH and RYLIE are all seated together at a table. They are speaking with each other animatedly as the lights come up but they are not yet audible. The GEOLOGY MAJOR is also in the cafe.

NARRATOR: The back roads of America's Midwest—the state and U.S. roadways that haven't been turned into super-highways—are dotted with roadside cafes. Often old wood-framed two-stories, these drinking and eating places are not particularly oriented towards the traveler, but function as "spots" where varied locals come together to socialize late at night or on weekends. Often they bear no name, simply a sign that says "Bar" or "Cafe" or "Eat." Many travelers who do wind up on these "back roads" view the cafe with some apprehension, concerned about getting too close to "crazy locals."

GEOLOGY MAJOR: Hanging out with your kooky friends again, Holiday?

NARRATOR: In fact they are typically very peaceful places. They are a kind of public surrogate living room and though someone might get a little out of hand once in a while like the rockhead Knox student who harassed Holiday at "The Moon," nothing more than that usually happens and remarkably diverse local groupings hang out at relative ease. At "The

Moon" farmers, factory workers, mental patients, Knox students all manage to overcome "town-gown" antagonisms. "The Moon" is about 12 miles northeast out of Galesburg on the way to Galva on Illinois Route 27, an old two-laner. It's just about a mile and a half away from Western Illinois State Mental Hospital—walking distance. Why is it called "The Moon"? No one knows for sure. Some say it came from the asylum. You know, "lunacy" and all that. The two establishments—the asylum and the cafe—opened around the same time—back in the late '30s. Others say it came from what has long been the region's favorite card game—Hearts—from the game's expression "shoot the moon." Still others say it derives from a long tradition of amateur piano players at the cafe who liked to play and sing the old song "East of the Sun (And West of the Moon)." No one quite knows. But it's been "The Moon" for as long as most anyone around here can remember.

HANNAH: *(Singing aloud)* "East of the Hump and Left of the Moon…"

TED: No, no, no, Hannah, darlin'. That's "*West* of the Moon"…The song goes "East of the *Sun* and *West* of the Moon…"

RYLIE: Maybe Hannah is singing a different song.

HOLIDAY: I like it. Yeah. I like it. "East of the *Hump* and *Left* of the Moon…" What do you think, Paul? Are we the left of the moon or what?

HELLER: We're certainly crazy enough.

RYLIE: You teach Greek philosophy, Professor Heller?

HELLER: Please, Rylie, call me Paul. Paul Heller. That's my name. Please call me Paul.

RYLIE: Did Plato have a last name?

HELLER: Now, no one ever asked me that before, Rylie.

TED: Well, did he?

HELLER: No. He didn't. He's just Plato…and Socrates is just Socrates and Aristotle is just Aristotle. No last names. None that I know of.

HANNAH: Moses, too…and Abraham. I mean God has no last name either.

HOLIDAY: Everyone just calls me Holiday.

TED: Names are kinda funny altogether. Ellie used to say that.

HOLIDAY: Actually, words are kinda funny. Don't you think?

RYLIE: They are funny. Very funny. And I don't know very many.

HANNAH: Are you gonna be fired, Professor Heller…I mean…Paul?

HELLER: I think so, Hannah. I think so.

TED: I mean why? What in the hell did you do? All ya did was to try and get Holiday reinstated. What's so bad about that? Jesus. I told Holiday she was gonna get hurt. Now you're gonna get fired. It's ugly, Mr. Heller. It's too damned ugly.

HELLER: Yes, it's very ugly and it's very crazy, Ted.

RYLIE: They say we're all crazy. "Crazy" is a funny word, Professor Heller… I mean, Paul.

HELLER: It's a funny word, Rylie…a funny word.

HANNAH: Are you crazy, Paul?

TED: Don't ask Heller that.

HELLER: Why not, Ted? Yes. I'm crazy, Hannah. I think I'm quite crazy.

HOLIDAY: But he's a good person…a very good person. Like all of you. A very good human being.

RYLIE: Are all crazy people good, Holiday?

HOLIDAY: No way, Rylie. No way.

TED: But I think all good people are crazy. At least these days.

HELLER: Well put, Ted…well put.

HANNAH: Are you a socialist, Paul? A communist? Are you a leftist? My father was a communist.

HELLER: I dunno, Hannah. I dunno. Maybe just a little "left of the moon." More mad than progressive. More insane than insightful. More crazy than commie. But yes, Hannah, "left of the moon." I would say so.

RYLIE: Holiday, what will you do when you go home?

HANNAH: Yeah, Holiday, will you write to us?

HOLIDAY: I'll send you all chocolates. How about that?

TED: But what will you do, Holiday?

HOLIDAY: I'll get a job. When I was in high school I worked in a beauty parlor. I can probably get that job back.

HELLER: Holiday, you've got to find another college so you can finish your degree.

RYLIE: Yeah, Holiday. The professor is right.

HOLIDAY: Maybe next year. We'll see.

RYLIE: Are you very sad, Holiday?

HOLIDAY: I'll miss you all.

RYLIE: When will you come to see us?

HOLIDAY: Oh, I dunno. In a while…Listen, Paul, a lot of students are talkin' about you giving the senior convocation address next May.

RYLIE: What's that, Holiday? What's that? What's a "con-vo-cation"? That's a funny word.

HOLIDAY: Well, the college has four or five cap and gown events each year. Y'know faculty gets all dressed up in these formal outfits and everyone has to go…They hold 'em at the gym. Different people give speeches …like addresses at them. One of 'em is called the Senior Convocation. The senior class selects the speaker for that one. It's usually a stodgy old favorite-type professor. But I've heard lots of kids talkin' about you, Paul. That would be great. It's in May. I'd come back for that. I'll tell ya. I'd wanna be there for that one.

HANNAH: Could we come, Holiday?

HOLIDAY: I don't see why not. I think it's open to people from the community. And even if it isn't I could get y'all an invite from the senior class board. I bet I could.

TED: I ain't been back at Knox since Ellie died. Not since I left there at 5 o'clock that Thursday and found her at home dead. Ain't been on the campus since then. Ain't seen Otie play ball. Ain't seen nothin' at Knox since my Ellie died…since my Ellie bled to death.

HANNAH: I ain't been at Knox since my family burnt up. I ran screaming to the roof of the main building. All the students circled the building… remember, where Lincoln and Douglas had debated…and looked up at me. And I screamed louder and louder. I ain't been there since, Holiday.

RYLIE: I ain't been into Galesburg since they raped me…since the boys stripped me and walked me down Main. I ain't stepped foot in Galesburg at all since that day. I used to go to Knox before that and sit on the front lawn and read poems…like I was a student or something. But not since they ripped my clothes off. I ain't even been in Galesburg since then.

HELLER: If I speak…if the senior class asks me to speak—I would love to have you there…in the front row…with me. Us crazy people need to stick together. And when I finish speaking I want you all up on the stage so we can sing "East of the *Hump* and *Left* of the Moon" together. Okay? Will you do it for me and for Holiday?

Scene 4

It's Senior Convocation Day at Knox College. The faculty in cap and gown at the gym are painted on a backdrop. In the front row of the audience are TED, RYLIE *and* HANNAH. *The* GEOLOGY MAJOR *is also in the audience.* HOLIDAY *is at a rostrum, stage right;* HELLER *sits stage left in cap and gown. Freeze.*

NARRATOR: It's May 1963. Knox College Senior Convocation Day. Professor Paul Heller has been fired. He will not return to Knox in the fall. His wife, Ruth Heller, left Paul in early March, returning to New York City with their two children. In April, Paul suffered what was called "a slight nervous breakdown." He was hospitalized for eight days at St. Mary's Hospital in Galesburg. The Holiday Hill incident triggered a small movement at Knox and about 30 other Midwestern colleges in opposition to dormitory hours and other discriminatory regulations against women. It received some national press coverage. Paul *was* selected by the senior class to deliver the address at today's convocation. Several key members of the administration including the President, Dean of Faculty, Dean of Students, Dean of Women and others have made plain that they will boycott today's event. Paul has spoken to Holiday by phone a few times since she left. They spoke last about two weeks ago when she received the invitation to introduce him at the convocation. Paul has been out to "The Moon" a dozen times since November. Ted Little, Hannah Cohen and Rylie Shall continue to live at the state mental hospital and regularly visit "The Moon." In about six months, John F. Kennedy will be shot dead in Dallas by Lee Harvey Oswald. Lyndon Johnson will escalate the Vietnam War and the '60s will begin in earnest. That full-blown attempt to change American society will, of course, fail. Nixon will return; be forced to resign in disgrace, but Ronald Reagan will be in the wings waiting to bring America back to its senses; to make America sane again. It is May 1963. All this has yet to happen. But somehow on this ordinary day in this very ordinary Midwestern town the failure that is the '60s is already known, is already felt. For no one has figured out how to mobilize the madness that inevitably accompanies genuine progressivism in our American culture. Certainly not Professor of Greek Philosophy Paul Heller.

(*HOLIDAY breaks freeze.*)

HOLIDAY: Professor Paul Heller got himself thrown out of this place in one year. I'm impressed—it took me three years. Now, I'm real proud of the Knox College students and the seniors in particular who had the guts to break with bullshit tradition and challenge some heavyweight powers-that-be around this place and select Paul Heller as your speaker here today. You all know that Professor Heller went to bat for me when I was expelled last fall for breaking curfew…on a regular basis. And what he found out was that a lot of people around here weren't practicing what he was trying to teach in his philosophy classes. And that pissed Paul Heller off. Now Paul Heller is no angry young man. He's a damned scholar and a good teacher. (*Aside.*) And he's not so young. But he's no political radical. He never claimed to be. And I might as well say it right now. He never laid a hand on me. This isn't about sex. A lot of these pompous administrators who are boycotting today's convocation have been hanky-pankying it up with co-eds—including me—for a long time.

But not Paul Heller. We never had no sex. Even though we kinda dig each other. A lot of people think I was out gettin' laid late at night when I broke curfew. Actually most of the time I was at "The Moon Cafe" doing my homework and hangin' out with my friends Ted Little, Rylie Shall and Hannah Cohen. They're right down here in the front row. No. Paul Heller never laid a hand on me. That's how crazy the son of a bitch is. Like he once said about himself, he's "more crazy than commie." I don't know what all of this stuff means on a grander scale. I know I'm workin' in Sally's Beauty Parlor in South Chicago. I know Heller's got no job and no wife and he spent a week or so crazy as a bedbug over at St. Mary's a couple of months ago. And I know Rylie got raped and Hannah's family got burned to death, and Ted's wife, Ellie, bled to death. I know all that. But I don't know what any of it means—if it means anything at all. But I know that Paul Heller is a decent guy, and I know the president of this school is a prick who fucked me in his office when I was a *17-year-old sophomore*. I dunno know what it all means, but ya can tell some differences. I had a dream the other night. In it John F. Kennedy had his head blown off and Jackie was spread-eagled across the back of their limo screaming for the FBI. I hope it's just a dream. But what happened to Rylie and Hannah and Ted and Paul wasn't no dream. There's a big rally comin' up in Washington, D.C. this August— a civil rights rally. Dr. King's gonna talk. I think I'll go. I'm not sure why. Maybe Paul Heller will meet me there and we'll rent a cheap motel room and we'll fuck like crazy. Maybe not. Anyway, he's a good dude. Here's Paul Heller.

GEOLOGY MAJOR: Right on, Holiday!

(Loud applause as HELLER approaches the rostrum.)

HELLER: *(He looks long and hard at HOLIDAY; embraces her. She sits.)* I'm no great public orator like Socrates is said to have been. Some people might say that I've corrupted the minds and morals of the youth like the old Athenian did. But nothing could be further from the truth. Actually you all have corrupted my mind and my morals…and I cannot thank you enough for it. I am, no doubt, a madman. And Dostoevsky and other literary geniuses notwithstanding, there is nothing the least bit glorious in being mad. Ask Rylie Shall and Hannah Cohen and Ted Little, my dear friends. For *madness,* whatever its genetic, biochemical or early childhood causes may be, is, as well, a decision to withdraw from the utter ugliness that is life in our rather sick culture. And that withdrawal is terribly painful. What I have learned from all of you, and most particularly Holiday, is that if mad I am then mad I must be. And mad I am. I am a teacher with a Ph.D. in philosophy. A student, a scholar who reads the philosophical fragments of Parmenides and Heraclitus The Obscure in the original ancient Greek. I am well-versed in the use of language if not so skilled in oration. But, as my friends at "The Moon" have taught me, language is funny. And as you students are fond of quipping, "not funny ha-ha but funny peculiar." It has been observed that a peculiar feature of our language is that we use the same language to tell the truth as we do to lie. Language can express who and how we are and it can obscure who and how we are. Language can expose the madman and it can hide him. I am a philosopher; a professor. I always appeared sane enough if, perhaps, a bit esoteric. Why? In part, because my language convinced the world. My pain, my torture, my insanity, all hidden behind language. Then Holiday said, "I don't wanna be a wise-ass, but don't you teach morality?" And somehow I could no longer hide my madness. And Rylie and Hannah and Ted exposed their madness to me; their clear, unembarrassed decision to withdraw from so ugly a world and I could no longer hide my madness. So now I invite them to join me here onstage before you. Please, Rylie, Hannah, Ted…come up here with me.

(They come up to the rostrum.)

RYLIE: We're gonna sing a song we wrote. It's like different words for that old song…you might know it…the one "East of the Sun and West of the Moon." Well…this was Hannah's idea originally…we wrote something called "East of the *Hump* and *Left* of the Moon." It sounds a little bit the same…but it's really different. Anyway, here it is.

(RYLIE hands pieces of paper to TED, HANNAH and HELLER.)

HANNAH: This song is dedicated to Holiday Hill.

TED: And my darlin' Ellie.

RYLIE: And all the poor farm girls.

HANNAH: And my family that got killed in the fire.

(They sing, raucously, almost as if they were drunk.)

East of the "hump"
And left of "The Moon,"
We're all leavin' Galesburg
And not a moment too soon.
Everyone says we're mad
As if that was somethin' bad
But we had a little life together
Doin' a play
With our darlin' Holiday.

East of the "hump"
And left of "The Moon,"
You might not get these words
But it's a mighty nice tune.
Professor Heller's a helluva guy
But now it's time to say goodbye.
East of the "hump"
and left of "The Moon."
East of the "hump"
and left of "The Moon."

(They all laugh wildly and "moon" the faculty. Freeze.)

NARRATOR: Rylie Shall wrote those words; her only poem. She died two
years later when she was hit by a truck in downtown Chicago where she
had moved when she left the mental hospital.

Hannah Cohen returned to New York City in 1965, went back to
school at CCNY and joined Youth Against War and Fascism.

Ted Little went with Holiday to the 1963 March on Washington and there
joined the Southern Christian Leadership Conference (SCLC).

Holiday Hill works to this day as a hairdresser in South Chicago.

Professor Paul Heller has effectively disappeared from the face of the
Earth. Some people claim they have heard him on radio voiceovers.

And, in what might be the most encouraging indicator of the potential for human change, I am told that the "welcome wagon" in Galesburg no longer speaks of their "railroad hump." The message of our play? Well…

(*NARRATOR sings.*)

East of the "hump"
And left of "The Moon"…

(*NARRATOR continues singing the melody as the words become gibberish.*)

))》

The Store:
One Block East of Jerome

Although the current version of *The Store: One Block East of Jerome* was not written and performed until 1995, its story and its lead character, Carmela Petrelli, have deep roots in Newman's life and art.

Carmela first appeared in a short story (also named "The Store: One Block East of Jerome") which Newman wrote in 1957 as an undergraduate. She reappeared in "Mr. Hirsch, The Whore and Mr. Wittgenstein All Died Yesterday," a story by Newman published in 1966 in *Promethean,* a literary magazine of the City College of New York, where Newman was a professor of philosophy at the time. It is quite a remarkable piece, one that has been out of print for over 30 years. Like much of Newman's literary work, it is hard to classify—part fiction, part memoir, part philosophical discourse.

"Mr. Hirsch, The Whore and Mr. Wittgenstein All Died Yesterday" contains the seeds of no less than four future Newman plays. It is where the candy store owners Hirsch and Hoffman, later brought to the stage in Newman's 1986 play *Mr. Hirsch Died Yesterday,* first appear in print. The "whore" of the title is Carmela, and while the details differ somewhat, the essence of her narrative remains unchanged in the nearly three decades between published story and performed play. The *Promethean* piece also makes reference to Newman's dismissal from Knox College in 1963, an event that was the inspiration for *Left of the Moon.* And it contains an extensive discussion of Ludwig Wittgenstein, the brilliant philosopher around whom Newman's farce *Outing Wittgenstein* centers.

The character of Carmela is a composite of a number of young women Newman knew growing up in the Bronx in the 1940s and early '50s. Carmela first appeared onstage at the Castillo Theatre in 1991 in the first production of *The Store: One Block East of Jerome,* which grew out of discussions and improvisations with a group of Castillo artists/activists, including Madelyn Chapman, Nancy Green and Diane Stiles. This early version of the play consisted of three stories told by three women drinking in a bar, one of whom was Carmela (played in the 1991 production by Janet Weigel). The other two characters were Dawn, an African American woman with a retarded child, and Paula, a former waitress and aspiring artist, who at the end of the play, as a way of being giving to Carmela, strips for her. Carmela appears again onstage in *Dead as a Jew (Zion's Community)*, a transitional work by Newman which includes within it versions of *Mr. Hirsch, The Store* (now minus Dawn and Paula) and *No Room for Zion* (produced at Castillo under Newman's direction in 1989). In the 1995 version included here, Paula re-emerges as the feminist scholar Professor Paula Brownell.

Not only has Carmela long been an important part of Newman's life and art, but the questions Carmela's story raises about the organization of sexuality in our society have been of central concern in Newman's personal, political and therapeutic work. The productions of *The Store* at Castillo have been among the theatre's most controversial. It's not simply that the play contains nudity. It's that *The Store* ruthlessly examines nudity itself—how and for whom and under what conditions women take their clothes off.

Newman, of course, is not alone in this concern. Over the last two decades a number of women performance artists have used their bodies (mostly through solo performance) to challenge the "male gaze"; that is, the male-imposed objectification of the female body and the violence against and humiliation of women that are an integral part of our society. Their primary approach—pioneered by Carolee Schneemann in the 1960s—is to expose the male gaze by using the grotesque to rip through the veils of romanticism which obscure the oppression of women.

Newman takes a different approach. For Newman the male gaze is difficult to challenge precisely because it is so insidious and ordinary; it is projected in virtually every billboard, magazine cover, television commercial, movie, and love song—not to mention every sexual relation, inside marriage and out. We have all (male or female, gay or straight) been organized by this male-determined way of seeing. Newman starts from where people *are* (not where they "should" be, or where he would like them to be) and then works to create a performatory experience that radically challenges their assumptions. Thus in *The Store,* the male gaze is, in the beginning, assumed; everyone in the audience wants Carmela to strip, even as that wanting makes us uncomfortable and/or furious. Rather than using the alienated and grotesque to critique the male gaze, Newman (here, as in virtually all of his work) uses the banal and ordinary—and then explodes them.

Nor does Newman leave the audience (and reader) with exposé or critique alone. There is the hint, at least, of a possible reconstruction of our sexual attitudes. As Carmela tells her story it becomes obvious that she cannot change; society's prevailing sexual hypocrisy has destroyed her capacity to develop. She is able, however, through her narrative, to give Paula what she needs to break out of repressive middle-class feminism. Carmela is—like Emmy Strait and Holiday Hill—the catalyst/organizer character who makes possible the development of others, in this case Paula.

Structurally, *The Store* builds on the use Newman made of video in *Left of the Moon.* As in that play, the video element in *The Store* is one of the narrative elements and establishes a connection/tension with the stories enacted onstage. In both the 1995 and 1997 productions, video interviews with professional strippers were conducted. Excerpts from these interviews were included in the production as part of Paula's lecture that opens the play. These documentary video clips tell much the same story of humiliation that Carmela expands upon in the "fictional" part of the play. They become one of the play's narratives and establish a structural tension with both Paula's lecture and Carmela's story.

While there are many ways of approaching the script of *The Store,* a significant dimension is opened up if the producers arrange their own interviews. This activity is not only invaluable to the actresses in the process of developing their characters, but connects the production to the broad community of women who strip for a living.

D.F.

The Store: One Block East of Jerome was first produced at the Castillo Theatre in 1991. The version presented here was produced at the Castillo Theatre (Fred Newman, artistic director; Gabrielle Kurlander, producing director; Diane Stiles, managing director) in New York City on March 24, 1995. The cast, in order of appearance, was as follows:

PAULA BROWNELL . . . . Nancy Green
VIDEO INTERVIEWS. . . . . Angel Carter, Angie Z., Tanya J., Juliana Francis
CHLOE . . . . Bette Braun
ELVIRA . . . . Kathy Fiess
CARMELA PETRELLI . . . . Madelyn Chapman
OFFSTAGE VOICES . . . . Roger Grunwald, David Nackman,
Marian Rich, Bette Braun, Kathy Fiess

Fred Newman, director; Diane Stiles, producer; Joseph Spirito, set design; Charlotte, costume design; Jessica Massad and Beth Peeler, lighting design; Michael Klein, sound design; Barry Z Levine and Fred Newman, video design; Barry Z Levine and Diane Stiles, cinematography; Brenda Ratliff, production stage manager.

*Find out just what people will submit to, and you have found out the exact
amount of injustice and wrong which will be imposed upon them; and these will
continue till they are resisted with either words or blows, or with both. The limits of tyrants are proscribed by the endurance of those whom they oppress.*

FREDERICK DOUGLASS

Carmela Petrelli, played brilliantly in this production of *The Store: One
Block East of Jerome* by Madelyn Chapman, will not submit to the exploitation and vicious oppression of women in our culture. And in our postmodern, post-progressive, post-revolutionary society the individual's unwilling-
ness to submit must include the shocking recognition that she will surely be
destroyed. Carmela Petrelli is a stripper, not a revolutionary. She is a working-class woman who has been raped by her world: her family, her friends,
her community. But she will not submit passively. She will expose the
hypocrisy of a violent world by making The Man see Himself for the
degraded Humiliator that He is. It is, as she sees it, all she can do. It is the
only way, from her point of view, to not submit completely. Paula Brownell,
played wonderfully by Nancy Green, is an academic looking for a life. She
finds it in the tragic world of striptease. It is not filled with meaning; it is
merely alive. This is, after all, a postmodern world and the opportunities for
heroine-ism are few.

 The Store: One Block East of Jerome is dedicated to my big sister Pearl,
who taught me to love and respect women.

MARCH 1995

CHARACTERS

PAULA BROWNELL
ELVIRA
CHLOE
CARMELA PETRELLI

Offstage voices
STAGE MANAGER
JOEY CONIGLIARO
GUYS
GIRLS CHORUS
MARVIN K.
MRS. PETRELLI
MR. PETRELLI
UNCLE GUS

On video (documentary)
STRIPPERS

NOTE:
This play contains both live scenes and video sequences.

Scene 1

The stage is dark. A dressing room, backstage at the "Kit-Kat" Club, a strip joint on 47th Street in New York City. A huge dressing mirror and a dressing table dominate the altogether seedy room. An exit onto the strip stage area is clearly demarcated upstage. The actual strip stage is not seen, but light from the strip show spills out through this exit during performances, and strip show music is heard. Downstage left is a lectern lit simply, classroom-style, from above. Video monitors, right and left of the stage, are dark. PAULA BROWNELL, a New School professor, enters and crosses slowly to the lectern.

PAULA: *(Speaks academically though hesitantly—haltingly, shyly)* Good evening, ladies and gentlemen. I'm Dr. Paula Brownell. Welcome to tonight's lecture on the sociology and psychology of the female stripper. I've been here in the Department of Gender Studies at the New School for 12 years now. I received my Ph.D. in anthropology from the University of Wisconsin some…oh…15 years ago. My dissertation was on feminist values in early patriarchal cultures. Over the last five years or so I have become increasingly interested in women's attitudes toward female nudity and exhibitionism and, two years ago, I received a small grant to study the sociology and psychology of women who take their clothes off professionally…for a living—i.e., strippers.

As a part of this study I have video-interviewed dozens of professional strippers. In a few minutes I want to show you parts of some of those interviews. First a brief history of the striptease.

(While PAULA talks, still images appear on the monitors.)

While the intentional, self-conscious displaying of various parts of the female body is, no doubt, as old and as pervasive as sexuality itself, the public and/or theatrical form of this activity is associated, at least here in America, with Burlesque. As far back as the middle of the 19th century so-called "Living Models," semi-nude women in still, classical poses, appeared onstage in New York City under the sponsorship of

one Dr. Collyer. (We do not know what he was a doctor of. We do know
he was a man.) By the 1860s naked or near-naked women began to
move onstage. A leader in this *movement* was Adah Isaacs Menken, an
early women's rights advocate who popularized cigar smoking, dress
reform and free love—often with distinguished male American
authors. Mary Garden contributed substantially to striptease. A significant singing actress, Garden semi-stripped in doing "The Dance of the
Seven Veils" in a production of Strauss' *Salome*. The well-known Theda
Bara did the Salome dance in an early silent movie, and the famous
French music hall star Gaby Delys was the first to strip in a Broadway
show—*Stop Look and Listen* in 1915 to the words of Irving Berlin.
Berlin, author of "God Bless America" and "White Christmas," in the
days before "political correctness" wrote:

(Reads from piece of paper.)

"Take off a little bit,
If that don't make a hit,
Take off a little bit more.
Take off a little bit.
Don't let it drag on the floor.
The doctor, the lawyer, the Indian Chief,
Will always look longer
When dresses are brief.
Take off a little bit.
If that don't make a hit,
Take off a little bit more."

By the 1920s and '30s stripping, which had been one small element of
Burlesque, had taken over the whole show. In New York City, the
world-famous Minsky's presented an all-stripper show. With Ann Corio
and Gypsy Rose Lee leading the way, hundreds of "artistes"—as they
now called themselves—Margie Hart, Bonnie Kerr, Sherry Britton,
Rose La Rose, Carmen Bridges, Lili St. Cyr, Lotus Dubois, Amber
Halladay, Val de Val, Sally Rand, Princess La Homa and thousands of
others took over the stage as Burlesque died. By the 1960s stripping
had become a component of the burgeoning sex industry. By the '70s,
'80s and '90s, in keeping with postmodern values, stripping became

substantially less theatrical—though still for many, dance-like—and more and more it was simply hard-core sexual turn-on.

Always the object of outraged citizenry and opportunistic politicians, striptease and sexually erotic performance nonetheless remains a well-entrenched part of American culture, attracting audiences—mainly, though not exclusively men—from across the socio-economic spectrum. But who are the strippers? Where do they come from? Nowadays in a crossfire between feminism on the left and fundamentalism on the right, how do they view themselves and their work? The best way to find out, in my opinion? Let them speak for themselves.

(Videos are four- to five-minute interviews, which begin with a freeze-frame of the stripper and a short introduction by PAULA, *e.g., "That's Angel. She's 50 and..." The video ends.)*

PAULA: I have an interview today with Carmela Petrelli at the Kit-Kat Club up on 47th Street. She's their star performer. I've been trying to speak with her for months. Come with me. It's a live show. *(Laughs self-consciously at joke.)* Believe it or not, I've never done an interview at one of these clubs before.

*(*PAULA *crosses to the door of the dressing room as a video of 42nd Street environment plays on the monitors.)*

Scene 2

Two strippers, CHLOE *and* ELVIRA, *getting ready to go on.* CARMELA *enters. There is a general hubbub.*

STAGE MANAGER: *(Offstage)* Chloe and Elvira, you're up next. *(As* CHLOE *and* ELVIRA *exit onto "strip stage" to music,* PAULA *knocks on the door.)*

CARMELA: Come on in, it's open. *(*PAULA *enters.* CARMELA, *dressed in street clothes, sits down and is taking off her hat.)*

PAULA: *(To* CARMELA*)* Hi. I'm Paula Brownell...from the New School. We've spoken on the phone several times. It's great to finally meet you in person.

CARMELA: *(Points to available seat for* PAULA *to sit in)* Oh yeah. I'm sorry I had to cancel so many appointments. I've been really busy. My oldest kid is graduating from college and I've been a little sick. Nice to meet ya. *(They shake hands; an awkward pause.)* Well, how do we do this? Whattya wanna know about, Professor?

PAULA: How are you feeling *today*? Are you better now? Are you still sick?

CARMELA: Oh, the usual…my left knee hurts…and, uh, well, I'm a little despondent. Ya know, *(becomes reflective)* hey, I was despondent long before I knew what in the hell that word meant. I *still* don't know exactly what it means. *(Laughs.)*

PAULA: Well, what's it like…this despondency? I mean, how does it feel?

CARMELA: I get this feeling; it begins as a little pain in the pit of my stomach and, well…next thing ya know it sorta spreads out like vinegar all over my body. Ever since I was 12 or 13 I felt this way a lot. Despondent, a doctor I went to once called it. But to me it was like somethin' empty and kinda slimy inside that kept on growin' and growin'. *(CARMELA is pensive; an uneasy pause.)* Would you like some coffee? *(PAULA nods yes; CARMELA reaches over for a coffeepot and two cups; pours the coffee.)* Y'want milk?

PAULA: *(Shakes head "no"; takes sip of coffee)* Well…what were you like as a child? Can I call you Carmela?

CARMELA: Oh sure, Professor. That's what everyone calls me.

PAULA: Call me Paula, please.

CARMELA: Yeah, Paula, yeah. Well, I guess I was a pretty happy little kid…ya know when I was about eight or nine. Hey. For a long time the happiest day of my life that I could remember—this'll sound silly to ya, Paula— was when I was about eight-and-a-half and I got to say "Ring-o-levio-cork-cork-cork" out loud for the first time.

PAULA: What's that? What did you say?

CARMELA: You know the game, "Ring-o-levio"? Well, I won't go into the whole thing but it's kinda a tag game and when ya catch the other guy ya gotta say "Ring-o-levio-cork-cork-cork" three times. I mean it's not a big deal but as a real little kid I couldn't get it…I mean I couldn't say it.

It was kinda like that old song my father once taught me, "Maresy doats and doesy doats and little lambsy divy." 'Member dat song? Hm. I ain't thought about dat for a long time. But yeah, I was pretty happy as a little kid. Yeah. I hadda take care of my brat brother a lot…that was a pain in the ass. He's three years younger. He's still kind of a pain in the ass. I mean he's grown up now…he works in a drug store down on Houston Street. But he's still a pain in the ass. He never can do nuttin' for himself. He'll come to my house and say, "Carmela, can ya get me a beer?" I mean he's closer to the kitchen than me and he comes over all the time. But ya know, he's spoiled…like a man, he's spoiled. My older brother was different…a little. But he got killed in Vietnam. Yeah, I was a pretty okay kid, ya know. *Den I grew tits*! Huh. Dey made quite a difference. Ya know…I mean you're a woman…you know how the whole body changes with tits. Actually everything changes with tits. Like, we useta hang out at this candy store on DeKalb Avenue, a block east of Jerome, up on Gun Hill Road in the Bronx. All us kids. Boys and girls. Even when we was 11, 12. Kids I went to Public School 90 with. We horsed around at the candy store on DeKalb. Funny. Der was candy stores on every damned corner of Gun Hill from DeKalb all the way east. Every store had some kids hangin' out. It was nice. You'd get home from school, maybe run some dumb errands for your mother and then hang out at the store. Nobody ever minded. We'd give some people a hard time once in a while…you know, we'd get a little rowdy. But nobody ever really got pissed off. Then came the tits and it all changed. Like Joey, for example, Joey Conigliaro.

PAULA: Who was Joey? Who was Joey Conigliaro?

CARMELA: Joey was the dumbest kid in the fourth grade. Ugly, too. He was a pain in the ass, ya know. But nobody bothered with him. I mean, he wasn't worth it. People sorta let him be. But then, suddenly, it's five years later. Joey's still dumb and still ugly and still a pain in the ass. But Joey C. grew a big cock and some other muscles too and now he thinks he's hot shit. So Joey Conigliaro thinks he can do whatever the fuck he wants; especially with the girls. Big changes…big fuckin' changes. (*Lighting changes;* CARMELA *walks to the mirror.*)

JOEY: (*Offstage*) Hiya, Sweetheart.

CARMELA: Whattya lookin' for Joey? Whattya doin' your "hi sweetheart" bullshit for?

JOEY: *(Offstage)* Hey, sweetheart…I ain't lookin' for nuttin'. Whaddya mean, what'm I lookin' for?

CARMELA: You sonofabitch, you sonofabitch; always lookin' at me, talkin' to me like you wanna put your fuckin' hand on my pussy.

JOEY: *(Offstage)* Carmela Petrelli. The second smartest girl in fourth grade at P.S. 90. Is dat a way to talk? Does your mother and father know you use that kinda language? *(Lights change back; CARMELA returns to her chair.)*

CARMELA: Big changes. I mean we'd always touched each other before. It was okay. It was playin'.

PAULA: You mean like spin the bottle? Kissing games?

CARMELA: No. No. Not just spin the bottle. Whatever. Johnny on the pony. Taggin' games. Touchin'. Yeah it was kinda sexy…for young kids. But it was touchin'…it wasn't grabbin'. It wasn't no asshole like Joey C. tryin' to rub his new cock against my ass. But that all changed with tits. Everyone started talkin' different, too. Talkin' phony. Like everyone was in da movies…bad movies. I think I remember thinkin' dat when kids started talkin' that way they was only jokin'. I mean, I guess I did it too. Jokin'. Nervous like. 'Cause now we had tits and cocks and asses and we didn't know what to do with 'em…in a way. So we was jokin' to begin with. But then guys like Joey, that asshole…and Eddie Pelligrini, another creep (when *he* was nine), start gettin' carried away. I mean they ain't playin' and yeah I guess they're angry 'cause of how we treated them when dey was younger and now they're gonna "get even." So, suddenly, everyone's not jokin' anymore. I don't know when it happened. Like one day that's how we are…no more playin' …no more jokin' around. No more horsin' around. Now it's all makin' out. And then the older folks at the candy store and old Mr. Hirsch, the owner, they don't like us no more. Suddenly we got tits and pricks and balls and asses and they don't like us no more. Big fuckin' changes. Yeah. Big fuckin' changes. Yeah. Dat's when I started gettin' this vinegar feelin'.

PAULA: So now we're talking about your adolescence. What happened? What were your teenage years like? Early sexual experiences?

CARMELA: It ain't no more ring-o-levio-cork-cork-cork…that's for sure. But we're still hangin' out at da candy store. A little later at night maybe; after dinner. Same old crowd. Only now it's darker and a little scary. One night I come walkin' along DeKalb towards Gun Hill and the candy store and my girlfriends and some of the guys are sittin' on car fenders or standin' up against buildings makin' out or, a lotta times, *makin' out* like they're makin' out…ya know the old movie actin' bit. And the guys…even the guys with girls…are jumpin' all over ya with their eyes. It ain't even like they ain't got someone with 'em, it's the scene now. It's how we are with each other. I don't think no one likes it. Maybe Joey C. and Eddie P. like it…ya know, de assholes. But I don't like it. I hate it. I think most of us hate it. But now it's how we are with each other. Yeah…we're…adolescents, teenagers…shit, we got tits and asses. (*CARMELA goes to the mirror.*)

JOEY: (*Offstage*) Hey, Carmela…I ain't never seen an ass like that. How come you don't share it with us, you bitch? Your ass and your pussy too smart for the rest of us?

CARMELA: (*Tough*) Joey, you sonofabitch, my ass was smarter than your head when we was seven.

JOEY: (*Offstage, nasty*) Is it smart enough for my prick?

CARMELA: Now I hadda act tough 'cause I was scared. Other guys started chimin' in…even guys I liked.

GUYS: (*Offstage*) Yeah, Carmela. How smart *is* dat ass of yours? (*Laughter.*) How smart is it? You a smart ass, Carmela? You some kind of smart ass?

CARMELA: (*Stays at mirror; looks back towards* PAULA) I went into the candy store and I sat down at the counter, ordered a cherry coke and began sippin' it real slow. The fear slowly turned into this knot in the pit of my belly and den the waves of vinegar started spreadin' across everything …my ass, my pussy, my legs, arms…everything. Despondency. I'm sittin' there in a goddamn candy store on the corner of Gun Hill Road and DeKalb Avenue in the Bronx drinkin' a cherry coke and I'm gettin' despondency. And in my head I'm hearin' fuckin' voices...like a bunch of crazy girls in a weird chorus saying:

GIRLS CHORUS: *(Offstage, using shrill voices)* GIRLS LIKE US ARE A DIME A DOZEN. GIRLS LIKE US ARE A DIME A DOZEN. GIRLS LIKE US ARE A DIME A DOZEN.

CARMELA: I'm feelin' like shit...I mean I'm really feelin' sick. I'm sittin' there and I know...I fuckin' know that I can't be lettin' assholes like Joey Conigliaro get to me...*but they are; they are*. And my cherry coke is about finished and I'm numb; vinegar numb. I don't feel hardly nuthin' but the vinegar now. So I pay for my coke; and I get off the counter stool real slow and I walk outta the candy store *(walks slowly to PAULA)*, turn left, back onto DeKalb. Everybody's still hangin'. And I walk slowly right at Joey C. and I grab his big fuckin' hand *(grabs PAULA's hand; acts out the following scene with PAULA; PAULA is paralyzed)* and, right in front of everybody, I put it under my dress and right smack on my pussy. And I make him squeeze it...squeeze it hard. And den I make his hand pull down my panties...right der in front of everybody and I make him squeeze my pussy even harder. Now my panties are down around my knees; my dress is up...I'm holdin' it up and fuckin' Joey C. is squeezin' my pussy hard as can be. Nobody's sayin' a fuckin' word...not one fuckin' word. But in my head dese crazy voices are screamin' louder and louder:

GIRLS CHORUS: *(Offstage)* GIRLS LIKE YOU ARE A DIME A DOZEN. GIRLS LIKE YOU ARE A DIME A DOZEN.

CARMELA: *(PAULA and CARMELA sit; CARMELA pulls up her panties)* Yeah. Tits changed everything. *(Big laugh.)* After that night I think I musta fucked everybody...everybody but Marvin K. This crowd on the corner of DeKalb and Gun Hill was *fast*...but Marvin K. was *slow*. Marvin K. was smart as could be...the bastard was takin' calculus as a fuckin' high school sophomore. He could figure de square root of anything but he couldn't figure out how to get his hand on tits or pussy. I mean he wasn't bad to look at, but he had no muscle; no cock, if ya know what I mean.

(Lighting changes; PAULA and CARMELA freeze.)

JOEY: *(Offstage)* You ain't fucked Carmela, Marvin? Whattya mean you ain't fucked Carmela? Marvin, goddamn it, everyone's fucked Carmela.

MARVIN K.: *(Offstage)* Joey, I haven't. I haven't fucked anybody, Joey. I haven't fucked anybody.

JOEY: *(Offstage)* Well, you gotta fuck Carmela then.

MARVIN K.: *(Offstage)* Why, Joey? Why do I have to fuck Carmela?

JOEY: *(Offstage)* Oh, Marvin…with your brain and my cock we could rule de world.

MARVIN K.: *(Offstage)* Thanks a lot, Joey, but I've got my own cock, thank you.

JOEY: *(Offstage)* But you ain't usin' it, Marvin; you ain't usin' it!

(Lights change; pause.)

PAULA: What happened with Marvin?

CARMELA: One Saturday, late afternoon-early evening in March, I think, Marvin got to use his cock. I sucked him off in the back seat of Joey C.'s father's car…parked about halfway down the block between DeKalb and Rochambeau on Gun Hill…right by the churchyard. After dat I'd give him a blow job every week or so and he got me through high school. I mean after the tits, the vinegar and all those cocks, I couldn't think good no more. So Marvin got me through. It was kinda crazy. I kept fuckin' everybody else, but Marvin and I had this kinda *special* suckin'-tutorin' relationship.

PAULA: A sucking-tutoring relationship?

CARMELA: Yeah, it was like being married in a way. So Marvin's over my house one Sunday afternoon. He's gettin' me ready for the English Regents…tellin' me de plots of all these books I ain't ever read. We're in my bedroom…actually I remember I gave him a blow job between *Great Expectations* and *Moby Dick*…ain't that funny…it's really true. Yeah. So we're lying on the bed and I hear my mother's voice. Company's over the house…I mean the whole family…aunts, uncles, my grandfather…my mother's father; my grandmother…yeah, everybody.

(CARMELA goes to mirror.)

MRS. PETRELLI: *(Offstage)* Carmela. Come in here for a moment, sweetheart.

CARMELA: *(To PAULA)* I had told my mother never to call me sweetheart no more, but…what can ya do? She's your mother. Ya know what I'm sayin'?

PAULA: Yes…I understand. My mother is the same way.

MRS. PETRELLI: *(Offstage)* Carmela, baby. Come in here…just for a moment.

CARMELA: So I tell Marvin to relax…he don't need this Italian *famiglia;* he's got *mishpucha* problems of his own at home…I tell him to cool out on the bed and read a good book or somethin'…I'll be right back. I come out into de living room; Uncle Bobby, the fuckin' letch, squeezes my ass and I give him a filthy fuckin' look. Den my father, who's drunk as a motherfucker, puts his arm around my shoulder with his knobby fingers practically touchin' my right tit.

MR. PETRELLI: *(Offstage)* Carmela, Carmela. Everybody wants you to do that dance you did in the school play in de third grade. You remember, baby? You remember?

CARMELA: Whatayou crazy, Papa? I was a child. Dat was 10 years ago. I was seven. Papa, stop treatin' me like a little girl.

UNCLE GUS: *(Offstage)* Yeah, Carmela. Remember? You bent over and showed us your cute little ass. Remember?

CARMELA: *(To PAULA)* That's Uncle Gus…he was a fuckin' sex maniac. *(Back to mirror.)* And the men in my family…my uncles and cousins, my father, my grandfather…suddenly, der all screamin'. I can't believe it. It's like the corner. It's like the fuckin' corner. And my aunts and grandmothers and my mother and girl cousins, they're standin' there, too, with stupid little smiles on their faces, kinda shakin' their heads watchin' these men tellin' me to show 'em my ass. I couldn't believe it. And I'm startin' to get numb. Ya know…the vinegar is rollin' all over my insides; into my nostrils and under my eyelids. And the next thing I know I'm standin' on the big round mahogany table…*(She begins to performs a strip)* and I'm unbuttoning my blue chiffon blouse. And everyone's gotten silent…nobody, not nobody is makin' a move to stop me. And now my blouse is off and I'm standin' there in my bra and tight skirt; high heels; no stockings... "Ya wanna see my ass? I'll show ya my ass." And I unbutton the three buttons on the skirt and pull it down real slowly. So now I'm in my bra and panties and pumps. They're all just lookin'. Nobody says a word. And I start screamin', "GIRLS LIKE ME ARE A DIME A DOZEN. GIRLS LIKE ME ARE A DIME A DOZEN." I unfasten my pink bra and let it hang for a few seconds on my shoulder. Then I lean forward and it falls off and there are my tits, right out there in the living room for the family to check out. The men's eyes are bulgin' outta their fuckin' heads. I bend over real slowly like I was goin' to touch my toes in gym class... and I point my panty-covered ass right at my father and uncle... then I put my two thumbs under the elastic of my panties and I start to take 'em off. Nothing. Not one fuckin' word. They can see my asshole now and I'm rollin' down my panties... they're almost down to my knees and I'm spreadin' my legs a little so they can see my pussy loud and clear. My panties drop to my ankles; I stand up straight; I turn around and give 'em all a bird's eye view of my cunt.

"You dumb fucks, I ain't your little baby. I'm Carmela, the fuckin' whore. I'm a fuckin' whore, daddy. Here's my pussy. Ya wanna eat it?" Then I bend over, pulled up my panties, climbed down from the table ...(*CARMELA returns to PAULA*) and walked slowly into my bedroom where Marvin, the prick, was fast asleep. And nobody said one fuckin' word. Not one fuckin' word.

About a year later, one day after a blow job, Marvin asked me to marry him. I had two kids in three years; then he ran off with this blonde he met in his speech class at Hunter College—when it was still up in de Bronx. I started strippin' for a livin' about a year or two later. When I look back on it I think I always wanted to strip. When I first started workin', people would say to me, "Ain't it hard to take your clothes off? Ain't it hard to strip?" I took to sayin', "Shit no. Strippin' is easy. Life is hard." Pretty smart ass, huh. Yeah, I'm pretty smart ass.

PAULA: That story really makes me angry, Carmela. I grew up very religious. Catholic. This awful society is filled with phony religious people... hypocrites... who talk their asses off about God but they're all ashamed of ...pussy. But if there is a God, then he or she *made* pussy. Jimmy

Swaggart isn't the only phony white preacher lookin' at dirty pictures. I mean, Bill Clinton is probably sitting in the front row of some seedy strip house right now in Little Rock or Washington, D.C. whacking off.

CARMELA: Hey, I ain't so angry no more. That kind of anger don't give me shit. It didn't put no food on the fuckin' table for me and the kids. It don't pay no bills. Listen. I respect your anger, Professor, but I don't get nuttin' from it. Hey look, I stripped and tricked right through the sixties, ya know. Everyone was talkin' "sister" this and "sister" that. Dese middle-class ladies…no offense, no offense…was takin' off der bras and burning 'em. I thought it wasn't a bad act, ya know. Heh. A couple a times they came to joints I was workin' with picket signs sayin' somethin' like "STOP THE PORNOGRAPHY," "STRIPPING EXPLOITS WOMEN." Ya know, stuff like that. And when I walked outta da door of the club after my act, these "sisters" looked at me like I was a piece of shit. Hey, listen here, Professor, I think the whole world sucks. I'm pissed about that. I'm witcha. And if 10 of us broads caught Joey C. or Marvin alone one night in a dark alley I'd be the first to kick his balls in. I mean, men ain't exactly been my best buddies. But I'd rather let 'em see my tits and my pussy for a paycheck then have 'em rape me in the streets or, even worse, have 'em strip me and fuck me for free in some bullshit relationship. Dat angry "lemme tell ya how fucked up de world is," honey, it ain't nuthin'. It's bullshit. It ain't even as real as tits and cocks and pussies and asses…Hey, listen to me bein' some kinda philosopher. Huh…I mean, you're the professor. (*Laughs.*)

PAULA: But how do you feel about taking your clothes off and *showing* yourself to all those men. How does it feel to *show* yourself to them?

(*ELVIRA and CHLOE run in from the strip stage, naked and making much noise.*)

CARMELA: (*Jokingly*) Quiet, you two. Can't ya see I'm talkin' with the professor? Paula, this is Elvira and her sister Chloe. This is Professor Paula. She's interviewin' me!

(*ELVIRA and CHLOE say hello shyly.*)

CARMELA: Now be a little quiet.

(*ELVIRA and CHLOE go off to dress.*)

CARMELA: Listen, Paula. I'm on in a few minutes. You mind if I dress while we talk?

PAULA: Oh no. Not at all.

(*CARMELA takes off her panties and puts on G-string, etc.; the costume for her act.*)

CARMELA: Now, what were you askin'?

PAULA: How does it feel to *show* yourself to all those men? Showing your breasts, your vagina, your ass. Isn't it humiliating?

CARMELA: I can tell you ain't no stripper, Paula. I can tell just from how you talk, cause you're talkin' about *showin'* pussy, *showin'* tits, *showin'* ass. But, honey, I've been in this business a long time, and I can tell ya... strippin' ain't no fuckin' *showin'* It's lettin' 'em see ya. It's exposin' a nipple here and some pussy there. Sometimes ya let 'em see the whole thing for a few seconds. But, honey...you don't *show* 'em shit. This ain't kid stuff. This ain't ring-o-levio-cork-cork-cork. This ain't show and tell. This is tease his dumb cock. Clinton and the rest of them guys out there are just a bunch of hard-ons. If we tickle his balls maybe we ladies can get a little somethin'. But you can't *show* that motherfucker nuttin'. You can't *give* that fuckin' asshole nuthin'. He's just a blind dick, honey. This whole fuckin' society is just a blind dick. Ya wanna fight it? Suck on it...and once in a while maybe give the dirty bastard a little teeth. Ya know...sneak in a bite. But at the first sign that he's noticing that you're hurtin' him, smile pretty and lick him under the balls. But hey, honey,...Paula, de golden rule...I just made this up... DON'T EVER *SHOW* HIM NUTHIN'. 'Cause if you show him, he'll think you're sayin' dat you got somethin'. And when he thinks...when the man thinks that we women think we got somethin', they get angry and they take their big cocks and they whack us. Hey, I'll *show* you who I am. I'll *show* my kids. I'll *show* people I love everything I got—every hair on my pussy, every pimple on my nipple. Yeah. But not the man. I don't show him shit. Not the man! Strippin' is my way of not showin' the man shit. You understand, Paula? Can you understand that?

STAGE MANAGER: *(Offstage)* Thirty seconds, Carmela.

CARMELA: That's me, Paula. That's me. That's my act. Hey, nice meetin' ya, Professor Paula. Nice meetin' ya. You're alright, darlin'. Take a good look at yourself. You're alright.

PAULA: Yeah, nice meeting you. Good luck, Carmela. Good luck. *(Softly.)* Good luck.

(CARMELA exits to the strip stage; PAULA sits in silence, listening to the strip music. Then she rises and walks slowly to the mirror and strips. When she finishes, lights fade out.)

))))

Sally and Tom
(The American Way)

Book and lyrics by Fred Newman, music by Annie Roboff

The issue of racism in America has been central in all Newman's work, literary and otherwise.

A key premise of the political movement he leads is that the broad masses of the African American population—permanently relegated to the back of the socio-economic bus—have the least stake in the status quo and are therefore in the best historical position to lead a movement for revolutionary transformation. Given this strategic perspective, everything that Newman's political movement/development community has created—including his plays—can be understood, at least in part, as an effort to create an environment in which the Black community can provide such leadership to the American people as a whole.

The very first play Newman helped to create, *A Demonstration: Common Women, the Uncommon Lives of Ordinary Women,* had at its core a confrontation between Black welfare mothers and white lesbian feminists. The second play he helped to put together and direct, *From Gold to Platinum* (1986), had as one of its major conflicts the mistrust between Black and white revolutionaries during a futuristic second American Revolution. The first play Newman wrote, *Mr. Hirsch Died Yesterday,* culminates in a struggle over identity between a white Jewish man and a Black lesbian, both of whom have the same history. The first visitor Lenin receives in *The Collected Emotions of V.I. Lenin* is a Black auto worker from Detroit, who has come to see for himself if Lenin is really "the same color as the boss." In *Billie & Malcolm: A Demonstration* every one of the main characters has died as a consequence of racism. While *Still on the Corner* focuses on the issue of "homelessness," the not-so-subtle subtext of the play (as it is on the streets of Manhattan's Upper West Side) is that the homeless are mostly African American and their middle-class neighbors are primarily Jewish. The unanswered questions of race relations continue to be asked in various ways in Newman's recent work: *What is to be Dead? (Philosophical Scenes), Coming of Age in Korea* and *Stealin' Home.*

The centrality of the struggle against racism in Newman's creative (and political) life was expressed at a stormy forum in Harlem in 1991 which had been organized to address the controversy stirred up by Castillo's first production of *Billie, Malcolm & Yusuf* (which later became *Billie & Malcolm: A Demonstration*). Responding to the objection that as a white man and a Jew, he neither had the right nor was qualified to make a play about Malcolm X, Newman replied, "As a Jew...the issue of white supremacy, the issue of racism, the issue of the exploitation and murder of African American people, is *my* issue. I'll stand here from now until the moment I drop dead insisting I must speak about it. No serious playwright in America today can work without devoting her or his creative energies to the issue of racism. If you're not writing about that, you're a bullshit artist—that's the kind of artist you are."

In *Sally and Tom (The American Way)* (1995), Newman takes us back nearly 200 years to examine the institutions and attitudes that have shaped America's particular brand of racism. The musical explores the contradiction at the heart of America: even as Americans made one of the world's most democratic revolutions, they preserved that quintessentially undemocratic institution—slavery. Many of the most democratically-minded of our "Founding Fathers" were, like Thomas Jefferson, slave owners. Jefferson seemed to embody the contradiction; the author of the Declaration of Independence which declared that "All men are created equal," he was opposed to slavery "in principle" yet his own wealth and privilege depended on it. While he led the fight to add the first Ten Amendments, the Bill of Rights, to the Constitution to guarantee citizens the freedoms of speech, press, religion, assembly, the right to a fair and speedy trial, and the right to bear arms, he never challenged the Constitution's denial of citizenship, indeed of full personhood, to African Americans.

Jefferson's political/ethical contradictions were exacerbated (and personalized) by the apparent fact that for 30 years he lived intimately with his slave Sally Hemings and had five children with her. There are some historians who insist—despite seemingly overwhelming evidence, including the testimony of some of their children, that a sexual relationship between Jefferson and Hemings could never have happened. Yet whatever the "truth" about "Sally" and "Tom" may have been, such a liaison is emblematic of the thousands of intimate sexual relationships between slaves and their owners that did exist throughout the South, and is made all the more dramatic by this particular slave owner's radical political views and the seminal role he played in American history. Theirs was a love affair crying out for dramatization, yet aside from the Merchant-Ivory film *Jefferson in Paris*, which depicts the beginnings of their relationship, no American author had brought the story of "Sally" and "Tom" to the stage before.

Sally and Tom (The American Way) is the first of Newman's musicals to use the parallel narrative/cubist structural approach that characterizes most of his non-musicals. The parallel narrative is embodied in and articulated by the character of Madison Hemings, one of Sally and Tom's sons, who emerges from the audience after the first scene to comment on the action and tell his version of the story. In this sense, Madison Hemings plays much the same role as the Narrator in *Left of the Moon*: his is the (Black) voice of history. However, unlike the Narrator in *Left of the Moon*, who for the most part is kept distinct from the characters and action onstage, in the last scene of *Sally and Tom* all the characters join Hemings "in history." There they can reflect on and talk about their lives from a point of view (and a basis of equality) denied them in life.

Paradoxically, not only does *Sally and Tom* bring Newman's "developmental" structure to the musical, at the same time it marks a major advance in Newman and Roboff's mastery of traditional musical theatre technique.

In their previous musical, *Still on the Corner*, the songs were used for all sorts of purposes—exposition, character revelation, comic relief. With *Sally and Tom*, for the first time Newman and Roboff use the unique element of the musical—its songs and duets—as the primary means by which the conflicts are advanced and the relationships developed.

At the top of the play the journalist James Callender provokes James Madison into a rage with a song (the lyrics of which were actually penned by John Quincy Adams) mocking Jefferson. Callender, Sally Hemings, Jefferson and Madison Hemings each reveal their (political/ethical/emotional) conflicts through song. The audience experiences the political relationship between Jefferson and Madison not through anything either of them say, but through the duet "Is it Constitutional?" The passionate (and passionately conflicted) love between Jefferson and Sally Hemings is explored not primarily through their dialogue but through the two painfully beautiful duets, "Enslaved by the Color of our Skin" and "The Coward's Song." The conflict between Jefferson and Callender comes to a climax in the duet "Rich and Poor Hypocrisy." The final scene brings together—and, in typical Newman fashion, leaves *un*resolved—each of the play's relationships and conflicts in a weave of song involving all the characters. In short, the songs are the dramatic action.

Sally and Tom diverges from/develops the American musical tradition in some interesting and significant ways. One example is in the structure. The story, set in America around the turn of the 19th century, could not be resolved there. In fact, to this day the contradictions and conflicts examined in *Sally and Tom* have not been resolved "in life." So Newman, rather than imposing a false resolution, brings all his characters together to converse (musically, of course) on the subject of America's unfinished business: the race question. The setting of the final scene in history (not "in the past") and the deliberate refusal to resolve dramatically what has not yet been resolved in history are, as this collection demonstrates, nothing new for Newman. It is new to the American musical stage, however. From *Oklahoma* to *Fiddler on the Roof,* the American musical is full of "dream sequences" but contains no "history sequences." Like the American theatre in general, the musical, despite its much-heralded showmanship, is psychologically oriented.

Newman's orientation, political in the broadest sense, is very different. The centrality of political concerns in *Sally and Tom* further distinguishes it from most other American musicals. Only *1776* by Peter Stone and Sherman Edward and *Cabaret* by John Kander and Fred Ebb attempt, as does *Sally and Tom,* to construct a musical play around political conflicts.

It is also an explicitly didactic play—didactic not only in the old agit-prop and Brechtian sense of teaching a political/ethical lesson (which it does), but didactic also in the strictly pedagogical sense of teaching American history (which it also does). Didacticism (of any type) is a major taboo in the American theatre (musical and otherwise), considered by commercial producers and theatre professors alike to be the polar opposite of entertainment and therefore to be avoided at all costs. Didacticism is also quite rare in Newman's plays. He has repeatedly made clear that he doesn't believe the theatre can effectively teach a lesson; what it can do, he says, is provide an experience. Yet within the overwhelmingly musical experience of *Sally and Tom* there are obvious didactic elements.

The emergence of didacticism in *Sally and Tom* is perhaps to fill the audience in on a period of American history with which most contemporary Americans are only vaguely familiar. Thus, for example, the character James Madison says to his good friend and political ally Thomas Jefferson: "That

Constitution is what we have, Thomas. It represents, together with the Bill of Rights, its first 10 amendments, the best of what we've created." Surely Jefferson, who fought long and hard for its passage, was aware that the Bill of Rights consists of the first 10 amendments to the Constitution. The audience, however, may not be. Similarly, *Sally and Tom* starts with a monologue delivered by James Madison which fills the audience in on the political fights of the early Republic from a distinctly Democratic-Republican perspective. Later, the teaching of American history (and, in particular, African American history) is taken up by Madison Hemings as he chats directly with the audience about his parents' relationship, the presidential elections of 1796 and 1800, the revolution in Haiti, and the Virginia slave revolt led by Gabriel Prosser, among other historical events relevant to the play's story.

The political didacticism comes primarily at the end, although the author's opposition to slavery and sympathy for the Democratic-Republicans in their fight with the Federalists is clear throughout. It is from the location of history, however, that the political and social repercussions of the compromises made and betrayals perpetrated during the early years of the Republic can most clearly be seen by both the characters and the audience. So it is that the final scene is filled with political conversation, including James Madison's sad comments to the audience at the very end, which deliver the sobering message of *Sally and Tom* and bring it to a close.

Interestingly, the play's didactic elements—whether providing historical background or political commentary—are contained primarily in the spoken word, while it is the songs which reveal character and move the story along. This reliance on song as the medium of dramatic action puts *Sally and Tom* in the tradition of the European opera and the American musical and distinguishes it from Brecht's dramaturgy, in which the story is told in dialogue and the songs are a distinct non-dramatic element designed to comment on the play's action and "teach the lesson."

Perhaps it is the beauty of the music that makes *Sally and Tom (The American Way)* such a powerful refutation of the American theatre's deep-rooted bias against didacticism. *Sally and Tom* is, among many other things, living proof that didacticism and entertainment are not necessarily incompatible.

D.F.

Sally and Tom (The American Way) was first produced at the Castillo Theatre (Fred Newman, artistic director; Gabrielle Kurlander producing director; Diane Stiles, managing director) in New York City on December 8, 1995. The cast, in order of appearance, was as follows:

JAMES T. CALLENDER . . . . David Nackman
JAMES MADISON . . . . James Hay
MADISON HEMINGS . . . . Marion "Doc" Davis
SALLY HEMINGS . . . . Monica J. Palmer
THOMAS JEFFERSON . . . . Robert Turner

Fred Newman and Gabrielle Kurlander, directors; Diane Stiles, producer; Dan Belmont, musical director/keyboards; Eugene B. Grey, guitar; Don Hulbert, flute; Madelyn Chapman and Gabrielle Kurlander, choreography; Joseph Spirito, set design; Sheila Goloborotko, scenic design; Charlotte, costume design; Jessica Massad, lighting design; Michael Klein, sound design; Barry Z Levine, video design/cinematography; Brenda Ratliff, production stage manager.

Sally and Tom is, among other things, a play about love; not merely a story of two people (the required number in our culture) in love, but a play about what love is. It reminds us, hopefully, of the rather startling fact that we humans can, apparently, love under almost any circumstances. In dire poverty, war, violent revolution, concentration camps, slavery, etc., we are nevertheless able to be deeply and emotionally touched by another. Che Guevara suggested that the "true revolutionary" is "guided by great feelings of love." I think he was not "ridiculous" in saying so. Sally and Tom's "love affair" does not hide the ugliness of slavery and exploitation. Rather, their capacity to touch, to love each other, makes the pain that we humans cause each other all the more poignant and tragic. In a sense, all love is tragic in a world so dominated by the injustices of one human being (or group(s) of human beings) to another.

Sally and Tom (The American Way) is dedicated to Anne Bettman and Gino Parente, two comrades who, unlike so many others, never gave up the struggle. You will always be loved.

DECEMBER 1995

CHARACTERS
(in order of appearance)

JAMES T. CALLENDER
JAMES MADISON
MADISON HEMINGS
SALLY HEMINGS
THOMAS JEFFERSON

NOTE:

A compact disk of musical selections from the original 1995 Castillo production can be obtained from the Castillo Cultural Center, New York.

Act I, Scene 1

The stage is dimly lit; a Richmond, Virginia street scene in 1802. Upstage is a large wall (the front of The Richmond Recorder *newspaper office).* JAMES T. CALLENDER *leans drunkenly on the wall.*

JAMES MADISON *is seated downstage, holding a copy of* The Richmond Recorder *and reading* CALLENDER'S *"Sally" story with obvious distress and agitation. He finishes, looks around and pensively and angrily speaks. Throughout his speech,* CALLENDER *pastes on the wall enlarged headlines from* The Recorder *denouncing Thomas Jefferson.*

MADISON: As I am James Madison, a Virginian and a lifelong friend of my mentor and neighbor from Monticello, Thomas Jefferson, now the third president of the United States of America, I will avenge him! Jefferson, who in the spring of 1776, some 26 years ago, authored America's Declaration of Independence. *(Thoughtfully.)* My God, can it really be that long? Indeed…it was another century. Jefferson, with an eloquence matched by no other American revolutionist, called for "…life, liberty and the pursuit of happiness." Some 11 years later, in 1787, Alexander Hamilton and I led the passage of the Constitution which formed our Republic; which limited the powers of our states even as it guaranteed, in the Bill of Rights, liberty and equality to them—and to the American people. *(More agitated.)* But oh, how quickly that liberty corroded in the 1790s; during Washington's eight years in office and John Adams' four years as president. The vicious Alien and Sedition Acts virtually made all criticism of government criminal. The Federalists, the party of centralized power, and its leaders, Hamilton, Washington and Adams, did not want a presidency—they really wanted a monarchy. The opposition party, the true party of democracy and liberty, the party of Thomas Jefferson, James Monroe and myself, James Madison, the Republican Party…we knew how critical the election of 1800 would be. A new century was at hand. Adams was up for re-election. He had narrowly beaten Jefferson in 1796. Jefferson spent those next four years as vice-president under Adams holding his breath and his tongue lest he himself be imprisoned under the reactionary provisions of Alien and Sedition. It was not simply Jefferson's political career at stake in the election of 1800—it was the fate of our young Republic; the fate of American liberty. AND HE WON. WE WON. What a day that was. After 35 votes in the House of Representatives *(aside)* (caused by the Republican scoundrel Aaron Burr reneging on his promise to graciously accept the vice-presidency when he and Jefferson tied—due to a mistake!—in the electoral college), after 35 votes America's very spirit of liberty, Thomas Jefferson, was finally our president.

How we did celebrate…And now, only two years later, this. *(He holds up the newspaper.)* Dammit, I told Jefferson that Callender was a liar and a cheat—a blackmailer with whom he should never work; someone who would betray him any time he had the chance; a drunkard, a wife-beater, a derelict, a blackguard, a yellow journalist with no scruples. And I told Thomas that he was in danger of being compromised by his bizarre (though no doubt meaningless and insignificant) relationship with his young Hemings slave. There is always a James T. Callender around who derives special gratification from destroying a great man. Happily in 1800 it was Hamilton, Washington and especially John Adams who suffered from Callender's poison darts. But now, here in September 1802, it is my dear friend, Thomas Jefferson, whom Callender seeks to destroy. The turncoat, the ingrate.

(CALLENDER approaches MADISON. He looks hungover and sleazy, and has an irritating laugh. He interrupts MADISON.)

CALLENDER: Mr. Madison. Mr. Madison, good afternoon, sir. What brings you to Richmond on this lovely late summer day?

MADISON: James T. Callender. James T. Callender. You dog. You swine. You betrayer. You uncouth liar. How dare you speak to me. *(MADISON looks away with utter disdain.)*

CALLENDER: *(Mockingly)* Mr. Madison. How ungenerous. You and Mr. Monroe and our dear president, Mr. Jefferson, did not hesitate to speak to me and encourage me with money when I wrote the truth of Hamilton and John Adams. Now, sir, you no longer wish to speak with me? Am I not properly aristocratic—is my blood not blue enough—for such dignified preachers of democracy as you and the president? (*Angrily.*) When I asked that you sponsor me to become Postmaster of Richmond I was condescended to, but never encouraged. (*Back to mocking.*) Did not my words attacking Adams in 1800 secure the job of president for Thomas Jefferson? Indeed, everyone knows they did. And that you and your friend Jefferson paid me for them. Now when I speak the truth of Jefferson, you hypocrite, you look down your Republican nose at me. I told you not to take James T. Callender lightly. I forewarned you. Now Jefferson will be destroyed. Everyone is speaking of the great Jefferson's affair with Sally Hemings, his Black concubine.

MADISON: I warn you, Callender, you have gone too far. You will wind up in prison again. Only this time you won't have Thomas Jefferson and Monroe and myself to get you out. Beware, Callender, we shall place you in the dungeon forever.

CALLENDER: And on what grounds, Mr. Madison, on what grounds? You and your Republican president, the holier-than-thou Thomas Jefferson, who has preached the doctrine of freedom of speech and criticism— will he jail me for telling the truth of his un-Christian affair? Is there no end to your hypocrisy? (*He laughs playfully, though maniacally.*) Oh, have you read John Quincy Adams' little poem about your friend? His dear parents, John and Abigail, who both feel understandably betrayed by their former comrade-in-arms, must be delighted with their son's poetic attack on the Monticellan rogue. Let me sing it for you, Mr. Madison. Let me sing it for you. (*MADISON walks snobbishly away, but CALLENDER follows him and sings, to the tune of "Yankee Doodle."*)

Of all the damsels on the green
On mountain, or in valley
A lass so luscious ne'er was seen
As Monticello Sally

Yankee doodle, who's the noodle?
What wife were half so handy?
To breed a flock of slaves for stock
A blackamoor's the dandy

Search every town and city through
Search market, street and alley
No dame at dusk shall meet your view
So yielding as my Sally

Yankee doodle, who's the noodle?
What wife were half so handy?
To breed a flock of slaves for stock
A blackamoor's the dandy

When press'd by loads of state affairs
I seek to sport and dally
The sweetest solace of my cares
Is in the lap of Sally

Yankee doodle, who's the noodle?
What wife were half so handy?
To breed a flock of slaves for stock
A blackamoor's the dandy

She's black you tell me—grant she be—
Must colour always tally?
Black is love's proper hue for me—
And white's the hue for Sally

Yankee doodle, who's the noodle?
What wife were half so handy?
To breed a flock of slaves for stock
A blackamoor's the dandy

You call her slave—and pray were slaves
Made only for the galley?
Try for yourselves, ye witless knaves—
Take each to bed your Sally

Yankee doodle, who's the noodle?
What wife were half so handy?
To breed a flock of slaves for stock
A blackamoor's the dandy

MADISON: *(Points his cane menacingly)* Stop it, Callender. Stop it. You have libeled and slandered our president and my friend; you have besmirched the name of the great hero of the American people. Stop it, or I'll have you locked up.

CALLENDER: Libel? How have I libeled? Slander? No, sir. Only the truth. *(He grabs MADISON's newspaper.)* Here's what I wrote of your hero. *(He reads.)*

"It is well known that Jefferson, whom it delighteth the people to honor, keeps and for many years has kept, as his concubine, one of his slaves. Her name is Sally Hemings. By this wench Sally, our president has had several children. There is not an individual in the neighborhood of Charlottesville who does not believe the story, and not a few who know it. Mute! Mute! Mute! Yes, very Mute! will all those Republican printers of biographical information be upon this point." *(He returns the newspaper to MADISON.)*

Libel? What libel? It is all true and you know it, Mr. Madison, you know it!

MADISON: Who paid for this filth, Callender? Who paid you? You mercenary. Good day, sir. You'll live in hell before the decade is done.

CALLENDER: And Mr. Jefferson shall join me there? Yes, he shall. For he has sinned far more than I. *(CALLENDER laughs maniacally.)*

(MADISON exits, leaving CALLENDER laughing and alone onstage. CALLENDER takes a bottle of whiskey from his pocket and drinks. He sings.)

("I'm a Yankee Doodle Mercenary")

Tommy Jefferson came to town
Riding a Monticello pony.
Everyone thought the world of him
But really he's a phony.

Tom's been sleeping with his slave,
Since he came back from France.
He is surely too depraved
To have his fame enhanced.

I wrote those words in 1802
In a Federalist paper of a friend I once knew,
To the tune of the "Doodle" it shook the Republicans,
Mainly the Virginians, Monroe, Madison and Jefferson.

I'm James T. Callender, a muckraking guy.
I'll bury Tom Jefferson and I'll tell you why.
He thinks that from heaven his person was sent
To be young America's third president.

I'm a scoundrel, they say.
I'd do anything for pay.
But I'm tellin' the truth;
Jefferson is a liar, we should burn him in fire.
He's not the American way.

James T. Callender came to town
Writing for the money,
Shot down Adams and Washington
Now he's after the Monticello phony.

Jimmy Callender knows the power
Of the yellow press.
Everyone hates J.T.C.
For making such a mess.

I have the feeling I'm gonna die young
Without any money, completely unsung.
Still someday they'll croak 'cause the words that I wrote
About Sally and Tommy, all the world will take note.

I'm a scoundrel, they say.
I'd do anything for pay.
But I'm tellin' the truth;
Jefferson is a liar, we should burn him in fire.
He's not the American way.

I'm a scoundrel, they say.
I'd do anything for pay.
But I'm tellin' the truth;

Jefferson is a liar, we should burn him in fire.
He's not the American way.
No!
He's not the American way.

(*CALLENDER staggers offstage humming "Yankee Doodle Dandy" and laughing wildly.*)

Act I, Scene 2

MADISON HEMINGS jumps up from the front row of the audience and onto the stage.

HEMINGS: (*With a distinct Southern accent*) Were you listenin' to those two white men fighting? When white folks fight it's always about who sinned the most. Who's the worst sinner. Who is the biggest sinner, Callender or Jefferson? (*Laughs a friendly, but slightly bitter, knowing laugh.*) Well, I suppose it's hard to say. Hard to say. Sure as hell, they've both done a lot of sinnin'. (*Checks out the audience.*) Now y'all may wonder who I am and where I came from. Actually that scene you just saw was from September 1802 in Richmond, Virginia. I wasn't even born until 1805. But I've been lookin' to catch up with those two—James Callender and James Madison—for a long time; a real long time. Y'know, Jimmy Madison wrote himself a constitution in 1787. And Jimmy Callender wrote himself that nasty piece about Tom Jefferson in the *Richmond Recorder* in 1802. I wrote a little bit myself in 1868, right after the Civil War when we was finally freed. I'll read y'all a little bit. (*Pulls out a document; sits down, puts on his glasses, and reads.*)

"I was named Madison by the wife of James Madison who was afterwards president of the United States. Mrs. Madison (who was named Dolley) happened to be at Monticello at the time of my birth, and begged the privilege of naming me, promising my mother a fine present for the honor. She consented, and Mrs. Madison dubbed me by the name I now acknowledge, but like many promises of white folks to the slaves she never gave my mother anything. I was born at my father's seat of Monticello in Albemarle County, Virginia, near Charlottesville, on the 19th day of January, 1805.

"Of my father, Thomas Jefferson, I knew more of his domestic than his

public life during his lifetime. He was the quietest of men. He was
hardly ever known to get angry. His general temperament was smooth
and even; he was very undemonstrative. He was uniformly kind to all
about him." *(Takes off his glasses; puts down the book and stands.)*

Yeah, I'm the livin' proof; the product—with my sisters and brothers—
of Thomas Jefferson and Sally Hemings' longtime relationship. Were
you watchin' those two white Jimmy's spittin' at each other? You'd
never guess my mama Sally Hemings and the rest of the slaves was the
real victims, now would ya? Callender's exposin' the great man, my
daddy, and Madison's protectin' him. Well, what about my mama?
What about my brothers and sister and Grandma Betty and the rest of
the Hemings slaves? What about millions of Black folks, some in slavery at the time and many more dead from the voyages over? What
about Mr. Madison's constitution that didn't say we wuz real people at
all? What about Callender callin' my mother a whore? Yeah...There
was lots a' sinnin' goin' on. Still is, I fear. Still is...even if we are eman-
cipated nowadays. *(Directly to the audience.)* So...now you know who I
am—kinda an invisible man in this here play. I guess I know something
about that. My name? Well, that's a little hard to say. *(Warm laugh.)*
Maybe y'wanna call me Madison Jefferson. Now, there's a helluva
name for ya. Madison Jefferson. Huh, I guess that's my real name.
(HEMINGS sings.)

("I'll Always be Thought of That Way")

My real name is Madison Jefferson,
But no one's ever called me that.
The illegitimate son of my master Tom Jefferson,
But I've had to keep it under my hat.
Sally Hemings was my Black mama.
She was the president's concubine,
So my real name is Madison Jefferson.
But no one's ever called me that,
No one's ever called me that.

Mama was known as "Dusky Sally,"
Was his woman for over 30 years.
She was the real mistress of Monticello Valley,

But lived her life with a slave woman's fears.
Mr. Jefferson told her that he loved her,
But he would never ever set her free.
So my real name is Madison Jefferson,
But no one's ever called me that,
No one's ever called me that.

Sally Hemings did you lust for him so?
Sally Hemings you would never let him go.
Could there be a love between you two
Or was the hatred of the master
Too much in you?

I got named by Dolley Madison,
She was James Madison's wife.
But I'm a Hemings, not a Jefferson,
And I've been so all my life.
My real name is Madison Jefferson,
The bastard child of Mr. Thomas J.
But, my slave name is Madison Hemings.
I guess I'll always be thought of that way.
I guess I'll always be thought of that way.

(As HEMINGS finishes the song the scene changes to a room in Monticello in 1789. SALLY HEMINGS and THOMAS JEFFERSON are busily unpacking— they returned only a few days ago from Paris via Norfolk. They both lift up a large, antique, ornate French picture frame and pose—freeze— inside it. As they freeze HEMINGS enters by a door, looks at them frozen and speaks.)

HEMINGS: That's my "mom and dad." *(Warm laugh.)* It's 1789 now and they just got back from France. That's where Mr. Jefferson and Sally Hemings started, huh...lemme see "...pursuing happiness" together. *(Warm laugh.)* Yes, sir. In Paris for six years Mr. Jefferson had himself some "life, liberty and pursuit a' happiness." His dear wife Martha, whom he loved a good deal, had died just about three years before he went over to Europe as the American ambassador to France. Once there, he had a big old love affair with an aristocratic and beautiful lady named Maria Cosway; he supported Lafayette and the French revolutionists; he watched the stormin' of the Bastille and…he slept with my mama, Sally, for the first time. Sally was there tendin' to his youngest daughter—also named Maria—and he and my mama—well she was a free lady in France, ya know, but she was only 15—they lay together. She came back to America with child—my brother, Tom, who later on disappeared mysteriously. Mr. Jefferson had got called back by President Washington to be his Secretary of the State.

(SALLY and JEFFERSON break their freeze, put away the frame, and continue unpacking.)

So it was in 1789 and "my folks" was back at Monticello even though the Master himself was in Philadelphia a lot. That's where the nation's capitol was then. And he started changin' after he got back. He started becomin' more of a politician up in Philadelphia. When he was younger he was a powerful voice against the sin of slavery—even though he was a slave owner. He was a staunch abolitionist even if he was also a hypocrite. I mean he was a kindly slave master—but he was still a slave master. Still, he favored the abolition of slavery. There was no doubt about that. But up in Philadelphia, as Secretary of State, with Adams and Hamilton and Madison and Monroe—and those "George Washington princes," as they were called—it seemed to me he got more interested in political power. But, listen, I'm gettin' way ahead of myself.

SALLY: *(She speaks [performs] as an exaggerated Black slave child)* Master Jefferson, did your dead wife and my white half-sister, Martha Wayles, help you to unpack like I do? Did she, Master Jefferson? Was she as good a "wife" as I am?

JEFFERSON: Sally, I wish you wouldn't speak that way. You're not really a little girl anymore. You're soon to be a mother and, Sally…you're not my wife. You must understand that, Sally. You really must.

SALLY: Yes, Master, I understand. But this baby I'm a carrying is gonna be free at 21, right, Master? You gonna keep your promise, right, Master? And you gonna let my older brother James be free real soon, ain't that right, Master? You gonna keep all them promises you made to me in Paris, yes y'are, Master?

JEFFERSON: Yes, Sally. Of course, I am. I would never break my promises to you. You're only 17, Sally, and you will come to learn who I am as you get older. I never break my promises, Sally, never.

SALLY: Is you gonna keep your promise to your dead wife? Is you never gonna marry again, Master? (*She laughs childishly.*) Then I'll be your wife, Master Jefferson.

JEFFERSON: I'll have no wife, Sally. I fear I'll be married only to our new nation.

SALLY: Is it my nation, too, Mr. Jefferson? Is it a nation for us slaves, too, Master? Is it?

JEFFERSON: That's a hard and fair question, Sally. Slavery is a sin, an evil. But perhaps for the moment a necessary evil. Do not worry about it, Sally. I will always take care of you.

(*SALLY continues to unpack. JEFFERSON crosses left and sings.*)

(*"Jefferson's Declaration"*)

My name is Thomas Jefferson
From Monticello and,
In youth a revolutionist,
Now I need to tend my lands.

Washington brought me back from France
To be Secretary of State.
When George requests I can't say no
For our duty is too great.

Still I wish I could retire
To family, books and plantation.
Shall I satisfy my passion's fire
Or serve my fledgling nation?

When Martha Wayles, my darling wife,
Died birthing our sixth child,
I vowed to marry nevermore
So our love wouldn't ever be defiled.

But sex and appetite were roaring in my soul;
In Paris I lay with Sally Hemings,
Beautiful and droll.
My dead wife's Black half-sister
Was sleeping in my bed,
She was a young Black child,
'Twas rape, my conscience said.

Back in America,
Where slavery persists,
Black Sally kisses me,
But Washington insists.

That, I am Thomas Jefferson,
I wrote the Declaration
And I must support the slavery
That unifies our nation.
That unifies our,
Unifies our,
Unifies our nation.

(As JEFFERSON finishes, SALLY crosses right. She sings.)

("I'll Never be Free")

SALLY:

I've been a house slave all my life,
A Black half-sister of the master's dead wife.
I went to Paris with Mr. Jefferson's daughter,
Spent many long weeks on becalmed waters.

In Paris they was makin' a new revolution.
My big brother James said we had a solution.
Ya see, in France he and I were free as birds,
But I slept with Mr. Jefferson, was taken by his words.

I'll be TJ's concubine all my life;
He ain't gonna take another white wife.
But I've never been free on American soil,
In Mr. Jefferson's bed is where I toil.

I'm Sally Hemings, and I'll never be free
Of Mr. Thomas Jefferson's slavery.
I'm Sally Hemings, and I'll never be free
Of Mr. Thomas Jefferson's slavery.

I'm stayin' with my master until he dies,
Livin' with a man who's livin' his lies.
The great Thomas Jefferson, framer of democracy,
He'll live eighty years plus with his lily-white hypocrisy,

HEMINGS and SALLY:

Oh, yeah.

SALLY:

I'll be TJ's concubine all my life;
He ain't gonna take another white wife.
But I've never been free on American soil,
In Mr. Jefferson's bed is where I toil.

I'm Sally Hemings, and I'll never be free
Of Mr. Thomas Jefferson's slavery.
I'm Sally Hemings, and I'll never be free
Of Mr. Thomas Jefferson's slavery.

HEMINGS and SALLY:

Oh, yeah.

Act I, Scene 3

A Monticello sitting room. JEFFERSON is working at his desk. SALLY is sewing. HEMINGS is reading way off to one side of the stage. There is a knock on the door. SALLY gets up to answer, but HEMINGS gets there first. He is still invisible, but he opens the door. It is MADISON. He and SALLY look surprised. They don't know how the door opened. They freeze. HEMINGS closes his book and moves "invisibly" to center stage.

HEMINGS: It's early summer, 1795. Still 10 years to go before I'm even born. *(Laughs.)* But mama's in her twenties now. She's had two more children with Master Jefferson—my brother Beverly and sister Harriet—and a miscarriage. Mr. Jefferson, now in his middle fifties, is "temporarily

retired" from political life. But things is heatin' up around the question
of who's gonna succeed General George Washington as president of
the United States. Washington was elected for his two terms unani-
mously. George was a mighty popular man. After all, he won the revolution. John Adams from Massachusetts was Washington's vice-president and he expected to be elected after Washington retired. Now Mr.
Adams was a great revolutionist, too. But he was kind of peculiar. Old
Ben Franklin once said of John Adams *(with "white" Northern accent)*,
"Always an honest man, often a great one, but sometimes absolutely
mad." *(Warm laugh.)* Well, when General Washington made plain that
he wasn't goin' to run for no third term, Adams thought that he should
be elected…unanimously. But Mr. Jefferson and Mr. Madison and Mr.
Monroe—the so-called Republicans—thought there had to be a real
election, otherwise things looked too much like monarchy, ya know.
Two parties had by then sprung into existence—the Federalists of
Hamilton and Adams and the Republicans, Mr. Jefferson's outfit. Now
y'all remember those ain't Mr. Lincoln's Republicans—they didn't
come around until much later in the 1850s. Mr. Jefferson's Republicans
are the ones that eventually became the Democrats. I know it's a little
confusin' but that's American politics. Anyway, it's 1795, the presidential election is comin' up in about a year. You recognize Mr. Madison
(points to him), don't ya? He and Mr. Jefferson talk a lot. He's over here
at Monticello often. He lives at a place called Montpelier. It's the next
plantation over. *(Stage whisper.)* I think he's here today to get my father
to run against John Adams again next year.

(SALLY, JEFFERSON and MADISON break the freeze.)

MADISON: Sally, my dear. How are you? *(SALLY nods.)* And the children, how
are they? *(SALLY nods; she's obviously more mature.)*

SALLY: And how are you, sir? And Mrs. Madison?

(A quick freeze.)

HEMINGS: *(Rushes in with stage whisper.)* That's Dolley Madison, his wife.
She's the one who's gonna name me Madison.

(Break freeze.)

MADISON: Fine, thank you, Sally. Just fine.

JEFFERSON: (*Stands and shakes hands with MADISON*) Hello, James. Good to see you. Would you like some brandy? (*MADISON nods.*) Sally, would you get us some brandy? (*SALLY nods and exits.*) I was actually just writing to you. But it's very good to see you in person, James. What brings you? Some scheme or another? (*Laughs.*) I was just re-reading that marvelous Constitution you wrote. (*Reflecting.*) Is it possible that it was only eight years ago that you and Hamilton were still working together at the constitutional convention? My God. These past five years have been trying. The Federalists have no faith in the common man and, therefore, none in liberty.

MADISON: That Constitution is what we have, Thomas. It represents, together with the Bill of Rights, its first 10 amendments, the best of what we've created. It is the Republic. These are terrible times, Thomas, terrible times, my friend. The Federalist financier and fornicator, Hamilton, wants to be royalty. And Adams…and even Washington …are more often with him than against him. To hold these 13 states together there must be liberty. That's what they demand. That's what we promised them.

JEFFERSON: Yes. And the Constitution is our guiding light; our test; our country's bible. Drink up, James. We mustn't become so despairing. We're very young, Mr. Madison, very young indeed, as countries go. Be of better cheer. We shall bury these Federalist fools. Drink and be more merry, James Madison. (*He begins to sing "Is it Constitutional?" JEFFERSON sings it lightly, with a sense of humor; mockingly. MADISON sings it seriously, although he lightens as the song progresses.*)

("*Is it Constitutional?*")

The country's very young, dear James,
Without too much tradition.
So when we wish to find
The correctness of a position
We have to ask in a proper way
That's duly institutional.

MADISON:

> Is it Constitutional?
> Does it pass the test?
> Is it good for all Americans?
> Does it serve us best?
> It must be Constitutional, Tom,
> To be American law.
> That's what the states agreed to,
> We mustn't make them sore.

JEFFERSON:

> I've thought a good deal lately
> About aliens and sedition,
> About Hamilton's obnoxiousness
> And Adam's pious tradition.
> We must destroy them, Madison,
> In a manner restitutional.

MADISON:

> But is that Constitutional?
> Mustn't we be fair?
> Even if they're truly traitors
> Is their danger present and clear?
> It must be Constitutional
> To be American law.
> That's what the states agreed to,
> We mustn't make them sore.

JEFFERSON and MADISON:

> You and I believe in independence
> Even states rights don't offend us
> If states do right by folks.
> But our Constitution,
> You know it must define us,
> Connect us and refine us
> As good Americans all.

JEFFERSON:

> And slavery, Mr. Madison,

What do we say of that?
It's such a terrible compromise
Yet it makes the economy fat.
I say we live with it, my colleague,
Though ever under perusal.

MADISON: *(Looking at SALLY)*
But is it Constitutional
To make someone a slave,
To rob her of her very soul
From birth time to the grave?

JEFFERSON and MADISON:
It must be Constitutional
To be American law.
That's what the states agreed to,
We mustn't make them sore.

You and I believe in independence
Even states rights don't offend us
If states do right by folks.
But our Constitution,
You know it must define us,
Connect us and refine us
As good Americans all.

So, it must be Constitutional
To be American law.
That's what the states agreed to,
We mustn't make them sore.

Yes, it must be Constitutional
To be American law.
That's what the states agreed to,
We mustn't make them…
Mustn't make them…
Mustn't make them sore.

(Vaudeville-style ending, in harmony.)

Act II, Scene 1

HEMINGS sits on a stool in the same room at Monticello as the last scene. There is a terrible thunder and lightning storm outside; it is visible through the window and very audible. The room is quite dark. Seated are SALLY and JEFFERSON, in a freeze. HEMINGS is idly and unself-consciously singing "My Real Name is Madison Jefferson..." He notices the audience.

HEMINGS: Well, Mr. Madison did get Mr. Jefferson to run for president in 1796 against old Johnny Adams—the Federalist—and that's how my daddy got to be vice-president. He came in a close second to Adams and back in those days that's who they made the V.P. My father hated it. He called it the biggest do-nothin' political job ever invented by man. *(Laughs.)* Now, Mr. Jefferson never even campaigned in 1796. He stayed here in Monticello the whole time. But by the election of 1800, four years later, he was rarin' to go against Adams again for the presidency...and he beat him bad. There was that little fuss with Aaron Burr that James Madison told y'all about earlier on but that finally got worked out and my father, Thomas Jefferson, became in the year of our Lord 1800, the third president of the United States. It was a dirty campaign. Those folks who say filthy, name-callin' elections didn't start till much later in American history just don't know what in hell they is talkin' about. The Adams-Jefferson race in 1800 was as dirty as they come. Now the capitol moved to Washington, D.C. that year and even though it wasn't all built up yet my father lived there while Mama, of course, stayed in Monticello. *(He stands.)*

Those was especially hard times for Black folks down South. White folks was reactin' to us real bad. In 1800 the free Black Gabriel—his former master's name and his slave last name was Prosser—attempted a slave insurrection in Richmond on August 30th. Twenty-five slaves and free Blacks were hanged by Governor James Monroe. I mean, President Jefferson had to cool his old friend Monroe out. He was gonna kill more. My father said of these slave insurrectionists; he said, "They are not felons but persons guilty of what the safety of society, under actual circumstances, obliges us to treat as a crime, but which their feelings may represent in a far different shape." And a way down in the Caribbean, Toussaint L'Ouverture and the Black masses were destroying and overthrowing the French colonists. All together, white hysteria toward Blacks seekin' freedom was mighty high. Mr. Jefferson actually worked for awhile on a plan for the deportation of Black Americans to Sierra Leone—but abolition or deportation would have also meant the end of his Monticello way of life—the life he wanted to return to when he was done with the presidency in 1808.

And in the middle of all that—in 1802—that whole business with Callender exposin' my mother and father's "affair." *(Thoughtfully.)* But ya know somethin'—it's kinda funny—all that stuff sorta brought my folks closer to each other. Sally Hemings spoke to Thomas Jefferson, her slave master, lover and president, convincin' him to spare many Black folks in response to the Gabriel rebellion. And he did. No, he never did free the slaves like they say Mr. Lincoln did. He used the successful rebellions against France in the Caribbean to help him peacefully purchase Louisiana—the French didn't want another war on the American continent. Mr. Jefferson was a shrewd politician. But he never freed the slaves, either all of us slaves or even his own slaves at Monticello. Thomas Jefferson was a hard man to love—and yet a hard man to hate.

(Lights up on SALLY *and* JEFFERSON *as the storm continues to rage.)*

SALLY: Is this Callender business going to hurt you real bad, Mr. President?

JEFFERSON: I believe we will weather it, Sally.

SALLY: You know him, Master?

JEFFERSON: Too well, dearest Sally…too well. I supported his writing when he worked for the Republican press. Abigail Adams is convinced I was behind his slanders against John two years ago. I fear she will not forgive me. Never.

SALLY: Were you?

JEFFERSON: Yes and no.

SALLY: *(Tauntingly)* It's always "yes and no" with you, Mr. Jefferson. It's always "yes and no." It makes you a hard man to love.

JEFFERSON: I do believe in liberty and compromise, dearest Sally.

SALLY: But you also stand for slavery, Thomas. You also stand for slavery. *(Sings.)*

("Enslaved by the Color of our Skin")

This heart of mine,
Would that it was free to
Beat for you.
This love of mine,
Would that it could only be true.

This passion for you,
Would that it came from only
My desire.
Enslaved to thee,
Would that my love came truly from me.

But I hate the hypocrisy in you,
When we touch where's the democracy in you?
Adore every gentle bone in you,
But in your arms I feel the throne in you.

Still I will stay with you,
Never ever run away from you.
Our tragic love,
Enslaved by the color of our skin,
Depraved by the odor of "the sin."

Yes, I will stay with you,
Never ever run away from you.
Our tragic love,
Enslaved by the color of our skin,
Depraved by the odor of "the sin."

JEFFERSON:
But whatever can I do my love?
I was born to be above.
And even though you are a slave, my love,
I'll give you everything I have.

SALLY:

You will never understand, my love.

JEFFERSON:

I will always be your man, my love.

SALLY:

No! You will always be my master.
Forever after, in the hatred of our love.

SALLY and JEFFERSON:

Enslaved by the sadness of our love.

(There is mad banging and screaming at the window. It is CALLENDER. *Musical introduction to "Rich and Poor Hypocrisy" begins.)*

CALLENDER: *(Yelling)* Jefferson, goddamn you, Jefferson. Are you in there? Are you in there with your Black whore? Are you in the lap of your shady Black bitch? Jefferson, Jefferson.

*(*JEFFERSON *moves* SALLY *[toward the invisible* HEMINGS*] and opens the window.* CALLENDER *is near death, soaked, inebriated. He sings.)*

("Rich and Poor Hypocrisy")

You are the winner, Mr. Jefferson.
Before it begins, you've already won.
You are the winner, Mr. Jefferson.
You will go on, my life is done.

I'm just a poor man of common blood.
You're an aristocrat, an American god.
I have a big mouth and make a loud noise,
But though you are quiet, you have the rich voice.

I helped you win in eighteen - o - o.
I muckraked John Adams with you in the know.
Now you and old Johnny no longer talk,
But you will be friends again when my bottle's long corked.

JEFFERSON:

You'll never know
Exactly what makes me go

Forward to build a better world
For common folks, decent and true, unlike you,
For common folks, decent and true.

You cause me shame;
You senselessly slander my name.
Yes, you will lose, not because I am rich,
You'll end up in a ditch, 'cause you choose
To turn human life into a game.

CALLENDER:

Yes, it's a game
Because you have the fame
And I'm locked in jail,
While you condescendingly bail me out
For a night. I'm a dread sight,
Not fit for a woman
On a Saturday night.

JEFFERSON:

I have no pity
For a blackguard like you from the city,
Who will defame anyone for a dollar or two.
You deserve, Mr. Callender, a turn of the screw
I hope you are through…

CALLENDER:

No, I'm not through.
Someone always will do what I do
For a living, to crucify you.
No, I'm not through.
Someone always will do what I do
For a living, to crucify you.

JEFFERSON:

I'll be redeemed even though
You have schemed
Mr. Callender, yes, I will win.
I'll be redeemed even though

You have schemed
Mr. Callender, yes, I will win.

(JEFFERSON slams window on CALLENDER.)

JEFFERSON: *(Hysterically)* That scoundrel! Imagine that slime coming to my home. Coming to Monticello. I will destroy him! *(JEFFERSON is very hysterical.)* Are you alright, Sally? Are you alright? *(He goes over to HEMINGS.)* Jupiter, see to it that Callender is thrown off the plantation. Quickly. Quickly, Jupiter, quickly.

(HEMINGS tries to indicate that he is not Jupiter, but, of course, JEFFERSON cannot hear him. Finally HEMINGS goes out the door, shaking his head in disbelief. JEFFERSON sits. SALLY comes over to him to comfort him.)

SALLY: Be calm, Master Jefferson. Be calm, Thomas. You'll bring on another deadly migraine. Be calm.

JEFFERSON: That impudent betrayer. That hypocrite. I will not have to destroy him. He will destroy himself. Oh, Sally, I did not wish for you to be a witness to all this.

SALLY: I have always been a witness to this, Thomas Jefferson. I have always been a witness to all this. Your passion to win is deep in you, Master Jefferson. It is, perhaps, covered by your gentility. But your "yes and no-ing" is not a sign of indecision. It is, rather, your politic. It is, my dearest Thomas, your desperate need to win. You are a man of profound passion. I have experienced it since I was a child. And I love your passion even though it could never truly be for me—nor, for that matter, mine for you. I remind you of all that you hate about yourself—your unprincipled cowardice, even as you remind me of all that I hate in myself, my unprincipled willingness to sell myself for a little privilege. I fear, Mr. President, that this may prove to be "the American way."

JEFFERSON: You have always been smarter than me, Sally. You have always been smarter than me.

SALLY: I am not smarter than you, Thomas, merely smarter than you could ever imagine me being.

JEFFERSON: I'll never leave you, Sally.

SALLY: Nor me you, Thomas Jefferson. Nor me you. If we are not made for each other it is only because we could not be. But we will live out our years in love…and in slavery. Maybe a better day will come for our children…and maybe not.

JEFFERSON: The world is for the living, Sally. We can take it only as far as we can.

SALLY: When I first heard you articulate that philosophy many years ago in Paris, I thought then what I still think: it is a philosophy of the privileged, Thomas Jefferson.

JEFFERSON: One of my privileges is to spend a lifetime with you, Sally Hemings—it is a great privilege. (*JEFFERSON weeps and sings.*)

(*"The Coward's Song"*)

Sally, I adore you.
Sally, ever more
I'll be with you.
In the twilight of our days,
We'll find the ways.

Love me if you're able.
Hold me, how I need you.
Hate me not
For what I'll never be.
I can't set you free.

I'm a coward.
Not proud to be,
A coward, letting them
Slander you, my love.
I can't protest
Too much invested
In my name.
It is my shame,

My Sally,
I will never leave your side,
But we must hide
Our tragic love affair.

SALLY:

You're telling me that we must lie,
And let me tell you why,
I'm your slave and not your passion,
Our love is never the fashion.

JEFFERSON:

I'm a coward.
Not proud to be,
A coward, letting them
Slander you, my love.
I can't protest
Too much invested
In my name.
It is my shame,

My Sally,
I will never leave your side,
But we must hide
Our tragic love affair.

(*They embrace.*)

Act II, Scene 2

The stage is abstract; avant-garde; no recognizable place. HEMINGS *is alone, in modern dress. He is, obviously, far more angry.*

HEMINGS: We is all dead now. Jimmy Callender didn't last but 10 months after his 1802 attack on Jefferson. He was found dead in three feet of water in the James River in the summer of 1803. No one knows how it happened. My father "weathered the storm" and won his re-election in 1804. He returned to Monticello in 1808 and lived there with my mama—and his other slaves—until he died on July 4th, 1826—the very same day as John Adams died up in Massachusetts. Now ain't that patriotic? They did become friends again—as Callender said they would—in their last 10 years. Mama, Sally Hemings, lived for a decade after Jefferson died. She was freed in 1827 by Jefferson's daughter, Martha. In 1836 both she and James Madison passed on. I myself lived to be 72—died of consumption in 1877. Yeah, we're all dead now. We can all see each other for who we were. And we can all see what's happened in America—maybe a lot better than all you livin' folks. Maybe not. The dead tend to be somewhat conceited. *(SALLY enters.)* There's my mama now. She's a mighty beautiful 222 years old, don'tcha think? "Dusky Sally." *(Warm cynical laugh.)* She made quite a fuss, quite a fuss. Hello, Mama. How is you today? *(SALLY nods.)* How's Dad? How's Mr. Jefferson?

SALLY: Oh, about the same, son. He's been dead 169 years, but everyone—includin' himself—is still protectin' him.

HEMINGS: Some things don't seem to change, Mama. Some things don't seem to change.

SALLY: I did the best I could, Madison...my son.

HEMINGS: You did good, Mama. You did good. Ain't your fault, Mama. It ain't your fault.

("The American Way")

SALLY: *(Sings)*
　　Madison Hemings, you were freed at 21
　　Just because you was Thomas Jefferson's son.
　　I got that promise from the master;
　　I couldn't make it happen any faster.

HEMINGS:
　　We've come a long, long way,
　　But have we gone anywhere?
　　It's another day,
　　But not a night without fear.
　　We are not yet free,
　　There's still slavery.

It seems like hatred of darkness
Is still the American way.

When we were still in chains
We could not conceive
That this awful pain
Might never be relieved.
We are not yet free,
There's still slavery.
It seems like hatred of darkness
Is still the American way.

The American way
Looks okay in the day,
But the American night,
What a terrible fright.
The American way,
The American way,
It seems like hatred of darkness
Is still the American way.

SALLY:

Thomas Jefferson was our founding father
And, Madison, I was your Black slave mother
Lived in the mansion, had a better life,
But I never got to be the master's wife.

HEMINGS:

We've come a long, long way,
But have we gone anywhere?
It's another day,
But not a night without fear.
We are not yet free,
There's still slavery.
It seems like hatred of darkness
Is still the American way.

The American way
The American way

The American way
The American way
The American way
The American way
It seems like hatred of darkness
Is still the American way.
It seems like hatred of darkness
Is still the American way.

HEMINGS and SALLY:
Oh, yeah.

(*Blackout. A storm begins and when lights come up again JEFFERSON, MADISON and CALLENDER are also onstage. JEFFERSON is next to HEMINGS so that HEMINGS is between his parents, SALLY and JEFFERSON. HEMINGS turns to JEFFERSON.*)

HEMINGS: Father.

(*JEFFERSON moves his head in simultaneous recognition and denial.*)

SALLY: You mustn't say that, Madison. You know you mustn't.

HEMINGS: It's over 200 years, Mama. It's time we tell the damned truth.

SALLY: No one wants to hear it, Madison—not white or Black. No one wants to know about it. No one really wants to know the truth. Some say the storm is frozen. To me it just gets darker and darker. (*The stage is getting darker and darker.*) Everyone's a politician nowadays, Madison. And everyone is usin' hate to grab a little somethin' for himself. It's the politics of hate, Madison. It's the hatred of darkness, like you sing about, becoming the darkness of hatred.

HEMINGS: But, Mama, I am angry and hateful. I am. I'm sorry, Mama, but I am angry.

SALLY: I know, Madison. And no one can hardly blame you. You hate us all. I understand that.

(*HEMINGS confronts CALLENDER and sings.*)

("The Beginning of America's Night")

HEMINGS:

    Mr. Callender, Mr. Callender,
    I've always wanted to meet you.
    You've slandered both my parents
    And I think I'd like to beat you.

    Mr. Callender, Mr. Callender,
    You wrote your words in yellow.
    You are a racist through and through,
    A most despicable fellow.

CALLENDER:

    Madison Hemings, Madison Hemings,
    You are such a stupid guy.
    You hate me for speaking the truth
    When Jefferson was the liar.

    The bastard Jefferson raped your mom
    When she was just a child.
    He's still the aristocrat,
    Your people still reviled.

HEMINGS:

    Listen, Mr. Jimmy Callender,
    What you say is a ploy
    Because you're the kind of political hack
    Who uses truth to destroy.

JEFFERSON: *(Singing to CALLENDER)*

    You'll never know
    Exactly what makes me go
    Forward to build a better world
    For common folks, decent and true, unlike you,
    For common folks, decent and true.

HEMINGS: *(To JEFFERSON)*

    Listen, Dad, you make me mad,
    And you made my people bastards.

Callender's a slimy dude
But don't be so self-righteous.

SALLY: *(To JEFFERSON)*

I hate the hypocrisy in you,
When we touch where's the democracy in you?
Adore every gentle bone in you,
But in your arms I feel the throne in you.

HEMINGS:

You're my mother, I respect you,
But there are those who might suspect you
Of using the little power you wield
To hurt the Black man in the field.

MADISON:

It must be Constitutional
To be American law.
That's what the states agreed to,
We mustn't make them sore.
It must be Constitutional
To be American law.
That's what the states agreed to,
We mustn't make them sore.

MADISON and JEFFERSON: *(As they do a dance)*

You and I believe in independence
Even states rights don't offend us
If states do right by folks.
But our Constitution
You know, it must define us,
Connect us and refine us
As good Americans all.

HEMINGS:

The Constitution compromised my soul
To keep the southern states in the fold.
And now we must engage the hate
That you founding fathers gave the states.

CALLENDER: *(Maniacally)*

> Yes, indeed, it's a sorry state.
> This is America's political fate.
> My harsh writings in Black and white
> Were just the beginning of America's night.

(Storm reaches a crescendo; CALLENDER comes center stage, laughing more maniacally than ever; "leads" the company even though they are not "following" him.)

ALL:

> Indeed, indeed, it's a sorry state.
> This is America's political fate.
> My [his] harsh writings in Black and white
> Were just the beginning of America's night.

ALL: *(Sotto voce, minus SALLY)*

> Yes, indeed, it's a sorry state.
> This is America's political fate.
> My [his] harsh writings in
>   Black and white
> Were just the beginning of
>   America's night.
> Yes, indeed, it's a sorry state.
> This is America's political fate.
> My [his] harsh writings in
>   Black and white
> Were just the beginning of
>   America's night.

SALLY: *(spoken)* No one wants to hear it, Madison—not white or Black. No one wants to know about it. No one really wants to know the truth. Some say the storm is frozen. To me it just gets darker and darker. Everyone's a politician nowadays, Madison. And everyone is usin' hate to grab a little somethin' for himself. It's the politics of hate, Madison. It's the hatred of darkness, like you sing about, becoming the darkness of hatred.

ALL: *(Including SALLY)*

> Yes, indeed, it's a sorry state.
> This is America's political fate.
> My [his] harsh writings in Black and white
> Were just the beginning of America's night.

(The company keeps singing/screaming to end of song. Then they all freeze. The "Star Spangled Banner" begins, in an electrified, distorted version à la Jimi Hendrix. MADISON speaks.)

MADISON: There are crimes so hideous that they cannot be forgiven; pain so overwhelming that it cannot be forgotten; humiliation so deep that it never recedes; constitutions so fundamentally mistaken that they cannot be corrected by amendments.

America is that most frustrating of human experiences—near perfection with a fatal mistake. And those of us who founded this country must ultimately come to terms with the fact that our creation was not equal to its vision. We failed. The inhumanity of slavery will, perhaps, never be overcome within our white and male-dominated revolutionary American culture. No reparation could be sufficient and yet no reform will succeed. For in the final analysis, we simply did not create a society in which all men and all women are equal. Frankly, as history reveals, we did not even come close.

(Lights dim to darkness. The "Star Spangled Banner" plays to conclusion.)

))))

What is to be Dead?
(Philosophical Scenes)

The key to *What is to be Dead? (Philosophical Scenes)* (1996) is to be found in its subtitle.

This play is best approached (by the reader, by the audience member, by director and performer) as a series of philosophical conversations. The topic of each is provided in the text: Existentialism; Identity; Meaninglessness; Being and Nothingness; Sex and Death; Postmodernism. Each can stand on its own. (Brecht had wanted the same for the scenes of his plays.) One need not know what was said in "Meaninglessness," for example, to understand and appreciate the conversation in "Being and Nothingness," although taken together they enrich each other. At the same time *What is to be Dead?* functions as a drama, exploring a number of richly interrelated relationships and bringing to the stage some of Newman's most interesting stage characters. The particular artistry of *What is to be Dead?* lies in the fact that it is a series of autonomous philosophical dialogues which also gracefully unfold into a play.

In this regard *What is to be Dead? (Philosophical Scenes)* comes the closest of any of Newman's plays to the work of George Bernard Shaw, although Shaw obviously had more faith in the power of ideas than Newman does. As in all Newman's plays, here it is the *activity* of the conversation (the dialectic) that is of value, not the ideas separated (abstracted, alienated) from that activity.

For 30 years the doing of philosophy and of politics have been inseparable activities for Newman. Over these last three decades he has been engaged in nothing more and nothing less than the excruciating and sometimes exhilarating business of creating environments—political, therapeutic, cultural—where the 2,500-year-old philosophical assumptions that overdetermine how we do politics, psychology and culture can be called into question. It should come as no surprise, then, that this most explicitly philosophical of his plays continues to explore many of Newman's ongoing political concerns.

As in *Mr. Hirsch Died Yesterday,* written 10 years earlier, in *What is to be*

Dead? Newman uses African American and Jewish characters to investigate the philosophical and political implications of identity. The conflicted historical relationship between these two oppressed peoples—which have both, in different ways and with different degrees of success, turned to identity politics as a response to oppression—provides fertile ground for this exploration.

All the characters in *What is to be Dead?* are gay; the play was originally written for a June (Gay Pride Month) production at Castillo. While the focus here isn't on gay identity, as it is in *Outing Wittgenstein, What is to be Dead?* utilizes a "coming out" scene to turn assumed identities upside down.

Like *Lenin's Breakdown, What is to be Dead?* is very much a post-communist play. The parallels it sets up between late 19th-century Russia and late 20th-century America are made all the more stark by the fact that the Russian Revolution failed. From our vantage point in history we know that Rivin is right when he advises his Bolshevik sister, "Get what you can now out of his [Lenin's] sad eyes. Soon enough, I fear, they will turn colder and colder and his successor, I suspect, will have no eyes at all." The intervening century has not come up with a cure for Rivin's sickness. Instead the disease has become more pervasive and far more advanced.

Finally (and here the distinction between philosophy and politics, method and content, becomes considerably blurred), this play is full of dead people. *Lenin's Breakdown, Outing Wittgenstein, Billie & Malcolm: A Demonstration,* and the last scene in *Sally and Tom (The American Way)* also contain "dead" characters. In *What is to be Dead?* just what Newman means by "dead" is more ambiguous than ever. These dead people are not in "heaven" (as in *Billie & Malcolm*), nor are they neatly in "history" or "memory" (as in *Lenin's Breakdown* and *Sally and Tom*). They are simultaneously in history and society, now and then, here and there, alive and dead. Those who find contradiction uncomfortable may be driven to distraction by *What is to be Dead?* The play *is* a contradiction—characters who are and aren't, settings that are where they are and also somewhere else, lively conversations and warm relationships soaked in a deep despair.

Anyone looking for answers will not find them here. The action of the play is, among other things, a prolonged *asking* of the question: "What is to be dead?" It attempts no answer. At most, the experience of the play may assure us, as Walt Whitman did in "Song of Myself" some 150 years earlier,

"Has any one supposed it lucky to be born?/I hasten to inform him or her it is just as lucky to die, and I know it."

The thread of common concerns and themes evident in Newman's plays, as well as the clear patterns of character construction/deconstruction and dramatic structure in his work brings to mind Heiner Müller's remark that "…you always write the same play, [only] with different material."

Yet comparing *Mr. Hirsch* and *What is to be Dead?* also throws into sharp relief the development of Newman's playwriting craft. Both plays are concerned with identity, with an exploration/critique of the conventional concept of self. Not surprisingly then, both plays offer examples of Newman's approach to character as other-than-a-specific-one. In *Mr. Hirsch* the two characters with the same history (Fred and Freda) confront each other over the issue of identity. In *What is to be Dead?* the character as other-than-a-specific-one is approached much more casually. There is no explanation of (or fight about) how Sprintze could also be Mrs. Golub or how Pearlie could be Hinda. They just are. Rivin (a Jew) and Sam (an African American), whose stories and attitudes—separated by more than 100 years—parallel each other so closely, may very well be not two different people with the same history but the *same* person with two different histories. The nature of the individual is no longer, as it was in *Mr. Hirsch*, the focus of the play. Instead, Newman's fluid, emergent, transforming vision of the (un)self is taken for granted and is simply a part (a significant part) of the play's philosophical investigations into the identities of "dead" and "alive."

Both plays tell the same story (in the case of *What is to be Dead?* it is hardly a story at all) from different points in history. *Mr. Hirsch* presents the same story twice, consecutively. *What is to be Dead?* not only weaves the two narratives together in a series of alternating scenes in which the characters (and their stories) gradually merge; as these two sets of characters/stories come together, they coexist with/are the same as a series of related philosophical dialogues.

What is to be Dead? is the most layered of Newman's plays to date. It contains within it virtually all of Newman's philosophical, political, and dramatic concerns presented within his most nuanced dramatic structure.

D.F.

What is to be Dead? (Philosophical Scenes) was first produced at the Castillo Theatre (Fred Newman, artistic director; Gabrielle Kurlander producing director; Diane Stiles, managing director) in New York City on June 7, 1996. The cast, in order of appearance, was as follows:

SAM . . . . Doug Miranda
RIVIN . . . . Kenneth Hughes
PEARLIE/HINDA . . . . Gloria Strickland
SPRINTZE/MRS. GOLUB . . . . Marian Rich

Fred Newman, director; Jim Horton, producer; Joseph Spirito, set and scenic design; Charlotte, costume design; Beth Peeler and Charlie Spickler, lighting design; Michael Klein, sound design; Barry Z Levine, video design/cinematography; Brenda Ratliff, production stage manager.

A NOTE FROM THE AUTHOR

What is to be Dead? (Philosophical Scenes) is about many things; one important thing it's about is family and, in particular, the relationship between brothers and sisters. My own sister Pearl (I come from a family of four boys and one girl) has played a critical role in my life. As the only girl, the middle child of five in a working-class family in which both parents died relatively young, Pearl became the surrogate mother (especially to me, the youngest, some 15½ years her junior) and the cohesive force of the family. I was the official rebel and Pearl, perhaps sometimes unwittingly, nurtured that rebelliousness. For she herself is a rebel. But like so many working women of her generation (she is now 76), she had little opportunity for higher education and a career. She married young; looked after a husband injured in World War II; raised her own family (plus me); and continues even now to work at relatively low paying, labor intensive sales jobs. Some "outsiders" might think she "failed" in her raising of me. Of course, she and I know better. My big sister is a rebel "in the closet." She made it possible for me to "come out." I dedicate this play to her and to all the other rebels who have not had the opportunity to live their lives fully.

JUNE 1996

CHARACTERS
(in order of appearance)

SAM

RIVIN

PEARLIE

SPRINTZE

HINDA

MRS. GOLUB

Scene 1: Existentialism: past and present

The entire set is a dingy "underground"/shelter setting; the right half of the stage is a Russian turn-of-the-century scene, the left a contemporary inner-city scene. Each side has a small table. Seated at the Russian table is RIVIN *(who calls himself Raskolnikov), the underground man; at the other table is* SAM, *a street person. Each has a stack of papers before him; presumably their own writings. They hold the papers (perhaps) as they "read" (speak) their own words.*

RIVIN: I am a sick man…I am a wicked man. An unattractive man. I think my liver hurts. However, I don't know a fig about my sickness, and am not sure what it is that hurts me. I am not being treated and never have been, though I respect medicine and doctors. What's more, I am also superstitious in the extreme; well, at least enough to respect medicine. (I'm sufficiently educated not to be superstitious, but I am.) No, sir, I refuse to be treated out of wickedness. Now, you will certainly not be so good as to understand this. Well, sir, but I understand it. I will not, of course, be able to explain to you precisely who is going to suffer in this case from my wickedness; I know perfectly well that I will in no way "muck things up" for the doctors by not taking their treatment; I know better than anyone that by all this I am harming only myself and no one else. But still, if I don't get treated, it is out of wickedness. My liver hurts; well, then let it hurt even worse!

I've been living like this for a long time—about 20 years. I'm 40 now. I used to be in the civil service; I no longer am. I was a wicked official. I was rude, and took pleasure in it. After all, I didn't accept bribes, so I had to reward myself at least with that. (A bad witticism, but I won't cross it out. I wrote it thinking it would come out very witty; but now, seeing for myself that I simply had a vile wish to swagger—I purposely won't cross it out!) When petitioners would come for information to the desk where I sat—I'd gnash my teeth at them, and felt an inexhaustible delight when I managed to upset someone. I almost always managed. They were timid people for the most part: petitioners, you know. But among the fops there was one officer I especially could not stand. He simply refused to submit and kept rattling his sabre disgustingly. I was at war with him over that sabre for a year and a half. In the end, I prevailed. He stopped rattling. However, that was still in my youth. But do you know, gentlemen, what was the main point about my wickedness? The whole thing precisely was, the greatest nastiness precisely lay in my being shamefully conscious every moment, even in moments of the greatest bile, that I was not only not a wicked man but was not even an embittered man, that I was simply frightening sparrows in vain, and pleasing myself with it. I'm foaming at the mouth, but bring me some little doll, give me some tea with a bit of sugar, and maybe I'll calm down. I'll even wax tenderhearted, though afterward I'll certainly gnash my teeth at myself and suffer from insomnia for a few months out of shame. Such is my custom.

And I lied about myself just now when I said I was a wicked official. I lied out of wickedness. I was simply playing around both with the petitioners and with the officer, but as a matter of fact I was never able to become wicked. I was conscious every moment of so very many elements in myself most opposite to that. I felt them simply swarming in me, those opposite elements. I knew they had been swarming in me all my life, asking to be let go out of me, but I would not let them. I would not, I purposely would not let them out. They tormented me to the point of shame; they drove me to convulsions, and—finally I got sick of them, oh, how sick I got! But do you not perhaps think, gentlemen, that I am now repenting of something before you, that I am asking your forgiveness for something?...I'm sure you think so...However, I assure you that it is all the same to me even if you do...Not just wicked, no, I never even managed to become anything: neither wicked nor good, neither a scoundrel nor an honest man, neither a hero nor an insect. And now I am living out my life in my corner, taunting myself with the spiteful and utterly futile consolation that it is even impossible for an intelligent man seriously to become anything, and only fools become something. Yes, sir, an intelligent man of the 19th century must be and is morally obliged to be primarily a characterless being; and a man of character, an active figure—primarily a limited being. This is my 40-year-old conviction. I am now 40 years old, and, after all, 40 years—is a whole lifetime; after all, it's the most extreme old age. To live beyond 40 is indecent, banal, immoral! Who lives beyond 40—answer me sincerely, honestly? I'll tell you who does: fools and scoundrels do. I'll say it in the faces of all the elders, all these venerable elders, all these silver-haired and sweet-smelling elders! I'll say it in the whole world's face! I have the right to speak this way, because I myself will live to be 60. I'll live to be 70! I'll live to be 80!…Wait! Let me catch my breath.

You no doubt think, gentlemen, that I want to make you laugh? Here, too, you're mistaken. I am not at all such a jolly man as you think, or as you possibly think; if, however, irritated by all this chatter (and I already feel you are irritated), you decide to ask me: what precisely am I?—then I will answer you: I am one collegiate assessor. I served so as to have something to eat (but solely for that), and when last year one of my distant relations left me 6,000 rubles in his will, I resigned at once and settled into my corner. I lived in this corner before as well, but now I've settled into it. My room is wretched, bad, on the edge of the city. My servant is a village woman, old, wicked from stupidity, and always bad-smelling besides. I'm told that the Petersburg climate is beginning to do me harm, and that with my negligible means life in Petersburg is very expensive. I know all that, I know it better than all these experienced and most wise counsellors and waggers of heads. But I am staying in Petersburg; I will not leave Petersburg! I will not leave because… Eh! But it's all completely the same whether I leave or not.

But anyhow: what can a decent man speak about with the most pleasure?

Answer: about himself.

So then I , too, will speak about myself.

(Lights fade on Russian setting; come up on inner-city setting.)

SAM: I am a sick man…I am a wicked man. An unattractive man. I am sure I have AIDS. However, I'm not even sure what it is that hurts me. Y'know. I refuse to be treated—yeah, I refuse to be treated out of my wickedness. Yeah, I am a wicked man—a *homosexual,* a dope fiend, a nigger. Now I assume you liberals will not understand all of this; I assume you think I am "conveying the wrong message to others." But I am no message—I have no message—I send no message. My life, my sickness, my homosexuality, my Black ass, my AIDS is no damn message. Yeah. I know I am unattractive in this way. Ugly. Yes. I am ugly as sin. I like being ugly in your pretty and petty world.

I would like to tell you liberals, whether you do or do not wish to hear it, why I never managed to become even an insect. I have mostly wanted to be a roach—a cockroach. I have mostly wanted to die by being stepped on—from above. Squish. Then dead. Why? You ask why? You think it is because I wish to die quickly? To avoid pain? To avoid my wretchedness? Well, as usual, you are wrong. No. I wish to die like a cockroach so my death, my life, will have no meaning at all; will send no message. Ya see, even you animal-loving liberals—you whale lovers—show no concern for the roach. No pickets. You see no significance in the regular stomping out of roaches in the kitchens of our squalid homes. I want to die as a roach; squished out of existence in a moment, to deprive you of my havin' any significance, of my bein' a message. Yeah. I am a wicked man—a faggot, a nigger, a crack head, and I mean nothing—nothing at all. You will not "make something" of my life.

I have diabetes. I can barely walk. So I go to a clinic in Harlem near where I live. I call for an ambulette. I am told one is not available for 10 days. I say, "I need my shots." They say, "Ten days." Why, I ask? Why so long? They tell me, "The ambulettes go first to the AIDS patients." I will not tell them, "I have AIDS." Diabetes means less. I prefer it. I do not want to be your message, your meaning.

Now, you liberals, you readers of Dostoevsky, will call me a liar—what is your funny word?—disingenuous. *(Laughs.)* You'll say—*(in funny, white-sounding, high-pitched voice)* "He wants to be more significant than everyone else. He wants to be *especially* meaningful. That's what his denial, his desire to be a cockroach is really about." How clever you all are. How hip. How existential. Of course, you are right. I am really an egomaniac. I really think I am more significant than all of you and more significant than others with AIDS, other faggots, other dope fiends, other niggers. Yeah. You liberals got this one right. But so what? That's still not what you want me to mean. You don't want me to be too significant—just a little significant and, most importantly, to be *your* significance—to be significant for you or to you. So I aggravate you even if you are "on to me." For you cannot stand that I know that you are on to me. I have AIDS and it means nothing. Nothing at all. It don't mean shit. And you can't stand that I don't care 'cause you need me to care. Ya see the right-wingers don't care that I don't care. They don't care either. But you liberals got the carin' sickness. Shit. The carin' sickness is worse than AIDS. Kills more people. Got no cure either. But it don't make *you* ugly and it don't make YOU dead. But the carin' sickness killed more people than the plague. AIDS; AIDS ain't nothin' next to the carin' sickness. Say what, liberal? Oh yeah. I hear ya. Now you sayin' *(in liberal's voice)*, "Well you seem to have the caring sickness, too. You seem to care for us far too much." Yeah. I hear ya. This time you is partly right. I do cares for ya, liberal. But I don't pretend to care *about* ya. Dat's why y'all hate Farrakhan. And why ya hated Malcolm and Fanon. 'Cause they all said, "We don't care what you liberals think. We don't hate you…we even care *for* you…we just don't care about you. You don't *mean* nuthin' to us." And Farrakhan, hmm', he don't like me either. Why? 'Cause I don't care about nuthin'. He don't mean nuthin' to me either. And the Minister wants to kick my Black ass 'cause I don't care. But with all due respect, Mr. Farrakhan, I *don't* care. Funny thing, Mr. Farrakhan, you and the liberals, the white liberals you don't care about, *both* got the carin' sickness. Shit. I only got AIDS. I feel sorry for y'all but I don't care about you. I don't care about you and I don't care about me. But I don't care that I don't care. The right-wingers don't care outta hate; the liberals care for me out of guilt. Ya wonder why I'm not so high on white folks! That's one hell of a choice. Farrakhan cares *for* me outta "bow-tie" pride. But me, I just don't care. I don't even feel sorry for myself. I just don't care at all. Jesus, man, if I weren't a poor nigger and a faggot I'd be a goddamned existential hero! Who the fuck woulda believed there would be discrimination even in the "existential hero" business. *(Laughs into cough.)* The damned carin' disease adjusts everything. Even me. *(Pointing to RIVIN.)* He was never adjusted. Back then the world was too ugly, too despairing, too fearful to adjust to. So those poor folks, those poor Russians eventually made a goddamned revolution "to change the world." But only a fool tries to become something; only a fool—or an opportunist—tries to change the world. Nowadays we adjust to everything. No more fear, no more trembling, no more—what's the word—*angst,* no more revolution...just bein' adjusted. *(Laughs into coughing.)* I don't *wanna* be adjusted but I am. The damned carin' disease adjusts everything. *(Points to RIVIN.)* Back then the world was uncarin'. You could be an existential hero, a genuine madman. Back then AIDS woulda been a bona fide apocalypse; it could have been what ignited the goddamned Russian Revolution which, we all know, failed anyhow. But AIDS coulda been a first rate tragedy that moved fools to try to do something. Not now. No way. Nowadays—we adjust. But I don't wanna adjust; I don't want to be cared for; I don't want to be someone's message. What can a sick and wretched man do in such a well-adjusted world? He can merely get on with it, I guess. He has no meaning. What can a decent man talk about? Nothing. Not even himself. He can simply move from moment to moment. Life is meaningless. Why? Because we have all adjusted. And, I'm sick of it. But I am adjusted, too. You liberals won the day. Now the political reactionaries are taking over 'cause you liberals won and anything goes. We will adjust to that, too, I guess. Meanin' don't mean a damned thing no more.

Scene 2: Identity

A modest working-class contemporary inner-city apartment, SAM's sister PEARLIE's home; decorated with nationalist icons; pictures, etc. PEARLIE is sitting on a couch reading. There is a knock at the door. She opens the door and SAM stands in the doorway totally disheveled.

SAM: Hey, Pearlie. How ya doing, Babe? *(Pause.)* Oh, hey, I'm sorry, kid. It ain't Pearlie no more, right? What's it now, sis? Teluma? Is that it? Teluma. I like that new name. You say it's African, huh. Teluma. Shit. I got me a damned sister named Teluma. How ya doin', T-E-L-U-M-A? *(Reaches to kiss her; she pulls away.)*

PEARLIE: You smell like shit. When'd you last take a shower?

SAM: Hey, I don't want no shower, T-E-L-U-M-A.

PEARLIE: It's TAKUMA...and you know it...and you STINK. Go take a goddamned shower, brother.

SAM: TAKUMA! Oh yeah. Yeah, I forgot…really I did, Pearlie. Those African names is hard, y'know. Dey sound funny. TAKUMA. I like it, baby sister. It's cool, TAKUMA. Sounds goddamned authentic, y'know.

PEARLIE: It was our great grandmother's name, big brother…now get your Black ass cleaned up or get the fuck outta my house. *(Walks stage left and gets a big black towel that she throws at SAM.)*

SAM: You gonna throw out your big brother if'n he don't take no shower? That's the kinda sister you gonna be? Dat how you treat a sick African brother? *(Mocking.)* Is you anti-gay, Pearlie…oh, I'm sorry, TAKUMA.

PEARLIE: No, I ain't anti-gay, I'm anti-dirt. *(Pause. Looks at him more tenderly. Sighs.)* How are ya feelin' anyway? You been in the hospital again? How's ya T-count? You heard a' this new drug? I read about it in the *City Sun*. How the hell are ya, man? You look like shit warmed over. Go take a goddamned shower and I'll fix ya some breakfast. *(Walks over to closet and gets a pair of her sweats; throws them at him.)* Here's a pair of my sweats. Go shower and put 'em on. God, you stink bad.

(SAM walks slowly to offstage bathroom; PEARLIE goes to onstage kitchen to get pan, etc. She turns on the radio, tuned to a Black station. Shower water sound begins; blackout. After 25 seconds, lights up with wet-haired SAM at kitchen table in sweats and PEARLIE serving him eggs and toast.)

SAM: What you been up to, Pearlie? What you tryin' to be nowadays?

PEARLIE: Listen, Sam, I'm just trying to be who I really am…an African woman.

SAM: Now, how come you work so hard at tryin' to be who you really is? And why are you so damned proud to be who you simply is? I'd think it would make more sense to be proud of who in the hell you aren't. Y'know. What you made of yourself. Yeah, Pearlie, what d'you thinka that?

PEARLIE: I think that's a lot of your bullshit white philosophy. But no amount of that shit can cover up your Black ass, my brother. You still sleepin' on those damned streets 'cause you a Black man in racist America.

SAM: Now wait a minute, Pearlie…

PEARLIE: TAKUMA!

(SAM stares at her.)

SAM: ...I thought I was on those streets because I'm a lazy good for nothing. Ain't that what you been tellin' me for 10 years now, Pearlie?

PEARLIE: Yeah, my brother, but lazy good for nothin' *white* folks ain't where you are.

SAM: Oh, but they are, Pearlie. They are on the streets. We is knockin' on death's door, my sister. And there ain't no goddamned difference between dead Black and dead white. Pearlie, we all smell the same when we're dead. And as me and those ugly *white* faggots get closer we smell more and more alike. We all stink like shit. Ya see, Pearlie, it don't mean shit when you about to become shit. No. I ain't got no identity, baby. I don't want no identity. This is a kinda freedom I got now, Pearlie. Y'all gotta adjust to me.

PEARLIE: Maybe so, Sam. But for those of us still livin' ya gotta decide who y'are. And I'm an African...TAKUMA, an African woman. Y'know Sam, in a certain way I almost agree with you. I mean if ya look forward sometimes there ain't nothin' to see but death. So I choose to look backward to where I come from—and I come from Africa, Sam. I come from Africa. We all eventually go back to the earth, Sam. So it's where we come from that counts.

SAM: Hey, I hear ya, Pearlie—TAKUMA *(said for the first time almost seriously)*—I hear ya, sister. But nuthin' counts. And that's the good news. We're a funny kind of animal, Pearlie. Even before we got AIDS; even before we got the liberal carin' sickness; from almost the very beginnin' us crazy humans done had the countin' disease. That's why I want to be a roach, sister. Ya see, in a way, I wanna go back to my roots, too. I wanna go back to not countin', Pearlie. Does that make any sense to ya?

(PEARLIE is crying; she reaches out for SAM's hand.)

PEARLIE: *(Sadly and passionately)* Ya counts to me, Sam; ya counts to me.

SAM: I know, my little sister. I know, Pearlie. And it makes me feel bad and sad 'cause I'm gonna be dead in a little bit. *(Stands and kills a roach on the floor by stomping on it. They both freeze, staring at each other.)*

PEARLIE: *(Breaks the sad silence)* I gotta go to a meetin', Sam. We're havin' a big welcome back from Africa celebration for Minister Farrakhan, next month. You gonna hang around here for a while?

(SAM nods yes.)

SAM: My social worker might be comin' over to give me a check.

PEARLIE: Mrs. Golub?

SAM: Yeah, I told her I'd be here. Y'mind, Pearlie? *(PEARLIE shakes her head.)* I could meet her downstairs in the streets.

PEARLIE: I don't mind, Sam. Stay as long as ya like. When you leave, just close the door—it'll lock by itself. *(Starts toward the door; comes back and kisses SAM.)* Now, you take care, Sam. Take care.

SAM: I'm good, Takuma. I'm good. *(Sinks into the couch as PEARLIE exits.)*

Scene 3: Meaninglessness

1903 in St. Petersburg, the modest apartment of RIVIN's sister SPRINTZE, filled with books and Bolshevik icons. There is a knock on the door. It's RIVIN (who calls himself Raskolnikov). SPRINTZE waits for the correct—coded—knock. None comes. RIVIN keeps knocking. She goes to the door and whispers angrily.

SPRINTZE: Who's there? Who is it?

RIVIN: It's Raskolnikov. Open up. It's your brother Rivin. It's not the police. Open up, Sprintze. Goddamn it…open up.

(SPRINTZE opens the door and lets RIVIN in.)

SPRINTZE: *(Whispers)* What are you doing here?

RIVIN: I don't know. I am here.

SPRINTZE: It's dangerous for me. Don't you care?

RIVIN: What are you doing now? Why is it dangerous?

SPRINTZE: These are revolutionary times. You know that. But you don't care about me. You don't care about anything or anyone except yourself.

RIVIN: I do not care about myself. I care about nothing. Everything is meaningless. Nothing can be done, Sprintze, nothing can be done. Why do you risk your life? The Czar is no good. But you people, you socialists, you revolutionaries are no better. You are no better; I am no better. Chernyshevsky was a fool; spending 25 years in Siberia for writing an awful novel. A fool. Tales about new people. What new people? He was a fool. Then your hero Lenine writes an even more awful book with the same stupid title. *What is to be Done?* Nothing. Nothing is to be done. Only a fool thinks he can do something. Only a fool thinks he can be something or someone.

SPRINTZE: Why are you here? What do you want? For 10 years now I have listened to your dead talk; your Dostoevskian despair, your nihilistic nonsense. You have wasted your brilliant mind, your genius, on self-serving empty phrases. *You* can do nothing. Lenine and the Russian masses, the proletariat and the peasantry can do much. And they will. And Lenine will lead them. And you…you will still be underground pretending to see the future when, in fact, you are too dead to even see the present. *You* are a fool, Rivin or Raskolnikov—as you stupidly call yourself—pretending to be a philosopher and wasting your life.

RIVIN: No, Sprintze. We are *all* wasting our lives—our wretched lives. We are pretenders—the pretending species. We cannot stop pretending. We are doomed, all of us, to eternal pretense. No insect ever declares its own authenticity. Only us phonies, us fools, us pretenders, do that. Your Lenine might well succeed one day. After all, Russia is a cesspool; the Czar and his ministers are madmen. The Queen and her mystical lover, Rasputin, are more stupid than can be imagined even in a world more imbecilic than can be believed. No. Your Vladimir Ilyich Lenine might succeed. Maybe one day Russia, the darkest of all countries, will become the enlightened, social-ist state that you dream of, my dearest sister Sprintze. But it will grow dark again. Everything grows dark again. Socialism will fare no better than Moses or Jesus or Mohammed. It will be corrupted because we are a cor-ruption—pretending eternally that we can be other than a corruption. Socialism, Sprintze, is already—here in its earliest moments—as much a "commodified product" as anything your Mr. Marx writes of in his pompous puffery about Kapital. Progress! Historical progress! (*Laughs.*) There is no progress. Not for us. Not for pretenders like us.

SPRINTZE: Well, then are these words you tell me also pretense?

RIVIN: Of course they are. It is you who insists I am a genius. I am just another man making noises, Sprintze. Another fool. More a fool than others, thinking, perhaps, that my passion in seeing what a fool I am makes me less a fool. But, of course, it doesn't. Maybe they will make statues of Lenine one day. And then, someday, they too will crumble and everyone will rejoice like the fools that we are. *(Laughs.)* Heh, heh. Don't let them frighten you, Sprintze. Everything bad that could happen has already happened. We have nothing to lose...only because we have nothing to gain.

SPRINTZE: *(Very angry and confrontational)* I think you are crazy...Rivin. A genius, no doubt. And, as well, a fool. Indeed, a philosophical fool. For even if everything you say is true we must still figure out what is to be done. We must still figure out—so long as we have chosen to stay alive and *obviously* both you AND me have made that choice—we must figure out what to do given this dreadful picture you so beautifully paint. If there is nothing to choose between your ceaseless philosophizing and my ceaseless politicizing then so be it. LET'S NOT CHOOSE BETWEEN DIFFERENT VIEWS OF THE WORLD. Perhaps there are no real choices, no better views. They are all, let us agree, phony. Then we must *still* consider the difference between your phony choices, your view and my phony choices, my phony view. *(Pause.)* How easy it is to be negative—critical and philosophically correct. How easy to call Lenine just another phony ideologue. Oh yes. You are right, Rivin. Ideology oversimplifies life and your brilliant negativism exposes the limits of ideology. But no one—no one—is guided by your stupid philosophical truth; your negative insights. Ideology over-simplifies, distorts. Yes, I understand. But we must have ideology to move ahead. And socialism, social democracy, Lenine is our best ideological bet, my brilliant brother, Rivin, my underground man "Raskolnikov."

RIVIN: *(Breathing heavily)* You are a very bright woman, Sprintze...very intelligent. For you have identified a real meaning for the stupid question: what is to be done? What does it mean? It means this: given that we foolish humans seemingly cannot go forward without ideology and that ideology so distorts the human situation then how can we go forward without the ideology ultimately destroying us?

(Long pause.)

SPRINTZE: I believe in Lenine.

RIVIN: I envy you. I know him to be a fool.

SPRINTZE: Rivin, enough already. You must rest. You'll stay a few days? You do not look well. How is your liver?

RIVIN: I am sick…as always. *(He is breathing heavily.)*

SPRINTZE: We have talked too much.

RIVIN: No. No, dearest Sprintze. You are the only one I can talk to anymore.

SPRINTZE: I must go to a cell meeting. Here is the knock *(raps 1,2,3,—4)*. Do not let anyone in unless they knock properly.

RIVIN: You let me in.

SPRINTZE: I am your sister. You are my brother.

RIVIN: *(Laughs)* I would have thought that meant nothing to either of us.

SPRINTZE: *(Laughs)* We are silly fools. On this, perhaps, we agree. *(Puts on her coat; RIVIN lies down tiredly on couch. She kisses his forehead.)* Rest, Rivin, rest. *(Exits.)*

Scene 4: Being and nothingness

One hour later. RIVIN is still asleep. There is a "proper" knock on the door; RIVIN does not move. Then a louder knock; two times more. Finally RIVIN awakens, goes to the door and opens it. HINDA (played by the actress playing PEARLIE), an old family friend, once an orthodox Jew, now a Bundist, stands at the door.

HINDA: Rivin? *(With wonder.)* What are you doing here?

RIVIN: Hinda? Is it really you? I haven't seen you in years. Come in. Come in. *(She enters.)* I was just visiting Sprintze. She went off to *(whispers half mockingly)* one of her meetings—you know. I was very tired and she urged me to stay and rest for a while. I fell asleep. *(They stare.)* Do you want something? A glass of wine? (*Looks for wine.*) Where does she keep wine? (HINDA *finds it.*) Where are glasses? (HINDA *finds them;* RIVIN *pours; they stare.*) What have you been doing? Are you still in school? Look at you, Hinda, you're all grown-up.

HINDA: I finished school over five years ago, Rivin.

RIVIN: You did good? (*Laughs.*) Of course you did. You were always a wonderful student. (*Pause.*) You are married?

HINDA: No.

RIVIN: You are political…like, uh, Sprintze.

HINDA: I am political but not like Sprintze. I am a socialist but not a social democrat. I am with the Jewish Bund.

RIVIN: You are still orthodox?

HINDA: No. My family is dead. I am a socialist but still very much a Jew. I could never give that up, Rivin. (*Pause.*) Sprintze tells me you have gone underground; that you have abandoned everything. You do not look well. You have no color. Your old liver ailment is still with you?

RIVIN: I'm afraid so, Hinda. I am sick and…yes, I am also wretched. I am underground but unlike Sprintze I have no purpose for being so. I have no purpose at all.

HINDA: You are still a Jew.

RIVIN: I am not a Jew. I am still persecuted like one, but I am not a Jew anymore. I have neither a history nor a future, Hinda. I live for nothing for there is nothing to live for. Sprintze and I spoke of Lenine's new book, *What is to be Done?* A stupid book named after Chernyshevsky's silly novel. For me there is nothing to be done. I merely exist.

HINDA: When we were young together your parents were so wonderful and optimistic. Every one of us children envied you and Sprintze because your mother and father were so alive, so funny, so warm, so caring. And you, Rivin, you were the oldest boy in our crowd; so brilliant, so talented. You played music. You wrote poetry. You read Talmud. I looked up to you. No! I adored you. How could this have happened? What happened to you, Rivin?

RIVIN: *(Walks away a little)* It's good to see you, Hinda. I do not wish to fight with you. But for me—for me, the question is, how come nothing has happened to you? Why are you—and Sprintze—still children—beautiful children dreaming hopefully to change the world, socialists of varying stripes but still infants pretending that you can make a better world; searching to discover what is to be done? *(Smirks.)* Are you also like Sprintze a lover of Lenine?

HINDA: No. I am not. In fact, Mr. Lenine is causing me and the Bund much grief these days. He is insisting that we all must join the RSDLP—you know, *his* social democratic party. He says we can go no further together in coalition. He says there must be a centralized cadre; a single fist and a single mind—and, of course, it is his. And, as well, he is causing grief for me and Sprintze, our friendship. She deeply admires him and respects him—and follows him. I think he is clever and that he has suffered—his brother was murdered by the Czar, you know—but I am wary of him and his politics. He is an atheist. I am a Jew.

RIVIN: Why are you still a Jew? What does it mean that you are a Jew?

HINDA: It's where I come from, Rivin. Without it, I mean nothing. My hopes are for the future. But me, the one who hopes, comes from the past. And it is a Jewish past, a Jewish history. Without it, I am like you; nothing.

RIVIN: *(Ever so slightly critical; almost angry)* And so you *use* being a Jew to keep you from seeing that you are *nothing*? We are all nothing, Hinda. Perhaps we Jews are "the chosen" nothing. You, no doubt, are as committed to being chosen as *(pause)*... Mr. Lenine is. He also believes, I assure you, that he has been chosen to lead the starving and struggling masses of the Russian people out of captivity; out of bondage. Your pharaoh is his Czar. Your Moses is his Marx. Your phony Talmud is his phony "scientific socialism." Your god is his godlessness. There is no difference, dearest Hinda. You do not wish to follow him because you already follow another Man—equally tight-fisted and tight of mind. But there is no one to follow. We are quite alone, Hinda. And there is no place to go. So there is no need to have come from anywhere. Your Jewishness is a toy that you will not let go of.

HINDA: And what of *your* past? What have you done with it? This rebellion of yours seems to me as authoritarian as Lenine's. He selects which parts of history he is interested in; you deny it all. His followers heed everything he says; yours too. Only he has many followers. You have only one; *you*. But the dogmatism is the same, Rivin, you are an anti-Leninist—but you are much like Lenine; a man too focused on himself.

RIVIN: *(Laughs)* You are right. You're right. But I do not impose me or, for that matter, anybody else, on others. I do not believe in gods precisely because I know how easy it is to be one. A socialist Jew, Hinda, whatever could that mean? How could so brilliant a woman as you be a socialist Jew?

HINDA: Jewishness is my connection to the past; socialism my hope for the future. Together they define me; not unconflictedly, Rivin. But I think I tolerate conflict better than you. Even as a young man you craved consistency. Apparently you have found it—even if you have given up your life to do so.

RIVIN: And where is the woman, Hinda? Where is the woman in you—the socialist part or the Jewish part?

(Pause.)

HINDA: Sprintze and I are lovers. *(Long silence.)* Does that matter to you, Rivin?

RIVIN: I think it might, Hinda. I think it just might.

HINDA: I'm glad. I'm glad something matters to you. How does it matter?

RIVIN: I feel old feelings and old judgments. This news raises for me a kind of moral response that I have not felt in years; a repulsion that is utterly foreign to my current life. I suddenly have pictures in my mind of the two of you naked together and I am at once vaguely excited and nauseated by them. I am surprised. And I am surprised that I am surprised. Nothing has surprised me in a decade.

(The door opens, SPRINTZE enters; she pauses at the doorway; looks at HINDA who nods almost imperceptibly. She goes to HINDA and they embrace.)

RIVIN: I think I am jealous…But I will get over it.

SPRINTZE: *(Lovingly)* How are you, Hinda?

HINDA: I am good. Rivin and I have been, uh, "catching up."

SPRINTZE: I met Lenine today—personally—for the first time. Just an hour ago I was talking with him. His eyes looked at me and beyond me at the same time. He is a strange looking man. One of those people who looks like he is supposed to look. *(Laughs quietly.)* I asked him, Hinda, why he feels so strongly that the Jewish socialists—the Bundists—must abandon their Jewishness. He said we must all give up our pasts if we are to truly create a new human being—a socialist human being. He said it is not negating your past but fully using it to create something qualitatively new. When he said this his eyes looked sad, and I trusted him.

HINDA: I don't think I can give up my Jewishness.

RIVIN: But you have given up your womanliness.

SPRINTZE: *(Defensively)* But it is not the same.

HINDA: No, Sprintze. Rivin is right. It is the same. I must live with this inconsistency. My love for you is greater than my love for socialism. In any event I can have both. But my love for socialism is not as powerful as my Judaism. I don't know why. Perhaps it is spiritual; perhaps cultural. I don't know.

RIVIN: Judaism is your man, Hinda. Don't you see? And socialism is just another man—at that, a Christian man. You will not give up your man. Marx will not replace Moses. But for me, I see no difference between them; or Lenine or Christ. Yes. I am momentarily jealous of you and Sprintze. But I feel nothing for those living and dead phallic icons. Get what you can now, Sprintze, get what you can now out of his sad eyes. Soon enough, I fear, they will turn colder and colder and his successor, I suspect, will have no eyes at all…*(Pause.)* I cannot stay. I must go. Maybe I will see you both again. Maybe not.

(RIVIN puts on his coat. The three embrace)

Scene 5: Sex and death

PEARLIE'S apartment in Harlem, 1996. SAM is back in his old, dirty clothes. He is folding PEARLIE'S sweats and putting them neatly on a chair. There is a knock on the door. SAM opens the door. Enter MRS. GOLUB (played by the actress playing SPRINTZE), SAM'S social worker.

SAM: Mrs. Golub. Good to see ya. I was just gettin' ready to leave. Come on in.

MRS. GOLUB: Hello, Sam. How are you doing?

SAM: Oh, I'm doin' okay, Mrs. Golub. Can't complain. Nobody really cares anyway...y'know.

MRS. GOLUB: Now let's not get into that conversation again, Sam. I never know whether you think people care too much or too little.

SAM: Both, Mrs. Golub, both. *(Laughs.)*

MRS. GOLUB: How's Takuma...I mean Pearlie, doing?

SAM: Oh, she's okay. She's off at a Farrakhan meeting. She'll be back in a little while. Maybe you'll catch her.

MRS. GOLUB: Farrakhan's been getting an awful lot of publicity lately, Sam. What do you think of him these days?

SAM: Well...I respect him. But I think he's too much like all you white liberals—don't be offended, Mrs. Golub—he's got his own version of the carin' sickness—not to mention the countin' sickness. He cares too much and he thinks things count too much, for my blood—sick as it is. But he's okay. He's doin' his thing. A lot of Black folks like him.

MRS. GOLUB: Well, not many white folks like him, Sam.

SAM: Well, Mrs. G, white folks didn't create him to like him.

MRS. GOLUB: What's that supposed to mean, Sam?

SAM: You know, Mrs. G, the white folks—most particularly the liberals—needed a Black man they could justifiably hate. I mean *(sarcastically) after all the liberals have done for us* in the '60s, they was pissed off when some of us niggers started doin' "our own thing." Thought we was ungrateful, uppity. But it wouldn't do to hate all of us or even most of us—wasn't politically correct for a liberal to be a racist—so they had to create a popular icon who they could justify hatin'. I mean Farrakhan was a small-time preacher before the liberals got ahold of him. And the more the liberals hated him the more Black folks liked him. Now the liberals care too much but they ain't dummies. So they musta known that the more they was hatin' him, the more popular he was becomin'. Yeah. They was makin' him that way; popular and okay to hate. Those liberals are clever. A liberal can get away with hatin' Farrakhan.

MRS. GOLUB: *(Somewhat condescendingly)* Now, Sam, don't you think that's a little paranoid? A little conspiratorial?

SAM: No. No, Mrs. Golub, I don't. Whenever you liberals don't like something or don't agree with something, you call it conspiratorial. That's clever, too. I'm impressed. Actually it's the liberals and Mr. Farrakhan who do that about the best. I'm tellin' ya. I'm tellin' ya, white liberals and Farrakhan are very much the same. That's probably part of why they hate each other so much. But no, I ain't paranoid, Mrs. Golub. I'm a sick and dying man. I got AIDS. But I don't care about the Minister a whole lot more than I care about liberals... *(charmingly)* present company excluded.

MRS. GOLUB: Now, Sam, I know you hate me, too. *(Little laugh.)*

SAM: Not at all, Mrs. Golub. I don't hate you at all. *(Pause.)* You a socialist. Right, Mrs. Golub?

MRS. GOLUB: Yes, I am, Sam; a democratic socialist.

SAM: Oh, yeah, you mean you're not a communist.

MRS. GOLUB: That's right, Sam. My folks were communists, but they left the party when Stalin made his deal with Hitler in the late thirties.

SAM: Then you must know somethin' about this demonization business we was jest talkin' about. That's what the old social dems—really they was liberals—did with Lenine. The turned him into a demon so they could hate him while they abandoned socialism. Now you know that began long before Stalin took over. It's the liberal social dems that made Lenine and communism into a dirty word long before the commies went really nasty. Now you must know all this, Mrs. Golub. You're an old leftist. (*MRS. GOLUB nods.*) Actually, old Joe Stalin—miserable fuck that he was, pardon my language, Mrs. Golub—was just the sick child of this Lenine demonization business. You white folks better watch out for Farrakhan's successor. Someday you all gonna wish old Farrakhan was back. I won't be around to see it. But it'll be funny as hell. Shit. (*Laughs somewhat maniacally into a heavy cough.*)

MRS. GOLUB: (*Concerned*) You okay, Sam? We've been talkin' too much. (*SAM continues to cough. Lies down on couch.*) You want some water, Sam? Are you okay? (*SAM's coughing grows more violent. He is becoming sicker. MRS. GOLUB is getting more and more nervous. She is leaning over him on her knees.*) Sam, speak to me, speak to me!

SAM: (*Barely audible and coughing*) I think...I think I'm dyin', Mrs. Golub. I think I'm dyin'.

MRS. GOLUB: Let me call a doctor, Sam. (*Moves to get up; he grabs her arm.*)

SAM: No. No doctor. Mrs. Golub. No doctor. No treatment. If I'm dyin', I'm dyin'. (*Pause.*) Maybe I'm not. I don't see my life flashin' before me. So maybe I'm not dyin'! Actually...man, this is weird...I got a hard-on a mile long—hard as stone. My dick ain't been this big in years. And I ain't been turned on by no woman for decades. This is fuckin' weird, Mrs. Golub.

MRS. GOLUB: (*Looks hard and incredulously at SAM's crotch*) Sam, this is crazy. This is crazy.

SAM: (*Desperately*) Gimme a blow job, or a hand job, Mrs. G. It's a dyin' man's last request.

MRS. GOLUB: SAM, THAT'S INSANE. I CAN'T GIVE YOU NO...UH, BLOW JOB. ARE YOU CRAZY? YOU GOT AIDS. I CAN'T DO IT, SAM.

(*SAM coughs intensely.*)

SAM: Please, Mrs. Golub. I ain't never asked you for nothin' like this before and I'll never ask you for nuthin' again. Just touch my dick some way or another. Please, Mrs. Golub. Please.

(She slowly places her hand on his pants, his crotch. SAM's coughing changes to gradual moaning. She bends over and puts her face [mouth] on SAM's penis. He groans more and more. Suddenly the door opens and there stands PEARLIE. She sees MRS. GOLUB "down on" SAM.)

PEARLIE: Sprintzy…What the hell's going on?

(MRS. GOLUB stands up, humiliated. SAM turns over on the couch.)

MRS. GOLUB: Takuma…uh, Pearlie…uh, Hindy…Hindy…uh…shit…I thought he was dyin'…oh God…he got…uh…very aroused…uh… very hard…and, uh…he asked me to touch him…um…I thought he was dyin'…oh, shit…I'm sorry, Pearlie…uh, Hindy. *(Moves to embrace PEARLIE.)*

PEARLIE: That's okay, Sprintzy. That's okay. Don't be so upset. Don't be so upset. It's no big deal. *(MRS. GOLUB cries hysterically; PEARLIE comforts her saying "Sprintzy" again and again. Then she looks up.)* How are you, Sam? You okay?

SAM: I'm okay, Pearlie. I don't think I'm dyin' just yet. I'm okay. *(Pause.)* Who's Sprintzy, who's Hindy? How come you call Golub Sprintzy? And how come she's callin' you Hindy?

PEARLIE: She and I been lovers for years.

SAM: *(Incredulous, disbelieving)* SHIT. And you never told me! Goddamn. My sister and my social worker been sleepin' together for years and no one ever told me. Goddamn it.

PEARLIE: Well, it's nice to see there's somethin' you care about, Sam.

SAM: *(To MRS. GOLUB)* Ain't this some violation of social work ethics, Mrs. Golub?

PEARLIE: Sam…the woman was just givin' you a blow job. And you think us bein' lovers is unethical. Shit. Men.

MRS. GOLUB: Besides, Sam, my personal life ain't none of your damned business.

SAM: *(Standing)* Well, she's my sister.

PEARLIE: Would you two cut it out.

SAM: *(Shakes his head, sort of agreeing with* PEARLIE*)* How long you been together?

MRS. GOLUB: Let's see…almost 100 years now. Ain't that right, Takuma… Hindy?

PEARLIE: Yeah, Sprintzy, I think we got an anniversary comin' up. Yeah. I think we slept together for the first time in the late summer, 1896. In St. Petersburg.

SAM: What in the hell you two talkin' about? Are you crazy or somethin'? Eighteen ninety-six? Neither of you were alive in 1896. What's wrong with you two?

PEARLIE: What in the hell you know about bein' alive, Sam? You ain't been alive for years.

MRS. GOLUB: And what do you know about being dead, Sam? Nothin'. Not a damn thing.

PEARLIE: And what do you know about the difference between dead and alive? Zip. Sam, you don't know shit about this stuff.

(Pause.)

SAM: *(Incredulous)* So are you all dead or alive? What are you sayin'? Am I dead or am I alive? Or am I dreamin'?

PEARLIE: Y'know, Sam, there ain't so big a difference between dead and alive as most people make out. Dyin' simply gets ya back to where you was before you was born. Y'ain't here no more. But then again even when you're alive y'ain't a lot a places. You're only where you are. Y'know what I mean, Sam?

SAM: But people don't live forever, Pearlie.

PEARLIE: But people do *live and die forever*. Now don't they?

SAM: What you mean, Pearlie?

MRS. GOLUB: Sam, how come you've suddenly become so unphilosophical?

PEARLIE: *(Laughs)* Yeah, Sam, how come? The question we is askin'…the topic we is talkin' about is what is to be dead? Wittgenstein, that white philosopher you like so much, said, "The best thing about dyin' is that we don't live through it." Smart for a white guy, I think.

SAM: So, you two sayin' you been together since 1896? Dat's what you're tellin' me?

MRS. GOLUB: Yeah. That's what we're tellin' ya. I mean Takuma and I have our differences. But who doesn't?

SAM: You two are crazy, ain't ya?

PEARLIE: No crazier than you, Sam. No crazier than you. You the only one around here allowed to be crazy, Sam?

SAM: TAKUMA. Hmm. My sister TAKUMA.

Scene 6: Postmodernism

The setting uses the elements from the Scene 1 set, modified to create a gay club. SAM and RIVIN are standing at the bar. They have obviously "just met." SAM and RIVIN are slightly better dressed.

SAM: You come here often? I don't think I've ever seen ya before.

RIVIN: No. I don't think I've ever been here before.

SAM: You sick?

RIVIN: Yeah. My T-count's pretty damn low. You?

SAM: Fer sure. Been four years now. Where you from?

RIVIN: Originally from Russia. Now I live with my sister in Brighton Beach. How about you?

SAM: Well, I'm on the streets a lot. Shelter sometimes. Every now and again I stay with my sister in Harlem. Y'wanna dance?

RIVIN: Sure.

(They move to the dance floor and begin dancing.)

SAM: What's Russia like?

RIVIN: Corrupt and crazy. Everything has fallen apart. Nationalists, communists, liberals. They all stink. Brighton Beach is better.

SAM: Lotsa queers?

RIVIN: Yeah. In Russia and in Brighton Beach. Is Harlem as scary as they say? I've never been there.

SAM: About the same as a lot of places. A little rough sometimes, especially for a faggot. (*Pause.*) Can I ask you somethin' personal. I mean I don't usually ask this kinda stuff when I'm pickin' someone up, but…uh…

RIVIN: Go ahead. No problem.

SAM: Well…how old are you?

RIVIN: Let's see…I'll be 121 in June.

(*SAM stops dancing. They stare at each other.*)

SAM: One hundred and twenty-one?

RIVIN: Yes. In June. June 12th.

SAM: How come you ain't dead?

RIVIN: I guess I will be soon…unless they got a cure ready for production.

SAM: No, motherfucker. I ain't talkin' about AIDS. I'm talkin' about 121. You don't look a day over 40. No one lives to 121. What's your fuckin' sister's name, brother?

RIVIN: What are you so crazy about?

SAM: What's her name?

RIVIN: Her name is Sprintze.

SAM: She a lesbo?

RIVIN: Yes. How did you know?

SAM: She got a lover named Pearlie…or Hindy?

RIVIN: Sure. Takuma's her new name. You know them?

SAM: Pearlie's my sister. Takuma's my sister.

RIVIN: No shit.

SAM: Your sister's a social worker?

RIVIN: Yeah.

SAM: She's my social worker.

RIVIN: Hmm. That's incredible. She used to be straight. She was married for years to a guy named Charlie...

SAM: Golub.

RIVIN: Yeah. That's right.

SAM: What is to be dead?

RIVIN: Oh, I guess it's kinda like before you was born. You just aren't *here* anymore.

SAM: Are you dead?

RIVIN: I think so.

SAM: But you are *here*.

RIVIN: I used to be there. That's where *here* used to be.

SAM: Did I know you back then?

RIVIN: Were you there?

SAM: No.

RIVIN: Then I guess not.

SAM: When did you die?

RIVIN: I don't remember.

SAM: You died of AIDS?

RIVIN: No. I died when my liver stopped working. There was no AIDS then. This time I think I'll die of AIDS.

SAM: You mean we die more than once?

RIVIN: Unless we're Christ, we do.

SAM: But we remember who we were?

RIVIN: Some people do.

SAM: I can't remember being anyone else.

RIVIN: Maybe you weren't. Maybe you just can't remember. We all forget things sometimes.

SAM: This is the craziest stuff I ever heard in my life.

RIVIN: I heard crazier... *(pause.)* Sam is your name?

SAM: Yeah. And yours...how d'ya say it again?

RIVIN: Rivin.

SAM: Rivin.

RIVIN: You got it.

SAM: Rivin, now that you...uh,...believe all this stuff about dyin'...does it change your...uh...attitude toward life?

RIVIN: Oh, yeah. I used to think that nothing meant anything. Now I don't think about those kinds of things. I used to be an underground man and think that nothing could be done. Now I don't think about those kinds of things. I used to be sick and wretched. Now I am just sick... Do you want to dance more?

(SAM looks hard at RIVIN.)

SAM: Yes.

(They dance slowly and sexually as lights fade.)

))))

Risky
Revolutionary

Risky Revolutionary (1996) is the love story of Fidel Castro, the leader of the Cuban Revolution, and Dr. Ernesto "Che" Guevara, the Argentine physician who helped lead the revolution in Cuba in 1959 and was killed in Bolivia in 1967 during an aborted attempt to spark a revolution in that country.

Of course it is not a typical love story. The love between these two men develops through the joint activity of working together intensely over an extended period of time to create something new—in this case, a new Cuba. This love between revolutionaries (very different from the romantic love set against the backdrop of a revolution portrayed in the Warren Beatty film *Reds*) has, to my knowledge, not been treated before on the American stage. It is touched on by Newman in *Lenin's Breakdown,* during the scene in which Trotsky speaks of his love for Lenin, but *Risky Revolutionary* is a full-blown political romance.

The love between revolutionaries shares characteristics with the camaraderie of soldiers under fire, with the profound sympathy that develops between collaborators in an artistic or scientific endeavor, with the sexual electricity of new lovers, with the calm devotion shared by members of a religious group who live their lives together in common purpose, and with the matter-of-fact intimacy of a longtime married couple. Yet it is none of these exactly. The director, performers and audience must find a way to complete this romance through performance.

Risky Revolutionary is also a love letter of sorts from Newman to Castro and the Cuban people. The warmth and intelligence with which the characters of Che and Fidel are portrayed is expressive of the respect and affection that the author feels for them. It is in the context of this sentiment (this revolutionary love, if you will) that Newman offers a critique of the Cuban Revolution. *Risky Revolutionary* is a plea to the revolution to overthrow itself and build a radically democratic, participatory socialism in its place. Because it is simultaneously a love letter and a critique, the script has been (and, I presume, will continue for some time to be) deemed offensive both by (some) supporters of the Cuban Revolution and by (some of) its enemies.

Beyond (or, perhaps more accurately, *within*) the specifics of Newman's critique, *Risky Revolutionary* contains his most complete theatrical articulation of his views on revolution. For Newman, as with his Che, any revolution which completely consolidates itself commits suicide. It is the emergent activity of mass transformation—not the leaders or institutions it creates—that makes revolution developmental. "You have grown old and successful," Che says to Fidel. "You must be overthrown. But only you can do it." It is the paradoxical failure of the successful revolutions of the 20th century to overthrow themselves that has made them vulnerable to being overthrown by their enemies. To remain revolutionary (emergent, transformative, developmental)—in the face of failure *or* success—one must, as Che puts it, incur the risk of seeming ridiculous.

"Any revolution which does not include the overthrow of our own ego is not, after all is said and done, a real revolution at all," says Che. The remark sums up Newman's philosophical/political life's work. The deconstruction of the ego—the isolated, alienated, atomized "self"—is integral to any revolutionary deconstruction/reconstruction of the larger society. Overthrowing economic and political systems while leaving culture and psychology intact has proven a disaster for revolution in this sad century. While Newman's radically revolutionary world view is implicit in all of his plays, it is the encounter between the 70-year-old Fidel Castro, the leader of one of the last surviving socialist revolutions, and the long-dead "risky revolutionary" Ernesto Guevara which provides the context for this political/philosophical conversation to take place onstage.

Structurally the two versions of the narrative are the Cuban Revolution as it actually exists (portrayed in the opening video sequences) and a second Cuban Revolution that could be (as portrayed in the closing video). The center of the play is the process of transformation between what is and what might be.

Newman's use of video in the body of *Risky Revolutionary* breaks new ground. In *Left of the Moon* and *The Store: One Block East of Jerome* the video became a part of the dramatic structure of the plays; in *Risky Revolutionary* the video becomes one of the characters. While this script can be performed with a live actor playing "Older Fidel Castro" onstage, the playwright prefers, if it is at all possible, that Older Fidel be performed on videotape, talking to a live Che through a monitor or monitors visible to both the actor and audience. Fidel, who is alive in the world, is on video; Che, who is dead in the world, is live onstage.

It is interesting to note that audiences who saw the 1996 production at Castillo, which I directed, frequently found Fidel, the character on television, to be "more real" than Che, the character being performed live onstage. This isn't surprising if you keep in mind that most Americans are much more used to watching television than they are to seeing a play. What is more "real" to most of us than a television show?

If it is possible to have the same actor play both the older Fidel and the dead Che (as was done with the 1996 Castillo production) then the play can provide yet another experience/meaning by raising the possibility that the two characters of Che and Fidel are, in fact, the same person, and that the action of *Risky Revolutionary* might be going on in Fidel's head. In addition to a conversation between Fidel and Che, the play then becomes an encounter between the risk-taking and conservative impulses active in all of us. Needless to say, it also provides the actor playing the two roles with the unique opportunity of acting "opposite" himself.

It is worth noting that the characters of *Risky Revolutionary* (like those of *Sally and Tom*) are all historical figures. That is, they are all (except the video newscasters) based on "real" people who played a role in the Cuban Revolution and/or in progressive Latin American politics.

D.F.

Risky Revolutionary was first produced at the Castillo Theatre (Fred Newman, artistic director; Gabrielle Kurlander producing director; Diane Stiles, managing director) in New York City on September 6, 1996. The cast, in order of appearance, was as follows:

FIRST NEWSCASTER . . . . Charlie Navarette
YOUNGER FIDEL CASTRO . . . . Omar Ali
SECOND NEWSCASTER . . . . Gilbert Arribas
THIRD NEWSCASTER . . . . Judith E. Taranto
ERNESTO "CHE" GUEVARA/OLDER FIDEL CASTRO . . . . Robert Morgan
RAÚL CASTRO . . . . Richard Rosario-Velazquez
ÑICO LÓPEZ . . . . Otto Sanchez
HILDA GADEA . . . . Cecilia Salvatierra
JESÚS MONTANÉ OROPESA . . . . Doug Miranda
MELBA HERNÁNDEZ . . . . Magdalena López

Dan Friedman, director; Brenda Ratliff, producer; Joseph Spirito, set and scenic design; Charlotte, costume design; Candace Carell, special makeup design; Charlie Spickler, lighting design; Michael Klein, sound design; Barry Z Levine, video design/cinematography; Ellen Korner, production stage manager.

CHARACTERS

ERNESTO "CHE" GUEVARA
RAÚL CASTRO
YOUNGER FIDEL CASTRO
ÑICO LÓPEZ
HILDA GADEA
JESÚS MONTANÉ OROPESA
MELBA HERNÁNDEZ
OLDER FIDEL CASTRO

On video
NEWSCASTER(S)
OLDER FIDEL CASTRO*

NOTES:
This play contains both live scenes and video sequences.

**If it is not possible for OLDER FIDEL, in his scenes with CHE, to be
performed on video, he can instead be played live onstage.*

Act I, Scene 1

The stage is completely dark, with video monitor(s) visible to the audience.

(Video #1)

NEWSCASTER: Dateline Havana, Cuba; October 15, 1967. After several days of contradictory reports in the international media, Cuban Prime Minister Fidel Castro went on national TV today to announce the death of Dr. Ernesto "Che" Guevara.

(Cut to YOUNGER FIDEL on TV.)

YOUNGER FIDEL: As you must have figured out, the reason for this address is the news that has been arriving from Bolivia since October 9, and that has appeared for the last few days in our press. I must begin by stating that we have become convinced that this news—that is, the news related to the death of Commander Ernesto Guevara—is, painfully, true.

NEWSCASTER: The Prime Minister went on to discuss in great detail the capture of Guevara, an Argentinean doctor, a leader of the Cuban Revolution and the head of a small internationalist band of guerrilla fighters in the Bolivian jungles, and his assassination by Bolivian troops while in captivity. As well he spoke of the various (and contradictory) reports and speculations that have been made worldwide about the circumstances of Guevara's capture, treatment and disposition after his death. Castro, obviously deeply saddened, concluded his remarks thusly:

YOUNGER FIDEL: Today, the Council of Ministers met and adopted the following resolution:

"Whereas: The heroic Commander Ernesto Guevara died fighting for the liberation of the peoples of Latin America at the head of the Liberation Army of Bolivia;

"Whereas: The people of Cuba will always remember the extraordinary service rendered by Commander Ernesto Guevara, both in our war of liberation and in the consolidation and advancement of our revolution;

"Whereas: His conduct embodies the spirit of internationalism that inspires the united struggle of the peoples;

"Whereas: His untiring revolutionary activity, which knew no borders, his communist thinking, and his unshakable determination to fight until victory or death in defense of the national and social liberation of the people of Latin America and against imperialism, constitute an example of revolutionary conviction and heroism that will last forever;

"Therefore be it resolved:

"First, that for 30 days, beginning with the signing of this resolution, the national flag be flown at half mast; and that for three days, starting at 12:00 midnight tonight, absolutely all public entertainment be suspended.

"Second, that the day of Che's heroic death in combat be declared a national memorial day, to that effect establishing October 8 as the Day of the Heroic Guerrilla."

(Video #2)

NEWSCASTER: Dateline Havana, Cuba; October 18, 1967. One million people gathered today at Havana's Revolutionary Plaza at a memorial rally for Che Guevara. Cuban Prime Minister Fidel Castro addressed the massive crowd:

(Cut to YOUNGER FIDEL at rally.)

YOUNGER FIDEL: I first met Che one day in July or August 1955. And in one night—as he recalls in his account—he became one of the future *Granma* expeditionaries, although at that time the expedition possessed neither ship, nor arms, nor troops. That was how, together with Raúl, Che became one of the first two on the *Granma* list. Twelve years have passed since then; they have been 12 years filled with struggle and historical significance. During this time death has cut down many brave and invaluable lives. But at the same time, throughout those years of our revolution, extraordinary persons have arisen, forged from among the people of the revolution, and between them, bonds of affection and friendship have emerged that surpass all possible description. Tonight we are meeting to try to express, in some degree, our feelings toward one who was among the closest, among the most admired, among the most beloved, and, without a doubt, the most extraordinary of our revolutionary comrades. We are here to express our feelings for him and for the heroes who have fought with him and fallen with him, his internationalist army that has been writing a glorious and indelible page of history. Che was one of those people who was liked immediately, for his simplicity, his character, his naturalness, his comradely attitude, his personality, his originality, even when one had not yet learned of his other characteristics and unique virtues.

(Video #3)

NEWSCASTER: Dateline Havana, Cuba; October 1, 1997. As preparations continued for a massive 30th Anniversary memorial of Cuba's heroic martyr, Ernesto "Che" Guevara, rumors mounted about the apparent absence of Cuba's leader, President Fidel Castro. Castro has not appeared at a public event for over a month; did not appear at an annual forum about Guevara's role as an international political revolutionary at the University of Havana last week and has not been seen on public TV for several weeks. Speculations about ill health—Castro just turned 70—have been denied. Some have insisted that the Cuban leader is having secret meetings with Latin American liberation groupings. The "official" rumor mills on Cuba last received this kind of attention some 32 years ago when Ernesto "Che" Guevara's whereabouts were unknown for almost two years prior to his assassination in Bolivia.

Act I, Scene 2

ERNESTO "CHE" GUEVARA lies on a funeral bier-type structure; the 70-year-old OLDER FIDEL CASTRO appears on the video screen, somewhat out of focus. Otherwise, the stage is empty; a void.

CHE: Where am I? How long have I been out? Am I in a hospital? I thought for sure I was a dead man. Who are you over there? *(Peers, then shouts.)*

FIDEL?! Is that you? How very old you look. Am I in Cuba? How could I be in Cuba? Is that really you, Fidel? What's happened?

(The video picture becomes focused and goes full face.)

OLDER FIDEL: You're a dead man, Doctor Che. It's 1997! You've been dead for 30 years.

CHE: What do you mean "a dead man"? Where am I if I'm dead? How can I be dead? What are you talking about? I was seriously wounded in the legs. I was burning up with fever. I was captured, then they mutilated me and shot me in the chest. Then I remember nothing. Where am I, Fidel? Why do you look so old? Where am I? 1997? Did you say that? 1997! Where have I been? In a coma for…30 years! That's crazy… medically impossible. Fidel, tell me, what's going on?

OLDER FIDEL: You died in Bolivia. They ambushed you. They shot off your legs. They destroyed your weapon. They cut off pieces of your body. Then, once captured, they killed you. They shot you through the heart and lungs.

CHE: Yeah, I think I remember all that.

OLDER FIDEL: Then they buried you. Then they dug you up. Then they incinerated you. We never saw your body, Che. But we knew. You were dead! Thirty years ago. You're a dead man, comrade Che, a dead man.

CHE: So where am I now? *(Sarcastically.)* What is this—*heaven*? Are you dead, too, Fidel? Are we both in *heaven*? What's going on Fidel… what's going on?

OLDER FIDEL: I am not dead. I am 70 now. Old, but still the leader of the Cuban Revolution. The world has changed, Che. The world has changed dramatically. It is older. But Cuba survives; our revolution goes on, Che. *The Soviet Union has collapsed.*

CHE: *(Incredulously)* What? The Soviet Union collapsed? Are you kidding?

OLDER FIDEL: I wish. No. I'm not kidding.

CHE: When?

OLDER FIDEL: Almost a decade ago now.

CHE: There is no Soviet Union?

OLDER FIDEL: It is back to being Russia. There is still a Communist Party of Russia. It is the second strongest party; it gets about 40 percent in the national elections.

CHE: There are elections? In Cuba, too?

OLDER FIDEL: Yes. In Russia. Not in Cuba.

CHE: And Vietnam?

OLDER FIDEL: *(Enthusiastically)* We won! Vietnam is unified. The U.S. imperialist army was run out of the country. The communists control everything now.

CHE: And Africa? Latin America?

OLDER FIDEL: Not good, Che. Not good. Neo-imperialism dominates. Can you believe it? Mobutu is still in power in the Congo.

CHE: *(Disbelieving)* Mobutu is still in power?

OLDER FIDEL: The U.S. still controls Latin America—politically, economically; except, of course, Cuba. We've had very hard times; especially since the Soviet Union fell. But we have survived.

(Pause.)

CHE: But, Fidel, where am I? Comandante, what is going on here?

OLDER FIDEL: I don't know much more than you, Che. Last month I had a dream about you. It was not *so* shocking. I have dreamt about you often. But I hadn't dreamt of you for quite a while. The next night…another dream. Every night, another dream. Then, about a week ago, the dream seemed to say, "I must go and find Che." Two nights ago, in the dream, a voice told me where to go to find you. As you know, I have always listened to dreams. So I came here, where the dream told me to come.

CHE: But where is here, Fidel?

OLDER FIDEL: I'm not sure. I came to the opening session of the U.N. General Assembly. I wasn't going to come, but the dream said I should.

CHE: How are relations with the U.S.?

OLDER FIDEL: Worse than ever.

CHE: So we are in New York?

OLDER FIDEL: I think so.

CHE: What do you mean, "You think so"?

OLDER FIDEL: I remember landing at Kennedy. I remember our U.N. ambassador picking me up in a limousine. He said we were going to the Waldorf, you know, the fancy hotel. I protested, as I usually do. He insisted. "For security reasons," he always says. I remember seeing a sign that said "Van Wyck Expressway." Next thing I was here and you (*hesitates*)... "awoke."

(*They stare at each other incredulously.*)

CHE: What are we to do?

OLDER FIDEL: Can you walk?

(*CHE steps down from the funeral bier. He walks tentatively and then more securely.*)

CHE: Yes. I can walk. I feel fine.

OLDER FIDEL: Good.

CHE: But where should we walk to, Fidel?

OLDER FIDEL: I don't know, Ernesto. I don't know.

Act I, Scene 3

RAÚL CASTRO and CHE, as young men, sit and talk with youthful animation.

RAÚL: He will be here any moment now.

CHE: I am eager to meet your brother, Raúl. I hope we get along.

RAÚL: You will, Che. I know you will. You will love him. I know.

CHE: But he is not a communist.

RAÚL: It will make no difference. Wait and see. He is a great man; the most, the most... attractive man I have ever known.

CHE: I believe you, Raúl. I believe you.

(*Enter* YOUNGER FIDEL. RAÚL *and* YOUNGER FIDEL *embrace with much love.*)

RAÚL: Comandante, Fidel, this is Ernesto Guevara de la Serna.

(*YOUNGER FIDEL and* CHE *shake hands.*)

CHE: It is an honor to meet you.

YOUNGER FIDEL: Likewise. Raúl has told me a good deal about you. You are trained as a doctor? That could prove useful.

CHE: Useful? In what way?

YOUNGER FIDEL: To our revolution. (*Laughs.*) There is no other way. There is nothing else to *use* someone or something for.

CHE: You are right…what shall I call you…Fidel, comrade?

YOUNGER FIDEL: Whatever you choose, *Doctor Guevara*. (*Laughs.*) What do I call you?

CHE: You call me "Che." Raúl calls me Che. We are friends. It is a term of affection in Argentina…where I am from…where I was born. Its origins, I think, are Italian.

YOUNGER FIDEL: "Che." Yes. "Che." It fits you, I think. I will call you Che, too. Then you should call me Fidel (*pause*)…Che, Che Guevara…you are a communist?

CHE: Yes. I am.

YOUNGER FIDEL: Are you a revolutionary?

CHE: I am.

YOUNGER FIDEL: We are here in Mexico preparing to invade Cuba to conduct a guerrilla war to overthrow the fascist dictator Batista and his Washington, D.C. imperialist backers…Will you join us as doctor to the invasion force?

RAÚL: Fidel! You have only just met him…

CHE: I will join. Of course, I will join.

YOUNGER FIDEL: Good. *(With some irony.)* The duty of the revolutionary is to make the revolution…right, *Dr.* Che?

CHE: Right, comandante Fidel. We will be comrades. We will fight and, if need be, we will die for the Cuban Revolution.

YOUNGER FIDEL: I believe you, Dr. Che. I trust you. I like your smile. It cares for people. You will be, I suspect, more than our doctor in short order.

CHE: I will be whatever you ask of me, comandante.

RAÚL: Che has studied Marx and Lenine. *(Enthusiastically.)* He is a good teacher…a great teacher. He speaks the language of the masses.

YOUNGER FIDEL: If what he teaches helps the Cuban people to grow I wish to learn it all.

CHE: I will learn from *you*, Fidel. I am not a man of the books. I am a man of action. I believe in revolutionary guerrilla warfare. You will teach it to me in Cuba…in the making of the Cuban Revolution.

(YOUNGER FIDEL and CHE embrace.)

YOUNGER FIDEL: "Che." A good name. It suits you very well indeed.

Act I, Scene 4

CHE is on the empty stage of Scene 2. OLDER FIDEL is on the video screen.

OLDER FIDEL: You *remember* when we met…in Mexico…in July of 1955?

CHE: *(Laughs)* It was the most extraordinary moment of my life. How could I forget? It was love at first sight. We were both in our twenties and you were so beautiful.

OLDER FIDEL: You, too, Che. You too…And now you are dead and I am old.

CHE: But our love has made a difference. What did we used to say *(thinks)* …Ah, yes…"At the risk of seeming ridiculous, let me say that the true revolutionary is guided by a great feeling of love." You remember, Fidel …do you remember?

OLDER FIDEL: *Our* love guided us. From '56 when we sailed to Cuba on the

Granma to the day in '65 when you left me, Che. Our love inspired the Cuban people.

CHE: You have still not forgiven me for "leaving you"—as you call it? The revolution needed me elsewhere—in Africa…in South America. I did not leave you, Fidel. You are still angry. What did you say to me then? What was it? The last time we spoke in Havana? Ah—I remember. You said, my "love of being risky often guided me to being truly ridiculous." *(Laughs.)* A good joke, comandante, even if spoken in a lover's rage. What did Ñico and the others call me—the risky revolutionary!

OLDER FIDEL: I was, perhaps, more right than wrong, Dr. Che, my dearest friend. History has proven me right.

CHE: *(Almost angrily; certainly competitively)* History does not prove one right or wrong. You are still more a bourgeois romantic than a Marxist revolutionary, my comrade. History proves nothing for it is never over.

OLDER FIDEL: Perhaps. But it is all but over for us.

CHE: You seem more dead than me.

OLDER FIDEL: You never got to be 70, Ernesto.

(*CHE wanders upstage looking off in "the void."*)

CHE: Do you remember the first wedding—with Hilda in Mexico. August 1955. You remember? It was August 19th. A hot day—a very hot day.

OLDER FIDEL: I did not go to the ceremony. Or the celebration. Who was the bourgeois romantic then?

CHE: Yes, comandante. I recall that you were not there.

Act I, Scene 5

*The same room as in Scene 3 (*RAÚL's *room). Talking, drinking and slightly high on tequila are* CHE, RAÚL, ÑICO LÓPEZ, HILDA GADEA, JESÚS MONTANÉ OROPESA *and* MELBA HERNÁNDEZ.

JESÚS: *(A toast)* To Hilda and Che; a South American sister from Peru and a South American brother from Argentina; joined together in marriage *(the crowd cheers)*, both married as well to the world revolution and, in particular, the Cuban Revolution. Salut. Venceremos. *(All cheer. Then, patronizingly)* Melba, my dearest comrade and my darling wife, make a toast to Che and Hilda.

MELBA: *(Shy)* No, no, no, Jesús. You have put it so eloquently. You speak for both of us. We are a couple.

HILDA: *(Teasing her)* Melba, Melba, we have just recently spoken of this: We women must speak for ourselves. I would love to hear your words. What Jesús said was beautiful, but I want to hear from you, Melba.

MELBA: *(Lifts her glass)* To my new friends and comrades, Hilda and Che. To a long and wonderful marriage.

ÑICO: *(He is young and poor and macho; less middle-class than the others)* Like el comandante Fidel, I will be married only to the revolution. Oh...I love Hilda and Che and Jesús and Melba. Yeah, sure. But marriage— *(laughs)* the ball and chain—is not for me. *(Laughing.)* I am married to Fidel.

RAÚL: *(Teasing, making a joke)* Careful, my comrade Ñico. You'd better not let his mother and father—my mother and father—hear that kind of talk.

ÑICO: No, Raúl, I do not sleep with him. But I will live and die with him. That is even closer.

JESÚS: You are still so young, Ñico. Marriage is for older men—like me and Che.

RAÚL: Che is only 27.

ÑICO: Yes. And I am already 21.

RAÚL: And Fidel is 29!

ÑICO: But he will never marry. I tell you, he is married only to Cuba and to the revolution. El comandante is no bigamist! *(Laughs.)*

CHE: Why must it be one or the other? Married to a partner—a man or a woman—and married to the revolution. Why not both? Bigamy, comrade Ñico, is a piece of capitalist ideology. It is really about property rights. But I do not *own* either the revolution or comrade Hilda. I have more than enough love for both of them...and even much more than that. There is no competition *here*. Competition is still another bourgeois idea, Ñico. Sometimes I think Fidel himself is too competitive. Sometimes he seems more like a baseball player still and less like a revolutionary leader.

(There is a sudden and somewhat prolonged silence in the room.)

RAÚL: With all due respect, comrade Che, Fidel is always the revolutionary leader.

HILDA: Che meant no insult, Raúl. You know that. He loves Fidel madly... even though they have only recently met. He loves Fidel more than he loves me.

JESÚS: And Fidel loves him. I have never seen el comandante trust another so much in so short a time.

ÑICO: But, Che, isn't some amount of competition a good thing? In making revolutionary decisions, military decisions, mustn't we look carefully at *competing* ideas and choose the correct one? Perhaps, my dear comrade, you are not in this way competitive *enough*. Perhaps that is why you are so...risky. Sometimes too risky. You are always courageous. You never spare yourself. But sometimes you do not take a moment to consider another course of action; a "competitive" idea or plan.

RAÚL: Che, you have trained young Ñico well in the dialectic. You are indeed a risky revolutionary.

MELBA: To Doctor Che Guevara—a loving and a risky revolutionary. Long life, Che Guevara. Long life, risky revolutionary. *(They all cheer as HILDA and CHE embrace.)*

Act I, Scene 6

CHE is on the empty stage. OLDER FIDEL is on the video monitor.

CHE: Why did you not come to my wedding?

OLDER FIDEL: You might as well ask me why I did not come to your death. When you leave me, I cannot come to you.

CHE: *(Adamant)* I did not leave you!

OLDER FIDEL: You still have not learned what Ñico, our departed young comrade, tried to teach you back in Mexico. What you do, dearest comrade, is not just what you *intend* it to be. It is many other "competing" things as well. You did not *intend* to leave me. But you did leave me. You are the bravest, the most courageous, most beautiful man I have ever known. You never think of yourself. But in not thinking of yourself sometimes you also do not think of others.

CHE: *(Visibly hurt)* I do not think of others? That is a painful charge, my beloved comandante—a painful charge.

OLDER FIDEL: Others needed you! I needed you. The Cuban Revolution needed you—needed *our* love.

CHE: From the very beginning—in Mexico, in 1955, I asked only one thing of you. You *must* remember. I told you then I would give everything for the Cuban Revolution, including my life. And I did. I asked only that when the time came to make revolution in South America I must go. In 1965 that time came. I am an internationalist, Fidel. You've always known that.

OLDER FIDEL: *(Forcefully) The time hadn't come.* You decided the time had come. And you were wrong. The whole Bolivian adventure was too risky. Why can't you see that? It did not inspire revolutions; it demoralized the masses. The people respond to *success,* not martyrdom!

(Longish pause.)

CHE: And has Cuba's "success" inspired the world's masses? Did the Soviet "success" inspire the masses? You do not seem "inspired," my beloved Fidel. You seem tired. You seem old beyond your years.

OLDER FIDEL: *(Thoughtfully)* Then perhaps we both failed. Neither martyrdom nor success has changed the world; has produced international socialism, international humanism. Perhaps together we could have found something else. But we did not have the chance. You left me. *(OLDER FIDEL sobs.)*

CHE: I am very sad. I have hurt you terribly. In my deep love for you I have unintentionally betrayed you.

OLDER FIDEL: I fear we have betrayed each other, Che. And, in the process, we have, perhaps, betrayed the people…of Cuba, of Latin America, of the world.

CHE: *(Whispers)* But history is not over, Fidel. And you are still alive.

OLDER FIDEL: I cannot escape, Che—any more than you could. The CIA has tried to kill me many times. They no longer have to. Like vultures, they simply await my death. You did not live long enough, dearest comrade. I have lived too long.

CHE: Why do you suppose your dream told you to find me? What could I possibly do for you? Think about that. What do I know how to do better than you, comandante?

OLDER FIDEL: What, Che? I don't know. What are you thinking about? You have something on your mind? What is it? Tell me.

CHE: I am the *risky revolutionary*. Perhaps I can help you to take a revolutionary risk. It is all that I know. It is all that I can do.

OLDER FIDEL: What are you thinking of? There are no revolutionary situations, Che. This is 1997. There were virtually none in 1967 as it turned out. Now it is even worse. You are being ridiculous, Che. There are no risks to be taken.

CHE: I know of one. I know of a revolutionary situation; a revolutionary risk waiting to be taken.

OLDER FIDEL: Where? How could you know? You have been dead all these years.

CHE: I know. I know.

OLDER FIDEL: Where? Tell me where?

CHE: CUBA! We must make the revolution again, Fidel. You must be overthrown. But only you could do it. I did not have a beloved leader in Bolivia. That was the difference. You are that beloved leader in Cuba. You were *then* and you are *now*. But you have grown old and successful. You must be overthrown. We shall do it again, my dearest comrade. We shall do it again. That is the meaning of your dream, my brother, my beloved brother.

OLDER FIDEL: You are crazy. That is ridiculous!

CHE: Precisely! The true revolutionary must be ridiculous. Being ridiculous is no risk. What is risky is not being ridiculous. "Let me say, at the risk of being too much in love with you, that the true revolutionary is guided by great feelings of ridiculousness." One, two, three—many Cuban Revolutions.

OLDER FIDEL: I don't believe this.

CHE: You don't have to believe it. We will perform it in Act II.

("The Internationale" plays.)

Act II, Scene 1

The "void" set. The funeral bier is gone. CHE *is seated at a small writing table downstage left. He is reading papers aloud.*

CHE: *(Reads)* July 6, 1956. Dear Mom,

> Some time ago—quite some time ago—a young Cuban leader invited me to join his movement, a movement which sought the armed liberation of his country. Of course, I accepted. Dedicated to physically preparing those young men who would go back to Cuba, I spent the last few months maintaining the myth of my professional post. On July 21 (when I hadn't been home for a month, because I was on a ranch outside the city), Fidel and a group of comrades were arrested. Our address was in his home, so we were all eventually caught in the round-up. I had documents accrediting me as a student of Russian at the Mexican-Russian-Cultural Exchange Institute, which was enough for me to be considered an important link in the organization, and news agencies that are friends of Dad's made a hullabaloo all over the world. That was a synthesis of past events; future ones are divided into two groups: mid-term and immediate. In the mid-term future, I'll be linked to Cuba's liberation. I'll either triumph with it or die there...I can't say much about the immediate future, because I don't know what will happen to me. I'm in the judge's hands, and I may easily be deported to Argentina if I don't get asylum in another country, which would be good for my political health. Whatever happens, I must meet my new destiny, whether I remain in this prison or go free...We're on the eve of

declaring a hunger strike in protest against the unjustified arrests and the torture to which some of my comrades were subjected. The group's morale is high. If for any reason (and I don't think this will happen) I can't write again and have the misfortune to lose, look on these lines as my farewell—not very grandiloquent, but sincere. I have gone through life searching for my truth by fits and starts and now, having found the way and with a daughter who will perpetuate me, I have come full circle. From now on, I wouldn't consider my death a frustration, but, like Hikmet, "I will take to my grave only the regret of an unfinished song."

(Picks up another letter.)

April 13, 1965. Dear Fidel,

Recalling my past life, I believe I have worked with sufficient integrity and dedication to consolidate the revolutionary triumph. My only serious failing was not having had more confidence in you from the first moments in the Sierra Maestra, and not having understood quickly enough your qualities as a leader and a revolutionary. I have lived magnificent days, and at your side I felt the pride of belonging to our people in the brilliant yet sad days of the Caribbean [missile] crisis. Seldom has a statesman been more brilliant than you in those days. I am also proud of having followed you without hesitation, of having identified with your way of thinking and of seeing and appraising dangers and principles. Other nations of the world call for my modest efforts. I can do that which is denied you because of your responsibility at the head of Cuba, and the time has come for us to part.

(OLDER FIDEL appears on video screen.)

OLDER FIDEL: Why are you reading *that* letter?

CHE: It is the letter I sent you when...

OLDER FIDEL: *(Interrupting)* I know what it is. It is your farewell letter to me; from 1965. Why are you reading it now? Are you going to leave me again?

CHE: I am not leaving you, Fidel. I will never leave you again. *(His voice and manner lighten.)* Still, my dearest comrade, I cannot "come with" you to Cuba. I am dead, after all. There cannot be a *physical* relationship— straight or gay—between a 70-year-old and a dead person. It would be too morbid. Look, Fidel, we are still materialists—even if we are dialectical materialists or, perhaps more accurately, ridiculous materialists.

OLDER FIDEL: We exist together only here, you think?

CHE: I think. In this play we are together. In history we will always be together. In "life"—as they say—we are not. The second Cuban Revolution must take place in life, in your life—in Cuba.

OLDER FIDEL: *(Smiling)* Everyone will know you are with me in this invasion and "second revolution"—as you call it. I could never do this without you, Che. It is too absurd; too risky; too ridiculous. The name and spirit of Ernesto Guevara—the risky revolutionary—is written all over this plan. People everywhere—but especially people in Cuba—will know: Dr. Che will be with us in spirit even as he was in life on the *Granma* in 1957. *(Pause; still somewhat suspiciously.)* So tell me why you were reading those letters—these farewell letters.

CHE: *(Picks up pen and paper)* Because I want to write another letter; not a farewell letter. A letter to let the world know of our deepened love for each other.

OLDER FIDEL: This crazy revolution you have convinced me to lead—the overthrow of myself—will be a final testament to our love. No letter will be needed.

CHE: *(Puts down pen and paper)* Perhaps you are right, *comandante.*

OLDER FIDEL: El comandante, indeed! *You* are the leader this time around, *Dr. Che Guevara.*

CHE: No, Fidel. You are more the leader now than ever. Any revolution which does not include the overthrow of our own ego is not, after all is said and done, a real revolution at all. This second Cuban Revolution will complete your great work and will cement our beautiful love affair. For to liberate the human spirit is as important as to liberate the human body and mind.

OLDER FIDEL: Those are very beautiful words, Ernesto.

CHE: You are still a beautiful man, 70-year-old Fidel Castro. *(OLDER FIDEL laughs.)* I am sorry I will never get to love your body; to touch you sexually. *(Takes a speech pose.)* "Let me say, at the risk of seeming ridiculous, that the true revolutionary is guided by great feelings of sexuality."

OLDER FIDEL: *(Mock shock)* Dr. Che Guevara, no wonder the North American "flower children" loved you so. You are gay, Che. You are truly gay.

CHE: I love you, Fidel, in every way. You will free the people of Cuba of all prejudice and bias this time; a complete liberation. Civil rights and human rights and democratic rights for all.

OLDER FIDEL: *(Laughs)* Che's gay revolution. *(Chiding.)* Weren't you my Marxist-Leninist educator?

CHE: Che and Fidel's gay revolution. Even the educators must be educated. *(They laugh romantically.)*

(Video of OLDER FIDEL fades. Enter HILDA, MELBA, JESÚS, ÑICO, RAÚL from one side of stage, and YOUNGER FIDEL from opposite side of stage.)

MELBA: We have come to your wedding. *(Toasts.)* To Che and Fidel, our beloved leaders.

JESÚS: She now toasts everywhere!

RAÚL: So here is where you are Fidel, my dear brother. Comandante. We have been looking all over for you for days now. Where exactly are we?

YOUNGER FIDEL: Where exactly are we? I do not know. We are so many different places all at once, Raúl. We are so many different things all at once.

ÑICO: *(To CHE; still very macho)* I am dead, too—as you know, comrade Che. I died in battle like you.

HILDA: *(Speaks quietly to CHE)* Our dearest daughter died last year, Che—of cancer; at 39; like her father—the same age.

CHE: I know, Hilda. I know.

MELBA: We are all much closer to being dead nowadays. *(Toasts.)* To Fidel and Che and the Cuban Revolution—which will never die.

JESÚS: What are you two up to? You two always have a scheme.

CHE: We are planning another revolution, Jesús.

(Everyone laughs.)

JESÚS: Another revolution? Not in Bolivia, I hope?

(Everyone laughs even louder.)

CHE: No, comrade Jesús. Not in Bolivia. In *Cuba*!

(No laughter.)

RAÚL: In Cuba? What do you mean, in Cuba?

ÑICO: Who do we overthrow?

CHE: Fidel. El comandante.

ÑICO: There you go again, comrade Che. What are you, a counter revolutionary? *(Laughs.)*

HILDA: The revolution has been made in Cuba, Che. Fidel, what is your beloved comrade talking about?

YOUNGER FIDEL: He is talking about a second Cuban Revolution; a democracy revolution; a cultural liberation; a human rights revolt.

RAÚL: *(Deeply concerned)* You mean like Gorbachev? Like the Soviet Union? Won't that destroy our revolution, Fidel?

CHE: We must do it ourselves now or the CIA will do it after Fidel is dead. Lenine *died* in '24. Fidel *lives* in '97. Don't you see, Raúl?

RAÚL: Do we not trust the Cuban people to carry on after my brother's death?

ÑICO: Yes, Che. What has happened in Russia and elsewhere could *never* happen in Cuba.

CHE: Like I could *never* be trapped in the jungles of Bolivia with no support from the people?

JESÚS: True. Fidel is not Gorbachev. Fidel could never be accused of betraying the Cuban Revolution.

CHE: Exactly, Jesús. It would not be a betrayal. Quite the contrary. To leave the Cuban people disarmed against so-called "democratic" imperialists would be a betrayal.

YOUNGER FIDEL: Like the Americans have created Yeltsin, the drunkard, as the "democratic" leader of the Russian people. We want no Yeltsin in Cuba. We must prepare the Cuban people to take control when I am gone. And we must do it now.

HILDA: And our policy on civil rights, on human rights and, in particular, our opposition to homosexuality, to gayness has been wrong, Fidel. Is that what you are saying?

YOUNGER FIDEL: Yes, Hilda. We have not done enough in the struggle against racism and sexism and bias of all forms. Why? Because while we have fully mobilized the Cuban people to participate in the economic process we have not done the same in the political process. We communists must *lead* the world in advocating and practicing democratic participation; not follow the limited and coercive "democracy" of capitalist society. All power to the people must mean all political power to the people.

RAÚL: Fidel, with all due respect, isn't this too risky? Far too risky.

CHE: Nothing is too risky, Raúl, except not taking risks.

MELBA: I think Che is right. We have not had a discussion such as this in years. *(Toasts.)* A toast to our discussion.

YOUNGER FIDEL: Our second revolution is already underway. *(Laughs.)*

ÑICO: This is Che's idea. I can tell. But, Fidel, isn't he being too risky again? After all, he has nothing to lose. He is dead. No offense, dear comrade Che. No offense. But we are materialists.

CHE: But you are also dead, dear comrade Ñico. We revolutionaries mustn't let being dead conservatize us. You are right, Ñico. I am sometimes too risky. But Fidel is not. When our ideas and our spirits are married we reduce this risk of excessive riskiness. And with all of your support it is reduced almost to zero.

RAÚL: The Cuban Communist Party will have trouble with this.

YOUNGER FIDEL: With all due respect to our beloved party it has always been the Cuban people with whom we must dialogue and who must make our revolution. They have done so for 40 years and must do so for 400 more.

RAÚL: *(To YOUNGER FIDEL)* You know I would follow you anywhere. I always have. I always will.

(MELBA begins to make a toast.)

JESÚS: Melba, can I make a toast sometimes?

HILDA: We women will never catch up, comrade Jesús. But yes, why don't you make a toast.

(Everyone laughs.)

JESÚS: *(Playfully)* Hilda…are you being patronizing?

HILDA: Probably, Jesús. Probably.

JESÚS: To Fidel and Che and the glorious Cuban people. One, two, three… as many as we need…Cuban Revolutions!

(They all toast and cheer.)

ÑICO: Now let's get down to business. How do we make our second revolution?

(They talk excitedly.)

Act II, Scene 2

Video monitor comes on.

(Video #4)

NEWSCASTER: Dateline, Havana, Cuba. October 8, 1997. In an astoundingly atypical public relations extravaganza, President Fidel Castro, missing from public view for weeks, landed in Havana harbor on this the 30th anniversary of the Day of the Heroic Guerrilla. With a multiracial, multi-gender band of some 40 Cubans and other Latin Americans, el presidente arrived on a *Granma*-like yacht called *Risky Revolutionary*. Cuban military and police forces appeared initially to not know who was on board and looked to be apprehending them. But immediately upon recognizing the great Cuban revolutionary leader, comandante Fidel, they laid down their arms. President Castro then unfurled a parchment declaring victory for Cuba's second revolution—

civil, human and democratic rights for all. Interviewed just after he landed, an exuberantly youthful President Castro spelled out exactly what this meant:

(Cut to a youthful, invigorated OLDER FIDEL.*)*

OLDER FIDEL: Free elections will be held within six months for every office in Cuba including, of course, the office of president. No one needs to be thrown out of office more than me. *(Laughs.)* All Cubans 15 years and older—15 is how old our revered hero Ñico López was when he became a guerrilla fighter in Cuba's first revolution—will be allowed to vote *and* to hold office. The only condition for running is support for socialism here in Cuba and worldwide as declared in our Constitution. All those who do not support our way of life have already "run"—to Miami; thanks to the imperialists! And a new human rights code is hereby adopted outlawing all bias and prejudice based on race, gender, sexual preference and/or any other identity. We are all Cubans. We are all citizens of the world.

Now some people will wonder where these changes—these ideas— have come from. Some will say the CIA. But no Cuban will wonder. No true socialist will wonder. We all know. I have been to see the doctor. And these are the doctor's orders. Long live the Cuban Revolution; long live socialism; and long live my lover, Ernesto Che Guevara. Venceremos.

(OLDER FIDEL *then enters from upstage and appears—live, for the first time —onstage.* MELBA *runs onstage, drink in hand and toasts.)*

MELBA: Long live Fidel; long live Che; long live the Cuban people; long live socialism. They are one.

(Slow fade to black; "Internationale" plays.)

))))

Coming of Age in Korea

Book and lyrics by Fred Newman, music by Annie Roboff

Coming of Age in Korea (1996) is the fourth musical by the team of Fred Newman and Annie Roboff, and by far the most conventional piece they've written to date.

It grows directly out of that subgenre of American musicals which deal with American GIs and Asian women, from *South Pacific* (1949) to *Miss Saigon* (1991); like them it is a romantic love story—actually three love stories. The relationships between Sal and Suzie, Frankie and Kim, and Walter and Florence are among the most tender and humane young loves ever brought to the American stage.

Coming of Age is also a "buddy" story, a musical centered around three young men—one African American, one Cuban-American, one Jewish—getting to know each other and themselves in the context of the United States military. Here again the play draws on a number of influential precedents, from Maxwell Anderson and Laurence Stallings' *What Price Glory?* (1926) to Neil Simon's *Biloxi Blues* (1986). The friendship among Sal, Frankie and Walter—which the video prologue lets us know will last throughout their lives—is deep, matter-of-fact and rooted in American working-class decency.

Coming of Age in Korea is also subtly, but definitely, a play about the Cold War. Other plays and movies which examine that era do so either as anti-Communist melodramas (probably the most successful of these being the film *The Manchurian Candidate*) or as liberal indictments of the injustices committed against America's dissidents (such as Eric Bentley's 1972 off-Broadway hit *Are You Now or Have You Ever Been?*). *Coming of Age in Korea* (a joking reference to Margaret Mead's landmark anthropological study, *Coming of Age in Samoa*) does not deal directly with the politics of the era. It simply presents some theatrical "snapshots" of two formative years in the lives of three working-class American kids "coming of age" in the 1950s while serving in the U.S. Army, and in doing so reveals a social and political environment which made it impossible for these young men ever to grow up.

The progressive impulses of Sal, Frankie and Walter are expressed throughout the script, as is their working-class empathy with the impoverished and colonized Korean people. Yet the polarized political environment of the time made it impossible for them to translate those impulses and that empathy into a coherent working-class politic—or even a helpful explanation of the world. They returned to an America in which any political or ethical expression of their working-class-ness was stigmatized as "un-American." They thus found themselves trapped in a political culture that denied the validity of their experience. The most disturbing, and most meaningful, aspect of this denial, and of *Coming of Age in Korea,* is that Sal, Frankie and Walter are the same (emotionally, intellectually, politically) at the age of 60 as they were at 19. They are frozen in that horrific moment in 1954 when the sexist, racist arrogance institutionalized in the U.S. military occupation of Korea results in the rape and murder of "Little Kim"—a horror which they have absolutely no means to address.

The video segment at the beginning and end of the play is essential to making this statement. In the 1996 production at the Castillo Theatre, which was directed by Newman, the segment was made to resemble a crudely produced "home movie." Its deliberately dull amateurishness was intended to indicate a great deal about the post-Korea lives of Sal, Frankie and Walter. It is the showing of *exactly the same video* at the top *and* close of the play which is the "developmental" or "cubist" aspect of this production. Viewed after seeing the body of the play, the video, at first perhaps merely boring, now becomes painfully sad, transforming the totality of the production.

The story which unfolds between the two showings of the video is, taken by itself, Newman and Roboff's most conventional musical—and perhaps the most conventional of all Newman's plays. Its plot is linear; its characters are well-drawn and clearly defined individuals; the songs, as in *Sally and Tom (The American Way),* skillfully develop character, reveal relationships and move the plot along; there are no catalytic characters and no radical transformations or shifts of identity. Thus it is the video segments—the prologue and epilogue—which make *Coming of Age* a distinctly Newmanesque piece.

There are autobiographical elements in the play. Newman was a U.S. soldier in Korea when he was 19. Like the character Frankie, he testified on behalf of a friend who was being court-martialed; thanks to his testimony, the friend was acquitted. A number of the characters are based on people

Newman knew. Newman never had a relationship with a Korean woman, as Frankie does with "Little Kim," although brutal crimes such as Little Kim's rape and murder occurred with disturbing frequency and continue to take place. (During the production at Castillo, an American GI in Korea was arrested for the murder of a young Korean prostitute and three American soldiers were on trial for the rape and murder of a 12-year-old girl in Guam.)

"The world keeps sinnin'/And I don't get it," Frankie sings in the play's final sequence. Indeed, that, as much as the violence itself, is the tragedy of this play.

D.F.

Coming of Age in Korea was first produced at the Castillo Theatre (Fred Newman, artistic director; Gabrielle Kurlander producing director; Diane Stiles, managing director) in New York City on December 6, 1996. The cast, in order of appearance, was as follows:

SAL CASTRO . . . . Robert Morgan
FRANKIE GREENBERG . . . . Shawn Lipenski
WALTER SHELTON . . . . Will Parker
FLORENCE SHELTON . . . . Meredith Wright
KIM (ON VIDEO) . . . . Elyse Mendel
SUZIE (ON VIDEO) . . . . Rosa Goldstein
JOEY (ON VIDEO) . . . . David Nackman
ANN (ON VIDEO) . . . . Ellen Korner
MAGGIE (ON VIDEO) . . . . Magdalena López
RAFAEL (ON VIDEO) . . . . Omar Ali
EDDIE (ON VIDEO) . . . . Rafael Mendez
ELLY (ON VIDEO) . . . . AnaMaria Correa
BACKUP VOCALS (ON VIDEO) . . . . Ellen Korner, Meredith Wright
COLONEL NELSON . . . . Damian Buzzerio
SERGEANT BOND . . . . Doug Miranda
SUZIE . . . . Donna Ong
LITTLE KIM . . . . Vivian Bang
MAIL CALL VOICE . . . . Roger Grunwald
BACKUP VOCALS (OFFSTAGE) . . Shawn Lipenski, Donna Ong, Meredith Wright
RADIO ANNOUNCER . . . . David Nackman

Fred Newman, director; Diane Stiles, producer; Dan Belmont, musical director/keyboards; John Putnam, guitar; Damon Banks, bass; Lonné Moretton, choreography; Joseph Spirito, set design; Elena Borstein, scenic design; Charlotte, costume design; Charlie Spickler, lighting design; Michael Klein, sound design; Barry Z Levine, video design; Diane Stiles, still photography; Ellen Korner, production stage manager.

Coming of Age in Korea is a musical drama about three young working-class American soldiers who meet in Korea in the 1950s and together go through some of the "rites of passage" to adulthood. It is, as well, a tragic story of a Korean child/young woman who is the victim of a horrendous piece of "ugly Americanism"—gang rape and murder by senior U.S. officers.

There is another tragedy here. For in the highly political environment of the early stages of the "Cold War," Frankie, Sal and Walt are confronted with the hideous inexplicability of Little Kim's violent murder. Frankie and Walt sing of how they will, perhaps, never understand it. And they do not. Instead, these three decent young men are frozen forever in the tragic moment. Sal's "Don't sweat it" obviously will not suffice—even for Sal! They go on with their lives—they marry, get jobs, have families. But not only do they never forget Suzie and Little Kim, the incomprehensibility of their experience condemns them to permanent infantilism. Just as the beautiful and innocent Little Kim is not allowed to grow beyond her teenage years by the vicious action of Col. Nelson, so Frankie, Sal and Walt are permanently paralyzed by such unexplainable ugly Americanism.

The great Heiner Müller, the recently deceased (and, perhaps, as he would have it, the last) German playwright, speaks of the past half century as a "frozen storm"—progressivism and humanism destroyed by greed (the greed of progressives and humanists, as well as of others). It is the impact of this almost unspeakable failure of humanism and progressivism on the quite ordinary lives of working people (millions of Rwandans, Eastern Europeans, Chinese, Koreans, as well as Frankie, Sal and Walt) that consumes me and finds expression in *Coming of Age in Korea*.

While the play is not fully autobiographical, I spent 16 months as a soldier in Korea in 1954 and 1955. Many of my own youthful experiences are incorporated into the play. When William Lederer and Eugene Burdick's extraordinary book *The Ugly American* came out in 1959, it helped me to put together some of the jagged pieces of my Korean experiences. But it did not serve to "thaw me out." Whatever growth and development I have experienced I owe to the thousands with whom I have worked in creating a developing humanistic community over these past three decades. To all of them, and the billions of hours of ordinary work they do so willingly and well (represented in this production by our hardworking stagehands who, in the half light of history, make the stage spin), I dedicate this play with all my love.

DECEMBER 1996

CHARACTERS

COLONEL NELSON

SERGEANT BOND

WALTER SHELTON

FRANKIE GREENBERG

SAL CASTRO

SUZIE

LITTLE KIM

FLORENCE SHELTON

On video
KIM (Frankie's daughter)
SUZIE (Frankie's granddaughter)
JOEY (Frankie's son-in-law)
ANN (Frankie's wife)
MAGGIE (Sal's wife)
RAFAEL (Sal's grandson)
EDDIE (Sal's son)
ELLY (Sal's daughter-in-law)

Offstage
MAIL CALL VOICE
RADIO ANNOUNCER

NOTE:
This play contains both live scenes and video sequences.

Act I, Scene 1

The following scene takes place entirely on video. The setting is a working-class apartment, the occasion is WALTER, FRANKIE and SAL's "40th anniversary" party. Present (or arriving) are: WALTER, FRANKIE and SAL (at 60); FLORENCE (also 60); FRANKIE's wife ANN (at 60); FRANKIE's daughter KIM (at 35); FRANKIE's granddaughter SUZIE (at 15); SAL's wife MAGGIE (at 60); SAL's son EDDIE (at 40); KIM's husband JOEY (at 35); EDDIE's wife ELLY (at 40); and EDDIE's son RAFAEL (at 18).

SAL: *(To FRANKIE)* Hey man, where's your grandkid Suzie? Y'know she's my lover girl. Where is she?

FRANKIE: Don't sweat it, man. She'll be here any minute with her mother and father. So ya better behave yourself.

SAL: How dey doin? How's Kim and Joey gettin' along? Dey doin' okay?

FRANKIE: Yeah, man. Don't sweat it. They're doin' okay now.

SAL: Would you stop sayin' "don't sweat it"? Geez, I'm sorry I taught you that expression way back when in Korea.

FRANKIE: You taught me that? When? Bullshit.

(Mock fight between FRANKIE and SAL.)

WALTER: *(Intervenes in fight)* What's wrong with you two hoodlums? I can't leave you alone for a minute. If ya don't behave yourselves I'll get Florence over here.

(SAL and FRANKIE feign fear and "break it up.")

FLORENCE: Did I hear my name? You need me for something, Walter?

SAL: Don't sweat it, Florence. Everything's cool.

(Enter KIM, JOEY and SUZIE; ANN welcomes them.)

KIM: Hi, Mom.

SUZIE: Hi, Grandma.

JOEY: Hello, Mama Ann.

ANN: Hello, Kim darling. Hi, Suzie, how's my sweetheart? Hi, Joe, good to see ya.

(*The three,* KIM, JOEY *and* SUZIE, *make their way to* FRANKIE.)

KIM: Hi, Dad, how are ya, love?

FRANKIE: Hi, Kim, baby. Hi, Joey (*shakes hands*). Hiya, little Suzie. (*He hugs his granddaughter.* SAL *grabs her away for a hug.*)

SUZIE: Uncle Sal. How's my love?

SAL: Careful, darlin', Aunt Maggie'll hear you.

MAGGIE: (*Coming over*) No sweat, Suzie. Everyone knows you're his number one gal.

RAFAEL: (*To* SAL) Would you leave Suzie alone? I told ya I was gonna marry her.

EDDIE: (*Embracing* SUZIE) Don't worry about these two Latin lovers, Suzie.

WALTER: Hey, Eddie, what're you?

EDDIE: (*Jokingly*) I got a college degree, Walt—somethin' neither my father nor my son has. I'm a middle-class, middle-aged, civilized kinda guy (*he grabs* ELLY)—ain't that right, Elly darlin'? (*He grabs* MAGGIE.) Ain't that right, Mom?

MAGGIE: Walter…he's a Latino letcher.

ELLY: You better believe it, Walt.

(*They all laugh.*)

MAGGIE: Florence—is Sammy comin' today?

FLORENCE: (*A little hesitantly*) No. He's out of town. He and his wife send their love.

SAL: What's his new wife's name again?

FLORENCE: Susan.

SAL: She comes from a lotta money, yeah?

FLORENCE: She's a good person, Sal. She's just not so comfortable with us low lives—y'know.

SUZIE: *(Pointing to SAL, WALTER and FRANKIE)* Did you three sing yet? I wanna hear ya sing that fifties stuff.

KIM: Suzie, you ain't been hearin' it for 40 years.

FRANKIE: *(Jokingly)* I never knew ya didn't like it, Kim. My own daughter don't like my singin'. Geez.

WALTER: She don't like your voice, Frankie. It's too damned white.

SAL: Yeah, Frankie. I been meanin' to talk to you about that for 40 years now.

ANN: Would you three clowns sing already?

WALTER: We wrote a new song for our 40th anniversary.

ELLY: You guys have known each other 40 years? Let's see…Since 1954?

SAL: Can you believe it?

FRANKIE: Yeah, Elly. Don't sweat it, Sal. Don't sweat it.

FLORENCE: Just sing, you three, just sing.

(They come together; do "doo-wop" sounds and moves; sing.)

("1954")

FRANKIE, SAL, WALTER:
> I'll bet you'd never believe,
> I'll bet you couldn't conceive,
> That we were once nineteen;
> It was a mighty strange scene.

> Way back in 1954,
> Right after the Korean War,
> The mambo sound was just begun
> And Uncle Miltie's number one.

WALTER:

> 'Cause there were drive-in flicks
> And pick-up sticks
> McCarthy craze
> And Willie Mays
> In 1954.

FRANKIE:

> Presley moved his pelvis
> Which is why
> They called him
> Elvis
> In 1954.

SAL:

> Hula hoops,
> Balls off stoops
> And don't forget those doo-wop groups
> In 1954.

FRANKIE, WALTER:

> Adam Clayton Powell,
> Mel Allen
> For White Owls
> Made the city roar.

SAL:

> The Tito Puente sound,
> Tony Bennett came around
> In 1954.

WALTER:

> They still said "Negro" in that time.

FRANKIE:

> I first discovered lemon and lime.

SAL:

> I'm drinkin' rum and usin' coke,
> And Richard Nixon's still a joke.

FRANKIE, SAL, WALTER:

>We joined the Army, went away.
>We met in Pusan-by-the-Bay.
>Three guys from old Nueva York
>Just learnin' how to walk and talk.
>Way back in 1954.

Act I, Scene 2

Pusan, Korea, 1953. Lights up on COLONEL NELSON's office. NELSON is in front of a mirror, primping and preening à la George Patton. There is a knock at the door.

NELSON: *(Sternly, authoritarianly)* Come in!

(*SERGEANT BOND enters.*)

BOND: I have the three men you wanted to see, sir. Whenever you're ready.

NELSON: Bring them in, Sergeant. Right now!

BOND: Yes, sir.

(*BOND exits and returns with PRIVATES SAL CASTRO, WALTER SHELTON and FRANKIE GREENBERG. The men stand in front of NELSON's desk.*)

NELSON: Don't you men know how to salute?

(*They all belatedly and nervously salute; NELSON returns salute.*)

NELSON: Sergeant Bond, these are the three men—that is the *only* three men in the whole of headquarters company—who didn't have V.D. in last week's "short arm" inspection, right?

BOND: Yes, sir. That's correct, sir.

NELSON: *(Sarcastically)* Well, that's very good, gentlemen. Alright, now let's get down to it. How come, how come no V.D.? What's your "problem"? Y'all homos?

WALTER: *(Steps forward)* I'm married, sir. And Florence—that's my wife—would have my head if I slept with another woman.

NELSON: How old are you, Private…*(he reads name tag)* Shelton?

WALTER: I'm 19, sir.

NELSON: When did you get married?

WALTER: Florence and I got married when we were 17—actually she'd just turned 18...sir.

NELSON: Ain't that a little young, soldier? Was she pregnant?

WALTER: No, sir. We never had sex 'til we were married, sir. And both our families approved of the marriage...sir.

NELSON: What about you, Private *(reads name tag)* Greenberg?

FRANKIE: *(Hesitantly, shy)* I've never had sex, sir.

NELSON: Why is that, private? You a homosexual or somethin'?

FRANKIE: No, sir. I just...I just never did it.

NELSON: This some kinda moral position? You're Jewish, right?

FRANKIE: Yes, sir.

NELSON: Is this a Jewish kinda thing?

FRANKIE: Maybe...I dunno, sir.

NELSON: *(Turning quickly to SAL)* And you, Private...*(reads name tag)* Castro, *(sarcastically)* are you a virgin, too?

SAL: No, sir. No way, sir. I'm Cuban. I sleep pretty much with everything that moves...I mean, the female things...but I'm careful, sir!

NELSON: You're kind of a wise-ass, Castro. Isn't that right, Sergeant Bond?

BOND: Yes, sir. But he's been no problem, Colonel Nelson.

NELSON: Not yet, Bond. Not yet. *(Pause.)* You three bunk together, right?

SAL, WALTER and FRANKIE: *(Together)* Yes, sir.

NELSON: How come?

SAL: Well, sir, we got here the same day two months ago and when we got to Quonset 7—that's where we were assigned—the only three bunks empty were in the corner so we grabbed 'em...sir.

NELSON: You're all from New York City, right?

SAL: Yes, sir…But different neighborhoods.

NELSON: But now you're all livin' in the same neighborhood.

WALTER: Yes, sir.

NELSON: How do you like it, Greenberg?

FRANKIE: I like it fine, sir. Walt and Sal are good guys.

NELSON: I don't like it when different kinds of people live together. I don't trust it. I don't trust you three hangin' out together—sleeping together.

SAL: We just wanna be a honor to your company, sir.

BOND: Don't speak to the Colonel unless you're spoken to, Private Castro.

NELSON: You're the ring leader, Castro, right?

SAL: Well, I'm a little older than Walt and Frankie. I'm almost 20…sir.

NELSON: Some ugly Korean bitch is gonna stick the clap on you, Castro. Take my word for it.

SAL: Don't sweat it, sir. It'll never happen. Y'got my word.

BOND: Don't disagree with the Colonel, Castro. Don't be a wise-ass in here.

NELSON: Wait and see, Castro. This place'll wear all your asses down. Now get the hell out of here. I don't trust New Yorkers—any kind. Never have. Never will…Dismissed.

(The three privates salute and exit.)

BOND: Anything else, Colonel?

NELSON: Keep a close eye on those three. I'd like to make 'em eat shit. No offense, Bond, but I don't like Negroes, Latinos and Jews hangin' out together. I liked the Army better when it was segregated, Sergeant Bond.

BOND: Yes, sir. I hear ya, sir.

NELSON: But you don't agree, right, Sergeant?

BOND: Ain't my place to agree or disagree, sir.

NELSON: You're an old Army man, Sergeant. I like you.

BOND: Thank you, sir. Thank you. Is that all, sir?

NELSON: Yes, Sergeant.

(*BOND salutes and exits, leaving NELSON alone. He goes to the mirror and continues to primp and preen. He sings.*)

(*"I Was Never Meant to Lead These Kind of Men"*)

I was never meant to lead
These kind of men.
I came to the Army way back when
A soldier was white,
A crusading knight,
And not a member of a minor race.
It seems to me that I have lost my place.

I'm just old-fashioned
And I'll never like
Spics, niggers and kikes
Thinking they're all alike.

No. I'm not a bigot,
Just proud of my past.
This coming together,
It never can last.

I was never meant to lead
These kind of men.
I came to the Army way back when
A soldier was white,
A crusading knight,
And not a member of a minor race.
It seems to me that I have lost my place.
I was never meant to lead these kind of men.

Act I, Scene 3

Outside NELSON's office. SAL, WALTER and FRANKIE are talking together.

SAL: That crazy son of a bitch Colonel Nelson was chewin' our asses out for not havin' the goddamned clap. That bastard is wacko, man—*loco, muy loco.*

WALTER: Well, Sal, he's white, y'know. *(To FRANKIE.)* No offense, Frankie. But I don't think of you as white…y'know, you're a Jew…that's kinda different.

SAL: Yeah, Frankie. And besides…you're a virgin. *(He laughs playfully.)*

FRANKIE: Don't sweat it, Sal. Don't sweat it.

SAL: Who taught you that? Who taught you to say "don't sweat it"?

FRANKIE: You did, Sal. *(Sarcastically, playfully.)* You know you're like a father to me.

WALTER: But Nelson is right, Sal. You better look out or you'll wind up with the clap. *(Pointing to SAL's crotch.)* You're gonna wear that little fucker out.

FRANKIE: Yeah, Sal…you're gonna mess up our perfect record.

SAL: Don't sweat it, guys. No way, Josés. Ain't none of us gonna get the clap. Us Latins are careful with this shit. You stick with me you'll be fine. Most of these other guys with the clap…I mean they're mainly white dudes from the sticks and they treat their women bad. So women try to give 'em the clap. Hey. Not me. I like these Korean girls. I respect 'em, y'know.

WALTER: I hear ya, man. We ain't no shit-head ugly Americans, Sal.

FRANKIE: These people been fucked with enough—y'know what I mean? Y'hear what I'm sayin'?

SAL: *(Joking)* You some kinda Jew communist, Frankie? You related to them Rosenbergs?

FRANKIE: Shit. That Julius Rosenberg looks like my father. And my father couldn't steal no atomic bomb secrets if his life depended on it.

WALTER: I don't think they did it. They're gettin' framed. They're gonna fry 'em but they're gettin' framed.

SAL: I dunno nothin' much about this political shit. I know there's a moustachioed bastard down in Cuba named Batista who's runnin' the place and no one likes his ugly ass. I got a cousin down there studyin' to be a lawyer in Havana—a dude named Fidel—who says he's gonna get rid of the son of a bitch Batista someday. But I dunno—he says a lotta things.

WALTER: I don't think Nelson likes the Army bein' integrated. He's probably a member of the KKK and a goddamn Yankee fan. No Blacks playin' at the stadium. Now the Dodgers—that's my team: Jackie and Campy—they're the best.

FRANKIE: But the Yankees always beat their asses.

WALTER: Well, they got all the money. I think Mantle, Martin and "Whitey" Ford put on white hoods before the opening of the Series and scare the shit outta my bums. Anyway, wait 'til next year.

SAL: Mays make 'em all look like shit. Willie's the best. He must have some Latin blood in him.

WALTER: No way, Sal. He's just a sharecropper's kid from Alabama. Black through and through. Did you see that catch he made against Vic Wertz in the Series this year? Shit. He's the best. Sal's right.

FRANKIE: I'll bet Mays eats chicken soup with matzo balls. He is the best. He does it all.

SAL: Hey, man. How many more days before we rotate back home? What's the count, Walt?

WALTER: Four-twenty-four. And not one day more.

SAL: *(He calculates)* Sixty-three days in Korea. 424 to go. And I still ain't got the clap. That's unbelievable. I must be a goddamn genius. *(Sings.)*

("Don't Have the Clap")

We're like three Latins
From Brooklyn, Bronx and Manhattan
Here in Korea
Lookin' out for gonorrhea.
Three young wise-asses

Representin' New York's masses
Here in Pusan,
Tryin' to get it on
Without it fallin' off.

Don't have the clap,
Not caught in
That not so tender trap.
Not the clap,
V.D.'s not my thing.
No, not the clap,
Clean as a whistle,
Still a guided missile
Tryin' to keep it on.

SAL, FRANKIE, WALTER:

We're not clappin' it,
We're not clappin' it,
We're not clappin' it,
No, not at all.

WALTER:

We're three young privates
Havin' fun
Tryin' to jive-it.

FRANKIE:

Colonel don't like us,
Wishes he could straight out strike us.

SAL:

Three young wise-asses
Representin' New York's masses
Here in Pusan,
Tryin to get it on
Without it fallin' off.

Don't have the clap,
Not caught in
That not so tender trap.

Not the clap,
V.D.'s not my thing.
No, not the clap,
Clean as a whistle,
Still a guided missile
Tryin' to keep it on.

Don't have the clap,
Not caught in
That not so tender trap.
Not the clap,
V.D.'s not my thing.
No, not the clap,
Clean as a whistle,
Still a guided missile
Tryin' to keep it on.

SAL, FRANKIE, WALTER:
We're not clappin' it,
We're not clappin' it,
We're not clappin' it,
No, not at all.

Act I, Scene 4

Same setting as Scene 3. BOND enters.

BOND: What are you three meatheads up to?

WALTER: Just waitin' 10 minutes for the chow line to form, Sergeant Bond.

BOND: Y'ain't got nothin' better to do than wait around, Private Shelton?

SAL: We was just discussin' military strategy, Sarge.

BOND: I'll bet, Castro. I'll bet. Castro, why don't you and Shelton go into the mess hall and see if they need some help. I needa talk with Greenberg for a minute.

WALTER: Sure thing, Sarge.

SAL: But couldn't we just listen a little to what you're gonna tell Frankie? I'm sure it would be most instructive, Sergeant.

BOND: Get outta here, Castro, before I send ya off to clean latrines for a year, ya Cuban meathead.

SAL: Don't sweat it, Sergeant Bond. I'm gone.

(*WALTER and* SAL *move away quickly, but continue to lurk and listen at a distance.*)

BOND: Listen, Greenberg, you seem like a good kid. Why are ya hangin' around with a Latin meatball like Castro?

FRANKIE: Sal's my buddy, Sarge. And he's a good guy.

BOND: But he don't know nothin' about the ways of the Army, Greenberg. He's a street punk. How come you ain't in college, Greenberg? You look like a college type.

FRANKIE: I went to City College of New York for one semester, Sergeant Bond. I did bad, fell in love, the girl's family *busted* it up. So I *joined* up.

BOND: Well, Greenberg, the Army's a good place to *grow* up. I came in when I was 18, during World War II. It's an okay life. But ya gotta pick the right people to learn from. I could teach ya a lotta stuff, Greenberg. Maybe I ain't got no crystal ball or college degree, but I know the ropes. I can teach ya how to march and make out in this "school of hard knocks."

FRANKIE: Hey, I appreciate it, Sergeant Bond. I wanna learn. And you seem like a good guy to learn from.

(*"Coming of Age in Korea"*)

BOND: (*Sings*)
Did you ever read
The book by Margaret Mead?
It's called
Coming of Age
In Samoa.
They say the book is read
By every college head.

It turns a novice
To a genuine knower.

But since you made the choice
To leave your college voice
And get smart
Here in the U.S. Army,
I'll be your swami,
My kosher salami,
And you'll be
Comin' of age in Korea.

Comin' of age, 'cause life's a stage,
Comin' of age in Korea.
Comin' of age, 'cause life's a stage,
Comin' of age in Korea.
Comin' of age, 'cause life's a stage,
Comin' of age in Korea.
Comin' of age, 'cause life's a stage,
Comin' of age in Korea.

I'll teach you sex and vice
And how to suck on ice
As you are
Comin' of age in Korea.
So my young soldier boy,
This learnin's such a joy
You'll be
Comin' of age in Korea.

Since you made the choice
To leave your college voice
And get smart
Here in the U.S. Army,
I'll be your swami,
My kosher salami,
And you'll be
Comin' of age in Korea.

BOND, FRANKIE, WALTER, SAL:

Comin' of age, 'cause life's a stage,
Comin' of age in Korea.
Comin' of age, 'cause life's a stage,
Comin' of age in Korea.
Comin' of age, 'cause life's a stage,
Comin' of age in Korea.
Comin' of age, 'cause life's a stage,
Comin' of age in Korea.

Act I, Scene 5

Same set as Scenes 3 and 4. At the end of the song, BOND *exits.* SAL, WALT *and* FRANKIE *are laughing and jiving around when* SUZIE *and* LITTLE KIM *walk on accompanied by offstage whistles.* SUZIE *is dressed like a prostitute;* LITTLE KIM *is in child-like clothing (maybe Catholic school dress).*

WALTER: *(Looking at* SUZIE*)* Wow. That's a fine lookin' woman.

SAL: You want her, Walt?

WALTER: Hey, Sal, I told ya, I'm faithful to Florence. Besides, she'd kill me.

FRANKIE: This Florence seems like quite a girl, Walt.

WALTER: Oh, she is, Frankie. I've known her since I was 12. We both grew up in Brooklyn—right near Ebbets Field. Florence always took good care of me. When I was about to do somethin' crazy with my buddies, she'd stop me. She's real smart. We're gonna spend our lives together.

SAL: *(Looking at* SUZIE*)* Well, then I guess she's all mine. *(He approaches* SUZIE*.)* Hiya, darlin'. *(Patronizingly.)* You speakie English?

SUZIE: I speak English, GI. You speak English?

SAL: *(He laughs)* Whoa. I like that. A wise-ass—and a beautiful ass, too.

SUZIE: Watch your language, soldier boy. This is my kid sister with me.

SAL: Excuse me. Excuse me. My apologies. What's your name?

SUZIE: Suzie's my name. And yours?

SAL: Sal's my name. *(He turns to LITTLE KIM.)* And what's your name, little darlin'?

SUZIE: She don't talk to strangers, soldier boy.

SAL: But you do, don't ya, Suzie? What you doin' here in the compound?

SUZIE: I'm a secretary for Major Collins over in battalion supply. I keep tabs on the condoms. It's a full-time job.

SAL: You are a wise-ass. Is that your only line of work, Suzie?

SUZIE: I do whatever I have to to make a living. There's a lotta mouths to feed in my family.

SAL: Maybe we could…ah, get together some time?

SUZIE: Where's your family from, Sal…I mean, originally?

SAL: From Cuba. You heard of Cuba?

SUZIE: Yeah. I heard of Cuba.

SAL: But I was born in the USA. *(Jokingly.)* You heard of the USA?

SUZIE: Yeah, I'm acquainted with Uncle Sam.

SAL: Well, I'm his cousin Sal.

SUZIE: You a nasty son of a bitch, Sal, who beats up women?

SAL: No, no, no, no, no, Suzie. I'm not. I treat women right. I treat 'em real good.

SUZIE: Well, maybe we'll get together, Sal. Come by Major Collins' office some time. Don't forget to salute.

SAL: *(Laughs)* I'll salute *you*, Suzie Wise-ass. I'll salute you.

(*SUZIE and LITTLE KIM walk away. SUZIE salutes and they exit.*)

FRANKIE: That was slick, Sal. I'm impressed. She's some good-lookin' woman.

SAL: She's a prostitute, Frankie. Just a prostitute.

WALTER: But she's real smart, ain't she?

SAL: Prostitutes ain't no dummies, Walt. Just 'cause you spread your legs don't mean you ain't got no brains.

FRANKIE: And the little sister is beautiful, too.

SAL: She'll be whoring in a year.

WALTER: She didn't look like no whore to me.

SAL: Dat's de only way to make money over here, Walt. The Japs, the Commies, and Uncle Sam been kickin' the shit outta these people for a long time, man. They ain't got shit. It's a fuckin' shame, but that's the deal. Whorin's their major industry.

FRANKIE: How do you know all this stuff, Sal?

SAL: I ain't no dummy either, Frankie. Uncle Sam's been kickin' the shit outta Cuba for a long time, too.

WALTER: Uncle Sam's a regular ass-kicker, ain't he, Sal?

FRANKIE: But he's our boss; he's our boss. And his whip is Colonel Nelson.

WALTER: That Simon Legree is a real bastard.

FRANKIE: We better look out for him.

SAL: Yeah. We better.

WALTER: I bet Suzie and Sal gonna make it together.

FRANKIE: Maybe the bell's will be ringin' for Suzie and Sal. Y'know that old song?

SAL: Don't sweat it. Never happen, GI. Never happen. I ain't gettin' hitched to no prostitute.

FRANKIE: (Sings) The bells are ringin' for Suzie and Sal…

WALTER: Y'all look out for V.D., my Cuban friend. We got a reputation goin' here.

SAL: Don't sweat it, good buddies. Don't sweat it.

(Short musical reprise of "Don't Have the Clap.")

Act I, Scene 6

In a poor Korean hut. SUZIE and LITTLE KIM are sitting on a straw bed together.

LITTLE KIM: Who was that nice Cuban man you were talking to, Suzie?

SUZIE: He's just another GI, darling—just another soldier boy lookin' to have some fun.

LITTLE KIM: Are you going to marry an American soldier some day, Suzie?

SUZIE: No, Nabyah. They don't wanna marry someone like me. They all got gals back home in the U.S. of A. Nice gals. *(Laughing.)* Not like me.

LITTLE KIM: You're the nicest gal I ever knew, Suzie. And the best big sister in the world. *(They hug.)*

SUZIE: Well, little darling. Bein' a prostitute ain't so terrible. As the Americans say, it's an honest profession...and an old one.

LITTLE KIM: A lot of Korean woman are prostitutes aren't they, Suzie? I don't think I want to be a prostitute. I want to be a nurse.

SUZIE: When you were young, darlin', I hoped when you grew up we'd have more money. It was during the big war. I wished the Americans would win and throw the Japanese out. And they did. But now the Americans turn out to be almost as bad to us as the Japanese were and we are still living in dirt and squalor. So we are prostitutes.

LITTLE KIM: But I don't think I would like men touching me in that way.

SUZIE: As long as they don't hurt you it isn't so bad. It gives them pleasure. The Americans are all like little boys. They are silly but some of them are generous.

LITTLE KIM: Will I have to become a prostitute soon?

SUZIE: Yes, Nabyah, you will. You are very beautiful. You'll make a lot of money for our mother and father and our brothers and sisters.

LITTLE KIM: Will you always be with me, Suzie?

SUZIE: I'll always be with you. We'll always be together. Suzie and her little sister, partners.

LITTLE KIM: Then I won't mind being a prostitute, Suzie. We'll be partners.

(They embrace and SUZIE sings.)

("Maybe")

SUZIE:
> Maybe
> When you were
> A baby
> I'd kiss you
> Little doll
> In a splendid world.
> But
> That was just a dream.
>
> Maybe
> When you were
> A child
> I'd touch you
> You smiled
> In a splendid world.
> But
> That was just a dream.
>
> But what's a woman for,
> Except to be a whore,
> To sleep with any man
> Who works for Uncle Sam?
> What's a girl about
> To lay her body out,
> To make the GI's sigh
> While you hide the eyes that cry?
>
> Maybe
> When you were
> So small
> I'd hear you,
> Little dear,
> In a splendid world.

But
That was just a dream.

Maybe
When you were
Tiny
So lovely,
Tiny sister,
In a splendid world.
But
That was just a dream.

But what's a woman for,
Except to be a whore,
To sleep with any man
Who works for Uncle Sam?
What's a girl about,
To lay her body out,
To make the GI's sigh
While you hide the eyes that cry?

Now
Our life's no lovely dream
Just a dreadful, awful scream
In a darkened, blackened night.
Life's not what it seemed.

(Instrumental)

But what's a woman for,
Except to be a whore,
To sleep with any man
Who works for Uncle Sam?
What's a girl about,
To lay her body out,
To make the GI's sigh
While you hide the eyes that cry?

But what's a woman for,
Except to be a whore,

To sleep with any man
Who works for Uncle Sam?
What's a girl about,
To lay her body out,
To make the GI's sigh
While you hide the eyes that cry?

Act I, Scene 7

Split stage. On one side, FLORENCE *is dressed in a halter top on a hot summer day in Brooklyn, writing a letter to* WALTER. *On the other side,* WALTER *is sitting with* FRANKIE *and* SAL *when mail call brings him still another letter from* FLORENCE.

FRANKIE: How many letters ya gonna get today, Walt?

SAL: Maybe 10. Shit, Walt, I ain't got a letter for three months. How come Florence don't ever write to me?

WALTER: Well, I wrote her about you and Suzie.

SAL: *(Mock annoyance)* What did you tell her about me and Suzie? It ain't nothin' but good sex. You tell Florence that?

FRANKIE: Don't sweat it, Sal. Walt's tellin' Florence the real deal—"the bells are ringin' for Suzie and Sal." I mean Little Kim relates to you like her big brother.

SAL: She's a good kid. I don't want her to get hurt. Hey, next time me and Suzie go out drinkin', maybe you and Little Kim'll join us? Dat be nice.

FRANKIE: Hey, man. She's too beautiful for me. Besides I don't think she's kosher.

WALTER: *(To* FRANKIE*)* C'mon, man, go out with Little Kim. You're the only two virgins left in Korea. You'd make a beautiful couple.

SAL: Hey, Walt, what's the magic number? How many days left?

WALTER: Two-twenty-nine—ain't that fine—two hundred and twenty-nine. Can ya dig it? Two-two-nine.

FRANKIE: We've been in this hell hole over six months now. Hey, guys, maybe it's time for an R&R to Tokyo. Whattya think?

WALTER: Hey, I've been writin' to Florence about that. She's savin' some bucks so she can come over to Japan and see me for a week. Why don't y'all come along? We'll have a ball. Sal, you can bring Suzie.

SAL: I ain't bringin' Suzie to Japan. There's lotsa good Japanese girls I ain't tried out yet.

OFFSTAGE VOICE: Mail call!

(*WALTER runs off.*)

OFFSTAGE VOICE: Shelton, Shelton, Vorrick, Shelton, Shelton, Grazelli, Shelton…that's it.

(*WALTER returns with lots of letters. He sits on a cot and opens one of them. On the other side of the stage, FLORENCE sings.*)

(*"Dear Walter"*)

FLORENCE:
Dear Walter,
Sittin' here in my halter, whew.
It's hot out
So I'm not out
Sitting on the couch
Where you used to slouch.

Dear Walter,
Before you went away
It was a helluva day
Remember?
My sister Jill
She fell down on the hill.

Dear Walter,
Are ya faithful to me
In Korea?
Can I see ya?
You're my man,
In Japan

Let's make it happen
With an R and R plan.

Went out
Don't pout
Hot dog
Sauerkraut
When you get back
I'm gonna shout.
Dear Walter,
Mama says hello
So does Uncle Joe.
Remember
My cousin Jack?
Well, he just got back
From Hackensack.
Hey Walter,
What can I say?
Aunt Lorraine's
Still drivin' a bright yellow hack.

Dear Walter,
Are ya faithful to me
In Korea?
Can I see ya?
You're my man,
In Japan
Let's make it happen
With an R and R plan.

Dear Walter,
Are ya faithful to me
In Korea?
Can I see ya?
You're my man,
In Japan
Let's make it happen
With an R and R plan.

Act I, Scene 8

A ballroom/bar at the Ga-jo-en, an R&R hotel in Japan. Music is playing. SAL, FRANKIE, WALTER and FLORENCE enter and sit at a table together.

SAL: You're a mighty fine looker, Florence. Mighty fine.

WALTER: Whattya all wanna drink? I'm buyin'.

FRANKIE: You have a good effect on this guy, Florence. He ain't bought in six months.

WALTER: Now that ain't true, Frankie.

FLORENCE: He was probably savin' up for me comin' over here to Japan on this R&R.

WALTER: Yeah. That's right. So now that we're here, I'm buyin'.

SAL: I already asked them to bring over a bottle of champagne. This is our first get-together. We're gonna have many more. Lotsa reunions.

FLORENCE: That's how come you guys gotta take care of each other. We wanna be drinkin' together 40 years from now.

FRANKIE: Don't sweat it, Flo. We're the three musketeers.

SAL: Yeah. Frankie here's the world's only Hebrew musketeer.

FLORENCE: And y'all take particularly good care of my baby. *(She reaches out for WALTER's hand. He seems a little embarrassed. SAL and FRANKIE jump up and jokingly embrace WALTER.)*

WALTER: Alright, you two, cut it out.

SAL: He don't never do nothin' wrong, Florence. Everyone likes Walter.

FLORENCE: What about Colonel Nelson?

FRANKIE: Well, he don't like nobody, Florence. He's bad news.

FLORENCE: Well, he must really hate the three of you hangin' out together. Walt always manages to get in trouble when I ain't around.

WALTER: Hey, that ain't true no more, darlin'. Shit, I'm a married man now.

FLORENCE: I know. I'm your wife. Be careful, baby. You're still a Black man in a white man's Army.

(She turns to FRANKIE and SAL, who are still standing and sings.)

("Take Care of My Baby")

Take care of my baby,
Bring him home to me.
You're his pals, so maybe
You see what I see.
Take care of my baby,
I wanna spend my life with him.

Take care of my darling,
He's the nicest kinda guy.
My life's a movie he's the star in,
Please don't ask me why.
Take care of my darlin',
I need to have him come back home.

You two guys seem
So mighty sweet,
Some gal's gonna love you
And you're gonna give 'em both a treat.
Let me repeat:

Take care of my baby,
Y'all get back safe and sound.
Take care of yourselves,
So we can hang around.

Take care of my baby,
I wanna spend my life with you.
So take good care of my baby,
So take good care of my baby,
So take good care of my baby,
So take good care of my baby,
And he'll take care of you.

Act II, Scene 1

Inside Quonset #7. It's the dead of night, and FRANKIE *and* SAL *are "fixing up"* WALTER'S *bunk to make it seem as if he's in it.*

FRANKIE: Shit. I can't believe that Walt didn't make that flight back to Kimpo in Seoul. He's in big, big trouble now.

SAL: I told ya we shouldn't of left him and Florence alone in that hotel room in Tokyo at the Ga-jo-en. Those two are crazy in love. I knew they'd miss the bus to the airport.

FRANKIE: Whattya mean you knew? Ya never said a word. Walt's in big fuckin' trouble. He's AWOL right now. Colonel Nelson's gonna throw the book at him.

SAL: Don't sweat it, Frankie. We'll cover for him. Just fix up his bed. Make it look like he's in it. We'll tell everyone he came back with us.

FRANKIE: *(Panicked)* But what if he doesn't show up tomorrow? We'll all go to jail. Shit. I don't wanna go to the goddamn stockade.

SAL: Hey, man, stop your whinin'. We gotta cover for him. He's our buddy ...and besides we promised Florence. You remember?

FRANKIE: Yeah. You're right, Sal. I'm sorry. I guess this time Florence got Walt *into* trouble.

SAL: No sweat, man. We'll just get him *outta* trouble.

Act II, Scene 2

A waiting room outside of the court-martial room. FRANKIE, SAL *and* WALTER *are pacing, awaiting the verdict.*

WALTER: *(Nervously)* Whattya think, Sal? Whattya think? Y'ever been in-volved in a court-martial before?

SAL: Well, y'heard what that asshole Colonel Nelson said: he's gonna send all of us to the stockade for a decade—you for being AWOL and us for lyin' through our teeth coverin' for ya. So—no sweat, Walt—we'll all still be together, even if it's in jail.

FRANKIE: Ya think Sergeant Bond's helpin' us out? He's been in there testi-fyin' for over half an hour now.

SAL: I dunno, Frankie. You're the one he likes. He's your swami. I hope so.

WALTER: Ya know, you guys didn't have to do this. Shit, when I heard that racist Nelson tell ya that if you was perjurin' yourselves you'd go to jail with me, I almost shit in my pants.

SAL: No sweat, man. It's that new West Point Lieutenant Jasiota's word against mine and Frankie's. I mean who would you believe? (*Laughs.*)

FRANKIE: Sal, you're crazy. You are crazy!!!

WALTER: I think you two'll be okay. Nelson really hates me and my Black skin. I ain't gonna let you guys do time for me. I was AWOL. I'll pay the price. I'm never goin' home. I'll never leave this fuckin' Korea. (*Sings.*)

(*"You're a Dead Man, Walter"*)

That racist's gonna get me,
Gonna lock me up for good.
That bastard's gonna jail me,
Gonna spend a decade choppin' wood.
Hey, Florence, can ya hear me?
I'm never comin' back
To that old neighborhood.

Colonel is a white man.
He hates me being Black.
A middle of the night man,
I ain't never goin' back.
Hey, Florence, can ya hear me?
I'm never comin' back
To that old neighborhood.

You're a dead man, Walter.
You're a dead man, Walter.
You're a dead man, Walter.
You're a dead man, Walter.

You're a dead man, Walter.
You're a dead man, Walter.

Hey, Florence, can ya hear me?
I'm never comin' back
To that old neighborhood.

(As the song ends BOND *enters the waiting room.* NELSON *stands in the doorway glowering. The three privates freeze in anticipation; a two- or three-second pause.)*

BOND: *Not guilty, Shelton.* You're all not guilty. I told 'em that Castro here was a congenital liar, but that Greenberg was as honest as Moses. So they must be tellin' the truth.

*(*NELSON *slams the door. They all shake hands.)*

WALTER: Wow!!! Not guilty. I don't believe it. Thanks, Sergeant Bond. Thanks.

BOND: Hey, don't thank me, Shelton. Don't thank me. These two guys got ya off. They saved your ass.

FRANKIE: Unbelievable. Un-fuckin'-believable.

SAL: *(Cool)* I told ya we'd get him off. I never sweated it—not for a minute.

(The three embrace.)

BOND: Now get back to work, you three meatheads.

SAL: Don't we get time off to deal with all this anxiety?

BOND: Listen, Castro, get your ass back to work immediately or I'll make you think the stockade is a vacation in Bermuda.

WALTER: *(To* BOND*)* I always figured you didn't like me, Sergeant Bond.

BOND: You're a Black man, Private Shelton. And so am I. I ain't gotta like ya. I know what it is to be Black and I take care of my own...Now get the fuck outta here.

*(*WALTER *heads off with* FRANKIE, *followed by* SAL. BOND *stops* SAL.*)*

BOND: Good work, Castro. Y'got balls. I know this was your scheme. I respect ya. Y'took care of ya buddy. It's a good thing y'got Greenberg in there.

(*SAL simulates a salute. BOND simulates a salute back. SAL exits.*)

Act II, Scene 3

SAL, SUZIE, LITTLE KIM and FRANKIE are seated at a table in a run-down Pusan Korean night club. Loud music is playing.

SUZIE: So you two clowns got Walt off! Incredible. Everyone's talkin' about it. Colonel Nelson is pissed off. Especially at you, Frankie. My boss, Major Collins, told me that Nelson said you'd better look out. He's gonna have your ass if it's the last thing he does. Be careful, Frankie. Be careful. Colonel Nelson's a nasty ass son of a bitch. And he's outta his mind.

SAL: Don't sweat it, Suzie. Don't sweat it. It was Frankie's word against that asshole West Point Lieutenant Jasiota. And Frankie's got the look of an angel. Look at that sweet face. (*Playfully.*) I won't let 'em hurt ya. Frankie, I won't let 'em hurt ya. (*Kisses him.*)

FRANKIE: (*Laughingly*) Cut it out, Sal. Cut it out. (*To SUZIE.*) Sal's the one who made this happen. He's the real hero, Suzie. My knees were shakin'. Sal's a damned good man. Ya got a good man here, Suzie.

SUZIE: I know it, Frankie. He makes out like he's tough. But he's as tender as a teddy bear.

SAL: Would you two stop it already? (*Points to LITTLE KIM.*) Now there's the beautiful person around here. She has the soul and innocence of a beautiful young child. Ain't that right, Little Kim darlin'? You'll always be a little child.

(*"Little Kim's Song"*)

LITTLE KIM: (*Sings*)
Oh, yes, I'm still a little child,
And I don't think
I ever want to grow.

I wish to stay a wild flower
And there's nothing more to know.

I sing,
I dance,
But I'm afraid that forever
May be coming to an end
And I'll never be
A little child again.

A woman's life is very hard
In a land that's not our own
Where a flower
And a child
Cannot grow
Any more.

So I'm afraid that forever
May be coming to an end
And I'll never be
A little child again.

(At the end of the song, SAL hugs LITTLE KIM.)

SAL: *(To FRANKIE and LITTLE KIM)* Now why don't you two go take a walk and get to know each other a little better? Y'know what I'm sayin'?

FRANKIE: You want to, Little Kim? It's warm out.

LITTLE KIM: Sure, Frankie. Let's take a walk.

SAL: Now you behave yourself, Greenberg. *(Joking.)* You're a tough old GI and she's just a little girl.

LITTLE KIM: Hey, Sal. I ain't *that* little no more. And Frankie's not so tough.

SAL: Since when do you talk back to your Uncle Sal?

LITTLE KIM: *(Hits SAL playfully in the belly; SAL pretends he's hurt)* You need a nurse?

SAL: Frankie, get her outta here before I give her a spankin'.

LITTLE KIM: Yeah, Frankie. Let's take a walk. I'll tell ya about this partner-ship that Suzie and I are settin' up.

(*FRANKIE and LITTLE KIM exit.*)

SAL: (*To SUZIE*) Now, I know you got the cutest kid sister in the whole world, but you're kinda cute yourself, little Suzie. Y'wanna dance?

SUZIE: Yeah, Romeo. I wanna dance. I sometimes think maybe I wanna dance with you forever.

SAL: Careful, Suzie Wise-ass. There's danger in them there words.

(*They go to the dance floor. They start dancing and then sing.*)

(*"It's Simply Absurd"*)

SAL:

I'm a guy who don't love easy.

SUZIE:

I'm a gal who lives too hard.

SAL:

I'm a guy who's kinda crazy.

SUZIE:

I'm a gal with a helluva bod.
So it's extraordinary, don't you think,
That we might have fallen in love?

SAL:

Don't you say it, baby.
Please don't use the word.

SUZIE:

I'm a gal who sleeps with everyone.

SAL:

Hey, I'm a guy who does the same.

SUZIE:

But you're not simply anyone,

SAL:

> And Anyone's not your name.
> And it's extraordinary, don't you think,
> That we might have fallen in love?

SUZIE:

> Don't you say it, baby.
> Please don't use the word.
> You and me fallin' in love
> Is simply absurd.

TOGETHER:

> But here we are huggin' each other
> For a moment in space,
> Hangin' on for dear life together
> Before leavin' this place.

(They dance.)

SAL:

> I'm a guy who don't love easy.

SUZIE:

> I'm a gal who lives too hard.

SAL:

> I'm a guy who's kinda crazy.

SUZIE:

> I'm a gal with a helluva bod.

TOGETHER:

> So it's extraordinary, don't you think,
> That we might have fallen in love?
> Don't you say it, baby.
> Please don't use the word.
> You and me fallin' in love
> Is simply absurd.

Act II, Scene 4

Outdoors; a beautiful Korean early evening landscape. FRANKIE *and* LITTLE KIM *are walking/talking.*

FRANKIE: What kinda partnership you and Suzie gettin' into?

LITTLE KIM: Oh, nothing really. It's just a little joke Suzie and I made up. It just means that I'm ready to start "working" for a living.

FRANKIE: What d'ya mean, Little Kim? What kinda work?

LITTLE KIM: You know, Frankie. What kind of work is there for me?

FRANKIE: *(Panicked pause)* I thought you was gonna become a nurse?

LITTLE KIM: It takes too much time and costs too much money. The family needs help from me right now.

FRANKIE: I don't want you to be no prostitute, Little Kim. What does Sal say?

LITTLE KIM: Oh, y'know Sal. He says y'do what you have to do—y'know, don't sweat it.

FRANKIE: You'll get hurt, Little Kim. Suzie's tough. She can handle it. But guys'll take advantage of you. I know they will.

LITTLE KIM: Suzie says she'll start me out with an easy clientele—mainly older officers.

FRANKIE: Officers! Older officers! I'll bet they're the fuckin' worst. Pardon my language, Little Kim.

LITTLE KIM: I'll be okay, Frankie. You're goin' home pretty soon now. You'll find a nice American girl—a nice Jewish girl—and forget all about me.

FRANKIE: Never happen, Little Kim. Never happen.

(They embrace and kiss, then sing.)

("What is it Called?")

LITTLE KIM:
I never felt this way before,
To be with another as if he were me.

I never thought I could adore
In the way that I do you.

But what is it called?
What is the word?
We might be too young to say,
But this is the first
This wonderful burst
Of joy
Is all for you.

FRANKIE:

I've heard them say, this is the way
That you first fall in love on a sunny spring day,
But I never thought there was wonder like this
In the magic of a kiss.

But what is it called?
What is the word?
We might be too young to say,
But this is the first
This wonderful burst
Of joy
Is all for you.

TOGETHER:

But what is it called?
What is the word?
We might be too young to say,
But this is the first
This wonderful burst
Of joy
Is all for you.

Act II, Scene 5

Split stage. On one side FLORENCE is at home writing. On the other is the interior of Quonset #7. FRANKIE, SAL and WALTER are sitting around awaiting mail call. A radio is playing.

SAL: What's the count, Walt? How many days to the big R—the big rotation?

WALTER: We still gotta thirty-three-it, Sal—y'can almost see it. Thirty-three days to go, Sal, and look out New York City, here we come. I'm Brooklyn bound.

SAL: Yeah. Goin' home to Nueva York!

FRANKIE: *(Pause. FRANKIE is pensive)* You just gonna dump Suzie? Hey. That ain't right man. You two love each other.

SAL: Don't sweat it, Frankie. That's how it is, man. We never made no promises we didn't keep. We took good care of each other. Hey. I ain't never got the clap. But that was for now—not forever. Suzie'll be okay.

FRANKIE: Well, I don't wanna leave Little Kim. I think I love her. *(He sulks.)*

SAL: Hey, man, I think ya love her, too. I love her. And I love Suzie. But love ain't marriage, man. Love ain't forever, Frankie. We come from different worlds. We're still kids, Frankie. And so are they. We're far away from home. Like you say, kid, "It isn't kosher." Suzie and Little Kim are beautiful people. I'll never forget 'em. But y'going home in 33 days.

FRANKIE: I dunno, Sal. I dunno.

OFFSTAGE VOICE: Mail call…Shelton, Shelton, Grombowski, Mathers, Castro and Greenberg, Edwards…that's it.

(FRANKIE, SAL and WALTER look at each other shocked. They run offstage and return immediately. FRANKIE and SAL open a letter from FLORENCE as she—on the other side of the stage—sings.)

(Reprise: "Take Care of my Baby")

FLORENCE:
You two guys seem
So mighty sweet,
Some gal's gonna love you
And you're gonna give 'em both a treat.
Let me repeat:

Take care of my baby,
Y'all get back safe and sound.

Take care of yourselves,
So we can hang around.
Take care of my baby,
I wanna spend my life with you.

So take good care of my baby,
So take good care of my baby,
So take good care of my baby,
So take good care of my baby,
And he'll take care of you.

(At the end of the song, a radio announcement interrupts.)

RADIO ANNOUNCER: We interrupt this program to bring you a late breaking news story from *Stars and Stripes News*. A 16-year-old Korean girl was apparently gang-raped and killed this afternoon at a hotel in downtown Pusan. "Little Kim," as she was apparently known, was pronounced dead on arrival at Pusan General Hospital. Three U.S. Army officers were arrested by U.S. military police in connection with the rape/murder. The three men claimed that the *murder* was actually committed by a fourth officer who was with them, Colonel John Nelson. Colonel Nelson is being sought after for questioning at this time. If anyone has information... *(WALTER turns off the radio.)*

FRANKIE: *(Screams madly and continuously)* Noooooo. Noooooo. Noooooo.

SAL: Walter, you stay with Frankie. I'm gonna go find Suzie. I'll be back as soon as I can. Don't let him outta your sight. You understand me?

WALTER: Yeah, Sal. I understand ya. *(He grabs FRANKIE in an embrace.)*

Act II, Scene 6

Inside NELSON'S darkened office, NELSON is disheveled and insane. BOND is shaking him; trying to bring him to his senses.

BOND: What happened, sir? What in the hell happened?

NELSON: I KILLED THE LITTLE BITCH. I KILLED A LITTLE GIRL. I FUCKED HER AND THEN I KILLED HER.

BOND: What happened, Colonel? Why did you kill her? What did she do? What happened, sir?

NELSON: *(Hysterically)* There were four of us. She was beautiful. I went last. I fucked her last. She started sobbing. I said, "Why are you crying?" She kept crying, more and more. I told her to stop. I screamed at her. She was saying something. I said, "What are you saying?" She sobbed, "Frankie, Frankie…" I said, "Who's Frankie? Frankie who?" She said, "Frankie Greenberg…I need you, Frankie…Frankie Greenberg." I went crazy. I began to hit her. I couldn't stop. And she kept screaming for Frankie Greenberg. I killed her. I killed her. I couldn't stop.

BOND: Y'gotta turn yourself in, Colonel. Come with me. I'll bring you down to the compound MPs. That's what you have to do, Colonel.

NELSON: *(Becoming strangely calm)* You're right, Sergeant Bond. You're right. Give me a minute to fix myself up, Sergeant. *(BOND doesn't leave.)* Sergeant, wait outside for me. I'd like a minute or so alone.

BOND: Sir, I don't think…

NELSON: *(Interrupting)* That's an order, Sergeant. I'll be out in a minute.

BOND: *(Reluctantly)* Yes, sir. I'll be right outside, sir…you've done a really bad thing, Colonel. You're a sick man…sir. A sick man.

(NELSON stares blankly as BOND exits. He crosses slowly to his desk, opens a drawer, takes out a pistol. He goes to the mirror and looks blankly at himself.)

("The Colonel's Good-bye")

NELSON: *(Sings)*
I look at you
And I can't stand
The sight of me.
There's nothing left
But emptiness,
The middle-of-the-night of me.

Once upon a time
There was a child
In me,

A young boy
Playing in the grass
Who loved a mom,
Who loved the sight of me.
But that's all past.

Now I am old.
I have no face.
I have no heart.
I have no place.
I'm lookin' at my death
And not my life.
Now I need to
Say to me "Good-bye."

I'm just a memory.
I'm sayin' "Good-bye."

(*NELSON slowly lifts the pistol and shoots himself in the head. BOND rushes
in and stands contemptuously over NELSON's body.*)

Act II, Scene 7

Inside the darkened Quonset #7 WALTER is still holding FRANKIE.

("I Don't Get It")

FRANKIE: *(Sings)*
The world keeps spinnin'
With me upon it.
The world keeps sinnin'
And I can't stand it.

Sal tells me,
"Hey, man, don't sweat it."
I say, "Okay,"
But I don't get it.

Walt and Flo,
They'll be alright.

I'll keep on walkin'
Through the night.

The world keeps sinnin'
And I don't get it.
I think perhaps
I never will.

How could such a child die?
How could such a child die?

The world keeps spinnin'
With me upon it.
The world keeps sinnin'
And I can't stand it.

Sal tells me,
"Hey, man, don't sweat it."
I say, "Okay,"
But I don't get it.

Walt and Flo,
They'll be alright.
I'll keep on walkin'
Through the night.

The world keeps sinnin'
And I don't get it.
I think perhaps
I never will.

How could such a child die?
How could such a child die?
I could never tell you why.
I could never tell you why.

WALTER:
The world keeps spinnin'
With me upon it.

The world keeps sinnin'
And I can't stand it.

Sal tells me,
"Hey, man, don't sweat it."
I say, "Okay,"
But I don't get it.

Little Kim and Frankie,
They'll never make it.
Flo 'n' I, we'll keep on walkin'
Through the night.

The world keeps sinnin'
And I don't get it.
I think perhaps
I never will.

How could such a child die?
How could such a child die?

The world keeps spinnin'
With me upon it.
The world keeps sinnin'
And I can't stand it.

Sal tells me,
"Hey, man, don't sweat it."
I say, "Okay,"
But I don't get it.

Little Kim and Frankie,
They'll never make it.
Flo 'n I, we'll keep on walkin'
Through the night.

The world keeps sinnin'
And I don't get it.
I think perhaps
I never will.

WALTER and FRANKIE:

> How could such a child die?
> How could such a child die?
> I could never tell you why.
> I could never tell you why.

Act II, Scene 8

The video sequence from Act I, Scene 1 repeats.

SAL: *(To FRANKIE)* Hey man, where's your grandkid Suzie? Y'know she's my lover girl. Where is she?

FRANKIE: Don't sweat it, man. She'll be here any minute with her mother and father. So ya better behave yourself.

SAL: How dey doin? How's Kim and Joey gettin' along? Dey doin' okay?

FRANKIE: Yeah, man. Don't sweat it. They're doin' okay now.

SAL: Would you stop sayin' "don't sweat it"? Geez, I'm sorry I taught you that expression way back when in Korea.

FRANKIE: You taught me that? When? Bullshit.

(Mock fight between FRANKIE and SAL.)

WALTER: *(Intervenes in fight)* What's wrong with you two hoodlums? I can't leave you alone for a minute. If ya don't behave yourselves I'll get Florence over here.

(SAL and FRANKIE feign fear and "break it up.")

FLORENCE: Did I hear my name? You need me for something, Walter?

SAL: Don't sweat it, Florence. Everything's cool.

(Enter KIM, JOEY and SUZIE; ANN welcomes them.)

KIM: Hi, Mom.

SUZIE: Hi, Grandma.

JOEY: Hello, Mama Ann.

ANN: Hello, Kim darling. Hi, Suzie, how's my sweetheart? Hi, Joe, good to see ya.

(The three, KIM, JOEY and SUZIE, make their way to FRANKIE.)

KIM: Hi, Dad, how are ya, love?

FRANKIE: Hi, Kim, baby. Hi, Joey *(shakes hands)*. Hiya, little Suzie. *(He hugs his granddaughter. SAL grabs her away for a hug.)*

SUZIE: Uncle Sal. How's my love?

SAL: Careful, darlin', Aunt Maggie'll hear you.

MAGGIE: *(Coming over)* No sweat, Suzie. Everyone knows you're his number one gal.

RAFAEL: *(To SAL)* Would you leave Suzie alone? I told ya I was gonna marry her.

EDDIE: *(Embracing SUZIE)* Don't worry about these two Latin lovers, Suzie.

WALTER: Hey, Eddie, what're you?

EDDIE: *(Jokingly)* I got a college degree, Walt—somethin' neither my father nor my son has. I'm a middle-class, middle-aged, civilized kinda guy *(he grabs ELLY)*—ain't that right, Elly darlin'? *(He grabs MAGGIE.)* Ain't that right, Mom?

MAGGIE: Walter...he's a Latino letcher.

ELLY: You better believe it, Walt.

(They all laugh.)

MAGGIE: Florence—is Sammy comin' today?

FLORENCE: *(A little hesitantly)* No. He's out of town. He and his wife send their love.

SAL: What's his new wife's name again?

FLORENCE: Susan.

SAL: She comes from a lotta money, yeah?

FLORENCE: She's a good person, Sal. She's just not so comfortable with us low lives—y'know.

SUZIE: *(Pointing to SAL, WALTER and FRANKIE)* Did you three sing yet? I wanna hear ya sing that fifties stuff.

KIM: Suzie, you ain't been hearin' it for 40 years.

FRANKIE: *(Jokingly)* I never knew ya didn't like it, Kim. My own daughter don't like my singin'. Geez.

WALTER: She don't like your voice, Frankie. It's too damned white.

SAL: Yeah, Frankie. I been meanin' to talk to you about that for 40 years now.

ANN: Would you three clowns sing already?

WALTER: We wrote a new song for our 40th anniversary.

ELLY: You guys have known each other 40 years? Let's see…Since 1954?

SAL: Can you believe it?

FRANKIE: Yeah, Elly. Don't sweat it, Sal. Don't sweat it.

FLORENCE: Just sing, you three, just sing.

(As the video characters begin "1954," SAL, WALTER AND FRANKIE come onstage. They begin singing the song to live accompaniment. Sound on video fades out, though picture stays up. They sing song to completion.)

(Reprise: "1954")

FRANKIE, SAL, WALTER:
> I'll bet you'd never believe,
> I'll bet you couldn't conceive,
> That we were once nineteen;
> It was a mighty strange scene.
>
> Way back in 1954,
> Right after the Korean War,
> The mambo sound was just begun
> And Uncle Miltie's number one.

WALTER:

> 'Cause there were drive-in flicks
> And pick-up sticks
> McCarthy craze
> And Willie Mays
> In 1954.

FRANKIE:

> Presley moved his pelvis
> Which is why
> They called him
> Elvis
> In 1954.

SAL:

> Hula hoops,
> Balls off stoops
> And don't forget those doo-wop groups
> In 1954.

FRANKIE, WALTER:

> Adam Clayton Powell,
> Mel Allen
> For White Owls
> Made the city roar.

SAL:

> The Tito Puente sound,
> Tony Bennett came around
> In 1954.

WALTER:

> They still said "Negro" in that time.

FRANKIE:

> I first discovered lemon and lime.

SAL:

> I'm drinkin' rum and usin' coke,
> And Richard Nixon's still a joke.

FRANKIE, SAL, WALTER:

> We joined the Army, went away.
> We met in Pusan-by-the-Bay.
> Three guys from old Nueva York
> Just learnin' how to walk and talk.
> Way back in 1954.

))))

Stealin' Home

Stealin' Home (1997) is a paean to baseball and a meditation on the possibilities and pitfalls of "integration" in American society.

It is the first of Newman's plays to give expression to his lifelong passion for sports, particularly for baseball. The "boys of summer" played a big role in Newman's life from an early age. (He lived in a building so close to Yankee Stadium that he and his friends could watch the game from his rooftop.) In those days—before superhighways and super salaries (the 1940s and early '50s)—many of the ballplayers still lived, at least during the season, near the stadiums where they played. For a while Mr. and Mrs. Yogi Berra lived in a neighboring building, and as a boy Newman sometimes delivered groceries to the great Yankee catcher and his wife. Later on Newman sold souvenirs outside the stadium. His allegiance to the Yankees didn't, however, blind him to the historic and moral significance of Jackie Robinson and the Brooklyn Dodgers, the Bronx Bombers' longtime rivals. Newman, who was 12 years old when Robinson broke the color barrier in baseball, dedicates *Stealin' Home* to "...the real Jackie Robinson, who helped me (as much as anyone) to live through a painful childhood."

Given the centrality of baseball in American culture, there are surprisingly few baseball plays—the musical *Damn Yankees* (1955) with music and lyrics by Richard Adler and Jerry Ross and a book by George Abbot and Douglass Wallop, and Joe Mantegan's *Bleacher Bums* (1977), a play about Chicago Cubs fans, are among the notable few. Even in film, the quality baseball movie has been slow to appear. During the last 15 years films such as *Bang the Drum Slowly, The Natural, Field of Dreams, Bull Durham,* and *Eight Men Out* have brought some depth to the genre. Yet none of these, whether onstage or celluloid, is as poetic a tribute to the game as *Stealin' Home*. The drunken reflections of the character Pee Wee on the nature of baseball are, without question, the most poetic stage language yet written by Newman.

Despite the play's loving tribute to the national pastime, its major concern is not the game. *Stealin' Home* is not fundamentally a baseball play. Like all Newman's work for the theatre, it is a *political* play. Baseball, precisely because it has played such a prominent role in America's self-image, is a useful metaphor for the larger culture and society. The integration of base-ball (within a few years of the integration of the armed forces), had a pro-found impact on Americans, Black and white. Baseball was *the* American game, and it had, since the failure of Reconstruction, always been strictly segregated. When, in response to the racist taunts of white fans, the Dodgers' captain Pee Wee Reese, a white Southerner, put his arm around Jackie's shoulder as they left the field together, the image became part of America's memory of itself. In that moment, Reese said: We're on the same team and that's more important than the fact that we have different colored skin. What was true of the Brooklyn Dodgers was also true—or could be true—of the United States of America.

The breaking of the color barrier in baseball is the point of departure for an examination of integration and its impact on the Black community. Covering some 48 years of history in seven scenes, Newman has the myste-rious character Sojourner (whose name, and truth-telling function, evoke Sojourner Truth, the early 19th-century former slave who became an aboli-tionist and feminist) confront Robinson with some hard cultural and politi-cal questions. Can we become part of the "big leagues" without losing who we were before being let in? Does the Black community as a whole benefit from a few Blacks winning access to money and fame? Does the answer lie in making the system more inclusive or must the totality of society be changed before equal opportunity is possible for the Black masses? What is the relationship between color and class in America? The questions Sojourner forces Jackie—and the audience—to consider are not easy to answer. She has her opinions (often seeming to contradict each other), but as in most Newman plays no authorial answers are imposed. The asking of the questions is the action of *Stealin' Home,* which in typical Newman fash-ion has virtually no plot.

The play's plotlessness is emphasized by its obliqueness. Newman goes out of his way to avoid the moments of high drama, of glorious victory or painful defeat. We do not see, for example, Robinson crossing the color line; there is no scene of the Dodgers' oh-so-sweet victory over the Yankees in the 1955 World Series; Robinson's departure from baseball is skipped over, as are the death of his son due to a drug overdose, and his own death at the age of 53. The play's seven scenes depict conversations during the off moments of an extraordinary life. *Stealin' Home* is a play that begins in the middle and stays there. Periods of intense conflict, occasions of victory and defeat, are not, usually, times for conversation. They tend to be flashes of polarized emotionality when thought is reduced to the categories of "right" and "wrong." Newman's tendency to value conversation over drama, which has been evident in his work from the beginning, reaches its fullest realization so far in *Stealin' Home*.

The agent of these conversations, Sojourner, represents the merging of two other types of characters to be found in Newman's plays. She bears some resemblance to the catalytic characters—Emmy Strait in *Billie & Malcolm*, Holiday Hill in *Left of the Moon*, and Carmela in *The Store*—who make it possible for other characters to change and develop. While neither Jackie nor Pee Wee changes or develops as a result of Sojourner's interventions, she *is* the cause of virtually every conversation in the play, and conversation, Newman maintains, is the mundane developmental activity of everyday life. The characters onstage might not develop, but it doesn't follow that they are not creating an environment conducive to the development of the performers and/or the audience.

Sojourner is, at the same time, a descendant of the Narrator in *Left of the Moon* and of Madison Hemings in *Sally and Tom (The American Way)*. She is the embodiment of history, but unlike the Narrator in *Left of the Moon*, who stands outside the action, or Madison Hemings in *Sally and Tom*, who stands with one foot in the action and one foot outside, there is no dualism about Sojourner. She is most definitely a character(s) *in* the play—the character without whom very little would happen. At the same time, it becomes increasingly obvious as the play progresses that her questions, her opinions, her overview, her very presence, cannot be explained or justified in realistic terms. She is history not as an abstraction, not as something other than everyday life, she is the history that is continuously among us.

This aspect of Sojourner becomes apparent in the last scene, which transforms the entire play. It tells the whole story of Jackie Robinson's life over again—but it is a very different life, lived in a very different America. Jackie Robinson becomes one character with two different histories. As a philosopher, a political theorist and a therapist, Newman believes that the present determines the past and not the other way around (as is assumed in a linear, cause-and-effect world view). Newman has always been fond of the rope as a metaphor for history—you shake the end and the entire shape of the rope changes. Thus our actions have an impact on everything that preceded them. *Stealin' Home* is structured like that rope. The last scene shakes out the whole play. Jackie Robinson lived out certain choices. He could have made others which might have brought about very different results.

Stealin' Home has had one production at the Castillo Theatre under the direction of Laurence Holder, in February of 1997. Newman wrote the play and Castillo produced it to commemorate the 50th anniversary of Robinson breaking the color barrier in 1947. The production received a great deal of publicity, both in the print media and on television, as a sports play. Those who wrote about it chose to ignore its politics and its provocative sexuality. But everyone who wrote about the production has made favorable mention of the play's ending. One critic called scene seven "every baseball fan's dream."

When near the end of the play Jackie asks Sojourner how he could be living out a very different reality, she replies, "I want your life to be happier. I want it to turn out better than what the books say about you."

In a very fundamental sense, that is why Fred Newman wrote the play— and why he writes all his plays.

                                                                        D.F.

Stealin' Home was first produced at the Castillo Theatre (Fred Newman, artistic director; Gabrielle Kurlander, producing director; Diane Stiles, managing director) in New York City on February 7, 1997. The cast, in order of appearance, was as follows:

PEE WEE .... David Nackman
SOJOURNER/MISS SOJOURNER/SALLY SOJOURNER .... Lisa Colbert
JACKIE ROOSEVELT ROBINSON .... Emmitt H. Thrower
RECORDED VOICES ... Laurence Holder, Kenneth Hughes, Roger Grunwald

Laurence Holder, director; Ellen Korner, producer; Joseph Spirito, set and scenic design; Charlotte, costume design; Charlie Spickler, lighting design; Michael Klein, sound design; Barry Z Levine, video design/cinematography; Kenneth Hughes, production stage manager.

A NOTE FROM THE AUTHOR

Written, in some ways, to provoke, *Stealin' Home* does not, I hope, offend. It is, of course, not a play about the real Jackie Robinson, but is based on my Jackie Robinson. To a large extent, that distinction—between the real Jackie and my (or your) Jackie—is one very tragic theme of the play. For ultimately there was no "real" Jackie Robinson; there were only the subjective images of this extraordinary athlete and social symbol who broke baseball's vulgar color barrier in 1947.

To me, as a lonely 12-year-old, Robinson was far more a profound subjective experience than a real person in my sad childhood. And so it was for millions, young and old. To me and, no doubt, so many others, Jackie and his "boys of summer" were the joy of childhood that was nowhere to be found in my own unhappy youth. My father, who died suddenly in 1945 at 51 years of age, left a gaping hole in my life and a frightening emptiness in my home. Baseball, in general, and Robinson's Dodgers, in particular, filled it. Growing up in the Bronx, literally in the shadow of Yankee Stadium, I was, of course, a Yankee fan. But the Yankees were too close to home to be fully exotic. Besides, they won all the time...and besides, the Dodgers were in the National League...and besides, the Yankees were too white. Jackie Robinson's Dodgers (unlike Mantle's bourgeois Bronx Bombers) were joy incarnate. He and they lived in my fantasies.

Life is far more joyous now, but Jackie is still there exciting me. He is one of the great loves of my life, although we never actually met. I mean no offense to those who knew the real Jackie well. But I will not now or ever give up my Jackie Robinson. *Stealin' Home* is simply its current form.

FEBRUARY 1997

CHARACTERS

Stealin' Home has three characters and several offstage voices. The characters are JACKIE ROOSEVELT ROBINSON, a Black baseball player; PEE WEE, a white baseball player; and a Black woman variously identified as SOJOURNER, MISS SOJOURNER, SALLY SOJOURNER, etc. She is sometimes a waitress, sometimes a lover/prostitute to PEE WEE and sometimes a sportswriter. Whether she is one character or several is left purposely ambiguous.

The ambience (the sound and look) of the play is Williams (Tennessee)/ Wilson (August)-esque between 1949 and 1997.

This play is lovingly dedicated to the real Jackie Robinson, who helped me (as much as anyone) to live through a painful childhood.

NOTE:
The sports writer Red Smith is quoted at the top of Scene 3.

Scene 1

The year is 1975. PEE WEE, *a white man in his fifties, is seated at a table in a modest bar. He has been drinking heavily and speaking for a long time.* SOJOURNER, *his prostitute/friend, a Black woman in her forties, returns to the table, touching* PEE WEE *caringly as she does. He slowly notices her return and continues speaking.*

PEE WEE: You have no idea just how Black Jackie Robinson was. And how big he was. I seen him, in person, for the first time at the Dodgers spring training camp in Santo Domingo in 1946. The son of a bitch was built like a goddamned football player—which he…which he was in college. His size, his bigness, and his blackness and his speed—mostly his quickness—and, well, his extraordinary good looks together with that phony soundin' name—*Jackie Robinson*—well…he was kind of a walkin', talkin' cliché. Y'know what I mean, Sojourner? He was jest too perfect. And all my innermost feelings and fantasies about bein' Black—the almost sexual desire to be such a man and at the same time the repulsion I felt—as a redneck Southerner from Louisville, Kentucky—to the frightening ugliness of his blackness—all those passions were triggered by this perfectly chiseled ebony Black god of a man. When I first saw him stark naked in the clubhouse that spring I quickly became aware that I could not take my eyes off of him. I got scared that Walker and Stanky and other southern white teammates were lookin' at me lookin' at him. So I'd turn away real fast. But my eyes kept comin' back to him. Y'know automatic like. I couldn't keep 'em off of his body, his beauty, his blackness. I think that part of what made him such a great base runner is that people—other players, mainly white guys at first—were hypnotized by him. They couldn't stop lookin' at him. They couldn't move. He paralyzed 'em. Man…Jackie was Black. He was the fuckin' ace of spades. Black Beauty. The Black Knight come to Ebbets Field, Brooklyn, New York City. I ain't never seen nothing like him—before or since. *(Drinks slowly.)* Baseball's a real funny game. It's down and dirty like

five-card stud. Never was no college sport really. Just crazy workin'-class
stiffs who had some athletic skills and didn't want to work for a livin'!
That's who played baseball mainly since about 1900, I guess. White
guys—lotsa nuts and weirdos—playin' the world's slowest movin'
game. Lotsa guys who never could stand still for a minute, doin' very little for a couple of hours every day; waiting for the pitcher to throw, the
batter to swing. Watchin' the ball move gracefully through the air or on
the ground; breakin' at the crack of the bat to cut across that little ole
ball's path and feeling the thump of it in your leather glove; squeezin' it;
holdin' it; it ain't nuthin' but pure sex. Crazy white guys playin' with a
hard little ball. Yeah. That's baseball. One of them baseball writer guys—
college types who couldn't even spit far enough to play the game—once
wrote this article in the *New York Times* about baseball's "metaphysics."
(He laughs.) Can you believe that? Well, it's the *Times*, ya know, big
words and all. But what this dude with thick glasses—this writer—what
he said was exactly true. He said, "the thing about baseball is that there
ain't no clock on it. Every game could go on forever. Guys could keep
hittin' 'em where no one is. Pitchers could all lose the plate. And the
game could go on and on—maybe forever." It's a slow game—could
last an eternity maybe. But it's a game you can live in; a game you can
lose yourself in completely. It's a lot better than life in that way. Y'see,
basketball, football, hockey, tennis, and all them others are faster than
life. But not baseball. When it's real good it's like sex—slower than life;
much, much slower. So for the first 60, 70 years or so it's mainly about
dumbass bigoted white dudes playin' a game that's more beautiful than
any painting in the goddamned museum. Oh, yeah, I guess the owners
were makin' some bucks. But mainly they were millionaires like
Wrigley, the chewin' gum magnate, and Ruppert and Busch, the beer
bosses who had made big money elsewhere and bought themselves a
baseball team. And us players didn't make shit. But it didn't make no
difference. It beat the hell outta workin' and the grass was green, the
dirt was soft, the sky was blue—it was like bein' in the country—and
the ball and the players were all lily white. And then, along comes the
blackest man who ever lived: Jackie Robinson. For about a decade I
watched that son of a bitch shower every day for half the year. He was
beautiful. I ain't never had the hots for no man. But Jackie Robinson?

I'd a lay in bed with him butt naked forever. I sometimes get a hard-on just thinkin' about him. (*He drinks more.*)

SOJOURNER: (*In a high-pitched voice with a Southern accent*) You always tell me that your name is Pee Wee? What kind of a name is Pee Wee? What position did you play anyway? (*She doesn't let him answer.*) I heard of Jackie Robinson. Yeah. I heard of him. First Negro—uh, Black man— to play major league baseball, that's what you been sayin', huh? Ain't that right? I never knew him myself, personally, but I sure as hell heard of him. So you had the hots for him, huh? Yeah. Black men can get ya that way. They're mighty beautiful...but some of 'em is mighty mean. Was Jackie Robinson mean? Pee Wee, was he mean, huh? Now c'mon, tell me, what position did you play? And Jackie Robinson, where did he play? Was he a pitcher or somethin'? I don't know much about base- ball. Saw kids playin' in the fields when I was a youngster. But I ain't never seen no professionals playin'. No, Pee Wee, I ain't got no deep love for that game of yours. But I know a few things about Black men. I even loved some like you is in love with your Mr. Jackie Robinson. So, c'mon, tell me your position, Pee Wee. And Robinson's. Where did he play? He was a pitcher, wasn't he?

PEE WEE: No, little lady, Jackie Robinson was no pitcher. I was the short stop and the captain of the Brooklyn Dodgers. When Jackie Robinson first came up to the show in '47 he played first base. He was rookie of the year and we got back to the World Series. Lost to the damn Yankees again. Next year Robinson was moved to second base and he and I made up the best double play combination in all of baseball. We wuz good, little lady. We wuz as good as they come.

SOJOURNER: Now, what in the bejesus is a "double play combination"? Sounds like some dirty sex trick that I must a done a million times but never called by that funny name. What in the hell is a double play, Mr. Pee Wee?

PEE WEE: Well, little lady, in baseball, mostly ya make just one out at a time. It's a slow game, like I told ya. But once in a while you can make two... and when you do, they call that a double play—ya get two outs instead of one. Now mostly that happens on a ground ball with a man on first ...and usually that ground ball is to the middle of the infield...and who covers the middle is the shortstop and the second baseman. So they call those two dudes "the double play combination," ya see. I was the shortstop and Jackie Robinson was the second baseman. And, for a minute, we were the best in the world…I do believe…the very best in our day. Me 'n' Jackie. I'd go into the hole between short and third…backhand that hard grounder, jump high in the air and fire one to Jackie who just barely touched second base. Then he jumped high—kinda pirouetted like a beautiful Black ballet dancer, high above the spikes of the runner slidin' in and threw a perfect strike over to first base. Big old Gil Hodges, with his pink-white hands the size of a lobster, would grab that throw from Jackie and, little lady, there was two outs. It was real beautiful; real fine. And Jackie was right in the middle. Black and quick as the night. Smilin' real mean-like, lookin' down at some poor white son of a bitch that had tried to spike him just a second before and in that funny little squeaky clipped voice of his sayin', "Sorry, honky." *(He laughs; imitates JACKIE.)* "Sorry, honky." Oh, yeah, he could be a mean son of a bitch alright. But, god, he was beautiful…and sexy.

SOJOURNER: I don't think I quite get it, Mr. Pee Wee—where did you get that name?—but it sure does sound like good sex to me. I like when a man or a woman touches me real slow and watches me real hard when I start to come. Yeah, it's like we're doin' a dance together; a hot, sexy slow dance, Mr. Pee Wee. Ya right. Good sex is slower than life and it's beautiful. Jest the two of us sweatin' on each other and playin' with our hot parts; touchin', lickin', movin' every which way. Yeah…alright. It's a double play. I think I'm gettin' your drift. This baseball shit is kinda sexy, Mr. Pee Wee, kinda sexy.

PEE WEE: Yeah, it's sexy alright. And Jackie Robinson was the king and the queen all rolled into one. Y'see, little lady…a double play is like an orgasm. Everything is goin' slower than molasses. The game is always real slow. Players primpin' and preenin', scratchin' at their crotches, suckin' their tobacco and spittin' five feet; it's all foreplay, little lady, and it's gotta be slow—you know—foreplay's gotta be slow to be any good. And just when everything has gotten so slow that you can't imagine it goin' any slower…it happens. And it's faster than light. *Pshawww.* It's hot. A flash…and then it's done and it's back to slower than slow.

And it's that slow to fast and then back again that makes it so damned hot…so sexy. And no one went from slow to fast and back again like Mr. Jackie Robinson. Nothin' was so sexy, so hot, such a turn-on as Mr. Jackie Robinson stealin' home.

SOJOURNER: Stealin' home? What in the hell is stealin' home, Mr. Pee Wee? What in the hell is stealin' home?

Scene 2

1949. A bright sunny day at Ebbets Field. The crowd roaring. Stage empty. JACKIE slides into home plate downstage right. OFFSTAGE UMPIRE screams "Yer out!" JACKIE jumps up, shakes and wipes off dirt. He walks a few steps away from the OFFSTAGE UMPIRE.

JACKIE: *(Mumbling)* You blind son of a bitch. He never put that ball on me. You can't see shit over that damned beer belly you got there. *(JACKIE turns back in the direction of the UMPIRE and yells.)* Ain't you never seen no one steal home, Mr. Umpire? You been spendin' too much time watchin' these slow ass white dudes. You ain't never seen my kinda speed, Mr. Umpire. This is Black speed.

OFFSTAGE UMPIRE: Get outta here, Robinson. Go back to the cotton fields and the Negro Leagues. That's where your Black ass belongs. Yer out.

JACKIE: *(Getting angrier)* What did you say to me, you racist son of a bitch? At Negro League games they'd put dark glasses on your fuckin' head and have ya sellin' pencils, your blind honky ass fartin' away from all that beer.

OFFSTAGE UMPIRE: You're outta the game, Robinson. No nigger talks to me like that. Go take a goddamned shower, you mean-spirited Black son of a bitch.

(JACKIE begins to move menacingly toward the OFFSTAGE UMPIRE when he is grabbed from behind by a much younger [than in Scene 1] uniformed PEE WEE.)

PEE WEE: Okay. Okay. Cool down, Jackie, cool down. If you keep yellin' at Fatso the league will fine your ass 1,000 big ones. C'mon. Go take a shower. What were you tryin' to steal home for anyway? We're up four runs. Y'took the bat outta Furillo's hands. Did you have a green light from Dressen?

JACKIE: Pee Wee, I always got a green light to steal. That's how come the money-hungry bastard O'Malley's sellin' all these tickets these days— to watch me steal—and to watch you and me make those beautiful double plays. One day that cheap son of a bitch is gonna take the Dodgers right outta Brooklyn to make more money. Wait and see.

PEE WEE: The Dodgers outta Brooklyn? You crazy, Jackie? Shit. No one else would have us. We're the last of the old-style dirty ass teams and with your Black ass added to the mix, ain't no tellin' what in the fuck we are. Old man Rickey is one smart son of a bitch. We could only get away with this in Brooklyn, USA.

(By now, JACKIE and PEE WEE are "at the shower"—off the field—continuing their conversation. JACKIE is slowly taking off his uniform.)

JACKIE: I'm tellin' ya, Pee Wee, it's a new day comin' for baseball. The second half of this old 20th century baseball's becomin' nuthin' but big business. With night ball and TV and all it's becomin' more and more about money. Shit. That's how come they're lettin' me and Satchel and a few other Black guys play. These owners didn't suddenly become moral, Pee Wee. Shit. It was mainly the communists pushin' for the integration of baseball and since when do millionaires listen to commies? No. There's money to be made by integratin' baseball right now. And this park is too small for Moneybags O'Malley. I tell ya before the '50s are over, we'll be outta Brooklyn. Take my word for it, Pee Wee. Take my word for it. Now you and me will probably wrap up our careers here in New York. But these owners are lookin' for bigger markets. Shit, Pee Wee, there ain't no major league baseball team in all of California and people movin' out there by the millions. Wait and see, Pee Wee, wait and see.

PEE WEE: Well, Mr. Robinson, you are the college man. You know all about this economics shit. I'm just a dumb redneck from Kentucky who can pick up ground balls better than most and bunt better than almost anyone. Baseball's all I know, Jackie. And I'll keep playin' it wherever and with whoever I can until they throw me out...I hope the National League office don't fine your ass too much for that little incident with Fatso out there. What did he say to ya? He musta hit a nerve...I thought you was out myself.

JACKIE: Of course I was out. I didn't get a good enough lead. But that son of a bitch told me to go back to the cotton fields and the Negro League. I don't ever want to hear that overstuffed bastard talk about the Negro Leagues. Gibson, Cool Papa and the rest of the guys ain't never gonna get a chance to play here; ain't never gonna get no chance to make even a few real bucks playin' this damned game. And they're the best. The Monarchs could ass whip any team in the majors. And Satchel. Shit. He's the best pitcher ever lived. They finally let him in last year in Cleveland. Y'know how old he is, Pee Wee? The son of a bitch must be almost 50. And he wins 14 big ones for the Indians and they grab the American League pennant. Can ya believe him? I couldn't hit the fucker worth a damn over in the Negro League. He winds up slower than shit. Makes the ball look like it's comin' at ya faster than lightning. Y'ever hit against old Satchel, Pee Wee, in one of them exhibition games?

PEE WEE: Yeah. Yeah. About a dozen times. The best I ever got was a walk. I slouched over real low and got a couple of calls. He's mean, Jackie. I ain't never seen no one better.

JACKIE: Well, I hope the goddamned Yankees make it back to the Series this year so we can finally whip their asses. You think those racists in the Bronx ever gonna sign up a Black player? Probably not, Pee Wee. Probably not. How many times you lost to them in the Series, Pee Wee? How many times?

PEE WEE: Just once before '47, Jackie *(laughs)*...when we both lost. Back in 1941; just before the war.

JACKIE: Jesus, that seems a long time ago, Pee Wee. A million years ago. Before the war. Nineteen forty-one. That was my senior year at UCLA. That's when I met Rachel. We was married right after the war in '46.

PEE WEE: How's Rachel doin'?

JACKIE: She's good...like always.

PEE WEE: I bet you don't get on her the way you do those umpires, Mr. Robinson. Mr. Jackie Roosevelt Robinson.

JACKIE: No way, Pee Wee. I save that anger for you white folks at the ball park. My family don't need me to be no nasty-assed fuck. Besides, Rachel would throw my Black ass out of the house. I don't mess around with straight-A, straight-laced Miss Rachel.

PEE WEE: *(He has begun to take off uniform also)* C'mon, I'm gonna go grab a beer. Have one with me.

JACKIE: Nah. I gotta go home. I don't drink no beer anyway. Y'know that.

PEE WEE: C'mon, Jackie. Ya got some time. Ya finished work a little early today anyway. *(They laugh.)* I'll buy ya a root beer. Just an hour or so.

Scene 3

1951. JACKIE and PEE WEE sit at a table in a bar, in darkness.

OFFSTAGE MALE SPORTS WRITER: …the Brooklyn Dodgers are tied with the Phillies in the bottom of the twelfth inning. It is 6:00 p.m. on an October Sunday, but the gloom in Philadelphia's Shibe Park is only partly due to oncoming evening. The Dodgers, champions-elect in August, have frittered away a lead of 13 1/2 games, and there is bitterness in the dusk of this last day of the 1951 baseball season. Two days ago, the New York Giants drew even with Brooklyn in the pennant race. Two hours ago, the numbers went up on the scoreboard: New York 3, Boston 2. The pennant belongs to the Giants unless the Dodgers can snatch it back. With two out and the bases full of Phillies, Eddie Waitkus smashes a low, malevolent drive toward center field. The ball is a blur passing second base, difficult to follow in the half-light, impossible to catch. Jackie Robinson catches it. He flings himself headlong at right angles to the flight of the ball, for an instant his body is suspended in midair, then somehow the outstretched glove intercepts the ball inches off the ground. He falls heavily, the crash drives an elbow into his side, he collapses. But the Phillies are out, the score is still tied. Now it is the fourteenth inning. It is too dark to play baseball, but the rules forbid turning on lights for a game begun at two o'clock. Pee Wee

Reese pops up. So does Duke Snider. Robin Roberts throws a ball and a strike to Robinson. Jackie hits the next pitch upstairs in left field for the run that sets up baseball's most memorable playoff.

(Lights up.)

PEE WEE: I can't believe you caught that goddamned line drive. I ain't never seen nuthin' like it. You wuz 10 feet away when you threw yourself at it.

JACKIE: I can't believe I caught it either, Pee Wee. It was kinda like a miracle. Like everything stopped. Like the ball waited for me to get there. It was kinda like a dream. I think we must be destined to win this year, Pee Wee. We'll take Durocher's and Stanky's bullshit Giants two out of three in the playoffs and then finally whip those Yankees' asses in four straight. Whattya think, Pee Wee? Whattya think?

PEE WEE: Could be, Jack. Could be. This is a funny game. Last year they said the Phillies was a miracle team—whiz kids and all that bullshit. But the fuckin' Yankees took 'em in four in the Series. The goddamned Yankees' miracles go on forever. They play in luck all the fuckin' time.

JACKIE: No, Pee Wee. This is our year, I tell ya. I feel it. When I caught that goddamned line drive, I felt it. I felt it, Pee Wee.

(SOJOURNER, a waitress, comes to the table.)

SOJOURNER: You boys want anything more?

PEE WEE: *(Pointing to JACKIE)* Y'all know who this here "boy" is?

(SOJOURNER stares hard, somewhat contemptuously.)

SOJOURNER: I give up. Who is he?

PEE WEE: This here is Jackie Robinson. About two hours ago, right across the street there in Shibe Park he just single-handedly beat your Philadelphia Phillies to tie us for first place in the National League. I do believe he made the greatest play in the history of baseball. Yeah, little lady, this here is Mr. Jackie Roosevelt Robinson.

SOJOURNER: *(Incredulously)* You're Jackie Robinson? *(JACKIE nods.)* No shit. How come you ain't gone back to Brooklyn yet?

JACKIE: Oh, Pee Wee and I decided to relax a bit and drive up in a couple of hours. Pee Wee's wife had brought her car down.

(*SOJOURNER turns to PEE WEE.*)

SOJOURNER: You Pee Wee? (*PEE WEE nods.*) The Philly players never come over here. I ain't never met no one famous before. I'm glad to make your acquaintance, Mr. Pee Wee and Mr. Jackie Robinson. Yeah, I'm mighty happy to meet ya. That was one hell of a catch. Everyone in the bar here, watchin' on TV, said they never seen nuthin' like it.

(*SOJOURNER puts out her hand and shakes with JACKIE.*)

JACKIE: What's your name, sister?

SOJOURNER: Sojourner. That's what they call me. Sojourner.

JACKIE: You from Philly, Sojourner?

SOJOURNER: Not originally. My family's from Savannah. Been north about 10 years now.

JACKIE: You follow baseball, Sojourner?

SOJOURNER: Jest a little, Jackie Robinson, jest a little. But I heard all about you. You is a hero—a genuine hero to our people.

PEE WEE: Mainly, he's one helluva baseball player.

SOJOURNER: With all due respects, Mr. Pee Wee, he's my hero. He's my people's hero.

JACKIE: You wanna sit for a little bit?

SOJOURNER: (*Agreeably*) I'm jest gettin' off a work in a minute. Yeah. I'd wouldn't mind joinin' ya. Y'all want something else before I go off?

JACKIE: No, Sojourner. We're set.

SOJOURNER: (*Turning away*) I'll see y'all in a few minutes.

(*JACKIE and PEE WEE nod; SOJOURNER exits.*)

PEE WEE: How come ya done that? I ain't never seen ya do anything like that before, y'know, "come on" to a woman.

JACKIE: I ain't comin' on to no woman, Pee Wee. She seems like a nice person. I think she's good luck, ya know. We gotta go with the signs this year. Sojourner's a lucky name. Maybe this sister's a lucky lady. *(Laughing.)* Hey, didn't you know I was a goddamn hero, Pee Wee? I don't think you know who you're hangin' out with.

PEE WEE: *(Laughing)* Fuck you, Jackie Roosevelt Robinson.

(They laugh and drink as SOJOURNER returns with her own beer.)

SOJOURNER: What you two "bums" laughin' about?

PEE WEE: Jackie here thinks that maybe you are a good luck sign, Sojourner.

SOJOURNER: I dunno. I ain't been good luck to no one before. Especially I ain't been no good luck to me.

JACKIE: You married, Sojourner?

SOJOURNER: I ain't got no man, Jackie Robinson. Got two small kids, though. Two boys. They're my men.

JACKIE: Where's the father?

SOJOURNER: Who knows? He's been gone three years now. I'm glad. He was a mean son of a bitch. Beat the hell outta me.

JACKIE: You're mighty pretty.

PEE WEE: Y'sure are, Sojourner.

SOJOURNER: *(She stands up arrogantly)* Hey, you two, don't come on to me. I ain't no whore. *(To JACKIE.)* You might be my hero but I ain't your whore. *(To PEE WEE.)* And I don't sleep with no white men.

JACKIE: Hey, hey, hey, hey. Sit down, little lady. We ain't comin' on to ya, Sojourner. We jest want to sit with you a while and talk. But you are mighty pretty.

SOJOURNER: *(She sits slowly)* You're mighty pretty, too, Mr. Jackie Robinson. Every Black girl I know is in love with you.

PEE WEE: Jackie here is the most faithfully married man I ever did know.

SOJOURNER: *(To JACKIE)* Is that true?

JACKIE: I believe so. Rachel and I been together almost 10 years now. Got us a couple of kids and another one comin'.

SOJOURNER: You could have pretty much any woman you'd want, Jackie Robinson.

JACKIE: I couldn't have you, Sojourner. You just told me so.

SOJOURNER: Oh, you could probably have me, too...if you really wanted me. I ain't no whore but I ain't about to say no to Jackie Robinson if he really wanted me.

PEE WEE: Whooo weee!

JACKIE: I want you, Sojourner. I want you to have some more luck in your life and to bring me 'n' Pee Wee here some good luck against the Giants and the Yankees.

(*SOJOURNER jumps into JACKIE's lap and kisses him passionately.*)

PEE WEE: Whoooo weeee!

SOJOURNER: You is my hero, Jackie Robinson. Maybe this is my lucky day.

PEE WEE: That's two great catches in one day. Maybe we do have a little destiny on our side this season, Jackie. Maybe so.

(*JACKIE gently puts SOJOURNER back in her seat.*)

JACKIE: (*Laughing*) You didn't see no flash bulbs goin' off, did ya, Pee Wee? No one took no pictures of that little scene, did they?

SOJOURNER: (*Jokingly*) Jackie Robinson...you think I'm trying to set you up? Never happen. Never happen.

JACKIE: No. No, I don't, Sojourner. I think you're a mighty pretty good luck charm. Yeah, Pee Wee, this is our lucky year.

(*Lights fade. OFFSTAGE ANNOUNCER is heard over crowd noises.*)

OFFSTAGE ANNOUNCER: (*Russ Hodges-like*) Okay...let's set the stage one more time. It's game three of the National League playoffs. The Dodgers are ahead four to two, with one out in the bottom of the ninth here at the Polo Grounds, New York City, home of the New York Giants. The Giants got two men on base and Bobby Thomson's at the plate. Dodger pitcher Ralph Branca has relieved starter Don Newcombe and the count is two and one on the Giants right-handed hitting left-fielder. Branca's takin' his time. He's ready. Here's the pitch. *It's a long fly ball to left. It's gone. It's a home run. The Giants win the pennant. The Giants win the pennant. The Giants win the pennant. The Giants win the pennant.*

Scene 4

1953. JACKIE and PEE WEE are in Junior's Restaurant in downtown Brooklyn, laughing hysterically. SOJOURNER, a waitress, comes to the table.

SOJOURNER: What you two *(sarcastically)* gentlemen laughin' about? What's so funny? You guys gonna lose to the Yankees again this year?

JACKIE: Listen, Sojourner, we are out here in Brooklyn and you ain't even supposed to think thoughts like that.

PEE WEE: Yeah, Sojourner. Everyone knows the Brooklyn Dodgers are the greatest team in all of baseball. And there's no goddamned way the Yankees are winnin' five straight.

SOJOURNER: Now if you are the greatest, how come they whip your asses all the time? *(Pause.)* Y'all know what they say on the streets, don't ya?

JACKIE: No, Miss Sojourner, what do they say on the streets?

SOJOURNER: They say you bastards choke. *(She pantomimes choking and makes a funny noise.)*

PEE WEE: What do you think, little lady? You think we choke?

SOJOURNER: Oh, I dunno. I ain't no expert. But it does look a little suspicious—don't you think?

JACKIE: How come y'all think we choke? How come the goddamned Yankees don't choke? What's so different about us, Miss Sojourner?

SOJOURNER: Well…for the last seven years *you've* been what's so different about us. Ain't that so, Mr. Jackie Robinson?

JACKIE: *(Thoughtfully)* And during those seven years that I have been in the major leagues the goddamned Yankees won the World Series five times and are goin' for number six this year. And they is the whitest team in baseball…and we is the Blackest. So what you saying, Miss Sojourner, what you sayin'?

PEE WEE: She's saying Black is best but Black is chokin'. Is that right, Miss Sojourner? Ain't that what you're sayin'?

SOJOURNER: I guess so. Maybe so. I guess that's what everyone is sayin'. The white team—the Yankees—ain't nearly so good as y'all but they don't choke.

JACKIE: Well, ya know what you can tell those folks on the street, Miss Sojourner?

SOJOURNER: What's that, Jack Robinson?

JACKIE: You can tell 'em that I think maybe they are right. I think we are the greatest and I think maybe we choke in the big games. I think we believe the white boys are always gonna find a way to win. They always have and they always will. They ain't no better than we are—no faster, no stronger, no smarter. But they always find a way to win. They have taught us we are losers and I expect that maybe we have come to believe it ourselves. And if you believe it, you've come a long way toward makin' it true. We is snake bit, Miss Sojourner. We are choke artists. Yeah, Miss Sojourner, maybe for now, Black is chokin'.

PEE WEE: You really believe that, Jackie?

JACKIE: I do, Pee Wee. I really do. Maybe it's gonna take some time to turn that around.

(Pause.)

SOJOURNER: And what were you two boys laughin' about so much?

PEE WEE: *(Laughs very hard)* Jackie and I pulled off a little "shadow ball" against Cincinnati today.

SOJOURNER: What's shadow ball?

JACKIE: You don't know shadow ball, Sojourner?

SOJOURNER: No, I don't, Jackie. What's shadow ball?

JACKIE: Well, over in the Negro Leagues we'd warm up shadow ball style. The fans loved it. The infielders would throw the ball around—around the infield; only we don't use no ball. (*Laughs.*) We just makin' believe we got a ball. But we do it so fast and so slick and so good that people can't tell the difference. It's a little game—a little show we do before the ball game begins, ya know, a kinda warmup.

SOJOURNER: Boys will be boys, won't they?

PEE WEE: Anyway, Jackie always said that someday we wuz gonna do a shadow ball double play in a real game.

SOJOURNER: Are you kiddin?

PEE WEE: No. No, no, I ain't kiddin'. We figured someday late in a game we'd be up eight or nine runs with a double play situation and we'd tell Gil over at first base, and give it a try. What the hell? If they catch us— what the hell—there would just be two more guys on base with one out or none out. Y'know what I'm sayin', Sojourner? We'd still have the big lead.

SOJOURNER: Boys will be boys.

PEE WEE: Well, Sojourner, today against Cincinnati we pulled it off. It was incredible. (*JACKIE and PEE WEE laugh—giggling—almost uncontrollably.*)

SOJOURNER: Well, what happened?

PEE WEE: (*He controls himself enough to speak*) Well, there's one out in the seventh and we're up by 10 runs. The Reds got a man on first. Big ole Ted Klusewski is up. He's a power hitter, a left-hander, home run or nuthin' kinda guy. Well...Jackie heads to the pitcher's mound to talk to Labine. I'm sayin' to myself, "What in the hell is he doin' at a time like this, talkin' with the goddamned pitcher?" when all of a sudden I see him motionin' to me and Hodges to come on over. So I trots to the mound. And Jackie in a whisper says, "Now's the time. If Klu hits a grounder to me or you, Pee Wee, it's 'shadow ball' time. A shadow ball double play time. All you gotta do is catch it at first, Gil. Don't drop that invisible ball." And Jackie laughs that pipsqueak little laugh of his. Well, me 'n' Gil look at him like he's crazy. But we nod and I head back to shortstop—tell the truth, hopin' big Klu puts one out of the park.

But he doesn't. Instead, he hits a sharp grounder just a hair to Jackie's right. Wouldn't ya know it—a perfect double play ball.

JACKIE: *(Excitedly)* Well, Sojourner, I moves two steps and pick it real clean. And I toss it to second base. At least I pretend to. Actually the ball is still in my glove—hidden. Well, Pee Wee grabs that imaginary ball, leaps in the air and fires it—pretends to—to first base like he was a playin' for the goddamned Black Yankees—it was as good a shadow ball pivot as I ever seen—Pee Wee, you sure you ain't Black? *(They laugh.)* Anyway, I hear the second base ump scream "Yer out" and I begin to giggle *'cause I'm still holdin' the ball in my glove!* Ole Klusewski is slowly truckin' down to first when Gil reaches out with his big mitt and "grabs the ball." Another great piece of actin' by a white man. Donatelli is umpirin' over at first and he screams, "Yer out" and I watch for a second as Pee Wee and Gil head for the dugout. Now I'm still standin' there with that ball hidden in my glove. In this kinda situation big Gil would normally either roll the ball toward the mound or flip it to Donatelli—it being the end of the inning. But, of course, he can't because he ain't got no ball. So he's just trottin' to the dugout. Now…I head off for the dugout and as I pass Donatelli I flip the baseball to him. And I give him my best smile. Well, Mr. Donatelli gives me the strangest look. Like he knows in a flash that he's been taken but it would be humiliatin' to expose it. So he just takes that ball. Rubs it for a second and slides it on over to the pitcher's mound. Donatelli's playing along with shadow ball! Incredible! Now everyone—all our guys and all the Cincinnati guys and the fans—everyone knows that somethin' funny is goin' on but no one can quite figure out what it was. *(Pause.)* So that's it. We did it. It's a shadow ball double play. Incredible.

(PEE WEE and JACKIE start laughing hysterically.)

SOJOURNER: You boys will be boys, now won't ya? I bet those Yankees don't play no shadow ball.

(PEE WEE and JACKIE stop laughing.)

PEE WEE: But there ain't no harm done, Sojourner. The Reds couldn't a won today. It's jest a little fun.

JACKIE: Yeah, Sojourner. What was the harm?

SOJOURNER: Well, someday, Mr. Jackie Robinson, someday in the middle of an important game—maybe even the World Series—Mr. Donatelli's gonna be umpirin' at home plate and you gonna have three balls and two strikes on ya with the bases loaded and that pitcher, that Yankee pitcher maybe, is gonna throw you a ball a way outside—too far outside to even get a bat on it—a ball all the goddamned way—ball four and a run is jest waitin' to score. And Mr. Donatelli's gonna scream out, "Strike three. Yer outta here, Mr. Robinson." And he's gonna give you a smile and a little nod and he's gonna whisper, "That was a shadow strike, Mr. Jackie Robinson. But you are really outta here." (*JACKIE and PEE WEE sit a little stunned.*) This is the big leagues, Jackie Robinson. Don't play no shadow ball over here. Our funnin' days are over, Mr. Jackie Robinson. It's kinda sad, I know. But we is gonna have to get whiter and whiter. Forget those wonderful days in the Negro Leagues, my friend. This is the big leagues. Now someday, maybe, most of the players might be Black. But the big leagues will still be white. And when we finally learn that then we won't be chokin' so much. You ain't invisible no more, Jackie Robinson. No more shadow ball. No more playin' around. Mr. Jack Roosevelt Robinson.

Scene 5

1969. JACKIE and PEE WEE haven't seen each other in many years. They are both way beyond their playing days and much older, wearing business suits. JACKIE is an executive with Chock Full o' Nuts and he appears sickly. PEE WEE is a sports announcer. They are in a bar/restaurant.

PEE WEE: (*Lightly, somewhat distantly, somewhat jokingly*) So you're a damned executive vice president now. Man, Jackie, you certainly have come way up in the world, a vice president of Chock Full o' Nuts coffee. Used to be baseball was chock full of nuts. Now we is executives with 'em. Playin' any shadow ball with the coffee beans, Mr. Robinson? (*Laughs.*)

JACKIE: No way, Pee Wee. No way. You remember what that pretty little waitress at Junior's told us so long ago? It's a white man's world, Pee Wee. And I'm playin' the white man's game. Shit, Pee Wee, even my hair has turned to white. (*He laughs.*)

PEE WEE: It made me real sad to hear about Jack, Jr. Y'got my flowers and the note, Jackie, didn't you?

JACKIE: Yeah, I got 'em, Pee Wee. Thank you. Me 'n' Rachel was very moved.

PEE WEE: How is Rachel and the other kids doin'?

JACKIE: They're doin' okay. We're carryin' on.

PEE WEE: And how are you feelin'? I read somewhere that you was sick or something.

JACKIE: Y'know me, Pee Wee. Just gettin' older. I got me some diabetes and my eyes ain't doin' too good. But I ain't complainin'. Ain't no use complainin'.

(*SOJOURNER, the waitress, comes to JACKIE and PEE WEE's table. She is wearing her hair in an Afro and radical garb of the era.*)

SOJOURNER: Can I get you two somethin' else?

JACKIE: No, thank you. We're fine.

PEE WEE: What y'oughta be gettin' is this man's autograph.

SOJOURNER: Oh, yeah? How come? Who is he?

PEE WEE: This is Mr. Jackie Robinson—the man who broke the color line in baseball and one of the greatest ballplayers in history.

SOJOURNER: (*She glowers at JACKIE*) And the man who ratted on Paul Robeson before the Un-American Activities Committee; and the man who's supportin' Richard Nixon and the war in Vietnam. No. I don't want his autograph. I don't even want no tip from y'all. I think he's a pig. Yeah (*turning to JACKIE*), I think you a goddamned pig who sold out yer own people for a soft fuckin' job.

PEE WEE: (*Irate*) You can't talk to Jackie Robinson that way!

JACKIE: Oh, yes she can, Pee Wee. She's got every right. Well, I'm a Republican, sister. What are you, a supporter of the Democratic Party?

SOJOURNER: No, Mr. Robinson. I'm a member of the Black Panther Party.

JACKIE: Well then, I take it you support communism. I don't. And I don't think Black folks gonna get anything outta communism. I think we're much better off supportin' the American way—and that's about makin' more money, and buyin' our own homes and sendin' our kids to college.

SOJOURNER: It's about bein' white! That's what you're really sayin', ain't it, Mr. Jackie Robinson?

JACKIE: Yes, it is. If us Black folks gonna make it, we're gonna have to get more white. I know all about racism, young sister. I had enough white spit spat at me to fill this here pitcher (*holds up water pitcher*). And I spoke out loud and clear about the evils of racism when Huey P. Newton was still shittin' in his diapers. I think the stuff I said about Robeson was too harsh and I regret it…and I've said so publicly. But I ain't no communist. I'm a Black man in white America and I want my family to have all they can. And to get ahead in America is to get white in America. There ain't no room for shadow ball or phony revolutionary parties. You just gonna get yourself hurt, sister, and y'ain't gonna win nuthin' for anybody—especially us Black folks. I learned this from a lot of people and a lot of experiences. But most especially from a Black sister—a waitress just like you—named Sojourner, many years ago in a restaurant in downtown Brooklyn.

SOJOURNER: Well, maybe it's time for your next lesson, Jackie Robinson. You ain't about bein' white. That's bullshit. You about bein' green. Green, like money is green. And my people, Afro-American people—we ain't just Black—we is mainly poor. And it's Toms like you with your readiness to be white who is keepin' us poor. You standin' tall behind that bastard neo-fascist Richard Nixon is sayin' it's alright for lots of Black folks to be poor so long as a few make a little money. And as long as you are one of 'em who does. No, Jackie Robinson, you ain't white. Lotsa white people are still poor and some white people are workin' their asses off to do somethin' about all this poverty. But not you, Jackie Robinson. You has become a symbol of what it means to sell out your own people. Y'know who's dying over there in Vietnam? Mostly poor people—poor Black, poor tan, poor yellow and poor white. Once upon a time they damn near court-martialed you for refusin' to sit in the back of a bus. Now, you is sittin' in the back of a limousine. That didn't happen 'cause you turned white, Robinson. You is still Black as the ace of spades. But now your soul is green. Now you is rich and you has forgotten what is means to be poor. You think Black Americans gonna get homes and jobs in the next 25 years? If you do, you is even dumber than I thought. No, poor Black America is gonna get poorer and poorer. We is goin' to prison not to the suburbs. We ain't gettin' into the backs of no limousines; we is barely able to find work drivin' those limousines. You is still playin' shadow ball, Jackie Robinson. Tricky Jack, pretendin' to be white, like tricky Dick pretendin' to be about democracy. He is about political power and money and he'd do anything to achieve it and retain it. And so are you. It's an insult to white folks to say you has become white. You is as green as…as a goddamned watermelon.

(*JACKIE collapses onto the table he has been sitting at, obviously very ill. PEE WEE jumps up to help him. He grabs him. He is hysterical.*)

PEE WEE: Jackie, are you okay? Jackie, speak to me, Jackie. What's happenin'? Someone call for a doctor. Please, get a goddamned doctor. This man is Jackie Robinson and he needs a doctor.

(*SOJOURNER stands above them, defiantly.*)

Scene 6

1975. The PEE WEE and SOJOURNER of Scene 1 in the bar. PEE WEE is quite drunk.

PEE WEE: He died just a few years after that. In 1972. Somehow I felt like I had let him down. I didn't take good care of him, Sojourner. I don't quite know what I mean. After all, as a vice president, he was makin' more money than I was. But, y'know, I was the captain and Jackie was my man—my second base man. And I just feel like I let him down. There was always too much pressure on him. Y'know he was amazin': an amazin' athlete; amazingly beautiful; a symbol and, oh yes, a great hero to his people. And he was a decent and loving person, a good family man. But he was kind of a child—like a man-child. And he failed a lot. I mean we all fail a lot. It's part of bein' human, ain't it? But this was Jackie Robinson. And he wasn't allowed to fail. There was just too much pressure on him. Way too much.

SOJOURNER: How old was he when he died, Mr. Pee Wee?

PEE WEE: He was just 52. Just 52 years old. And that beautiful Black body had completely deteriorated. Couldn't see outta one eye at all. Hands were shakin', walked slow and unsteady as could be. Like a child. And there wasn't no quickness left at all—except in his eyes, his beautiful cat-like eyes. They still jumped about like he was gettin' ready to steal home. Even the last time I seen him about a month or so before he passed on his eyes was quick. And I still couldn't take my eyes off of him. *(Pause.)* How long I knowed you, little lady?

SOJOURNER: A lifetime, Mr. Pee Wee…and I still don't really understand baseball. But I like makin' love with you…even if I am only your number two Black love.

PEE WEE: Hmmmm. Number two and number 42—that was Jackie's number, Sojourner.

SOJOURNER: Forty-two is a lucky number, Mr. Pee Wee.

PEE WEE: It wasn't so lucky for him, Sojourner.

SOJOURNER: Maybe someday you and he will run into each other again. Y'know what I'm sayin'?

PEE WEE: Naw. Jackie and me had our moment together. I'm just a little guy, Sojourner, who don't mean much historically speakin'. Just a slightly better than journeyman shortstop who finally won a World Series ring in 1955. That Black man playin' on the other side of second base—Mr. Jack Roosevelt Robinson—that's as close to history as I ever did get. I only got one face, Sojourner, just one ordinary white guy who wasn't even big enough for his mistakes to matter that much. But you and Jackie got many faces. You're both like history. Maybe you two'll meet again somewhere. I hope so. I do hope so. *(Pause.)* Hey, look, I'm too drunk to spend the night.

SOJOURNER: No, Mr. Pee Wee. You're too drunk not to spend the night. I'll go fix up the couch for you. *(She kisses him on the forehead.)* You're a good man, Mr. Pee Wee—wherever that funny name came from. What did you tell me once—somethin' about marbles? Naw. That can't be. I think Pee Wee means what you was jest sayin'. You is jest an ordinary, decent, white man. Jackie Robinson was no pee wee. He

was a Black giant. You is a white pee wee. And that's what I love
about you. (*PEE WEE has fallen fast asleep on the table.*) Yeah. Maybe I will
run into Mr. Jackie Robinson one more time. After that last nasty get
together we needs another moment or two.

(Fade to black with SOJOURNER's arm around a sleeping PEE WEE.)

Scene 7

*1997. JACKIE at 77 in a Dodger baseball uniform #42. SOJOURNER is a youthful
'90s Black woman reporter interviewing him.*

SOJOURNER: Mr. Robinson, this is the 50th anniversary of your coming into
baseball and your 36th year as manager of the Brooklyn Dodgers.
That's a long time. You saved baseball from its racist apartheid and you
saved baseball for Brooklyn. Your life is a great success story. How does
it look to you as you get ready to retire?

JACKIE: What's your name, sister?

SOJOURNER: Sally. My name is Sally, Mr. Robinson. Sally Sojourner. I cover
sports for *Essence* magazine.

JACKIE: They got a lot of women coverin' sports these days, don't they?

SOJOURNER: Not as many as they should have, but a lot more than they
used to have. So…Mr. Robinson…who have been your important
influences these past 50 years? I mean your life is filled with one extraordinary accomplishment after another: breaking the color line as a
player in '47; breaking the line again as a manager in '56 and then that
incredible public fight with O'Malley in '59 to keep the Dodgers here in
Brooklyn. And you winnin' it by becomin' baseball's first Black president and makin' Brooklyn the first franchise in major league baseball
history owned by community shareholders and then proceedin' to win
those seven straight World Series championships in the '70s and '80s.
It's been a hell of a life—a helluva run, Mr. Jackie Robinson—one helluva journey. And now that you're finally stealin' home for good, who
are the big influences?

JACKIE: Well…Rachel's always been there for me. Since we were married in

1946 she's been at my side day by day. No one could be more important. And then there's Pee Wee. Just an ordinary guy. Pee Wee was no
liberal crusader with me. And that's why I liked him—no, loved him,
so. Just a decent working-class man who could usually tell right from
wrong and always did right by me. He was my shortstop and we hung
out a lot together. (*Thoughtful pause.*) And then there's these people—
or maybe this person—that I keep runnin' into for a moment here and
a moment there. I don't even know her name sometimes. But on this
long journey of mine, she's always set me straight.

SOJOURNER: This person…or these people…it's always a woman?

JACKIE: It's always a Black woman. And I don't see her but once. And then
she's gone. Vanishes. Then she—or someone like her—might come
back again in a few years. But in that momentary appearance, she
speaks the truth. No. Wait. More important, she speaks to me honestly.
Like Rachel and Pee Wee, she ain't intimidated by me. Yeah. That's it.
She's a stranger but she talks to me real honest.

(*Pause.*)

SOJOURNER: I could be her, Jack Robinson. I could be her.

JACKIE: (*He looks at her carefully*) Yes. You could be her, Sally Sojourner. You
got a message for me?

SOJOURNER: No. I ain't got no message today. I just wanna make some
more sense out of your life. And I want your life to be happier. I want it
to turn out better than what the books say about you. You're a big man,
Jackie Robinson. But you lived your life in a small and narrow-minded
world. And you was doin' everything for the first time. You didn't know
how to do it. Y'got a lotta stuff all wrong. Not surprisingly. But ya did
good, Jackie Roosevelt Robinson. Ya did good.

JACKIE: (*He stares into her eyes*) You are her! Who are you?

SOJOURNER: Just an ordinary person who don't need or want anything from
ya. I just want ya to be more happy. That's what my piece for *Essence* is
gonna be about. "Jackie Robinson Finally Finds Happiness."

JACKIE: I've been too busy fightin' all my life to look out for happiness.

SOJOURNER: True enough. True enough. You've been too busy tryin' to be white.

JACKIE: (*Irate, but not nasty*) Now wait a goddamn second here. Wasn't it you who told me I had to be more white? That was your advice!

SOJOURNER: (*Laughs uproariously*) More white meant givin' up shadow ball in the major leagues. It didn't mean bein' a fool Republican and supportin' Richard Nixon. More white means giving up Black and white altogether. 'Cause as long as there's Black and white, Jackie Robinson, white's gonna win. Gettin' more and more white means givin' up color. Then you don't have to be the first everything. Then, maybe, you can be happy. I always thought it was a mistake to have the first Black baseball player be so talented an athlete as you. It should of been a more ordinary player. Y'know, like old Hank Thompson of the Giants or someone like that. First, it makes the racial point better. Baseball had to be integrated for all Black players—not just great ones. Second, it probably woulda produced less antagonism. And it wouldn't have ruined your career as an athlete by confusin' it with your career as a symbol quite so much. If you was just an ordinary super-star who come up 30 or so years later you'd be known as the greatest player ever lived.

JACKIE: And I'd a been a lot richer!

SOJOURNER: Yeah. Probably so. But don't go mixin' up white and green again!

JACKIE: You was that Panther, too, wasn't you?

SOJOURNER: Sorry about that... but I was pissed off at you.

JACKIE: (*With mock anger*) Y'almost killed me.

SOJOURNER: Oh, you was as healthy as could be. You'll live to be 100.

JACKIE: (*Thoughtfully*) Wait a second. Wait a second. I thought I did die way back then. I remember havin' real bad diabetes and then I got more and more blind and weaker and weaker. I thought I died back then. What in the hell is goin' on here?

SOJOURNER: That was your *first* life, Jackie Robinson. The *first* go around.

This is the *second*. D'you always have to go with being first? With what's first? Hey, sometimes number two is just fine.

JACKIE: *(Nodding)* Yeah. And sometimes plain old number 42 is just fine— ain't that right, Sojourner...Sally Sojourner.

SOJOURNER: Yeah...that's right.

(SOJOURNER flips a "shadow ball" to JACKIE. He "catches" it and flips it back. They play "shadow ball" as lights fade.)

))))

Carmen's Place (A Fantasy)

Book and lyrics by Fred Newman,
music by Fred Newman and Annie Roboff
With excerpts from *Carmen:* music by Georges Bizet,
words by H. Meilhac and L. Halevy, translated by
Deborah Green

With *Carmen's Place (A Fantasy)* (1997) Newman returns, 10 years after *Carmen's Community,* to Georges Bizet's opera *Carmen* and the questions of love and romance that it raises for contemporary society.

It is a very different Carmen that we meet here. Instead of the hooker and her tough—but wise—street cronies, the Carmencita of *Carmen's Place* is a waitress. Unlike Bizet's heroine or Newman's own earlier Carmen, both of whom lived on the social and emotional edge, Carmen Ortiz of *Carmen's Place* is a solid, hard-working member of the working class. Everything about her is stable. She's lived on Manhattan's upper West Side all her life. She's been at the same job for seven years and has had the same boyfriend—José Lugo, now a police officer—since they were both 10. Her idea of a good time is not a bullfight (or provoking a fight) but going to the "movies, and sometimes a play." Carmen's stability, and in particular the steadiness and supportiveness of her relationship with José, is fundamental to the play.

In *Carmen's Community* romantic love is critiqued for being destructive to women. The Carmen of the opera, attempting to play one man against the other, gets tangled up in the possessive assumptions of romantic love and is killed. The Carmen of Newman's earlier play refuses to accept the rules of romantic love and thus avoids destruction. *Carmen's Community* is, essentially, a deconstruction of Bizet's (and society's) romanticism.

Carmen's Place is not a critique, but an exploration of different ways of loving. It makes the claim—through all the main characters, but particularly through José—that love (even the love of a man for a woman) need not be predicated on the "owning" of the other's affection, time, or body. In *Carmen's Place* Newman proposes not that love is a many-splendored thing, but that it is *many splendored processes.* Each of the main characters in *Carmen's Place* loves each of the others. They love each other in very different ways, but none of these loves is deemed true or false, weaker or stronger, more or less passionate—and none of these loves is characterized by possessiveness. In effect Newman seems to be saying, "There are more loves, Bizet, than are dreamt of in your opera." In this sense *Carmen's Place* is a *re*construction of love(s). Not surprisingly, it is the sunniest, most upbeat, and least conflicted of Newman's plays.

Carmen's Place has a simple plot: the waitress Carmen and the opera singer Placido Quesara have a love affair and then end it when he moves on to another job. What *Carmen's Place* doesn't have is much dramatic conflict. José, Carmen's longtime boyfriend, says of the liaison: "So, yeah, I could be as jealous as the next guy. And Carmen is my whole life. But Carmen says that we mean forever. And I trust her. Always have. Always will...We've known each other since we were 10, and we loved each other from the moment we met. And it's never been me tellin' her what to do, or her tellin' me what to do. I'm just a simple Puerto Rican working-class guy but I got that straight." Officer José Lugo may be "simple" but he's no typical Puerto Rican working-class guy, nor is he a typical New York City cop, nor is he a typical contemporary man of any sort. He is what men *could* be if they were able to give up possessiveness in love. Perhaps this is why Newman calls the play a "fantasy."

Because José doesn't need to act out his jealousy, the play has very little conflict. The high drama is left to the opera sequences, which are far more distant, emotionally and stylistically, than they are in *Carmen's Community*. In the earlier play the 20th-century Carmencita and Don are so emotionally in tune with the 19th-century Carmen and Don José that the danger of violence and death haunts the play. However, Carmen Ortiz and José Lugo of *Carmen's Place* are on a different frequency altogether. They can appreciate the opera as a work of art from the olden days about old attitudes, but there is never any possibility of the characters feeling the possessiveness or acting out the violence of the opera.

The play's gentleness is reinforced by its structure. *Carmen's Community* doggedly cross-cut from tense scenes in the opera to tense scenes in the play, establishing a relentless momentum toward tragedy narrowly averted. In contrast, *Carmen's Place* floats from opera scenes (which, after all, are only rehearsals) to easygoing, loosely connected scenes of the contemporary characters, all joined harmoniously by Bizet's music and the music of Newman and Roboff. The cumulative effect is as close to that of a song cycle as it is to an American musical.

D.F.

CHARACTERS

KAREN ALLEN, a mezzo soprano from Montana
DON NOBLE, a tenor from Queens, NY
PLACIDO QUESARA, a baritone from Barcelona
CARMEN ORTIZ, a waitress at the Opera Diner, on 57th St. and 9th Ave.
JOSÉ LUGO, a police officer in the 57th St. and 9th Ave. neighborhood

Offstage
MAESTRO MALINI, a musical director from Milan
COOK

Act I, Scene 1

A rehearsal hall at the New York City Opera. Three chairs and a piano are on the stage, which is otherwise empty. An offstage sound booth, perhaps partially visible, houses MAESTRO MALINI, *an old-guard, old-world opera director who is not the least bit thrilled with having to do opera in English.*

KAREN ALLEN enters stage right. She is about 25 years old, a Midwestern American. She is simply dressed and obviously nervous. She looks around the empty rehearsal hall and is startled when an offstage voice with a thick Italian accent speaks her name.

MALINI: Is that Miss Allen? (*KAREN looks around startled and nods.*) I am Maestro Malini, the musical director. Good morning. Please have a seat. (*KAREN goes to piano and begins to play first four bars of the theme from "A Woman's Song." MALINI speaks sternly.*) I'm sorry, Miss Allen. You mustn't touch the piano. Union regulations.

(She jumps up.)

KAREN: Excuse me.

MALINI: Are you new in New York, Miss Allen?

KAREN: (*Nervously*) Oh, no, I've been here six years.

MALINI: Where were you before that?

KAREN: Montana.

MALINI: Montana?

KAREN: Yes.

MALINI: How did you get to New York?

KAREN: I won a Juilliard scholarship, Maestro Maloni.

MALINI: Malini, Miss Allen, Malini.

KAREN: Oh, I'm sorry, sir. *(Pause.)* Where are you from?

MALINI: I'm originally from Milano. But I have been here in New York for many years. *(Pause.)* Why do you ask? *(She doesn't answer.)* Are you very nervous?

KAREN: Yes. I've only done local work.

MALINI: Have you sung in English before?

KAREN: Oh, yes. Several times.

MALINI: And do you hate it?

KAREN: No, sir.

MALINI: Well, you should. Opera should be done in its native language.

KAREN: Yes, sir. *(Pause.)* But isn't it good for people to understand it?

MALINI: In opera you understand the music, not the lyrics. Have you never learned that, Miss Allen?

KAREN: I did have a teacher at Juilliard who used to say that a good deal.

MALINI: Well, he was right.

KAREN: It was a woman.

MALINI: Well, then she was right. *(Pause.)* Have you sung this opera before? Have you sung *Carmen*?

KAREN: Oh, yes, sir. Several times.

MALINI: Have you sung it in English?

KAREN: Yes, sir.

MALINI: Did you hate it?

KAREN: *(Pauses, then reluctantly)* No, sir. I really didn't.

MALINI: Good.

(*DON NOBLE enters stage right, and crosses to* KAREN.)

DON: Hello, my name is Don Noble. I'm playing Don José.

KAREN: Hi, I'm Karen Allen. I'm playing Carmen. *(Pause.)* I was just talking to Maestro Malini.

(DON looks around and sees no one.)

DON: Maestro Malini?

KAREN: He's in the booth.

DON: Hello, Maestro Malini.

(There is no answer.)

KAREN: I guess he must have stepped out for a second.

DON: Can he hear us?

KAREN: I guess so.

DON: Where are you from?

KAREN: Montana.

DON: Montana?

KAREN: Yes. But I've been in New York for six years. Where are you from?

DON: Queens. I've lived here all my life.

KAREN: In Queens?

DON: Well, that's where I was raised. I live in Manhattan now.

KAREN: Have you ever sung with the New York City Opera before?

DON: No. This is my first time.

MALINI: Is that Mr. Noble?

DON: Yes, sir. I'm Don Noble.

MALINI: You're from Queens?

DON: Yes.

MALINI: Have you met Miss Allen?

DON: Yes. We just met.

MALINI: She's from Montana.

DON: Yes, sir. I know.

MALINI: And you're from Queens?

DON: Yes, sir.

MALINI: Montana and Queens. And you're going to sing *Carmen* together. Hmmm.

(*PLACIDO QUESARA enters stage right.*)

PLACIDO: (*Loud, jovial, and self-assured*) Is that you, Maestro Malini? Are you hanging out in the booth again?

MALINI: Placido, you're still working at the New York City? Aren't you ever going to make it to a real opera house?

PLACIDO: (*Laughs*) No, Maestro. You and me are destined to do English opera together. At least here in America.

MALINI: Are you still thinking of going back to Spain, Placido?

PLACIDO: Maybe so, Maestro. Maybe so.

MALINI: How long have you been here now?

PLACIDO: It will be 10 years in October.

MALINI: Do you miss Barcelona?

PLACIDO: Oh, yes. I've been back only one time. How long have you been here, Maestro?

MALINI: Eighteen years. Eighteen long years. And I'm still doing English operas. (*Pause.*) Have you met your co-stars?

PLACIDO: No. (*He turns to* DON *and* KAREN.) I'm Placido Quesara. I'll be singing Escamillo. It's good to meet you.

DON: It's a pleasure to meet you. I've heard you sing.

KAREN: Yes, it's very good to meet you. I've heard you sing also.

PLACIDO: Is this your first time at the New York City?

(*DON and* KAREN *both nod.*)

MALINI: She's from Montana.

PLACIDO: Montana?

KAREN: Yes. But I've been in New York for six years.

PLACIDO: *(Turning to DON)* Are you from Oklahoma?

DON: No. Forest Hills.

PLACIDO: *(Laughs)* Montana, Barcelona and Forest Hills. That's some threesome. Do you think we can sing together?

MALINI: You three better get to know each other. I'll be back in a few minutes and we'll go to work.

(DON conspicuously lifts up a boom box. He turns it on and a taped accompaniment to "Montana, Barcelona and Forest Hills" begins. KAREN, DON and PLACIDO sing and dance.)

("Montana, Barcelona and Forest Hills")

KAREN:
Montana,
It's my home.
Grandpa Joe,
Top banana, so
I sang young.
Had a voice so big
And Mr. Juilliard said,
"Come to New York, kid."

DON:
Queens, New York,
Played at Forest Hills,
Hated Jets,
Loved Miss Beverly Sills.
Simple guy
Now I'm singin'
With a beauty from the West,
Big sky.

PLACIDO:

> I come from Barcelona,
> Studied opera in Verona.
> Thought I was the
> Best baritone
> In the world.

ALL:

> Doin' *Carmen*
> At the New York City
> Not the Met.
> And that's a pity
> But it's a job.
> So like Walter Mitty
> We're gonna make it
> A fantasy come true.

(They dance.)

> Doin' *Carmen*
> At the New York City
> Not the Met.
> And that's a pity
> But it's a job.
> So like Walter Mitty
> We're gonna make it
> A fantasy come true.
> We're gonna make it
> A fantasy come true.

(Dance is interrupted by MALINI's voice.)

MALINI: Alright, you three, I see you can sing and dance in America. Let's see what you can do in Spain. Placido, do you know Zuniga's part in the opening?

PLACIDO: Yes, Malini. Yes I do. Or at least I could fake it.

MALINI: Mr. Noble and Miss Allen, do you know your lines in Scene 1?

KAREN and DON: *(Together)* Yes, sir, we do.

MALINI: Okay, I'll do the soldiers, the town people and the cigarette girls. *(Pause.)* When you're ready, Placido.

(Overture. An imaginary barracks is to one side, with an imaginary cigarette factory in the distance. Spoken dialogue.)

PLACIDO as ZUNIGA: Don José, they say there are a lot of pretty women working in that factory there. Is that true?

DON/JOSÉ: Yes, sir. They also say that those cigarette girls are of very easy virtue!

PLACIDO as ZUNIGA: Yes. But at least they are pretty?

DON/JOSÉ: Sir, I wouldn't know. I don't pay attention to women like that. Well, here they come now. You can judge for yourself.

(Sound effect [perhaps MALINI's voice] of factory bell ringing; we imagine [or hear] the square filling with cigarette girls and soldiers coming out of their barracks. DON/JOSÉ indifferently busies himself with the "chain" on his "saber.")

MALINI as SOLDIERS/TOWNSPEOPLE: Here they come, those flirtatious factory girls, puffing away on their cigarettes! But we don't see "la Carmencita."

MALINI as CIGARETTE GIRLS: There she is! There she is! There is la Carmencita!

MALINI as SOLDIERS/TOWNSPEOPLE: At last! We've been waiting for you! Carmen, how long will you go on teasing us? When will you give us your love?

(Musical introduction: two bars of recitative, then aria.)

KAREN/CARMEN: *(With a glance at DON/JOSÉ, sings)*
When will I give my love?
Who knows, it's hard to say!
Perhaps not at all, tomorrow I may.
But one thing is sure: Not today!

("Habanera")

KAREN/CARMEN:

> Love is free as the wayward breeze,
> It can be shy, it can be bold.
> Love can fascinate, love can tease,
> Its whims and moods are thousandfold.
>
> All at once it arrives and lingers
> For just how long can't be foretold.
> Thus it deftly slips through your fingers,
> For love's a thing no force can hold.
>
> L'amour! L'amour!
> L'amour! L'amour!
>
> A heart in love is quickly burned,
> It knows no law except its own desire.
> If I should love you and you spurn me,
> I'm warning you, you play with fire!
> If I'm in love with you,
> Don't ever, ever try to spurn me.
> My friend remember, if I love you,
> you play with fire!
>
> Wait for love and you wait forever
> Don't wait at all, it comes to you.
> Try to grasp it,
> It's far too clever,
> It flies away into the blue.
>
> Love has so many forms and shapes,
> Each day it wears a new disguise.
> Think you've caught it and it escapes
> To catch you later by surprise.
>
> L'amour! L'amour!
> L'amour! L'amour!

(A pause. Imaginary soldiers surround KAREN/CARMEN, *who "looks" at*

them one by one. Then she "breaks through the circle" and goes straight to DON/JOSÉ, who is still busy with his "chain." Spoken dialogue.)

KAREN/CARMEN: Hey, friend, what are you up to?

DON/JOSÉ: I'm fixing the chain that holds my saber.

KAREN/CARMEN: *(Laughing)* Fixing the chain that holds your saber! Really, is that *all* you want to hold? Look! Here's something to hold on to!

(KAREN/CARMEN throws the flower in her hair at DON/JOSÉ and runs away. He jumps up. The flower has fallen at his feet. MALINI makes the sound of an outburst of general laughter. Imaginary factory girls surround DON/JOSÉ with KAREN/CARMEN singing "A heart in love is quickly burned…" The "factory bell" rings again. KAREN/CARMEN and her imagined friends run into the factory. Imagined soldiers go into guard house. DON/JOSÉ is left alone; he picks up the flower.)

DON/JOSÉ: What a hussy! The way she threw that flower at me—it hit me like a bullet! But how pretty and fragrant it is! And the woman…If there really are witches, she's certainly one!

(Sound effect by MALINI of offstage commotion, girls screaming.)

PLACIDO as ZUNIGA: What's going on over there? José, take two men into that factory with you and see who caused all that commotion!

(DON/JOSÉ takes two imaginary men with him and goes into the factory. Sound of cigarette girls shouting, taunting the soldiers, pushing each other out of the way. DON/JOSÉ collars KAREN/CARMEN and brings her onstage. PLACIDO as ZUNIGA speaks, KAREN/CARMEN sings.)

PLACIDO as ZUNIGA: What have you got to say?

KAREN/CARMEN:
Tralalalalalalalala
You can cut me or burn me,
and silent I'll stay.
Tralalalalalalalala
You may beat me or torture me,
It doesn't matter!

PLACIDO as ZUNIGA: Spare us your songs, and since you've been told to answer, answer!

KAREN/CARMEN:
Tralalalalalalalala
I will never betray
What I keep in my heart!
Tralalalala
There's one man I adore,
And for him I would die.

PLACIDO as ZUNIGA: Since that's your attitude, you can sing your song to the prison walls.

KAREN/CARMEN:
Tralalalalalalalalala
Lalalalalalalalala
Lalalalalalalalalalala

PLACIDO as ZUNIGA: *(To DON/JOSÉ)* Corporal, take her away!

MALINI as CIGARETTE GIRLS: Oh no! Not to prison! Not to prison!

(A brief pause. KAREN/CARMEN raises her eyes and looks at DON/JOSÉ. He turns, withdraws a few paces, then comes back to KAREN/CARMEN who has been watching him all the while. Spoken dialogue.)

KAREN/CARMEN: *(To DON/JOSÉ)* Where are you taking me?

DON/JOSÉ: To prison. You heard the order—I do as I'm told.

KAREN/CARMEN: Very well, but I know you'll help me escape no matter what your captain says—because you love me!

DON/JOSÉ: I? I, love you?

KAREN/CARMEN: Yes, José! The flower I just gave you, you know, the witch's flower—you can throw it away now. The spell is working!

DON/JOSÉ: Don't talk to me any more! You hear me? Say no more! I forbid it!

KAREN/CARMEN: *(Speaks, as music begins)* Very well, mon capitan, very well! You forbid me to talk, so I won't talk. *(Sings.)*

("Seguidilla" and Duet)

Close to the wall of Sevilla,
Lives my old friend Lillas Pastia.
I'll dance to a gay seguidilla
And I'll drink Manzanilla,
At the inn of Senor Lillas Pastia.
But when a girl goes out to dance,
She wants to have some company.
So I don't want to take a chance,
I'll take the man I love with me.
(Laughing) The man I love?
What am I saying?
I told him yesterday we're through.
My heart is free, longing for someone,
Eager for love with somebody new.
There are so many who adore me,
But I don't care for any one.
With one whole Sunday free before me,
Who wants my love? He'll be the one.
Who wants my heart?
Who comes to claim it?
Here is your chance, it still is free.
You can have it for the asking.
With my new love I'm on my way.
Close to the wall of Sevilla,
Lives my old friend Lillas Pastia.
I'll dance to a gay seguidilla
And I'll drink Manzanilla.
I will meet my love at Lillas Pastia's!

DON/JOSÉ: *(With severity)* Enough! For the last time, I forbid you to talk!

KAREN/CARMEN: *(Sings, with simplicity)*
Who said I spoke to you?
I sing for my own pleasure,
I sing for my own pleasure!
And I'm thinking!

Since when are people not allowed to think?
A certain young man's on my mind,
A certain young man's on my mind,
Who loves me, and I confess,
Yes, I confess that I could love him too.

DON/JOSÉ: *(Sings)*
　　Carmen!

KAREN/CARMEN: *(Pointedly)*
　　He's not a colonel or sergeant,
　　Really his rank is quite low.
　　He's only a corp'ral but
　　That's good enough for a Gypsy girl.
　　I'll be happy with him, I know.

DON/JOSÉ: *(Agitated)*
　　Carmen, I can bear it no longer!
　　If I free you, if I surrender,
　　Will you promise to keep your word?
　　And if I love you, Carmen,
　　Carmen will you love me?

KAREN/CARMEN:
　　Yes.

DON/JOSÉ:
　　At Lillas Pastia's?

KAREN/CARMEN:
　　We both will dance the seguidilla.

DON/JOSÉ:
　　I have your word?

KAREN/CARMEN:
　　And we will drink Manzanilla.

DON/JOSÉ: *(He "unties the rope")*
　　You'll keep your word!

KAREN/CARMEN:

Ah!
Close to the wall of Sevilla,
Lives my old friend Lillas Pastia.
We'll dance to a gay seguidilla
And we'll drink Manzanilla,
Tralalalalalalalala!

(Spoken dialogue.)

PLACIDO as ZUNIGA: *(Returns to DON/JOSÉ)* Here's the order; off you go now. And keep a good lookout!

KAREN/CARMEN: *(Aside, to DON/JOSÉ)* On the way I shall push you, as hard as I can…let yourself fall over…the rest is up to me.

MALINI: Bravo! Miss Allen. You sing very beautifully. I am pleased.

KAREN: Thank you, Maestro.

PLACIDO: Yes, you are excellent! I am very impressed.

KAREN: *(Shyly)* Thank you, thank you, Placido.

DON: *(Obviously struck by lightning)* That was fantastic!

PLACIDO: Your voice has the clearness of a big sky.

DON: Yeah. Like Montana.

PLACIDO: No, like Barcelona. *(They laugh.)*

MALINI: We'll take a half an hour here.

PLACIDO: You two want to grab some lunch at the Opera Diner?

KAREN: Yeah, sure.

DON: Yeah. Yeah.

(They exit.)

Act I, Scene 2

The Opera Diner. There's a counter and a couple of tables. CARMEN ORTIZ, *in a waitress uniform, stands behind the counter.* JOSÉ LUGO *sits on a stool at the counter; he wears a police uniform. The scene opens with no one else at the tables or counter.* COOK *is offstage.*

COOK: You wanted those french fries light?

*(*JOSÉ *nods to* CARMEN.*)*

CARMEN: Yeah, very light.

COOK: Who are these for? Your boyfriend, Carmen?

CARMEN: Yes.

COOK: Be ready in a minute.

JOSÉ: What time are you off tonight?

CARMEN: Oh about seven. Are you gonna pick me up?

JOSÉ: Yeah, maybe we'll catch a movie.

CARMEN: Okay. You want to eat first?

JOSÉ: Yeah. You wanna go out and grab a bite?

CARMEN: I could cook.

JOSÉ: You work too hard all day. We'll go out.

CARMEN: Okay, good.

JOSÉ: You working this Sunday?

CARMEN: *(Checking the schedule on the wall)* No.

JOSÉ: *(Laughing)* Let's get married Sunday.

CARMEN: *(Laughs)* I haven't sent out invitations.

JOSÉ: After 15 years, no invitations?

CARMEN: Has it really been 15 years? Time flies when you're having fun.

JOSÉ: We met when we were 10.

CARMEN: I was never 10.

JOSÉ: *(Romantically)* You'll always be 10.

COOK: Those fries are ready, Carmen.

(She exits and returns immediately with the fries.)

JOSÉ: Seriously, Carmen. Isn't it time to have a real talk about the wedding date?

CARMEN: I've been ready to marry you for 10 years. But I still feel like I have to wait awhile before we make it official. I want something more in my life before I say "I do."

JOSÉ: I want to be able to play baseball with our kids.

CARMEN: C'mon, we're only 25. We'll be married for 100 years.

JOSÉ: A hundred years? What will we do after that?

(CARMEN laughs as music begins.)

("We Mean Forever")

CARMEN: *(Sings)*
You and I,
We're all about forever.
'Til we die,
We'll never be apart.
We met when we were only ten,
Way back way back when,
And I knew
I could never be without you again.

JOSÉ:
You and me,
I agree we mean forever.
It's a lifetime
Never, never apart.
We met when we were very small
But even then we knew,
It all
Had to be
Forever.

CARMEN:
But I might need a minute
For myself
A minute for a fantasy
A moment just for me to be
Myself.

JOSÉ:
I can see
A reason for your moment
And though it frightens me,
I could never keep anything
From you.
So do what you must do.
We'll always be together,
Forever, together forever, together...

(As the song ends, PLACIDO, KAREN and DON enter stage right. They are talking quietly with each other.)

PLACIDO: *(Formally—like a European)* Table for three.

CARMEN: *(Stares at him)* Oh, sit anywhere.

(The three sit at a table center stage.)

DON: *(To PLACIDO)* Do you like America? Do you like New York?

KAREN: Are you lonely for Spain? Do you miss home?

PLACIDO: I do like America. And I love New York City. But yes, Karen, I deeply miss my home. Do you miss Montana?

KAREN: Yes, I miss its openness and its emptiness and its...

DON: *(Interrupts)* Big sky?

KAREN: Yes, Don, its big sky. But I've met wonderful people in New York. And things are getting better all the time.

DON: The sky is a little bigger in Forest Hills than in Manhattan.

PLACIDO: *(To DON)* You live here in Manhattan now, yes? Do you go to Forest Hills to visit your family often?

DON: Once in a while. Maybe I could bring the two of you to meet them someday soon. They're nice people. Even if they are Mets fans.

KAREN: We don't have a baseball team in Montana. At least not a major league team.

PLACIDO: I will never understand you Americans' love of baseball.

KAREN: It's a very beautiful sport.

PLACIDO: Yes? It seems so slow to me.

KAREN: It is slow. But in a city and a country where everything else is so fast, it's very beautiful.

DON: I never thought of it that way, Karen.

KAREN: (*Smiles. To* PLACIDO) Tell us about Barcelona. Tell us about Spain.

PLACIDO: Oh, Karen and Don, Spain is very old. Americans come to visit it as if it were a museum. And I love those Americans. I love Americans. But Spain is not a museum, it's my home. It is very old and in many ways very tired.

DON: Well, Forest Hills is a mite sleepy, but not quite tired.

KAREN: In Montana, the nature is very old, but the state is very young.

PLACIDO: In Spain the history is very old. And the people are more serene. You must come and visit us someday.

DON: (*To* KAREN) Yeah, maybe we could go together.

KAREN: (*Smiling*) Well, first we have an opera to create...and maybe a visit to Forest Hills.

(*They laugh as* CARMEN *approaches the table.*)

CARMEN: What can I get for you all?

PLACIDO: You have a special soup today?

CARMEN: Yes, we have Yankee bean soup.

DON: Placido, that's an American soup.

PLACIDO: Yes, Don, I've been here 10 years.

KAREN: Well, I'll have the Yankee bean soup and an iced tea, please.

DON: Me, too.

PLACIDO: *(To* CARMEN*)* Where are you from?

CARMEN: My family is from Puerto Rico, but I was born and raised on the West Side of Manhattan. Where are you from?

PLACIDO: From Barcelona, from Spain. Para mi tambien la sopa Yankee de habichuelas. *("I'll have the Yankee bean soup, too.")*

CARMEN: Te gustara. No es mala para una sopa Americana. *("You'll like it. It's not bad for an American soup.")*

*(*CARMEN *laughs and walks away from the table.)*

KAREN: What did you two say?

PLACIDO: Oh, I just ordered the Yankee bean soup, too. And the waitress said it wasn't bad for an American soup.

KAREN: That's nice. You must miss speaking Spanish.

PLACIDO: Yes, I miss a great deal about my home and my culture. I'm afraid I'll always be a stranger in America. *(Sings.)*

("A Stranger in America")

I'll always be a stranger in America,
Even though I love its magic energy.
Where I'm from there is a deep serenity
And a greater love for what things used to be.
España always sings its song to me,
Barcelona rising far above the sea...

The lights are wondrous in America;
In Spain the darkness rules the night.
There is a freshness in America;
Spain is an old world beyond its height.
España always sings its song to me,
Barcelona rising far above the sea...

The lights are wondrous in America;
In Spain the darkness rules the night.
There is a freshness in America;
Spain is an old world beyond its height.
España always sings its song to me,
Barcelona rising far above the sea…
España always sings its song to me,
Barcelona rising far above the sea…

(Music fades and CARMEN *returns with food.)*

PLACIDO: Thank you. Gracias. What is your name?

CARMEN: My name is Carmen. Carmen Ortiz. *(She turns to* JOSÉ.*)* And this is my boyfriend, Officer Lugo. *(He stands from his stool.)*

PLACIDO: Your name is Carmen? And your first name, Officer?

JOSÉ: My name is José.

PLACIDO: So you are Carmen and José?

CARMEN and JOSÉ: *(Together)* Yes.

PLACIDO: Well, my name is Placido Quesara and I am an opera singer. I play Escamillo in the opera *Carmen* which is going to open at the New York City Opera in six weeks and believe it or not, this is Karen Allen, who plays Carmen and Don Noble who plays Don José. Don, this is José. Karen, this is Carmen.

DON: Well, we appear to have a lot in common.

KAREN: *(To* CARMEN*)* How long've you worked here, Carmen?

CARMEN: Oh, maybe seven years now. But I've lived in the neighborhood all my life. So has José. We met when we were 10.

KAREN: Have you ever been to the opera?

CARMEN: No. José and I we don't ever go to the opera. We like movies, and sometimes a play.

DON: So you've never seen *Carmen*?

JOSÉ: Not in the opera.

PLACIDO: You should come and see the opera. You should be our guests at the opening.

CARMEN: Really?

KAREN: Yes. That would be very nice.

JOSÉ: It would be fun. I would like to do that. Do you want to, Carmen?

CARMEN: Yes, why not? What language is it in?

PLACIDO: I'm afraid it's in English.

JOSÉ: Well, that's good. We all speak English.

DON: Yes, that's right. We all speak English.

KAREN: Carmen is such a beautiful name. And it's a beautiful opera all about you.

CARMEN: This is wonderful. I love to do new things. I can't believe there is a new thing to do right across the street from where I've grown up.

PLACIDO: Life is short. It is good to do new things when we have the chance.

JOSÉ: Yeah, it's good to mix old things and new things.

("Just About Everyone Knows")

KAREN: *(Sings)*
    My name's Karen,
    I play "Carmen."

CARMEN:
    My name's Carmen,
    I serve coffee.
    Nice to meet ya.
    Ain't life a stitch?

KAREN:
    I'm a singer.

CARMEN:
    I'm a "flinger,"
    Chopsticks piano.

KAREN:

> Mezzo soprano.
> But I like ya.
> Ain't life a stitch?
> Life's a play.

CARMEN:

> Not for me.

KAREN:

> A great day.

CARMEN:

> I'm not free.

KAREN:

> Take a trip.

CARMEN:

> Where should I go?

KAREN:

> On a ship.

CARMEN:

> To a show.

KAREN and CARMEN:

> Life is so short,
> We better live it before it goes.
> Life is so short,
> As just about everyone knows.
>
> Life goes so fast,
> We better dig it before it's past.
> Life goes so fast,
> As just about everyone knows,
> As just about everyone knows.

DON:

> My name's Don,
> I play "José."

JOSÉ:

> My name's José,
> I'm a cop.
> Nice to meet ya.
> Ain't life a stitch?
> Walk a beat,
> Hurts your feet.

DON:

> Don't right wrongs,
> Just sing songs.
> But I like ya.
> Ain't life a stitch?
> Life's a play.

JOSÉ:

> Not for me.

DON:

> A great day.

JOSÉ:

> I'm not free.

DON:

> Take a trip.

JOSÉ:

> Where should I go?

DON:

> On a ship.

JOSÉ:

> To a show.

DON and JOSÉ:

> Life is so short,
> We better live it before it goes.
> Life is so short,
> As just about everyone knows.

ALL:

> Life goes so fast,
> We better dig it before it's past.
> Life goes so fast,
> As just about everyone knows,
> As just about everyone knows,
> As just about everyone knows.

(PLACIDO has been listening gleefully to the singing of the quartet and as the song ends with the four singers laughing, he motions for CARMEN.)

PLACIDO: *(In something of a stage whisper)* Would you like to come and see a rehearsal?

CARMEN: A rehearsal?

PLACIDO: Yes. I think you'd find it very interesting. And I would love to get to know you better. Do you work every day?

CARMEN: No, as a matter of fact, I'm off tomorrow.

PLACIDO: Wonderful. Come to a rehearsal tomorrow.

CARMEN: What time?

PLACIDO: I'll meet you at the Lincoln Center Fountain at 11 o'clock. Would that be good?

CARMEN: Yes, that would be good.

PLACIDO: And I'll take you to lunch afterwards?

CARMEN: Yes. I would like that.

PLACIDO: Till tomorrow then.

Act I, Scene 3

In the rehearsal hall chatting are KAREN, PLACIDO and CARMEN.

MALINI: *(With some hostility)* Young lady, are you in this opera? What are you doing here?

PLACIDO: Malini, this is a friend of mine. I've invited her to watch the rehearsal today. Stop pretending to be so nasty.

KAREN: Yes, Maestro. And her name is Carmen Ortiz. She lives in the community. And works as a waitress at the Opera Diner.

MALINI: Well, welcome, Miss Ortiz. Do you sell lasagna at your diner? (*CARMEN nods.*) I'll expect an especially large serving when I come by.

CARMEN: You got it.

MALINI: Okay, can we do some work today? We'll start with Act II, Scene 1. I'll do Zuniga and the chorus today, and we'll go right through, Karen, until you chase everybody out of the inn. (*Pause.*) Miss Ortiz, Mr. Quesara will have a chance to show off his beautiful baritone voice singing the "Toreador's Song." Do you know the opera?

CARMEN: I'm afraid not.

MALINI: Well, you must know the "Toreador's Song."

CARMEN: I don't think so.

MALINI: Well, at least you must know Quesara.

CARMEN: What do you mean?

PLACIDO: (*Feigning irritation*) Could we begin, Maestro?

MALINI: Okay, Placido. When you're ready, Miss Allen.

(*"Curtain up" on the "tavern of Lillas Pastia." KAREN/CARMEN is there with imagined Gypsy friends and soldiers.*)

(*"Gypsy Song"*)

KAREN/CARMEN: (*Sings*)
The stillness at the end of day
Is broken by a lazy jingle,
The sleepy air begins to tingle.
The Gypsy dance is underway!
And soon the tambourines of Spain,
And strumming of guitars competing,
Continue on and on, repeating

The same old song, the same old strain,
the same old song, the same refrain!
Tra lalalalalalala!

(*MALINI sings "Tra lalalalalala," or musicians play this vocal line.*
KAREN/CARMEN dances "with friends.")

The copper rings the Gypsies wear
Against their dusky skins are gleaming,
With red and orange colors streaming,
Swirling skirts billow through the air!
The music guides the dancing feet
With ever more compelling beat.
Quite timid first, but soon the master,
It drives them on, and growing faster,
It starts to rise and rise to fever heat!
Tra lalalalalala!

(*MALINI sings "Tra lalalalalala," or musicians play this vocal line.*
KAREN/CARMEN dances "with friends.")

The Gypsy men play on with fire,
Their tambourines loudly whirring!
The pulsing rhythm fiercely stirring
Enflames the Gypsy girls' desire.
Their passion carries them away,
Their agile bodies turn and sway
In burning frenzy and abandon.
On and on they dance, madly driven
Like a whirlwind no force can stay!
Tra lalalalalala!

(*MALINI sings "Tra lalalalalala," or musicians play this vocal line.*
KAREN/CARMEN dances "with friends." Spoken dialogue.)

MALINI as ZUNIGA: Your soldier boy—the one they sent to prison on account
of you—he's free now.

KAREN/CARMEN: Don José's free? (*Carelessly.*) Oh. That's nice.

MALINI as CHORUS: *(Offstage)* Hurrah! Hurrah for the Toreador! Hurrah! Hurrah for Escamillo!

MALINI as ZUNIGA: It's the winner of the Granada bullfights. *(To PLACIDO/ ESCAMILLO, who enters surrounded by an imagined cheering crowd.)* Will you drink with us, comrade? To your past and future triumphs!

("Toreador's Song")

PLACIDO/ESCAMILLO: *(Sings)*
> Thank you all, you gallant soldier-heroes,
> And in return I drink to you tonight!
> Long may you share a common joy,
> The thrill of the fight!
> Crowds are swarming in the great arena,
> Excitement fills the atmosphere.
> Ev'ryone waiting, loudly debating,
> Wild with impatience,
> They raise a thunderous cheer!
> Shouts and stamping become contagious,
> Till at last it's like a thunderstorm.
> Day of fame for men of soul courageous,
> Day of fame for men of heart!
> It's time, Torero, come on! On guard! Ah!
> Toreador, fight well and hard,
> Proud as a king!
> Yours is the ring!
> And, after you have won the victor's crown,
> Earn your sweet reward,
> Your señorita's love!
> Toreador, your sweet reward is love!
>
> *(MALINI sings or musicians play this vocal line.)*
>
> Toreador, fight well and hard…

PLACIDO/ESCAMILLO:
> All at once, the crowd is silent.
> What are they waiting for?
> And what is happening?

Breathless expectancy
Hushes the gallery
Through the gate the bull is leaping out into the ring!
Rushing on, he charges madly,
A horse goes under, dragging down a picador,
"Come on, Torero!"
They roar like thunder.
Then, like a flash, the bull turns 'round,
Charging once more!
The lances stab his bleeding shoulder,
And blind with rage he runs.
The sand is red with blood!
Clear the ring, ev'ryone take cover!
Just one man stands sword in hand!
It's time, Torero, come on! On guard! Ah!

(KAREN/CARMEN "refills" PLACIDO/ESCAMILLO's "glass." Spoken dialogue.)

PLACIDO/ESCAMILLO: *(To KAREN/CARMEN)* What is your name, señorita? When I fight again, your name will be on my lips!

KAREN/CARMEN: Carmen, Carmencita! It makes no difference. *(Pause.)* And now, gentlemen *(to imagined soldiers and PLACIDO/ESCAMILLO),* out with you! The chief of police wants the inn closed for the night!

MALINI: Okay, let's take lunch. I gotta make a phone call.

CARMEN: *(Applauds loudly)* That was beautiful! I have heard that music before, Maestro Malini. I didn't know it came from an opera called *Carmen.*

MALINI: Well, it's your namesake. I'll be back after lunch.

CARMEN: Karen, you sing so beautifully!

KAREN: Thank you, Carmen. I love playing a character with your name. Just since meeting you yesterday, I am thinking about her in a new way. She has become more real for me. And I want to come to know you better. I think there is no one named Carmen in all of Montana.

(CARMEN laughs.)

PLACIDO: But in Barcelona there are many Carmens. *(They laugh.)*

KAREN: I'll see you later. I have to put a quarter in the meter. *(Exits.)*

CARMEN: What a wonderful voice you have!

PLACIDO: I sang that especially for you.

CARMEN: Is this you speaking or Escamillo?

PLACIDO: *(Laughs)* I sometimes cannot tell the difference.

CARMEN: What happens in the opera?

PLACIDO: *(Thinks for a moment)* Oh, Don José is put in jail for letting Carmen escape. And while he's away, Carmen falls in love with me. Then Don José returns from prison and desperately wants to continue his love affair with Carmen. But she spurns him and he kills her. *(Pause.)* So, beware, Carmen.

CARMEN: That's a very heavy story.

PLACIDO: It happens.

CARMEN: My José would never kill me. He would never hurt me.

PLACIDO: No matter what you might do?

CARMEN: No matter what I might do. He is a wonderful, wonderful person. And a very unusual man.

PLACIDO: I'm afraid I'm not so unusual.

CARMEN: What does that mean? You would hurt me?

PLACIDO: I would never try to hurt you. But I think I could never let you go.

CARMEN: Let me go? I met you just yesterday.

PLACIDO: I know. But you are here. And you are looking for something. And I am a romantic figure, even if I can't make it to the Met. *(He laughs.)*

CARMEN: *(Laughing)* You are, indeed. You are very romantic, Placido. I will not hurt José. He is my dearest friend. I am not the Carmen of the opera. But I would like to get to know you. You are attractive and you are exotic. And I've never been close to a bullfighter.

PLACIDO: We will do something together then? Carmen and Escamillo?

CARMEN: Well, we will at least go to lunch together. And, I suspect, something will come of it.

PLACIDO: You are a little like the Carmen of the opera. You are brazen. You have a strong will. You desire to be free. But you are also nice. The Carmen of the opera is not so nice. I think I like you better, Carmen Ortiz. I think I like you better.

CARMEN: Well, then you'd better feed me.

(She takes his arm and they exit stage left.)

Act II, Scene 1

The fountain at Lincoln Center at dusk. KAREN is standing downstage right, as DON enters upstage left, humming the Dragoon D'Alcala song.

KAREN/CARMEN: *(Loud enough for him to hear)* Here he comes, my handsome soldier. (*DON/JOSÉ continues singing the song until he is standing next to KAREN/CARMEN.)* So, it's you! Just out of prison?

DON/JOSÉ: Carmen, I'd do it all over again if it were for you!

KAREN/CARMEN: You love me, then?

DON/JOSÉ: I adore you!

(Duet and "Flower Song")

KAREN/CARMEN: *(Gaily—she takes him by the hand)*
Now that you're here, I'll dance for you
For you alone, señor
And even more than that, I'll sing and play my music.
(She makes him sit on the edge of the fountain.)
You sit right here, Don José *(With serio-comic air)*
You're the audience!

(KAREN/CARMEN sings "Lalalalalalalala..." and dances. Near the end of the dance DON/JOSÉ indicates that he "hears a sound" in the background and stops KAREN/CARMEN.)

DON/JOSÉ:

> Just one moment, wait,
> Only one moment, I beg you!

KAREN/CARMEN: *(Surprised)*

> And just why, may I ask?

DON/JOSÉ:

> In the distance I hear…
> Yes, our bugles are blowing,
> Sounding the retreat.
> Now, don't you hear them too?

KAREN/CARMEN: *(Gaily)*

> Bravo! Bravo! That's even better!
> It's not so easy a thing to sing and dance without music,
> But now we have some music which has dropped from the sky.

(She resumes her dancing.)

> Lalalalalala.

DON/JOSÉ: *(Agitated)*

> You do not understand, my love!
> That was the signal,
> I must be back, in camp,
> In my quarters by night.

KAREN/CARMEN: *(Stupefied)*

> Back in camp? For the night?
> *(With an outburst)* Ah, how could I be so stupid!
> I took no end of pains.
> I tried my very best,
> My very, very best,
> To entertain señor!
> So I sang and I danced,
> (May heaven forgive me)
> I was almost in love!
> Taratata!
> He hears the blasted bugle!

Taratata!
Dear me, and off he goes!
Back to camp, stupid fool!
Here! *(pretends to throw his shako at him)*
Take your belt, your saber and your helmet,
And go back to your camp, my boy!
Hurry back to your quarters!

DON/JOSÉ: *(Sadly)*
You're very wrong, Carmen,
To mock me as you do!
It's painful leaving you,
No woman I have known
Has so affected me.
Never before, no never in my life,
Has any woman ever
Moved my soul so deeply!

KAREN/CARMEN:
It's painful leaving me,
No woman you have known
Has affected you.
Never before, no never in your life,
Has any woman ever
Moved your soul so deeply!
Taratata! "My God, retreat is sounding!"
Taratata! "I'm going to be late!
Oh, my God, there are the bugles,
I'm afraid I'll be late!"
So he forgets me, runs off,
That's the end of his love!

DON/JOSÉ:
And so, you don't believe my love is real!

KAREN/CARMEN:
I don't.

DON/JOSÉ:

Well then, you do not know!

KAREN/CARMEN:

What more is there to know?

DON/JOSÉ:

Listen to me!

KAREN/CARMEN:

You'll keep them waiting!

DON/JOSÉ: *(Violently)*

Yes, I say you will!

KAREN/CARMEN:

No, no, no, no!

DON/JOSÉ:

I want it so!

(He draws from the vest of his "uniform" the flower which KAREN/CARMEN threw at him and shows it to her.)

("Flower Song")

Through ev'ry long and lonely hour
In prison there, I kept your flower,
and though its bloom was swiftly gone,
Its haunting fragrance lingered on.
In the darkness, as I lay dreaming,
Its perfume consoling, redeeming,
Recalled your image night and day,
And my despair would fade away.
At other times, I would berate you.
I swore to detest and to hate you!
Of what nemesis am I the prey?
What whim of fate sent you my way?
Then I knew I was lying:
There could be no doubt, no denying,
One burning hope was all I knew,

One sole desire inflamed my heart!
To see you, my Carmen,
To see you.
Carmen, the magic of your glances
Cast a spell around my heart,
Luring me on like an enchantress.
Oh, my Carmen!
You took possession of my heart!
Carmen, I love you!

(End of duet. Following is spoken dialogue.)

KAREN/CARMEN: You don't love me!

DON/JOSÉ: What did you say?

KAREN/CARMEN: No, no if you loved me, you'd prove it by coming away with me. You'd take me up behind you on your horse and carry me far across the mountains!

DON: *(Breaking out of character and lifting her up)* You got it, Karen! I'll carry you right out to Forest Hills and tell my mom and dad we're going to get married.

KAREN: *(Jokingly)* Don't you have loyalty to your company?

DON: I don't even have a company, but if I did I'd go AWOL for you. You're the best thing that's ever happened to me, Karen Allen. And I'm not going to lose you to Placido, Escamillo or anyone else. Besides he's got his own Carmen.

KAREN: He certainly seems to. And I'm worried about José.

DON: Me?

KAREN: *(Jokingly)* No. No, not you, you wise-ass! José, Carmen's boyfriend. They're a great couple and Carmen is a wonderful person. I just don't want to see anyone hurt.

DON: Well, you won't be hurt. I'll tell you that.

KAREN: I know. I love you. And besides, Forest Hills is exotic enough for me. I mean, after all...

DON: I know, I know, you're from Montana.

(They laugh, and exit downstage right arm in arm, laughing. Throughout the scene, CARMEN and PLACIDO have been standing watching them from upstage left. They come downstage and sit on the edge of the fountain.)

PLACIDO: *(Pointing to the exiting DON and KAREN)* Those two Americans really love each other.

CARMEN: I'm an American, too.

PLACIDO: You're a Puerto Rican.

CARMEN: But I'm an American also. A Puerto Rican American. *(Pause.)* And besides, you love Americans, Placido.

PLACIDO: You're right, Carmen. I do love Americans. Especially you.

CARMEN: These last several weeks have been wonderful.

PLACIDO: Is that all about me?

CARMEN: No, you silly baritone from Barcelona. It's all about lots of things, including you. It's about me and José discovering Don and Karen as friends. And the opera. It's like seeing a little bit of a new world. A world right across the street that I never knew was there. *(Pause.)* And yes, it's about you.

PLACIDO: But is all this over when the opera ends? Does Escamillo lose Carmen once again? Am I to be left alone in the bull ring?

CARMEN: You'll never be left alone, my friend. A man with an ego your size cannot be alone. Besides I will always be your friend.

PLACIDO: My friend! I want you for more than a friend.

CARMEN: And we are more than friends. And we will have this forever. But you will not possess me. Because I do not wish to be possessed. Because I will never leave José. And because you will never leave Placido and Escamillo and the opera. No small part of my love for you is your love for the opera. And to have learned that one can love in other ways, to have learned that from you means more to me than I can tell you. Maybe my love for José can mean something new for you. *(Sings.)*

("Many Kinds of Love")

Many kinds of love
Appear in many different ways.
Many kinds of love
Make up our many different days.
You and I have played,
Yet you and I have stayed
Much the way we were
When we began.

PLACIDO:

I'll never be the same.
I'll never love again
In quite the way I did
When you arrived.
I once survived
For me and only me
But now I plainly see
There's something else.

CARMEN:

How long have we belonged together?

PLACIDO:

I would answer "all my life."

CARMEN:

That's not me,
That you see.
I won't be
The "Carmen" of your play.
(Softly.) Yet you have changed my soul,
I now can play a different role.

PLACIDO:

You have changed me, too.
To have this love for you
Makes me something new,
Makes me someone who

Can sing a song
I never knew.

TOGETHER:

We never knew.

(They embrace and exit downstage right. After they exit, from upstage left come JOSÉ and KAREN to the same spot. JOSÉ is in uniform.)

JOSÉ: How's the singin' business goin', Karen?

KAREN: Oh, it's going well, José. The opening is a week from today, you know.

JOSÉ: *(Pulls out two tickets from pocket)* I know. It's my first opening.

KAREN: It means a great deal to me that you and Carmen will be there.

JOSÉ: *(Getting serious)* Yeah, it means a lot to me, too. *(Pause.)* What did you want to speak to me about?

KAREN: Well…*(pause)*…I know this is none of my business, but I wanted to talk to you about…you and Carmen. *(Pause.)* You know, I was wondering how you were doing *(pause)* with her getting to know Placido better …their becoming friends. I was wondering how you're handling that. Actually, I'm meeting Carmen here in about half an hour. We're going to go have a drink together. I was planning to talk with her about it, but I wanted to speak to you also. This might not be any of my business. If I'm out of bounds just tell me, but Don and I have really fallen in love with the two of you, even as we have fallen in love with each other over the last several weeks. And we don't want to interfere. You know, you don't interfere in Montana. But you also take care of your friends. And you and Carmen are good friends.

JOSÉ: Hey, listen, I don't think you're interfering. We feel the same way about you and Don, Karen. It's meant a lot to us to get to know you. Shit, I never thought I'd be a friend of anyone from Forest Hills, no less Montana, no less an opera singer. I'm just here on the streets to keep folks who are goin' to that opera house from bein' mugged. But you two, you two are great people. So, no, I don't think you are interfering.

KAREN: So how are you two doing? And, ya know, what are you feeling about this whole thing with Placido?

JOSÉ: Well, I'll tell you the truth, it's tough. In part because I really like Placido. The loudmouth son of a bitch is pretty romantic. And I could understand Carmen's feelings for the guy. I mean that don't make it easy. But Carmen's always been straight with me about how plain and unexotic I am. I'm no match for a toreador. So, yeah, I could be as jealous as the next guy. And Carmen is my whole life. But Carmen says that we mean forever. And I trust her. Always have. Always will. So I don't know what's goin' on between the two of 'em, but this ain't my case. And I ain't investigatin' it. We've known each other since we were 10, and we loved each other from the moment we met. And it's never been me tellin' her what to do, or her tellin' me what to do. I'm just a simple Puerto Rican working-class guy but I got that straight. *(Pause.)* And if I wasn't madly in love with Carmen, and didn't like Don and you so well, I'd think I'd fall madly in love with you. For one thing I always thought I'd love to go to Montana.

KAREN: How'd you learn to be like this?

JOSÉ: I don't know. I never learned much in school, but somehow I understand this. If you love somebody, you don't possess 'em. Maybe that's what the opera is about. You see what happens when people confuse loving with possessing. You wind up dead on the stage. Hope I don't run up there on opening night and keep Don from killing you. *(Sings.)*

("But I Know How to Love")

I'm just a simple man,
A proud Puerto Rican man,
A crazy New York Giant fan,
A cop who walks the beat,
My assets two good feet,
But I know, I know how to love.

I'm just plain ordinary,
I must confess.
Nothing extraordinary,
You'd never guess
Despite my meager manner
I know, I know how to love.

We met when we were ten.
We fell in love and then
Carmen taught me how to give.
She taught me how to live,
And so, I know how to love.

I'm just a simple man,
A proud Puerto Rican man,
A crazy New York Giant fan,
A cop who walks the beat,
My assets two good feet,
But I know, I know how to love.

(JOSÉ and KAREN embrace. JOSÉ starts downstage right.)

JOSÉ: Say hello to Carmencita for me.

(He exits downstage right as CARMEN enters upstage left. KAREN and CARMEN notice each other and wave as CARMEN continues walking downstage and sits next to KAREN.)

CARMEN: Karen, where do you want to go for a drink?

KAREN: Carmen, how you doin'? Let's sit here for a minute and talk.

CARMEN: Sure, it's gonna be a beautiful night. *(Pointing behind her.)* That's a great sunset.

KAREN: I was just talkin' to José.

CARMEN: José? Was he here?

KAREN: Yeah, I called him up and asked him to meet me here.

CARMEN: Oh, that's nice.

KAREN: I wanted to speak to him about the two of you and…*(pause)*… and Placido. I hope you don't mind, but I'm sure you could tell, I've fallen in love with the two of you, with you and José and I want to make sure no one gets hurt. Ya know, I don't want to interfere, but…

CARMEN: No, I don't think you're interfering. I think you're beautiful. Is José alright? Is he cool?

KAREN: Unbelievably so. I don't think I've ever known a man like José.

CARMEN: He's very special. *(Laughing.)* And you stay away from him.

KAREN: And what about Placido? Is he special, too?

CARMEN: No, he's delightfully unspecial. He's a real man. He's exotic. He plays a role and I want to perform with him. And it's been a great play. And I like him a lot. In fact, I love him. But Placido is not about forever. Placido is about Placido. And that's alright. He's wonderful to me. And I was lookin' for that kind of wonder. And now with you and Don and the opera... *(pause)* and Placido, I've found it. It feels as if it's filled an extraordinary void in my life. But it can never replace what José and I have made together.

KAREN: I feel some of that with Don. Our love creates a whole new part of me, but it doesn't negate me. I think I understand that void, that emptiness that you're talking about. I think it has to do with being a woman. I think it's about being who you are or being who a man needs you to be, but not being allowed to be both. I think that's something we both know about—that all women know about—whether you're from Puerto Rico or Montana.

CARMEN: I think you're right, Karen. *(Pause—then somewhat lightly.)* Maybe I can play in an opera called "Karen" someday.

("A Woman's Song")

KAREN: *(Sings)*
Women are lovers
In all kinds of ways—
Mothers of children,
Sweethearts in plays—
(But) men still possess us
For most of our days.
Women.

CARMEN:
Women are objects,
Forced into roles.
Men are the bodies,

Women the souls
Our beauty demeaned
Even as we're extolled.
Women.

TOGETHER:

We're mighty tough women,
Still there's a big void.
These guys want to own us,
Even if we're destroyed.
So you and me, baby,
We're doing our thing.

KAREN:

I'm at the opera
Watchin' you sing,
Both of us lookin'
For somebody's ring.
Women.

Act II, Scene 2

At the rehearsal hall. Present are KAREN, DON, PLACIDO, CARMEN and JOSÉ.

MALINI: I assume you are the real José.

JOSÉ: Me?

MALINI: *(Sarcastically)* Yes, sir. You're the only one here I don't know. You're Carmen's boyfriend?

CARMEN: Yes, Maestro Malini. He is my corporal.

JOSÉ: I'm not a corporal.

CARMEN: Quiet, José. It's from the opera.

MALINI: Well, welcome Mr. José. I've never had so many outsiders in my rehearsals, but I guess it's a good thing. I think it has brought us good luck. Placido, I have very good news.

PLACIDO: What is that, Malini? What is your good news?

MALINI: Oh, it's very good news, Placido. I have been asked to be musical director for next season's performance of *Carmen*—at the Met!

PLACIDO, DON and KAREN: *(Shouting)* Bravo! Bravo!

MALINI: They have already signed Don José and Carmen, but they have asked me to choose my own Escamillo. And I have chosen you, Placido.

DON, KAREN, CARMEN and JOSÉ: Bravo!

PLACIDO: That is wonderful, Malini. I cannot believe it. It seems too good to be true.

MALINI: It is true, Placido. We're finally going to the Met. *(Everyone is excitedly and animatedly congratulating PLACIDO.)* Finally, Placido, you can bring your wife and children to New York.

(Everyone goes silent and stares at PLACIDO who gives an elongated pantomime shrug.)

MALINI: Did I say the wrong thing?

PLACIDO: No, you did not say the wrong thing. It is very good news to share with my friends.

CARMEN: *(Grabbing PLACIDO's hands)* What is her name, you rogue baritone? And what are the children's names?

MALINI: Would you all mind if we did a little work today? We have an opening tomorrow. *(PLACIDO and CARMEN embrace.)* Let's do the final scene. I need one more look at it. Karen and Placido begin with the duet. I'll do Frasquita and Mercedes. Placido and Karen enter stage left.

(They move into stage positions. The opening music begins. The "setting" is a crowd scene taking place in a square in Seville, outside the bull ring. A bullfight is about to take place and there is great excitement in the imaginary crowd milling about. At last PLACIDO/ESCAMILLO appears, accompanied by a radiant and magnificently dressed KAREN/CARMEN.)

PLACIDO/ESCAMILLO: *(Sings)*
If you love me, Carmen
Then today, of all days,

You will be proud of me,
If you love me, if you love me.

(Duet)

KAREN/CARMEN:

    I am yours, Escamillo,
    And may God be my witness,
    I never loved a man with such passion before!

TOGETHER:

    How I love you, how I love you!

(PLACIDO/ESCAMILLO leaves. Following is spoken dialogue.)

MALINI as FRASQUITA: Carmen, a word of advice, don't stay here.

KAREN/CARMEN: And why, may I ask?

MALINI as MERCEDES: Don José is here! He's hiding among the crowd; look!

KAREN/CARMEN: Yes, I see him. But I'm not afraid of him. I'll wait for him here.

MALINI as MERCEDES: Carmen, believe me, take care!

KAREN/CARMEN: I'm not afraid of anything!

MALINI as FRASQUITA: Take care!

(The imaginary crowd enters the arena, and in withdrawing has "revealed" DON/JOSÉ, leaving him and KAREN/CARMEN alone downstage.)

(Duet and Final Chorus)

KAREN/CARMEN:

    José.

DON/JOSÉ:

    Carmen.

KAREN/CARMEN:

    Frasquita and Mercedes both told me you were near,
    That you would look for me.

And they even believe my life will be in danger.
But I have courage and decided to stay.

DON/JOSÉ: *(Gently)*

I do not mean you harm.
I beg you, I implore you,
What used to be is done,
The past is dead, it is over.
Yes, we'll start life anew.
It will be a new existence,
Far away, just you and me.

KAREN/CARMEN:

You are talking like a dreamer.
I won't lie, I won't pretend!
What was between us is over;
Once and for all this is the end!
You know, I never lie,
Once and for all, this is goodbye!

DON/JOSÉ:

Carmen, oh let me persuade you,
Yes, life is still before you.
I beg of you, please, come away with me,
For I adore you.
(Passionately) Ah Carmen, come away with me,
We both can be happy still!

KAREN/CARMEN:

No, I have made my decision,
And I know that this is the hour.
But come what may, I do not care, no, no!
No. I will not give in to you.

DON/JOSÉ:

Carmen, life is still before you…

KAREN/CARMEN:

There's no use at all imploring,
My heart holds no love for you.

No, my love for you is dead.
I will not hear what you say.
There's no hope for you.
My love is dead, you hope in vain.
I won't go with you,
Never will!

DON/JOSÉ: *(Anxiously)*
You don't love me at all?

KAREN/CARMEN: *(Tranquilly)*
I love you no more.

DON/JOSÉ:
But I, I love you more than ever.
Carmen, I worship and adore you!

KAREN/CARMEN:
What's the good of that?
Your words are pointless now!

DON/JOSÉ:
Carmen, Carmen, I adore you!
Alright, I will remain an outlaw,
I'll rob and steal for you.
I will do anything, yes, all you ask,
If only you will come with me Carmen!
Those golden days, have you forgotten them?
How much we loved each other!
(With desperation) O Carmen, do not leave me now!

KAREN/CARMEN:
Carmen will never yield!
Free I was born, and free Carmen will die!

*(Hearing the cries of the crowd in the amphitheater applauding PLACIDO/
ESCAMILLO, KAREN/CARMEN makes a gesture of delight. DON/JOSÉ keeps his
eyes fixed on her. When KAREN/CARMEN attempts to enter the amphitheater
DON/JOSÉ steps in front of her. Musicians play through chorus part.)*

DON/JOSÉ:

Is it he?

KAREN/CARMEN:

Let me go!

DON/JOSÉ:

That is your fine new lover
Applauded by the mob!

KAREN/CARMEN:

Let me go, let me go!

DON/JOSÉ:

Never, never, you will not run to him!
Carmen, I'll make you follow me!

KAREN/CARMEN:

Let me go, Don José, I'll never go with you!

DON/JOSÉ:

You're on the way to him, Carmen.
(*Furiously*) You love this man?

KAREN/CARMEN:

I love him!
Defiant in the face of death,
With my dying breath,
I shall love him!

(*KAREN/CARMEN again tries to enter the amphitheater but is stopped by DON/JOSÉ. Strains of "The Toreador's Song" are heard.*)

DON/JOSÉ: (*Violently*)

And so I have lost my salvation.
I am damned to hell, so that you
May run to your lover, you harlot,
And in his arms jeer at my despair!
I swear to God you shall not go.
I say, you are coming with me!

KAREN/CARMEN:

   No, no, I won't!

DON/JOSÉ:

   Once again, time is getting short!

KAREN/CARMEN: *(Angrily)*

   Go ahead, kill me at once!

   Or let me go inside!

DON/JOSÉ: *(Madly)*

   For the very last time, Carmen!

   Will you come with me?

KAREN/CARMEN:

   No, no! *(Tears a ring from her finger.)*

   Remember this ring?

   The ring that you once gave me! Here! *(Throws ring away.)*

DON/JOSÉ: *(Rushing toward KAREN/CARMEN)*

   By God, then die!

JOSÉ: *(Jumps in between KAREN and DON. In a theatrical voice)* I am a police officer. There will be no killing while I'm around. And no one will hurt Karen.

   (The whole cast begins to laugh uproariously. JOSÉ and DON embrace.)

MALINI: *(In a feigned "directorial" voice)* What kind of rehearsal is this? At the
   Met I'm sure they'll respect tradition. Officer José, you cannot interrupt
   a rehearsal.

JOSÉ: I'm sorry, Maestro. But I am trained this way. And I love Karen.

MALINI: You love Karen? I thought you were Carmen's boyfriend.

CARMEN: He is. But he loves Karen.

DON: And I love Karen, too.

MALINI: And Miss Allen, who do you love?

KAREN: *(Laughing)* I love Don…though not Don José.

PLACIDO: And I love Carmen, but I also love my wife and children.

(Reprise: "Many Kinds of Love")

ALL: *(Sing)*

> You have changed me, too.
> To have this love for you
> Makes me something new.
> Makes me someone who
> Can sing a song
> I never knew.
> We never knew.

MALINI: *(Applauds)* Bravo! Carmen and José, you have very beautiful voices. How would you sing the end of this opera?

KAREN: Yes, sing your duet.

ALL: Yes, please.

(Reprise: "We Mean Forever")

CARMEN: *(Sings)*

> You and I,
> We're all about forever.
> 'Til we die,
> We'll never be apart.
> We met when we were only ten,
> Way back way back when,
> And I knew
> I could never be without you again.

JOSÉ:

> You and me,
> I agree we mean forever.
> It's a lifetime
> Never, never apart.
> We met when we were very small
> But even then we knew,
> It all
> Had to be
> Forever.

CARMEN:

> But I just needed a minute
> For myself,
> A minute for a fantasy
> A moment just for me to be
> Myself.

JOSÉ:

> I could see
> A reason for your moment
> And though it frightened me,
> I could never keep anything
> From you.
> So you did what you had to do.

TOGETHER:

> Now we'll always be together,
> Forever, together forever, together…

MALINI: Bravo!

(Everyone applauds, in a kind of a ruckus.)

DON: Maestro Malini and Placido, let me take you out for a drink to celebrate the wonderful news. *(He puts his arm around PLACIDO and exits, leaving KAREN, CARMEN and JOSÉ.)*

KAREN: I like your ending better.

CARMEN: But you sing the opera so beautifully.

JOSÉ: It is a very beautiful opera.

KAREN: And you live your life so beautifully.

(They embrace.)

CARMEN: Go home and rest for opening night. We'll see you tomorrow.

(KAREN exits slowly as JOSÉ and CARMEN embrace.)

))))

Beyond the Pale

Life Upon the
Wicked Stage

*B*eyond the Pale (1996) and *Life Upon the Wicked Stage* (1997) were written under different circumstances and for a different audience than the rest
of Fred Newman's plays. While the other scripts in this collection were created with the audiences of the Castillo Theatre in mind and were first produced there, these two short works were written for and presented at
annual meetings of the American Psychological Association (APA).

In these plays Newman's three decades of innovative work as the
founder of social therapy, the cultural performatory approach to emotional
pain and psychopathology; and his experimental work as a playwright and
director are most explicitly connected. *Beyond the Pale* and *Life Upon the
Wicked Stage* are written with psychologists in mind. They are performances
of (as distinct from explanations of) social therapy and its conceptual
underpinnings.

To the extent that they are teaching/learning tools, of all Newman's
work for the theatre they come the closest to Brecht's learning plays
(lehrstücke). Unlike Brecht (and Augusto Böal), however, Newman offers
no "lesson" and constructs no framework for "solutions." His "learning
plays" (he prefers to call them "learning-leading-development" plays) are
instead philosophical conversations between and among some of his
favorite thinkers.

Referring to the comparison with Brecht's learning plays in *The End of
Knowing: A New Developmental Way of Learning* (Routledge, 1997),
Newman and his colleague Lois Holzman write: "...for Brecht, the learning
play was a political tool designed to teach the audience members (and the
players) a new, cognitive way of understanding (a Marxist and/or communist way of understanding) a somewhat traditional moral-social situation.
The learning-leading-development play is not designed to be cognitive at
all, and surely not to teach a new way of *looking* at things. Rather, it is used
to have people experience a new way of *doing* things. It is the performance
of performance."

Beyond the Pale is the simpler of the two plays. Its premise is a social therapy session with Lev Vygotsky, the early Soviet developmental psychologist, and Ludwig Wittgenstein, the Vienna-born philosopher. Their therapist for this session of "couple counseling" is Bette Braun, a longtime social therapist trained by Newman (and playing herself in the original production). Vygotsky and Wittgenstein have been major influences on Newman's work in psychology, and *Beyond the Pale* is a performance of their relational activity within social therapy. For an in-depth discussion of the influence of Vygotsky and Wittgenstein on the development of social therapy and an exploration of the implications of their work for the emergence of a postmodern, unscientific psychology, see *The End of Knowing,* cited above, as well as two other books by Newman and Holzman—*Unscientific Psychology: A Cultural-Performatory Approach to Understanding Human Life* (Praeger, 1996), and *Lev Vygotsky: Revolutionary Scientist* (Routledge, 1993).

Beyond the Pale was first presented in Toronto in August of 1996 at the 104th Annual Convention of the American Psychological Association as part of a symposium entitled "Performative Psychology Redux."

•

The setting of *Life Upon the Wicked Stage,* the longer and more complex of these two learning-leading-development plays, is a cafe in Geneva at which some of the seminal figures of the 20th century meet and talk, in various combinations. The exiled Russian revolutionaries V.I. Lenin and Leon Trotsky appear here in a very different setting, but with many of the same characteristics they displayed in *Lenin's Breakdown.* Lev Vygotsky also reappears, this time only 19 years old and paired off with Jean Piaget, a founding father of modern developmental psychology. Wittgenstein, who not only makes a reluctant appearance in *Beyond the Pale* but is the main character in Newman's 1994 farce *Outing Wittgenstein,* makes his third appearance in a Newman script—here on his way to fight in the First World War—and carries on conversations with both Franz Kafka and Sigmund Freud. Vygotsky and Piaget, who held very different views about the nature of learning and development, bring this string of fanciful philosophical conversations to an end by tap-dancing together—while disagreeing strenuously about the nature of the tap-dancing activity. The seven characters in *Life Upon the Wicked Stage* are played by two actors, whose transformation from character to character—by means of various costumes, wigs, beards, physical stances, facial expressions, etc.—is meant to be visible to the audience. The performance of the performance is central to the production.

Each conversation is introduced by offstage narration which connects the conversations to each other and to a late 20th-century audience presumably concerned with the failure of modernism (in all its guises) to sustain human development. For the second production of the play (performed at Performance of a Lifetime in November and December of 1997), Newman turned the narrator (originally a disembodied voice functioning as a deliberate residual of the academic paper) into Sir Malcolm Muckerex, the stuffy PBS-style television host who had first appeared in *Off-Broadway Melodies of 1592.* Muckerex is not, like Madison Hemings in *Sally and Tom,* the voice of history. He is, rather, the voice of an academic historian (or at least Newman's satirical take on an academic historian)—full of himself and totally unaware of the limitations and failures of his interpretive activity. Even as Muckerex serves as a link between the play and the audience, he is also a farcical embodiment of Newman's critique of the pomposity of academic discourse, and thus a friendly nod to the audience itself.

Life Upon the Wicked Stage contains a number of "inside" jokes; to be fully appreciated, they require some knowledge of history, psychology and philosophy. For example, the reference to the "seal car" of the Swiss National Circus in which Trotsky proposes to smuggle Lenin back into Russia is a play on the "sealed car" in which the Germans helped to smuggle Lenin into St. Petersburg in 1917. The argument between Vygotsky and Piaget over the name of the street where they are supposed to meet ("Stage Street" or "Zone Street") is based on one of the major differences between them. Piaget's view, which remains dominant in the field of developmental psychology, holds that human development takes place in a fixed set of predetermined stages. Vygotsky held to a more fluid, transformational view, maintaining that human development is a social/performatory activity with no fixed stages and no necessary limit. He called the social activity through which this open-ended development occurs the "zone of proximal development." The "language games" which Kafka mentions casually to Wittgenstein refer to a key concept in the philosopher's later writings. Although the jokes are made with a specific audience in mind, there is much to enjoy and learn from in these performances whether one gets the jokes or not.

Life Upon the Wicked Stage was performed in Chicago at the 105th Annual Convention of the American Psychological Association in August 1997, at a special session sponsored by the APA Committee on Film and Other Media. An audience of 450 psychologists saw the play, the largest audience for a single performance of a Newman play to date. It went on to a limited run at Performance of a Lifetime, the performance school that grew out of the Castillo Theatre in the SoHo area of Manhattan, in November/December of 1997.

Unencumbered by the need to tell a story or acknowledge any other theatre conventions in *Beyond the Pale* and *Life Upon the Wicked Stage,* Fred Newman, philosopher, simply brings us philosophical conversations. Writing of *Beyond the Pale* in *The End of Knowing,* Newman and Holzman summarize the spirit informing not only these two plays but all of Newman's work for the stage. "It is designed to remind us, through the performance of it," they write, "that we are *performers* of varied conversations—not truth workers or tellers, or object describers, but revolutionary tool-and-result activity makers."

D.F.

Beyond the Pale was first produced by the East Side Institute for Short Term Psychotherapy at the Castillo Theatre in New York City in August 1996. The cast was as follows:

BETTE BRAUN . . . . Herself
LEV VYGOTSKY . . . . Roger Grunwald
LUDWIG WITTGENSTEIN . . . . David Nackman

Fred Newman, director; Diane Stiles, producer; Charlotte, costume design. Presented in Toronto, Ontario at the 104th Annual Convention of the American Psychological Association on August 9, 1996 as part of a symposium entitled "Performative Psychology Redux."

CHARACTERS
(in order of appearance)

BETTE BRAUN
LEV VYGOTSKY
LUDWIG WITTGENSTEIN

BETTE BRAUN, a social therapist, is seated in chair in her office as LEV VYGOTSKY and LUDWIG WITTGENSTEIN enter. She rises to welcome them.

BRAUN: Good afternoon, gentlemen…Please, have a seat. *(They nod and sit.)* Well…What can I do for you?

(Pause.)

VYGOTSKY: *(Somewhat hesitantly)* Miss Braun…is that correct…is that how you say your name? Is it "Miss"?

BRAUN: Yes…That's fine, Dr. Vygotsky.

VYGOTSKY: *(Hesitant)* Well, Miss Braun, Dr. Wittgenstein *(gesturing to WITTGENSTEIN)*…Dr. Wittgenstein and I have a somewhat unusual… "presenting problem."

BRAUN: And what is that, Dr. Vygotsky?

WITTGENSTEIN: *(Clipped and critical)* He is too slow, Dr. Braun…too polite. Here's the problem. Vygotsky and I never knew each other when we were alive. He died in the '30s. I died in the '50s. *Now*…40 years later —*against* our will—we have been brought together—"synthesized"— by a number of people including, I am told, two Americans named Newman and Holzman, whom I understand trained *you* in this performatory therapeutic method you call social therapy.

VYGOTSKY: *(Calming WITTGENSTEIN down)* Don't be so harsh, Ludwig. Don't be so harsh. You see, Miss Braun, it's not that we don't like each other. Dr. Wittgenstein is a brilliant philosopher and he has written extensively about the philosophical foundations of psychology. We agree on a great deal.

BRAUN: Then what's the problem?

WITTGENSTEIN: *(Harshly)* The problem, Braun, is that we didn't agree to be put together.

VYGOTSKY: You know, Miss Braun, we each have our...well...our egos... and...well...

WITTGENSTEIN: Say it already, Lev. This is a short session! Spit it out, Lev.

VYGOTSKY: *(Shaking his head at WITTGENSTEIN)* Quiet, Ludwig. *(To BRAUN.)* Well...we feel we should have been asked before we were synthesized. Do you know what I mean?

BRAUN: I do. Dr. Vygotsky. I certainly do.

VYGOTSKY: *(Smiling and shaking his head somewhat shyly and childishly)* Call me Lev, Miss Braun. I prefer it.

WITTGENSTEIN: What? Miss Braun, Dr. Vygotsky is one of the great psychologists of our age. I hope you appreciate that. I do not think it appropriate for you to call him Lev!

VYGOTSKY: Ludwig, Ludwig. Still a stuffy Viennese aristocrat on such matters. *(To BRAUN.)* Call me Lev.

WITTGENSTEIN: *(Sighing disgustedly)* Oh—you communists! You communists. *(Facetiously.)* Braun, why don't you call him comrade? *(He turns away.)*

BRAUN: *(With a smile)* I see there are things you don't agree on. Lev...I like how that sounds...Lev, let me ask you this: How could Newman and Holzman and others have asked you two about how you felt about being "synthesized"? You were both dead long before they got together to write about you.

WITTGENSTEIN: *(Turning back toward BRAUN confrontationally)* Then they should have left us alone! Don't you postmodernists...that's the right word, isn't it...don't you postmodernists believe in "Rest in Peace"? No one understands what I was saying. No one even understood when I was alive. I want my work left alone. It is not systemizeable. It is not synthesizeable.

VYGOTSKY: I do not feel the same way that Dr. Wittgenstein does. I am eager to see my work continued...or "completed" as I sometimes used that term and concept. But I feel concerned that this synthesis with Wittgenstein's work might...er, well, shall we say...might water down what both he and I have to say.

WITTGENSTEIN: Might? No! Must! Synthesizing and systematizing are inseparable. My work is therapeutic. It is addressed to specific linguistic philosophical pathologies. It is not meant to be generalized upon. With all due respect, Dr. Vygotsky, you were a system builder; a brilliant one, no doubt, but still a systematizer. You are, after all, a Marxist. You were eager to create a systematic psychology. I was convinced there could be no such thing. We cannot be put together. We cannot be synthesized. Newman and Holzman are opportunists; frauds; phrase makers—not real thinkers. They make even more metaphysical mist than already exists. They are—shall we say—mystifiers.

VYGOTSKY: I am sorry, Miss Braun…

BRAUN: Please, Lev, call me Bette…if you like.

WITTGENSTEIN: *(Disgusted)* This is too friendly for my taste!

VYGOTSKY: *(Motions to WITTGENSTEIN to keep quiet)* I am not interested in insulting Newman and Holzman. I do not even know them…Bette. *(He stares at WITTGENSTEIN.)*

BRAUN: Perhaps, Lev, you are more concerned with…Dr. Wittgenstein than you are with Newman and Holzman?

(VYGOTSKY nods.)

WITTGENSTEIN: Is this a therapeutic trick, Dr. Braun? Are you trying to turn Vygotsky and me against each other to protect your mentors Newman and Holzman?

BRAUN: Not at all, Dr. Wittgenstein. You two are no more opposites— antagonists—than you are the same—synthesizeable. Putting you together doesn't make you one. From Newman and Holzman's per- spective—as I understand it—you two have always been together. It was only our individuated and institutionalized way of characterizing matters that appeared to separate you. In history, if you will, you are not simply related—you are relational—relational activity. Newman and Holzman didn't "bring you together"; societal, institutional labeling "kept you apart."

WITTGENSTEIN: This is a semantical trick, Braun.

BRAUN: Perhaps, Dr. Wittgenstein, it is a new language game?

VYGOTSKY: *(Laughs loudly)* That's a good one, Ludwig, don't you think? She …Bette…is clever. *(Laughs.)* A language game. *(To BRAUN.)* Did you make that up, Bette? This language game idea is a concept of yours?

BRAUN: No. No, Lev. It is Dr. Wittgenstein's.

VYGOTSKY: YES! Wittgenstein…was this in the *Tractatus*?

WITTGENSTEIN: No, Vygotsky. It was in my *Philosophical Investigations*— published after I died…and long after you died.

VYGOTSKY: And what is a language game, Wittgenstein? How is it played? What kind of play are we talking about here?

WITTGENSTEIN: *(Somewhat begrudgingly)* It is a philosophical game meant to help one see the activistic origins of language. Not so much to clarify the use of language in societal communication and surely not to expose the abstract propositional meaning of language—I rejected that stupid earlier idea of mine completely—but to show the…

VYGOTSKY: *(Interrupts)*…historical activity of language. Yes?

WITTGENSTEIN: You could say that.

VYGOTSKY: So then language…and/or the learning of language…is rooted in play; the playing of games.

WITTGENSTEIN: You have written a good deal about play, yes?

VYGOTSKY: I have.

WITTGENSTEIN: But play is not so systematic, Vygotsky. It is more cultural than scientific.

VYGOTSKY: That is certainly true. Many rules of play do not exist antecedent to the game but emerge in the playing of the game.

WITTGENSTEIN: Good. Very good, Vygotsky. Then games, including language games and, therefore, including language itself, are not systematic in the traditional sense of being understood or explainable in terms of pre-existing rules or laws?

VYGOTSKY: Play and work are quite alike in this way. They both create something qualitatively new in their process—something that wasn't there before and therefore cannot be understood simply in terms of things that were there before, i.e., reductionistically.

WITTGENSTEIN: That sounds a little too Marxist for me, Vygotsky.

VYGOTSKY: Use your own language, Ludwig. It makes no difference to me as long as we understand what language is—and what it isn't. Language—more precisely speaking (or writing)—doesn't express anything; thoughts, judgments, feelings, intentions, whatever. Rather, it completes the unified process that is thinking/speaking.

BRAUN: This is a very fine performance, you two. I am honored to watch Lev Vygotsky and Ludwig Wittgenstein working—and playing—together.

WITTGENSTEIN: A fine performance of what?

BRAUN: A fine performance of Lev Vygotsky and Ludwig Wittgenstein speaking to each other and creating a new understanding.

VYGOTSKY: Yes, it is, Ludwig. And I rather enjoy it. Moreover, I do not think either of us is "violated" in this process.

WITTGENSTEIN: It is clever, Braun, I grant you that. But, of course, it is a hoax. For as you and I both know I am not *really* Wittgenstein and he is not *really* Vygotsky...I assume you are really Braun.

BRAUN: You are right, Dr. Wittgenstein. But why must you *really* be Wittgenstein and he *really* be Vygotsky for Wittgenstein and Vygotsky to be working and playing together? Performance, after all, is always about being who we are not. And, Lev, isn't that what "learning which leads development" is all about?

VYGOTSKY: But that is for discreet individuals.

BRAUN: But can't others complete for us in the zone of proximal development—the ZPD?

WITTGENSTEIN: ZPD? Is this a concept of yours, Braun?

BRAUN: No. It isn't, Dr. Wittgenstein. It's Vygotsky's.

VYGOTSKY: What are you saying, Braun; that ZPD's might...might include *dead* people?

BRAUN: And why not? If it can include various people at differing levels of development then why not dead people? Isn't a ZPD more historical than societal?

VYGOTSKY: And performing is how we continuously *complete* and create culture?

BRAUN: Yes. Not a synthesis, an activity—a social relational *completion*; a revolutionary activity.

WITTGENSTEIN: *(Excitedly)* A new form of life—as I put it!

BRAUN: Yes, Dr. Wittgenstein, a new form of life.

WITTGENSTEIN: In your…social therapy…people actually create new *forms of life*?

BRAUN: Indeed. By "moving about and around"…old forms of life. If you will permit me, Dr. Wittgenstein, by moving about and around *alienated* forms of life.

WITTGENSTEIN: Oh, how you Marxists *fetishize* that word *"alienation."* (*BRAUN and VYGOTSKY laugh.*) So even though I am not *really* Wittgenstein and he is not *really* Vygotsky, we can further develop Wittgenstein and Vygotsky?

VYGOTSKY: And if we can, why can't Newman and Holzman?

WITTGENSTEIN: Who wrote this damned script anyway? Who created this play?

BRAUN: Newman wrote the script. We created the play.

VYGOTSKY: It's clever, Ludwig. It's clever.

WITTGENSTEIN: Perhaps, Lev. But, Braun, does it work when it isn't scripted?

BRAUN: I think so. That's my experience with it. Whether scripted or improvised we can always perform.

VYGOTSKY: It is at once a tool *and* a result, as I used to say. It is a *practice of method.*

WITTGENSTEIN: Practice of method. Did you make that up, too, Vygotsky?

BRAUN: No. That's Newman and Holzman's.

WITTGENSTEIN: I like practice of method. This approach is truly beyond psychology—beyond the pale.

VYGOTSKY: I came from beyond the Pale, Ludwig. I am a Russian Jew.

WITTGENSTEIN: I know, Lev. I know. My family abandoned Judaism. I was raised a Catholic—a wealthy Viennese Catholic.

BRAUN: I'm from Dayton…And we're all in Toronto. Labels are funny, aren't they? They can also be dreadfully destructive. Well, gentlemen, have I made the problem vanish? (*VYGOTSKY and WITTGENSTEIN laugh loudly. BRAUN stands; so do they.*) Good, because we are out of time.

(*They all turn to audience and bow.*)

))))

Life Upon the Wicked Stage was first produced by the East Side Institute for Short Term Psychotherapy on August 8, 1997. The version presented here was produced at Performance of a Lifetime in New York City in November 1997. The cast was as follows:

LEV VYGOTSKY, V.I. LENINE,
FRANZ KAFKA, SIGMUND FREUD .... Roger Grunwald

JEAN PIAGET, LEON TROTSKY,
LUDWIG WITTGENSTEIN .... David Nackman

SIR MALCOLM MUCKEREX (OFFSTAGE) .... Allen Cox

Fred Newman, director; Nancy Green, producer; Diane Stiles, production coordinator; Ann Amendolagine, tap choreography; Charlotte, costume design. Presented in Chicago, Illinois at the 105th Annual Convention of the American Psychological Association on August 16, 1997 at a special session sponsored by the APA Committee on Film and Other Media.

CHARACTERS

LEV VYGOTSKY
JEAN PIAGET
V.I. LENINE
LEON TROTSKY
FRANZ KAFKA
LUDWIG WITTGENSTEIN
SIGMUND FREUD

Offstage (taped)
ANNOUNCER
SIR MALCOLM MUCKEREX

Prologue

JEAN PIAGET and LEV VYGOTSKY sit frozen at a small cafe table as the song "Life Upon the Wicked Stage" from Showboat *plays. They slowly become animated, stand, and do a tap dance to the music. Then they sit, and engage in silent, animated conversation, until the music ends and the lights fade.*

Scene 1

ANNOUNCER: History Theatre. Your host: Sir Malcolm Muckerex.

MUCKEREX: The world is a wicked stage upon which we all perform our lives. The paradox of people trying to perform decent lives on a wicked stage sometimes becomes overwhelming. So with modernism, which in the early years of this century generated achievements of almost unbelievable magnificence, even as the stage for the remainder of the century was being built—a set for 50 years of devastating warfare. But although the stage is wicked it does not follow that life is wicked. Modernism's failure has been brought about by the inability of genius to make a better world for all. World War I, the War To End All Wars, turned out to be the beginnings of a new level of human atrocities. Yet the pre-World War I period was an exceedingly optimistic moment of great scientific, technological and humanist accomplishment. It was a time of great and powerful thinkers creating and dialoguing on great and powerful ideas. It was a time of exiles debating these great ideas within the growing intellectual urban centers. Often the setting for such dialogue was not the formal environment of the university, but the street cafe or the dingy, cigarette smoke-filled restaurant. These settings turned out to be the unknown and unheard-of sites of new developments; the wicked off-Main Street stages on which was exposed the paradox of the greatness of modernism and its inability to change a wicked world. A small sidewalk cafe in Geneva, Switzerland; the early summer of 1916.

(Enter LENINE and TROTSKY. They sit at the cafe table.)

LENINE: I did not know you would come here, Leon. I was led to believe you would remain in America until the time was ripe.

TROTSKY: The time might well be ripe today, Comrade Lenine. Combined and uneven development governs history all the time. And in a histori-cal moment such as this matters can leap forward in what we, overde-termined in our thinking by the temporal mode of society, call a week or a fortnight, Comrade Lenine.

LENINE: Yes, Comrade Trotsky, you are right—as always. I also think the conditions for revolution are more ripe than meets the eye. Though, as you know, I have never felt completely comfortable with your theory of combined and uneven development.

TROTSKY: And why not?

LENINE: I suppose I am not completely at ease with any *psychological* notion of development—not yours or Freud's or anyone else's for that matter. I am concerned that the historicalness, the sensuousness of Marx's notion of dialectics is in some ways corroded by these psychological notions of development that now consume so many bourgeois thinkers as well as yourself.

TROTSKY: Comrade Lenine, are you calling me a bourgeois thinker?

LENINE: Leon, Leon, don't be so sensitive. All of us are bourgeois thinkers. We live still in a bourgeois world. My concern is that our bourgeois thoughts not *totally* overdetermine our actions. I am constantly touched and motivated by the stories of Marx's reactions to the Paris Commune; his immediate and intense support for the communards in the face of his stern opposition before the commune began. So, in my view, must our actions be more determining than our words. Leon, I fear most of all the brilliance and purity of your thought. You might well be as much a danger for your being right about everything as other Bolshevik leaders are for being wrong about everything.

TROTSKY: Lenine, Lenine, Lenine, Marx was first and foremost a scientist.

LENINE: No. No, never. He was first and foremost a revolutionary.

TROTSKY: Well then, enough of this gibberish. What is to be done? The Western world is at war and so is Mother Russia. Our people are dying in droves. We cannot afford to sit here in a cafe in Geneva. I'm sure we both agree on that. What is to be done? I've come here from the Bronx, New York—in America—to find out what is to be done? My theory of combined and uneven development does not tell me that. You, my leader, V.I. Lenine, must do so.

LENINE: I do not know what to do. I sit here in Geneva day after day re-reading Hegel's *Logic* like a school boy preparing for an examination. But I do not know what to do.

TROTSKY: This must be a result of your extended stay in Western Europe. Everywhere there are brilliant theories of how to understand everything —but their world is not working. Not even the social democrats here know what to do. Kautsky creates theories, theories, theories, and betrayals in action every day. But we are Russians. We are making a revolution. You must know what to do.

LENINE: But I don't, Leon! I don't.

TROTSKY: Then you must return to Russia.

LENINE: Easier said than done, Leon. I am nowadays easily recognized even in disguise.

TROTSKY: *(Thinking hard)* Maybe I can help. I have a friend here in Geneva. He is a ringmaster in the Swiss National Circus and he told me yesterday, they are going to St. Petersburg next February.

LENINE: The Swiss Circus?

TROTSKY: Yes. I'm sure you've heard of them. They are famous the world over for their trained seals. He said he could get me or a couple of Bolshevikis back to St. Petersburg in one of the seal cars. It would be smelly but safe.

LENINE: *(Laughs)* And what will the headlines say: Lenine returns to St. Petersburg on seal train.

TROTSKY: You will make something positive of it, Comrade Lenine. You are our very best propagandist.

LENINE: I like it, Leon. I like it. You will put me in touch with your seal man.

TROTSKY: *(Nods)* Yes.

Scene 2

MUCKEREX: We choose to fictionalize matters altogether. We have our characters come together as their total historical becomings, rather than presenting them in their space-time straitjackets. Lenin and Trotsky abandoned their table at around 5:30 in the afternoon. They are quickly replaced on the historical performatory stage by Jean Piaget and Lev Vygotsky. They never met, you say? Good. Here they can meet! They were only 19, you say—both having been born the same year, 1896, but never having seen each other in their entire lifetimes? Again, you are right. But this is only a story.

Truth was a passion for our civilization in the early years of this century. But we now know that passion, not truth, ruled the day. Our postmodern story continues with the meeting of Piaget and Vygotsky in Geneva, 1916 on June 19 at 5:45 p.m.

(Enter JEAN PIAGET in his late teens, dressed like a student, carrying books. He sits down at the table and starts to read. LEV VYGOTSKY enters, also looking like a student. He looks around trying to find a seat and finally comes over to PIAGET's table, seeing no other place to be seated.)

VYGOTSKY: Might I join you? There appear to be no other tables available.

PIAGET: *(Stands and extends his hand)* Oh, of course. Please. My name is Jean Piaget.

VYGOTSKY: *(Shaking hands)* Thank you so much. I am Lev Vygotsky.

(They sit.)

PIAGET: I take it you are not from Switzerland.

VYGOTSKY: Oh, no. I am not from Switzerland. I am from Russia—Gomel. I am here on spring break from the university. And you?

PIAGET: Yes. Yes, I *am* from Switzerland, though also on spring break from the university. *(Pause.)* What is happening in Russia? Things seem so chaotic. I heard Lenine speak at a forum the other night. But I could tell nothing from what he said. He is such a fanatic. And there is a rumor going about that Trotsky is in the city. Do you follow Lenine or Trotsky? Are you a leftist? Or should I not ask?

VYGOTSKY: No, No. Please. It's quite alright. Yes, indeed I am a leftist—a Marxist. And I would say I follow Lenine and Trotsky and the Bolsheviki line. But I have not been active. I have been studying in school mainly. Trotsky is very popular in Gomel where there are many Jews. He is a Jew, you know.

PIAGET: I did not know. I am not so political. Switzerland is a peculiar place. In many ways we have no politics. We are a kind of permanent neutral state in Western Europe—a home to exiles of every variety. It makes us all too neutral in every respect. But what can I do? We are put wherever we are put. And our place on the world stage determines the role.

VYGOTSKY: Perhaps. Perhaps you are right. Perhaps my place in Russia makes me a revolutionary. But I do not feel comfortable with the passivity of your observation.

PIAGET: Nor do I. Nor do I. But I am afraid it's so. We are, after all, animals not unlike the lower phyla. We transform as they do. In stages. In accordance with relatively rigid biological laws. And, I suspect, laws determining stages of consciousness which we merely have not yet discovered.

VYGOTSKY: And culture?

PIAGET: Not so much of a factor, I think. *(Pause.)* But, listen, speaking of culture, I have two tickets to a play this evening. Chekhov. Do you like Chekhov? You must. *(Smiling.)* He is a Russian.

VYGOTSKY: I do like him very much. But I do know many Russians who hate him. Yes I would love to join you. It's nice of you to invite me. Maybe this bit of Russian culture can have more of an impact than you think possible. Where is the theatre? And when does the play begin?

PIAGET: It is at the Leo Tolstoy Theatre. Downtown. At eight.

VYGOTSKY: Really? I was there just yesterday. To a photographic exhibition. It's on that small curvy street, right off of the main square in the center of town...right next to the post office. Yes, I remember it well. It's on something called Zone Street, isn't that right?

PIAGET: You have a good memory, Lev Vygotsky. But actually that street is called Stage Street.

VYGOTSKY: No, no I am certain. It's Zone.

PIAGET: Lev, I have lived here all my life. It's Stage Street. I am absolutely certain. Stage. Stage Street.

VYGOTSKY: Do the tickets say? I am certain it is Zone, Jean.

(*PIAGET pulls out tickets.*)

PIAGET: It does not say. As you know, it is not a very formal theatre.

VYGOTSKY: Well, I am absolutely certain it is Zone Street.

PIAGET: (*Slightly frustrated*) Well, Vygotsky. You go to your Zone Street Theatre and I'll go to my Stage Street Theatre and if we both wind up at the same place, we'll see the play together. But now I must be going. I have a prior meeting. I hope we see each other again.

(*PIAGET exits.*)

Scene 3

MUCKEREX: The world of 1916 was a strange mixture of optimism and pessimism. In Europe, dying monarchism and unborn communism mixed to form a confusion that was not easily articulated. Real politics, which have no capacity to deal with the subtleties of history, resolves these contradictions by bureaucratic means and ultimately by the most extreme of bureaucratic moves—war. But those thinkers, famous and ordinary, for whom war was not a serious or moral solution—those who identified these confusions as more cultural or more psychological or more historical and less in terms of the game playing of nation states— they searched the fields of science and the humanities, of literature and music, of philosophy and theatre, more generally of culture, to better understand what was going on. Our table hosts still another conversation on that summer day in 1916.

(*FRANZ KAFKA is seated at the table as WITTGENSTEIN wanders aimlessly— with a knapsack on his back.*)

KAFKA: Ludwig. Ludwig Wittgenstein.

(*WITTGENSTEIN looks around bemusedly until he sees who is calling him.*)

KAFKA: Kafka. Franz Kafka. (*He stands, reaches his hand out to WITTGENSTEIN.*) We met at a conference on aeronautics…in Prague…last summer.

WITTGENSTEIN: I remember, I think. Franz…uh…

KAFKA: Franz Kafka. Do you *really* remember?

WITTGENSTEIN: (*Stiffens*) I do not lie, Mr. Kafka. I do not lie.

KAFKA: No offense, Wittgenstein. I mistakenly thought you were being polite. I should have known better. Please have a seat.

WITTGENSTEIN: I was looking for Freud…Sigmund Freud. Do you know him? We had an appointment. He is a friend of my sister, Gretl…we are all from Vienna.

KAFKA: I do not know him, though I have heard of him. He is becoming quite famous. (*WITTGENSTEIN sits.*) Perhaps we could chat until he arrives. What are you up to these days, creating model airplanes, are you?

WITTGENSTEIN: No. I have given up aeronautics. I am just now completing a tractatus which shows positively the precise nature of language.

KAFKA: Impressive, Ludwig. I am impressed.

WITTGENSTEIN: There is a problem, Kafka.

KAFKA: And what is that?

WITTGENSTEIN: Language is not precise.

KAFKA: Then what have you shown?

WITTGENSTEIN: Either that I am wrong or that one can show something to be precise which isn't.

KAFKA: Well, I guess everything can be bureaucratized—even language. Everything can be shown to be what it isn't. Using language is a kind of game, don't you think, Ludwig?

WITTGENSTEIN: A game? What kind of game? What is a game?

KAFKA: There are endless kinds of games. Some are very precise; follow very clear rules. Others are like randomly moving about in a complex maze with no rules at all.

WITTGENSTEIN: What are you doing now, Kafka?

KAFKA: Oh, I'm still working as an accountant. But I've begun to think more and more about writing stories.

WITTGENSTEIN: Then you think writing stories is like playing a game with language?

KAFKA: Perhaps.

WITTGENSTEIN: There will be no rules in your stories?

KAFKA: I hope not. The stories are all about the endless rules of our bureau-cratized lives. And the alienation and madness created by living in such a world. But I hope my stories do not create still more rules.

WITTGENSTEIN: I'm returning home to enter the Austrian Army. I think I will carry my tractatus with me and see how it appears to me by war's end.

KAFKA: I hope it is not filled with bullets by the war's end. This is a stupid war. A wholly rule-governed game played by bureaucrats with the lives of young men.

WITTGENSTEIN: I agree. But I feel morally bound to participate on the side of my homeland.

KAFKA: Wittgenstein, you have only the duty of genius to consider. Your genius. Do not let them turn you into cannon fodder.

WITTGENSTEIN: I am not so sure as you are, Kafka, as to the nature of life. I cannot even discern the nature of mathematics and language and they're infinitely less complex than life. In any event, my family, in par-ticular my father, who is a wealthy man in Vienna, needs for me to ful-fill this obligation.

KAFKA: Do not die Wittgenstein. It would be a great waste.

WITTGENSTEIN: When the war is over I will think more about games. *(Looks offstage and points.)* Oh, there's Freud looking through the window.

(KAFKA turns, looks where WITTGENSTEIN is pointing.)

KAFKA: I'll go now. I'll tell Freud where you are as I leave. Have a good… what does he call it…?

WITTGENSTEIN: I don't know.

KAFKA: …session. *(Stands and starts offstage. Turning back to WITTGENSTEIN.)* Take care, Ludwig Wittgenstein. Do not let them squish you out like a roach. Take care. *(He exits.)*

Scene 4

MUCKEREX: Does the world determine the mind or does the mind determine the world? Modern psychology is born in this paradoxical quagmire. It is an old paradox, to be sure, but it is a new day. The mind-body dilemma appears quite different when the bodies are creating great technology and building more and more sophisticated elements of the wicked stage while the mind stays relatively the same. Geneva, June 19, 1916; 6:31 in the afternoon.

(Enter FREUD. WITTGENSTEIN stands.)

WITTGENSTEIN: Dr. Freud. Over here.

(FREUD recognizes him and heads toward the table extending his hand.)

FREUD: Ludwig. Ludwig Wittgenstein. I've not seen you for years. You've grown up. I have regards from your sister Gretl whom I saw just last week. *(Sits.)* What have you been studying?

WITTGENSTEIN: I've been studying the philosophy of mathematics and the philosophy of language. Do you know anything of that, Dr. Freud?

FREUD: Not a thing, Ludwig. Not a thing.

WITTGENSTEIN: What then is the relationship of the language of our dreams, the language of our unconscious, as you have called it, and the language of everyday life?

FREUD: I would say it is the same language, only it is used differently. And the pictures it conjures up are not so constrained by the representations language has in real life.

WITTGENSTEIN: Well, would that not eventually make the language itself different?

FREUD: I would suppose so, Ludwig. I have not thought as much about it as I probably should. But it seems quite important. Since in my opinion the language and structure of the mind, both conscious and unconscious, determine our understanding of the world. It would be important to better understand the language of the mind as part of understanding the activity of the mind.

WITTGENSTEIN: But what if the mind has no language? What if the mind determines, amongst other things, the language that we use in life without itself having a language?

FREUD: That might well be what I am saying. The mind might not need language for it has no one to talk to, save itself. Representing it as an inner conversation might just be the language that we use in reality imposing itself on the mind.

WITTGENSTEIN: And, in turn, this understanding of the mind in conversation might in turn be imposing itself on reality.

FREUD: You are too clever for me, Ludwig.

WITTGENSTEIN: I do not mean to be clever.

FREUD: I know, but you are. Does it seem a curse to you?

WITTGENSTEIN: No, not a curse, but a burden. Would your method of analysis help?

FREUD: I fear not. Brilliance is not psychopathology.

WITTGENSTEIN: Yet brilliance perhaps creates more pain than stupidity. Brilliance abounds in Europe and more generally in Western civilization. And yet it appears to be of little value in making our world work.

FREUD: It's hard to live a good life on so wicked a stage.

WITTGENSTEIN: But how could it have gotten to be so wicked on your theory?

FREUD: We are wicked, Ludwig. Not only wicked, but wicked enough.

WITTGENSTEIN: So yours is a theory about the wickedness of men?

FREUD: No, Ludwig. Mine is a theory about the workings of the mind of man, which surely must include its capacity for wickedness.

Scene 5

MUCKEREX: And so we live our lives on our wicked stage. Our performances are constrained by the theatre space. Or so it appears. Sometimes the performance almost seems to go beyond the stage. Sometimes in a story. Sometimes in a life performance. Many doubt that it can. It is the old paradox in its latest form.

(VYGOTSKY seated at the table. PIAGET enters. VYGOTSKY notices him and waves to him to come sit.)

VYGOTSKY: Piaget. Good to see you. I was hoping you would be here again today. Please sit. I must apologize for my pig-headedness yesterday. You, of course, were right. The Tolstoy Theatre is on Stage Street. I have been obsessed lately with zones. I do not understand it. My apologies.

PIAGET: What precisely is a zone?

VYGOTSKY: I don't know. Though so far as I can tell, it is the opposite of a stage. If you could tell me then exactly what a stage is, it might help me understand better what I am thinking.

PIAGET: A stage is a point in a temporal line. It is then, following Kant, a unit of time, of succession, necessary for perception. It is the *a priori something that comes next* in our experience of the world.

VYGOTSKY: And what of the experience of the transition itself? Is there not danger here of an infinite regress—a kind of Parmenidian paradox?

PIAGET: Such is our limitation, Vygotsky. As scientists. As students of our own selves and our world, we are limited by such categories of perception.

VYGOTSKY: Again, Jean Piaget, limitation. I think a zone is perhaps a rejection of limitation. It is a place from which becoming—transaction— can be studied and, simultaneously, lived.

PIAGET: This seems too Hegelian for me. A practical use. Give me a practical example.

VYGOTSKY: *(Long pause, thinking)* Tell me the strangest thing you do—you know—something you don't tell anyone about. I will not laugh! Please.

PIAGET: *(Thinks hard)* I tap-dance!

VYGOTSKY: *You tap-dance, too?*

PIAGET: *You are also a tap dancer?*

VYGOTSKY: Incredible. This must be what made us attractive to each other at first sight.

PIAGET: You dance in public?

VYGOTSKY: *Never.* I am in the tap-dance closet.

PIAGET: Me too. Me too…You think, perhaps, a zone is where embarrassed tap dancers hide out?

VYGOTSKY: *(Laughs)* Could be, Jean. Could be…We continue. How do you tap-dance?

PIAGET: Am I to show you? Right here…in public? Are we coming out, Lev?

VYGOTSKY: Why not? Let us tap-dance together. *Piaget* and *Vygotsky*—the tapping thinkers.

(Music comes up on chorus of "Life Upon the Wicked Stage." They tap-dance for about 30 seconds.)

VYGOTSKY: *(Stops the dancing)* Now tell me, Piaget, what have we just done? Let us study the relationship between what we have done and our characterization of what we have just done.

PIAGET: I have actually thought about this often…My understanding is that tapping begins in the feet. The feet move first and the rest of the body follows.

VYGOTSKY: Aha! To me nothing moves first. Everything moves at once; the body—not just the feet—taps. Our obsession with stages—with what comes first—distorts history where there is no beginning and no end. A zone, it seems to me, is a methodological construct for examining the processes of life and history as process. We must not make things stand still in order that they might be studied.

PIAGET: But what of objectivity, Vygotsky? The theatre, I must remind you, *was* on Stage Street. By the way, did you get to the theatre?

VYGOTSKY: No. I didn't. You neither? (*PIAGET shakes his head "no."*) I wound up at an informal discussion with Leon Trotsky at the Workers' Salon. He laid out his theory of combined and uneven development.

PIAGET: Did he tell you what is happening in Russia?

VYGOTSKY: No. He did not.

PIAGET: I went to have dinner with my mother and she would not permit me to leave. Besides, I was angry at you and didn't want to see you.

VYGOTSKY: We'll be talking about zones and stages for the rest of our lives, Piaget...you think?

PIAGET: But we will, I fear, never explain our strange meeting yesterday.

VYGOTSKY: Maybe it needs no explanation. We lived it. And we can communicate it to others as a story rather than an explanation.

PIAGET: *Piaget* and *Vygotsky*—the tap-dancing thinkers.

(*They laugh, and return to the table. "Life Upon the Wicked Stage" music plays again, and they converse animatedly with each other. Near the end of the song they again perform a tap dance, after which they embrace and bow.*)

))))

Salvador
(Fictional Conversations)

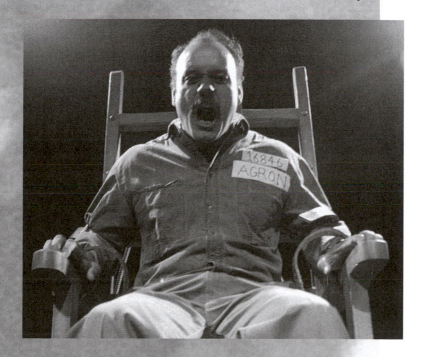

Salvador (Fictional Conversations) (1997) is, in my opinion, Newman's greatest love story to date.

It is the tale of a rather unlikely pair: Salvador Agron, an impoverished Puerto Rican kid from the barrio sentenced to the electric chair for the death of two white youths during a gang rumble, and Nancy Peck, a child of the middle-class, tree-lined, liberal streets of Queens, New York. What brings them together is politics. Each is profoundly affected by the social upheavals of the 1960s which create a space in history, temporary and remarkable, where these two people can fall in love.

Like *Risky Revolutionary* before it, *Salvador* is the story of two people struggling to change the world and in the process of that joint activity discovering their passionate love for one another. One of Newman's most original (and lovely) contributions to American dramatic literature is his portrayal onstage of love between political activists, who have largely been ignored, ridiculed or trivialized—depoliticized beyond recognition—by other American playwrights.

Salvador and Nancy and the energy, tenderness and wonder of their relationship are brought to the stage in a series of short monologues and scenes, giving the play the feel of an artist's sketch—the sketch of a master who knows and loves his models. Indeed, *Salvador* is based on a "true story" of which the playwright was a part. Newman knew Agron well, helped to secure his release from prison in 1979, and was the younger man's therapist, political colleague, and friend in the years following his release. The character of Nancy Peck is based on the real-life Gail Peck, who played a leading role in the Committee to Free Salvador Agron and was, as a character puts it in the play, Salvador's "one and only real love." Gail Peck has been Newman's friend and colleague for nearly 25 years. *Salvador* is not only a play that explores the love between Salvador and Gail; it is also an extension of the love Newman feels for both of them, their relationship and for all the poor people of the world who, like Salvador, have never had a chance to tell their own story.

While the script itself (particularly its video segments) provides the background to Salvador Agron's life, touching on them here may be helpful for comprehending the life behind (or perhaps more accurately, *within*) the play.

Salvador Agron was born in Mayaguez in Puerto Rico, where he spent much of his early childhood in a poorhouse. He came to New York City to live with his mother, one of a million other impoverished Puerto Ricans who migrated north between 1949 and 1959. At the age of nine, Salvador was sent to a reform school in upstate New York. Returning to the city, where his mother had married a puritanical Pentecostal minister, Salvador soon found himself living mostly on the streets. (By the age of 14 he had given up the pretense of going to school.)

Agron became a member of a Puerto Rican street gang called the Vampires. In late August of 1959 he was arrested, along with 12 other Puerto Rican young men, after a rumble in Hell's Kitchen (then a primarily Irish and Italian neighborhood) left two young white men dead. The sensationalist and racist press tried and convicted the 15-year-old Salvador— identifying him as the sinister "Capeman" from the black cape he wore— long before his case ever reached judge and jury.

Sentenced to die in the electric chair when he was 16, Agron was the youngest person ever condemned to death in the history of New York State. After his case became a liberal cause célèbre, with the governor of Puerto Rico and Eleanor Roosevelt adding their voices to the chorus of protest against Salvador's electrocution, in 1962 his sentence was commuted to life in prison by Governor Nelson Rockefeller.

Functionally illiterate when he entered prison, Salvador used his years behind bars to educate himself. He learned to read and write, earned his high school diploma, went on to achieve an associate's degree, and was working on a B.A. when he was finally released in 1979. He also educated himself politically; his experiences on the street and behind bars, fueled by the radical spirit of the times, transformed Agron into a self-described communist.

In the late '70s Salvador was searching for a way to contribute to an international revolution of the poor and oppressed when he met Fred Newman. At the time, the pioneers of Newman's development community were busy building the New York City Unemployed and Welfare Council, a union for welfare recipients which was seeking collective bargaining rights for its members. Word reached Agron at Greenhaven Correctional Facility that Newman's followers were leftists you could trust, people who actually did what they said they would do. He contacted them and requested their help in winning his freedom.

Newman and his fellow activists responded by forming the Committee to Free Salvador Agron. The Committee, whose most active members came from the Unemployed and Welfare Council, succeeded primarily because it was able to mobilize broad support for Agron within the working-class Puerto Rican and African American communities. The radical attorney William Kunstler (the basis for a character in *Salvador*) was enlisted in the battle, and events unfolded roughly as they are depicted in the play. Once Agron's freedom was secured he became active in the political tendency led by Newman, but gradually fell victim to despair and self-destructive behavior. In 1986, at the age of 42, Salvador Agron died.

With the play's subtitle, ("Fictional Conversations"), Newman goes out of his way to emphasize that this is not the "true" story of Salvador Agron. Further, Newman does not believe there can be such a thing as a "true" story. It is one of many possible stories. In fact, it is *another* Salvador Agron story that motivated Newman to write *his* version of Salvador's life.

Some three or four years after Agron's death, the singer-songwriter Paul Simon asked to meet with Newman. Simon was thinking of writing a musical about Agron and wanted to learn from those most directly involved about the fight to free him from prison and the last 10 years of his life. Simon held meetings with Newman and a handful of others, including Gail Peck. As articles about Simon's *The Capeman* began appearing in the press emphasizing the sensationalistic and violent aspects of the story and name, Newman grew uneasy.

In a letter to Simon sent in July of 1997, Newman wrote: "My concern is that...*The Capeman* will serve not only to trivialize and thereby present a distorted picture of Sal; it will also serve to perpetuate the caricature of inner-city youth as wild, asocial, and even subhuman creatures."

This play is Newman's response, not to Simon's script per se, which he hadn't seen when he wrote *Salvador,* but to the commercialization of Agron's life. *Salvador (Fictional Conversations)* is Newman's counterpoint to that activity.

Newman's play does not glorify Agron; in fact, some have found Sal's character, as written here, unattractive, even offensive. If *Salvador* makes any political statement about Agron, it is about the corrosive effect of poverty on his life—and, by implication, on the lives of the tens of millions of others who find themselves at the bottom of the "New World Order."

Salvador (Fictional Conversations) juxtaposes 14 scenes for live actors with 11 video sequences. The first eight scenes are essentially monologues, short dramatic poems/character sketches, in which the four principal characters are introduced. Their lives then begin to interweave. In the last scene of the play the tone shifts abruptly to the fanciful and ridiculous, with Agron and Kunstler coming back from the dead. This scene liberates Agron from the burdens and restrictions he faced in life; the playful, joyous, naive Salvador of the last scene drives home the tragedy of his inability, in life, to overcome the debilitating effects of poverty. And, with its radical transformation of tone and content, this scene serves to undercut the tragic "resolution" of the previous one. Like the last scene in *Stealin' Home*, it challenges and changes everything that preceded it.

Structurally, *Salvador* is Newman's most "Brechtian" full-length play. While it tells a linear story spanning some 38 years, it does so not in the condensed and causal manner of the realistic "well-made play" but, like the plays of Brecht (and Shakespeare before him), by showing only those scenes in which decisions are made and/or key turns in the conflict take place. Newman's use of video here closely resembles the epic theatre technique of using film, slides, and projections to provide historical background and "open up" the dramatic action to the larger social, economic and historical factors shaping the story onstage.

The play ends, Newman-style, with its conflicts unresolved; in the final scene two "dead" people (Agron and Kunstler) converse with two "live" ones (Simon and Peck). Although the love of Nancy and Sal couldn't survive the destructive pressures of poverty, it does survive death.

Salvador (Fictional Conversations) was produced at the Castillo Theatre in September of 1997 under the direction of Newman and this writer.

D.F.

Salvador (Fictional Conversations) was first produced at the Castillo Theatre (Fred Newman, artistic director; Gabrielle Kurlander, producing director; Diane Stiles, managing director) in New York City on September 19, 1997. The cast, in order of appearance, was as follows:

EXECUTIONER (OFFSTAGE) . . . . Roger Grunwald
SALVADOR . . . . Rafael Mendez
RADIO ANNOUNCER (RECORDED) . . . . Kenneth Hughes
NARRATOR (ON VIDEO) . . . . Jeremy Black
A (OFFSTAGE) . . . . Randy Balan
B (OFFSTAGE) . . . . Doug Miranda
C (OFFSTAGE) . . . . David Nackman
NANCY PECK . . . . Diane Stiles
NANCY'S MOTHER (OFFSTAGE) . . . . Marian Rich
PAUL SIMON . . . . David Nackman
JUDGE HOFFMAN (OFFSTAGE) . . . . David Nackman
WILLIAM KUNSTLER . . . . Roger Grunwald
BAILIFF (RECORDED) . . . . Arthur Rubin
HARRY KRESKY (ON VIDEO) . . . . Himself
NEWSCASTER #1 (ON VIDEO) . . . . Andrew Chernack
NEWSCASTER #2 (ON VIDEO) . . . . Cecilia Salvatierra
NEWSCASTER #3 (ON VIDEO) . . . . Lisa Linnen
NEWSCASTER #4 (ON VIDEO) . . . . J.B. Opdycke

Fred Newman and Dan Friedman, directors; Jim Horton, producer; Joseph Spirito, set design; Charlotte, costume design; Charlie Spickler, lighting design; Michael Klein, sound design; Barry Z Levine, video design/cinematography; Brenda Ratliff, production stage manager.

Salvador Agron was my friend, my political associate and, for a time, my therapy client. I had worked with many others—most notably, Gail Peck, Harry Kresky, and members of the New York City Unemployed and Welfare Council (led by Alma Brooks, Neter Brooks, John Cummings, Vera Hill, James Scott and Lorraine Stevens) to free him from prison. He finally made it out (after complex legal and political hassles having to do with his so-called "absconding" depicted in my play) in early November of 1979. It was then that Sal and I became friends. He would come to my therapy office (then located at 102nd Street and West End Avenue) and we would walk together for an hour or so in Riverside Park. Sal would speak poetically and politically about himself. And he would ask me to do the same. And while our lives were quite different, there were many shared experiences—largely having to do with poverty and how we had each dealt with it.

The poor in America have no voice. Others (with a variety of agendas, from the ethically virtuous to the most morally and politically corrupt) will speak on their behalf. But the poor rarely, if ever, speak for themselves. Perhaps the unemployed councils of the 1930s were as close as they ever came. But it took a great depression, in which millions who had jobs rapidly became jobless, to make that happen. And as soon as union organizing began to gather momentum, the poor—the chronically poor—were left in their silent misery, even by the unions they worked so hard to create.

Poverty has always been related to in our society as having to do with a relatively small number of people and, at the same time, as a necessary evil of our system. These days crime is the issue of popular concern precisely because it addresses how poor people (mostly) interact with more affluent people (those who count). However, crime is not a problem in America! Crime is a troublesome solution of the poor to the pervasive and lonely problem of chronic poverty. But, in a way, crime is the least of it. Poverty pervades our entire culture; it undermines the moral integrity of our country. For while we may not all be poor, we all conspire to accept it. Unselfconsciously or consciously we seek to make the poor, and poverty, invisible.

The poor are, perhaps, America's most multi-racial, multi-ethnic, multi-aged grouping. In their diversity they reflect the American dream. In fact, however, they are the American nightmare. When will we wake up?

Sal and I grew up poor. In quite different ways our lives were determined by a desperate need for poor people to be heard. Paul Simon's *The Capeman* does not let Sal be heard—it is about Simon being heard. I unconditionally support his right to be heard. But I do not support his (or anyone's) continuing the ugly tradition of repressing America's impoverished. Hence, *Salvador*. For long before Sal was "The Capeman" he was a poor Puerto Rican child named Salvador Agron.

This play is dedicated to Neter Brooks, who died a few years ago. She was the president of the New York City Unemployed and Welfare Council. She was my friend. She was poor. She spoke with an eloquence that would have made Shakespeare envious. She was never heard!

As the title suggests, this play is a work of fiction. While it contains characters who are based on actual people (some famous, others not), some of whom were (and are) dear friends of mine, I make no claim that the play or the dialogues herein are factual.

SEPTEMBER 1997

CHARACTERS

SALVADOR
NANCY PECK
PAUL SIMON
WILLIAM KUNSTLER

Offstage voices
EXECUTIONER
RADIO ANNOUNCER
A
B
C
NANCY'S MOTHER
JUDGE HOFFMAN
BAILIFF

On video
NARRATOR
HARRY KRESKY
NEWSCASTER(S)

NOTE:
This play contains both live scenes and video sequences.

*The letter in Scene 10 and Salvador's testimony in Scene 12
are Salvador Agron's actual words.*

Scene 1

Lights up on a significantly oversized electric chair. Strapped into it is SALVADOR, *a working-class Puerto Rican man.* EXECUTIONER *and* RADIO ANNOUNCER *are offstage.*

EXECUTIONER: *(White working-class voice)* Do you have any last words?

SALVADOR: I always have words. You know that, you son of a bitch. How many words you want?

EXECUTIONER: You got one minute, Agron. Then you fry. One fuckin' minute. Then we're gonna burn your Puerto Rican ass to a crisp. One minute. Take it or leave it.

SALVADOR: Maybe I'll count to 60.

EXECUTIONER: I didn't know you could count, you dumb spic.

(SALVADOR begins to count in Spanish; he reaches 23.)

RADIO ANNOUNCER: We interrupt this show to bring you a special announcement. The governor has just signed into law the anti-capital punishment legislation—the so-called "Capeman Bill." All executions will be stopped immediately.

EXECUTIONER: Son of a bitch.

SALVADOR: *(Laughing maniacally)* I only knew five more numbers, you asshole.

EXECUTIONER: Listen, Agron, we're gonna fuck up the rest of your life so bad you'll wish you were dead.

SALVADOR: *(Laughs)* Meanwhile, you badass motherfucker, get these straps off of me. You heard the damned governor. No more fryin' dark meat. We're gonna make you a vegetarian, lard ass...and get your fuckin' hand off the lever, you gringo fuck.

Video #1: Documentary footage and still photos of the arrest and environment described by the NARRATOR.

NARRATOR: On the sultry summer night of August 30, 1959 there was a gang fight in a playground on West 46th Street between Ninth and Tenth Avenues. Two white youths—Robert Young and Anthony Krzesinski— were killed in the rumble.

The next day 13 Puerto Rican youth were arrested in connection with the deaths. Those rounded up were said to be members of Puerto Rican gangs, intent on avenging the beatings of Puerto Ricans who had ventured into what was then the primarily Irish and Italian neighborhood known as Hell's Kitchen.

Salvador Agron, the 16-year-old reputed leader of the Vampires, who was dubbed "The Capeman" by the press because he was identified as wearing a black cape on the night of the killings, was charged with first-degree murder. Agron, who was said to have stabbed the two with a foot-long, silver-handled dagger, was singled out by the press because of his angry and defiant attitude. On the night of his arrest he told reporters, "I don't care if I burn. My mother could watch me."

Oddly echoing the hit musical *West Side Story*, which had opened two years earlier, the West Side rumble fanned middle-class fears of "juvenile delinquency" and added to the resentment against the growing numbers of impoverished Puerto Ricans pouring into New York City— nearly one million in just 10 years.

In the days following the killings, New York City Mayor Robert Wagner summoned top city officials to discuss what he termed "the recent outbreaks of juvenile violence," and responded by assigning 1,400 cops, five percent of the entire New York City Police Department, to a special unit to fight juvenile crime.

After a trial that lasted four months, the all-white, all-male jury found Agron guilty. Agron was sentenced to the electric chair, earning the dubious distinction of becoming the youngest person ever sentenced to death in New York State.

Two years later his sentence was commuted to life in prison by Governor Nelson Rockefeller.

Scene 2

The stage is dark, except for a spot on SALVADOR. *Offstage voices and jail sounds are heard. Inmates are talking to* SALVADOR *(in the middle of the night) about the called-off execution. The voices are Black and Latino; they are whispering.*

A: Were you scared, Sal? Strapped in the fuckin' chair. Were ya scared?

SALVADOR: No, man, I wasn't scared. I ain't never scared. *(Pause.)* Of course, I was scared, you dumb motherfucker. Those straps were tight. I'd a had a hard time breakin' out of 'em.

B: Thirty seconds away from the big fry, Sal. Man, you are a lucky motherfucker.

SALVADOR: Yeah. Ya right. I'm a lucky motherfucker. Bet you guys thought you'd never hear my pretty voice again. Well, man. We got lotsa time to talk. Lotsa time. Thousands of nights to bullshit away the hours.

C: Yeah, Sal. Ain't that great?

SALVADOR: Yeah, Chickie, that's great. Really great.

B: You was wise-ass right to the end. You a ballsy motherfucker, Mr. Capeman—one ballsy spic.

SALVADOR: Yeah. That's me. I got balls. Big balls. Big hands and a big dick, too. Big Puerto Rican balls.

C: What ya gonna do now Sal, huh? What's next?

SALVADOR: I'm gonna settle down for a long stay. We all better do that. Now that they ain't fryin' more of us, they gonna keep us here forever. We better get some sleep.

A: Yeah, Sal. Pleasant dreams, man.

Video #2: Appropriate stills and clips. Statistics appear on screen as the NARRATOR *talks about them.*

NARRATOR: The death penalty has always been hotly debated in America.

The England that the American colonists rebelled against imposed the death penalty for some 200 crimes—including male homosexuality, petty theft and pickpocketing. English laws allowed for the execution of anyone over 10 years of age. This is what Thomas Jefferson and others had in mind when they added the Eighth Amendment to the Constitution, prohibiting "cruel and unusual punishment."

During most of American history, however, capital punishment was far from unusual. Like Salvador Agron, the vast majority of those condemned to death—whether white, Black, Native American or Latino —were poor. That no rich person has ever been executed in the entire history of the U.S. is the reality behind the grim joke, "capital punishment means those without the capital get the punishment."

In 1972 the Supreme Court ruled that the death penalty was "cruel and unusual punishment" in violation of the Eighth Amendment. The moratorium on executions lasted just four years, when a more conservative court modified the ban, allowing states to reintroduce the death penalty under specific circumstances.

Twenty years after that decision, 38 states impose capital punishment and 263 executions have been carried out, with hundreds more on death row. After the election of Governor George Pataki in 1995, capital punishment was reinstated in New York.

Scene 3

A lower middle-class bedroom in 1950s Queens, New York. NANCY, a teenager, is sitting on an oversized bed with a telephone. NANCY'S MOTHER is offstage.

NANCY: *(On telephone)* Did Bill touch you? *(Pause for response.)* Gloria, are you tellin' the truth? *(Pause.)* How far up? *(Pause.)* What did it feel like?

NANCY'S MOTHER: Are you off that telephone yet? What do you girls have to talk about? You haven't lived long enough to have done anything yet. You're only 16. Hurry up. I need the phone.

NANCY: *(Elongating the name)* Mom. Ten more minutes. C'mon. *(Pause, back into phone.)* Did you and Billy French kiss? *(Pause.)* Y'wanna go to the new Alexander's on Queens Boulevard? *(Pause.)* I can't make it until three. *(Pause.)* Right in front? *(Pause.)* Okay. At the bathing suit counter.

Video #3: Over audio of Doris Day singing "Que Sera, Sera" we see footage of: 1950s bathing suit parade; kids with hula hoops; child with Davy Crockett cap; Jackie Robinson in a Brooklyn Dodgers uniform; President Eisenhower playing golf; Levittown or another new suburban tract; Harry Belafonte; "juvenile delinquents" with ducktails; Palisades amusement park; a doo-wop group harmonizing on a street corner; and at the end, two 1950s teenagers, a boy and a girl, drinking the same ice cream soda from two different straws.

Scene 4

Back in NANCY's bedroom. She is, once again, on the telephone. NANCY's MOTHER is offstage.

NANCY: Paul asked me to go with him to Jahn's for an ice cream soda. *(Pause.)* Yeah, the short, funny lookin' kid…Paul, Paul Simon. He writes music, you know. Plays guitar. *(Pause.)* I don't care if I'm a foot taller than he is. He's cute. *(Pause.)* So he's square. I'm sort of square too. *(Pause.)* No. I don't care if I never get laid. Maybe I won't have sex until I'm married. *(Pause.)* No, Gloria, I never heard of Kinsey. What kind of report did he write? *(Long pause)* Really? Forty-two percent by the age of 17? He didn't speak to me.

NANCY'S MOTHER: Are you on that dammed phone again? Tell your friend Gloria she should wear less make-up. I saw her on the corner of Francis Lewis yesterday lookin' like a prostitute.

NANCY: Mom. We're talkin' school work. We're talkin' sociology. We're discussin' the Kinsey report.

NANCY'S MOTHER: Listen. Tell your sexy girl friend to learn how to type.

NANCY: My mom says you should learn to type. *(Laughs.)*

Video #4: Still of the young Salvador Agron under arrest dissolves into still of Senator John F. Kennedy on the campaign trail, which in turn dissolves into a close-up of Vice President Nixon smiling. The opening of the first televised Kennedy-Nixon presidential debate plays silently with the following narration.

NARRATOR: Shortly after Salvador Agron was sentenced to die in the electric chair, Vice President Richard Nixon and Senator John F. Kennedy held the first of their four televised debates, the first between presidential candidates to be broadcast on network television. On most of the important issues, the Republican Nixon and the Democrat Kennedy were in full agreement. They quibbled about tactics, most sharply what response to take towards China's claim to the small islands of Quemoy and Matsu.

Clip of an exchange between Nixon and Kennedy in one of their televised debates.

NARRATOR: The trial of Salvador Agron and the Nixon-Kennedy debates, each in its own way, brought the 1950s to a close. Something new was stirring in America.

Over the refrain of Bob Dylan's "Blowin' in the Wind"—a quick series of clips and stills: Kennedy's inaugural address "Ask not what your country can do for you, ask what you can do for your country"; the Reverend Dr. Martin Luther King, Jr. leading a civil rights march; American soldiers fighting in Vietnam; anti-war demonstration in the United States; a still of a Young Lord; fade out…

Scene 5

PAUL SIMON is sitting in a "hip" Queens bedroom on the telephone with a guitar.

SIMON: What ya mean, Artie? Ya don't know what parsley, sage, rosemary and thyme is? What's wrong with you? *(Pause.)* Don't they teach you nothing in college? *(Pause.)* Yeah. That's what I said yesterday. We need a hip, middle-class white sound. That's gonna be our niche, man. Simon and Garfunkel…No, man, I don't like Garfunkel and Simon. This ain't no Wall Street law firm. It's white singers doin' high-pitched vocals against the war to rip off the movement—kinda a Queens Boulevard version of Dylan. Sort of a non-violent revenge of the nerds, Artie. *(Pause.)* Oh, shit. My mother always used sage. *(Pause.)* Well, your mother never cooked very good. (*Pause.*) Well, yeah. I found rosemary in a hippie dippy feminine cook book. Artie, man, wake up. Long after Hendrix is dead from drugs and the Panthers are pussy cats we'll still be around. Middle-class nerds from Queens gonna be around long after West Village hipsters have gone back to Minnesota. Believe me, Artie. (*Pause.*) Yes, Artie, that's exactly what I'm saying! It's all about finding a niche. (*Pause.*) Yeah, the Beatles are good, but they're not American. Dylan's got that folk niche. The Beach Boys are Southern California. The Stones are crazy. Motown is Motown. But there's more middle-class nerds in this country than all those put together, Artie. Just a little hip looking, a little movement-identified, singin' for all those kids our age who really dig Frank Sinatra but can't let no one know about that. D'you understand, man? It's all about nerds hearin' sounds they can live with which makes 'em feel cool—not too cool, Queens cool. That's our sound, Artie. That's our sound. (*Pause.*) That's all the music business is! It's rip-off, pure and simple. The committed artists will be burned out or dead and we'll still be makin' it. Nerds want a cool sound and free verse lyrics to match. Believe me, Artie. Believe me.

Video #5: Starts with blackness on the screen.

Audio: In the darkness we hear Jim Morrison of the Doors in the middle of the song "The End" in which he says, "Father, I want to kill you. Mother, I want to fuck you..." and screams. Visual: Up on Morrison in the middle of a frenetic performance. Freeze frame. Overlay (words appear, no audio): Jim Morrison, 27, Heroin overdose, July 3, 1971.

Visual: Janis Joplin performing. Audio: Janis Joplin singing "Take Another Piece of My Heart." As she sings, "...Take it, if it makes you feel good." Visual: Freeze frame on Joplin in performance. Overlay (words appear, no audio): Janis Joplin, 27, Heroin overdose, October 4, 1970.

Visual: A dead male body floating in a swimming pool, cut to the early Rolling Stones singing "Satisfaction." Audio: Stones' "Satisfaction." Visual: Close-up of guitarist Brian Jones. Freeze frame. Overlay (words appear, no audio): Brian Jones, 27, Drowned due to drugs, July 3, 1969.

Visual: Jimi Hendrix performing at Monterey Pop Festival. Audio: Whatever he is singing/playing in the film. Visual: Freeze frame of Hendrix on his knees, playing his guitar. Overlay (words appear, no audio): Jimi Hendrix, 26, Suffocation due to drugs, September 18, 1970.

Over freeze frame of Hendrix burning his guitar, there is an audio of the character Paul Simon saying: "The committed artists will be burned out or dead and we'll still be making it…Believe me, Artie, believe me."

Scene 6

NANCY in an Upper West Side phone booth. It's the late '60s but she's still Queens-dressed, talking to her mother.

NANCY: Yeah, Mom, it's not a bad job. *(Pause.)* Yeah, that's right…I'm a typist…and I do a little filing. *(Pause.)* It's called the American Civil Liberties Union…Yeah…the ACLU. No, Mom, they're not all communists. They do some good things. And besides, I'm just a secretary. *(Pause.)* I like living on 93rd Street, just off Broadway. *(Pause.)* No, Mom, it's not a colored neighborhood. It's a multi-racial community. It's the Upper West Side. *(Pause.)* It's too expensive on the lower West Side. *(Pause.)* Yes, it's safe. It's safe, Mom. *(Pause.)* I know it's not Queens. That's why I moved here. *(Pause.)* Yes, Mom, I do like Queens. It was good enough for me. *(Pause.)* I love you and Dad…but I'm not 15 anymore. I wanted to live alone and in the city. *(Pause.)* No, I'm not a hippie…and I'm not a communist.

Video #6: Montage of video clips and stills of the riots of the late 1960s and early 1970s—burning buildings, cops busting heads, looters, police cars being turned over, National Guard soldiers marching through the ghetto, etc. The Rolling Stones' "Street Fighting Man" plays under visuals. Music fades down as the NARRATOR begins.

NARRATOR: In the late 1960s many of the social conflicts that had been reshaping America for a decade began to erupt in violence.

Faced with intensified police brutality, continued unemployment and poverty, and the frustration of the high expectations brought about by the civil rights and Black Power movements, working-class communities of color across the nation began to rebel. Beginning with Watts in 1965, over 100 American cities experienced major riots by the end of 1968. One hundred and eighty-nine people, the vast majority of them Black, were killed, 7,614 were wounded, 59,257 were arrested, and nearly $160 million worth of property was destroyed. Leaders like Malcolm X, the Reverend Martin Luther King, Jr., and scores of local and national leaders of the Black Panther Party were gunned down.

Anti-war protesters outside the 1968 Democratic Party convention in Chicago were brutally attacked by the police. In the spring of 1970 over a million college students across the country went on strike to protest the U.S. bombing of Cambodia. National Guardsmen, brought in to quell a student strike at Jackson State, a Black school in Mississippi, stormed the dormitories and killed two students. Within a few days, four white students at Kent State in Ohio were murdered by Guardsmen. In riots over the conversion of a park into a parking lot in Berkeley a protester was shot dead by the police. The armed wing of the radical movement—the Weather Underground—set off at least 250 bombs at military and government installations across the country.

Visuals freeze on protester throwing Molotov cocktail or holding a rifle aloft. "Street Fighting Man" comes back up.

Scene 7

The same setting as Scene 2, with a Mao poster on the wall. A, B, C are offstage; they are whispering.

SALVADOR: Chickie? You awake, Chickie?

C: Yeah, Sal. I'm awake.

A: That you, Sal?

SALVADOR: Yeah, man. It's me.

B: We gonna study tonight, Sal?

SALVADOR: Yeah, man. We study every night. Did y'all read Chairman Mao's "Combat Liberalism" like I told ya to?

A: I just could read a little.

C: I read the whole thing, Sal.

B: I read it already before…in the Panther newspaper.

SALVADOR: Chickie…what did it say? I mean not the exact words, but what's it got to do with liberals here in the U.S.? Y'know what I'm askin'? How do we combat liberalism?

C: Well, Sal, the one I remember best is how the liberals are always pattin' themselves on the back. Y'know what I'm sayin'? It's like they need us to be fucked up so they can do somethin' for us.

B: It's like white folks tryin' to know what it's like to be Black.

A: Or people outside tryin' to know what it's like to be inside.

SALVADOR: But what else can they do? Y'know. I mean no one decided what color to be born.

B: Yeah, man, but white folks, white liberals, make out like they really care— but they don't.

SALVADOR: How d'you know they don't really care, Blackie? How do you know? Maybe they just care the way white people care. Y'can't blame white people for that.

C: Maybe bein' liberal is being white and pretendin' to be somethin' else.

A: Yeah. Y'know. It's an attitude.

SALVADOR: But everyone's got attitudes. Not just white people. Mao wrote "Combat Liberalism" for yellow people—yeah, for Chinese communists. So it ain't Black and white or tan or yellow or red.

C: Yeah, I get it. We all pat ourselves on the back. That's it. Right, Sal?

SALVADOR: Yeah, Chickie. That's right. It's us communists who gotta combat liberalism in ourselves. We can't worry about the liberals or the white folks. We gotta worry about ourselves rippin' each other off. When we start gettin' off on bad-mouthin' white liberals we is bein' liberals tryin' to show off how Black we are.

B: Are you sayin' I'm a liberal, Sal?

SALVADOR: Yeah Blackie, that's what I'm sayin'. I'm combatin' your liberalism.

B: I don't appreciate that, man.

SALVADOR: I didn't say it for you to appreciate, man. You're my brother and my comrade and we gotta combat liberalism right here on the inside. Yeah, white liberals rip us off. But they ain't the same as communists, Blackie. When liberals, Black or white, pat themselves on the back its kinda like birds singin'—it's what they do. When communists, Black or white, pat themselves on the back that's liberalism and we gotta combat it.

C: I get it, Sal. Yeah, man. I get it.

A: But ain't white people the enemy?

SALVADOR: No, man. Rich people are the enemy. People gettin' rich offa all of us.

B: You really are a communist, man, ain'tcha?

SALVADOR: Yeah, Blackie, I really am. I really am.

Scene 8

The Chicago 8 Trial in 1969. WILLIAM KUNSTLER in argument with offstage JUDGE HOFFMAN.

HOFFMAN: Mr. Kunstler, you're not on trial here…yet. If you continue your showboating I will hold you in contempt of this court. Your eight defendants—the so-called Chicago 8—are in serious trouble. This was no college prank. It was organizing a full-blown riot…

KUNSTLER: Correction…your honor. The Chicago police and mayor Daley organized the riot. My clients and thousands of others were peaceably demonstrating. Demonstrating. That's an inalienable right guaranteed by the Constitution of the United States of America…and the last I heard Illinois was one of those states, your honor.

HOFFMAN: Yes, it is. And Illinois and Chicago have laws which govern the holding of those demonstrations. For example, Mr. Kunstler, permits are required and obeying the orders of the local police is demanded.

Mr. Davis, Mr. Hoffman, Mr. Dellinger, Mr. Seale and the rest did not have permits and not only didn't follow the orders of the Chicago police but urged many others not to.

KUNSTLER: Your honor, the millions of Americans and millions more the world over who saw that police riot on TV did not see it happening in Illinois or Chicago. They saw it happening in America. And they were shocked that police gone wild and beating women and children can happen in America—the land of freedom and free political expression.

HOFFMAN: And those millions of people are who you're posturing for right now, Mr. Kunstler. You've been a lawyer long enough to know what every junior high school student in this country knows: there are federal laws, there are state laws and there are local laws and you have to obey all of them. And failing to recognize that in your defense is not fair to your clients. You are not giving them their best shot legally. You are showboating your own agenda, your anti-American agenda to make a political statement.

KUNSTLER: And so were they, your honor. They bravely ran that risk on the streets of Chicago last August. Because they are patriots. Daley and his boys in blue are the anti-Americans. My point is known to every sixth grader: The Constitution guarantees civil rights and human rights even when—indeed, especially when—local laws and local authorities violate them. My clients were not in Chicago, Illinois; they were in the United States of America asserting the rights that millions of Americans have fought and died for.

HOFFMAN: Chicago, Illinois is not on trial, Mr. Kunstler.

KUNSTLER: It should be…your honor.

HOFFMAN: And should I be on trial too, Mr. Kunstler?

KUNSTLER: I didn't say that, your honor. But it should be pointed out to the jury that they have no obligation to make their decision based on the laws of Illinois or Chicago. By the Constitution of the United States of America—where this trial is being held!—they are free to vote their conscience independent of what the laws say. Your honor, I demand that you so instruct them.

HOFFMAN: Mr. Kunstler, you are in contempt of this court.

KUNSTLER: Your honor, you are in contempt of American democracy and American justice.

Scene 9

Greenhaven Prison visiting room. SALVADOR *(in prison garb) is seated center stage.* NANCY PECK *is holding a large green pass and standing center stage right; she is obviously looking for someone.*

SALVADOR: You Nancy Peck?

NANCY: Yes. Yes, I am. You're Salvador?

SALVADOR: Yeah, I'm Salvador Agron. Call me Sal.

NANCY: Okay, Sal. It's nice to finally meet you. You write very interesting letters.

SALVADOR: Yeah, Nancy. You, too. You're very nice lookin'. Even better than the pictures you sent. You're very pretty.

NANCY: *(Embarrassed)* Oh, that's nice of you to say. Thank you, Sal. It's great to meet you. *(Long uneasy pause.)*

SALVADOR: You wanna know anything about me, I mean you got any questions you was savin' for us meetin' in person? Like, did I kill those kids?

NANCY: *(Embarrassed)* Well you told me a lot about yourself in those letters and in your poems. I like your poems. Are there other things you think I should know about?

SALVADOR: Well, I'm a communist. Does that bother you? Are you a communist or a liberal? I mean, I don't care but it would be good to know which. You still work at the Civil Liberties Union?

NANCY: No. Not anymore. I work with a welfare union now...it's called the Unemployed and Welfare Council. We do welfare advocacy, but we're also looking to get union recognition, welfare center by welfare center. I sent you some materials about the union in the last packet. Did you read it?

SALVADOR: Yeah, I read it all. It's a good idea. I like the stuff you send. I think

I like those people you're working with. They seem like communists to me. (NANCY *laughs nervously.*) Hey, you don't gotta say. It's a hard word to say in America. It's easy for me. I don't live in America. I live in prison. It's easier to be a communist. But the stuff you sent don't read like no liberals. And you look too nervous to be a liberal. I like that. Yeah. I like you. You're not cool. When my friend Jackie put me on to you people she said they're the only leftists that could get me outta here. Jackie's no bullshit artist. So I believe her. I don't trust the traditional Left. They don't like me too much. I'm a communist, but I say whatever's on my mind. Y'understand, I don't dig party line. Y'got a party line?

NANCY: Not really. Not a hard line. I'm not Communist Party and I'm not a Trot...or a social dem. No labels really.

SALVADOR: But a communist! That's good. A sort of independent communist...And you're from Queens, right?

NANCY: I grew up there. I live in Manhattan now...Upper West Side.

SALVADOR: And you and your people think ya can get me outta here? It's been a long time y'know. I been in here almost 20 years...but you know all about me. I can tell you done your homework. Y'got good lawyers? (NANCY *nods.*) Y'ever worked with prisoners before? (NANCY *shakes her head.*) Good. That's good. Y'gotta boyfriend?

NANCY: (*Embarrassed*) Why do you want to know?

SALVADOR: I think I'd like to be your boyfriend.

NANCY: We just met, Sal. I hardly know you.

SALVADOR: You ever go out with anyone famous?

NANCY: (*Laughs*) Well, I had a few dates with Paul Simon. Y'know, the folk singer. He grew up in Queens. We went to the same high school. But that was a long time ago...before he became famous.

SALVADOR: Oh yeah. I hearda him. I like his music. Who's the guy sings with him? Garfunkel, right? Yeah, they're good. Music's a little white...but shit, that's cool, they're white. He seems a little nerdy, but hey, nerds got a right to live, too. So you went out with Paul Simon, yeah. I'm impressed.

NANCY: Well…it was just three or four dates and we were very young…and it was a long time ago, Sal.

SALVADOR: You think I'm famous?

NANCY: Yes. I do.

SALVADOR: Well, maybe we could have some dates.

NANCY: That might be nice, Sal.

SALVADOR: C'mon over here with me. *(They move upstage right.)* Would you pull your skirt up and your panties down so I can see your pussy?

NANCY: *(Shocked)* Do what, Sal? What did you say?

SALVADOR: Pull up your dress and pull down your panties so I can see your pussy. I wanna jerk off…y'know masturbate. Ya turn me on.

NANCY: Are you kidding, Sal? Y'mean right here in public?

SALVADOR: Y'mean you'd do it in private?

NANCY: Well, I don't know…but here in public. I don't know if I could, Sal.

SALVADOR: This is as private as it ever gets for me…except when I'm alone in my cell…Look around. Everyone else is doin' some kind of sex here in this visiting room…in public. I'd really like to see your pussy. I'll bet it's a beauty. It won't take but half a minute or so. What d'ya say? Lemme see.

(A longish pause. Then NANCY slowly lift up her skirt and pulls down her panties. SALVADOR, with his back to the audience, masturbates while counting in Spanish and panting excitedly. He reaches orgasm at "23" as lights fade.)

Video #7: Medium shot of attorney HARRY KRESKY standing in front of a banner reading "Committee to Free Salvador Agron." Close-up of KRESKY as he begins to speak.

KRESKY: I'm Harry Kresky, one of the attorneys representing Salvador Agron. We are happy to announce that after 18 years of incarceration, in preparation for his release from prison, Mr. Agron has enrolled in the Educational Release Program at the State University of New York at

New Paltz. When he entered prison, Mr. Agron could neither read nor write. While behind bars he not only taught himself those skills, but went on to get his GED and then earned a college associates degree in liberal arts. Mr. Agron intends to use the Education Release to complete his college education while attending classes at New Paltz during the day and returning to Fishkill Prison at night. This marks an important milestone in the process of Mr. Agron's return to society.

Quick fade.

Scene 10

NANCY's apartment on the Upper West Side. She's in a bathrobe, reading a book. It's late at night. The doorbell rings. NANCY looks through the peephole and opens the door. It's SALVADOR.

NANCY: Sal! What in the hell are you doin' here?

SALVADOR: Quiet. *(Holding a finger to his mouth.)* Lemme inside. You alone?

NANCY: *(Ushering him in)* Yes. I'm alone. But what are you doin' here?

SALVADOR: I escaped. I absconded. I was in class at New Paltz and I decided to split. I needed to see you. I had to get out.

NANCY: Won't they come here right away?

SALVADOR: I don't think so. They'll probably wait till morning. Y'know, all the paperwork and shit. I'll be out of here by mornin'. You'll be safe. I'm sure I wasn't followed. Can I get a big hug? I don't escape from prison every day.

(They embrace.)

NANCY: Sal, you were gonna get out soon. You were comin' up for parole. I'm scared Sal. I'd never tell you what to do, baby. But I'm frightened for you. Where are you going to go?

SALVADOR: I'm gonna head out west…southwest. Head to Mexico and maybe find a way to get to Cuba from there.

NANCY: Can you get into Cuba?

SALVADOR: I dunno. But I can try.

NANCY: You'll need some clothes and some money. I'll call someone.

SALVADOR: I'm sure you're tapped.

NANCY: It's only a few blocks away. I'll walk over.

SALVADOR: Let's wait about a half hour or so.

NANCY: Okay. You hungry?

SALVADOR: Yeah, baby. *(She goes to get him some food. He picks up a record album of Paul Simon's* Graceland.*)* What's this? A new album by your old boyfriend? Oh yeah. This is that *Graceland* album he made in South Africa. The man's got a way with other people's music. Lotta the brothers were pissed off about it. They don't like him rippin' off African music. I told 'em...man, he's a liberal. That's what he does. I kinda like his sound...in a way. Maybe he made some money for some poor Black South Africans.

NANCY: I heard he made a deal with the ANC to cover his white liberal ass.

SALVADOR: Well, shit. The official communists been known to make a few deals in their day. *(NANCY brings him a sandwich and a beer and sits on his lap.)* Maybe your old boyfriend'll write some music about me someday. Like, y'know, that TV documentary they did last winter. Well, maybe Simon will do a musical about me. There's lotsa Puerto Rican sounds he could rip off.

NANCY: Yeah. And that liberal nerd'll probably call it something like *Capeman.*

SALVADOR: Now don't go ultra-left on me, baby. That would be the money makin' name.

NANCY: Well...I'd sue the nerdy son of a bitch.

SALVADOR: Hey, hey, hey, Queens girl. It ain't no crime to be a nerd. Who ya gonna hire, William Kunstler? Get him another two million in free publicity? That's who made it off of the movement—the white liberals—not the brothers, not the sisters, not the political prisoners. They're still rotting in their cells, but the white liberals, huh. More power to 'em.

They make us look like chumps. No, baby, if your lover boy Paul does something with me, try to get some of the action, baby. Give him the inside story on my cock. I mean, don't take this too personal, Nancy darling…don't take this too personal. Ha, ha, ha. *(They laugh; then hug; he peeks under the robe and they kiss passionately.)* Okay, darling Nancy. Run over and get the money and clothes. Be careful. When you get back I got a letter I wrote you last night. I wanna read it to ya then I wanna fuck all night. Then, when the sun comes up I'm gonna leave. We'll see each other again. Don't worry.

(The lights dim. NANCY exits and SALVADOR lies down. NANCY returns in an overcoat carrying a suit for SALVADOR. She takes off the coat. She is wearing only her underwear. She sits down on the bed and slowly removes her bra and panties as SALVADOR sits up and reads his letter/poem.)

Dear Nancy,

I am presently writing because what I feel is real. I want you to know that presently I got my jockey shorts on with a top red t-shirt laying on my bed side ways writing to you. I feel sexual all over. From my toes to my head. Sex is a beautiful reality. I love sex very much—I love your sexuality completely. I can feel your wet flesh mixing with mine—you inside of me. Yes—in this state of ecstasy we are, indeed, completely surrendering to each other. We are one flesh.

I want to take you right now and strip your clothes slow till you stand in front of me in your little bikini panties. I gently bring you close to me and with my mouth and lips remove your soaked dark blue panties— then, I let you strip me while I am finally in my dark blue jockeys, bikini style with a big juicy bulge in my male panties. You then begin to pull them off me with your teeth—we are both on the bed when this is going on. The mirrors on the ceiling reveal our nakedness, our wicked and beautiful shame. My cock is hard as steel. Sexually, we are made for each other. I do love you.

Video #8: Still of SALVADOR surrounded by police officers.

NEWSCASTER: Good evening. In the news tonight, convicted murderer Salvador Agron, the notorious "Capeman" convicted of the stabbing deaths of two youths in a gang fight in New York City nearly two decades ago, was recaptured today after escaping from an Educational Release program in upstate New York. Agron, whose death sentence was commuted to life in prison in 1962, fled the New Paltz campus of the State University of New York four days ago and apparently returned to the neighborhoods where he grew up in the 1950s.

Agron, who was unarmed at the time of his apprehension in Arizona, was returned tonight to the Fishkill Correctional Facility.

Scene 11

Dutchess County court house. NANCY is seated stage left. Center stage is the defendant's table. SALVADOR is seated. KUNSTLER and SIMON are standing right of the defendant's table chatting. BAILIFF is offstage.

KUNSTLER: *(Shaking SIMON's hand warmly)* It's good to see you Paul. Good to see you. You've been taking a lot of flak for that *Graceland* album. I myself love it, beautiful music. Some people just don't appreciate all you've done for civil rights, Paul.

SIMON: Well, you know all about that, Bill.

KUNSTLER: Yeah, Paul, but lawyers are used to that…What are you doin up here?

SIMON: I come to hear you whenever I can, Bill. And I'm always lookin' for a good idea for some music. How in the hell are you gonna get Agron off? He did, after all, abscond.

KUNSTLER: Well, between me and Sal I think we have a chance. He's a bright and charismatic guy—musical material if I ever saw it.

SIMON: Well if you get him off it'll make a damned good scene.

KUNSTLER: I'll do my best, Paul. Listen, I gotta talk to Sal for a moment before we begin. Nice seein' ya again. Take care. Don't let our unappreciative liberal friends get to you.

(They shake hands and SIMON sits "in the crowd" stage right. NANCY glowers at him and he doesn't notice her. KUNSTLER sits down next to SALVADOR.)

KUNSTLER: How ya doin', Salvador? *(SALVADOR nods.)* Okay. We went over the whole thing yesterday. Just be calm and follow my lead.

SALVADOR: I've had some new ideas…some new thoughts since yesterday. I'm sure you'll pick up on 'em when I testify.

KUNSTLER: Wait a minute, Sal. We don't need no new ideas. And we haven't even decided if you're going to testify yet. Remember what we said yesterday—that I'll decide that during the trial based on how things are going.

SALVADOR: I wanna testify.

KUNSTLER: Look Sal, it's gotta be my call. That's how I work.

SALVADOR: With all due respects, Mr. Kunstler, I do the time, I do the trial. You're supposed to be workin' for me, not me for you.

KUNSTLER: Sal, this is no time for you and me to be having a fight.

SALVADOR: I agree. I'll testify.

KUNSTLER: Hey listen, man, I think you'll be a great witness. I just want to reserve the right to not use you if I don't need you.

SALVADOR: Y'mean if you've already won it. Hey, man. I don't mind you bein' a star. I know your style. I just wanna be a co-star. That's my style. I'm gonna testify.

KUNSTLER: *(Stares at SALVADOR)* What if I don't let you?

SALVADOR: I'll fire you…right on the spot. I'll defend myself.

KUNSTLER: You're crazy, man.

SALVADOR: I've heard that before. By the way…who was that you were talkin to? *(He points to SIMON.)* Him, over there, who is that?

KUNSTLER: That's Paul Simon, y'know, the folk singer.

(SALVADOR looks at NANCY. He points to SIMON. She nods and makes a face. He smiles broadly.)

SALVADOR: *(To KUNSTLER)* We understand each other?

KUNSTLER: I've been fired before, Salvador.

SALVADOR: Not the way I'll fire you.

KUNSTLER: I don't think we'll have a problem.

SALVADOR: *(Extends his hand to shake with KUNSTLER)* Good. Let's win it together.

BAILIFF: Please rise everyone. The Honorable Albert Rosenblatt presiding.

(Everyone stands.)

Video #9: Stills and clips to illustrate the various trials.

NARRATOR: One of the ongoing contradictions of American political life is that despite its deep-rooted tradition of democracy, the U.S. establishment has a long record of using the legal system to prosecute, jail and even kill those it perceived as political threats. These political trials, which have most often been disguised as criminal proceedings, have invariably been directed against progressive activists.

In 1918, at the height of World War I, Eugene Debs, leader of the Socialist Party, was arrested for speaking out against American involvement in the war and sentenced to 10 years in federal prison. While in prison he ran for president of the United States and received a million votes. Debs' conviction was only one of hundreds obtained under blatantly unconstitutional "anti-sedition" laws.

In 1920 Bartolomeo Vanzetti and Nicola Sacco, Italian immigrants and anarchist activists working in the Boston area, were arrested and charged with the death of a security guard killed during the robbery of a payroll truck. Although the evidence against them was entirely circumstantial, they were convicted and condemned to die. Sacco and Vanzetti were electrocuted in 1927.

In 1950 Julius and Ethel Rosenberg, two working-class Jews and Communist Party members from New York's Lower East Side, were arrested and charged with being Russian spies who had "stolen the secret of the atomic bomb." Despite obvious holes in the government case, the Rosenbergs were convicted of treason and went to the electric chair.

In 1968, in a trial that became a flash point in the political and cultural struggles of the 1960s, seven anti-war and counterculture leaders were charged with inciting the nationally televised riot that took place outside the Democratic Convention in Chicago. The Chicago Seven—which included Abbie Hoffman, Rennie Davis and Dave Dellinger—were defended by the flamboyant civil rights attorney William Kunstler. They were all convicted, although their convictions were later overturned.

In the late '60s and early '70s hundreds of Black Panther Party members and leaders—including Huey P. Newton, Bobby Seale, David Hilliard, and Ericka Huggins—were arrested and prosecuted on numerous charges trumped up by the FBI and local police. Scores of others were murdered in shoot-outs provoked by the authorities.

Scene 12

Dutchess County courtroom, several hours later. BAILIFF *is offstage.*

KUNSTLER: *(Stands)* I'd like to call for our final defense witness Mr. Salvador Agron.

(SALVADOR crosses downstage center, and puts his hand on the Bible.)

BAILIFF: Do you promise to tell the truth, the whole truth and nothing but the truth, so help you God?

SALVADOR: I do, I surely do. Si.

KUNSTLER: Mr. Agron, would you tell the jury, in your own words, how you understand your being on trial here today?

SALVADOR: First, before we go into anything about my "absconding" from the Fishkill Correctional Facility's work release program, let me say that I have been in prison since the age of 16 when I was but a child "with the mentality of a 12-year-old." About the crime which I am accused, charged, indicted and convicted, I did not commit such acts—this may sound preposterous to some, but it is the truth. However, we will not deal with that aspect of the matter—I'll reserve such knowledge for a future new trial in a court of law. This is my right as a human being.

Presently I am in the Dutchess County Jail in Poughkeepsie, New York. I was held in Auburn State Prison from the 11th of May, 1977 until today [May 18]. At one o'clock two sheriffs from the Dutchess County Transportation came to pick me up and, as of yet, I do not know why I am here and no commitment papers have been given to me nor have I been informed of any charges. However, here I am in the county jail. This system is beginning to function more like Nazi Germany each day. I gather (without being informed) that I will be charged with "escape" from Fishkill, or for "absconding" from work release, or perhaps the charges will get so outrageous until I am charged with "running away from New Paltz College." Which will it be? A "crime" has been committed by Salvador Agron. The scene of this alleged "absconding" ("escape" or "crime") was New Paltz College—I demand that the Town of New Paltz take legal jurisdiction for this ridiculous charge so that they may be the ones to look silly before the nation.

Why did I abscond from the program?

Behavior modification began to be applied to me, but being that I am somewhat of a psychology student myself and have taken courses in abnormal psychology and other psychological approaches, I was able to intelligently identify why my grades were dropping as a problem being caused by the negative pressure that was intentionally being applied by my tormentors at Fishkill. At times I would come in and encounter verbal abuse. However, this I could handle in that I trained myself as a child when I used to play the Dozens. The Dozens is a game in which one tries to beat the other fellow verbally, vulgar and abusive. One just says the worst about another's mother. When guards get too abusive with their tongue I just look right into their eyes. This usually lets them know that if they persist they will find my fist on their jaw! One officer would usually say to me, "See how nice we treat you—you murder us and we sent you to college." I had to stop him one day, "I think that is enough of that 'murder' nonsense—murderers are you and those who like you have killed many innocent people in the past of which I know about. So, please, stop using the term before we have a misunderstanding." At this he would walk away and mumble, "I think he had too much to drink at the college today." I never, as a personal policy, play (verbally or physically) with correction officers because familiarity in this case would breed only more contempt than I already have for them.

Thursday, 20th of April, I appeared before the nurse, lieutenant, and sergeant that composed the adjustment committee—the charges were read and I looked at all three and said, "Go on, do your thing…" I was told that I had to spend Saturday and Sunday locked up in a room. I hit the desk with my ring, got up and walked out. That night I could not sleep, but I knew that a new struggle was flaming in my heart and that I would take flight for a while till I got my head back together, turn myself in and protest the conditions at the Fishkill Behavior Modification Program. I did not escape or abscond from the College of New Paltz or my education. But I merely ran for my sanity and life. I may be radical, militant, revolutionary and whatever else correctional officials and newspapers may label me but I am not a low down capitalist pig or capitalist liar!

Hasta la victoria siempre.

Video #10: A medium long shot of HARRY KRESKY *and the 36-year-old* SALVADOR AGRON *surrounded by a crowd of supporters from the Committee to Free Salvador Agron, mostly members of the New York Unemployed and Welfare Council, who traveled up to Poughkeepsie by bus for the trial. They are holding a press conference on the steps of the Dutchess County Court House. Camera moves to a close-up of* KRESKY *and* SALVADOR, *who are standing side-by-side with* KRESKY *slightly in the foreground.* KRESKY *speaks.*

KRESKY: Naturally, we are all very happy that the jury returned a verdict of not guilty in the case. My colleague, William Kunstler, conducted a political defense, and to their credit, this multi-racial group of working- and middle-class people from Dutchess County understood that Salvador Agron, a Puerto Rican from New York City, was a political prisoner.

That Mr. Agron fled from the Educational Release Program was never in dispute. But we were able to show the jury that the conditions under which Mr. Agron was forced to live—by day, attending classes on the beautiful New Paltz campus, then returning every night to the oppressive, racist and brutal conditions of Fishkill Prison—were so contradictory, that Mr. Agron was literally being driven insane and had no choice but to flee.

But despite being found not guilty by a jury of his peers, the parole board has remanded Salvador to the Bronx Psychiatric Hospital. This is clearly an abuse of power by the parole board designed to further punish Mr. Agron for his political views.

We intend to fight this decision in court, and we are confident that Mr. Agron will soon win his freedom.

SALVADOR: I want to say that I agree with everything Harry just said. I'm grateful to him and the rest of the defense team for the hard, smart work they did to win this case.

This fight for justice has been supported by many people. But in my mind what clearly stands out is the support that I received from the underclass, the poverty-stricken unemployed and welfare recipients. And it was this underclass that gave inspiration to the working class, students, prisoners and middle-class people to come to my support.

This is the way I wanted it and, being that I am one of the billions who belong to this underclass, I was proud of my people, poor as they are, when they stood up in my support. My commitment is—and always will be—to the poor of this earth, 'til poverty is clothed in gold apparel.

When I am freed, I look forward to returning home and living a normal life with my most wonderful girlfriend, Nancy. Thank you.

Fade to black.

Scene 13

NANCY and SALVADOR's West Side apartment, about a year after SALVADOR's release.

SALVADOR: *(Obviously depressed)* Nancy, I can't write no more. I can't fuck no more. I feel like shit. I look like shit. Whatsa matter with me, Nancy? I think I'm dyin' of freedom. I can't stand it. I lost the struggle. Too much dope and no struggle. What's goin' on, Nancy? What's goin' on?

NANCY: You're killing yourself, Sal.

SALVADOR: Why? Shit, I ain't no killer. I ain't never killed anyone before. You know that.

NANCY: 'Cause they brainwashed you, Sal. For almost 20 years. They made it impossible for you to think of anything but yourself. That's what you had to do to survive. And you did it, Sal. You worked as hard as anyone ever has to create a new person—a new Salvador Agron who could survive the brutality of being inside. But that new Salvador can't survive outside. You've got to do it all over again—create still another Salvador Agron—to make it out here.

SALVADOR: *(Crying)* I can't do it, Nancy. I can't do it. I'm too tired.

NANCY: You won't do it for me?

SALVADOR: I can't. I don't hate you. I love you. I hated the prison. I hated the brutality.

NANCY: What are you saying, Sal; you are truly motivated by hate and not love? Didn't Che say that the true revolutionary is guided by feelings of love?

SALVADOR: *(Jumps up angrily)* Che did not spend 18 years in prison!!! He did not grow up in a poor house in Mayaguez! Salvador, the revolutionary, is not guided by hatred. But long before I was a revolutionary I was poor. And the poor hate. And now I am poor again and my hatred has returned. I cannot stand my hatred. Sometimes…sometimes I even hate you for not being poor. You who have given me everything. How could I hate you? But I do. I hate you because I am poor.

NANCY: The dope is killing you.

SALVADOR: You're right. The dope in this country is to kill the poor. And I am no different than all the others. The brutality of the prison made me loving. But now I am poor again and the hatred is creeping through my veins. I did not kill when I was 15. But I wanted to. Now I will kill. I will kill myself because I cannot stand being poor. Can you understand that Nancy? Can you understand!!! Are you afraid of me?

NANCY: I could never be afraid of you, Sal. You would never hurt me. But I am afraid for you. You are killing yourself. I cannot understand what it means to be poor. I am not one of those phony liberals who claim to understand poverty and race by sleeping with it. I have never been poor. And my love is for you—not your poverty. No. I do not understand your poverty and your hatred. But I do understand that you are killing yourself and that you are coming to hate even me. And I cannot live with that. What did the woman in *Butch Cassidy and the Sundance Kid* say? I am just an ordinary woman. I will wash your clothes and do all the ordinary things that a lower middle-class woman from Queens can do. Our love has been this ordinary woman's special moment in an otherwise very ordinary life. You are as close to the extraordinary as I will ever be. I will not stay around and watch them kill you—watch you kill yourself. I will not let you hate me. What we have had has been far too wonderful for that...so I am leaving, Sal. All I've ever had that is special is your love. And I am far too ordinary and far too selfish to give that up. (*They embrace passionately as stage darkens.*)

Video #11: The following sequences are set up as three separate newscasts with different newscasters, each in a typical television newsroom. Clips and stills to illustrate the news should be used as possible and appropriate.

Title on screen: April 22, 1986

NEWSCASTER #1: Salvador Agron, who gained notoriety more than a quarter of a century ago as the "Capeman," died today. In 1959 Agron, who was the leader of a Puerto Rican gang and who wore a red-lined black satin cape, plunged a dagger into two rival gang members in a Hell's Kitchen playground. After serving 20 years in prison, a major campaign on his behalf resulted in his release on parole in 1979. Agron, who was 43, was living with his mother in the Bronx at the time of his death.

Title on screen: September 4, 1995

NEWSCASTER #2: William Kunstler, the gravel-voiced radical lawyer whose long wild hair symbolized his permanent rebelliousness and kinship with unpopular people and causes, died today. From the early days of the civil rights movement Kunstler was a champion of the Left. Early in his career he defended the Reverend Martin Luther King, Jr., and at the time of his death he was the defense attorney for suspects in the 1993 World Trade Center bombing. The son of a prominent New York physician, Mr. Kunstler was born in 1919, and graduated from Princeton University in 1941. After serving in the Pacific during World War II, he earned his law degree from Columbia in 1949. Other of Kunstler's notable clients included: Congressman Adam Clayton Powell, Jr.; Stokely Carmichael, leader of the Student Nonviolent Coordinating Committee, who popu-

larized the slogan "Black Power"; Bobby Seale, a leader of the Black
Panther Party; anti-war priest Daniel Berrigan; and Salvador Agron, the
Puerto Rican gang leader who later became a political activist. Kunstler
was also one of the attorneys for prisoners charged in the 1971 rebellion
at Attica Prison, in which more than 40 inmates and corrections officers
were killed. Kunstler, who lived in Greenwich Village, was 76.

NEWSCASTER #3: Paul Simon's long-awaited musical, *The Capeman,* is set to
open on Broadway in January under the direction of Mark Morris, the
"bad boy" of modern dance. With 30 new songs by Simon—including
salsa, doo-wop, plenas and gospel tunes—and a book by West Indian playwright Derek Walcott, the musical is the true story of Salvador Agron, the
Puerto Rican gang leader who committed two brutal murders in New York
City in 1959. Agron, who became a writer while in prison, was dubbed
"The Capeman" because he wore a cape while committing his crimes.
Salsa heartthrob Marc Anthony portrays the teenage Salvador, and Ruben
Blades plays the older Agron. Simon told Arts and Entertainment News
that he has been working on the musical for over seven years.

Close-up of actor playing PAUL SIMON.

PAUL SIMON: It was always a story that fascinated me. I saw in the New York
of those times this dangerous shadowy figure, the fear of gangs and
juvenile delinquents. It's a story where music enhances the telling.

NEWSCASTER #3: The musical extravaganza has a cast of 40. The previews
are set to open on Broadway at the Marquis Theatre on December 1st.
The show officially opens on January 7th.

Scene 14

SIMON's posh office. NANCY rings the bell and SIMON lets her in.

SIMON: Hi. Nancy Peck? (*NANCY nods.*) Please come in and have a seat.
(*She enters and sits.*) Thank you so much for coming. As I wrote to you
in my letter, I am researching Salvador Agron's life for a musical called
The Capeman that I hope to open on Broadway in a couple of years.
Everyone I talk to mentions "Nancy" as Sal's one and only real love…
Do you mind if I call you Nancy?

NANCY: You don't recognize me, do you?

SIMON: Y'know, I think maybe I do. You were up at the Dutchess County courthouse…at Bill Kunstler's "absconding trial." Weren't you?

NANCY: Yeah. I was there. I looked at you. But that's not where I know you from.

SIMON: Oh no? Where do you know me from?

NANCY: You and I dated for about a month when I was 16, in Queens. I was Nancy Green then. (*SIMON stares hard at NANCY.*)

SIMON: (*Incredulous*) Nancy Green. Nancy Green? Oh God, yeah, Nancy Green. Holy shit. I do remember. And you wound up as Sal Agron's girlfriend? That's like no degrees of separation. Little Nancy Green.

NANCY: No. Little Paul Simon.

SIMON: (*Laughs*) You're right. Little Paul Simon. I don't believe this. This is incredible.

NANCY: I want you to give up this project, Paul. I owe it to Sal. I can't tell you how important this is to me. Please give up the project, Paul. For old times in Queens, Paul. Y'know, as a favor. One nerd to another.

SIMON: (*Laughs*) Jesus. Now I do remember. You are Nancy Green! Y'haven't changed a bit. Still a dumb ass straight shooter. Yeah. We always had something in common. We both knew we were nerds even before hardly anyone know what a nerd was.

NANCY: You've come a long way for a nerd, Paul. So, whattya say? Drop the project. "Nerdify" someone else's life. Like Bill Kunstler or someone like that.

SIMON: Listen, Nancy I'll cop to bein' a nerd but I ain't stupid. There's millions of bucks tied up in *The Capeman* project already and investors all over the place. I understand where you're coming from, Nancy. But, I can't do it. I really can't.

NANCY: At least drop the name. The "Capeman" shit needs to stop.

SIMON: Listen Nancy…I really wish I could, but frankly…it's the money making name. It really is.

NANCY: You're the second person to tell me that. When *Graceland* came out Sal and I talked about the possibility of you rippin' off his life someday in some kinda music thing. I was real angry about the prospect of it. And Sal tried to cool me out. He said "Capeman" was the money makin' name. Same thing you just said. Then he told me to grab some of the action. He said I should tell you all about his cock for some dollars.

SIMON: Sal was a smart man.

NANCY: No. Sal was a poor man.

SIMON: Okay. Okay, Nancy. But he had a good business mind.

NANCY: He never made a penny off his notoriety…or his cock. But he wanted me to. 'Cause he loved me. Well, I don't want to. But even more, I don't want you to. I like your music. So did Sal. But I don't like what you stand for. 'Cause you ain't really rippin' Sal off, you're rippin' me and all of us nerds off. I ain't talkin' on Sal's behalf. I'm talkin on behalf of the nerds of the world. So, one more time, Paul, drop the name…drop the fuckin' name.

SIMON: *(Laughing)* I can't do it Nancy Green. I can't do it. *(NANCY pulls a pistol out of her handbag and points it at SIMON's head.)* What are you crazy? Now I see what you two had in common. Put that gun away and get the fuck outta here.

NANCY: No, Paul. This is gonna be the nerd news story of the decade. QUEENS CUTIE KILLS SIMON FOR FAILING TO PAY FOR ICE CREAM SODA 40 YEARS AGO.

SIMON: What are you talkin' about? I paid.

NANCY: Bullshit. Okay, the last date…when I told you I wasn't gonna see you anymore, you made me pay for myself.

SIMON: Okay. Okay, I'll pay you a lot for a sexy interview. A million dollars plus …what…40 cents for the soda. Alright? Now put that damned gun down.

NANCY: Change the name.

(Ghost-like, KUNSTLER and SALVADOR enter. SALVADOR is wearing his black cape. He grabs the gun from NANCY.)

SALVADOR: Didn't I tell you to not go ultra-left on me about this? Jesus, Nancy...did he really not pay for the ice cream soda?

KUNSTLER: Sal and I have been watching, Paul. And I must say even I was a little put off by your calling it *my* "absconding trial."

SIMON: Well, that's what you always called it, Bill.

SALVADOR: *(To NANCY)* Were you really gonna shoot him? *(Turns to KUNSTLER.)* Bill, you probably coulda gotten her off all together. I mean, this middle-class feminist stuff plays well in court these days.

NANCY: What are you two doin' here? And how come you're hangin' out with Kunstler?

SALVADOR: What I'm doin' here is lookin' after you. That's what I do full-time nowadays. Kinda like a guardian angel. You're still lookin' beautiful, baby. But I guess you'll always be a white middle-class nerd. Well, at least y'aint no liberal. But don't take this too personal. Y'know what I'm sayin? Oh yeah, Bill over there and me became good friends since he croaked. The class stuff don't mean all that much once yer dead.

KUNSTLER: Yeah. Sal and I are kinda like twin stars...permanently.

SALVADOR: Now the man made ya a nice offer. A million and 40 cents for the true story of my cock. Grab it, Nancy. Grab it. *(Turns to SIMON and walks slowly downstage, modeling the cape. He motions to SIMON to come to him, which SIMON hesitantly does.)*

SIMON: What, do you want to sell me something?

SALVADOR: The cape, man...the cape. I'll sell ya the actual cape for uh... let's see...50 bucks.

KUNSTLER and NANCY: *(Astonished)* SALVADOR!!!

))))

A CHRONOLOGY OF CASTILLO THEATRE

September 1984
The Learning Play of Rabbi Levi-Yitzhok, Son of Sara, of Berditchev
by Dan Friedman, directed by Lou Rackoff

January 1985
The Medea Project by Eva Brenner, Candido Tirado and Heiner Müller
directed by Eva Brenner

March 1985
King Without a Castle by Candido Tirado, directed by Guillermo Gentile

September 1985
We Are written and directed by Probir Guha

October 1985
A Way Out of No Way by Julie Johnson, directed by Charles Turner

February 1986
Hoodoo Revelations by John Patterson and various authors, directed by Miguel
Valdez-Mor

March 1986
A Demonstration: Common Women, the Uncommon Lives of Ordinary Women
by William Pleasant and Fred Newman, directed by Fred Newman

June/September 1986
From Gold to Platinum by Fred Newman, William Pleasant, and Dan
Friedman, directed by Fred Newman

October 1986
The Collected Emotions of V.I. Lenin by Dan Friedman and Fred Newman
directed by Fred Newman

November 1986

    A Storm Blowing From Paradise (The Decadence Show) written and directed by Eva Brenner

December 1986

    Mr. Hirsch Died Yesterday written and directed by Fred Newman

March 1987

    Carmen's Community written and directed by Fred Newman, with excerpts from *Carmen,* music by Georges Bizet, words by H. Meilhac and L. Halevy

May 1987

    Explosion of a Memory (Description of a Picture) by Heiner Müller (New York premiere), directed by Joseph Szeiler

September 1987

    Müllerschmerz/Müller's Pain by William Pleasant, directed by Fred Newman

May 1988

    Demonstration! by Fred Newman and William Pleasant, directed by Fred Newman

September 1988

    What do you see when you open your eyes in the morning? written and directed by Walter Redweg

September 1988

    Demonstration! by Fred Newman and William Pleasant, directed by Fred Newman, Aaron Davis Hall, City College of New York

October 1989

    The Task by Heiner Müller (American premiere), directed by Eva Brenner Stephan Muller, William Pleasant

October/November 1989

    No Room for Zion (A Kaddish by a Communist Jew) written and directed by Fred Newman

    Müllerschmerz/Müller's Pain by William Pleasant, directed by Fred Newman

    Carmen's Community written and directed by Fred Newman, with excerpts from *Carmen,* music by Georges Bizet, words by H. Meilhac and L. Halevy

June/December 1990
The Collected Emotions of V.I. Lenin by Dan Friedman and Fred Newman directed by Fred Newman

December 1990
No Room for Zion (A Kaddish by a Communist Jew) written and directed by Fred Newman

February 1991
Our Young Black Men are Dying and Nobody Seems to Care written and directed by James Chapman

March 1991
Mr. Hirsch Died Yesterday written and directed by Fred Newman

March 1991
The Store: One Block East of Jerome written and directed by Fred Newman

April 1991
Amandla! by Vernelle Edwards, directed by Salaelo Maredi, Henry Street Settlement, Louis Abrons Arts Center

April 1991
Our Young Black Men Are Dying and Nobody Seems to Care written and directed by James Chapman

November 1991
Billie, Malcolm & Yusuf written and directed by Fred Newman

February 1992
The Resurrection of Dark Soldiers written and directed by William Electric Black

April 1992
Carmen's Community written and directed by Fred Newman, with excerpts from *Carmen,* music by Georges Bizet, words by H. Meilhac and L. Halevy

May 1992
Dead as a Jew (Zion's Community) written and directed by Fred Newman

September 1992
Mitote by Maisha Baton, directed by Lorna Littleway

October 1992

> *Explosion of a Memory (Description of a Picture)* by Heiner Müller, directed by
> Fred Newman

November 1992

> *Off-Broadway Melodies of 1592 (The 400th Anniversary of the Centennial
> Celebration of Columbus' So-called Discovery of America)* book by Fred
> Newman, music and lyrics by Fred Newman and Annie Roboff, directed by
> Fred Newman

January 1993

> *Billie & Malcolm: A Demonstration* written and directed by Fred Newman

March 1993

> *It's Going Around* by Yosef Mundy (American premiere), directed by Fred
> Newman

May 1993

> *Yes! We Have No Bananas and Other Contradictions in the Life of Ludwig
> Wittgenstein* written and directed by Fred Newman

June 1993

> *Outing Wittgenstein (or Sunday in the Park with Ludwig)* by Fred Newman
> directed by Dan Friedman and Mary Fridley

October 1993

> *Olivia's Opus* by Nora Cole, directed by Herman LeVerne Jones

November 1993

> *Still on the Corner* book by Fred Newman, music and lyrics by Fred Newman
> and Annie Roboff, directed by Fred Newman

January 1994

> *The Governor of Jericho* by Yosef Mundy (American premiere), directed by
> Yosef Mundy

> *The Task* by Heiner Müller, directed by Fred Newman

February 1994

> *Billie & Malcolm: A Demonstration* written and directed by Fred Newman

March 1994

> *Lenin's Breakdown* by Fred Newman and Dan Friedman, directed by Gabrielle
> Kurlander

April 1994
Who Will Dance With Pancho Villa? (Only a Crazy Revolutionary) by John and Gabriel Fraire, directed by Fred Newman

June 1994
Outing Wittgenstein written and directed by Fred Newman

June 1994
Mortality Waltz written by Robert Lanier, directed by Mark Greenfield

August 1994
Kansas on my Mind by Fred Newman, music and lyrics by Fred Newman and Annie Roboff, directed by Fred Newman

September 1994
Red Channels by Laurence Holder, directed by Fred Newman

November 1994
Left of the Moon written and directed by Fred Newman

December 1994
Still on the Corner book by Fred Newman, music and lyrics by Fred Newman and Annie Roboff, directed by Fred Newman

February 1995
Billie & Malcolm: A Demonstration by Fred Newman, directed by Gabrielle Kurlander

April 1995
The Store: One Block East of Jerome written and directed by Fred Newman

May 1995
Carmen's Community written and directed by Fred Newman, with excerpts from *Carmen,* music by Georges Bizet, words by H. Meilhac and L. Halevy

June 1995
Outing Wittgenstein by Fred Newman, directed by Mary Fridley

September 1995
A Season in the Congo by Aimé Césaire, directed by Fred Newman

October 1995
Controluce conceived by Graziella Martinoli and Fred Newman, directed by Graziella Martinoli

December 1995

    Sally and Tom (The American Way) book and lyrics by Fred Newman, music by Annie Roboff, directed by Fred Newman and Gabrielle Kurlander

February 1996

    F by Laurence Holder, directed by Fred Newman

    Left of the Moon by Fred Newman, directed by Laurence Holder

March 1996

    Hamletmachine by Heiner Müller, directed by Fred Newman

May 1996

    Galileo by Bertolt Brecht, directed by Fred Newman and Gabrielle Kurlander

June 1996

    What is to be Dead? (Philosophical Scenes) written and directed by Fred Newman

July 1996

    A Season in the Congo by Aimé Césaire, directed by Fred Newman, SERMAC Festival, Fort-de-France, Martinique

September 1996

    Risky Revolutionary by Fred Newman, directed by Dan Friedman

October 1996

    Hot Snow by Laurence Holder, directed by Gabrielle Kurlander

December 1996

    Coming of Age in Korea book by Fred Newman, music and lyrics by Fred Newman and Annie Roboff, directed by Fred Newman

February 1997

    Stealin' Home by Fred Newman, directed by Laurence Holder

April 1997

    medeamaterial by Heiner Müller, directed by Stephan Suschke

    An Obituary—Heiner Müller: A Man Without a Behind by Fred Newman with texts by Heiner Müller, directed by Fred Newman and David Nackman

June 1997

    Dinner at Vic's by Dave DeChristopher, directed by Mary Fridley

September 1997

Salvador (Fictional Conversations) by Fred Newman, directed by Fred Newman and Dan Friedman

November 1997

The Store: One Block East of Jerome by Fred Newman, directed by Madelyn Chapman and Nancy Green

January 1998

Satchel: A Requiem for Racism by Fred Newman, directed by Fred Newman and Dan Friedman

April 1998

Carmen's Place (A Fantasy) book by Fred Newman, music by Fred Newman and Annie Roboff, directed by Gabrielle Kurlander, with excerpts from *Carmen,* music by Georges Bizet, words by H. Meilhac and L. Halevy

May 1998

The Mission by Heiner Müller, with original music by Fred Newman, directed by Fred Newman

RECOMMENDED READINGS

Brenner, Eva. "Theatre of the Unorganized: The Radical Independence of the Castillo Cultural Center." *The Drama Review.* Fall (T135), p. 28-60, 1992.

McConachie, Bruce and Friedman, Dan. *Theatre for Working Class Audiences in the United States, 1930-1980.* Connecticut: Greenwood Press, 1985.

Monges-Rafuls, Pedro R. "Fred Newman: A Man of Many Ideas." an interview in *Ollantay Theater Magazine.* Volume V, No. 1 (Winter/Spring 1997).

Newman, Fred. *The Myth of Psychology.* New York: Castillo International, 1991.

_____. "Surely Castillo is Left—But is it Right or Wrong? Nobody Knows." *The Drama Review.* Fall (T135), p. 24-7, 1992.

_____. *Let's Develop! A Guide to Continuous Personal Growth.* New York: Castillo International, 1994.

_____. *Performance of a Lifetime: A Practical-Philosophical Guide to the Joyous Life.* New York: Castillo International, 1996.

Newman, Fred and Holzman, Lois. *Lev Vygotsky: Revolutionary Scientist.* London: Routledge, 1993.

_____. *Unscientific Psychology: A Cultural-Performatory Approach to Human Life.* Connecticut: Praeger, 1996.

_____. *The End of Knowing: A New Developmental Way of Learning.* London: Routledge, 1997.

ABOUT THE PLAYWRIGHT

Fred Newman is the artistic director of the Castillo Theatre in New York City, where he has directed many of his own plays, as well as the work of Bertolt Brecht, Aimé Césaire, Laurence Holder, Heiner Müller, and Yosef Mundy.

In addition to his work in the theatre, Fred Newman is the founder of social therapy, a cultural-performatory method for curing emotional pain and psychopathology which is practiced in a number of cities throughout the United States. He has been a practicing therapist for 25 years, and is the host of a weekly call-in radio show on WEVD-AM—"Let's Develop!"—which is heard on Sundays at noon throughout the New York metropolitan area. Newman is a founder and co-executive producer of the All Stars Talent Show Network, an anti-violence program for youth, which uses Newman's performatory developmental approach in all aspects of its program.

Newman received a doctorate in the philosophy of science from Stanford University in 1962. In addition to his plays, he is the author of *Performance of a Lifetime: A Practical-Philosophical Guide to the Joyous Life, Let's Develop! A Guide to Continuous Personal Growth, The Myth of Psychology,* and co-author (with Lois Holzman) of *The End of Knowing: A New Developmental Way of Learning, Unscientific Psychology: A Cultural-Performatory Approach to Understanding Human Life,* and *Lev Vygotsky: Revolutionary Scientist.*

ABOUT THE EDITOR

Dan Friedman is the resident dramaturg at the Castillo Theatre in New York City where he has worked closely with Fred Newman for nearly 15 years.

He received a doctorate in theatre history and dramatic literature from the University of Wisconsin in 1979, and is co-editor (with Bruce A. McConachie) of *Theatre for Working Class Audiences in the United States, 1830-1980.* He is an assistant professor in the Department of Speech Communication and Theatre Arts at Queensborough Community College in New York City. Friedman is the author of 10 plays and conducts an ongoing playwriting workshop at the Performance of a Lifetime school in New York City.